Foundations
of
Program
Evaluation

This book is dedicated to three pioneers who
constructed many of the theoretical foundations
on which program evaluation now rests:

Michael S. Scriven, for his work on value theory,

Donald T. Campbell, for his work on
epistemology and methodology,
and

Carol H. Weiss, for her work on
how social programs change and how social research is
used in this process.

Foundations
of
Program
Evaluation

Theories of Practice

William R. Shadish, Jr.
Thomas D. Cook
Laura C. Leviton

SAGE Publications
International Educational and Professional Publisher
Newbury Park London New Delhi

For information address:

SAGE Publications, Inc.
2455 Teller Road
Newbury Park, California 91320

SAGE Publications Ltd.
6 Bonhill Street
London EC2A 4PU
United Kingdom

SAGE Publications India Pvt. Ltd.
M-32 Market
Greater Kailash I
New Delhi 110 048 India

Printed in the United States of America

Library of Congress Cataloging-in-Publication Data

Shadish, William R.
   Foundations of program evaluation : theories of practice / by
William R. Shadish, Jr., Thomas D. Cook, and Laura C. Leviton.
      p.   cm.
   Includes bibliographical references and index.
   ISBN 0-8039-3551-X   —ISBN 0-8039-5301-1 (pbk.)
   1. Evaluation research (Social action programs)   I. Cook, Thomas
D.   II. Leviton, Laura C.   III. Title.
   H62.S433   1991
   361.6'068'4—dc20   90-43944
                                                                      CIP

FIRST PAPERBACK PRINTING, 1995

                    00   12   11   10   9   8

Sage Production Editor: Judith L. Hunter

Contents

Part V. Conclusions

Preface

We want this book to counter the belief that program evaluation is just applied social science methodology. We want to present the intellectually challenging problems raised in program evaluation and to show how evaluation theory has progressed in addressing these challenges. Finally, we want to make the case that evaluation theory needs to be even more thoroughly grounded in empirical research than is the case today.

This book should be instructive to several audiences. One is students of evaluation. Most texts lack detail about the theoretical history of the field, and about reasons for changes in theory. They leave unclear how and why modern practice has evolved as it has. Though all evaluation texts discuss methods, few are comprehensive about the contextual matters that shape and constrain method choices — about how social programs originate, operate, and change; how evaluative information is used; how program efforts and outcomes might be valued; how the different kinds of knowledge evaluators construct might be justified; and how studies might be conducted that are genuinely sensitive to practical trade-offs. Our presentation should help all students see evaluation as an important, practical enterprise that is theory-based and linked to substantive issues in the other social sciences.

Our second intended audience is practicing evaluators in government, universities, local service agencies, or consulting firms. They will not find in this book yet another faddish recipe for doing evaluations. Instead, they will find concepts, principles, and issues that enlarge their options for planning and executing evaluations. To be sure, their options are never as many in practice as in theory. Once the guiding evaluation questions, budgets, and time lines have been set — usually by persons other than the evaluators themselves — these constrain what is then possible in an evaluation. Nevertheless, many choices still remain, and this book will inform practicing evaluators about them. We also hope to expose practicing evaluators to evaluative assumptions and procedures from different substantive fields than their own. Much evaluation practice is sector-specific, in education, mental health, job training, public health, and the like. Many sector-specific evaluation practices have evolved in response to unique circumstances within a particular sector. But this will not be the case with all practices, and even those that are products of past accommodation might not be as appropriate today as yesterday. Thus there may be much to learn from knowing about the theories and practices undergirding evaluation in fields other than one's own. Indeed evaluation may already be too sectorally fragmented. Psychologists and educators in evaluation gravitate toward the American Evaluation Association, economists and political scientists toward the American Association of Public Policy and Management, and health researchers toward various associations in health education, epidemiology, biostatistics, or public health. Such fragmentation is regrettable. These groups have a common latent commitment to the general concepts specified in, say, Scriven's *The Logic of Evaluation* (1980; see Chapter 3 of this volume). We hope the variety of sectoral perspectives we consider will prompt evaluators to appraise their own practice in more critical fashion.

A third audience for this book is evaluation policymakers — those who set policy priorities about the conduct of evaluation. They have impact on a number of key issues. First, how much evaluation should be done? They have considerable latitude in determining the budget officially earmarked for evaluation, and in defining how research and development funds are used. Second, which types of programs or questions should be emphasized in evaluation? Evaluation questions could emphasize description or explanation, the targeting or quality of services, program effects on individuals, families, schools, or neighborhoods, etc. And the object being evaluated could be a local project in one particular city, or a national program dispersed across many cities, or even a national policy that has given rise to many different programs all with similar purpose, perhaps to improve the academic performance of small children or encourage work participation by the unemployed. Decisions about such fundamental policy matters often predate each evaluation assignment, so evaluators are often constrained by them. Yet casual observation of evaluation policies in federal, state, and local government, and in operating social agencies, suggests that they vary considerably and are often poorly thought through. This book will help policymakers identify a range of options for evaluation policy, and understand how better to choose among them.

Our fourth intended audience is scholars, students, and teachers from related fields who seek an introduction to the intellectual history, achievements, and debates in program evaluation. Evaluating programs is closely related to policy analysis, for programs are a primary mechanism for policy implementation (Nathan, 1989). So policy analysts must be able to analyze program evaluations to understand where and why a particular policy was more or less successful.

Evaluating social programs also has implications for social theorists. Programs reflect, mostly implicitly, substantive theories from the social sciences. These theories are not blueprints for program design, but they do suggest ideas worth considering by those responsible for program design and change. There can be no theory-free program design, so evaluations often provide partial probes of theoretical ideas. While this book is not about those substantive theories themselves, it will help audiences learn about how evaluators understand and assess those theories.

Many factors gave rise to this book. The most salient was a class taught by the second author called "Models of Evaluation," in which each week students examined the evaluation theory proposed by a different person. The exercise was enormously educational, both for its breadth of perspective and because it tied evaluation theory to real people and the ideas that run through their work even outside of evaluation. In some senses, the class was about intellectual biographies and the forces that led evaluation theorists to the views now associated with their names. When the present book was available in draft form, the first author used it in a class that was divided so that there was one small group for each theorist. Each group read their theorist's original work as well as our chapter presentation of it, and used that theorist's approach to plan and conduct an evaluation. Seven quite different evaluations of the same program were generated, and the class members came to see that the evaluation theory one chooses has an important effect on the kinds of questions one chooses to answer and the types of methods one uses.

A second source of this book is our years of personal involvement with many other evaluation theorists. The prefaces of Cook and Campbell (1979), Cronbach (1982a), and Lincoln and Guba (1985) informally chronicle the dialogues that stimulate theorists to think about the relation of their own work to that of others, and to explain and resolve the similarities and differences in them. Yet in most of the forums where scholars meet, such as at annual association meetings, they rarely discuss in a sustained fashion the merits of ideas, and they seldom resolve differences. Perhaps public forums are showplaces for what we believe rather than marketplaces for productive dialogue. Perhaps it is most likely with books, which we can study at length, that we can clarify, if not resolve, theoretical differences.

Another influence was our own writing on evaluation theory, especially coping with challenges from other evaluators. Several years ago we considered writing a book expanding a theory we had developed (Cook, Leviton, & Shadish, 1985), but we decided that effort ought to be preceded by thorough study of what others had already said. This book is that study. Having now completed it, we can say without hesitation that the book on our own theory that we had planned will be quite different—if we ever complete it—and will be much better informed about the issues and positions we need to consider.

In this book we present the theories of seven evaluation theorists, and then criticize each one from different perspectives. This proved to be more difficult than we first imagined. It is hard to reconstruct what authors said, and harder still to reconstruct what they meant. Michael Scriven (1986b) notes:

> What is said is only a first indication of what is meant. . . . When the author is not available, then we must have recourse to the construction of what we can call PLOTs (for Possible Lines of Thought), with little commitment to the claim that one of these was in the author's mind (i.e., that they are truly reconstructions). . . . In the absence of the author, the context can sometimes provide enough clues to pin down meaning, but the general emphasis . . . shifts from blaming to investigating. Even when the author is present, what happens when the challenge is laid down is that the author thinks up answers and these are not always properly thought of as something the author had in mind when the argument was put forward in the first place. Thus a typical investigation is creative and not just analytic. (p. 22)

Our reconstructions of others' works are investigative and creative in exactly these senses. We will inevitably be wrong in how we have re-created parts of any theory. Although we solicited critical feedback from all these authors, they did not all respond to our reconstructions with the same degree of detailed commentary.

Writing this book renewed our sense of the importance of sustained study of original works. Time and again we found ideas we thought we had invented that other theorists has elaborated long before us; we also found cogent arguments for positions we had been inclined to dismiss given their inconsistency with our own position; and we sometimes found we had inadvertently distorted others' arguments to fit them into our own neat but partially inaccurate pigeonholes. We also came away from studying others' writings with a renewed sense of the complexity of argument in evaluation. These theorists are smart people who would not be saying what they are without good reason. Our book is not an adequate substitute for reading their work; we hope it whets the appetite but does not assuage it. Nevertheless, we have tried to present each theorist's work as accurately as we could, and to make our praise and criticism as explicit and justified as possible.

We should also comment on what we do and do not mean by claiming that this book is about foundations of program evaluation given that in the final analysis we are antifoundationalist. Epistemology teaches that firm foundations will never be achieved, not if *foundations* means solid, reliable, never-changing knowledge bases that will always support us. We should, of course, search for such foundations, even if we never find them; our focus in this book is on that search. But the foundations we locate are imperfect and will change over time. Each time we rebuild, we hope we make something stronger. But the job of making firm foundations is never done, and we do not claim to have done so. What we do claim, however, is that we have identified some of the crucial questions and issues around which the search for foundations in evaluation might fruitfully be centered.

We completed this book with help and support from many colleagues and friends. The seven theorists in this book gave helpful and often detailed feedback. Our presentation of their work is much better for it, though they might disagree with some of our interpretations and criticisms. Various students and colleagues contributed to this book in ways they may not even realize, including Len Bickman, Dick Bootzin, Bob Boruch, Maria Doherty, Roberta Epstein, Mike Hendricks, Tara Davis Knott, Ken Lichstein, Mel Mark, Chip Reichardt, Roger Straw, Sara Thomas, and Bill Trochim. We are particularly grateful for the close critical reading given this book by Mary Church, Lee Clark, Connie Clay, Steve DePaola, and Lori Hartman. Our editor at Sage, Deborah Laughton, was patient and helpful as we tried to bring this book to fruition not too far past our deadline.

William Shadish's work on this project was partially supported by a Centers of Excellence grant from the State of Tennessee to the Psychology Department at Memphis State University. Thomas Cook's work on this book was partially supported by the McArthur Foundation Research Program on Successful Adolescent Development Among Youth in High-Risk Settings, by a year as a visiting scholar at the Russell Sage Foundation, by the Center for Urban Affairs and Policy Research at Northwestern University, and by the Center for Applied Psychological Research at Memphis State University. Laura Leviton's work was supported in part by the Health Policy Institute of the University of Pittsburgh.

Finally, once again, we want to thank our ever-patient spouses, Betty Duke Shadish and Fay Lomax Cook. We have thanked them in a number of book prefaces, so this acknowledgment might sound perfunctory. We hope not. We trust that they still believe it when we say we could not have done this without their support. For years they have been the (ever marginally changing) foundations on whom we counted for much of the quality in our lives.

William R. Shadish, Jr.
Thomas D. Cook
Laura C. Leviton

Acknowledgments

We are indebted to several publishers for permission to reprint extensive excerpts of earlier works by and about the theorists discussed in this volume. We also want to thank the theorists themselves for granting permission to reprint this material.

D. T. Campbell, "Reforms as Experiments," *American Psychologist*, 1969, Vol. 24, 409-429. Copyright 1969 by the American Psychological Association. Reprinted by permission.

D. T. Campbell, *Methods for the Experimenting Society,* paper presented at the annual meeting of the Eastern Psychological Association, New York, and at the annual meeting of the American Psychological Association, Washington, DC, 1971. Reprinted by permission of the author.

D. T. Campbell, "Assessing the Impact of Planned Social Change," *Evaluation and Program Planning*, 1979, Vol. 2, 67-90. Copyright 1979, Pergamon Press plc. Reprinted by permission.

D. T. Campbell, *Methodology and Epistemology for Social Science: Selected papers.* E. S. Overman (Ed.), Copyright 1988, University of Chicago Press. Reprinted by permission.

H. T. Chen & P. H. Rossi, "The Theory-Driven Approach to Validity." Reprinted with permission from *Evaluation and Program Planning*, Vol. 10, 95-103, Copyright 1987, Pergamon Press.

L. J. Cronbach, "Course Improvement Through Evaluation," *Teachers College Record*, Vol. 64, 672-683. Copyright 1963 by Teachers College Record. Reprinted by permission of the publisher.

L. J. Cronbach, S. R. Ambron, S. M. Dornbusch, R. D. Hess, R. C. Hornik, D. C. Phillips, D. F. Walker, & S. S. Weiner, *Toward Reform of Program Evaluation.* San Francisco: Jossey-Bass, 1980. Reprinted by permission of the publisher.

L. J. Cronbach, *Designing Evaluations of Educational and Social Programs.* San Francisco: Jossey-Bass, 1982. Reprinted by permission of the publisher.

P. Horst, J. N. Nay, J. W. Scanlon, & J. S. Wholey, "Program Management and the Federal Evaluator," *Public Administration Review,* Vol. 34, 300-308. Reprinted by permission of the publisher.

P. H. Rossi, "The Iron Law of Evaluation and Other Metallic Rules," paper presented at Rockefeller College, State University of New York, Albany, April 17, 1985. Reprinted by permission of the author.

S. Salasin, "Experimentation Revisited: A Conversation with Donald T. Campbell," *Evaluation*, Vol. 1, 7-13. Copyright 1973 by the Minneapolis Medical Research Foundation, Inc. Reprinted by permission of the publisher.

M. S. Scriven, *Value Claims in the Social Sciences*, publication no. 123 of the Social Science Education Consortium, Purdue University. Copyright 1966 by M. S. Scriven. Reprinted by permission of the author.

M. S. Scriven, *The Logic of Evaluation*. Copyright 1980 by Edgepress. Reprinted by permission of the publisher.

M. S. Scriven, "Evaluation Ideologies," in G. F. Madaus, M. Scriven, & D. L. Stufflebeam (Eds.), *Evaluation Models: Viewpoints on Educational and Human Services Evaluation* (pp. 229-260). Copyright 1983 by Kluwer Academic Publishers. Reprinted by permission of the publisher.

M. S. Scriven, *Probitive Logic,* paper presented at the First International Conference on Argumentation, Amsterdam, 1986. Reprinted by permission of the author.

R. E. Stake, "To Evaluate an Arts Program," in R. E. Stake (Ed.), *Evaluating the Arts in Education: A Responsive Approach* (pp. 13-31). Columbus, OH: Merrill, 1975. Copyright by R. E. Stake. Reprinted by permission of the author.

R. E. Stake, "The Case Study Method in Social Inquiry," *Educational Researcher*, Vol. 7, 5-8. Copyright 1978 by the American Educational Research Association, Washington, DC. Reprinted by permission of the publisher.

R. E. Stake, "Program Evaluation, Particularly Responsive Evaluation," in W. B. Dockrell & D. Hamilton (Eds.), *Rethinking Educational Research* (pp. 72-87). London: Hodder & Stoughton, 1980. Reprinted by permission of the publisher.

R. E. Stake, "Case Study Methodology: An Epistemological Advocacy," in W. Welch (Ed.), *Case Study Methodology in Educational Evaluation*. Copyright 1981 by the Minnesota Research and Evaluation Center, Minneapolis. Reprinted by permission of the publisher.

R. E. Stake, "Constructivist Reality," March 14, 1989, unpublished. Reprinted by permission of the author.

R. E. Stake & J. A. Easley, *Case Studies in Science Education*. Champaign: University of Illinois, Center for Instructional Research and Curriculum Evaluation, 1978. Reprinted by permission of the author.

R. E. Stake & D. J. Trumbull, "Naturalistic Generalizations," *Review Journal of Philosophy and Social Science*, Vol. 7, 1-12. Copyright 1982 by the College of Education, Arizona State University. Reprinted by permission of the publisher.

M. Strosberg & J. S. Wholey, "Evaluability Assessment: From Theory to Practice in the Department of Health and Human Services," *Public Administration Review*, Vol. 43, 66-71. Copyright 1983 by the American Society for Public Administration. Reprinted by permission of the publisher.

Carol H. Weiss, *Evaluation Research: Methods for Assessing Program Effectiveness* © 1972, pp. vii, 1, 3, 4, 6, 9, 13, 19, 21, 25, 28, 50, 60, 66, 68, 88, 126. Reprinted by permission of Prentice-Hall, Inc., Englewood Cliffs, NJ.

C. H. Weiss, "Utilization of Evaluation: Toward Comparative Study" and "Evaluating Educational and Social Action Programs: A Treeful of Owls," in C. H. Weiss (Ed.), *Evaluating Action Programs: Readings in Social Action and Education*. Boston: Allyn & Bacon, 1972. Reprinted by permission of the publisher.

C. H. Weiss, "Where Politics and Evaluation Research Meet," *Evaluation*, Vol. 1, 37-45. Copyright 1973 by the Minneapolis Medical Research Foundation, Inc. Reprinted by permission of the publisher.

C. H. Weiss, "Improving the Linkage Between Social Research and Public Policy," in L. E. Lynn (Ed.), *Knowledge and Policy: The Uncertain Connection*. © 1978 by the National Academy of Sciences. Reprinted by permission of the publisher.

C. H. Weiss, "Policy Research in the Context of Diffuse Decision Making," *Journal of Higher Education*, Vol. 53, 619-653. Copyright 1982 by Ohio State University Press. Reprinted by permission of the publisher.

C. H. Weiss, "Evaluating Social Programs: What Have We Learned?" Published by permission of Transaction Publishers from *Society*, Vol. 25, No. 1. Copyright © 1987 by Transaction Publishers. Reprinted by permission.

C. H. Weiss & M. J. Bucuvalas, *Social Science Research and Decision-Making*. Copyright © 1980 Columbia University Press. Used by permission.

J. S. Wholey, *Evaluation: Promise and Performance*. Copyright 1979 by The Urban Institute. Reprinted by permission of the publisher.

J. S. Wholey, *Evaluation and Effective Public Management*. Copyright © 1983 by Joseph S. Wholey. Reprinted by permission of Scott, Foresman and Company. Reprinted by permission of the author.

J. S. Wholey, M. A. Abramson, & C. Bellavita (Eds.), *Performance and Credibility: Developing Excellence in Public and Nonprofit Organizations*. Copyright 1986 by Lexington Books, D. C. Heath and Company. Reprinted by permission of the publisher.

J. S. Wholey, J. N. Nay, J. W. Scanlon, & R. E. Schmidt, "If You Don't Care Where You Get to, Then It Doesn't Matter Which Way You Go," in G. M. Lyons (Ed.), *Social Research and Public Policies: The Dartmouth/OECD Conference* (pp. 175-197). Copyright 1975 by Dartmouth College. Reprinted by permission of the publisher.

J. S. Wholey, J. W. Scanlon, H. G. Duffy, J. S. Fukumoto, & L. M. Vogt, *Federal Evaluation Policy: Analyzing the Effects of Public Programs*. Copyright 1970 by The Urban Institute. Reprinted by permission of the publisher.

Chapter 10 is a heavily revised version of a chapter by Thomas D. Cook and William R. Shadish, Jr., that appeared originally in the *Annual Review of Psychology*. It has been adapted, with permission, from the *Annual Review of Psychology*, Vol. 37, © 1986 by Annual Reviews Inc.

PART I

Introduction

1

Social Program Evaluation: Its History, Tasks, and Theory

We can evaluate anything—including evaluation itself. But this book is about evaluating social programs. Social programs, and the policies that spawn and justify them, aim to improve the welfare of individuals, organizations, and society. Hence it is useful to assess how much any social program improves welfare, how it does so, and how it can do so more effectively.

The need for such feedback is pressing because we have few clear, agreed-upon criteria for judging the worth of social activities. What, after all, is the "improvement of welfare"? Whatever it is, it is not as clear or widely accepted as the profit criterion we use to evaluate business activity in the private sector. Even in the rare social program where most of the interested parties think the same criterion is most important, it will rarely have the convenient properties of profit—its simple metric in dollars and cents, or its plasticity for combining outcomes as disparate as the number of people employed, the average hours worked, and the volume of goods shipped. Finally, most of us have an intuitive sense of what money "means," and of the value of different sums of money. This is less often true with social program outcomes. The intuitive meaning and comparative worth of different amounts of family cohesion, social mobility, or relative deprivation are not readily apparent. Moreover, in day-care centers, school reform, or job training, complete monetarization of important outcomes is rarely possible. Criteria other than profit must be justified, measures other than money must be constructed, and means of finding improvements must be developed.

For the last 20 years, practitioners and scholars in program evaluation have addressed these and related tasks. At first, they borrowed concepts and practices from other fields, especially from the academic disciplines in which they were trained. But as experience with program evaluation accumulated, evaluators adapted those concepts and methods, invented others, and combined them in new ways of practicing evaluation. More than anything else, social program evaluation is a practice-driven field. Its greatest need is for advice about how to perform its special professional tasks.

Program evaluation is like medicine or engineering in emphasizing the practical. Nonetheless, all three fields rely heavily on theories that are not immediately practical. Physicians learn about basic anatomy and physiology not for tools of practice, but to understand the systems in which their practice occurs, influencing what is possible or efficacious. Engineers learn about physics not for rules about building rockets but because physics gives them concepts they need to understand and solve problems in their work. Similar observations hold in other practice-driven fields. They draw much basic theory from other disciplines, but use this knowledge and their own problem-solving experiences to develop specialty theories specifically adapted to the practical demands of their work. It would be a serious mistake to suggest that medicine or engineering could do without such basic theories. It is just as serious a mistake to overlook the importance of theory in program evaluation. The major purposes of this book are to suggest some necessary basic theories underlying practical program evaluation and to review some existing approaches to evaluation with these theories as a comparative standard.

Most current books on evaluation give theory short shrift. Instead, they mostly tend to be atheoretical listings of methods rather than theory-based prescriptions about how and when various methods should be used in practice. Such books can be misleading in the practices they prescribe. They can overlook important options that a complete theory would contain, recommend practices that are ill suited to situations evaluators face, and fail to tell evaluators about why certain practices are worth adopting over alternatives. Of course, evaluation has moved toward greater theoretical breadth and sophistication over the last two decades, and many topics raised in this book have been debated by others. But few evaluation texts contain detailed theoretical rationales for their practice prescriptions. Even the best of them are not as comprehensive as they might be in the theoretical matters they address (Cronbach, 1982a; Cronbach et al., 1980; Rossi & Freeman, 1985). We hope this book lays the groundwork for developing the next generation of evaluation theory.

THE CONTEXT AND HISTORY
OF SOCIAL PROGRAM EVALUATION

Intrinsic to evaluation is an idealized problem-solving sequence for (a) identifying a problem, (b) generating and implementing alternatives to reduce its symptoms, (c) evaluating these alternatives, and then (d) adopting those that results suggest will reduce the problem satisfactorily. For millennia, humans have been doing these tasks to identify options for improving their lives. From an evolutionary perspective, a noncognitive form of evaluation must have been involved in "inventing" *Homo sapiens*. To survive changes in their environment, species must (a) detect the change, (b) generate mutations to reduce any danger, (c) evaluate whether a given mutation reduces the problem, and (d) store genetic information about options that work in the new environment. In evolutionary biology, evaluation is not a cognitive process, as it is in social affairs. In evolutionary biology the criterion for success is clear: Does a morphological change raise the likelihood of passing on the genes responsible for the change? In social affairs we rarely have such clear and urgent criteria.

In this evolutionary conception, the third task is most explicitly evaluative. But its efficacy depends on other tasks being done well. What good is a fine evaluation of an important attempt to solve a trivial problem? What good is a fine evaluation of a puny attempt to solve a serious problem? What good is a fine evaluation of a program that solves a serious problem if the results are not stored and used to ameliorate the problem? Evaluation is just one part of a complex, interdependent, nonlinear set of problem-solving activities. Such evaluations have always been with us and always will be, for problems will always occur, solutions will always need to be generated, tests of their efficacy will need to be done, and the test results will have to be stored if they are to help.

In social life most decisions involve more foresight, planning, and reflection than in biological evolution. Planful social evaluation has been noted as early as 2200 B.C., with personnel selection in China (Guba & Lincoln, 1981; Wortman, 1983b; but see Bowman, 1989). Evaluations during the last 200 years have also been chronicled (Cronbach et al., 1980; Madaus, Stufflebeam, & Scriven, 1983; Rossi & Freeman, 1985; Weiss, 1978). Our concern is with evaluation theories and practices after about 1960, especially concerning the assessment of social policy. Those efforts have intellectual roots in earlier work, especially by Tyler (1935) in education, Lewin (1948) in social psychology, and Lazarsfeld (Lazarsfeld & Rosenberg, 1955) in sociology. They also have roots in the rapid economic growth in the United States after World War II, in the interventionist role that the U.S. federal government took on in social policy during the 1960s, and in the increasing numbers of social science graduates who became interested in policy analysis, survey research, field experiments, and ethnography. All this set the stage for modern program evaluation.

The 1960s and the Great Society

Modern social program evaluation emerged in the 1960s. Its growth is largely due to the social programs initiated under President Kennedy and expanded under Presidents Johnson and Nixon. Social programs were launched in education, income maintenance, housing, health, and criminal justice, primarily in the hope of protecting Americans against the negative effects of poverty. Most programs were launched with high hopes, great dispatch, and enormous financial investment. Bell (1983) estimates that the dollars spent on all public social programs, from social security through public aid programs, increased from $23.5 billion in 1950 to $428.3 billion in 1979—an increase of 1,800% before inflation is considered, ·600% after inflation. As a percentage of the gross national product, funds for social welfare programs doubled during that time. Social insurance programs, primarily social security, accounted for most of this, going from $5 billion to $160 billion between 1950 and 1979. Spending on all public aid programs, such as Aid to Families with Dependent Children (AFDC) and food stamps, increased from $2.5 billion to $40 billion; spending on public health and medical programs such as Medicaid and Medicare increased from $3 billion to $87 billion. Even adjusted for inflation, this financial investment is large by any standard.

These huge investments raised important issues. Congress is concerned with holding the recipients of federal funds accountable for their disbursement, especially with estimating expenditure patterns and preventing inappropriate payments. But Congress also cares that programs bring about some of the expected effects while avoiding important negative side effects. Until the social programs of the 1960s, these congressional functions existed more on paper than in practice. The rapid growth of federal funding for social programs, media reports of fraud, abuse, and mismanagement, and popular apprehensions about the legitimacy of social welfare programming led many in Congress to want more teeth in these oversight and accountability functions. These concerns increased over time, as did defense budgets, inflation rates, and deficits. In such an environment, proponents of social programs faced more calls to show that program funds had been spent as intended and in ways that caused desirable results.

Other political concerns also pushed toward evaluation. Some observers thought that some local projects were being implemented in ways that did not respond to federal intents (Cronbach et al., 1980; Cumming, 1976; House, 1980). Federal and state administrators and legislators wanted more leverage over these projects to ensure that the federal will held more sway. Conversely, others saw the new federal initiatives as threatening local control; they wanted to document beneficial effects from locally controlled social programs (Feeley & Sarat, 1980). Both groups assigned evaluation a role — to control local variation in one case and to glorify it in the other.

Other concerns were managerial. Massive federal involvement in social welfare was a new phenomenon; few managers had experience with it. It was a formidable task just to learn which activities were actually implemented under a new social program. Since such implementation is a precondition for program effectiveness, managers wanted such data to manage programs better and to respond to varied information requests from Congress, administration executives, local constituencies, and media professionals (Wholey, 1983).

Other concerns were intellectual. Social critics quickly saw that some social programs had problems. They sought to discuss the process of solving social problems that undergirded the design of these programs, and to critique old assumptions and develop new ones. To do this they wanted assessments of how well programs were doing, data about why successes and failures occurred, and identification of nongovernment paths through which the goals of social programs might be obtained. These aims transcended the evaluation of individual programs, but evaluation of each program was necessary input.

Who Would Respond to These Concerns?

The public sector lacked sufficient established mechanisms to respond to these concerns. Social programs lacked the well-developed roles and professions that provide this feedback in the private sector. Independent accountants from certified firms regularly check company books to determine profits and tax liabilities. Their results are made public so that stockholders and IRS officials can judge how well corporate obligations are met. Sometimes they provide such data for individual offices or divisions in a company, to diagnose problems and achievements so as to improve operations. Management consulting firms also try to improve organizational functioning; their work is broader than accounting and not restricted to auditing financial records. Many corporations have their own research and development departments charged with basic research, product development, and test marketing. In the private sector, these three functions — summarizing achievements, improving operations, and designing new products — are generally recognized as important, evaluation-dependent activities. It is no accident that professional accountants, management consultants, and research and development specialists evolved to do them.

The public sector employs some specialists to serve these three functions — auditors at the Internal Revenue Service and the U.S. General Accounting Office, economists in executive branch agencies, planning and systems analysts in the Department of Defense, and budget specialists everywhere. But they were overwhelmed when it came to providing feedback about social programming. Too few personnel existed in government to meet the demands for evaluation; many were often in the wrong departments. For example, planning and systems analysts were mostly in the Department of Defense prior to the Johnson administration. The government either had to move these people — hard to do when demands on Defense were also increasing — or look outside itself to managers of private sector corporations for organizational expertise; to financial experts for accounting, planning, budgeting, and auditing; and to academicians for scientific methods for evaluation.

In addition, skills of existing government employees were partly irrelevant to giving feedback about social programs. Planning and systems analysts could forecast the effects of new initiatives, but had little training for providing retrospective, grounded evaluations of the operations and consequences of existing social programs (Wholey, Scanlon, Duffy, Fukumoto, & Vogt, 1970). Economists could easily analyze the cost-benefits of a water project, but had less idea how to measure social outcomes such as increased family stability or education. Consequently, existing methodologies in accounting, auditing, surveying, and forecasting yielded less confident conclusions in the social sector. Moreover, strong theories in physical science aid problem solving in engineering programs, and similar theories in biological sciences aid medicine, but few strong theories exist in the social sciences. This made the design of social programs for social problem solving more difficult.

By the late 1960s, demand for feedback about social programs exceeded the supply of personnel with appropriate skills. That demand swept into evaluation many graduates of professional schools and social science departments. Graduate education rapidly expanded during this period. From 1955 to 1974, annual U.S. production of M.A. and M.S. degrees rose 479%, from 58,000 to 278,000; the number of doctorates rose 375%, from 8,800 to 33,000 (Keller, 1983). Increased doctoral production in social sciences (mostly economics, education, political science, psychology, and sociology) was even more dramatic. Between 1960 and 1970 alone, U.S. doctoral production in these disciplines increased 333%, from 2,845 to 9,463; between 1950 and 1986 doctoral production in social science increased 895%, from 1,469 to 13,153 (U.S. Bureau of the Census, 1951, 1962, 1972, 1989). Employment in academia did not keep pace with this rapid increase. From 1955 to 1974, faculty in U.S. colleges and universities increased 238%, from 266,000 to 633,000 (Keller, 1983). Data about increases in social science faculty during this period are more difficult to locate, because early Census Bureau reports did not always identify social scientists as a separate category. But we do know that from 1965 to 1985, social science faculty increased 228%, from 42,283 to 96,300, with most of this increase taking place by 1980 (U.S. Bureau of the Census, 1972, 1989). Professional evaluation became a viable career alternative to academic employment. Thus evaluation met a need of the day, and a supply of labor existed to conduct its tasks, which led to a profession of evaluation.

The Structural Base of
the Profession of Evaluation

Evaluation is a profession in the sense that it shares certain attributes with other professions and differs from purely academic specialties such as psychology or sociology. Although they may have academic roots and members, professions are economically and socially structured to be devoted primarily to practical application of knowledge in a circumscribed domain with socially legitimated funding (Austin, 1981). Professionals have somewhat greater constraints than academics about which tasks they can undertake, and they tend to develop standards of practice, codes of ethics, and other professional trappings. Program evaluation is not fully professionalized, like medicine or the law; it has no licensure laws, for example. But it tends toward professionalization more than most disciplines.

Probably the key impetus to the establishment of professional evaluation was federal legislation mandating it and supplying funding for it. We can trace this development only inexactly. Weiss (1987b) claims that "the first Federal program to require evaluation was the juvenile delinquency program enacted by Congress in 1962" (p. 40), but funding for this evaluation was modest by later standards. Wholey (1986b) says that "program evaluation has been an important component of Federal employment and training programs since the Manpower Development and Training Act of 1962, [and] an important component of Federal antipoverty programs since the Economic Opportunity Act of 1964" (p. 6). Wholey and White (1973) describe the educational evaluation requirement generally referred to as "Title I" as the "grand-daddy" of them all — referring to Senator Robert Kennedy's 1965 evaluation rider to the Title I (compensatory education) section of the Elementary and Secondary Education Act (House, 1980). This act (now called Chapter 1) provided major funding for evaluation. Another oft-noted milestone was the 1968 federal RFP

(Request for Proposal) for evaluating Head Start (Wortman, 1983b); the Office of Economic Opportunity (OEO) supported 13 university-based evaluations of Head Start as early as 1966 (Wholey et al., 1970). Also in 1968, Stanford Research Institute got funds to evaluate the Follow Through program (Wholey et al., 1970). Boruch and Cordray (1980) found 119 federal education statutes using the word *evaluation* between 1968 and 1978 — and their sample did not exhaust all education statutes.

Evaluation quickly spread to other social sectors, especially at the federal level (Comptroller General, 1980a, 1980b, 1980c). Wholey et al. (1970) note that Congress earmarked funds for evaluations, or otherwise authorized them, in (a) the 1967 amendments to the Economic Opportunity Act for Community Action Programs and for Job Corps, (b) the 1967 Child Health Act, (c) the 1967 Elementary and Secondary Education Amendments, (d) the 1967 Partnership for Health Amendments, and (e) the 1968 Vocational Rehabilitation Amendments. In 1967, the assistant secretary for planning and evaluation in the Department of Health, Education and Welfare (HEW; now Health and Human Services, or HHS) was given responsibility for departmentwide improvements in evaluation. In the same year, the Community Action Program funded an impact evaluation of its own programs. By 1968, Congress had funded evaluation in HEW under 11 pieces of legislation, and OEO had a well-developed evaluation plan to evaluate Head Start, Upward Bound, the Community Action Program, neighborhood health centers, and family planning and legal services programs.

Many of these mandates were accompanied by funds specifically appropriated for evaluation. How many dollars were allocated and spent at federal, state, and local levels is unclear. Wholey et al. (1970) report that in fiscal year 1969, $17 million was obligated to federal evaluation contracts and grants (as opposed to demonstration projects) for 12 programs in four federal agencies. By fiscal year 1972 this figure increased to roughly $100 million (Buchanan & Wholey, 1972): $8 million in the Manpower Administration of the Department of Labor, $11 million for education in HEW, $2.5 million for child development in HEW, $25.8 million for health services in HEW, $6-7 million for drug abuse and alcoholism in HEW, $11 million for crime control in HEW, $25 million for income maintenance in HEW, and $10 million for housing in the Department of Housing and Urban Development. HEW alone spent about $40 million a year on evaluation between 1978 and 1980 (Wholey, 1983), and more than $50 million in 1980 (Abramson & Wholey, 1981). Over all federal agencies, $177.8 million was obligated for evaluation in fiscal years 1975-1977 (Abramson, 1978; cited in Cronbach et al., 1980). Finally, a U.S. General Accounting Office (1982) survey of federal evaluative activities (excluding both Defense and all funds for audits and routine management information) found "228 separate evaluation organizations, employing about 1,400 highly trained professionals and spending about $180 million in fiscal year 1980" (p. ii), producing 2,362 evaluations. These figures are not always mutually consistent. What is clear is that a good deal of federal money was being spent on evaluation.

In addition to federal dollars, state and local funds finance evaluations, but how much is not clear. Wholey and White (1973) claim local evaluation accounted for most Title I evaluation expenditures, and exceeded federal Title I evaluation funds. Similarly, in mental health, the National Institute of Mental Health spent $11 million between 1969 and 1981 evaluating community mental health center (CMHC) programs (Williams & Light, 1982); local CMHCs supplemented this with between $3.7 million and $24.3 million per year on self-evaluation between 1976 and 1980 (Neigher, 1982).

These funds were earmarked for evaluation. If one adds federal investment in demonstration projects and applied research, some of which is evaluative, federal investment in evaluation for 1975-1977 exceeded $3 billion (Abramson, 1978; cited in Cronbach et al., 1980). Clear financial, legislative, and administrative incentives were present for people to do evaluations.

The 1980s saw declines in evaluation funding and activities. Cronbach claims the decline began in the late 1970s and was in full swing by the 1980s, given momentum by budget cuts of the Reagan administration. Federal evaluation offices were hit hard. Evaluation-related "fiscal measures" at the Department of Education's Office of Planning, Budget, and Evaluation (OPBE) declined 62% in constant dollars between 1980 and 1984 (Cordray & Lipsey, 1987). OPBE conducted 114 evaluation studies in 1980, but only 11 in 1984. Funding for statistics in OPBE was down 8% in 1984 compared with 1980, and personnel declined by 12% (Cordray & Lipsey, 1987). In 1984, $111 million was available to assess the results of all domestic programs. The decline slowed in the late 1980s. Funds for evaluation decreased 37% from 1980 to 1984 (in constant dollars), but fell only 6% from 1984 to 1988. Manpower dropped proportionally. Professional evaluation staff decreased 52% from 1980 to 1988 in 15 evaluation units, 12% of which occurred between 1984 and 1988 (U.S. General Accounting Office, 1988). Some signs of decline continue today. However, lively evaluation activity continues on many fronts, often linked to substantive disciplines rather than to organizations with the word *evaluation* in their names. These include the growing use of passive longitudinal data systems like the National Assessment of Educational Progress, evaluations of large-scale health promotion and disease prevention programs

(Braverman, 1989), international evaluations (Conner & Hendricks, 1989), and evaluations of poverty and labor force participation programs. Despite declines, therefore, much evaluation is probably still occurring.

The funding and activity described above gave evaluation credibility. Wholey and White (1973) say of the effects of mandated local evaluation in education, "The major impact of all this local Title I evaluation activity has been an increasing acceptance of evaluation; 'Evaluation' is now a household word among educators" (p. 73). Federal initiatives did more than give credibility. Much as clinical psychology became a profession through federal initiatives after World War II (Sarason, 1981), so evaluators received the necessary institutional support for a new profession responsible for certain tasks (feedback about social programs) in a sector (public social programming), with a funding base (reimbursement for evaluative functions) and social legitimation (through government need for evaluation) (Austin, 1981). Without this support, evaluation might exist only as a small, applied academic discipline, like community psychology (Heller & Monahan, 1977) or clinical sociology (Glassner, 1981).

Responses by Evaluators

Professionalization of evaluation. Professions require a unique and transmittable knowledge base. The early knowledge base of evaluation borrowed heavily from existing methods and theories in nearly all social sciences. More specialized knowledge bases emerged as experience with evaluation increased. Explicating these evaluation-specific knowledge bases is the core of this book. To develop and transmit this knowledge, some universities started evaluation centers or degree-conferring programs (Evaluation Research Society, 1980). Wortman (1983a) claims the first of these programs began admitting students in 1973 — presumably referring to the Northwestern University doctoral and postdoctoral evaluation training program, where he was a faculty member. Other universities trained evaluators in related doctoral programs. For example, between 1966 and 1986 the Center for Instructional Research and Curriculum Evaluation (CIRCE) at the University of Illinois produced 49 doctorates specializing in measurement and evaluation. Many professional evaluators do not have doctorates, but most have at least master's degree training in related fields, such as public administration (Shadish & Epstein, 1987).

Another indicator of professionalization is creation of yearbooks, societies, journals, and professional standards (Austin, 1981). The field's yearbook was the *Evaluation Studies Review Annual,* first published in 1976 (Glass, 1976) and each year after until 1987 (Shadish & Reichardt, 1987). Evaluation journals exist for the field at large (*Evaluation Review,*

Evaluation Practice, Evaluation and Program Planning), and for specific sectors (*Evaluation and the Health Professions, Evaluation and Educational Policy*). In 1976 two professional societies were founded — Evaluation Research Society and Evaluation Network; in 1985 they merged to form the American Evaluation Association, with about 3,000 members and annual meetings attended by 500-1,000 people (American Evaluation Association, 1986). Finally, the field developed standards for practice that imply minimal levels of competence for evaluators (Rossi, 1982b).

Diversity of professional practice. Evaluators responded to government requests for evaluation in three ways (Cook & Buccino, 1979). First, some contract research firms quickly specialized in bidding for evaluations. Some grew to include 800 Ph.D.-level professionals. In 1970 more than 300 firms were qualified to receive federal evaluation RFPs (Wholey et al., 1970). Second, university researchers won evaluation contracts and grants, consulted with contract research firms, and developed evaluation theory and methods. Third, specific evaluation offices were established in federal, state, and local agencies to respond quickly and pointedly to managers' information needs.

Across these settings, evaluators did an enormous number of studies. The U.S. General Accounting Office compiled a three-volume index of completed federal evaluations, and found 5,610 of them between 1973 and 1979 (Comptroller General, 1980a, 1980b, 1980c). Aaronson and Wilner (1983) found 3,027 local mental health center evaluations — a nonexhaustive sample from the Databank of Program Evaluations at UCLA. The validity of these figures is unclear, and depends on how evaluation is defined. But clearly tens of thousands of evaluations may have been done.

These evaluations were diverse in many ways. They were diverse in the level of government to which they responded. Some responded to federal mandates; an example in education is the evaluation of the national Follow Through program (House, 1980). Others responded to such state mandates as Chapter 328 of the Laws of 1976 of the State of New York authorizing mental health evaluation (Landsberg, Neigher, Hammer, Windle, & Woy, 1979). Still others responded to local project managers; an example is the locally controlled community mental health center evaluations mandated by the 1975 amendments to the Community Mental Health Centers Act (Cook & Shadish, 1982). Evaluators were also diverse in their substantive areas, including education, public health, criminal justice, medicine, labor force participation, income support, nutrition, traffic safety, international aid, mental health, and many other sectors. Indeed, a major task for evaluators is keeping up with the accomplishments in these areas (Light, 1983; Shadish & Reichardt, 1987).

But more than anything, evaluators were so diverse in the activities they conducted that it is often hard to see what those activities share. Some evaluators constructed management information systems (MIS) to provide timely data about program operations; mental health evaluators were even told that "an MIS is prerequisite to undertaking formal program evaluation" (Landsberg et al., 1979, p. 5). But other evaluators ignored this supposed prerequisite entirely. Others conducted case studies and participant observation in the traditions of sociology and anthropology (Guba & Lincoln, 1981). Some evaluators did huge social experiments in which units were randomly assigned to different treatments, as with the New Jersey Negative Income Tax Experiment (Rossi & Lyall, 1978) or the Manhattan Bail Bond Experiment (Ares, Rankin, & Sturz, 1963; Botein, 1965). All this diversity led one reviewer to say, "Evaluation — more than any science — is what people say it is; and people currently are saying it is many different things" (Glass & Ellett, 1980, p. 211).

Diversity was also fostered by funding agencies that demanded different activities under the rubric of evaluation. Evaluators responded with different disciplinary frameworks and methods, and the programs studied had substantive theoretical ties to many different social science and professional fields. This diversity continues to the present day, making it difficult for evaluators to agree on what the practice of evaluation should be, and why. Such differences of opinion are reflected in lively debate about evaluation definitions, models, and methods, debates that have intensified as experience in evaluation has grown (Cook & Reichardt, 1979; Glass & Ellett, 1980; House, 1980; Lewy & Shye, 1978; Madaus, Scriven, & Stufflebeam, 1983; Stufflebeam & Webster, 1981). Gradually, comprehensive theories of social program evaluation tried to integrate this diversity into a coherent whole to help practitioners understand the field and improve their practice.

From Diversity to Integration in Evaluation Theories

What do we mean by theory? No single understanding of the term is widely accepted. *Theory* connotes a body of knowledge that organizes, categorizes, describes, predicts, explains, and otherwise aids in understanding and controlling a topic. Theories do this many ways, such as searching for invariant laws, using definitions and axioms to deduce testable propositions, and describing the causal processes that mediate a relationship (Reynolds, 1971). Our conceptualization is closest to this last kind (Bhaskar, 1979, 1982). The ideal (never achievable) evaluation theory would describe and justify why certain evaluation practices lead to particular kinds of results across situations that evaluators confront. It would (a) clarify the activities, processes, and goals of evaluation; (b) explicate relationships among evaluative activities and the processes and goals they facilitate; and (c) empirically test propositions to identify and address those that conflict with research or other critically appraised knowledge about evaluation.

Toward unique evaluation theories. As evaluation matured, its theory took on its own special character that resulted from the interplay among problems uncovered by practitioners, the solutions they tried, and traditions of the academic discipline of each evaluator, winnowed by 20 years of experience (Shadish & Reichardt, 1987). Out of this developed a specialty-centered theory. As a specialty, evaluation is most like methodological specialties — ethnography, psychometrics, experimental design, or survey research. But even the narrow specialty of psychometrics uses many kinds of theory — not just statistical theory but also theory about the nature of data (Coombs, 1964) and the role of measurement in applied decisions (American Psychological Association, 1985). Ethnography aspires to broader goals, so it needs a broader theory base about what questions to ask, how to implement studies, and what the researcher's role is in those studies. Evaluation may be the broadest methodological specialty. Its theory includes a vast array of decisions about the shape, conduct, and effects of an evaluation. Evaluation theory is about methods, but not just methods. To inform evaluators about choosing methods, it needs to discuss philosophy of science, public policy, value theory, and theory of use.

Without its unique theories, program evaluation would be just a set of loosely conglomerated researchers with principal allegiances to diverse disciplines, seeking to apply social science methods to studying social programs. Program evaluation is more than this, more than applied methodology. Program evaluators are slowly developing a unique body of knowledge that differentiates evaluation from other specialties while corroborating its standing among them. Evaluation is diverse in many ways, but its potential for intellectual unity is in what Scriven calls "the logic of evaluation" (see Chapter 3), which might bridge disciplinary boundaries separating evaluators.

Developmental trends in evaluation theory. Early theories were based on little experience and so were naive about how research fits into social policy. For example, early theories were more concerned with methods than with the politics of applying methods in field settings, partly because the methodological problems were so pressing that it took time for political factors to make their full force known. As experience with evaluation accumulated, however, this kind of craft knowledge was gradually incorporated into the theoretical literature. Hence some early theories in this book may strike the reader as naive given what is known today — unavoidable in an account of the intellectual history of a field.

The field's first theoretical integration was by Suchman (1967), whose ideas overlapped with the more influential views of Campbell (1969, 1971). Both were more interested in summarizing achievements of existing programs in the public sector for policymakers than in collecting information to help practitioners at the local level. Their greatest interest was in evaluating demonstrations of new ideas that might be incorporated into existing or new programs. Reform, testing bold new approaches, was the watchword; evaluating marginal change in existing programs was less prized; evaluating local practice for local reasons was mostly ignored.

Over time, evaluation theories changed and diversified to reflect accumulating practical experience. Exclusive reliance on studying outcomes yielded to inclusive concern with examining the quality of program implementation and the causal processes that mediated any program impacts (Sechrest, West, Phillips, Redner, & Yeaton, 1979). Exclusive reliance on quantitative studies yielded to including qualitative methods (Guba & Lincoln, 1981). Using policymakers as both the source of evaluation questions and the audience for the results yielded to consideration of multiple stakeholder groups (stakeholders are those who have a stake in the program or its evaluation) (Weiss, 1983a, 1983b). Concern with methodology gave way to concern with the context of evaluation practice and to fitting evaluation results into highly politicized and decentralized systems (Cronbach et al., 1980). Today, modern evaluation theories cover more topics, have a better sense of the complexities that plague evaluation practice, and better integrate the diverse concepts, methods, and practices that span the field (see, e.g., Cronbach, 1982b; Rossi & Freeman, 1985).

Our review of theory in this book. This book documents and analyzes these kinds of changes in evaluation theory. We intentionally show the field's theoretical development by describing and analyzing seven theories that were constructed between about 1965 and 1990. Through this vehicle we show how assumptions and prescriptions have changed about five fundamental issues that undergird practical program evaluation:

(1) *social programming:* the ways that social programs and policies develop, improve, and change, especially in regard to social problems

(2) *knowledge construction:* the ways researchers learn about social action

(3) *valuing:* the ways value can be attached to program descriptions

(4) *knowledge use:* the ways social science information is used to modify programs and policies

(5) *evaluation practice:* the tactics and strategies evaluators follow in their professional work, especially given the constraints they face

We refer to these five fundamental matters repeatedly throughout this book. They justify the need for five theoretical bases essential to a good theory of evaluation. Consequently, these five theoretical bases are the core topics of a critical analysis of evaluation theory presented in Chapter 2.

We apply this critical framework to the work of seven evaluation theorists whose writings are scattered across journals and books in many areas. Consequently, many evaluators have not read most of these works, and so may not be as well grounded as they could be in the scholarly thinking of the field (Shadish & Epstein, 1987). By summarizing each author's major points, often verbatim, we offer evaluators the chance to study a broad sample of theoretical writings in the field. More important, our critical analysis of each theory helps clarify its strengths and weaknesses and why it differs from other theories.

Why do this? First, many agreements may emerge across theorists concerning the logic and practice of evaluation. For example, most theorists profess dedication to using evaluation for social problem solving, and all imply that their evaluative practices are improvements over gossip and other informal means of evaluating programs. Such agreements are especially important because they have emerged despite radical disagreement among theorists on many matters. Also, critically appraised commonalities have helped set standards for practice, such as the Standards for Evaluation Practice (Rossi, 1982b). Careful analysis may reveal other commonalities.

Second, disagreements among theorists invite attempts to explain and resolve them, and help identify ambiguities in current knowledge and practice. An example is the dispute between advocates of qualitative and quantitative methods for evaluation. One group feels that qualitative methods best serve evaluators in most cases (Guba & Lincoln, 1981; Stake, 1978); they criticize those they believe prefer quantitative methods (Boruch & Cordray, 1980). Both groups include reasonable and informed scholars; attempts to resolve their differences have advanced understanding of method choices in evaluation (Cook & Reichardt, 1979).

Third, critical analysis reveals areas not addressed well by any theorist. Cronbach, for example, found that few extant theories of evaluation emphasized generalizability or cogently discussed the relationship between evaluation and policy-making (Stanford Evaluation Consortium, 1976). In his effort to resolve this problem, Cronbach began by surfacing these underemphasized concerns (Cronbach et al., 1980). We hope this book will identify other omissions.

Fourth, we hope to demonstrate how evaluation theory evolved in response to experience in doing evaluation. Experience is the major means by which theorists ground their writings. Early theorists were disadvantaged compared to later ones because there was less experience to form the empirical content of their theories. In the 1960s, Campbell (1969) could reasonably think that experimental methods should be widely adopted in field settings to identify effective solutions to social problems. Subsequent experience, however, led to frank acknowledgment of difficulties with field experiments. So other theorists developed theories that place lower value on causal statements (e.g., Cronbach, 1982a). Early theorists are also influenced by experience, and their pronouncements are not cast in stone. Campbell's current theory of evaluation places less stress on experiments and more on mutual criticism of knowledge claims, which he thinks is inadequately practiced in social science (Campbell, 1979b, 1986b, 1987a). Through reflections on such changes in practice and theory, we vicariously benefit from others' experience without recreating their mistakes.

Why write about evaluation theory? Why not write another book on evaluation methods? The most widely used textbooks (e.g., Cook & Campbell, 1979; Rossi & Freeman, 1982, 1985, 1989; Rossi, Freeman, & Wright, 1979), kits (e.g., Herman, 1987; Morris, 1978), and sourcebooks (e.g., Brinkerhoff, Brethower, Hluchyj, & Nowakowski, 1983) in program evaluation deal primarily with methods. Books on evaluation theory — as this one is — have never been as popular (Cronbach et al., 1980). The popularity of methodological books is no surprise, given that program evaluation is a pragmatic activity. Evaluation practitioners need to act and need tools to use in their daily work. Methods texts are their essential references.

Why, then, write about evaluation theory? We do so because there is an imbalance in evaluation between the great attention to methods and the small attention to theoretical issues that guide method choice. No method is appropriate always and everywhere. Always using just one method, such as experiments or case studies, leads to such problems as producing less useful data or reporting inaccurate findings. Evaluation theory tells us when, where, and why some methods should be applied and others not, suggesting sequences in which methods could be applied, ways different methods can be combined, types of questions answered better or less well by a particular method, and benefits to be expected from some methods as opposed to others. Evaluation theories are like military strategy and tactics; methods are like military weapons and logistics. The good commander needs to know strategy and tactics to deploy weapons properly or to organize logistics in different situations. The good evaluator needs theories for the same reasons in choosing and deploying methods. Without thorough grounding in evaluation theory, the evaluator is left to trial and error or to professional lore in learning about appropriate methods. Such on-the-job training is partly feasible for evaluators who remain many years in one place (say, a local mental health center evaluator who stays in the same position for years), but can be fatally impractical for evaluators whose responsibilities change rapidly and dramatically (for example, an evaluator in a private sector research firm with contracts from diverse sources to evaluate different programs).

At the same time, however, all evaluation practitioners are nascent evaluation theorists. They think about what they are doing, make considered judgments about which methods to use in each situation, weigh advantages and disadvantages of choices they face, and learn from successes and failures in their past evaluations. In fact, the pragmatic concepts developed in practice probably constitute the most important basis for academic theories. This book is meant to encourage the theoretical dispositions of practitioners by expanding their repertoire of methods, challenging the assumptions behind their methodological and strategic decisions, and creating a broader conceptual framework for them to use in their work. Readers should finish this book with increased ability to ask and answer key questions such as these:

(1) *social programming:* What are the important problems this program could address? Can the program be improved? Is it worth doing so? If not, what is worth doing?

(2) *knowledge use:* How can I make sure my results get used quickly to help this program? Do I want to do so? If not, can my evaluation be useful in other ways?

(3) *valuing:* Is this a good program? By which notion of "good"? What justifies the conclusion?

(4) *knowledge construction:* How do I know all this? What counts as a confident answer? What causes that confidence?

(5) *evaluation practice:* Given my limited skills, time, and resources, and given the seemingly unlimited possibilities, how can I narrow my options to do a feasible evaluation? What is my role — educator, methodological expert, judge of program — worth? What questions should I ask, and what methods should I use?

Books on methods rarely answer these questions, because the questions are mostly not methodological. These questions, and attempts to answer them, are the stuff of theory. These questions do not always have one correct answer. The answers often vary from situation to situation, and depend on factors that evaluators can only partly control, such as resources, skills, constraints imposed by funding agencies, and time frame. But even in such cases, by the time readers have finished this book they should better understand the contingencies that bear upon the answers to these questions.

2

Good Theory for
Social Program Evaluation

Judging the merits of evaluation theories requires specific description of the things such theories ought to do and the issues they ought to address competently. The linchpin of our argument is that the fundamental purpose of program evaluation theory is to specify *feasible practices that evaluators can use to construct knowledge of the value of social programs that can be used to ameliorate the social problems to which programs are relevant.* This description has five components — practice, knowledge, value, use, and social programming — and implies that an evaluation theory should have a knowledge base corresponding to each component.

This chapter describes these components in detail, but they are briefly described as follows. The *social programming* component concerns the nature of social programs and their role in social problem solving. It deals with the internal structure and functioning of programs, their relationship to other institutions, and the processes through which programs and their components can be changed to improve program performance. The *knowledge* component is concerned with what counts as acceptable knowledge about the object being evaluated, with methods to produce credible evidence, and with philosophical assumptions about the kinds of knowledge most worth studying. The *value* component concerns the role that values and the process of valuing play in evaluation. It deals with which values ought to be represented in an evaluation, and how to construct judgments of the worth of social programs. The *use* component concerns how social science information can be used in social policy and programming. It deals with possible kinds of use, relative weight to be given to each kind of use, and what evaluators can do to increase use. The *evaluation practice* component concerns the things evaluators do as they practice their profession. It deals with the role of evaluators in relating to program stakeholders; how to decide which questions to ask; where one gets questions from; and what methods to use given priorities among questions, the issues about which uncertainty is greatest, and constraints of time, financial resources, staff skills, and procedural standards (Cook & Shadish, 1986; Shadish & Reichardt, 1987).

Every comprehensive evaluation theory will be better if it explicitly describes and justifies each of these five components. But the fifth component — evaluation practice — is most important because evaluators have to practice in a context where leisurely reflection about theoretical alternatives must yield to action within constraints. Even so, in using existing theories of practice, practitioners implicitly accept the assumptions built into them about social programming, knowledge construction, valuing, and use. It is better that this be explicit. Some theorists are explicit about particular components, such as Weiss (1977b) about use, Campbell (1977) about knowledge construction, and Scriven (1980) about valuing. Yet no theory we review deals explicitly and in detail with all five components. Hence we will describe and analyze the assumptions about social programming, use, valuing, knowledge construction, and evaluation practice that each theorist has made or assumed. We turn now, however, to an extended discussion of the five components, since they are our critical tool for analyzing evaluation theory. Each section begins with a summary table that is then discussed in detail.

THE SOCIAL PROGRAMMING COMPONENT
OF EVALUATION THEORY

Program evaluation assumes that social problem solving can be improved by incremental improvements in existing programs, better design of new programs, or terminating bad programs and replacing them with better ones. If these conditions do not hold, evaluation cannot achieve its purpose. Theories of social programming, therefore, must show if and how these things can be done.

Based on our experience and some of our past writing (Cook, 1981; Cook et al., 1985; Shadish, 1987b), we can divide the relevant territory into three elements:

- internal program structure and functioning
- external constraints that shape and constrain programs
- how social change occurs, how programs change, and how program change contributes to social change

The internal structure of a program includes its staff, clients, resources, outcomes, administration, internal budget allocations, social norms, facilities, and internal organization. Internal structure also involves how these

TABLE 2.1 A Summary of the Social Programming Component

The issues: How can social programs contribute to social problem solving, and how can programs be improved in this task?

Knowledge bases: This component describes
  (1) how programs are structured internally, what functions they fulfill, and how they operate;
  (2) how the external context shapes and constrains the program; and
  (3) how social change occurs, how programs change, and how program change contributes to social change.

A better theory of this component
  (1) discusses all three elements;
  (2) recognizes that
      (a) authority for starting, changing, and ending programs is diffuse,
      (b) heterogeneity results from implementing multiple programs under any social policy, multiple projects in each program, and multiple elements in projects, and
      (c) the value of evaluation depends on how well other problem-solving activities are done — clear definition of an important problem, generation of a bold set of potential solutions, faithful implementation of any particular solution, and targeted dissemination of information about results; and
  (3) identifies key concepts or leverage points for improving program capacity to address social problems.

things are combined in a program model that relates inputs to activities to outputs (Chen & Rossi, 1987; Wholey, 1979). Knowing internal structure helps evaluators to ask questions about such matters as whether actual structure meets intended structure, or about strengths and weaknesses in ongoing structure and functioning.

Programs do not operate in a vacuum. They affect and are affected by other social, political, and economic institutions and activities. Among these are external funding sources, pressure from political constituencies and program stakeholders, availability of local resources such as transportation systems, and the political and economic values of society. Context plays an enormous role in shaping programs, particularly during implementation, as local interests change program design in ways that we are only beginning to understand (Pressman & Wildavsky, 1984). Even in older programs, administrators respond to contextual matters when considering which program improvements are desirable from political, economic, administrative, and logistical perspectives.

Knowing internal and external structures tells one little about changing them; in fact, structure can be so stable that conscious attention to change is required. Programs can change by introducing incremental improvements in small practices, by adopting or adapting demonstration projects that are more effective than existing ones, and by radical shifts in values and priorities. Evaluation needs to understand these matters if it is to contribute to change in a purposeful way.

A theory can deal well or poorly with these three elements. Better theories should be more *comprehensive*, more *accurate in their content*, and should *prioritize* more acutely those things worth attending to. Is current evaluation theory about social programming comprehensive? We think not. Most evaluators attend more to internal structure and functioning of programs than to external context or to program change (Bickman, 1987). Evaluation practice can suffer as a result. The program itself may be well understood, but its role in society and policy may not be. For example, a problem in the adoption of Fairweather's (1980) Lodge — an effective project for treating persons with chronic mental disorders — was that the evaluation focused mostly on the Lodge rather than on the fit of the Lodge to its political-economic environment. Consequently, it has not been widely adopted relative to other settings for these patients (Shadish, 1984).

Better program theory also has descriptively accurate content. At a minimum, it must accommodate the following. First, in the United States, beginning, improving, or terminating social interventions occurs in a political system and economic marketplace in which authority to act is diffuse. Changes in social programs result from thousands of accumulated small inputs. No single authority can radically change a program. Second, social programs are characterized by considerable heterogeneity of local implementation. "Programs" (e.g., the Community Mental Health Center Program) are funding and regulatory umbrellas for diverse local "projects" (e.g., local mental health centers) that provide service. Projects are composed of service and administrative "elements" (e.g., intake, day treatment, psychotherapy, prevention). Homogeneously implemented programs, such as social security money that is distributed relatively uniformly across the nation or a public health program that delivers inoculations, are rare. But the diverse structure of most social programs, coupled with diffuse authority for action, produces heterogeneous program implementation even when central authorities want uniform implementation. Third, the worth of evaluation depends on how well other social problem-solving activities are executed — problem definition, solution generation, solution implementation, and dissemination of results. Successful completion of each activity is thwarted in a political system where problem definition is more a political than a technical exercise, where radical ideas about solutions occur less often than minor variations in the status quo, and where adopting successful solutions is dependent on practical feasibility and professional discretion as much as on efficacy (Cook et al., 1985; Shadish, 1984).

Good program theory also *prioritizes* by identifying and justifying key leverage points for improving programs. Wholey (1979), for example, says that programs can improve when managers are ready to manage for results; he assesses this readiness and helps those managers who meet this criterion. Rossi and Freeman (1985) say that there is no one key to meaningful change in social programs; rather, different evaluations will be useful at different stages of program development. Hence their recommendations depend on whether the target is an innovation, an adjustment to an existing program, or an established program. The justification for such priorities is crucial to making the case that the priorities make a real difference in social problem solving, and to suggesting which priorities are better and worse, because different authors have different priorities.

Does a better theory of social programming make a difference? "Good" program theory makes a real difference to evaluation theory and its practice. Consider, for example, the implicit program theory in Scriven's work. In discussing why a curriculum developer prepares a new book, Scriven (1972a) says, "He is presumably doing what he is doing because he judges that the material being presented in the existing curriculum is unsatisfactory" (p. 126). In Scriven's theory, society is as devoted to such rational problem solving as is Scriven himself:

> Business firms can't keep executives or factories when they know they are not doing good work and a society shouldn't have to retain textbooks, courses, teachers, and superintendents that do a poor job when a good performance is possible. The appropriate way to handle anxiety of this kind is by finding tasks for which a better prognosis is possible for the individuals whose positions or prestige are threatened. (p. 125)

Weiss (1981b) presents a different view that challenges whether Scriven gives a descriptively accurate account of how programs work. She faults evaluators who assume

> that organizations make decisions according to a rational model: define problems, generate options, search for information about the relative merits of each option, and then, on the basis of the information, make a choice. As our colleagues who study organizations tell us . . . this is a patently inaccurate view of how organizations work. When we implicitly adopt this as our underlying theory of organizations . . . we inevitably reach distorted conclusions. (pp. 25-26)

Scriven's theory predicts that the best new textbook would be chosen. If so, the evaluator designs the evaluation to find the best book. Weiss's theory says other motives also drive textbook adoption, including profit, perks, desire to keep a used-book market viable, and personal contact with authors. Weiss would study these contextual factors more intently than would Scriven. The evaluator who follows Weiss's advice will produce an evaluation that is more realistic about how programs change.

Early evaluators assumed evaluation would identify solutions to be widely disseminated and uniformly adopted in local projects across the nation. But this proved difficult. For example, a "planned variations" evaluation was once done to estimate the relative efficacy of each of three types of Follow Through programs at multiple sites around the country. When evaluators examined actual program implementation, they found more variability within the three types than between them. Had evaluators known that programs are so heterogeneous, they might have planned for heterogeneous rather than homogeneous implementation, or focused on better describing and explaining implementation. Later evaluation theories took such considerations into account (Cook & Walberg, 1985), developing finer pictures in which heterogeneity plays a greater or lesser role depending on the political system in a country (some centrally planned systems might have more homogeneous implementation), the policy sector (heterogeneity is less an issue with SSI payments compared with education programs), and relevant practitioners (Public Health Service personnel are trained toward uniform implementation of medical technology).

For all these reasons, evaluation theory must deal with the historical and political origins of a program; its structure, governance, and funding; the ways it is implemented; its context; and available leverage for changing it. Otherwise, the theory is deficient and may lead evaluators to assume unrealistic or illogical links between social programs and problems (Bickman, 1987; Shadish, 1987b) or to assume mistakenly that certain parts of programs can be changed (Cook et al., 1985).

THE KNOWLEDGE COMPONENT
OF EVALUATION THEORY

Why employ professional evaluators to study social programs? Why not rely on gossip, cronyism, newspaper reports, or lobbyists? Do evaluators offer different or better knowledge than what is already available? A theory of knowledge addresses such questions. Evaluators claim to provide knowledge that is especially worth having, often characterized as scientific. All evaluators seem to share this assumption and related ones — that conflicts between common sense and the systematic observations of evaluators should generally favor the latter, or that some methods for constructing knowledge are better than others. But much dispute lurks

Table 2.2 A Summary of the Knowledge Component

The issues: Is anything special about the knowledge evaluators construct, and how do they construct such knowledge?
Knowledge bases: This component describes
  (1) ontology, the study of the ultimate nature of reality;
  (2) epistemology, the study of the nature, origins, and limits of knowledge; and
  (3) methodology, the study of techniques for constructing knowledge.
A better theory of this component
  (1) addresses all three elements;
  (2) recognizes that
      (a) no paradigm of knowledge construction is best because significant difficulties plague all epistemological and ontological approaches,
      (b) in methodology, all methods are not equally good for all tasks, so the task is to sort out strengths and weaknesses of methods for different purposes, and
      (c) no method is routinely feasible and unbiased, so no study is ever free of flaws;
  (3) helps evaluators prioritize the kinds of knowledge to construct, how much uncertainty reduction is needed, and what methods to use given available tasks and resources.

behind this united front. We will find many disagreements in this book about the kinds of knowledge evaluators should construct, and how they should do so. Theory of knowledge helps us understand and resolve such disputes.

Theories of knowledge make three kinds of assumptions:

- *about ontology:* What is the nature of reality?
- *about epistemology:* What are the justifications for knowledge claims?
- *about methodology:* How do we construct knowledge?

Terms like *ontology* and *epistemology* bore many evaluators, because they conjure up images of sterile philosophical debates. Yet evaluators probably know more about theories of knowledge than about any other theories because of methodology. Evaluators care deeply about such matters as experimental and quasi-experimental design, assessment, case study methods, survey and sampling techniques, data analysis, and methods for question generation. They often know about these methods in detail—for example, that quasi-experimentation deals with interrupted time-series designs, regression discontinuity designs, and nonequivalent control group designs; and that variations on nonequivalent control group designs include nonequivalent dependent variables and reversed treatment implementations (Cook & Campbell, 1979). All evaluators must be familiar with such methods to do their work, which is why so many evaluation books are about methods. By comparison, most evaluators see debates about ontology and epistemology as tangential to their work. Yet many key arguments in evaluation – like debates between Campbell and Cronbach about the kinds of causal knowledge that are possible and worthwhile – are as much epistemological and ontological as they are methodological. So most evaluators are already familiar with these topics in the implicit sense that they continually have to resolve such debates in their daily work.

Ontology concerns common and pervasive attributes of being, such as whether things we experience are real or not. The recent popularity of qualitative evaluation (Guba & Lincoln, 1981; Lincoln & Guba, 1985; Patton, 1980) acquainted many evaluators with ontology's more conspicuous issues. For instance, most evaluators know of Heisenberg's uncertainty principle: Measuring either the position or the motion of atomic particles precludes simultaneous accurate measurement of the other (Davies & Brown, 1986). Some theorists use such controversies to make radical constructivist claims that question the existence of reality (Lincoln & Guba, 1985). If reality did not exist, concepts such as causality and validity would have meanings that are radically different from those we now give them. Validity might be what each individual decides it is.

Epistemology is the study of the characteristics of and standards for knowledge. Knowledge, for example, can be about different topics. Knowledge about generalizability concerns extrapolating from specific observations to constructs, places, people, and times with similar and dissimilar characteristics. Causality concerns whether A caused B (causal inference) and how that happened (causal mediation). Construct validity speaks to the accuracy of labels for causes, outcomes, and the things in between. Evaluators also want to know about the certainty they can place in knowledge, and so require standards for what is to count as acceptable or exemplary knowledge. An example is Campbell and Stanley's (1963) standard that "*internal validity* is the *sine qua non*" (p. 5) of good research. Campbell and Stanley outline a host of standards to use in judging internal validity.

Better theories of knowledge comprehensively address their ontological, epistemological, and methodological assumptions. Few theorists do so for ontology and epistemology (Campbell, 1969, 1971, 1977, 1988; Guba & Lincoln, 1981; Lincoln & Guba, 1985). We prefer comprehensive theories to a narrow focus on methods. Narrow theories run two risks. First, by their silence they leave evaluators to their own wits in sorting out confusing ontological, epistemological, and methodological debates, increasing the likelihood that no resolutions occur. Second, they may commit sins of omission or commission, especially in methodology, as when narrow advocacy of one method limits the applicability of a theory.

Good knowledge theory also needs accurate content, and should probably take into account the following. First, in epistemology and ontology there are many losers but few clear winners. Logical positivism probably counts in the loss column; even its proponents stopped advocating it by the 1940s (Meehl, 1986). But there is no consensus replacement for it (Brown, 1977; Machan, 1977; Morgan, 1983), since significant difficulties plague all epistemologies and ontologies. Any theorist who claims to have the answer is almost certainly wrong. Second, not all methods are equally good for all tasks. So it is folly to prescribe one method for all evaluations, and evaluation theory must sort out the relative strengths and weaknesses of different methods for specific tasks. For example, the original quasi-experimental evaluation of Head Start (Cicirelli & Associates, 1969) used a covariance analysis to adjust for selection biases between treatment and nonequivalent control groups. Campbell and Erlebacher (1970) point out why this is incorrect. Subsequent analysts (e.g., Rindskopf, 1981) have used linear structural modeling techniques to remedy some but not all of the problems (Cronbach, 1982a; LaLonde, 1985; Murnane, Newstead, & Olsen, 1985; Reichardt & Gollob, 1986). This sorting out of strengths and weaknesses is an essential theoretical job. Third, no method is routinely feasible and unbiased, so no study is ever free of flaws. Hence evaluation theories rely more on research syntheses or systematic programs of research than on single studies, hoping that many heterogeneous studies will minimize the biases due to any one study (Campbell, 1987a).

Good knowledge theory also identifies key priorities for knowledge construction. Early evaluation theorists, for example, thought it most important to assess program effects as opposed to, say, implementation or needs. But over the years this prioritization diminished. Similarly, early theorists placed a high premium on rigorous scientific standards for judging the certainty of results; later evaluators thought it more important to produce useful knowledge for policymakers. Finally, theorists differ in the methods they recommend. For example, Stake tells evaluators to use observation, inspection of records, and open-ended interviewing most of the time; Campbell prefers experimental methods. Both give epistemological reasons for their preferences. Good knowledge theory is partly about justifying such priorities.

Does good theory of knowledge make a difference? When Campbell and Stanley (1963) say that internal validity is the sine qua non of good research, they highlight the priority they assign to causal inference: "Internal validity is the basic minimum without which any experiment is uninterpretable: Did in fact the experimental treatment make a difference in this specific instance?" (p. 5). They contrast this with external validity—whether the causal inference could be generalized to other populations, settings, treatments, and measures. They want to be certain first that a program works before generalizing it to a place where it might have no effects or harmful ones. Campbell's thinking had great impact on evaluation in the 1960s, so his preference was widely adopted in evaluation.

Cronbach (1982a) directly challenges Campbell on this: "Evaluators need not and ought not sort inferences into a more honored category of causal statements and a less honored category of correlational statements" (p. 140). Cronbach argues "that internal validity is of only secondary concern to the evaluator" (1982a, p. 112). For him, relevance to decisions in circumstances not studied — one part of Campbell's external validity — is most important. Cronbach objects to the apparent triviality of research emphasizing internal validity, and resists applying the word *cause* to the results of such research at all:

> I consider it pointless to speak of causes when all that can be validly meant by reference to a cause in a particular instance is that, on one trial of a partially specified manipulation *t* under conditions A, B, and C, along with other conditions not named, phenomenon P was observed. To introduce the word *cause* seems pointless. Campbell's writings make internal validity a property of trivial, past-tense, and local statements. (1982a, p. 137)

Cronbach offers a different notion of cause: "Progress in causal knowledge consists partly in arriving gradually at fuller formulations" (1982a, p. 139) of relationships among variables, the nature of the manipulation, the conditions surrounding it, and the characteristics of outcomes. "The effect of an intervention depends on initial conditions, and . . . without a close analysis of those conditions one's experiment teaches nothing" (1982a, p. 128). Because it is so hard to specify all these conditions accurately, Cronbach saw little reason to place causality on a pedestal in the pantheon of evaluation gods.

Cronbach also questions the authoritativeness of the randomized experiment, pointing out that its key benefits often are thwarted in implementation. To make his point he assembled information from often obscure sources to criticize a favorite example of those advocating experiments, the Manhattan Bail Bond Experiment — an experimental group of subjects recommended for pretrial release without bail and a control group not recommended. Cronbach claims that the mystique of randomization made readers overlook serious flaws in the experiment's execution; in his opinion, citing it as an exemplar is justified only by overlooking the weakness (perhaps falsity) of the evidence it produced. Despite the severe biases Cronbach found, he agreed the study had an impact despite its flaws as an experiment: since "internal validity cannot be claimed for its main conclusions, that the randomized design added little force to the conclusions"

(1982a, p. 144). And "inferences from loose, biased, and poorly described contrasts loomed as large in reports and must have carried as much weight in the bail reform movement as those meeting Campbell's strict standard" (p. 149). Cronbach prefers to gather policy-relevant information by scientific methods as much as possible, but with randomization as one of many standards of science, not always the highest priority.

More extremely, Lincoln and Guba (1985, 1986) premise their radically different theory of evaluation almost entirely on arguments that there is no reality beyond what we each construct, so causality, generalizability, and truth have little useful meaning for them. They advocate nearly exclusive use of case study methods as best suited to capturing the idiosyncratic richness of each person's reality. If Lincoln and Guba's (1985) arguments are accurate, they have important implications for evaluation practice.

Theories of knowledge make another difference that is closely tied to practice. Methods with different strengths and weaknesses will often yield different or contradictory results in evaluations of a single program. Trend (1979) describes the contradictory outcomes of evaluations of a housing project yielded by quantitative and qualitative methods. The program was effective or ineffective, depending on how it was evaluated, leaving Trend to explain the discrepancy. The resolution of such common discrepancies is partly a theoretical matter concerning general strengths and weaknesses of methods.

In summary, if evaluators claim to construct knowledge that is special or authoritative, then a theory of knowledge construction must be explicit in evaluation theory. This component helps evaluators to place abstract epistemological debates into practical context, to reach conclusions about epistemological assumptions in their own work, to see connections between those assumptions and the methods they use, and to assess the worth of various methods for constructing particular kinds of knowledge.

THE VALUE COMPONENT
OF EVALUATION THEORY

Early evaluators mostly ignored the role of values in evaluation — whether in terms of justice, equality, liberty, human rights, or anything else. Scriven (1966, 1983a, 1983b) suggests that such evaluators believed their activities could and should be value-free. But it proved to be impossible in the political world of social programming to evaluate without

Table 2.3 A Summary of the Valuing Component

The issues: Values are omnipresent in social programming. How can evaluators make value
    problems explicit, deal with them openly, and produce a sensitive analysis of the value
    implications of programs?

Knowledge bases:
   (1) metatheory, the study of the nature of and justification for valuing;
   (2) prescriptive theory, theories that advocate the primacy of particular values; and
   (3) descriptive theory, theories that describe values without claiming one value is best.

A better theory of this component
   (1) describes all three of these elements;
   (2) recognizes that
      (a) no prescriptive theory is widely accepted as best,
      (b) all prescriptive ethics are underjustified, and selecting one involves trade-offs
          about which few stakeholders agree, and
      (c) descriptive theories are more consistent than prescriptive theories with the social
          and political organization of the United States, which is based upon fostering a
          pluralism of values that compete against each other in social and political arenas;
   (3) clearly states its priorities about which kinds of values to attend to, and why.

---

values becoming salient. Social programs are themselves not value-free.
For example, Fairweather's (1980) Lodge program was not widely implemented partly because its implicit values were inconsistent with profit in
the free marketplace and professional control over mental health (Shadish,
1984). Second, evaluative data about program effects relative to needs,
about expenditures and implementation relative to congressional intent, or
about fraud and abuse enter policy debates to influence decisions about
programs. Those decisions, involving distribution of social resources, are
matters of values and ethics. Third, data do not speak for themselves, but
are interpreted in terms that invoke values. For instance, Cook et al. (1975)
found that *Sesame Street* teaches some alphabet skills to economically
disadvantaged children who view the show regularly. But the disadvantaged watch the show less often than affluent cohorts, who learned even
more skills. So *Sesame Street* increased the gap in skills between these two
groups. Are the gains of disadvantaged children worth widening the gap
between them and advantaged children? There is no easy answer to such
value dilemmas. Fourth, an implicit notion that evaluation serves the
"public good" runs through most evaluation, yet the concept is rarely
explicated. Little agreement exists among evaluators or others about what
the concept means. Since it is implicitly central to evaluation, it deserves
more attention. Theories of valuing help evaluators to make such value
problems explicit, deal with them openly, and produce a sensitive analysis
of the pros and cons of results.

Theories of valuing can have three elements (Beauchamp, 1982):

- *metatheory:* the study of the nature of and justification for valuing
- *prescriptive theory:* theory that advocates the primacy of particular values
- *descriptive theory:* theory that describes values without advocating one as best

Metatheory describes how and why value statements are constructed, for example, analyzing the meaning of key terms, the structure or logic of valuing, and the nature of justifications for values. In this book, Scriven has the only metatheory. He argues that evaluation ought to be about constructing value statements; he analyzes the meaning of key terms having to do with values; and he describes a logic for constructing value statements about anything. The logic involves (a) selecting criteria of merit that something must do to be good, (b) setting standards of performance about how well it must do on the criteria, (c) measuring performance on each criterion and comparing it to standards, and (d) synthesizing results into a value statement. The logic allows evaluating such diverse entities as curricula, word processors, teachers, and social programs. It is a technology, a tool that is neutral with respect to any particular ethic or morality. Scriven claims it unites all evaluative work, and we tend to agree. But even if he is wrong, without a metatheory for constructing value statements, it is unclear how evaluators can state or justify a conclusion that a program is good or better than something else.

Some theorists promote particular values—a prescriptive theory of valuing. House (1980) does this when he concludes that evaluators should follow Rawls's theory of justice, prioritizing in the interests of the economically and politically disadvantaged. Bunda (1985) takes the prescriptive approach a step further and examines what variables would be studied in three kinds of educational programs depending on which system of ethics one used. Depending on the theory, evaluators would have different conceptions of programs, and would use different dependent variables.

The justification and internal explication of prescriptive theories usually have been carefully worked out over centuries of philosophical thinking. For example, Rawls premises the priority he gives to the disadvantaged on an initial assumption that the ideal decision maker is blind to his or her own economic, social, and political conditions (for example, blind to whether or not his or her parent will leave a large inheritance). Evaluators can assess those assumptions prior to using them in evaluation. The relationships of prescriptive theories to each other and to issues in philosophy have also been explored, so the relative strengths and weaknesses of each approach are known. For example, those who know

Rawls's theory of justice will detect that Scriven's definition of "need" — central to his theory — implies endorsing assumptions of egalitarian theories of ethics that are not obvious. Prescriptive theories give evaluators a critical perspective and intellectual authority that descriptive theories cannot match. They broaden evaluators' understanding of good social programs by broadening their understanding of what is good for the human condition generally.

Most evaluators use descriptive valuing: They describe values held by stakeholders, determine criteria they use in judging program worth, find out if stakeholders think the program is good, and see what they think should be done to improve it. The claim is not that these values are best, but that they are perceptions of program worth that are grist for the mill of decision making. Descriptive valuing is implicit in most evaluation theory, even though the word *values* may never be used. Stakeholder-based approaches are descriptive approaches because they solicit information about stakeholder interests in the program and its evaluation (Bryk, 1983). Similarly, Wholey uses a version of this approach even though he never mentions values. Other theorists who discuss values explicitly, such as Stake, say evaluators should study values descriptively because we do not have a correct prescriptive theory, and because the evaluator should not impose one ethical view on a program in a political system characterized by value pluralism. Descriptive values are easily constructed by contacting stakeholders; no special training in ethics is needed. All this makes descriptive valuing more practical than prescriptive valuing.

Good value theory comprehensively discusses its stance on these things. Only Scriven gives extensive attention to values, and then only to metatheories. No evaluation theorist does descriptive, prescriptive, and metatheorizing explicitly and systematically. Yet evaluators acknowledge that values deserve more attention (House, 1980). Nearly all the theorists in this book agree that evaluation is about determining value, merit, or worth, not just about describing programs. But few theorists do more. They rarely even deal with related topics, such as cost-benefit and cost-effectiveness analyses, to develop statements about utility based on scaling outcomes in monetary terms. These analyses deal explicitly with valuing, and most theorists ignore them.

Good value theory has descriptively accurate content. Since most evaluation theories have little content about values, they fail this test straight away. But some theorists struggle with valuing. For them, the following minimum criteria ought to be part of a good theory about valuing in evaluation. To begin with, just as in epistemology, in prescriptive value theory there are no clear winners. In ethics, utilitarian theories (roughly, theories aiming to produce the greatest good for the greatest number) compete with deontological theories (doing one's duty), and both compete with virtue theories (emphasizing characterological propensities to act properly). Egalitarian theories of justice (emphasizing equality) compete with libertarian theories (emphasizing liberty), and the list goes on (Beauchamp, 1982). Philosophers simply disagree on which theory is best. A theory about prescriptive values that fails to mention this fact is deficient. In addition, the choice of prescriptive ethic involves trade-offs. For example, Rawls's theory of justice focuses on the material needs of the disadvantaged, which libertarians will object might require them to sacrifice resources their theory says they can keep (for example, giving up more or all of an inheritance to taxes). Any theory advocating a particular ethic should outline such gains and the losses, and consider if it is worth alienating stakeholders who may object to the losses. Finally, the social and political organization of the United States reflects a conscious effort to foster a pluralism of values that compete against each other in social and political activity. When evaluators describe this plurality of values, and provide results that bear on those values, they increase the chances that the information will be perceived as fairly reflecting the interests being debated. Conversely, advocating a prescriptive ethic, and gathering data on that basis, will not reflect this plurality well, and the likelihood that the information will be perceived as fair will be decreased, thus making it less credible in policy. Descriptive theories are more practical than prescriptive theories in this sense.

Good value theory clearly states its priorities concerning which kinds of values to study, and why. One choice is whether descriptive or prescriptive theories have priority. Since descriptive theories are more politically and socially practical in a system of pluralistic interests, we assume that descriptive values ought to have priority most of the time in evaluation. Any theory that prioritizes on prescriptive theories has the heavy burden of justifying why. In either case, the theory must justify selections within descriptive or prescriptive theories. Within prescriptive theories, Rawls's theory of justice is only one of many theories; one alternative, for example, is Nozick's (1974) procedural theory of justice. Justice is just one important moral issue raised in social policy; others are human rights, liberty, freedom, equality, and utility. Value theories must tell the general orientation to be taken (descriptive or prescriptive), the particular values preferred in each orientation, and justification of those choices.

There are many different ways to do descriptive valuing. Stake tries to give all values a hearing by consulting with all stakeholders. This uses resources that could be spent elsewhere in evaluation, so other evaluators choose only a few stakeholders from which to construct descriptive values. Cohen (1983) says that each stakeholder group should have its own evaluator to represent it, but this is not very practical. Wholey gives priority to program managers. Many evaluators give priority to elected representatives, because no other group is so politically validated to represent wide interests.

Does good theory of valuing make a difference? The differences between prescriptive and descriptive valuing are driven home by House's (1980) claim that prescriptive ethics are integral to evaluation. He begins his argument by saying:

> Evaluation is by its nature a political activity. It serves decisionmakers, results in reallocations of resources, and legitimizes who gets what. It is intimately implicated in the distribution of basic goods in society. It is more than a statement of ideas; it is a social mechanism for distribution, one which aspires to institutional status. Evaluation should not only be true; it should also be just. Current evaluation schemes, independently of their truth value, reflect justice in quite varying degrees. And justice provides an important standard by which evaluation should be judged. (p. 121)

He examines different prescriptive ethics for their suitability to evaluation, and settles on Rawls's theory of justice. From Rawls, he draws implications for how evaluations ought to be done, especially regarding the needs of the disadvantaged.

House's position has elicited strong reactions from evaluators who were probably advocating descriptive approaches. Kenny (1982) complains:

> I am very suspicious of those who say they are speaking for the poor or disadvantaged when they themselves are not poor or disadvantaged. It strikes me that the highest form of elitism occurs when persons unchosen by the disadvantaged say that they speak for the disadvantaged or they say that they take the disadvantaged's interests into account. Let us be concerned, but let us remember that we can speak only for ourselves. (pp. 121-122)

Having the disadvantaged speak for themselves is descriptive valuing. Wortman (1982) responds to House:

> Most modern evaluators are concerned with the fairness, justice, and ethical conduct of the government. However, most of this work is done by contract from the government and for the government. There is little opportunity to negotiate agreements, and all audiences are assumed to be represented by this legitimate authority. For the evaluator to challenge this except in clear legal and ethical violations of conduct would be foolhardy. (p. 124)

Wortman endorses the political legitimacy of government authority given the political process — also descriptive valuing.

Consider the practical payoff of descriptive valuing in more detail. If the values of a particular stakeholder group are not considered, that group may feel morally and politically slighted and may be uncooperative with the work and critical in subsequent debates. If a group's values are misunderstood, group members may see the evaluation as less relevant than otherwise. House, Glass, McLean, and Walker (1978) claim that this happened with the Follow Through evaluation. Program developers said evaluation measures did not tap the constructs they thought the program would change. Parents said they had been excluded from decisions about the evaluation, so it did not reflect their interests. Consequently, the evaluation had less credibility with these stakeholders.

In all of these forms, value theory is necessary to evaluation theory. It helps evaluators understand what steps to undertake to make value statements about programs, to see value judgments implicit in their work, to place recommendations about ethics and values in a common perspective within which to contrast and compare them, and to make decisions about implementing those recommendations in their work. Without this component, evaluators may not understand, or even detect, the values that permeate their work.

THE USE COMPONENT OF EVALUATION THEORY

Evaluators hope that their work is useful in social problem solving. By contrast, basic researchers often disclaim any intention to be useful to decision makers, policymakers, program managers, or other stakeholders. Society justifies large funding for evaluation partly expecting that some more or less immediate payoffs will accrue. If evaluation is not useful, those funds could be used for more programs, for reducing the deficit, or for other alternatives that might yield more immediate results. Thus evaluators need a theory to tell how, when, where, and why they can produce useful results.

Theories of use have three elements:

- a description of possible kinds of use
- a depiction of time frames in which use occurs
- an explanation of what the evaluator can do to facilitate use

Consider different kinds of use. Early evaluations aimed to show which programs worked. The implicit assumption about use was that policymakers would eliminate ineffective interventions and replace them with better

Table 2.4 A Summary of the Use Component

The issues: How can evaluators produce results that are useful for social problem solving?
Knowledge bases:
  (1) a description of possible kinds of use;
  (2) a depiction of the time frames in which use occurs;
  (3) an explanation of what the evaluator can do to facilitate use under different circumstances.
A better theory of this component
  (1) addresses all three of these elements;
  (2) recognizes that
    (a) use of evaluative results can threaten entrenched interests,
    (b) certain types of information are harder to use than others (for example, it is hard to use results to start or end social programs because those programs as a whole rarely start or end),
    (c) the slow, incremental nature of policy change implies that instrumental use is also slow and incremental,
    (d) policymakers often give ideology, interests, and feasibility a higher priority than evaluation results,
    (e) using evaluation results is not a high priority for many practitioners who assume the efficacy of what they do, and
    (f) different activities facilitate different kinds of use, but limited time and resources make it hard to do them all;
  (3) identifies key choices that evaluators must make in deciding how, when, where, and why to try to produce useful results.

ones. This is instrumental use: making direct decisions about changing programs based on evaluation results. But over time evaluators found that other kinds of use also occurred. Sometimes results were not used instrumentally to make changes, but they still affected how people thought about an issue. Theorists call this "conceptual use" (Leviton & Hughes, 1981), "enlightenment" (Weiss, 1977b), or "demystification" (Berk & Rossi, 1977). All believe that this form of use is legitimate. Sometimes evaluation results were used to persuade people of a position already taken. At first evaluators dismissed such use as less scientifically legitimate — it seemed more like lobbying than scientific reasoning. But presenting evaluative data in policy debates is always partly an exercise in persuasion. Evaluators themselves engage in this kind of use when they argue that their approaches to particular studies are compelling, or that their interpretations are authoritative. Eventually all three of these uses (instrumental, conceptual, persuasive) have found a place in evaluation.

Second, evaluators began to see that different kinds of use occur in different time frames. The early hope was that use would occur quickly, leading to immediate program changes and improvements. But evaluators found that sometimes changes in programs did not show up for years, until policy circumstances allowed adoption of a new intervention (Polsby,

1984). They found that people who read evaluation results were conceptually influenced, but did not have much latitude to make changes that later proved feasible (Weiss & Bucuvalas, 1980). Hence evaluators granted legitimacy to long-term use, even though it moved away from the hopes for short-term use that initially drove the field.

Finally, because use is central to justifying the field, evaluators quickly realized that they needed plans to facilitate use. The early hope was that use would happen with little effort because evaluation results were compelling, because stakeholders eagerly awaited scientific data about programs, or because policy-making was a rational problem-solving endeavor. If those hopes were realistic, the evaluator's job would be simple: Produce results and wait for users to arrive at the doorstep. But those hopes were dashed, because evaluation results were seldom compelling relative to the interests and ideologies of stakeholders, stakeholders usually regarded scientific input as minor in decision making, and problem solving is far from a rational endeavor. If evaluations were to be used in such an environment, evaluators had to take active steps toward that end. Largely through trial and error, evaluators developed ways to do so.

A good theory of use comprehensively discusses possible kinds of use, time frames in which use occurs, and things evaluators do to facilitate use. Debates about use occurred early in evaluation's history, so comprehensive discussions of use have appeared (e.g., Leviton & Hughes, 1981) that have been adopted by some evaluation theorists (e.g., Rossi & Freeman, 1985). But most theorists discuss their favorite kinds of use in detail while minimizing alternatives. Some theorists have no explicit theory of use at all, and have flawed implicit theory.

Good theory of use has descriptively accurate content. Evaluators have learned much about obstacles to short-term instrumental use (Weiss, 1972a, 1972b) — with implications for accomplishing the purpose of the field and for the credibility of the claim that evaluation provides society with short-term return on its investment. One obstacle is that evaluative results often threaten entrenched interests. Evaluation always has an adversarial relationship with some parties to public debates; its findings do not enter debates as uncontested nuggets of truth. A second obstacle is that social programs *as a whole* (as opposed to projects or elements) rarely die or get replaced. When they do, it is mostly for political or economic reasons, not because they were evaluated negatively. Hence evaluative information about *program* effects does not affect policy quickly. A third obstacle is that service deliverers engage in practices for reasons besides efficacy, such as convenience, habit, and security. A fourth obstacle is that political decision making is a slow process, and change is almost always incremental. A fifth obstacle is that policymakers and managers use information in many ways. Although political decision makers appreciate information about program performance (Weiss & Weiss, 1981), they must attend to conflicting values, interests, and expediency; and they have less power to modify programs than outside observers might think. Constraints are imposed upon them by past decisions and current fiscal realities, and by the political realities of social programming. A sixth obstacle is that even if an innovation is highly successful, local personnel may still not adopt it. Potential adopters of an innovation do not learn about it through journals, books, or in-service training, since not all professions require in-service training and few practitioners cite scholarly journals as influencing their practice (Barlow, 1981; Barrom, Shadish, & Montgomery, 1988). Textbooks for practitioners in social service fields contain information about major evaluations, but these take time to be known (Leviton & Cook, 1983).

Evaluators have learned much about what to do to facilitate use. Helpful activities for instrumental use include identifying users early in the evaluation; having frequent contact with users, especially during question formation; studying things that users can control; providing interim results; translating findings into actions; and disseminating results through informal meetings, oral briefings, media presentations, and final reports with brief and nontechnical executive summaries. Each of these activities also aids conceptual use even when the user cannot act on results. Conceptual use can also be facilitated by challenging fundamental assumptions about problems and policies, and by circulating results through the network of scholars, policymakers, and interest groups concerned with the issue.

Good theory of use identifies key choices that evaluators must make about how, when, where, and why to produce useful results. Although some conceptual use accompanies instrumental use, evaluations that produce the latter will sacrifice some of the former. For example, studying interventions that policymakers control increases instrumental use but restricts the range of options to those that most resemble what already exists. These may be the least likely to challenge fundamental assumptions about social problems and solutions. A good theory makes such trade-offs explicit, and justifies the choices made.

Does good theory of use make a difference? In his seminal article "Reforms as Experiments," Campbell (1969) proposes the short-term instrumental use of evaluation results, advocating an "experimental approach to social reform, an approach in which we try out new programs designed to cure specific social problems, in which we learn whether or not these programs are effective, and in which we retain, imitate, modify, or discard them on the basis of apparent effectiveness on the multiple imperfect criteria available" (p. 409). At the time, this seemed reasonable to many evaluators. Evaluation would provide the data about effects, and policymakers would use those data to decide.

Weiss (1973b) counters that, contrary to Campbell's hopes, "devastating evidence of program failure has left some policies and programs unscathed, and positive evidence has not shielded others from dissolution" (p. 40). Even if evaluation shows a program is ineffective,

> a considerable amount of ineffectiveness may be tolerated if a program fits well with prevailing values, if it satisfies voters, or if it pays off political debts. What evaluation research can do is clarify what the political trade-offs involve. It should show how much is being given up to satisfy political demands and what kinds of program effects decision-makers are settling for or foregoing when they adopt a position. (p. 40)

All this led Weiss to emphasize conceptual use and activities that facilitate it.

Neither Weiss nor Campbell is as comprehensive as Rossi, who finds a place for all kinds of use in his theory. Rossi contends that sometimes Weiss is right to stress enlightenment, but that evaluation need not give up instrumental use entirely just because some of Campbell's implicit assumptions were not realistic. Rossi points to Wholey as a model for instrumental use, and he outlines conditions under which evaluators should pursue Wholey's approach. Rossi's theoretical comprehensiveness, coupled with solid grounding in empirical findings about use, gives evaluators better advice than a narrower theory could.

Evaluation has some examples of use gone awry that we could better predict with good theory of use. Salasin (1980) describes locally controlled community mental health center (CMHC) evaluations that were intended partly to increase local short-term instrumental use by tying evaluation to local CMHC managers. The premise was that managers would request information that they were particularly likely to use and to trust because they supervised its gathering. This approach did produce short-term instrumental use, but the information needs of managers revolved around billing, reporting, and public relations, so this approach underemphasized the effect of the local program in addressing social problems (Cook & Shadish, 1982). Too much emphasis on local instrumental use, undisciplined by knowledge of political and organizational constraints that shape the questions asked, risked trivializing evaluation by destroying the distinction between evaluating a program and constructing a management information system within it.

Such experiences led evaluators to increased humility about the use of their work, and about the small role social science information plays in social problem solving (Lindblom & Cohen, 1979). It also prompted them to explore the problem in more detail, leading many theorists to set the goal of facilitating use as the major agenda in their work. All these theorists are skeptical that major instrumental use occurs often for changing programs, but they are exploring circumstances that foster it without sacrificing a connection to social problem solving (Leviton & Boruch, 1983). They study how social science information is used by policymakers (Weiss & Bucuvalas, 1977; Weiss & Weiss, 1981) to learn how to take advantage of those uses. They explore how use is promoted by a focus on questions about program implementation to help managers target the program effectively, and about the effects of robust practices that can be adopted during practitioner training and development.

Hence a theory of use is a necessary component of evaluation theory. It helps evaluators assess the role of new information in decision making and in shaping practice, to know what information is more or less effective for such purposes, to understand the role scientific information plays in an interest group democracy where certain freedoms are inconsistent with naive conceptions of how science should influence policy, and to decide what kinds of use they want their work to facilitate. Without such a component, evaluators risk producing information that cannot be used.

THE PRACTICE COMPONENT
OF EVALUATION THEORY

Practitioners are action oriented. If they rely on theories of evaluation at all in their work, it is to find pragmatic concepts to orient them to their task and to suggest general strategies and some practical methods to implement those strategies. They want useful advice about how to make their decisions given the constraints under which they work. Theories of practice — the most essential component in theories of evaluation — address this need.

Theories of practice discuss the essential decisions in any evaluation (Shadish, 1986b; Shadish & Epstein, 1987). They have elements that address the following:

- whether or not an evaluation should be done at all
- what the purpose of the evaluation should be
- what role the evaluator ought to play

Table 2.5 A Summary of the Practice Component

The issues: Practicing evaluators need pragmatic concepts to orient them to their task and to suggest general strategies; they need practical methods to implement those strategies within the constraints under which they work.

Knowledge bases: This component addresses
   (1) when an evaluation should be done,
   (2) what the purpose of the evaluation should be,
   (3) what roles the evaluator ought to play,
   (4) what types of questions should be asked,
   (5) what design will be used, and
   (6) what activities will be carried out to facilitate use.

A better theory of this component
   (1) addresses all these elements;
   (2) prescribes various options that can be implemented, given various constraints under which evaluators work;
   (3) clarifies the logical and logistical contingencies among these decisions; and
   (4) suggests priorities in general and in different situations.

- what questions will be asked
- what design will be used
- what activities will be carried out to facilitate use

Theories of practice depend on the other four components of evaluation theory, because the content of the above list is drawn partly from the other components. Theory of knowledge covers methodology; choice of method depends on assumptions about the strengths and weaknesses of methods, and about the kinds of knowledge most worth constructing. Theory of practice is similarly dependent on theory of valuing. Choice of a particular descriptive or prescriptive approach to valuing influences the questions asked and the variables measured. With a descriptive approach, an evaluator will let stakeholders heavily influence question formation and decisions about dependent variables; this might not be done with a prescriptive approach. Theory of use has implications for how to facilitate use in practice. Similar connections hold between theory of social programming and theory of practice. Evaluators who believe that short-term incremental change can lead to worthwhile improvement in a program's capacity to address social problems may undertake evaluations with that purpose.

Yet theory of practice is more than just the sum of content from the other components. Its primary purpose is to prioritize that content given the limited time, resources, and skills that constrain any given evaluation — *which* methods to choose from those possible, or *which* questions to ask. Theory of practice deals with the following decisions. First, an evaluator must decide whether to do an evaluation at all. Some evaluators have little choice, being told by an employer to do so. Other evaluators have more latitude in making the decision. Some academic evaluators decide to evaluate (or not) out of intellectual curiosity, out of interest in a basic research question addressable by evaluation, or out of a desire to publish in the area. Other considerations also enter the decision. Scriven tells evaluators to consider if the benefits of the evaluation exceed its costs. Wholey asks if management will make changes if findings are provided. Nearly everyone asks if the evaluation can be done in a worthwhile form given available resources. Those who fund evaluation consider whether the money would be better spent on other things, such as more social programming.

Second, if an evaluation is to be done, it could be done for different purposes. Scriven identifies two alternatives—formative and summative evaluation. Formative evaluations improve program performance by influencing immediate decisions about the program, especially about how its component parts and processes could be improved. Summative evaluations judge program worth by assessing program effects in light of relevant problems. This dichotomy oversimplifies, as any simple dichotomy is bound to do. It emphasizes short-term rather than longer-term or conceptual uses, for example.

Third, evaluators can take on different roles. Most early evaluators were social scientists who were used to pursuing questions out of personal curiosity rather than to satisfy needs of clients or interests of stakeholder groups, to having freedom of inquiry in topics and methods, to being responsible to scientific peers rather than to evaluation funders, and to letting the marketplace of ideas use results rather than taking an active part in promoting use. These role assumptions were not always functional in the world of evaluation. Even those evaluators who remained in academia modified the traditional role somewhat, seeing themselves as methodological experts giving competent consultation to clients, as educators of evaluation clients about social programs, as servants of the "public interest" who owe no allegiance to the interests of stakeholders, or even as judges of program worth who use the security of academia to safeguard against being co-opted by stakeholders. Evaluators in policy or program settings, or in the private sector, began to see themselves as servants of program managers or program stakeholders, as facilitators of program change, or as part of the program team. In the latter roles, responsibility to a specific program, its staff, and stakeholders often takes precedence over traditional role behaviors of scientists.

Fourth, evaluators can ask questions about (a) intended or actual clients, their needs and desires; (b) program inputs, such as budget and staff; (c) internal structure and processes of the program, including activities, internal organization, and program model outlining the relationship among these things; (d) variables outside the program that affect it, such as legislation, regulations, or local political and organizational support; (e) changes in clients or society; and (f) costs and benefits of the program. The specifics of each of these questions can be drawn from such sources as stakeholder information needs, past research and theory, and pending decisions or legislation.

Fifth, the evaluator must design the study. This includes selecting methods — inspection of program records, on-site observation, sample surveys, interviews with stakeholders, program monitoring, client needs assessments, experimentation and quasi-experimentation, metaevaluation, secondary analysis, causal modeling, and meta-analysis, to name a few. Design also includes identifying variables to be measured — inputs, program implementation and activities, or outcome. Breaking this down even further, measures of outcome can be drawn from program goals, anticipated side effects, relevant legislation, social science theory, ethical theory, or management expectations.

Finally, the evaluator must decide how to facilitate use. Minimally, the evaluator places results in public forums such as books, journals, or popular media. Extensive user contact also facilitates use by allowing the evaluator to identify users early, to ask about how information could be used, to keep in contact during the evaluation, and to provide interim results. Use can be aided by final reports that include executive summaries and action recommendations, and by using oral briefings and other supplements to final reports.

Few theories of evaluation practice are comprehensive. Since few of them are equally explicit about all of the other four components of theory, their prescriptions for practice often borrow heavily from one component but are poorly grounded in another. For example, Scriven takes a metatheory of valuing and combines it with a theory of knowledge emphasizing critical realism and questions about needs and program effects, but leaves out most theories of use and social programming. Stake uses descriptive valuing, emphasizes local program improvement from theory of social programming, stresses conceptual use, and says little about theory of knowledge. No theorist builds explicitly on strong analysis of all four of components.

Comprehensiveness has another implication for theories of practice: They must include advice about *what* to do and *how* to do it. When Campbell (1969, 1971; Campbell & Stanley, 1963) discusses methods for causal inference, he tells the evaluator how to use experiments or selected quasi-experiments to do this. When Wholey (1979, 1983) tells the evaluator to provide quick, sequentially better evaluation results to managers, he gives them the details of evaluability assessment, rapid feedback evaluation, and performance monitoring to implement that advice. Other theorists err by not elaborating how to implement their prescriptions. The mistake is not serious if the method is common and easily accessible; but it is often fatal for novel prescriptions. Scriven's (1976b) goal-free evaluation has been widely criticized for lack of operations by which to conduct it; it may be less widely used as a result. He tells you what to do but not how to do it. Creative practitioners may invent means of doing it, but it is doubtful this occurs often.

Good theory of practice has descriptively accurate content. This is largely ensured if the theory has accurate content in the four component theories — use, valuing, knowledge, and social programming. In theories of practice, the term *accurate* also takes on the connotation of *realistic*. Some theories of practice fail to give operations that can be implemented given the constraints under which evaluators work. Many evaluators, for example, do not have the skills or background to implement linear structural modeling programs. A similar criticism of randomized experiments focuses on the practicality of denying access to eligible clients of a program. Practicing evaluators need to know the resources required to implement different methods, especially relevant methods, and the quality of information yielded by each.

A descriptively accurate theory of practice also explicates connections among the decisions that evaluators face. A decision to evaluate for one particular client — say, program management — influences the kinds of questions asked. Management is more responsible for program improvement than for policy decisions about programs, and so is more interested in questions about program improvement than in whether the program as a whole is effective. Similarly, choice of question might lead to selecting some methods over others. If the question has to do with problem prevalence in a population, most methodologists might recommend a sample survey. Even the choice of role constrains practice; evaluators who see themselves as methodological experts may be less likely to worry about whether or not results get used.

Good theory of practice — more than anything else — is about *setting priorities* and the trade-offs that go with doing so. The very point of the theory is that practice cannot be comprehensive because of limited time, resources, staff, interests, and skills. Practice is about making constrained choices with a realistic understanding of losses and gains. Theory of practice must clearly identify those constraints and help practitioners sort through options to find the feasible few. This is usually done through heuristic devices to guide choices. These heuristic devices have qualities we associate with the notion of a schema from cognitive science. Schemas are organized, relatively stable frameworks of concepts, connections among concepts, slots for categorizing input, and prescriptions for actions. Once learned, schemas organize and make sense of experience. When a situation does not fit well into the schema, it is adjusted or a new schema is learned. As with schemas generally, evaluators have a limited number of heuristic devices to use in practice. They continue to apply those concepts routinely until the fit between them and the situation is so poor that a change must be made.

Heuristic devices in theories of practice are of two kinds: focusing devices and contingency devices. Focusing devices reduce the scope of possible activities by focusing attention on some things rather than on others. They tell evaluators to use some subset of roles, questions, methods, or practices. An example is Scriven's goal-free evaluation; he tells the evaluator to ignore program goals, to avoid contact with management, and to identify program effects relative to social needs. Stake's responsive evaluation tells evaluators to be responsive to the program by observing it passively and in its natural state, and to avoid introducing treatments, raters, or questionnaires into it. Campbell's experimenting society focuses attention on cause-and-effect questions, experimental methods, and a direct problem-solving view of social change. The advice does not vary over evaluators, programs, or situations; rather, the evaluator's attention is focused on a limited, tractable set of tasks.

Focusing devices always succeed partially because their recommendations are always realistic for some evaluators in some settings. But they are inherently limited because they tell evaluators about only part of the total picture. If a more complete theory of practice is better than a less complete one, then focusing devices are not a good answer to the problem of setting priorities. A more desirable solution is the use of contingency devices. Focusing devices were common during the 1960s and 1970s, but recent theory makes more use of contingency devices. Contingency devices specify practices that vary depending on situations. Rossi's tailored evaluation attends to level of program development, telling evaluators how to vary their practices depending on if the program is a new innovation, an ongoing program, or a modification to an ongoing program. Cronbach agrees, but presses evaluators toward giving more attention to those uncertainties with greatest significance for policy, if they can be investigated cost-effectively. In these cases, the questions asked, methods used, and anticipated uses vary depending on the situation. Contingency devices allow evaluators to exercise a wider array of skills in a wider array of situations than focusing devices allow. But contingency devices have problems, too. They are more complex than focusing devices, and require evaluators to possess more skills. Further, no single heuristic device captures all the complexities of practice, so it helps to use more than one device in a theory of practice — increasing complexity more. Finally, in simplifying complex input, heuristic devices risk oversimplifying and so painting an inaccurate picture of practice.

Cronbach, faced with this array of possibilities and constraints, claims that evaluation practice is more art than science. The possible choices are so vast as to require seasoned judgment and virtuosity in combining them, and each evaluation occurs within so many unique circumstances that the combinations are rarely the same over time or place. Hence even the best theories of practice do not try to specify rules for good practice completely. Most use a limited number of heuristics to organize the options into a tractable few.

Does good theory of practice make a difference? Yes; it helps evaluators sort through the discrepant advice that different theorists give about practice. Wholey (1979), for example, tells evaluators to use the following four steps of his sequential purchase of information:

> Evaluability assessment clarifies the extent to which evaluation information is likely to be useful and suggests changes in program activities and objectives which could improve program performance. Rapid feedback evaluation provides preliminary evaluations as by-products of the data collection and analysis needed in designing full-scale evaluations that will be worth their cost. Performance monitoring provides the program performance information that program managers need to set performance targets, to test alternative ways to meet or exceed performance targets, and to document the feasibility and cost of improving program performance. Intensive evaluation provides more conclusive evidence on the effectiveness of program activities when such information is needed for specific policy or management decisions. (pp. 202-203)

But Stake (1978) prescribes a quite different approach that relies heavily on case study methods:

> Most case studies feature: descriptions that are complex, holistic, and involving a myriad of not highly isolated variables; data that are likely to be gathered at least partly by personalistic observation; and a writing style that is informal, perhaps narrative, possibly with verbatim quotation, illustration, and even allusion and metaphor. Comparisons are implicit rather than explicit. Themes and hypotheses may be important, but they remain subordinate to the understanding of the case. (p. 7)

For logical or logistical reasons, both sets of advice cannot be followed concurrently. One example is logically contradictory advice. Wholey (1983) suggests working with managers to specify goals and objectives;

Scriven (1976b) says to avoid both managers and goals. Logically, the evaluator cannot do both. Another example concerns discrepancies that are practically inconsistent. Campbell (1969) says to use experimental methods or some high-quality quasi-experiments; Stake says to do nonexperimental case studies. Limited resources generally preclude the evaluator from doing both in any given study.

Surveys of evaluators suggest that their practices are influenced by theory. Although they learn from on-the-job experience, discussions with colleagues and clients, observations of other evaluations, graduate school training, reading, and workshops, they rate new ideas in the field as the most influential factor in the changes they have made in their work (Shadish & Epstein, 1987). The theoretical orientations these evaluators endorse are also statistically related to the use of practices consistent with those theories.

Of all the components, evaluation theory is better if it contains a complete, accurate, and realistic theory of practice. Such a theory lists the tasks that evaluators must do, the options for doing them, the resources required for each, the trade-offs among them, and the justifications for choosing one over another in particular situations. Practicing evaluators need such a discussion to avoid doing evaluations that are incomplete, impractical, or technically inferior.

THE REST OF THIS BOOK

Our vehicle for discussing evaluation theory is the work of seven evaluation theorists from the last 25 years. We devote one chapter each to Michael Scriven, Donald Campbell, Carol Weiss, Joseph Wholey, Robert Stake, Lee Cronbach, and Peter Rossi, in that order for reasons discussed shortly. The first part of each chapter uses extensive quotation from each theorist's original work to present his or her theory as faithfully as we can to the spirit of the work. We identify the concepts each explicitly uses in dealing with each component, or suggest those that may be implicit in his or her theory, although we try to label it as such when we do so. The second half of each chapter examines how each theorist deals with the five theoretical components.

Our Selection of Theorists

It is worth commenting on how we chose these seven theorists, and why, because the reader might have made other choices. We selected theorists who had written broadly about issues in evaluation, excluding those who mostly write about, say, methodology, as do many econometricians who do evaluations (Stromsdorfer & Farkas, 1980). We tended to include theorists who had been in evaluation for a while, mostly because they have experienced the diversity of growth in approaches in evaluation as it tried to cope with the harsh lessons of field research over the last decades. We selected authors in part to illustrate our view of the historical development of evaluation theory. We also chose theorists to reflect diverse positions in evaluation, omitting some theorists who elaborate positions initially outlined well by earlier theorists. All these decisions were partly arbitrary, so we omit from this book a number of good theorists whom others might have included.

This latter point deserves more comment. Program evaluation is a changing, dynamic field. New theorists constantly emerge whose work could be included in a book like this, such as Chelimsky (1987a, 1987b, 1987c), Hausman and Wise (1985), Haveman (1987), Lincoln and Guba (1985), Nathan (1989), and Patton (1988). If a second volume like this were written, they would be prime candidates for inclusion. But omitting such theorists does less *conceptual* harm than one might think. The issues raised by our theory — about use, valuing, social programming, knowledge, and practice — are broader than the work of any one theorist. The reader who learns to think in these terms, who can criticize any theory (or any evaluation!) from this perspective, is better equipped to understand the merits of new and emerging theories than is a reader who is simply coached about who is currently saying what. This is not just a book that describes evaluation theory; it is about *how to think about* evaluation theory. Moreover, new theorists do not always provide new answers to fundamental problems in the field. Their contribution is sometimes to combine old answers in new ways, to popularize an established point, or to show how an old idea applies in a new context. Such theorists make novel contributions, of course — indeed, we regret we cannot include all the novel contributions of the many bright theorists in evaluation. But still, newer theorists inevitably have a conceptual debt to the ideas of past theorists. There may be diminishing overall yield from new theories as time passes and an area matures.

It is probably also worth mentioning criteria we did not use in selecting theorists. We did not select these seven theorists as being the *most* influential in the field. Some of these theorists have been more influential and others less so, both relative to each other (Shadish & Epstein, 1987) and relative to theorists we did not include (Smith, 1981). Finally, these seven people might not necessarily see themselves primarily as either theorists or evaluators. One reviewer of a draft of this book said he did not think of some of them as being evaluators as much as "public administrators, interventionists, problem-solvers, solution-seekers," nor so much theorists as people with "a philosophy, orientation, bag of lessons learned over the years." Yet whether or not they intended to be evaluation theorists is beside the point. Along with a few other people whose work we could have included, these seven are viewed as evaluation theorists in the field. We cannot imagine writing a book on evaluation theory that did not include them or colleagues like them.

Order of Theory Presentation:
Three Stages of Evaluation Theory

The order in which we present these theorists illustrates our perception of the evolution of evaluation theory in three stages. Scriven and Campbell represent the first stage. As two of the earliest theorists in the 1960s, they provided concepts and methods particularly for valuing and knowledge construction. They advocated a rigorous scientific search for effective social interventions to solve social problems. But discontent with first-stage approaches led to a search for alternatives, represented by Weiss, Wholey, and Stake. These theorists illustrate an explosive growth of alternatives in the 1970s, and a special concern with being more realistic about the nature of social programs and about how social science concepts and findings are used in policy. Finally, a third stage of theory was devoted to integrating these alternatives into a coherent approach to evaluation, represented by Cronbach and Rossi. We describe these stages in more detail in material preceding the chapters themselves.

Stage theories oversimplify complex arguments. They imply continuous progress that belies the starts and sputters that actually characterize the development of evaluation theory. Also, the stages are not mutually exclusive; later theorists absorbed parts of previous theorists' work, rejected other parts, invented new parts, and made their own errors. Some theorists resist classification into one stage. For example, Wholey and Weiss briefly endorsed Campbell's approach, but most of their subsequent efforts to generate useful, politically realistic theories have dramatically modified or departed from Campbell. Similarly, when first-stage theories were dominant, Cronbach (1963) foreshadowed his contributions 20 years later, though the latter contributions were more comprehensive, better informed, and might not have been possible during the first stage. In some respects Cronbach and Weiss are closer in spirit than Cronbach and Rossi. We categorize Cronbach and Weiss in different stages to acknowledge Cronbach's explicit appeal to the defining features of third-stage theorists — use of contingency devices, and specific efforts to incorporate the work of preceding theorists. Finally, it would be wrong to infer that the third stage is the ultimate possible achievement in evaluation theory. Third-stage theorists disagree with each other, so that more integration is still needed; alternatives (additional second-stage theories) continue to be generated that existing syntheses must take into account; and even the best third-stage theories need improvement, especially in the degree to which each is buttressed by empirical evidence — the latter being mostly lacking in all theories of evaluation.

Despite the oversimplifications, these stages accurately reflect general trends in the field:

- Evaluation started with theories that emphasized a search for truth about effective solutions to social problems.
- It next generated many alternatives predicated on detailed knowledge of how organizations in the public sector operate, aimed at producing politically and socially useful results.
- It then produced theories that tried to integrate the alternatives generated in the first two stages.

PART II

Stage One Theories: Bringing Truth to Social Problem Solving

The first stage of evaluation theory emphasizes social problem solving and scientific rigor, with particular emphasis on valid causal knowledge about effects of social programs. The intellectual tenor of this stage is epitomized by the two theorists we cover next, Michael Scriven and Donald Campbell. They stress rigorous epistemological and methodological standards for evaluation logic and practice. Scriven, the philosopher, tells us more about valuing, and Campbell, the self-made epistemologist, tells us more about knowledge construction.

THEORY OF SOCIAL PROGRAMMING

Consistent with the social climate of the 1960s, these theorists searched for immediately implementable solutions to social problems. They assumed that significant problem amelioration might occur as a result of social programs. Behind these aims are implicit assumptions that (a) interventions would be implemented and evaluated in unambiguous ways, and (b) evaluated "successes" would be adopted by policymakers, service deliverers, and program managers, thus (c) significantly ameliorating the social problem. To do this, Scriven and Campbell searched for novel interventions that, if effective, could be adopted—if not now, then in the future. Theories of social programming during this stage, then, emphasized finding and evaluating *manipulable* solutions to social problems, often on a demonstration basis.

THEORY OF USE

The dominant assumption about use in this stage might be called "naive instrumentalism." Neither Campbell nor Scriven discusses use extensively, so we must infer the following two crucial but implicit characteristics. First, feedback about program effects would be used by policymakers and managers to maintain or expand effective programs and to make radical changes in ineffective ones. Second, evaluators would have to do little for such use to occur. Scriven treats use the way *Consumer Reports* does — stakeholders notice and use information as they see fit, given their judgment about how well it meets their needs. Campbell assumes that policymakers use data to improve programs, but expresses reservations because pressure on them can discourage use or encourage misuse. He advises evaluators to monitor how results are actually used and to protect the truth even if only in debates with scholars. Campbell fears that active evaluator efforts to promote use will compromise the standing of findings.

THEORY OF KNOWLEDGE CONSTRUCTION

The hallmark of first-stage theorists is the priority they give to truth. Scriven and Campbell have written more extensively about epistemology than have other evaluation theorists. Both are sophisticated realists; they believe a reality external to the knower probably exists, though it may never be known perfectly by observers. They think it possible to construct more or less valid knowledge about reality. But bias is a constant threat, so each emphasizes bias control. Scriven writes about controls that guard against the evaluator being co-opted; for Campbell the controls lie in knowledge of multiple validity threats, use of experiments, and intense public debate of knowledge claims. Scriven and Campbell hold evaluative knowledge to the highest standards, preferring the strongest methods whenever feasible.

THEORY OF VALUING

To Scriven and Campbell, a valuable social program solves important social problems. Part of the evaluator's task is to help render that value judgment, though Scriven is more explicit and detailed on this point than Campbell (or any other theorist). Scriven constantly contends that the purpose of evaluation is to construct value statements, that evaluation cannot be value-free, and that value statements are matters of fact, not opinion. Scriven's logic of evaluation is his method for doing this. It says evaluators should assess how much the thing being evaluated meets important needs, particularly in comparison to alternatives for meeting those needs. Then a single value judgment should be rendered about its worth. Campbell's theory implicitly follows much of this logic. Like Scriven, he compares the effects of programs to controls or comparison treatments that might accomplish the same ends. Scriven argues that such comparisons are key, because the choice is rarely between doing something and doing nothing; it is usually between doing one thing and doing another. These authors part company when at the fourth step in Scriven's logic; Campbell makes little mention of synthesizing results over outcomes to create a single judgment of worth. He prefers stakeholders to make their own integrations, but does once call for more scholarly work on summary utility judgments.

EVALUATION PRACTICE

First-stage theorists assess program effectiveness at solving social problems. They advise evaluators to maintain distance from stakeholders so as to avoid compromising the evaluation's integrity. Campbell emphasizes experimental methods as the core of practice, since he believes they render the best data about program effects. Scriven shares Campbell's interests in assessing effects, and expresses a theoretical preference for experiments; but in practice he gives them a lower priority because of their infeasibility in many settings. He allows a broader array of methods, even inventing some himself (e.g., the *modus operandi* method). For Scriven, the evaluator should strive vigorously to find the truth about the program no matter where the search leads. While Campbell writes about bias control through experimental methods, Scriven writes about such extradesign procedures as metaevaluation and organizational arrangements that remove evaluators from program advocates and detractors. Scriven and Campbell differ in some of their methodologies, with Campbell being more traditionally scientific than Scriven, yet the two theorists' work has the same summative goals and a similar logic.

3

Michael S. Scriven:
The Science of Valuing

KEY TERMS AND CONCEPTS

Evaluand: The thing being evaluated.

Cost-Free Evaluation: Evaluation should not be done unless it yields benefits exceeding costs.

Goal-Free Evaluation: Requires evaluators to ignore goals, and to match effects of evaluands against needs of those whom evaluands affect.

Summative Evaluation: Designing and using evaluation to judge merit.

Formative Evaluation: Designing and using evaluation to improve the evaluand.

Metaevaluation: Evaluating evaluations.

The Logic of Valuing: Four steps in constructing a value statement: select criteria of merit, set standards of performance, measure performance, and synthesize results into a value statement.

Key Evaluation Checklist: A list of dimensions and questions to guide evaluations.

BACKGROUND

At the 1981 Evaluation Research Society meeting, a speaker referred to Scriven as "our philosopher," a label that Scriven "modestly and immodestly agrees to, noting that he is the only philosopher we have" (Stake, 1982c, p. 12). He took his Ph.D. in philosophy from Oxford University in England. He has held positions at the University of Minnesota, Swarthmore, Indiana University, University of California at Berkeley, University of San Francisco, and University of Western Australia. He has written extensively in philosophy of science, particularly about the logic of science, causal inference and explanation, and values in science. His contributions to evaluation are similar — explication of the logic and philosophy of evaluation, with a practical bent.

Scriven is one of the earliest of modern evaluation theorists, writing since the 1960s. His article "The Methodology of Evaluation" (1967, 1972a) was the most cited educational evaluation article of the 1960s (Smith, 1981). His ideas are novel and productive, and he has a talent for labeling his concepts. Along with Campbell, Scriven has affected how we talk about evaluation more than any other theorist. The terms *formative* and *summative* evaluation — part of the everyday vocabularies of evaluators (Wortman, 1975) — were introduced in the Scriven (1967, 1972a) article. *Goal-free evaluation* and *metaevaluation* are also terms known by most evaluators; the list could go on (*evaluand, cost-free evaluation*). Of course, Scriven (1976b) refers to the term *metaevaluation* as an "opaque neologism for which I apologize" (p. 133); presumably he would say the same about his other neologisms if pressed. But, as he notes, the ideas behind the terms were novel and so deserved special attention: "As a matter of terminology, I think that novel terms are worthwhile here, to avoid inappropriate connotations" (1972a, p. 126). Scriven's ideas are seminally important to the field, and may still not be fully appreciated.

OUR RECONSTRUCTION OF
SCRIVEN'S THEORY OF EVALUATION

Evaluation as the Science of Valuing

Most evaluators acknowledge that evaluation assigns merit or worth, but they rarely discuss values more deeply. Scriven is the most forceful and persistent advocate of this position. He wants evaluation to be the science of valuing: "Bad is bad and good is good and it is the job of evaluators to decide which is which" (1986a, p. 19). He criticizes other evaluators for "*defining* evaluation as, for example, the provision of information to decision-makers. Evaluation is what it is, the determination of merit or worth, and what it is used for is another matter" (1980, p. 7).

Scriven believes that empirical facts should inform debates about values, and help decide which values are preferred (1966, 1983a, 1983b). He calls for increased empirical scrutiny of justifications for moral claims: "It should be clear from these analogies that the question of justification is itself largely a question for the social sciences, whether or not it has previously been accepted as part of their province" (1966, p. 24). He believes values can be investigated and justified empirically, that "the facts/value distinction is a bogey man" (1981a, p. 278), and that "the arguments for keeping science value free are in general extremely bad" (1969, p. 36) because scientific work has value implications whether intended or not. So, "evaluation research must produce as a conclusion exactly the kind of statement that social scientists have for years been taught is illegitimate: a judgement of value, worth, or merit. That is the great scientific and philosophical significance of evaluation research" (1974, p. 4).

Scriven argues that value statements are similar to other scientific constructs: "Value, worth, quality, and merit are simply constructs from observable variables, just as aptitudes and achievements and motivation and anxiety are" (1986a, p. 39). Establishing the validity of value claims is similar to establishing the validity of other scientific constructs. Scientific constructs are not directly observed, but are "indirectly demonstrated or inferred from the results of tests" (1986a, p. 39). Values are a special case of scientific constructs:

> The value of programs, the merit of teachers, the quality of products are simply theoretical constructs that can be indefinitely unpacked into factual implications, tied into the net of our concepts and needs and environment, and used like any other constructs in the practical or intellectual world. It is not possible to have accepted the role of empirical constructs in science and have any arguments against the role of value constructs. (Scriven, 1986a, p. 41)

Appealing to construct validity (Cronbach & Meehl, 1955), Scriven argues that the validity of a value claim is a matter of joining factual claims with a network of knowledge claims and searching for consistencies.

Appreciating this position requires knowing Scriven's epistemological beliefs. He is a "postpositivist," rejecting positivistic ideas that reality is directly perceived through sensations and perceptions without mediating theories and without perceptual distortion, that scientific constructs should be operationalized directly in observables, and that empirical facts are the sole arbiter of valid scientific knowledge (Feigl, 1969). He acknowledges that no single scientist ever observes "reality" completely and undistorted, but rather observes through biased perceptual filters. Using multiple perspectives helps construct a more complete picture of reality. He calls this *perspectivism*, differentiated from a relativism: "Perspectivism accommodates the need for multiple accounts of reality as perspectives from which we build up a true picture, not as a set of true pictures of different and inconsistent realities" (1983a, p. 255). He rejects the idea that there is no reality or that it is not possible to describe reality:

> If it were really the case that there is no objective superiority of some descriptions above others, then there could be no discipline of physics any more than evaluation. . . . Although we may reject the existence of a single correct description, we should not abandon the idea that there is an objective reality, though it may be a very rich one that cannot be exhaustively described. (Scriven, 1983a, p. 239)

There are no bias-free building blocks of knowledge. Rather, "knowledge has a netlike structure in which all parts are connected to all other parts more or less directly" (Scriven, 1986a, p. 40). All units of knowledge depend on other units in the net, sharing meaning, evidence, method, or topic with them. Changing the status of one unit implies changing the status of other dependent units. Valid scientific knowledge is not as contingent on empirical observation as it is on consistency with the network in which it is embedded:

> When we find discrepancies between our predictions/inferences from one part of the net — and our observations — themselves dependent on other parts of the net — we have to go back and look for the most appropriate adjustments to be made in the elements of the net. Perhaps we shall have to change theoretical axioms, perhaps reject some previous observations, perhaps rethink some inference or assumption. The net is thus not divided into the certain and the speculative, and indeed it is not even divided sharply into observable elements and theoretical elements. (1986a, p. 40)

Here Scriven brings value claims into the net:

> In fact, the net is not even divisible into factual and value elements because concepts like true and false ... are not sharply distinct from correct and incorrect, right and wrong, valid and invalid, sound and unsound, good and bad, proper and improper. It is of the essence of knowledge that the factual is connected with the evaluative because the distinction between knowledge and mistaken belief is itself evaluative. (1986a, p. 40)

Value claims "are supportable in principle by a mixture of factual claims and other value claims; and value claims are refutable in the same way as all other claims, theoretical or observational" (1986a, pp. 40-41).

When Scriven discusses empirical and scientific investigation of theoretical and observational claims, including value claims, he has in mind an "*intensely* practical" exercise (1986b, p. 1) intended to make a plausible inference. While he would welcome development of a logic or a scientific method that guaranteed a valid answer, he is pessimistic this goal could be achieved for most important knowledge claims. He wants to develop a "probative" logic that can be applied to evaluative logic as a special case. *Probative* means a model of "practical . . . reasoning of the kitchen, surgery and workshop, the law courts, paddock, office and battlefield; and of the disciplines" (1986b, p. 1). In these latter situations, as in evaluation,

> it is enough . . . that the indicators point a certain way, and that there are none so strong pointing the other way. . . . Reasoning is a practical matter; it cannot wait on the progress of science any more than accounting can attend the elimination of problems in the foundations of mathematics or speaking can attend the formalization of linguistics. (1986b, p. 30)

So the science of valuing must attend more to the probative logic of practical reasoning, to establishing the plausibility of its findings about value, than to adherence to any particular method. This is not license for sloppy reasoning; Scriven is quite concerned with bias control in probative reasoning.

Scriven's theory of evaluation practice follows from these notions about the empirical status of values. We will elaborate that theory of practice in a later section on Scriven's logic of valuing. But first we consider preliminary matters about the context of a science of valuing.

The Social Need for a Science of Valuing

Society requires a science of valuing because it requires systematic, unbiased means of knowing if its products, personnel, and programs are good. Scriven wants evaluation to have this function. He argues that evaluands (his word for the things being evaluated) are good if they meet important needs, and that evaluators should look "for the need that is best matched by the actual performance and the performance that best matches some group of needs" (1981b, p. 130). Lacking such a mechanism, society has no systematic means of allocating social resources; waste, fraud, and incompetence would go undetected; and social and consumer needs would be filled haphazardly.

Scriven sees evaluation as serving the interests of all those affected by the entity being evaluated. He calls this a consumerist ideology: "The essential point of the consumerist ideology in evaluation is that all parties affected by something that is being evaluated should be taken into account" (1983a, p. 249). Scriven does not mean serving only the person who directly consumes the product. Rather, he means something like the "public interest" (1976a, p. 220):

> It is crucial to see that the evaluation point of view is not the manager's point of view, and is not simply the consumer's point of view; it is a point of view which should stand above identification with either of these parties, but make clear to each the importance of the other. (1980, p. 103)

He elaborates:

> The doctrine refers to the ultimate purchaser of whatever it is that is being evaluated. That is not always the same as the ultimate consumer or user or beneficiary; those who pay for research on radical mastectomy or optimal diets for astronauts, i.e., all of us, do not all expect to use the results of the research. Nor can those results be said to provide a benefit to all taxpayers in the sense of providing something which they value, perhaps because of direct pay-off for a relative or for the society as a whole. There are a good many taxpayers who value neither relatives nor the common good. (1976a, pp. 218-219)

Scriven aims to serve the public interest in evaluation, not the interests of any particular group.

Cost-free evaluation. Although the public interest demands evaluation, it is not justified in each instance. Referring to "cost-free evaluation" (attributed to Daniel Stufflebeam), Scriven says that "evaluations . . . should meet the standard of providing a positive cost-benefit balance" (1976a, p. 217). Evaluators should demonstrate to "the ultimate purchaser of whatever it is that is being evaluated" (p. 218), and to "a number of other parties involved with an evaluation" (p. 219), that the fiscal benefits of the evaluation will probably exceed the costs of doing an evaluation. If not, "the evaluation should not be done" (p. 220).

Formative and summative evaluation. Evaluations can be designed and used in two ways to make social programs and social products more responsive to social needs:

> Evaluation may be done to provide feedback to people who are trying to improve something (formative evaluation); or to provide information for decision-makers who are wondering whether to fund, terminate, or purchase something (summative evaluation). (Scriven, 1980, pp. 6-7)

Both formative and summative evaluation have an important place in Scriven's evaluation, but he prefers summative when a choice must be made (1986a). Reacting to Cronbach's (1963) advocacy of formative evaluation over summative, Scriven says:

> Thus, it may even be true that "the greatest service evaluation can perform is to identify aspects of the course where revision is desirable" (Cronbach, p. 236), though it is not clear how one would establish this, but it is certainly also true that there are other extremely important evaluation services which must be done for almost any given curriculum project or other educational innovation. And there are many contexts in which calling in an evaluator to perform a final evaluation of the project or person is an act of proper recognition of responsibility to the person, product, or taxpayers. (1972a, p. 125)

Even when formative evaluation is undertaken, it should be in the service of summative evaluation: "Good formative evaluation normally involves giving the best possible simulation of a summative evaluation" (1974, p. 9).

Practical trade-offs often force the evaluator to choose between formative and summative evaluation. Inherent difficulties in formative evaluation, such as requiring knowledge beyond knowing that something worked, prevent one from doing a good job at it. Hence Scriven prefers summative:

> There is often an urgent necessity to choose between sound summative evaluation and relatively unreliable and more expensive formative evaluation. It is fairly easy to evaluate teachers on the basis of their success, where one can get appropriate comparison groups set up; but it is not a consequence of the validity of this evaluation that one can give any advice whatsoever to the teachers who perform less well as to how to improve their performance. The reason for this is not only that the best approach to summative evaluation is often holistic; it is also that we lack the grounded theory to provide the appropriate explanations. (1983a, p. 247)

Recently, Scriven (1986a) has elaborated some of these points, softening the distinction between formative and summative evaluation, so that summative evaluation can improve the overall evaluand by replacing weak components. But Scriven's fundamental preference for summative evaluation remains intact.

Avoiding Bias

Scriven wants to minimize the many biases that can intrude when one is constructing value statements (1972b, 1973, 1976b, 1983a). He is not saying biases can be avoided; rather, the evaluator can be explicit about biases and establish safeguards against undue or unacknowledged bias. These safeguards should be part of the code of practice that guides evaluation. The safeguard he recommends depends on the source of the bias, and he always recommends multiple safeguards.

Some biases stem from organizational and administrative arrangements and require cognate safeguards. Examples include evaluators who elevate management interests above others, who develop divided loyalties between the evaluand and funder, who belong to the staff of the agency being evaluated (internal evaluators) and have difficulty being objective, and who are co-opted by the agency being evaluated and become program advocates (Scriven, 1976b, 1983a). Solutions include organizational and administrative arrangements granting independent funding, administrative independence, and emotional distance from an agency (Scriven, 1976b). Scriven says that "it is extremely difficult to dismiss the arguments for external evaluation" (1976b, p. 125). He suggests rotating evaluators through tours of duty in different locations every few years, like in the armed forces or diplomatic corps, to discourage their co-optation into local structures.

Another common bias is the tendency to judge the program using goals that program management and staff use. The evaluator's job, according to Scriven, is to locate any and all program effects, intended or not, that might help solve social problems. Goals are a poor source of such effects. Goals are often vaguely worded to muster political support, and rarely reflect side effects that are difficult to predict. Program management and staff may have a particularly biased view of goals. For example, to look successful they may nominate feasible goals and avoid more important goals that are hard to achieve. From the beginning, the evaluator must struggle to avoid such biases:

> The crucial time to insulate the . . . evaluator is, fortunately, that time when it is easiest, namely, when forming the overall picture and preliminary hypotheses and questions that emerge as the evaluation design. (Scriven, 1974, p. 61)

Scriven advises evaluators to conduct "goal-free" evaluations (also called "needs-referenced" evaluation; 1980, p. 103). Goal-free evaluators begin evaluations "totally blind" (1976b, p. 137) to stated goals: "In evaluation, blind is beautiful. Remember that Justice herself is blind, and good medical research is double blind" (1973, p. 322). Goal-free evaluation is like double-blind methodologies used in medical studies, where neither the patient nor the physician knows which drug is which, nor which drug will produce which effects. In goal-free evaluations, not only the patient and the physician, but also the experimenter, does not know what effects to expect. The goal-free evaluator avoids contact with program staff who bias the conceptualization of the evaluation questions:

> The goal-free evaluator is totally insulated from any direct contact with project people at all, is not allowed to talk with them about goals nor vice versa, is not allowed to get long histories of the project, and so on. He doesn't, in fact, communicate with the people that run it. (Salasin, 1974, p. 10)

Goal-free evaluation "will make the observer-evaluator struggle hard to find any and all effects, without prejudice, since his or her reputation is on the line" (Scriven, 1976b, p. 137). Evaluators "have to *discover* what effect" the program has, and match "their effects against the needs of those whom they affect" (Scriven, 1983a, p. 235). Perhaps neither goal-free nor needs-based evaluation is the most accurate label. The former omits the connection to needs, and the latter does not emphasize discovery of effects. "Needs-based, effect-discovery" evaluation is accurate, but without the elegance and memorability of Scriven's neologism. Goal-free evaluation is probably most similar to Stake's case study approach to evaluation in emphasizing discovery; but Scriven differs from Stake in prioritizing on effects and in matching effects to needs.

The Key Evaluation Checklist
and Metaevaluation

After data have been collected, analyzed, and synthesized, the evaluator can bias the evaluation when writing the final report. Scriven suggests making such biases explicit by making drafts of the report available to critics prior to final printing:

> In particular, this has to mean that preliminary recommendations from the evaluator are going to be circulated to all affected for response, that (company) time will be arranged for discussion by those affected with each other and then — with their counter-recommendations, if any — there will be appropriate arrangements for a convergence meeting. Preferably there should be a neutral party present at that meeting whose recommendations will be attached unedited to the evaluation if it is to have external circulation or is being done for an external client such as a funding agency. (Of course, the counter-recommendations of the affected parties should also be attached unedited to any such report.) (1976a, pp. 220-221)

Auditing a final report is a special case of *metaevaluation* (Scriven, 1969) — controlling bias by making sure "the evaluators get evaluated"

(Scriven, 1976b, p. 126). Scriven recommends that evaluations be evaluated using his standard evaluation concepts and methods. To do so, evaluators can use the Key Evaluation Checklist (1980, pp. 113-116) (see Table 3.1), which is normally applied to evaluating social programs, but which the metaevaluator applies to evaluating evaluation. The metaevaluator would ask who the client is for the evaluation, what the need is for evaluation, and what it will cost, how it is implemented, what effects it might have, and so forth. The checklist has appeared in several forms (Scriven, 1974, 1980, 1981b, 1983a); the version in Table 3.1 is adapted from the 1980 work (the 1974 version was the "thirteenth iteration"; 1974, p. 11).

Scriven's (1983a) "multimodel" of evaluation deserves mention here, both because it follows from the Key Evaluation Checklist and because its fundamental function seems to be bias control. Evaluation is *multifield*, concerned with programs, products, proposals, personnel, plans, and potentials; *multidisciplinary*; with *multidimensionality* of criteria of merit; needing *multiple perspectives* before synthesis is done; *multilevel* in the "wide range of levels of validity/cost/credibility among which a choice must be made in order to remain within the resources of time and budget" (1983a, p. 257) and in the different levels of analysis, evidential support, and documentation appropriate in different circumstances; using *multiple methodologies, multiple functions, multiple impacts, multiple reporting formats*: "Evaluation is a multiplicity of multiples" (Scriven, 1983a, p. 257).

The Key Evaluation Checklist instantiates the multimodel by portraying multiple dimensions that evaluators must consider in doing evaluations, and evaluators should consider and use multiple approaches to assessing each dimension. This emphasis on multiplicity is epistemologically motivated to construct a picture of truth from multiple vantage points — consistent with Scriven's perspectivist epistemology. The more different the vantage points taken, the better the picture of the truth that is constructed:

> If we were searching for truth, we would realize that radical perspectives often uncover the truth and can demonstrate it to the satisfaction of all panelists. And we would realize that establishment-selected judges are likely to be blind to some of the more deep-seated biases of the institution. (Scriven, 1983a, p. 251)

The multimodel of evaluation encompasses much of Scriven's past writings on evaluation. Goal-free evaluation, metaevaluation, and formative and summative evaluation are all component parts of a multimodel to reduce bias in evaluation.

Table 3.1 Scriven's Key Evaluation Checklist

(1) *Description:* What is to be evaluated?

(2) *Client:* Who is commissioning the evaluation?

(3) *Background and context* of the evaluand and the evaluation.

(4) *Resources* available to or for use of the evaluand, and of the evaluators.

(5) *Function:* What does the evaluand do?

(6) *Delivery system:* How does the evaluand reach the market?

(7) *Consumer:* Who is using or receiving the (effects of) the evaluand?

(8) *Needs and values* of the impacted and potentially impacted population.

(9) *Standards:* Are there any preexisting objectively validated standards of merit or worth that apply?

(10) *Process:* What constraints/costs/benefits apply to the normal operation of the evaluand?

(11) *Outcomes:* What effects are produced by the evaluand?

(12) *Generalizability* to other people/places/times/versions.

(13) *Costs:* Dollar versus psychological versus personnel; initial versus repeated; direct/indirect versus immediate/delayed/discounted.

(14) *Comparisons* with alternative options.

(15) *Significance:* A synthesis of all the above.

(16) *Recommendations:* These may or may not be requested, and may or may not follow from the evaluation.

(17) *Report:* Vocabulary, length, format, medium, time, location, and personnel for its presentation need careful scrutiny.

(18) *Metaevaluation:* The evaluation must be evaluated, preferably prior to (a) implementation, (b) final dissemination of report. External evaluation is desirable, but first the primary evaluator should apply the Key Evaluation Checklist to the evaluation itself. Results of the metaevaluation should be used formatively but may also be incorporated in the report or otherwise conveyed (summatively) to the client and other appropriate audiences. ("Audiences" emerge at metacheckpoint 7, since they are the "market" and "consumers" of the evaluation.)

SOURCE: Adapted from Scriven (1980, pp. 113-116).

The Logic of Evaluation

Scriven wants to give practical advice "to clarify the underlying logic of evaluation, in a way that will improve practice" (1980, p. 117). If evaluation theory "doesn't come up with those practical recommendations, spelled out in detail, it is rightly regarded as no more than philosophical musings" (1986a, p. 29). He starts with a logic of evaluation: "The most common type of evaluation involves determining criteria of merit (usually from a needs assessment), standards of merit (frequently as a result of looking for appropriate comparisons), and then determining the performance of the evaluand so as to compare it against these standards" (1980, p. 18). This definition suggests three key activities — criteria determination, setting standards, and measuring performance. Criteria determination identifies the dimensions on which the evaluand must do well to be good. Standards of merit tell how well the evaluand must do on each dimension to be good — one can use absolute standards such as the certain minimum safety level that all automobiles must attain, or comparative standards comparing the evaluand to available alternatives. Assessing performance requires measuring the evaluand and comparing the results to the standards of merit. Scriven adds two corollaries to this logic. Prior to the three activities, the evaluator selects an object to be evaluated. After the performance tests, the evaluator summarizes results in an evaluative judgment. Scriven's practice of evaluation stems from this logic. Hence we now examine it in more detail.

Choice of Object

For Scriven, the choice of evaluand is secondary to the logic of evaluation. If asked what can be evaluated, he says: "Everything. One can begin at the beginning of a dictionary and go through to the end, and every noun, common or proper, calls to mind a context in which evaluation would be appropriate" (1980, p. 4). He bemoans the fact that evaluation is associated with social programs, because distinctions between program evaluations and other evaluations are artificial:

> Evaluating programs, particularly if one is interested in improving them, sometimes involves personnel evaluation. For one of the improvements that one must sometimes recommend is a change in the personnel. The same essential involvement sometimes occurs with product evaluation, as drug programs, for example, require one to look at the materials used. (1986a, p. 14)

His cursory treatment of choice of evaluands is a deliberate attempt at "broadening the horizons" and "unpacking the logic of all types of evaluation" (1980, p. 6).

But in most of Scriven's writings, he uses two examples of evaluands. The first is consumer products; he refers to *Consumer Reports* as a good model for evaluation. The second is educational evaluation, but he treats educational evaluation much like product evaluation (1973). He discusses small components of educational programs that resemble products in being relatively small, contained units, such as teachers or textbooks. But he assumes his theory is broad enough to apply to all evaluands: "The concept of 'product,' as used here, is very broad, covering processes and institutions as well as technical devices" (1974, p. 7).

Whatever the object is, it serves a critical function in Scriven's theory: It is the major source of questions to ask. The goal-free evaluator ignores program goals in formulating questions, looking for all possible important effects that the evaluand might have. But this universe of possible effects is large, so how is the evaluator to narrow this range to a more tractable number (Scriven, 1973)? Scriven says that the evaluand provides this information: *"The data on the treatment is what cuts the problem down to size.* I have the knowledge about probable or possible effects of treatments like that, from the research and evaluation literature and from my experience, that enables me to avoid the necessity for examining all possible variants" (1973, p. 322). In education, for example, the goal-free evaluator infers potential effects from sample materials, descriptions by observers of classroom process, information on treatment length, teachers' handbooks, and tests. Staff are not always ignored: "When the field staff do not know the goals of the program, except in the most obvious and general sense, and are only allowed to talk to the program's clients rather than program staff, then they are much more likely to pick up on other effects" (1983a, p. 237). To find unintended side effects of the evaluand, "one uses the needs of the patient — or client, or consumer, or user, or student" (1983a, p. 235), seeing if the evaluand had any effects that meet these needs.

Criteria of Merit

The starting point for constructing criteria of merit is an understanding of the evaluand:

> Once one understands the nature of the evaluand, . . . one will often understand rather fully what it takes to be a better and a worse instance of that type of evaluand. Understanding what a watch is leads automatically to understanding what the *dimensions* of merit for one are — time-keeping accuracy, legibility, sturdiness, etc. (Scriven, 1980, pp. 90-91)

If *dimensions* is synonymous with *criteria* (Scriven, 1986a), this implies that criteria of merit stem from descriptors of the evaluand — but not just any descriptor. Criteria of merit are the subset of descriptors "that are merit-connected" (1980, p. 49). To identify merit-connected dimensions, a descriptor must be joined to a needs assessment, for "nothing will have any value" (1974, p. 12) if it is not needed. Criteria of merit are descriptors of an evaluand that bear on its capacity to meet needs: "The engines that drive evaluation . . . should be viewed as studies of needs *or* wants *or* ideals that are appropriate for the particular evaluand" (1980, p. 90).

Needs are costs: "A needs assessment essentially looks at the costs of a failure to meet certain standards, and the evaluation is predicated upon a decision about the point at which these costs become excessive" (1980, p. 91):

> Roughly speaking, needs are met by anything which yields performance above what is to count as a minimum satisfactory level in a particular context; wants come into play from that point on, though they are of course subject to certain types of corrections based upon ignorance, or carelessness about ethical obligations; and finally we drive towards ideals, realizing that they will infrequently be attainable, providing only a direction for improvement. (1980, p. 91)

A need is always a presumption; it relies on "presumptive or prima facie inference. . . . It creates a presumption, which is potentially attackable, rebuttable — and often defensible" (1980, p. 25). For example:

> We have good reason to suppose that . . . the physically handicapped need access to school buildings in order to acquire any substantial level of educational achievement. But the matter can be disputed, and if evidence can be brought to show that they can do at least as well by studying at home — the social interaction losses not being significant — then our conclusions about good design of school buildings will have to be modified. (1980, p. 93)

The need is a presumed cost to society and the individual of denying the handicapped access to education in school buildings. The relevant criteria of merit are all characteristics of school buildings that influence access for the handicapped — the conjunction of school building characteristics with the need of the physically handicapped for education. Because this need is only a defensible presumption, it can be disputed.

Scriven's concept of need is catholic and admits many determinants:

> In scoring need, the following should be taken into account: the number of people involved, social significance (compensatory justice or some other factor), urgency, possible multiplicative effects (for example, the need for tool skills is not just a function of immediate utility but also of how much other accomplishments depend on them). (1974, p. 13)

This approach allows evaluators with diverse conceptions of need (or justice or ethics or value) to practice their craft under a common logic. Those who believe that the needs of the disadvantaged should be paramount can use that as a criterion; those who prefer to judge programs by their ability to create the greatest total good for the greatest number can do so.

Sometimes a formal needs assessment is available. Often, product developers do one during product development. The evaluator may use that information. But the evaluator should sometimes do an independent needs analysis:

> It is of course ludicrous to assume either that managers (or those who employ them) always do needs assessment, or always do valid needs assessments, or that any such needs assessments, even if done and valid, will still be valid years later when the time has come to evaluate the program. Needs change, not only because we come to recognize new ones, but because programs come and go, population demographics change, the state of the economy varies, and the extent to which needs have been already met varies. Hence up-to-date needs assessment – or something equivalent to this, such as the functional analysis that is often a surrogate for needs assessment in the case of product evaluation – is an essential part of any serious evaluation. (Scriven, 1983a, p. 235)

The product developer does a needs assessment as the first step in product development, but the program evaluator may not want to do it first. The goal-free evaluator aims to find effects whether or not they meet needs. Doing a needs assessment can distract from this primary task. But having identified effects, the evaluator searches for needs that those effects might meet, which can be done after the evaluation. As goal-free evaluators accumulate experience, they will bring some knowledge of relevant needs to a particular evaluation; this knowledge will affect question formation.

Scriven does not much discuss methodologies for needs assessments. He notes:

> They do not always require large-scale surveys or detailed testing. One of the most straightforward procedures for doing needs assessment, although it is sometimes thought of as excessively a priori, is based upon an analysis and consequent definition of function. In a recent issue of *Consumer Reports*, for example, a quite good evaluation of barbecue sauces was done, which began with a "needs assessment" of the functional analysis kind: A good barbecue sauce should not be so strongly flavored as to obliterate the flavor of the meat itself, nor should it be so mild as to add nothing. (1981b, p. 131)

Scriven characteristically prefers exploring the logical requirements of the task, rather than relying on formal methodologies that may not be needed in specific cases (1972b).

Standards of Merit

Next, the evaluator creates standards of acceptable performance on criteria of merit. Standards are constructed by comparison: "It is a principal maxim of product evaluation as expounded here that it is very rarely useful unless comparative, and that even what appears to be evaluation of isolated products virtually always turns out to be implicitly comparative" (Scriven, 1981b, p. 136). Comparisons can be with another product or program that could meet the needs, or with a set level of performance. For instance, the evaluator can compare a car's repair record to a minimally acceptable standard (e.g., results from a needs assessment about minimum bumper crash absorption) or to the records of other cars. Scriven prefers the latter option since it adds information to the former option that consumers need if they are to choose: "It would be totally misleading for an evaluator to recommend purchase of an automobile or to say that is was a good automobile when in fact it was the worst available for the money, although it would in fact do what was necessary and could be purchased by using up all the resources available" (1981b, p. 137). He adds that "evaluation is usually supposed to serve decision making, and decision making is choosing between alternatives, and if evaluation does not look at the comparative merits of the alternatives it is not serving decision making" (p. 137).

For Scriven, consumers need to know about "critical competitors" (1981b, p. 137)—feasible options likely to meet their needs. So one compares a Honda Accord with a Toyota Camry, but not with a Lincoln Continental or a Jeep. Critical competitors are not always obvious; the evaluator must be creative in identifying them. For example, "when Consumers Union tested rug cleaners, instead of falling into the natural trap of only comparing products which were called rug cleaners by their manufacturers, they ran all of those against each other *and* against a general purpose laundry detergent, Tide. An appropriately diluted sample of Tide turned out to beat the specialty rug cleaners" (1981b, pp. 141-142). Scriven relates the case of insufficient elevator capacity in a school building, which upset those waiting. One need might be for more elevator capacity, with the critical competitors being more elevators or more visible indicators of elevator location. Both these options were too costly. The consultant solved the problem by installing mirrors near the elevators into which students could gaze, distracting them from their impatience—the consultant satisfied a more basic need. A final example is a computer-assisted program package compared to a traditional programmed textbook; the latter did as well at a fraction of the cost.

Assessing Performance

Scriven avoids detailed discussion of methods for this step. He says the appropriate design is one "that will lead (or will probably lead, or in the weakest case may lead) to an answer to a particular question. The criteria of merit for a good assessment plan are the cost and time and resources needed for the investigation, the probability of getting an answer at all, and the probability that the answer is correct; usually some trade-offs have to be made" (1980, p. 45). The design is driven by the question, the certainty of the answer provided by the design is only one consideration in choosing a design, and sometimes the evaluator cannot provide a good answer to the questions.

What are the questions of interest for Scriven's evaluator, and what designs are appropriate for each? In addition to questions about needs, these include

> pre-evaluative questions, evaluative questions, and non-evaluative questions, *all of which* may be a part of an evaluator's job to answer. In saying that a question is non-evaluative, we're not saying that it is no business of the evaluator, only that it cannot be the main business of the evaluator. These other questions have often an important ancillary role, but they do not in themselves require an answer that is evaluative. (Scriven, 1980, p. 46)

The central — and only strictly evaluative — questions in evaluation are variants on "Is the evaluand good?": How good is it? How much is it worth? What components of it are good? In what respects is it good? Is it good compared to alternatives? and What combination of it and its alternatives is worth most? (Scriven, 1980). Since these are variants on cause-effect questions, he favors methods yielding confident answers about effects:

> One way or another, it must be shown that the effects reported could not reasonably be attributed to something other than the treatment or product. No way of doing this compares well with the fully controlled experiment, and ingenuity can expand its use into most situations. (1974, p. 16)

However, Scriven is not as vigorous an advocate of experimental methodologies as is Campbell. First, Scriven emphasizes relevance to the evaluative question over routine adherence to method. He sometimes prefers a poorer answer to the right question: "Crude measurements are not as good as refined measurements, but they beat the hell out of the judgements of those with vested interests" (1983a, p. 253). For example, about site visit evaluations of educational programs, Scriven observes:

> Such obvious devices as setting up a suggestion box on the campus during the site visit, providing an answering machine to record comments by those who wish to call them in anonymously, or careful selection of the most severe critics of the institution from among those who are interviewed are practices that one rarely if ever encounters. (1983a, p. 252)

Second, practical constraints mean that "we must frequently face the need to do the best we can with nonexperimental data" (1976c, p. 102). He advises the evaluator to develop fallback options to deal with this situation; "the order of preference in evaluation design begins with the truly experimental, moves after that to the quasi-experimental, then moves to the *modus operandi*, and only finally moves to a descriptive *ex post facto*" (Salasin, 1974, p. 16).

Modus operandi (MO) is a method Scriven (1976c) developed for inferring cause when better methods are not practical. The MO method borrows from detective work — a detective compares clues from a crime to a known pattern of clues left by various suspects, eliminating those criminals whose MO (method of operating) does not fit the observed pattern. When an effect is observed, the evaluator may be able to list possible causes and check for the presence of these causes, hoping to find that only one was present. If many causes are present, the evaluator notes the pattern of evidence that each cause would leave if it was the active causal agent, narrowing causal inference to the cause indicated by the pattern of evidence that was found.

The choice of methods for answering strictly evaluative questions hinges on prior knowledge, constraints, and the relevance of the method to the question. Early in an evaluation, the evaluator might have little prior knowledge to allow for quick and precise tests of specific effects. Broad correlational methods might be appropriate at this stage to identify candidates for more rigorous tests. Scriven did this in evaluating Title VII:

> We use the first year to identify by correlation analysis the best looking candidates for good programs. In the second year, we focus on them and really look to see if we can find anything in them that might be exportable. In the third year, we export it and see if it'll work in a different environment. (Salasin, 1974, p. 16)

But Scriven wants evaluators to know the limits of their work, and to acknowledge when the methods used do not clarify a product's effects: "If there is some doubt, for example, whether the results were due to the treatment . . . then the merit of materials must be judged less positively" (Scriven, 1974, p. 18).

Scriven discusses other (not strictly evaluative) questions for which the above methods are less appropriate — preevaluative and quasi-evaluative questions (1980). Preevaluative questions describe the evaluand and its circumstances, so the evaluator can properly label the cause. These are construct validity questions (Cronbach & Meehl, 1955) of the form, What is the evaluand? But they include other descriptive questions as well, such as, Who values the evaluand? Quasi-evaluative questions concern the factors that cause an evaluand's effects, or that could be manipulated to change those effects. Such causal explanation questions are of the form, What makes the evaluand good? and What will make it better? These questions serve formative evaluation, but Scriven's preference for summative evaluation leads him to give such questions lower priority than strictly evaluative questions.

Scriven is ambiguous about the importance of preevaluative and quasi-evaluative questions. The goal-free evaluator should focus mostly on identifying and comparing program effects to standards of merit. One need not ever address pre- or quasi-evaluative questions to do so; and the evaluation need not include recommendations for remediation (quasi-evaluative questions) — "They do not follow automatically from the conclusions of all evaluations" (Scriven, 1983a, p. 259). But the Key Evaluation Checklist (KEC) lists pre- and quasi-evaluative questions as "necessitata" (Scriven, 1983a, p. 258), suggesting that "competent evaluation must cover each of these points" (1974, p. 7). Scriven also says that description and process are among "the many dimensions that must be explored prior to the final synthesis in an evaluation" (1980, p. 113), and "it is relatively rarely that one can afford to dispense with at least a quick professional check on each of the checkpoints mentioned" (1983a, p. 258) in the KEC, often iteratively:

> One can't answer all the questions that come up under each of the early headings in adequate detail until one has studied some of the later dimensions; and, having studied them, one must come back and rewrite an earlier treatment, which will in turn force one to refine the later analysis that depends on the former. In designing and in critiquing evaluations, as well as in carrying one out, one is never quite done with this checklist. (1983a, p. 258)

So while the goal-free evaluator prioritizes on needs and effects, that evaluator must also study the other dimensions on the Key Evaluation Checklist. How much? Scriven is unclear. Presumably the evaluand should be described enough to be identifiable and discriminable from other entities. Presumably the evaluator ought to note causal mechanisms that mediate effects if they are known from previous work or from observation:

> The present thesis is that the search for explanations of performances, whether they are defined by reference to an evaluative or a purely descriptive scale, is not the professional turf of the evaluator; it is a standard type of problem for any social scientist. But the converse applies; since evaluators are often well-trained social scientists, they are no worse-equipped to do such an investigation than others and may sometimes be the best choice for the job. In taking it on, however, they not only change hats but they abandon an area which is extremely

short-handed, and the decision should be made carefully and consciously, not because it "all seemed like part of the same problem." (Scriven, 1980, p. 80)

Scriven has little to say about specific methods for answering pre- and quasi-evaluative questions. In one instance, he notes that "process observation is necessary" (1974, p. 16). Even his most expansive lists are brief, noting that the methods range "from participant observation to teacher interview to sampling from a list of educational variables" (1973, p. 323), and include "interviews, opinion surveys, and reporting" (1980, p. 49). It is characteristic of Scriven's theory that he devotes more attention to assessment of effects than of process. The goal-free evaluator's central task is finding effects; methods for doing so are the most important thing.

Emphasis on strictly evaluative questions does not require substantive theory about the functioning of the evaluand:

> There's absolutely no need for the theory. When you're evaluating television sets, you do not need to know the difference between a capacitor and a transistor. You only need to know the difference between a good and a bad picture. (Salasin, 1974, p. 13)

Substantive theory is relevant to quasi-evaluative questions, and to re-mediating a deficient evaluand by explicating the processes that mediate its bad effect. But even here, substantive theory is not necessary to remediation:

> Many remedies emerge without benefit of theories. . . . Nor does this occur only through accidental discovery. There is a systematic process for discovering remedies — part of it mechanized in antibiotic and other areas of drug research — which uses analogies, variations, and successive approximations to hunt them down. Or one may go after them using Polya-type problem-solving approaches, e.g., by working outward from a definition of the solution, an approach which one might call the attempt to generate a theory of the remedies instead of a theory of the problem. For example, a remedy for the deficit spending of a toll-bridge has often been found in conversion to one-way collection of a double toll. This is a highly ingenious remedy, but it doesn't come from a theory. (Scriven, 1980, p. 88)

Substantive theory is not necessary for summative evaluation, not the only route to remediation, and not the only means of guiding formative evaluation (Scriven, 1986a). Given Scriven's pessimism about the strength of current substantive theories, he may not see substantive theory as a practically desirable route to remediation.

Synthesizing Results

At this point the evaluator will have many data. One option is to present these results to the client to make sense of them, but Scriven prefers that the evaluator sum the results into a final evaluative judgment:

> It's his task to try very hard to condense all that mass of data into one word: *good*, or, *bad*. Sometimes this really is impossible, but all too often the failure to do so is simply a cop-out disguised as or rationalized as objectivity. (1971, p. 53)

This synthesis is not just statistical, but evaluative. A multivariate analysis of variance could provide a summary of the statistical significance of the effects of two educational programs, but Scriven (1974) requires that the summary also tell if it represents "an educationally significant result" (1974, p. 17).

How does he recommend that this be done? Using the Key Evaluation Checklist in synthesizing results, the evaluator assesses the presence and nature of the information about the evaluand called for in the first 14 categories of the checklist. All this information must be present "in order to provide a firm basis for a conclusion of merit when considering an educational product" (Scriven, 1974, p. 11). The evaluator can then assign a numerical index of merit to each category. For the "need" category of the 1974 checklist, Scriven (1974, p. 13) suggests using a needs assessment to determine where the need met by the evaluand falls on the following scale:

maximum priority, a desperate need   4
a need of great importance   3
a probably significant need   2
a possibly significant need   1
no good evidence of significant need   0

Scriven (1974) suggests similar scales for other KEC categories. A tabular or graphical presentation of these numbers quickly summarizes the merit of the evaluand.

Scriven would not stop at this exhibition of performance, for that would be "passing the buck to the non-professional, and represents far less than the appropriate response by a professional evaluator" (1983a, p. 248). Next one must summarize data over dimensions. Cost-benefit analysis does this by translating all inputs and outputs into monetary units (Scriven, 1983a), yielding a single cost-benefit ratio that summarizes net fiscal gains or losses. The "weighted sum" method (Scriven, 1981b, 1983a) could also be used, which

> consists of identifying the desirable functions or qualities, assigning them weights depending upon their importance, doing performance testing to discover the extent to which each of these functions or qualities are present in each of the critical competitors, assigning a point score to each critical competitor on each of these dimensions to reflect its performance (such as on a scale of one to ten), multiplying the weights by the scores, and summing the results for each critical competitor. We then identify the product with the highest score as being the best buy. (1981b, p. 162)

Problems exist in selecting and justifying weights, in assuming linearity and additivity, and in assigning some dimensions a critical status prior to summing (Scriven, 1981a). Hence "absent a precise formula, there is a great deal of intercase and interjudge variation in the way the elements are weighted and interacted" (1986a, p. 27). New information, new products, new perspectives on the effects of a product, new uses that are discovered for a product, and other perturbations during the analysis all force the evaluator to redo the summary many times (Scriven, 1981b, 1982). Different weighting systems, or different judges of the same data, can produce discrepant overall evaluations that must be remedied (Scriven, 1981b). Therefore, "expect to redo everything several times. Accept no solution about which you feel the least doubt as you reflect on it" (Scriven, 1982, p. 93).

OUR ANALYSIS OF
SCRIVEN'S THEORY OF EVALUATION

Scriven is the first and only major evaluation theorist to have an explicit and general theory of valuing. His logic of evaluation — selecting criteria of merit, setting standards, and assessing performance — is always implicit in evaluation but rarely appreciated by evaluators. He teaches evaluators to ask "What must this object do to be good?" to give program effects explicit social meaning. The power of Scriven's logic is best acknowledged by noting that it structured the present book — establishing criteria of merit for evaluation theory, describing theories on those criteria, and comparing theories with each other and with the lessons of the last 20 years.

Theory of Valuing

Scriven's logic as a metatheory of valuing. In Chapter 2, we distinguished among (a) metatheories about the nature of and rationale for valuing, (b) descriptive theories about values people hold, and (c) prescriptive theories about which values should have priority. Scriven's logic is primarily a metatheory in the analytical philosophy tradition. His logic can be found in general form in other treatments of value theory by philosophers:

> Evaluation consists in bringing together two things: (1) an *object* to be evaluated, and (2) a *valuation*, providing the framework in terms of which evaluations can be made. The bringing together of these two is mediated by (3) a *criterion* of evaluation that embodies the standards in terms of which the standing of the object within the valuation framework is determined. (Rescher, 1969, p. 72)

Rescher and Scriven use the word *criterion* to mean the same thing. Rescher's *valuation* is what Scriven means by *standards*:

> We shall refer to the systematic apparatus by means of which the realization of a value is assessed as a *valuation*. . . . A valuation may be *purely comparative* . . . or it may be *metric* and afford machinery for actually numerical measurements. (Rescher, 1969, p. 65)

Both Scriven (1966) and Rescher (1969) acknowledge the influence of Kurt Baier on their thinking about values.

Scriven's logic is compelling. In its bare-bones form, it is difficult to think of a value statement that could not be subjected to it. To reject the logic of valuing is to reject rational analysis of values entirely. Emotivists, for example, might say that values have nothing to do with evidence or rationality, that values are determined totally by personal preferences, and that no value statement is better supported than another (Ayer, 1936; Beauchamp, 1982; MacIntyre, 1981). No evaluation theorist in this book holds this position. All assume that evidence, logic, and rationality play a role in judging the value of social programs. They merely differ over how to implement Scriven's logic.

But Scriven has not presented just a bare-bones logic; he has fleshed out those bones in some objectionable ways. One objection is that Scriven's conception of needs implies a prescriptive theory of valuing, and that he disparages descriptive statements about what people think about the program. If this reading of Scriven is correct, this preference is insufficiently justified. If not, internal inconsistencies arise in his theory.

Unpacking the meaning of needs: the logic as a prescriptive theory. Prescriptive theories claim that some values have higher priority than others. The logic flirts with such prescriptions. Specifically, while the logic does not compel an evaluator to choose any particular criterion of merit, Scriven ties criteria to needs assessment. The leap from needs to prescriptive value theory is worth explicating. Contending that "even ethics itself had to be faced as a legitimate part of serious comprehensive program evaluation" (1983a, p. 234), Scriven refers to theories of justice as sources of criteria for evaluating social programs (1966, 1983a). Most pertinent, his definition of needs resembles the material principle of need that drives needs-based theories of justice (Rawls, 1971). Scriven says "a needs assessment essentially looks at the costs of a failure to meet certain standards, and the evaluation is predicated upon a decision about the point at which these costs become excessive" (1980, p. 91). Needs-based theories of justice use a similar definition: "To say that someone has a need for something is to say that the person will be harmed or detrimentally affected if that thing is not obtained" (Beauchamp, 1982, p. 241). But this latter prescriptive approach, a needs-based theory of justice, is just one theory of justice, and justice in turn is only one issue in ethics. Credible alternatives to Rawls (1971) exist, notably Nozick's (1974) libertarian theory. Moreover, while justice is a central moral concern in evaluation, so are human rights, equality, liberty, and utility. If one is to go the prescriptive route, all these topics could inform evaluation by suggesting a wider array of criteria of merit, and by providing perspective about the implications of the choice of any particular criterion (Bunda, 1985). Limiting evaluators to just one of these many prescriptive options is particularly problematic because none is widely accepted as best.

Many stakeholders in American social policy would dispute the assumptions and recommendations of needs-based theories of justice about redressing social inequities. One might dispute Rawls's assumption that reasonable people who knew nothing about their own fortuitous personal characteristics such as race, IQ, gender, family background, or special talents would opt to set up rules for justice that distribute resources evenly. They might prefer to take more risks in hopes of getting more resources. More important, the assumptions and recommendations of such egalitarian theorists of justice are probably not operational in U.S. social policy (Lindblom, 1977). When policy is being formed and implemented, participants in the policy process rarely seek to ensure that the needs of the most disadvantaged Americans are met before other needs. Lip service may be given to the "safety net" for the disadvantaged, but recent history suggests that policy may be shaped as much or more by defense policy, health care costs, taxes, and priorities that serve constituencies other than the disadvantaged. Selecting criteria of merit from needs-based theories of justice may result in evaluations that differ dramatically from the terms used in policy debates. This can minimize the usefulness of such evaluations.

Scriven could respond that his "presumptive" logic (1980) allows many criteria of merit to be selected, and that he is not committed to drawing criteria of merit from needs or from ethical theories at all. These two responses require different treatments. Scriven might allow evaluators to construct criteria from, say, Nozick's (1974) libertarian theory of justice, in which free choice is central and in which people can acquire, own, and distribute their wealth as they want if they follow agreed-upon rules and procedures — even if this results in inequities in wealth and income. Bunda (1985) discusses several ethical systems from which criteria of merit could be constructed. But the problems outlined in the previous paragraph occur in drawing criteria of merit from *any* prescriptive ethical theory.

On the other hand, Scriven's idea of presumptive need might allow drawing criteria from any source of needs, including stakeholder opinions. If Scriven intends this, it is inconsistent with his opposition to the "managerial" and "relativist" biases (1983a), which imply that all needs are not equal (or not all perceived needs are real needs). It is also inconsistent with this statement: "the needs assessment, the relevant professional standards, expert survey, functional or conceptual analysis, and so on. . . . To be sharply distinguished from a wants assessment ('market research') unless *no relevant needs* exist" (1983a, p. 259). Scriven seems to believe some criteria are more important than others, especially those drawn from material conception of needs.

Next we must address Scriven's rejection of a descriptive approach to values that selects criteria of merit from descriptions of values held by stakeholders. This is not the same as describing what stakeholders think about the evaluand; it is describing the evaluand in terms stakeholders understand. This approach identifies relevant stakeholder values, uses these to construct criteria and standards, and gathers and reports evaluative data in terms of those criteria. Unlike prescriptive valuing, the descriptive approach does not argue that any particular value should have priority. Most theorists have adopted a descriptive approach for two reasons. One is that the job of making value judgments belongs to citizens or their elected representatives, so that it is wrong to impose an ethical system by choice of criteria. The second is that couching value judgments in terms used by stakeholders facilitates use of evaluation in debates and decisions. Scriven seems to reject both these arguments. He rejects the argument "that it is the role of others to make appropriate normative, political and philosophical judgments" (1986a, p. 22; Scriven takes this quote from other authors but uses it in a manner consistent with our argument here); and he says that evaluative "conclusions will sometimes not reflect all of the values that will correctly enter into implementation decisions" (p. 23). He calls the purely descriptive approach "the 'lackey' view of evaluation research" (1986a, p. 23). That characterization conveys a sense of evaluator irresponsibility that is belied by the facts. In an interest group democracy like the United States, it may be very responsible to reflect the values held by stakeholders associated with a program in order to facilitate the use of evaluation results in policy-making. To the extent that serving the public good implies serving all the stakeholder groups that might be affected by the evaluand, it would seem sensible to speak to those groups to learn the criteria and standards to which they would hold the evaluand.

Our own view is that both descriptive and prescriptive approaches are required; no theorist has made an adequate place for both. We give priority to descriptive valuing, but would use prescriptive theories of valuing as a source of discipline about criteria and about ethical implications of certain choices. For example, if a U.S. senator asks if a program achieved its goal of deinstitutionalizing mental hospital patients, then it is responsible to answer that question. But it is also helpful and responsible to point out that the program is not meeting the needs of the deinstitutionalized patients who are now poor, homeless, and hungry. Both can be done responsibly.

The ambiguity of the public interest. Scriven frequently refers to the "public interest" (1976a, p. 220) or the "common good" (1976a, p. 219). This conception stands above and apart from the opinions held by stakeholders. Meeting social needs is as close as he comes to defining the public good. All the criticisms of the previous section apply to the notion of the public interest, as well. Here we raise a related but different criticism: The meaning attached to the "public interest" is far from clear.

Political scientists have debated the meaning of the term for years (Friedrich, 1962). Downs (1967) claims the public interest consists of the by-products of politicians trying to get elected. In seeking to increase their power, income, and prestige, politicians need votes, which they obtain by meeting the self-interests of their constituencies. The things they do to get those votes are the public interest. Downs is here at odds with Scriven, who says the public interest might differ from what voters want. Yet Downs's conception reflects the dominant understanding of public interest in political science — adherence to the structure and decision-making processes of a pluralistic, interest group democracy.

Schubert (1960) distinguishes among rationalist, idealist, and realist conceptions of the public interest. Rationalists postulate a common good defined by majority sentiments. The job of public officials is to execute this public will by translating it into government action. Idealists postulate a common good that is not isomorphic with public perceptions, but that arises from "whatever the still, small voice of conscience reveals to each official" (Schubert, 1960, p. 200). The public perception of the common good may be wrong, or the public may not have perceptions on some issues. The idealist conception of responsibility of public officials is to support the *true* interests of the public. Realists view all members of the policy-shaping community — political parties, public officials, voters in their many alliances — as interest groups. The common good is not an independent entity, not in the minds of the public or anywhere else. Rather, it is the result of the mediation of disputes among interest groups. Of these three, the realist position is probably most common in political science.

Scriven seems closest to the idealist conception. Since the idealist position is furthest removed from mainstream views in political science, Scriven's approach may seem somewhat naive to them. To the extent that this idealism is present to a lesser degree in all evaluation theorists, political scientists may find evaluation somewhat naive. More important, most evaluators give these matters little explicit attention. A theory of valuing for program evaluation should construct a cogent position about the nature of the public good.

Comparative and absolute standards of performance. Another problem in Scriven's operationalization of the logic is his advocacy of comparison with critical competitors as the most important standard of performance: "In short, virtually any serious product evaluation, formative as well as summative, must explicitly or implicitly refer to the available alternatives" (1981b, p. 137). But Cronbach (1963) disagrees:

> Ours is a problem like that of the engineer examining a new automobile. He can set himself the task of defining its performance characteristics and its dependability. It would be merely distracting to put his question in the form: "Is this car better or worse than the competing brand." (p. 676)

The difference between these theorists reflects their understandings of the purpose of evaluation. Cronbach emphasizes improving evaluands (formative) and Scriven emphasizes judging their merit (summative). Scriven (1981b) admits that in formative evaluation critical comparison is less necessary:

> Another line of thought which supported Cronbach in his push for noncomparative evaluation was clearly his interest in *explanations* of the performance of the evaluand, not merely the results of the horse race. But most product evaluations are aimed toward potential consumers — potential consumers who are not

principally interested in *understanding the reasons* for one product being better or worse than another; they are principally interested in finding out which products *are* better or worse than others, to guide their purchasing decisions. (p. 138)

Although Scriven thinks that information about critical competitors adds to the force of formative evaluation, and that seemingly noncomparative standards are implicitly comparative, when evaluation is to improve the evaluand, nothing in the logic of evaluation demands comparative information. But the risk is that "perfecting an intrinsically poor candidate is social as well as business nonsense" (1981b, p. 149). Comparative information helps avoid this risk.

Scriven's emphasis on comparative standards reflects the role of product evaluation in his theory. Consumers want comparative information on products. But product evaluation may not be the best model for Cronbach's educational evaluation. When we evaluate students, we are less concerned with their "purchase" than with improving their performance. Educational evaluators can improve the student for a year before a summative decision is needed about passing the student to the next grade. Where student advancement is made for social rather than educational reasons, the most important summative decisions are the rare ones about admission to high school, college, and graduate training. When evaluation of a curriculum or text is the issue, the product evaluation model may be more relevant. Even so, to the extent that product evaluation is not the best model for all evaluation, Scriven's relatively exclusive reliance on it is a problem.

Problems synthesizing results. Scriven is the only evaluation theorist to tell evaluators to integrate findings into a single, evaluative judgment about the worth of the evaluand. He recognizes that "sometimes this really is impossible" (1971, p. 53), and that methods for this task are not well developed, but says evaluators use this as a "cop-out" (p. 53) to avoid hard work. Cost-benefit methods are available (Levin, 1983), and the general "weight-and-sum" method is not difficult. Multiattribute utility theory or decision-theoretic approaches, which outline decision procedures in the face of multiple and sometimes conflicting input, could be adapted (Edwards, Guttentag, & Snapper, 1975). So Scriven is correct that it is not the methodological obstacles that retard this step, but ideological or theoretical biases of scientists against summative value judgments.

Even so, Scriven fails to appreciate the difficulties of credibly presenting a single summation in a context where multiple stakeholders weigh each finding differently. His cursory acknowledgment of "problems of justifying the actual weightings" (1981b, p. 162) understates the problem of finding a weighting system that is valid for all stakeholders. It may not be possible to obtain such a consensus without ignoring the objections of some groups to some weights (Shadish, Thomas, & Bootzin, 1982). Therefore, one can agree that evaluators ought not to "cop out" without also agreeing that this is best done by a single summary. One could construct several value summaries, each of the form "If X is important to you, then evaluand Y is good for the following reasons," where X is drawn from the interests of different stakeholders or from prescriptive theories. This would allow each group to see how its values and interests are affected, and might enlighten all participants about the value trade-offs in particular decisions.

A particularly frequent and vexing problem for weight-and-sum schemes is when a program reduces costs incurred by some recipients but increases the costs of others. Consider Scriven's (1980) example of a reading program:

> Intelligent consideration of the nature of reading programs yields the *dimensions* of merit. A study of what learners need to be able to read narrows matters down to a set of *standards* of merit on these dimensions of merit. (p. 93)

If "what learners need" is not singular, then multiple needs must be weighed. But what if they conflict? Consider the television program *Sesame Street.* At one level, the need is to improve the reading skills of disadvantaged children. Early evaluations suggested that *Sesame Street* met this need (Bogatz & Ball, 1971), but a later secondary evaluation (Cook et al., 1975) found that although the reading skills of disadvantaged children were improved, *Sesame Street* increased the gap between advantaged and disadvantaged children. What is the greater need: to increase reading skills of disadvantaged children or to narrow the gap? Or should both be equally weighted? If there is only one summary, this question must be answered, and the answer justified. While Scriven is correct that the justification could be constructed empirically based on the costs incurred by each choice, such study is not very feasible except in the long term and with controversy. In the short term in which most evaluators work, this answer is impractical. The best alternative is to use multiple summary statements reflecting differences of opinion about the costs associated with each choice. Scriven's contribution is his challenge to develop methods for synthesis; that he does not provide successful answers is inconvenient, but hardly reason for dismissing his challenge.

Theory of Knowledge

Scriven is an ontological realist who acknowledges our limited abilities to perceive reality. He believes that empirical study can yield valid knowledge of the world, but that the perspective of any single study is incomplete, so that multiple perspectives are needed. His primary concern is with making valid inferences about the things we are interested in, especially valuing. He welcomes any technique that practically aids this process.

Scriven's recent comments on knowledge construction (1983a, 1986a, 1986b) resemble our own views (Cook, 1985; Houts, Cook, & Shadish, 1986; Shadish, 1986a; Shadish, Cook, & Houts, 1986). Other theorists do not necessarily agree with him or us. Some theorists are more skeptical about the existence of reality, and about attendant concepts, such as causality (Guba & Lincoln, 1981; Lincoln & Guba, 1985). We share Scriven's concern about this relativist bias, but neither we nor Scriven have provided the detailed response that is badly needed to present a fair and balanced view of the issues involved. Scriven, as "our philosopher" (Stake, 1982c, p. 12), is in a good position to make such a response, but we cannot excuse ourselves on this account.

Scriven's realist stance, with the belief that some statements are more valid representations of reality than others, distances him epistemologically from the relativist end of the field and places him closest to Campbell. Both Scriven and Campbell are concerned more with practical inference than with the development of scientific theories about social programs. They share an interest in practical causal statements about what works, rather than in theories explicating deterministic causal laws mediating treatment and outcome (Cook & Campbell, 1979; Scriven, 1986b). They endorse similar tools for making these inferences, such as pattern matching and eliminating alternative explanations (Campbell, 1966; Cook & Campbell, 1986; Scriven, 1986b). Both prefer randomized experiments for assessing effects, although they differ as to when such methods are feasible; and both will accept the case study for causal inference under similar, limited circumstances (Campbell, 1975b; Scriven, 1976c). Finally, both are concerned with validity and with bias control.

Scriven's emphasis on bias control is very different from Campbell's. Both Scriven and Campbell believe that the most important biases are overlooked views that might change one's conclusions about program effects or value. Scriven emphasizes socio-organizational solutions, such as metaevaluation or goal-free evaluation, that bring many diverse perspectives to bear to identify biases. Campbell prefers to preclude bias a priori with design solutions whenever possible. He is more skeptical than Scriven that human reasoning can control bias, even when multiple perspectives are brought to bear. Scriven is more skeptical of methodology, preferring socio-organizational controls instead:

Allegedly serious discussions of current hot topics . . . frequently fail to identify the most crucial and questionable of the assumptions on which a position rests; or the critical alternatives to which it should be compared; or the agents who are ultimately responsible for the weaknesses or strengths of an approach; or the opportunity and other costs involved in its adoption/rejection; or the most significant of the possibilities or implications or potentialities or generalizations of the approach; or, for that matter, the known relevant and significant evidence. Consequently, they often fail to see that there is a significant reasonable alternative. There is no rule which avoids this mistake. (1986b, p. 16)

The last sentence shows that Scriven is skeptical that methodological rules can avoid these kinds of mistakes. He leans away from methodology and toward diverse critical perspectives embodied in socio-organizational remedies. Scriven's socio-organizational controls complement Campbell's quasi-experimental logic quite nicely. Particularly because quasi-experimentation has been abused by those who mindlessly apply the methods without applying the logic of bias detection underlying it, Scriven's controls are a critical addition to quasi-experimentation because of their greater strength in forcing evaluators to think about biases. Similarly, Campbell's threats to internal, external, construct, and statistical conclusion validities (Cook & Campbell, 1979) complement Scriven's socio-organizational methods that search for biases in report writing, co-optation, perspective exclusion, and value conclusions. More than any other theorists discussed in this book, Campbell and Scriven are devoted to inventing tools to aid bias control. Scriven's (1986b) foray into probative logic to guide argumentation is the most recent example. While other theorists, especially Rossi and Weiss, also use these tools, they have rarely been involved in inventing them.

Some theorists criticize Scriven and Campbell for prioritizing on knowing program effects. They deemphasize studies that narrowly focus on program effects, and prefer to gather data about not only effects but also costs, implementation, client characteristics, and causal mediating processes. The argument is that broad information is more useful to policymakers than is narrow historical information about whether or not a particular program worked at a particular time and place on a particular dependent variable (Cronbach et al., 1980). Scriven is somewhat less vulnerable to this criticism than is Campbell because the Key Evaluation Checklist lists as broad an array of questions as are listed by any other theorist. To the extent that Scriven really wants evaluators to be guided by the checklist — something currently unclear — he is not narrowly focused on effects. If we are wrong about his emphasis on the checklist, and if he really means to prioritize on effects as much as Campbell, then criticisms of this choice in the chapter on Campbell would also apply to Scriven.

Theory of Social Programming

Scriven's theories of valuing and knowledge are strong when assessed against either absolute or relative standards. In the former case, his theories are internally consistent, novel, and consistent with contemporary thinking. In the latter case, these theories stand up well in comparison to most other theorists in this book. These compliments do not extend to Scriven's theory of social programming, however, or to his theory of use. A good theory helps evaluation practice be responsive to the social needs that gave rise to the profession. Much of that need is for information that can be used expeditiously to ameliorate social problems. But Scriven's theory produces results that may not meet this criterion, mostly because social problems are usually not solved the way his theory implies.

An inadequate theory of social problem solving. Solving a social problem is aided by a sound understanding of how social problems are defined. Scriven defines problems as needs, but social problems are often defined in other ways. Consider Scriven's conception of why a curriculum developer prepares new textbooks: "He is presumably doing what he is doing because he judges that the material being presented in the existing curriculum is unsatisfactory" (1972a, p. 126). Such a product developer would probably be interested in an evaluation by Scriven, to know if his product is better than the existing one. Such interest would support the utility of Scriven's approach. But, given private sector economics of the production of textbooks in American society, it is more likely that the product developer is out to make money. Whether his product improves on the existing one may be an expendable consideration if the text sells well. If he is making a profit, he probably could not care less about Scriven's evaluation, or any evaluation that did not alert him to a decreasing market share. Current concerns in some areas about whether *any* textbooks are good suggest that such concerns are not misdirected. Problem definition in the public sector also appeals to criteria other than need, to political expediency and representing a pluralistic array of interests (May & Wildavsky, 1978; Polsby, 1984). Defining social problems on the basis of need is often the exception rather than the rule in policy-making. If so, information about which evaluands meet needs does not help policymakers who want to know which evaluands are fiscally feasible, politically attractive, and widely implementable — the main problems they may face.

Solving a social problem is also aided when one's theory is based on an accurate understanding of how social change takes place, so that one's proposed changes can realistically be implemented. Scriven's conception of social change may be unrealistic. He says that "the most obvious way in which an evaluation can save money is by killing off worthless enterprises" (1974, p. 92). But social programs are not killed off with meaningful frequency (Cook, 1981; Shadish, 1987b). Once initiated, they seem to have lives of their own. They marshal support from constituents who benefit from enactment of the program, and who may fight termination. After enactment, they gather new support from interest groups who find unanticipated benefits. Even when some people want to terminate a program, power to do so is spread widely over many actors, and getting them to agree is difficult. In those rare instances when programs are terminated, as during the Reagan administration, it is largely for political and economic reasons, not due to evaluation results. Scriven relies on the underjustified assumption that changes occur frequently enough to warrant the investment in summative evaluation.

Scriven offers few solutions to these problems. Consider his comments about allaying fears engendered by teacher evaluation:

> We cannot afford to tackle anxiety about evaluation by ignoring its importance and confusing its presentation; the loss in efficiency is too great. Business firms can't keep executives or factories when they know they are not doing good work and a society shouldn't have to retain textbooks, courses, teachers, and superintendents that do a poor job when a good performance is possible. The appropriate way to handle anxiety of this kind is by finding tasks for which a better prognosis is possible for the individuals whose positions or prestige are threatened. ... A little toughening of the moral fiber may be required if we are not to shirk the social responsibilities of the educational branch of our culture. (1972a, p. 125)

A little toughening of the moral fiber is an unlikely response from a social system responsible for seeing that not too many voters are unemployed, from a union that sees its power base threatened, or from a teacher who is told to find a new job. More likely, Scriven's evaluation will be shredded with great dispatch. Scriven recognizes the problem:

> Neither unions nor management would benefit from switching to an alternative approach since neither is rewarded for the replacement of bad teachers by good ones, and indeed would be heavily punished by the emotions, costs, and struggles that would be involved in a changeover. Only the children and the taxpayer are cheated and their representatives are not yet sufficiently sophisticated to speak up about the impropriety of this process. (1983a, p. 243)

He is correct that this failure is "so much the worse for students" and for "that style of management" (1981b, p. 139). Much social policy is so much the worse for the client, especially when the interests of a weak client conflict with those of more powerful stakeholders in the system (Shadish, 1984). It is unrealistic to construct evaluation theory around the hope that politically weak groups will develop sophisticated and powerful representatives, or that evaluations will be used by people with tough moral fiber and a devotion to the public interest.

It does matter what you evaluate: Products are not social programs. Scriven presents his theory of evaluation as impervious to context: "Evaluation is itself a methodological activity which is essentially similar whether we are trying to evaluate coffee machines or teaching machines, plans for a house or plans for a curriculum" (1972a, p. 123). That it is possible to lift evaluation out of context is beyond dispute: The existence of Scriven's theory is proof. But at what cost is it done? The cost is to limit the applicability of his theory of evaluation. More specifically, he focuses almost exclusively on product evaluation as a prototype for all evaluation, and he holds out *Consumer Reports* as a model for the conduct *and context* of evaluation:

> Product evaluation at its best is the most satisfactory type of evaluation currently practiced. Hence it is well worthwhile to examine it in some detail for the possibility of transferring its methods to other types of evaluation. Although it is perhaps somewhat simpler in principle than most other types of evaluation, for example, personnel and program evaluation, this in no way accounts for the difference in average quality. Personnel and program evaluation are usually done in ways that involve gross conceptual blunders. (1981b, p. 121)

Such a theory of evaluation may not transfer if the context of product evaluation is uniquely different from that of program evaluation. Product evaluation may not be "somewhat simpler" than program evaluation; it may be qualitatively different in important respects. Compared to social program evaluation, product evaluation involves different politics, has fewer problems involving heterogeneity and incompleteness of implementation, and appeals to different stakeholder motives and needs. A reasonable theory of product evaluation can teach us much about the logic of evaluation, but may be an inadequate theory of program evaluation because the contexts are so different. Although "everything" can be evaluated, evaluation may not be the same for everything.

Consider a few of the ways in which the context of product evaluation differs from that of program evaluation. In product evaluation, a clearly identified audience exists — the consumer of the product — whose interest in summative evaluation is clear; in program evaluation, the audience is diverse and vaguely specified, with diverse formative and summative interests in the social program. In product evaluation, the audience has a clear interest in the effects of a product; in program evaluation, some stakeholders have little interest in program effects relative to other questions. For example, debates about the content and implementation of family life curricula in schools are often of more concern to parents than information about whether such curricula would prevent teen pregnancy or AIDS. In product evaluation, many consumers will buy a product that is judged best; in program evaluation, taxpayers and their elected representatives buy a social program for reasons that go well beyond its effects. In product evaluation, use is clearly defined and easily measured by product purchase; in program evaluation, use is vaguely defined and difficult to measure — enlightenment, for example. This list could go on. Scriven's theory of evaluation is good in the context of product evaluation, but its fit in the social policy context is problematic.

The differentiated structure of social programs: policies, programs, projects, and elements. If you have used an Apple MacIntosh SE in Nedlands, Australia, chances are very good that when you use one in Inverness, California, you will have little difficulty, because the implementation of products is more uniform over sites and times than is the case for social interventions. Social interventions have structural and functional characteristics that bear on an evaluator's ability to control or change the intervention, and on the capacity of the intervention to respond to social problems. Specifically, interventions can be classified as policies, programs, projects, or elements (Cook, 1981; Cook et al., 1985; Cook & Shadish, 1986; Shadish, 1987b). *Policy* expresses intentions about the kinds of executive and legislative actions that have priority. Policy gives guiding assumptions and goals for many programs, and may be formally codified or informally expressed by policymakers in speeches, agendas, or expressions of support and opposition. *Programs* are administrative umbrellas for distributing and regulating funds under a policy. Programs rarely turn over entirely, for reasons cited earlier. They are mostly changeable at the margins, so a summative evaluation of a program will rarely if ever result in complete program replacement. Hence programs are different from products in ways that evaluators need to know when trying to change them.

Programs are not homogeneous. They consist of locally implemented *projects* where service delivery occurs (Cook et al., 1985). Projects can differ widely in character within the same program, because they are implemented under a national tradition of local control, service providers have discretion in the services they implement, and needs and demands change from place to place and over time at the same place. Like programs, projects have great staying power. Local community mental health centers, for example, may change parts of their internal functioning, but they rarely close shop completely in deference to some new project that wants the same funds, space, and resources. In these regards, projects are like programs and unlike products. Projects consist of many different service and administrative *elements*, and so are internally heterogeneous as well. Such elements usually affect fewer people with less impact than whole projects or programs, so changing an element usually results in less powerful problem amelioration than changing a project or program. But this weakness is partly compensated for by the fact that elements turn over at a more rapid rate. So elements offer more frequently occurring opportunities to introduce changes into a project.

Scriven's emphasis on product evaluation is an emphasis on elements rather than on programs or projects. In educational evaluation, Scriven uses "educational products" such as textbooks as evaluands, rather than evaluate the Title VII program as a whole or even the local Title VII office. Summative evaluation makes more sense for products and elements than it does for programs and projects, because the latter change so infrequently that they offer little practical leverage for change (Cook et al., 1985). But summative evaluations of textbooks are less likely to yield rapid or powerful problem resolution, since such elements have little coverage or impact compared with projects and programs. Scriven's theory implicitly endorses evaluating either elements and products that are weak but changeable or programs and projects that are strong but unlikely to change as a result of the evaluation.

An underdeveloped concept of disseminability. Scriven might be somewhat sympathetic to these criticisms. He says that if an evaluand produces no effects that are needed, it is not valuable; if it does produce needed effects, it is valuable. But an early version of the Key Evaluation Checklist put one other condition on evaluands without which they were not valuable. Evaluands could be valuable only if they were needed *and if they could be disseminated* (Scriven, 1974). Later versions of the checklist dropped this requirement; the 1980 version of the KEC has the evaluator describe the delivery system of a program, but does not require that a program have a viable delivery system in order to be valuable. Scriven never thoroughly returns to disseminability in subsequent work. He should do so, and should give it the same thorough treatment he gives such concepts as need and value. Disseminability is inherently a matter of social change. Studying this concept more would force Scriven to see that disseminating products in the marketplace is quite different from disseminating social programs and policies, and would force him to deal with the trade-off that disseminable interventions have smaller impact because their disseminability is partly due to their similarity to the status quo

(Shadish, 1984). Once one thinks this through, one sees that there are good reasons many evaluation theorists serve management information needs rather than social material needs (the former are problems faced by those who pay for evaluation), or emphasize formative over summative evaluation (it is practical to improve many interventions that will be around for a long while). In social policy, such considerations are critical if a theory of evaluation is to be practical in solving social problems.

This is not to reject summative evaluation or serving the public interest. We agree with Scriven that there are too few good, summative evaluations. Policymakers want them, and criticize evaluators for not providing them (Rayner, 1986). As Scriven (1986a) notes, some summative evaluations are potent in shaping policy—Murray's (1984) book on social welfare policy is a good example. We also agree that some evaluators focus so much on serving management interests that they lose sight of social problem solving (Cook & Shadish, 1982). The point is that his approach to evaluation has serious disadvantages for some important kinds of social problem solving, disadvantages that some alternatives in this book may not have.

Theory of Use

In distinguishing formative from summative evaluation, Scriven was the first major theorist to describe different kinds of use. This distinction advanced evaluation theory by crystallizing differences that have been explored in more detail since. But Scriven really has a theory of how evaluation results could or might be used rather than a theory of how use actually occurs in the real world. He says that evaluative information could be used immediately to replace some evaluands with better ones, or to improve evaluands. He does not show that this is how the use of evaluation actually occurs, or that the kind of use he favors is practical. As the reader can guess from the discussion of Scriven's theory of social programming, there is reason to think his theory of use is not practical, either.

A free-marketplace conception of how use actually occurs. We would speculate that Scriven's conception of use derives from product evaluation: The consumer will use information to dictate which product to buy, because that is the most efficient use of resources and because consumers seek to minimize costs while retaining quality. The product evaluator does not have to do much to facilitate such use other than place the information in a public forum. The market takes care of the rest.

If the social policy "market" does not work the same way as the product marketplace, the transfer of this logic to public sector use is flawed in several respects. The public sector is not driven by the same cost-efficiency incentives as the private sector (Lindblom, 1977). Rather than minimize costs, the public sector (in the United States) seeks maximum interest group participation in decision making. Program effectiveness in meeting needs is only one consideration in the adoption of a new program, often a minor consideration compared with politics, economics, or administrative constraints. Polsby (1984), for example, shows that superior social interventions are available for years before political, economic, and social conditions allow their use, and many never get used. Quirk (1986) calls this the "garbage can model" of policy. Proven interventions are thrown into the garbage can until one of them is coincidentally compatible with the current policy agenda. Most good ideas never get out of the garbage can, even if they are better than current policies.

Part of this difference between public and private sector use is the short life span of products compared with the long life span of programs. Consumer products turn over regularly; we buy new clothes and toothpaste often, and we buy cars and sometimes computers every few years. Only a few products have life spans longer than a decade. Moreover, changing toothpaste has little implication for changing anything else in life. When we use up our toothpaste, we can use new information to make a radical change in brand. If we buy a Waterpik and do not like it, we can discard it at little cost. Not so in policy-making. Programs and projects are long-term fixtures. Even when they are replaced or when they change at the margins, the opportunity for radical change is limited by the conservative nature of social change and by the tendency for social interventions to be highly connected to each other. Changing services offered in a mental health center can require considerable change in personnel, the amount of funds expended, needed intake procedures, and the desirability of the clients one attracts. The opportunities to use evaluative information in policy-making are inherently more limited than in product evaluation.

Second, in the marketplace the evaluator has to do little to facilitate use other than place the results in a publicly accessible outlet such as *Consumer Reports*. But simply placing program evaluation results in the *New York Times* is insufficient to facilitate use. Various "users" of social policy evaluations get information from an array of sources, including newspapers, intellectual magazines, executive summaries of evaluation final reports, oral briefings, scholarly publications, and gossip. No single outlet will do because, unlike in product evaluation, many diverse stakeholders are involved in social policy. Also, users often want more information about policies and programs than they want about products. It is often enough to know which car receives the *Consumer Reports* "Best Buy" appellation in the category of cars one wants. But even *Consumer Reports*, when it recently decided to look at poverty, used a descriptive, case study format with little summative component ("Life at the Edge," 1987). Scriven might respond that those reports were preevaluative, and did not offer evaluative judgments about poverty matters. Nonetheless, they did provide useful information for understanding poverty, information that may be critical to the policy process. But most policymakers or poor Americans may never notice these studies because simply placing them in *Consumer Reports* is inadequate to facilitate use in social policy-making. The evaluator must be more active in facilitating use in the public sector. Finally, when was the last time you saw a letter of hostile outrage to the editor of *Consumer Reports* about an evaluation of peanut butter or clear wood finishes? In contrast, read the letters to the editor sections of the issues subsequent to the poverty issues. Use of information about social policy is complicated by stakeholder values that are not as salient with products. The *Consumer Reports* model is insufficient to facilitate use in social policy.

A third problem with the marketplace model in the public sector is Scriven's equation of the consumer of evaluation as the public interest. Unlike a product consumer, "John Q. Public" is imaginary — one cannot talk to him to see how he would define problems, generate and implement solutions, choose criteria, set standards, assess performance, or synthesize and use results. All these activities are important to use. So Scriven's evaluation is relevant to a client who does not exist in an immediate or instrumental way. This abstraction makes it hard for Scriven to understand and respond to the needs and interests of stakeholders who do exist. Some remedies to this problem exist in his theory — allowing diverse stakeholders to respond to the report, and doing needs assessments. But these activities occur after the evaluation, the former by necessity and the latter by Scriven's recommendation. The conduct of evaluation is informed by neither.

The private sector, marketplace conception of use is not realistic to guide public sector use. Campbell has a similar theory of use. Both theorists have been criticized by subsequent evaluators for producing evaluations that were not used. It is difficult to appreciate the full impact of these criticisms without reading the work of Weiss, Wholey, and Stake, who made the development of a more realistic theory of use a high priority in their work.

Why prefer summative to formative? Scriven may overstate the case for preferring summative to formative. When evaluators must choose between formative and summative, they need decision rules to guide that choice. Scriven suggests several rules: Summative evaluation is usually cheaper (1983a), more reliable (1983a), and more essential to value statements (1980), and we lack theory to provide the explanations needed for formative evaluation (1983a). Yet summative evaluations may not be cheaper, given that a major argument against randomized experiments is that they are so expensive to mount; that the client will often spend a set dollar amount on evaluation, whether formative or summative; and that some ways of doing formative evaluations are probably cheaper than some ways of doing summative ones. Scriven could be implying that summative evaluations are more cost-effective, but that argument would be difficult to make.

Regarding the second argument, the reliability of methods for summative evaluation is questionable in practice (Cronbach, 1982a). We will discuss this in the chapter on Campbell, but Scriven implicitly acknowledges the point in advocating *modus operandi* when other methods of causal inference are impractical. Scriven says that "it is fairly easy to evaluate teachers on the basis of their success, where one can get appropriate comparison groups set up" (1983a, p. 247). Experience shows it is not easy to set up appropriate comparison groups or to evaluate teachers on their success, thwarting good summative evaluation. Randomized studies break down with attrition, and politics and educational organizations resist teacher evaluation. Witness the controversy over master teacher plans in states such as Tennessee. Teachers were pessimistic that a fair and valid teacher evaluation system could be found, and so initially stymied the legislation for fear that evaluation would compromise their interests in tenure and academic freedom. A plan was eventually passed, but opposition continued and a newly elected governor pledged to dismantle parts of it.

Scriven's third argument is that evaluation implies valuing. Since only summative evaluation is necessary to value statements, formative tasks are "not the professional turf of the evaluator" (1980, p. 80). But Scriven confuses defining a word with defining a profession. He is so concerned with explicating the science of valuing that he overlooks evaluation as a profession aimed at social problem solving. To say a thing is valuable is to give a summative evaluation; but it seems too concrete to limit the profession of evaluation to that, just as it would be too concrete to limit the profession of clinical psychology to the definition of psychology as a discipline — the scientific study of behavior. Formative evaluation, improving value, is obviously connected with tasks that professional evaluators are asked to do. Since Scriven (1972a, p. 125; 1980, pp. 6-7) explicitly recognizes that society needs both formative and summative work, and since he advocates empirical scrutiny of value premises (1966, 1983b), it would make more sense for these decisions to be a function of the relative social need for formative and summative evaluation. For instance, the social costs of not improving the value of existing programs and projects are probably high, since they will be with us a long time. If so, making program improvement a secondary task might even be unethical.

Scriven's final argument for summative evaluation is the lack of theory to provide appropriate explanations for formative evaluations. But he himself points out that formative evaluation does not require explanation or theory (1980, pp. 87-88). In fact, formative and summative evaluation are closely tied in many of his examples. Formative evaluation can be a summative evaluation of a subunit of the unit being evaluated, where a standard of performance is that the subunit improve the performance of the unit more than would another subunit. His recent explication of component evaluation and dimensional evaluation in formative evaluation is eloquent testimony to this point (Scriven, 1986a). He points out that summative evaluation of a component can have formative impact on the evaluand.

If we judged Scriven's theory to be summatively inferior to others for guiding professional evaluation, would the proper decision be to "kill off" his theory? No. The theory could be improved. In fact, Scriven will probably respond with clarifications or changes to address these criticisms. If so, when evaluating evaluation theory, he would do formative work.

Scriven overlooks some kinds of uses. Scriven's analysis leaves out an important class of use. Formative and summative uses are *instrumental* uses to produce immediate and direct changes in programs, assuming that short-term instrumental use is a preferred goal of evaluation. Cost-free evaluation is Scriven's statement of this assumption; Wholey's (1979, 1983) evaluability assessment is first cousin to cost-free evaluation, and has a similar goal of encouraging short-term instrumental use (Shadish, 1986b). Short-term instrumental use is laudable because the social funding of evaluation is not meant to promote academic theorizing; the field has an obligation to provide demonstrable and immediate return. But policy-makers will pay for evaluations that are not instrumental in the short term, such as analyses that enlighten them about the worth of policy options. If so, and if evaluators can provide such enlightenment, then a good theory of evaluation must discuss this kind of use. Such use requires somewhat different evaluation practices than instrumental use requires, as we will see with Weiss.

Theory of Practice

Problems with goal-free evaluation. Goal-free evaluation is a mainstay of Scriven's advice to practitioners. We agree with Scriven that goals are poor guides to program activities and effects. Management and staff may have biased views of goals. But it may be possible to improve goal-free evaluation or incorporate its positive features into improved hybrid models. Goal-free evaluation may be one of the least intuitive concepts in any theory. Evaluators have difficulty accepting the notion that they can, much less should, evaluate a program without knowing its goals. As a result, while most evaluators have heard of goal-free evaluation, they may not see it as central to their thinking about evaluation, and they still use goals as the most common source of dependent variables (Shadish & Epstein, 1987). Part of the problem may be that the label "goal-free evaluation" is unsatisfactory. It tells the evaluator only what not to do — do not look at goals, especially management and staff goals. But cognitive research shows that people do not think as well in terms of negatives (what not to do) as they do in terms of positives (what to do) (Graesser & Clark, 1985). Practicing evaluators might find a label more useful that orients them to what should be done — in this case, discovering effects, connecting effects to needs, and avoiding bias. Scriven's label "needs-based evaluation" captures one of these actions. To capture all three actions, one could say "effect-discovery, needs-based, bias-minimizing evaluation." Such a relabeling is unlikely to take place, with or without Scriven's blessing. We are reminded of Campbell's (1986a) effort to relabel internal and external validity to convey the concepts more accurately. That relabeling has not caught on, partly because, in some ways, these concepts are no longer Campbell's property to relabel. They belong to social science now.

We doubt that program management and staff have biases that are qualitatively or quantitatively worse than the biases of others. No stakeholder is bias free, including the evaluator. We cannot know that the evaluator's bias for needs-based theories of justice is more acceptable than management's bias for smoothly running operations without a priori setting up needs-based theories of justice as the preferred view. Since many groups have serious biases, avoiding only management and staff seems unfair to their legitimate interests when there are other legitimate ways to accomplish the goals of goal-free evaluation. To discover possible effects one can use the discovery-oriented methods Scriven suggests; his specific suggestions about inferring effects from a functional analysis are novel enough to continue to include them in the evaluator's repertoire. But one can also use past studies, stakeholder opinion, and social science theory — all of which reveal possible effects. Policy analysts explicitly use qualitative comparisons to other policies, other programs, other countries, and other practitioners to mitigate bias. These methods, coupled to meta-evaluative procedures (Cook & Gruder, 1978), guard the evaluator from being biased by the views of any one stakeholder group. In the spirit of the multimodel and perspectivist epistemology, are not evaluators better off using multiple methods to locate effects, assuming management and staff are not the only stakeholders with biases, and soliciting multiple perspectives to help avoid bias? A multiplist approach is better for bias control than goal-free evaluation because the fallible perceptual skills of a single evaluator will rarely be superior to those of multiple stakeholders. If Scriven disagrees, this implies a tension between goal-free evaluation and both the multimodel and the perspectivist approach.

Scriven might argue that multiple methods and perspectives are always preferable, but sometimes resource constraints limit evaluators to one thing, and that ought to be goal-free evaluation. We would argue the opposite. Under constraints goal-free evaluation should never be the only approach because it relies too heavily on one evaluator's limited perspectives. A number of alternatives might provide more information or could easily be adapted to do so, probably for the same cost. These include Stake's case study approach, which couples discovery methods with multiple perspectives, and Hendricks's (1981) service delivery assessment. Neither stresses effects or needs, but both could be adapted to do so with perspectivist advantages that goal-free evaluation lacks. With such alternatives, we are not sure what advantages are left for a strictly goal-free approach.

Choice of guiding model for practice. It may be that Scriven does not intend all evaluation practice to be goal-free. In discussing the third point of the Key Evaluation Checklist on the background and context of the evaluand, Scriven says "this checkpoint will be set aside in the early stages of an evaluation that is to have a goal-free phase" (1983a, p. 259), implying that some evaluations may not have such a phase. He also says about goal-free evaluation that "it seems a pity that one cannot suggest a new tool without the implication being drawn that one never uses anything else" (1974, p. 66). In discussing the merits of goal-free versus goal-based evaluation, he says that "both are part of good evaluation" (1974, p. 57):

> There is no need for program evaluation to be done on a wholly goal-free or wholly goal-based commitment. A mixture of the two — with some staff aware of goals and others, isolated from the first group, not aware of them — often works very well. A mode reversal is also possible, with the staff beginning their work in ignorance of the goals and proceeding as far as the preliminary report in writing; then being informed about the goals, and proceeding through such further work as may appear necessary at that point. (1983a, pp. 237-238)

Scriven (1974) says his advocacy of goal-free evaluation is partly intended to highlight an underemphasized concern in evaluation, but not to support goal-free evaluation exclusively.

Scriven may intend the Key Evaluation Checklist to be his general guide to practice, with goal-free evaluation being one instantiation of it. The checklist is more adaptable to evaluation practice over different situations. But this leaves two questions unanswered. First, when should the evaluator use the KEC in a goal-free mode? Presumably, when effect questions are the highest priority, when replacing the evaluand is preferable to improving it, when some chance exists that the evaluand can be replaced, or when instrumental use of results is expendable. Saying goal-free evaluation is not always the highest priority is the same as saying that effect questions are not always paramount, that sometimes it is important to know goals, that summative evaluation is not likely to result in replacing a program, or that improving the program may be important. Scriven needs to spell out when those times are.

Second, when not in a goal-free mode, how should the evaluator distribute resources over questions in the checklist, and choose methods to answer each question given the importance of each question and the available resources? If there are more than one possible combination of priorities among the items in the checklist, then sometimes the evaluator will prioritize on describing the evaluand, sometimes on describing process, and sometimes on formulating recommendations. Each combination is another instantiation of the checklist that is an alternative to goal-free evaluation. Each of the theorists in this book advocates a different combination of items from the checklist, along with recommendations for methods for answering those items. Potentially, the checklist implies a theory of evaluation much broader and more flexible than one would guess from reading Scriven. Lacking explicit instructions for operationalizing the checklist when not in a goal-free mode, the checklist endorses virtually any evaluative practice. We doubt Scriven intends this, so he should clarify the limits of the uses to which the KEC should be put.

Choice of audience. A related criticism concerns Scriven's selection of the audience for evaluation. He clearly prefers to serve the public interest: "Consumer-oriented evaluation is, on the whole, considerably more important than manager-oriented evaluation" (1983a, p. 233), but not without exception. For example, he notes exceptions to his general hard line against using management goals: "There is no argument for them in the evaluation context, *except* for providing managerial feedback and for providing meta-managers with some index of the success of their subordinates in projecting reasonable goals" (1983a, p. 233). This exception is not trivial. Wholey (1979, 1983) has built an entire evaluation theory on it, an approach that has been both popular and useful at the federal level. Maybe we need multiple models of evaluation, some for the consumer, some for management, and some for other contexts. The Key Evaluation

Checklist could guide such multiple models, but Scriven would have to admit formative evaluation to the honor role of evaluation practice.

Method choice. Scriven does not much discuss methods, trade-offs among those methods, or the feasibility of methods in field settings. He sees the fundamental issues in evaluation theory as logical and rational, not methodological. Hence his theory provides little guidance in selecting methods for practice. This leads to a common criticism of Scriven, that he provides few examples of implementing ideas like goal-free evaluation or *modus operandi.* This criticism is overstated—Scriven (1974) points to *Consumer Reports* to illustrate goal-free evaluation, and to other examples from social program evaluation. But he shows less concern for telling evaluators how to implement his ideas in practice than for suggesting the ideas in the first place. Despite his protestations (Scriven, 1974), the practicality of his ideas is still debatable. But since he makes so few methodological prescriptions, he rarely says anything wrong about methods. And his abstract approach does the field one important service. He counterbalances those theorists who emphasize methodology as central to evaluation, pointing out that decisions about methods are subject to the logic of evaluation, and that a primarily methodological evaluation theory cannot be a good evaluation theory. Still, a practical theory of evaluation must be better endowed with methods than is Scriven's.

CONCLUSION

Looking back on this chapter, our criticisms of Scriven's theory seem more salient than our respect. But of all the theorists in this book, we learned the most novel things from reading Scriven, especially about valuing. His work on valuing is complex, subtle, and so full of information that we learn new things each time we read it. One is surely deeply influenced by a theorist when one uses his concepts without any special effort. The logic of evaluation has found its way into several of our recent works, in the present book and in recent work on science evaluation and evaluating community psychology (Shadish, 1989, 1990). Read Scriven carefully and studiously about valuing. You will not see or do evaluation the same way again.

Yet much could be improved in Scriven's theory. His theory is philosophically strong, providing good conceptual structure for the field. It is weaker regarding using evaluation in improving social problem solving. Scriven's background suggests he was trained to be strong conceptually; but, unlike such theorists as Wholey, nothing in his employment situation forces Scriven to adapt to the realities of social problem solving. Other theorists, like Scriven, write theories that are often consistent with their educational and vocational backgrounds. These factors do not determine the theory they write, but disciplinary background and work settings seem to exert a profound influence on their ideas about evaluation.

We keep this observation in mind in the next chapter, on the theorist who is most like Scriven, Donald T. Campbell. Campbell is not a philosopher, but a psychologist. But he has impressive philosophical credentials in his own right, and, like Scriven, he is an academic. Should we be surprised that they have written evaluation theories that are similar in important respects? Like Scriven, Campbell emphasizes truth, bias control, measuring program effects, and solving social problems. Like Scriven's, Campbell's theory has difficulties regarding use of results in ameliorating social problems. But Campbell differs from Scriven in important ways, too. He has less to say about valuing, more about an ideal relationship between evaluation and society, more about methods for assessing program effects, and more about the nature of knowledge construction. Both Scriven and Campbell write theories that we might prefer in the best of all possible worlds. But that is not the world we live in.

4

Donald T. Campbell:

Methodologist of
the Experimenting Society

KEY TERMS AND CONCEPTS

Evolutionary Epistemology: Natural selection provides a metaphor for describing knowledge growth. When a problem of adaptation to the physical environment arises, randomly generated genetic mutations are "evaluated" to see if they improve the capacity to reproduce. Effective mutations are retained in genetic makeup; ineffective ones die. Effective learning in humans also depends on generating a wide and continuous range of novel potential solutions, on assessing effectiveness through trial-and-error elimination resembling natural selection, and on storing knowledge about effective solutions.

Internal Validity: The validity of a claim that A caused a change in B, with causation meaning the change in B would not have occurred without A. Campbell (1986a) renamed this "local molar causal validity" to highlight that causal claims are limited to specific local contexts actually studied and to variables in the grosser (molar) form in which they were manipulated or measured.

External Validity:	The warrant for asserting that findings of a particular study generalize to other persons, settings, and times. Campbell renamed this "proximal similarity" to emphasize that commonsense observed similarity between samples and populations is at stake, not inferences about unobserved theoretical attributes supposedly shared by samples and populations with distinctly different observed attributes.
Threats to Validity:	Plausible alternative explanations for claimed findings about covariation, causation, or generalization.
Randomized Experiment:	Units are assigned to treatment or comparison groups at random so that the expected pretest difference between groups is zero.
Quasi-Experiment:	A study that lacks random assignment but otherwise resembles an experiment.
The Experimenting Society:	An ideal society committed to experimenting with new reforms to discover effective ones that may merit widespread implementation.
A Disputatious Community of Truth Seekers:	Knowers organized around a focal topic and dedicated to open, mutually reinforcing but critical commentary on the procedures and assumptions undergirding any knowledge claim.

BACKGROUND

Donald T. Campbell received his bachelor's and doctoral degrees in psychology from the University of California, Berkeley, in 1939 and 1947, respectively. After some years at Ohio State University and the University of Chicago, he taught from 1953 to 1979 at Northwestern University, where he was the intellectual leader of a theory group interested in social science methodology and evaluation. He left Northwestern for Syracuse and is now at Lehigh University.

Campbell's works are widely influential in evaluation (Smith, 1981; Solso, 1987). Campbell and Stanley's (1963) *Experimental and Quasi-Experimental Designs for Research*, and its key concepts of internal and external validity, has been rated as more influential than any other evaluation work or concept (Shadish & Epstein, 1987). Yet Campbell's papers were mostly written for social science audiences, of which evaluators were but a part. Except for during the period 1968 to 1972, Campbell's interest in evaluation was secondary to his broader intellectual concerns with psychological theory, methods, sociology of science, and descriptive epistemology. In all these fields, he has received numerous prizes, awards, and other indications of the esteem in which his work is held (Brewer & Collins, 1981; Campbell, 1981a).

OUR RECONSTRUCTION OF CAMPBELL'S THEORY OF EVALUATION

The Intellectual Context

A retrospective analysis of an intellectual career can be so ill disciplined as to create continuities where a more faithful history would ascribe meaningful roles to chance, boredom, fitful stops and starts, or loose meanderings. In the case of a polymath like Campbell, these dangers are particularly acute, for in seeking continuity over a disparate set of aspirations and achievements, we risk finding explanatory concepts that are so general as to be vacuous.

Still, we think Campbell's intellectual career can be seen as a 40-year interest in describing and explaining how humans, including scientists and scholars, learn about the real world and how that learning might be improved. Campbell's main theoretical contributions to this are an evolutionary theory of knowledge growth (1960, 1974a) and a language for identifying and controlling systematic sources of bias that preclude true knowledge of manipulable causal factors (1957; Campbell & Stanley, 1963).

His concern with bias control is broad, both substantively and methodologically. One substantive interest is in visual illusions, where objective measurement shows that our senses can deceive us and that bias can predominate over veridical perception (Segall, Campbell, & Herskovits, 1966). A second concern has been with how lines of communication can bias messages (Campbell, 1959), including how cultural traditions are modified across generations (Jacobs & Campbell, 1961). A third interest has been in how external contexts affect stimuli interpretation (Campbell, Hunt, & Lewis, 1958; Campbell, Lewis, & Hunt, 1958); how internalized standards such as attitudes, expectations, and aspirations bias perceptions of how much individuals (Miller, Campbell, Twedt, & O'Connell, 1966) and groups (Brewer & Campbell, 1976; Campbell, 1965, 1967) differ from each other; and how they influence estimates of happiness (Brickman & Campbell, 1971).

These latter interests are less known than Campbell's methodological interests in biases in the collection, analysis, and interpretation of social data. His first four published papers dealt with this: One on indirect attitude assessment to control biases associated with direct assessment

(Campbell, 1950), the second on how ordinal position in a questionnaire affects responses (Campbell & Mohr, 1950), the third on whether or not fraternity leaders accurately assess their brothers' opinions (Hites & Campbell, 1950), and the fourth on interviewer bias (Wyatt & Campbell, 1950). Later contributions touch on bias arising from interviewer race (Rankin & Campbell, 1955), how items are worded (Campbell, Siegman, & Rees, 1967) or translated into another language (Werner & Campbell, 1970), how constructs are described and measured (Campbell & Fiske, 1959; Webb, Campbell, Schwartz, & Sechrest, 1966), how statistical controls inadequately adjust for partialed variables (Campbell & Boruch, 1975; Campbell & Erlebacher, 1970), how political interests of those commissioning research can influence results (Campbell, 1969), and how scholars come to hold the same shared set of false background beliefs (Campbell, 1986b).

Campbell is best known for his work on biases that arise in conducting cause-probing research in field settings. His language for this has become institutionalized. Most social scientists today recognize internal and external validity as cause-relevant validity types, and selection, history, and maturation as internal validity threats to be ruled out if causal inferences are to be plausible. He introduced these concepts in Campbell (1957) and fleshed them out in Campbell and Stanley (1963), where ruling out internal validity threats was linked to using experimental methods.

Since then he has identified more threats to unbiased inference (Cook & Campbell, 1976, 1979), clarified their meaning (Campbell, 1986a; Cook & Campbell, 1986), and devised more ways to rule them out in experiments (Riecken et al., 1974) and quasi-experiments (Cook, Campbell, & Perrachio, 1990). This methodological work on causation forged the strongest links between Campbell and evaluation practice. In asserting that evaluation is concerned with hypotheses about causation, and that randomized experiments and stronger quasi-experiments rule out many threats precluding causal inference, Campbell created a justification for preferring experimental methods in evaluation. This work on causal inference is only part of Campbell's concern with how to achieve true knowledge of the world. He postulates a real world, and has taken stands on many philosophical and epistemological questions (Campbell, 1974a, 1977). His special debt is to Popper, especially as concerns the logical impossibility of induction, the primacy of falsification in justifying knowledge claims, and the requirement that realism is a hypothesis, not a fact.

As a practicing scientist and evolutionary theorist, Campbell knows that science evolved in response to many forces other than philosophy. Since the 1970s he has been interested in using the history and sociology of science to describe how science approximates the truth because of — and despite—the passions of individual researchers and the organization of research communities. Campbell locates some sources of validity and invalidity, not in research design, but in the social organization of research. Here, too, Campbell sought to influence evaluation practice, urging development of public criticism in evaluation to scrutinize knowledge claims more intensely. He aims to create a "disputatious community of scholars" (Campbell, 1984a, p. 44), a field that eagerly seeks debate, includes dissenting opinions in reports, simultaneously funds multiple evaluations of a program instead of just one, and regularly resorts to reanalysis of others' evaluation data.

Hence Campbell could be called an evaluator, a general psychologist, a social psychologist, a methodologist for social sciences, a philosopher of science, or a metascientist. But whatever hat he wears, some version of two questions always animates him. How do humans achieve dependable knowledge of the world, especially about the consequences of their operations on it? And how might such processes be improved?

Describing and judging Campbell's work on evaluation is hard because of its connections with other parts of his intellectual life, and because the authors of this book are, in different ways, his students. To try to compensate for our biases we have tried to be extra critical, secure in the knowledge that few scholars are as explicit as Campbell about the need for peer criticism (Campbell, 1986b). To err toward excessive criticism is presumably what he would prefer.

THE HERITAGE OF SUCHMAN

Campbell (1984b) notes that his own career did not begin with a commitment to evaluation from which he then developed epistemological stances and methodological practices for which he is best known. Instead, he became an evaluator more by accident:

> Suchman's 1967 founding book on evaluative research cited my "experimental and quasi-experimental designs" as the appropriate methodological mode, I thus became overnight both a senior program evaluator by fiat, and one committed to an experimental epistemology and the theory of science shared by the physical sciences. (p. 13)

Suchman believed Campbell's work represented *the* model for evaluation because it detailed the most scientific option then available for causal research in field settings. Suchman (1967) wrote:

In our approach, we will make a distinction between "evaluation" and "evaluative research." The former will be used in a general way referring to the social process of making judgements of worth. This process is basic to almost all forms of behavior. . . . "Evaluation research," on the other hand, will be restricted to the utilization of scientific research methods and techniques for the purposes of making an evaluation. (p. 7)

Suchman defined evaluation as

the determination . . . of the results . . . attained by some activity . . . designed to accomplish some valued goal or objective. . . . This definition contains four key dimensions: (1) process—the "determination"; (2) criteria—the "results"; (3) stimulus—the "activity"; and (4) value—the "objective." The scientific method . . . provides the most promising means for "determining" the relationship of the "stimulus" to the "objective" in terms of reasonable "criteria." (pp. 31-32)

Suchman preferred a science-impregnated mode of evaluation for two reasons. First, he believed that evaluative studies conducted before 1960 collected data mostly from program participants, with no comparison groups for estimating how participants would have fared without the program. Second, he believed the reliance evaluators placed on program archives for outcome measures was misplaced given those sources' questionable validity and limited scope. Suchman wanted evaluators to develop their own measures and data that would meet higher standards.

Suchman (1967) wanted to improve experimental designs and quantitative measures in evaluations, but he knew that evaluation occurs in politicized contexts that offer little control compared to the more controlled settings in which experiments were first developed:

Operational programs are often highly entrenched activities based upon a large collection of inadequately tested assumptions and defended by staff and field personnel with strong vested interest in the continuation of the program as it is. It is obvious from this description that an evaluation which proposes to challenge the effectiveness of an established operational program poses a real threat to program personnel. Therefore, it is not surprising to note how rare and how difficult it is to conduct an evaluative study of an existing program. To a large extent such evaluations are limited to new programs which are still open to change. And yet the need for evaluation is undoubtedly greatest for established operating programs. (p. 142)

Here Suchman refers to themes that appear often in Campbell's writings: (a) the need for evaluations with cause-probing methods derived from experimental theory and practice; (b) the recalcitrance of administrators who fear independent and technically superior evaluations; and (c) the assumption that it is easier to evaluate pilot programs because, compared to current programs, fewer constituencies are involved in them or fight to preserve their immediate material interests.

Campbell and Stanley (1963)

Campbell and Stanley's classic *Experimental and Quasi-Experimental Designs for Research* attracted Suchman as a manual for scientific evaluation. It presents a theory of causation, justified and codified in terms of validity types and threats to validity. It outlines quasi-experimental designs that seem feasible for evaluation practice because they have been successfully implemented in field settings and do not depend on administratively problematic random assignment to treatments. Finally, most of the examples that Campbell and Stanley present in a positive light lead to defensible causal interpretations, suggesting that the designs in question are practical, grounded in a theory of causation, and valid in the results generated.

Random assignment is important in the theory of experimentation used in agricultural and social sciences. Campbell and Stanley explore the functions it fulfills and how they can otherwise be met. To them, random assignment promotes only causal inferences associated with identifying whether a manipulated change in one variable changes some other variable. As Campbell later noted, this corresponds in philosophy of science to a manipulability or activity theory of causation (Cook & Campbell, 1979). This theory differs from essentialist theories of causation that seek total prediction or explanation of a dependent variable. Manipulability theory seeks to estimate the marginal impact of an independent variable when other causes are held constant by the randomization procedure.

Random assignment can be used to pursue essentialist goals if the independent and dependent variables are chosen for theoretical relevance and if the theoretically implicated processes are extensively measured. But these are adjunct features of experiments in Campbell's view. Experimentation is nothing more than a way to arrange when and how treatments are delivered, when and how control groups are formed, and when outcomes are observed. Random assignment is concerned with whether manipulating A brings about B. If the As and the Bs are multivariate packages — as are social programs — then little explanatory or predictive knowledge results from random assignment alone. What can result is valid knowledge about whether or not variation in that treatment package leads to variation in a package called outcome (Campbell, 1969).

Manipulability is closely linked to popular conceptions of causation: what can be done to bring about positively valued results and avoid negative ones. For example, if you have a headache, take aspirin; to clean your hair, use shampoo. It is also linked to the concept of causation inherent in evolutionary biology. If the environment gets cold, then species that grow hair or modify their heart rates are advantaged; if new predators hunt only by day, then genetic variants facilitating night vision have a selective advantage. But the manipulability theory is not esteemed by scholars because the causal connections it finds are probabilistic and take the form "A caused B in the past" or "A often causes B," instead of the ambitious form "A always causes B."

Scholars who want full explanation or prediction prefer multivariate analytical methods or the discovery of generative processes (Cronbach, 1982a; Cronbach et al., 1980). In the multivariate case, preferred strategies focus on identifying causally efficacious parts of a molar treatment, the causally affected parts of a molar effect, and the pathways and contingencies through which cause and effect are related. Path analysis is often used in pursuing this purpose. In the second case, generative *mechanisms* are sought. So researchers ask how cholesterol causes heart attacks or how poverty in one generation causes poverty in the next—questions quite different from their manipulability counterparts: Does cholesterol cause heart attacks? Does poverty in one generation cause poverty in the next? Ironically, Campbell advocates one of the most scientific methods (the experiment) to support causal inferences of a type that scientists often do not prefer.

Campbell coined *internal validity* to refer to inferences about manipulable causal agents. Random assignment promotes internal validity because it falsifies many competing interpretations (Popper, 1968)—threats to internal validity—that could plausibly have caused an observed relationship *even if the treatment had never taken place*. Foremost among internal validity threats is selection: Groups exposed to treatments nonrandomly may differ in ways that mimic what treatment might achieve. Subcategories of selection include (a) selection-maturation (treatment groups may grow apart over time because they spontaneously mature at different rates) and (b) selection-history (treatment groups may differ over time because an event happened to the units assigned to one treatment but not the other). Campbell and Stanley (1963) list nine threats to internal validity. Their explication is one of Campbell's major contributions to social science and to evaluation.

To Campbell, internal validity threats are best ruled out through random assignment. Campbell and Stanley (1963) list forms of randomized experiments that are particularly feasible for field research. Since these are a small part of the repertoire of experimental designs and are invariably the simplest, Campbell and Stanley added little to scholarly thinking about randomized experiments. But they greatly contributed to quasi-experiments, systematically describing and evaluating novel designs without random assignment that incorporate other features that facilitate causal inference. Two features stand out. First is using pretest measures on the same scale as the posttest. Absent random assignment, pretests are indispensable. The more often they are collected, the better. A longer pretreatment time series helps estimate the likelihood of selection-maturation and statistical regression threats. Second is using maximally similar comparison groups as a no-treatment baseline (but not achieved through matching on fallible variables). Campbell and Stanley (1963) give researchers many quasi-experimental design options with pretests and control groups. In providing examples where each option leads to defensible causal conclusions, they empower practicing researchers to test causal hypotheses in field settings.

Campbell assigns higher priority to internal than external validity. Of what use, he asks, is generalizing a relationship if one doubts the relationship itself? But Campbell does consider external validity important. He coined the term and has explicated seven threats that can restrict a cause-effect relationship to specific groups, settings, times, or operationalizations of cause-and-effect constructs. In detailing ways to probe generalizability, Campbell and Stanley promote the hope that stable causal connections can be found that could be integrated into substantive theories and public deliberations about action.

Making the Case for Randomized Experiments

Suchman saw Campbell's work on quasi-experiments as legitimating a practical, scientific alternative to the randomized experiment. Ironically, one of Campbell's major concerns in the 1970s was to downplay quasi-experiments and make a three-part case for *randomized* experiments as the preferred method option. His first argument was that quasi-experiments lead to less certain causal inferences that can have mischievous consequences for decision making. Campbell and Erlebacher (1970) show in an evaluation of Head Start (Cicirelli & Associates, 1969) how statistical adjustment procedures fail to adjust for nonequivalence unless all differences that correlate with the dependent variable are fully known and perfectly measured. It was easy to make the case with the Head Start evaluation; the posttest measures were of academic achievement but the "pretest" measures were of family socioeconomic status, a poor proxy for a pretest on the achievement test. Indeed, Campbell and Stanley (1963) denounce as uninterpretable the design that Cicirelli used.

Campbell and Boruch (1975) attack the most widely used quasi-experimental design with identical pretest and posttest measures and nonequivalent treatment groups—a design that Campbell and Stanley discuss with optimism. Campbell and Boruch (1975) write:

> It may be that Campbell and Stanley (1966) should feel guilty for having contributed to giving quasi-experimental designs a good name. There are program evaluations in which the authors say proudly, "we used a *quasi*-experimental design." If responsible, Campbell and Stanley should do penance, because in most social settings there are many equally or more plausible rival hypotheses than the hypothesis that the puny treatment indeed produced an effect. In fact, however, their presentation of quasi-experimental designs could well be read as laborious arguments in favor of doing randomized assignments to treatments whenever possible. And admittedly, there are also encouragements to do the second best if the second best is all the situation allows. The arguments presented in this chapter continue the strategy of justifying randomized experiments by making explicit the costs in equivocality and the burdens of making additional estimations of parameters that result from a failure to randomize. We agree with those who say "Randomized experiments are expensive and difficult. Don't use them *unless you really need to.*" Our only disagreement may be over when it is that randomized experiments are actually needed. (pp. 202-203)

Campbell and Boruch worry about six biases that operate in the pretest-posttest, nonequivalent groups design: (a) regression artifacts due to using either matching or regression to create "equivalent" samples from different populations; (b) differential growth rates where the less advantaged change more slowly compared with the more advantaged—a situation inadequately modeled when fallibly measured pretest measures are the sole covariate; (c) increases in reliability over time, as happens in education as children mature; (d) higher reliability in scores of more advantaged control group members compared with more disadvantaged experimental group members; (e) floor and ceiling effects; and (f) feedback effects from social aggregation when children from advantaged backgrounds learn better vocabularies from schools and playmates, increasing gaps between themselves and disadvantaged students. Campbell and Boruch argue that statistical adjustments cannot deal with all of these threats, so that some of the initial group differences will not be fixed.

The second argument Campbell makes is to debunk claims about the limited applicability of random assignment. Campbell and Boruch (1975) refute this argument analytically and by presenting an inventory of completed experiments. A more comprehensive rebuttal is offered in Riecken et al. (1974). This monograph was prepared by a Social Science Research Council committee on which Campbell served. He drafted the section on quasi-experiments, and played a major role in the sections on strategies for overcoming obstacles to randomized experiments in terms of "cost, complexity, and delay in getting an answer" (p. 10). Advice is offered about persuading administrators to implement randomized experiments, assigning at random with few units, reducing attrition, and minimizing communication between persons in different treatments. The impression given by the book is that (a) the technical problems of random assignment can be circumvented, (b) random assignment is ethical since it distributes scarce resources by lottery, and (c) the major impediment to random assignment is the political will to make it routine.

Campbell's advocacy of the randomized experiment assumes that clearer causal inferences result from randomized experiments, and the benefits of these inferences outweigh additional financial or administrative costs incurred. He says:

> We would *improve* program evaluation if we were alert to opportunities to move closer to the experimental model. I think you will find a general consensus that 99 percent of our remediative programs have not been evaluated in an interpretable way. We cannot tell whether or not the programs have the intended effects or undesirable side effects. We don't have the evidence. Now we could partially improve that record if we were alert to opportunities to use improved scientific methods. But to create the increased alertness the methodologists have got to get down out of their ivory towers and produce practical how-to-do-it instructions. (Salasin, 1973, p. 7)

During the interview from which the above quote is taken, Campbell was asked what is sacrificed when quasi-experimental designs are used instead of experimental designs. He answered:

> What is sacrificed is clarity of inference on those points that we call "internal validity." There may actually be an advantage to the quasi-experimental design on external validity but in terms of asking the question "Did this change really have an effect here for these people," quasi-experimental designs are more equivocal. I think if you read my works carefully, you find that in presenting the quasi-experimental designs I made clear the threats to validity that they fail to control, and I suggest that we use common sense evaluations of the plausibility of those threats to decide whether the threats are relevant. One could also read my presentations of quasi-experiments as detailed, explicit arguments for randomized experiments. They can be read that way, and that is not a misleading way. (Salasin, 1973, pp. 7-8)

Campbell's third argument for randomized experiments is linked to his concern that bold innovations be tested in evaluation rather than modest variants on established practices. His argument can best be understood by an example he cites frequently. The New Jersey Negative Income Tax Experiment (Nathan, 1989; Rossi & Lyall, 1978) was designed in the 1960s to test whether guaranteeing an income to working poor families might be an alternative to welfare. The fear was that providing cash instead of services would undermine the work motivation of individuals and lead to a welfare life-style. The purpose of the experiment was to estimate how different income guarantees affect labor force participation. The basic idea was controversial. Some commentators believed it promoted the wrong values. Many bureaucratic and professional groups felt their own welfare would be compromised. Hence the hypothesis was tested as a demonstration, a trial run for a possible future program.

This demonstration allowed both testing a bold idea and assigning families to treatments at random. Guaranteeing incomes to some families but not others would have been impossible if the guaranteed income had already been national policy—then every eligible person would have access to it. But in a demonstration the treatment can be deliberately varied and withheld from some. Demonstrations promise a way to achieve clearer causal inferences (because of random assignment) and meaningful reform attempts (because of their lower political profile). They link bold ideas (blind variation of the evolutionary model) and rigor in evaluation (selective retention of the same model)—a happy marriage between Popper's (1968) call for boldness of conjecture and rigor in refutation.

Elsewhere, however, Campbell (1975a, 1979a) was more ambivalent about randomized experiments and produced arguments against his own position:

The critics taking what I am calling the humanistic position are often well trained in quantitative-experimental methods. Their specific criticisms are often well grounded in the experimentalist's own framework; experiments implementing a single treatment in a single setting are profoundly ambiguous as to what caused what; there is a precarious rigidity in the measurement system, limiting recorded outcomes to those dimensions anticipated in advance; process is often neglected in an experimental program focused on the overall effect of the complex treatment, and thus knowing such effects has only equivocal implications for program replication or improvement; broad gauge programs are often hopelessly ambiguous as to goals and relevant indicators; changes of treatment program during the course of an ameliorative experiment, while practically essential, make input-output experimental comparisons uninterpretable; social programs are often implemented in ways that are poor from an experimental design point of view; even under well-controlled situations, experimentation is a profoundly tedious and equivocal process; experimentation is too slow to be politically useful; etc. All these are true enough, often enough to motivate a vigorous search for alternatives. (1979a, p. 69)

By the early 1980s his optimism about demonstrations declined somewhat:

Most of what most governments offer in the name of "reforms" and "new programs" are symbolic gestures designed to indicate government awareness of problems and sympathetic intention, rather than serious efforts to achieve social change.... Due to competing needs and limited budgets, most of the few genuine novelties get drastically underfunded and have no chance of producing demonstrable effects. The legislative requirement that such so-called programs be scientifically evaluated becomes just more empty rhetoric, a token to indicate that the money is being spent responsibly. (1982, p. 118)

Keeping the Quasi-Experimental Pot Boiling

Campbell could not abandon quasi-experiments altogether, given his conviction that the political will to conduct randomized experiments was sometimes deficient, that implementing them was sometimes impossible, and that implementing them well was always difficult. Even in his most intense advocacy of randomized experiments, he notes that some kinds of quasi-experimental designs afford clear causal insights. In "Reforms as Experiments" (1969) he highlights two such designs. One is the interrupted time series, where an intervention begins abruptly and its effects are assessed by examining whether observations change in intercept or slope after the intervention. The string of pretest observations allows examination of secular trends prior to the intervention. Even here, Campbell stresses possible problems. The first is when archival measures are used for the outcomes and the record-keeping system changes when the intervention occurs; the second is when an irrelevant event occurs contemporaneously with the treatment. To minimize this last problem, he prefers complex forms of interrupted time series that use control series.

He also favors the regression-discontinuity design, where a treatment is assigned to units based entirely on a particular quantitative cutoff point. In this design the selection process is completely known; certain statistical analyses of this design yield unbiased estimates of effects (Trochim, 1984). Again, he acknowledges the limits of this design. One problem is the possible influence of the administrators' knowledge of the cutoff point on the scores individuals get; a second limit is that social allocation decisions are rarely made on the basis of quantitative scores alone.

Campbell is skeptical about the ability of any other quasi-experimental designs to rule out plausible alternative interpretations, however sophisticated and complex their statistical analysis might be.

In 1976 and 1979 Cook and Campbell extended this prior work on quasi-experimental designs, providing impetus to the case presented by Suchman but seemingly negated by Campbell's arguments for randomized experiments. Most of Cook and Campbell's points clarify and extend points made in Campbell's earlier work: (a) justifying experimental interventions in terms of a manipulability theory of cause, (b) systematizing practical lessons about implementing randomized experiments, (c) highlighting the special status of interrupted time series and regression discontinuity designs, (d) arguing the primacy of internal validity, and (e) emphasizing the difficulties of using statistical adjustments compared with random assignment or pretests and control groups.

Cook and Campbell added some new quasi-experimental designs and introduced new validity threats to systematize some ambiguities associated with randomized experiments, especially regarding "resentful demoralization," which can occur when controls feel treated like second-class citizens; "compensatory rivalry," which can arise if controls react to being excluded from the treatment by trying harder; and "compensatory equalization," which occurs when administrators allocate their resources to reduce inequities random assignment can cause. These additions implicitly question two contentions in Campbell's advocacy of the randomized experiment: whether the marginal benefits of randomized experiments in promoting causal inferences are as striking as Campbell claimed; and whether they are so large as to compensate for their greater costs. Whether intentionally or not, Cook and Campbell partly undermined Campbell's earlier rationale for randomized experiments at a time when this rationale was already under attack from scholars questioning all quantitative research in the human sciences.

Starting the Qualitative Pot Boiling

While he was being lionized as *the* father of scientific evaluation, Campbell wrote two papers about qualitative methods (1974b, 1975b; see also 1978) that were sometimes interpreted as renouncing experiments and advocating qualitative methods. Campbell became cited within evaluation as simultaneously legitimating hardheaded experimental methods *and* their "softer" qualitative counterparts. As background, Campbell's 1969 paper "Reforms as Experiments" was criticized by Weiss and Rein (1970), who encountered difficulties in mounting and experimentally evaluating a pilot project. Qualitative observations led them to question "black box" evaluations that do not inform researchers about (a) how well an intervention is implemented, (b) how well its evaluation is implemented, and (c) what unintended effects the intervention has. Campbell (1970) agreed with Weiss and Rein about the advisability of qualitative techniques in evaluation, endorsing the purposes they had specified for the qualitative methods. But he questioned if their critique went to the essence of experimentation; much of it dealt with generic attributes of poor research — relying on a single outcome measure, failing to measure process, using excessively nonequivalent control groups, and analyzing puny interventions reflecting administrators' exaggerated claims about project achievements. Campbell implied that better experimental design could have been achieved by Weiss and Rein, that the steps Weiss and Rein advocated should be built into all experiments. Building them in does not vitiate experimental designs; it complements them.

Campbell's writing on qualitative methods undermines naive advocates of quantitative research. He notes that quantitative measurement rests on qualitative assumptions about which constructs are worth measuring and how constructs should be conceived. He shows that different stakeholders prefer different outcomes; their understandings can imply different theoretical components and different operational representations. Even if they agree on an operationalization, they would still be likely to imbue it with their own theories of its factorial composition and relationship to other concepts.

Campbell never deviated from the postpositivist position that all measurement is theory-laden and that objective knowledge is impossible if it is understood as theory-neutral, pure glimpses into the social world. Objectivity is better understood as intersubjective verification of observations where the same observation is repeatedly made despite the use of many different measures. Campbell stresses the need for critical commentary on all measures, for measuring multiple constructs, for using multiple measures of any one construct, and for measuring process to get within the black box.

Campbell greatly values knowledge obtained directly from program participants, preferring their reports to those of social scientists because the impressions of program participants are more likely to be grounded in extensive program experience. He wants narrative program histories to be kept — preferably by different people with different presuppositions about the project's value — and he wants these histories included in final reports so they can be publicly criticized by interested parties.

Campbell is in favor of both quantitative and qualitative procedures; he wants the qualitative to complement rather than replace the quantitative. However, he does respond to the argument that qualitative methods can fulfill the same cause-probing function as quantitative methods, particularly experiments. His response is complex. From the Popperian falsificationist theory of knowledge growth he leans toward, the amount of uncertainty reduced about a knowledge claim depends primarily on the extent to which plausible alternative interpretations are ruled out. The crucial issue is ruling out alternatives; *how* they are ruled out is immaterial. With exceptions, he takes case studies to task for failing to rule out such alternatives (Campbell, 1975a, 1975b, 1979a). Campbell notes that many valid causal claims predate modern science; for example, rain facilitates crop growth, and external enemies induce in-group cohesion. Private insights and social discussion sometimes identify important causal hypotheses and produce evidence from experience that rules out alternatives. Campbell respects such prescientific social-evolutionary winnowing processes even though the knowledge achieved is likely to be in the naive form of "validated as true" rather than in the form he prefers: not yet shown to be false.

Campbell (1975b) maintains that discipline can be added to cause-probing qualitative studies through processes akin to the concept of statistical degrees of freedom. The key is to identify a pattern of results that would occur only if A were the cause, rather than B or C. Requirements for such pattern matching include explicit expectations about what a program is likely to achieve and about the pattern of results expected from plausible alternative causes, and high-quality measurement of processes and outcomes implicated in different patterns. In this connection, Cook and Campbell (1979) discuss how a nonexperimental science like astronomy achieves causal success. Discipline comes from precise point predictions unique to a theory and from observational tests discriminating between different magnitude estimates predicted from contending theories. Precise point prediction is rare in evaluation, where more promise inheres when pattern matching predicts a multivariate fit, a complex statistical interaction (Campbell, 1966). In all these cases the logic is the same: Incorrect theories are weeded out by showing that some of their implications are incommensurate with data. No experiments need be involved and quantification is not a requirement.

The practical issue is whether qualitative methods reduce as much causal uncertainty as do quantitative methods, particularly when qualitative methods are compared with the stronger experimental methods. Campbell does not deal with this in detail, but this passage gives a strong clue:

> So far, the qualitative-knowing alternatives suggested (e.g., Guttentag, 1971, 1973; Weiss & Rein, 1969, 1970) have not been persuasive to me. Indeed, I believe that naturalistic observation of events is an intrinsically equivocal arena

for causal inference, by qualitative or quantitative means, because of the ubiquitous confounding of selection and treatment. Any efforts to reduce that equivocality will have the effect of making conditions more "experimental." "Experiments" are, in fact, just that type of contrived observational setting optimal for causal inference. The problems of inference surrounding program evaluation are intrinsic to program settings in ongoing social processes. Experimental designs do not cause these problems and, in fact, alleviate them, though often only slightly so. In such protests, there often seems implicitly a plea for the substitution of qualitative clairvoyance for the indirect or presumptive processes of science. But while I must reject this aspect of the humanistic protest, there are other aspects of it that have motivated these critics in which I can wholeheartedly join. These other criticisms may be entitled "neglect of relevant qualitative contextual evidence" or "overdependence upon a few quantified abstractions to the neglect of contradictory and supplementary qualitative evidence." Too often quantitative social scientists, under the influence of missionaries from logical positivism, presume that in true science, quantitative knowing replaces qualitative, common-sense knowing. The situation is in fact quite different. Rather, science depends upon qualitative, common-sense knowing even though at best it goes beyond it. Science in the end contradicts some items of common sense, but it only does so by trusting the great bulk of the rest of common-sense knowledge. (1979a, pp. 69-70)

Here Campbell's honesty inadvertently undermines his own case for experiments and quantitative research. He prefers experiments, but acknowledges their imperfections and constructs one of the strongest cases to date that qualitative methods can yield valid causal knowledge. Such honesty is not welcomed by those who look to methodologists for reassurance and certainty in method recommendations.

Campbell admits that qualitative methods are useful for purposes for which experimental design is mute (unless additions are made to the measurement framework) — about the implementation of program services, the identification of side effects, and the explanation of causal processes. This raises the issue of whether the *marginal* advantages of experiments for identifying causal connections are enough to justify them if they are difficult to implement and can detract from the resources needed to study these other matters.

Campbell's analysis of the relationship between quantitative and qualitative research is like his analysis of the relationship between experiments and quasi-experiments. In each case he constructs a case of *relative* superiority; but he produces such a strong case for the inferior alternative and such a qualified case for the superior option that the marginal difference between the superior and the inferior *seems* minor. Moreover, if readers weight differently the criteria by which Campbell evaluates method choices, they might come to a different conclusion. If practicality is weighted more heavily than marginal gain in truth about causal connections, then quasi-experiments might be preferred over experiments. If knowledge about multiple types of variables is preferred over a marginal increment in the quality of causal knowledge, qualitative methods might be preferred. As a result, Campbell's methodological writings have been used to justify evaluation practice centered on randomized experiments (Riecken et al., 1974), quasi-experiments (Suchman, 1967), *and* qualitative case study methods (Yin, 1984).

Campbell the Visionary
of the Experimenting Society

Most evaluators view Campbell as providing and legitimating methods. However, his work has broader intellectual origins, containing a self-consciously critical and pessimistic but still utopian view of experimentation and evaluation. He describes the political and value context in which he wants his methodological work to be embedded. (We will discuss the limited meaning Campbell ascribes to utopia later in this chapter.)

Prelude: "Reforms as Experiments" (1969). This paper begins with Campbell proposing that

> the United States and other modern nations should be ready for an experimental approach to social reform, an approach in which we try out new programs designed to cure specific social problems, in which we learn whether or not these programs are effective, and in which we retain, imitate, modify or discard them on the basis of their apparent effectiveness on the multiple imperfect criteria available. Our readiness for this stage is indicated by the inclusion of specific provisions for program evaluation in the first wave of the "Great Society" legislation, and by the current congressional proposals for establishing "social indicators" and socially relevant "data banks." So long have we had good intentions in this regard that many may feel we are already at this stage. . . . It is a theme of this article that most ameliorative programs end up with no interpretable evaluation. (p. 409)

Throughout the article he gives a number of reasons to explain the absence of interpretable evaluations in the past. One is past dependence on fallible human testimonials:

> Human courtesy and gratitude being what it is, the most dependable means of assuring a favorable evaluation is to use voluntary testimonials from those who have had the treatment. If the spontaneously produced testimonials are in short supply, these should be solicited from the recipients with whom the program is still in contact. The rosy glow resulting is analogous to the professor's impression of his teaching success when it is based solely upon the comments of those

students who come up and talk with him after class. In many programs, as in psychotherapy, the recipient, as well as the agency, has devoted much time and effort to the program and it is dissonance reducing for himself, as well as common courtesy to his therapist, to report improvement. . . . Probably the testimonials will be more favorable as: (a) the more the evaluative meaning of the response measures is clear to the recipient—it is completely clear in most personality adjustment, morale and attitude tests; (b) the more directly the recipient is identified by name with his answer; (c) the more the recipient gives the answer directly to the therapist or agent of reform; (d) the more the agent will continue to be influential in the recipient's life in the future; (e) the more the answers deal with feelings and evaluations rather than with verifiable facts; and (f) the more the recipients participating in the evaluation are a small and self-selected or agent-selected subset of all recipients. Properly designed, the grateful testimonial method can involve pretests as well as posttests, and randomized control groups as well as experimentals, for there are usually no placebo treatments, and the recipients know when they have had the boon. (pp. 426-427)

A second reason for poor evaluations lies in the near omnipresent confounding of selection and treatment:

Another dependable tactic bound to give favorable outcomes is to confound selection and treatment, so that in the published comparison those receiving the treatment are also the more able and well placed. The often-cited evidence of the dollar value of a college education is of this nature — all careful studies show that most of the effect, and of the superior effect of superior colleges, is explainable in terms of superior talents and family connections rather than in terms of what is learned or even the prestige of the degree. Matching techniques and statistical partialings generally undermatch and do not fully control for the selection differences — they introduce regression artifacts confusable as treatment effect. (p. 427)

Campbell is explicit that "many of the difficulties lie in the intransigencies of the research setting and in the presence of recurrent seductive pitfalls of interpretation" (p. 409). He is also mindful that political problems lead to less interpretable results:

Decisions are made in a political arena, and involve political jeopardies that are often sufficient to explain the lack of hardheaded evaluation of effects. Removing reform administrators from the political spotlight seems both highly unlikely, and undesirable even if it were possible. What is instead essential is that the social scientist research advisor understand the political realities of the situation, and that he aid by helping create a public demand for hardheaded evaluation, by contributing to those political inventions that reduce the liability of honest evaluation, by educating future administrators to the problems and possibilities. (p. 409)

Campbell is sensitive to the problem faced by administrators who advocate specific reforms as certain to be successful:

> Given the inherent difficulty of making significant improvements by the means usually provided and given the discrepancy between promise and possibility, most administrators wisely prefer to limit the evaluations to those the outcomes of which they can control, particularly insofar as published outcomes or press releases are concerned. Ambiguity, lack of truly comparable comparison bases, and lack of concrete evidence all work to increase the administrator's control over what gets said, or at least to reduce the bite of criticism in the case of actual failure. There is safety under the cloak of ignorance. Over and above this tie-in of advocacy and administration, there is another source of vulnerability in that the facts relevant to experimental program evaluation are also available to argue the general efficiency and honesty of administrators. The public availability of such facts reduces the privacy and security of at least some administrators. . . . If the political and administrative system has committed itself in advance to the correctness and efficacy of its reforms, it cannot tolerate learning of failure. To be truly scientific we must be able to experiment. We must be able to advocate without that excess of commitment that blinds us to reality testing. This predicament, abetted by public apathy and by deliberate corruption, may prove in the long run to permanently preclude a truly experimental approach to social amelioration. (pp. 409-410)

Campbell seeks to create innovations on two fronts. The first is technical, to come up with research designs that promote clearer causal evidence; the second is political, to develop stances that program administrators can adopt to avoid the traps inherent in the advocacy required to get programs funded.

On the technical issues, in "Reforms as Experiments" Campbell pursues some familiar themes about the desirability of randomized experiments and of interrupted time series and regression discontinuity designs. As far as political stances are concerned, he says we should

> shift from the advocacy of a specific reform to the advocacy of the seriousness of the problem, and hence to the advocacy of persistence in alternative reform efforts should the first one fail. The political stance would become: "This is a serious problem. We propose to initiate Policy A on an experimental basis. If after five years there has been no significant improvement, we will shift to Policy B." By making explicit that a given problem solution was only one of several that the administrator or party could in good conscience advocate, and by having ready a plausible alternative, the administrator could afford honest evaluation of the outcomes. . . . Coupled with this should be a general moratorium on ad hominem evaluative research, that is, on research designed to evaluate specific administrators rather than alternative policies. . . . If we threaten this [the privacy

of administrators], the measurement system will surely be sabotaged in the innumerable ways possible. While this may sound unduly pessimistic, the recurrent anecdotes of administrators attempting to squelch unwanted research findings convince me of its accuracy. But we should be able to evaluate those alternative policies that a given administrator has the option of implementing. (p. 410)

The vision in "Reforms as Experiments" is of a rational society in which decisions depend on results of hardheaded tests of bold attempts to improve social problems. Campbell thought that the political will to generate important changes was present in the United States of 1969, as were the technical requirements for evaluating the effects of these changes. Missing was a genuine administrative commitment to implementing available experimental and quasi-experimental techniques. Could that society be experimental in the dual sense of cherishing both bold new ideas and their honest evaluation experiments?

"The Experimenting Society." "Reforms as Experiments" was the starting point for an extensive paper on the same topic: "Methods for the Experimenting Society" was presented at the American Psychological Association and Eastern Psychological Association annual conventions in 1971. The paper was not published in an authorized version until Campbell (1988) published a collection of his papers (with the editorial assistance of E. S. Overman). It was retitled "The Experimenting Society" and introduced as a utopian speculation to prepare for a future when social reform was higher on the political agenda. Campbell (1988) did not claim that his views were true or superior, saying, "I myself withhold full advocacy" (p. 292). He contended that his ideas were worth critical public scrutiny, and that it was to this end he published them.

Despite his 20-year ambivalence about publishing "The Experimenting Society," its continued attractiveness to him is suggested by his use of the term in the titles of several subsequent papers (Campbell, 1981b, 1987b; Tavris, 1975). Problematically, the 1971 and 1988 versions differ considerably. The earlier paper treats methodological issues in greater detail than does the later one. For historical continuity we should consider the earlier version, but for accuracy with the published record and fidelity to Campbell's reappraisal on his earlier ideas we should cite the 1988 version. To compromise, we deal more with the 1988 version, citing significant modifications that occurred.

"The Experimenting Society" begins with articles of faith about norms that should govern a society committed to experimenting with new reforms. Such a society will be one that would vigorously try out possible solutions to recurrent problems and would make hard-headed, multidimensional evaluations of outcomes, and when the evaluation of one reform showed it to have been ineffective or harmful, would move on to try other alternatives. (Campbell, 1988, p. 291)

Campbell acknowledges that no such society exists; in the 1971 draft he noted movement in that direction in Finland, England, Yugoslavia, Poland, Czechoslovakia, Chile, and the United States. He dropped these references later, providing only a brief description of the Czech mood in 1968. The experimenting society would be *active*: "explores possibilities in action (as well as, or instead of, in thought and simulation)" (1988, p. 293); it would be committed to *"action research"* (p. 293) rather than research to postpone action; it would be *honest*, committed to *reality testing* and avoiding self-deception and defensiveness, open in its self-presentation to the world; it should be *scientific* in valuing "open criticism, experimentation, willingness to change once-advocated theories in the face of experimental and other evidence" (p. 295); it should be an *"accountable, challengeable, due process society . . .* [with] public access to the records on which social decisions are made" (p. 295); it would be an *open society, decentralized* as much as possible, committed to *"means-idealism* as well as *ends-idealism"* (p. 296), and it will be a *"popularly responsive society"* (p. 296), a *"voluntaristic society,* providing for individual participation and consent at all decision-levels possible" (p. 296). Finally, it will be an *"equalitarian society,* valuing the well-being and the preferences of each individual equally" (p. 296).

Noting aspirations to experimentation in capitalist and communist countries, Campbell sees experimentation as a new ideology to bridge East and West. All countries make reforms to increase their fit to the world, reducing the roles of ideology or adaptations to a past and different world. Experimentation is here linked to a utopian vision of a pragmatic society in which evaluation plays a major role in determining which problem-solving strategies are worth retaining, abandoning, or further testing. In this utopia, "the job of the methodologist . . . is not to say *what is to be done,* but rather to say *what has been done"* (p. 297). Thus the most useful aspect of social science is its methodology; but Campbell believes that the design of innovations should depend on groups in the political process that are responsive to a wider range of interests and experiences than scholars. Campbell goes so far as to assert: "Even the conclusion drawing and the relative weighting of conflicting indicators must be left up to the political process" (p. 297). Why the reluctance to endorse social scientists as policy advisers?

Government asks what to do, and scholars answer with assurance quite out of keeping with the scientific status of their fields. In the process, the scholar-advisors too fall into the overadvocacy trap and fail to be interested in what happens once their advice is followed. . . . We social scientists could afford more of the modesty of the physical sciences, should more often say that we can't know until we've tried. (p. 298)

In both versions of "The Experimenting Society" Campbell acknowledges that social programs imperfectly incorporate substantive social science theories. In the early version he says that theoretical knowledge makes social scientists capable of "wise conjectures" and that "the methodological challenges of the experimenting society (require) appeals to the theory and content of the social sciences." In the later version he writes only that "the guesses of the experienced administrator and politician are apt to be on the average as wise as those of social scientists" (p. 298). Campbell has little faith in social science theories, so he wants evaluators to play a servant-methodologist rather than an advisory role. He thinks that role is more commensurate with democratic values.

In the early draft, the servant-evaluator had three major methodologies to use. The first was experimental. The second involved using social indicators, a theme Campbell takes up elsewhere (1976, 1984b). He stressed the need for data series relevant to a specific reform rather than developed for general monitoring purposes. He also stressed the need for multiple single indicators, all recognized as partially imperfect and partially relevant. He claimed that indicators will change in validity once they become the focus of decision making. In the early draft, Campbell said that indicators are less biased compared "to the interview biases of fear, courtesy and expectation which are apt to provide pseudo-successes in survey-research evaluations" (p. 28). He omitted this in 1988, pessimistically citing "a discouraging law that seems to be emerging: *the more any social indicator is used for social decision making, the greater the corruption pressures upon it*" (p. 306). Campbell (1984b) spells out the forms the corruption takes: the archived numbers deviate from what was observed, and the social processes being monitored change because monitoring is taking place. Examples from the field of mental health have been given by a student of Campbell (Ginsberg, 1984).

These archives were also to contain results of surveys routinely conducted to measure "general happiness and specific enjoyments, satisfactions with both the work day and recreational aspects of life" (Campbell, 1971, p. 30), measures of "not only pride in own achievement but also pride in family, community and national achievement. We must attempt to measure satisfaction with family and neighbor interactions as well as consumer satisfactions. . . . We should assess preferences, satisfactions and resentments with regard to the specific program and problem area" (p. 30). By 1988, for whatever reasons, the discussion of these subjective indicators is missing.

In the early version Campbell presented a third set of methods. Each month he wanted service agencies to report who they served and how much service they delivered, to conduct customer satisfaction reports and surveys of unsatisfied needs from potential consumers, and to use such information to decide budgets and agency expansion, reorganization, or elimination. Here Campbell specifically advocates using evaluation for accountability purposes; since he was elsewhere so negative about such purposes it is probably no accident that this section did not appear in 1988. Campbell discusses the practical, ethical, and bias-inducing obstacles to letting participants vote on their programs, detailing how to reduce these obstacles. He also details problems common to interviews and mail questionnaires for surveying participants, such as clients who exaggerate complaints to get more services, the possibility that a survey raises expectations that cannot be met, bandwagon effects due to knowing neighbors' opinions, and boredom of repeated surveys. Here Campbell exhibits his usual creativity for identifying validity threats, advocating remedies, and critically assessing his own proposals. The 1971 draft also has a much sharper concern for treating program clients as research collaborators rather than subjects, as indispensable experts about their needs and program experiences.

In both versions of the paper Campbell stresses the social organization of science more than its methods, though the analysis is more extensive in the later version. He wants science to foster open discussion and trenchant criticism from many substantive, epistemological, and methodological perspectives. The social organization and commitments of Polanyi's (1962) republic of science mirror the organization and commitments of the experimenting society. The organizations of science, society, and politics become as one. Campbell therefore stresses funding many smaller studies of a program, critically reanalyzing completed evaluations, and encouraging internal criticism of a program (e.g., by whistle-blowers) or an evaluation (e.g., by a dissenter from a research team). The 1988 section title "Getting Mutual Criticism and Competitive Replication into Social Experimentation and Program Evaluation" summarizes Campbell's belief that social arrangements for mutual criticism are as important as method choice in science.

In both versions of "The Experimenting Society" the norms of the society are identical with the fully lived norms of an open scientific *and* political system. Campbell sees evaluators at the core of this disputatious community of truth seekers. Yet the 1988 version is more tentative about the core idea, and more pessimistic about the quality of relevant social science theory and cooperation from bureaucrats and welfare professionals. The later version contains fewer suggestions about methods for evaluators to use and fewer exemplars of nations moving toward an experimenting society. Comparing the two drafts is sobering.

The 1971 vision of an experimenting society elicited commentary from many quarters, mostly critical. In the United States, Shaver and Staines (1971) questioned whether administrators or social scientists could be impartial, and whether administrators could adopt a tentative, uncommitted stance toward reform. Shaver and Staines said administrators must overadvocate programs to get programs approved. No overadvocacy, no program. Czech social psychologist Janousek (1970) wondered whether the experimental society would be too coercive, with individuals having little say in constructing reform. Zuniga (1975), a Chilean, questioned whether social scientists' orientation was problem centered rather than profession centered, so that their question and method choices would be sensitive to problems rather than professional norms. In keeping with his ideals about open critical commentary, Campbell facilitated the publication of these critiques of his (then still unpublished) "Methods for the Experimenting Society," using the critiques to make the final published version more tentative.

Campbell's ambivalence about "The Experimenting Society" is expressed in a 1983 commentary on it:

> When a year ago Euclides Sanchez and Gerardo Marin asked me to address this convention on the experimenting society, my first reaction was probably like yours: "The topic is outdated, a forgotten dream." But then I came to the realization that this was indeed an optimal time for such planning, that we would constitute here an excellent group of planners, and that a great deal of ambivalent critical reassessment was needed to replace our earlier over-optimistic advocacy. For the image of a truly experimenting society will turn out to be a perennially attractive vision that many have come to, and it will spontaneously revive again as social scientists attempt to advise governments that seem sincerely to seek progress. Moreover it is in periods like this, when governments are less interested in our services, that we have the time to plan, so that, when the public will to support such efforts returns, we will be readier than we were last time." (p. 1)

Campbell the Theorist of Science

Campbell is unique among evaluation theorists in favoring experimental methods in a self-consciously critical way, in linking his theory to sociopolitical norms like Polanyi's (1962) republic of science, and in

grounding his preferred methods and society in a systematic epistemological framework. His epistemological rationales avoid normative epistemology — theories of how we *should* learn — for skeptics convinced him
that all theory of knowledge presupposes knowledge. He endorses *descriptive* epistemology — describing and explaining the processes whereby
organisms (and scientists) learn about their world. Campbell wants descriptive epistemology to provide tentative guidelines for improving social science and evaluation practice (1987a). He endorses the utility of
common sense, practical knowing, and tradition; but he thinks science is
marginally more effective because of its norms about identifying and
publicly adjudicating threats to knowledge claims. These ideas are cogently discussed when Campbell (1974a, 1977) justifies why he is a
critical realist, why evolutionary epistemology is a comprehensive descriptive theory of knowledge growth, and why the sociology of science
might improve scientific practice (Campbell, 1987a).

Critical realism. Campbell postulates the existence of a real world beyond the minds of human knowers. He has written about physical entities
as ephemeral as candle flames and as unbreakable, immutable, and homogeneous in substance and color as adamant, the ideal metal of the Greek
gods (Campbell, 1977). He discusses such social entities as groups (1958)
and individual personality traits (Campbell & Fiske, 1959), relating
entitivity to criteria from Gestalt psychology — for example, common
fate, similarity, proximity, and good figure. Campbell's ontology includes
forces, too, including the "push-pull" forces of mechanics buttressing a
manipulability theory of causation (Cook & Campbell, 1979), emphasizing how these forces are complexly interrelated so that a full description
of reality entails higher-order statistical interactions (Campbell, 1987b).
He publicly acknowledges the possibility of latent powers that gradually
manifest themselves, as when genetic disposition controls physical growth
or unfolding brain structures control intellectual potential (1977).

Campbell is no naive realist, believing that our senses give direct access
to the real world. He writes about how evolution and cognitive structure
mediate false views of reality that visual illusions provide, and how all
knowledge is mediated by observers' theories. Visual illusions occur, he
contends (Segall et al., 1966), because our senses are rooted in presuppositions about the (past) world to which they adapted — a world that
contained fewer horizontal lines and sharp angles than today's carpentered
world and where greater utility inhered in seeing small objects move
within frames than our current world requires (Campbell, 1977). Without
this evolutionary and biological history, Campbell thinks we would not
see the lines in the Muller-Lyer illusion as so unequal, and we would not
see small objects move when the frame is manipulated in the Duncker rod

and frame illusion. The external world is fallibly interpreted by observers rich in suppositions from biological or individual histories that have more adaptive relevance to the past than to the present or future.

Given the impossibility of certain knowledge, the key issue for Campbell is how best to approximate truth. Like Hume, he assigns a minor role to induction; like Popper, he assigns a major role to a falsificationist deduction, arguing that we can construct reality tests to learn whether a proposition is probably false in the weak sense that no viable alternative interpretation of it is currently envisaged. Campbell and Stanley (1963) write:

> In a very fundamental sense, experimental results never "confirm" or "prove" a theory — rather, the successful theory is tested and escapes being disconfirmed. ... The results of an experiment "probe" but do not "prove" a theory. An adequate hypothesis is one that has repeatedly survived such probing — but it may always be displaced by a new probe. (p. 35)

Campbell is more explicitly fallibilist than Popper, perhaps because he deals more with examples from the social than the natural sciences. Falsification tests are themselves fallible, he argues, because social measurement is indirect, and social theories and hypotheses are squishy with many multivariate complexities, including those that arise when humans react to their worlds.

Campbell's discussions of measurement make particularly clear the fallibility of scientific knowledge. He rejects the logical positivists' definitional operationalism that an entity is equivalent to its measure (for example, IQ is what an IQ test measures — Campbell, 1969). Instead, he espouses multiple operationalism, the belief that many measures that differ in irrelevancies are needed to triangulate on a construct. Valid measurement also requires discriminating a construct from related but theoretically distinct concepts — for example, discriminating genuine rehabilitation in ex-criminals from their learning in prison how to avoid detection when committing crimes. From this conception of measurement arises the multitrait multimethod technique that requires convergent *and* discriminant validity as conditions for naming something (Campbell & Fiske, 1959).

Campbell (1969, 1986a) acknowledges that the treatments studied in program evaluation are more complex multivariate packages than manipulations in basic social science. He is not troubled that such complexity detracts from theoretical purity and from the likelihood of transferring a treatment effect to unstudied settings. This is because the relevant theories are so radically underspecified they cannot be adequately tested, and because complex treatments are the sum of causal forces that, taken singly, would be puny. When taken together they might have impact.

Campbell is a *critical* realist. He believes that analysis, commentary, and open learning from experience help us to learn about threats to valid inference and to develop methods that reduce their plausibility. Of course, we can examine only those alternatives currently identified as plausible. To reduce the likelihood of overlooking alternatives, he wants a public science in which contending parties compete to overthrow interpretations about, say, how an object should be named or whether a relationship is causal. There is no objectivity except that implicit in pluralist, critical assessments leading to intersubjectively verified inferences. For Campbell, knowledge is justified true belief. But he acknowledges that scientific groups (and their sponsors) share unacknowledged biases. The descriptive history of science (Feyerabend, 1975; Kuhn, 1970) has convinced him that such biases are so built into research that the relevant focal community often cannot detect them. Thus Campbell abjures all sure foundations of knowledge; he is antifoundationalist. But he still believes that organizing science into disputatious communities gets closer to truth than its major alternatives — self-criticism or scientific methods that rule out validity threats so automatically that practicing researchers no longer know the threats against which the procedures safeguard. Collective science complements self-criticism and methodological sophistication by forcing out more alternative interpretations and by providing more rigorous tests of knowledge claims.

Evolutionary epistemology. In Campbell's conception, largely borrowed from Darwin, three mechanisms are crucial once a problem of adaptation to the environment is detected. First is a mechanism to generate many different variations that potentially could solve the problem. In biological evolution, the random mutation of genes supplies variation, with randomness making the variants "blind" in not being specifically generated to solve the problem. In social evolution, variation stems from human creativity and social willingness to implement ideas that deviate from the norm. Second is a mechanism to select at least one variant that reduces the problem sufficiently. In biological evolution, selection occurs through the breeding advantage of individuals with a mutation that better fits the environment. These survive; others may die out. In social evolution, selection occurs through evaluations that tell how much a solution alleviates a problem. The third mechanism concerns retaining knowledge about effective variants. In biological evolution, retention is carried out by genetic changes passed on to subsequent generations. In social evolution, retention depends on deposits in libraries, computer memories, and folk wisdom, and on how easily relevant stored knowledge can be retrieved for use. The core notions are that blind variation and selective retention are especially fruitful, that no holds should be barred when identifying what might work, and that the latter depends on competition between theories to see which best explains some result. (In Campbell's case, the alternative theory is rarely a grand substantive theory, but rather individual nuisance factors of the type specified as threats to validity.)

Campbell knows that biological evolution does not match social evolution. Time frames are very different, and humans use more means to learn about the world. He values the biological model for its apparent success in macrobiology; its emphasis on radical, novel, and unforeseen variants; and its reminder of the nefarious effects of misconstruing or inadequately recording what works. So subtle and original is Campbell's writing on evolutionary epistemology that he is widely cited in philosophy as the major source of recent rejuvenation of thinking along these lines (Giere, 1985; Popper, 1972). We discuss Campbell's theory in two parts: its variation and selection components.

Campbell (1982) writes pessimistically about *variation* in social programs: "Most of what most governments offer in the name of 'reforms' and 'new programs' are symbolic gestures designed to indicate government awareness of problems and sympathetic intentions, rather than serious efforts to achieve social change" (p. 118). Realities demand that social programs be watered down to be funded. Only rarely does the political mood favor experimentation with bold alternatives to the status quo. Campbell believes that the Great Society, under Presidents Johnson and Nixon, was such a moment, even though the bureaucracy pursued agendas during that time that overlapped only partially with the national agenda. From this pessimistic analysis arises Campbell's preference for pilot programs, the best approximation to random mutations in biology. Concern with bold alternatives makes Campbell more explicit than other theorists about when evaluation is *not* worthwhile. He opposes evaluating anything that (a) is likely to be puny, or approved so that officials could say they were addressing a problem; (b) has components not likely to be transferable; (c) is still being implemented and so is making productive mistakes; or (d) involves explicitly evaluating officials, especially those who are not proud of their program. Campbell does not rely on social science theories for generating bold variants worth testing. He wants this role to be played by those who know a problem, by those who have made attempts to ameliorate it, by on-the-job invention, and by creative practitioner insight. He wants truly new ideas and will be promiscuous about their origin since social life cannot provide the dazzling sources of unimaginable variability that characterize random genetic mutations.

Selection is the second function in the evolutionary model. Here evaluation plays a special role, selecting variants that reduce the severity of a social problem. Campbell advocates experiments because they provide less ambiguous causal knowledge than the alternatives and so specify better the fit between the program and the target problem. As early as Campbell and Stanley (1963), he wrote:

> Underlying the comments of the previous paragraphs, and much of what follows, is an evolutionary perspective on knowledge (Campbell, 1959), in which applied practice and scientific knowledge are seen as the resultant of an accumulation of selectively retained tentatives, remaining from the hosts that have been weeded out by experience. Such perspective leads to a considerable respect for tradition in teaching practice. If, indeed, across the centuries many different approaches have been tried, if some approaches have worked better than others, and if those which work better have therefore, to some extent, been more persistently practiced by their originators, or imitated by others, or taught to apprentices, then the customs which have emerged may represent a valuable and tested subset of all possible practices. But the selective, cutting edge of this process of evolution is very imprecise in the natural setting. The conditions of observation, both physical and psychological, are far from optimal. What survives or is retained is determined to a large extent by pure chance. Experimentation enters at this point as the means of sharpening the relevance of testing, probing, selection process. Experimentation thus is not in itself viewed as a source of ideas necessarily contradictory to traditional wisdom. It is rather a refining process superimposed upon the probably valuable accumulations of wise practice. Advocacy of an experimental science of education does not imply adopting a position incompatible with traditional wisdom. (p. 4)

Campbell became increasingly concerned with factors other than chance and the technical limits of methods that reduce the quality of reality-testing. In selecting variants, interest relevance and action feasibility play significant roles (Campbell, 1977, p. 80). In the biological model selection is cruel; only the fittest survive. Social selection is also cruel. Bureaucratic and professional groups constrain the selection of variants and tilt evaluations to protect themselves against results that might harm them or cause them to lose their jobs.

Selection differs in the biological and social world because vicarious processes are more common in the latter. We learn what works by observing others or by thought experiments. We do not exclusively depend on direct experience. We can learn a room by looking at it rather than by directly exploring it as would be required if we were blindfolded (Campbell, 1977). In fact, Campbell admits that he has never done an evaluation. His relevant experience is vicarious, through talking to evaluators, reading about their successes and failures, and using others' critiques of his work.

In accord with evolutionary theory, Campbell suggests possible solutions that other (more cautious) scholars would consider premature. He published his work with a critical utopian flavor (Campbell, 1971, 1987a, 1988) hoping to see the ideas discussed rather than to see them accepted as "true" or acted upon in policy. For Campbell, as for Popper or Darwin, it matters not that conjectures are incorrect but only that they be bold and reflect different suppositions about solutions likely to be effective. It does matter to Campbell that claims about effective solutions be as true as possible. His work consistently reflects the duality of the evolutionary model: Suggestions for solutions should be bold and cannot be perfectly thought through; analyses of their efficacy should be based on the best available evidence. Anything goes in generating potential solutions; in evaluating them, multiple sources of evidence are relevant and only the best will do.

By the 1980s Campbell could reflect on his years of "trial and error" in evaluation and synthesize the lessons he vicariously learned watching evaluators work in social programs. These empirical lessons are worth storing to make future evaluations more productive. The lessons are contained in his paper "Can We Be Scientific in Applied Social Science?" (1984a). First is the problem of the greater equivocality of causal inference for research in policy settings. Second is the likelihood of greater extraneous biases entering into all discretionary judgments in research. Third is the mistaken belief that quantitative measures replace qualitative knowing instead of qualitative knowing being a prerequisite of quantification. Fourth is the error of specifying as program goals fallible measures that are open to bureaucratic manipulation. Fifth, a one decision/one research ideal was central to our original program evaluation model; Campbell now recommends decoupling research from a single decision. A sixth mistake was recommending to government external evaluation of programs rather than evaluation by the delivery team itself. A seventh mistake was calling for evaluation before programs were debugged. An eighth problem was recommending a single, national, once-and-for-all evaluation to settle an issue. The ninth mistake was overvaluing external validity over internal validity. Tenth was neglect of the fact that scientific truths are the collected product of a community of scientists (Campbell, 1984a).

This retrospective leads Campbell to some positive recommendations for evaluation. First is to move to a "*contagious crossvalidation model* of program evaluation" (1984a, p. 36). This entails government funding of diverse local programs addressing the chronic sores of society. After time for debugging, a subset of these programs may be proud enough to evaluate themselves however they want, with results being widely disseminated, even if they are probably bias riddled. Organizations that want to adopt evaluated programs are funded to do so. Serious summative evaluations are then carried out and restricted to the newly adopting sites. Results from these sites are widely shared and critiqued in the hope that

> by moving the primary evaluation to the dissemination stage, we are evaluating the transferable, borrowable aspects of the program. In the initial zeal of program development, exceptional success is frequently due to heroic 80-hour weeks on the part of the key staff and these are not aspects of the transferable program. We need to know about effectiveness for the program's routinized form. While the problem of generalizing in applied science is substantially different than in theoretical science, one essential of the "knowledge" produced is still reusability on different occasions and times. (1984a, p. 37)

Campbell's second suggestion involves competitive replication of policy-relevant pilot studies through simultaneous replication, data re-analysis, and dissenting reports from research team members. Third, he recommends *"writing up our evaluation reports for our fellow evaluation researchers* in and out of the universities" (1984a, p. 41) rather than writing them for the social policy world—he is so concerned with truth that he wants to avoid traps in writing reports for those whose interests dominate their concern for truth. Finally, Campbell counsels evaluators about *"avoiding 'ad hominem' and 'ad institutionem' research"* (1984a, p. 43), for corruption pressure is maximal when research aims to evaluate institutions, social organizations, or persons rather than programs.

Campbell is explicit that these four recommendations are not a complete, formal framework for improving evaluation. Rather, they are steps toward a more scientific applied social science based on a "mutually monitoring, disputatious community of scholars who listen carefully to each others' arguments and rebuttals" (1984a, p. 44). The creative angle in this paper is using concepts from sociology of science to devise social arrangements leading to less biased learning in applied sciences. Once again we see Campbell seeking out scholars with different intellectual interests and using their work to improve how we learn about social programs.

OUR ANALYSIS OF
CAMPBELL'S THEORY OF EVALUATION

Theory of Social Programming

Campbell presents three worlds of social programming—the current world, the current world as it can be modified marginally, and a radically different world that is utopian but worth critical scrutiny.

The current world. Campbell's description of the current world of social programming is quickly summarized. Evaluation helps select options that make a true difference to trenchant social ills. But the context surrounding social programs constrains their capacity for alleviating such ills. Inadequate public funding is one constraint. Another comes from legislators, bureaucrats, and professional service providers whose interests lead them to initiate programs for cosmetic reasons and to propose reforms that offend as few as possible. As a result, programs are often peripheral to clients' real needs. To protect their interests agencies tend to sponsor uncritical evaluations and to promote overly optimistic reports, neither of which promotes useful social knowledge. To Campbell, the major heroes of social programming are whistle-blowers who publicly oppose attempts to whitewash their programs.

We see here a quite negative assessment of the motives of major actors in social programming. Is this assessment warranted? Considerable literature and experience support Campbell's pessimism that client needs are not the primary driving force behind political and administrative behavior. Getting reelected and maintaining the agency budget are more powerful priorities. Of course, client needs play some role and can be an important motive for designing or evaluating social programs; entire fields, such as social administration and public policy, are predicated on helping managers help those in need. Campbell (1984b) himself notes that economic indicator data are routinely published and sometimes embarrass the very governments that fund them. Moreover, a few genuine countercases could help us to construct a contingency theory of when bureaucratic, professional, and client interests overlap. Agencies like Housing and Urban Development have been captured by those who provide services or control public housing; but in agencies like the National Institutes of Health or the Centers for Disease Control, client interests play a major role. Campbell does not explore factors that promote honest problem solving in government or elsewhere. Instead, he locates the capacity for significant change in demonstration projects and a hypothetical experimenting society, largely ignoring current social programs.

Other evaluation theorists struggle to discover leverage points for important social change in current programs, painting a world of social programming that is more differentiated and enlightened than the world Campbell portrays (Kelman, 1987). But it is a world where evaluation plays a marginal role in facilitating the marginal social changes that are the norm. Some programs serve millions of people and cost billions of dollars, so the sum of marginal changes may not be trivial in total lives influenced or dollars saved. Campbell is rarely concerned with these margins; bold conjectures and reforms interest him.

Bureaucratic and political interests do not preclude implementing social programs worthy of being called reforms. The social problems with which evaluators deal are recalcitrant, having withstood attempts to alleviate them. Fresh, novel thinking is particularly required. The spectacular practical successes of theory in physical and biological sciences incline us to look to social theory for such novelty. But Campbell is pessimistic that current social science theories can help design effective social programs. Given poor substantive theories and existing programs watered down to be politically and administratively acceptable, where in the current system can one make a difference?

Marginally modifying the current world. Campbell's answer is to develop focal indicators for continuous monitoring of program performance. This is not comprehensive advice and is likely to provide only indirect information about changing a program. The advice falls short because maintaining comprehensive indicators relevant to only a single program is expensive, and because of the corruptibility of indicators about which Campbell's pessimism has increased in his recent writings (e.g., 1984b, 1987a, 1988). Further, the distinction between program and individual performance is unclear in bureaucracies; high officials believe they will be held personally accountable for the performance of their programs. Program monitoring is inadequate by itself for reforming current programs.

Some of Campbell's advice about innovative pilot projects is relevant to current programs, particularly using experiments to examine modifications in a program, evaluating programs or elements that are effective and transferable, and using periodic client surveys to describe program elements that most and least satisfy clients. But Campbell does not develop these matters very thoroughly. Who can blame him, given his premise that studying ongoing programs holds less leverage for social change than studying pilot programs with assumptions that are different from the failed assumptions of current programs?

His major mechanism for studying bold change in society is the demonstration project. Initially, Campbell discussed demonstrations in isolation, arguing that their lesser political impactedness and the absence of the demand that all clients receive services make them more innovative and evaluable than existing programs. Campbell often cites the negative income tax experiments as his exemplar, yet their sad history gives us no cause to believe that bold experiments lead to widespread policy change or that interest groups do not interfere with demonstrations. Moreover, Cronbach (1982a; Cronbach et al., 1980) notes that many pilot studies are mounted by their developers, with atypical effort, defensiveness about results, and reduced likelihood of the achieved results generalizing to contexts where these qualities are in shorter supply.

Campbell recognizes these possibilities; in later writings he describes demonstrations somewhat differently. He is convinced that some variants invented by program personnel and their clients will be unique and effective. His "contagious crossvalidation model" aims to identify or stimulate such variants; it suggests a marginal reform of the current social programming, for many social programs are so decentralized that much local variability exists in services offered. Under the model, government first funds many smaller projects representing interesting and novel reform ideas within a program. The funded projects are developed without external evaluation pressure until the personnel are so proud of their achievements that they want to release them for adoption/adaptation. Summative evaluation is restricted to these second-stage sites, where the original developers are not present. Stated in evolutionary terms, stage one sites generate variation, while stage two sites aid selection. This contagious cross-validation model is Campbell's major strategy for reforming current programs at the margin.

The model assumes that second-stage pilots will be mounted in an atmosphere of lesser novelty and special attention than first-stage sites. Perhaps—but those who bring in new materials may still oversell them, overadvocate them, and treat them as successful, permanent institutions (Frankfather, 1982). The model also assumes that much heterogeneity exists or can be stimulated in a program so truly novel variants will be found. This hypothesis needs probing; most professional practice may operate from a restricted set of fashionable models. How many ways can one organize teachers, police officers, social workers, community action projects, community economic initiatives, or drug abuse centers? How much politically acceptable creativity in social programming is independent of currently preferred theories? We are not sanguine that there are thousands of blossoming flowers. A few may blossom, but locating them in existing programs is difficult, as is stimulating new demonstrations that might be incorporated in programs.

A third assumption of the model is that funding agencies can wait five years or so before getting evaluative feedback. Such time horizons are infrequent in many social sectors of the U.S. government, except perhaps in health. Indeed, something like this model is commonplace in the National Institutes of Health — the National Cancer Institute's model of multiphase research on cancer prevention specifies many types of studies to be conducted between origination of an idea and its implementation as policy. Most administrative time horizons in social welfare are shorter; it is rare for funds to be disbursed for a yield five years later.

Finally, the contagious cross-validation model assumes that openminded evaluators debate among themselves the strengths and weaknesses of programs and evaluations, insulated from corruption by tenured university positions. Important actors in social programming would probably attend to such debates if a mechanism existed for extracting consensus from them about classes of interventions that are most effective. But Shaver and Staines (1971) warn us not to expect noble, open, and scholarly behavior from evaluators, most of whom operate on soft money and cannot afford extensive debate or public criticism of their work. Even those tenured in universities might attend more to disciplinary agendas than to public interest (Zuniga, 1975). Further, who pays for such debates? Which evaluator is brave enough to endanger future contracts by engaging in public debates that make agencies seem to have paid for inadequate research or findings? These examples all illustrate the same point: a lack of fit between the current world of social programming and Campbell's major suggestion for improving that world.

Aspiring to a utopian goal. Rather than analyze the current world of social programming, Campbell constructs a counterfactual utopia, hoping that its institutions and assumptions will be critically discussed, will highlight the limits of the present, and will create the will to improve the future. This utopian "experimenting society" is Campbell's literary device (much as Voltaire used England or Montesquieu Persia) to confront our current smug assumptions about political stances for improving society. His utopia is a self-consciously optimistic vision that he has no illusions will occur soon. He pointedly calls for criticism of this vision and notes that it *"may lead you and I in the end to oppose the experimenting society"* (1988, p. 292). Hence criticizing its lack of realism about social programming is unfair, since he is so obviously pessimistic and realistic about its potentialities, viewing himself more as a revolutionary than as an optimist.

Nonetheless, especially since Campbell calls for such criticism, one must question whether this utopian vision is feasible in *any* plausible world or *any* plausible time frame. Campbell's counterfactual world is predicated on giving high priority to client needs, fundamental new solutions, honest reality testing, advocating the importance of problems rather than solutions, and open debate. Current priorities, and many priorities we can realistically imagine, are the opposite. Political and administrative convenience overpowers client needs; generally accepted ideas dominate novelty and boldness; defensiveness about program effects takes precedence over honest reality testing; and control over debates about problems and programs vanquishes openness. In the world as it is, Campbell wants evaluators to be sideline commentators, speaking truthfully to other social scientists but holding their tongues when co-opted evaluators and self-serving administrators create slanted evaluation reports. In utopia, evaluators function differently — as honest truth-telling servants to enlightened administrators who desire and debate the feedback.

Some readers might want Campbell to provide the intellectual bridges to get us from the counterfactual to the real world. They will look largely in vain. Campbell does not discuss why tomorrow's politicians and administrators should be different from today's, or how administrators can be committed to honest reality testing if they have to sell programs to get support. In "The Experimenting Society," Campbell acknowledges that he does not bridge his two worlds; but he asserts that bridges need to be built and his utopian writing furthers this process — an honest admission of current intellectual impotence.

Perhaps, as a literary device, the experimenting society does not need bridges. Voltaire did not describe how eighteenth-century France could become more like libertarian England in his *Lettres Philosophiques*; he only asserted the need for movement. Similarly, Campbell's utopia describes alternative political arrangements facilitating a more scientific society and a more enlightened approach to social programming, with honest evaluation at its core. His utopia is more an end worth discussing for the future than a blueprint for today. Still, his analysis would be more compelling if readers could see how to go from Campbell's counterfactual world to ours.

To be fair, we should not forget that most of Campbell's writing on evaluation occurred in the Johnson and Nixon years, when money for innovations was available and pilot programs were more frequent. But as these funds decreased, program designers and evaluators accommodated more to the status quo. In this atmosphere Campbell's doubts about "The Experimenting Society" increased, his influence on evaluation decreased (though it is still high), and rationales for evaluation arose predicated on studying minor improvements in current programs (e.g., Patton, 1978; Stake, 1980b; Wholey, 1983). We doubt the present relevance of Campbell's construction of social programs and their political context; but we are less sure of its future relevance, since Campbell is not writing just for today or for the United States. In a 1975 interview he said:

I admit to one thing. I have as yet no solution to the political dilemmas of corruption, which is why I don't think we are ready for the experimenting society. We social scientists must first develop recipes to solve the political aspects of program evaluation; we can't just blunder in with our 10-foot-shelf of methods and stop there. All we can do now, with full conscience, is dedicate ourselves to exploring all the possibilities for an experimenting society, even if in the end we recommend against it. After all, shouldn't the experts be the first to say it won't work, if in fact it won't? (Tavris, 1975, p. 56)

The problem is that even though Campbell's theory of current social programming is realistic, his theory of practice is based on a utopia that is less so. Since most evaluators live in the world of current programming, this puts them in a substantial dilemma.

Theory of Knowledge Construction

Campbell has few peers among social scientists when it comes to the erudition and subtlety with which he justifies his stances on constructing knowledge about entities, causal connections, generalization, and theoretical explanation. His stances on these issues are well grounded in epistemology and research on methods. Though Campbell cannot prove that an external reality exists, his arguments for such a world are detailed and public. His description of our existential predicament — never knowing what is true and imperfectly knowing what is false — is internally cohesive. His epistemological relativism, which postulates that knowledge is impossible without active knowers who bring their own expectations to bear, accords with findings in human cognition.

He yokes epistemological fallibilism to ceaseless effort to reduce the fallibility of all scientific inferences. He looks to philosophy and sociology of science, to research on research, and to public criticism of methods to develop ways to provide better approximations to truth, especially about entities and causal relations. To see him improving methods like this breeds optimism, as do the examples he presents of research conducted well.

Though he argues that no way of constructing knowledge is perfect, he denies that anything goes, or that all ways of learning yield equally strong inferences. His discussions of causal methods illustrate this, for he ranks choices from among randomized experiments, quasi-experiments, and nonexperimental studies. Careful readers come away from Campbell's epistemological writings with a thorough justification for particular method choices. Yet these justifications must seem daunting to evaluators who look to methodologists for blueprinted techniques to take off a shelf and plug into studies. Even though he favors randomized experiments, Campbell sees their shortcomings and identifies many steps required to circumvent them partially. He offers no easy answers about methods that can be implemented mindlessly.

The most impressive aspect of Campbell's epistemology is his evolutionary theory of knowledge growth. This descriptive theory purports to show how knowledge increases. If true, it would benefit science as a general case and evaluation as a specific case. But if the account is wrong or incomplete in important ways, we then must ask: Has his commitment to evolutionary epistemology led him to misjudge important aspects of evaluation?

There is little doubt that biological and scientific evolution overlap conceptually around clear problem description, heterogeneity in proposed solutions, the need for rigorous tests, and storing knowledge about successful variants. But there are also obvious differences between biological and social evolution. Campbell notes the most important ones — humans rely heavily on vicarious processes to select variants that work, and they are constrained in the range of variants they can generate for solving a social problem because of deficiencies in individual creativity and cultural prescriptions about *legitimate* change attempts. In science or evaluation there can be no blind variation if blind means "free of all constraints," "independent of prior knowledge," "indifferent to results," or "indifferent to expectations about results."

Dunn (1982) contends that Campbell's evolutionary theory underestimates the role of symbols and interests in social change. In biological evolution, selection criteria are linked to reproductive advantage. Otherwise a mutation is less likely to be passed on. In biology, problem definition is not problematic. A specific lack of fit to the material world is the problem — for example, an animal that is cold, or hungry — with obvious clues about criteria that meet the need. If the weather is colder, lack of body warmth is the problem; metabolic change and increased intelligence (that helps find shelter) are two possible biological answers. If the problem is that the food source on trees is getting scarcer because it is burrowing under the bark, then sharper beaks are a possible answer.

Social problem definition is more complicated. Social interests often define needs for reform efforts, furthering some stakeholders' interests over those of others. Dunn (1982) contends that the interests of the economically and politically powerful will be dominant. Campbell is mute about what social need is; he does not differentiate needs from wants, and he deals little with social processes whereby some needs or wants enter the political agenda while others do not. A complete analogy to biological evolution must deal with detecting social problems that are worthy of amelioration. Dunn thinks that the relevant social processes are more complex and important in their consequences than the relevant biological ones.

Problem definition leads to selection of some evaluative criteria. In biological evolution, the major criteria concern changes in reproductive advantage. With social programs, the mechanisms generating evaluative criteria are less clear; Campbell does not deal with them explicitly. He emphasizes that multiple criteria should be used in all evaluations. He sometimes calls for evaluators to be concerned with utility issues involving selecting and weighting outcomes (other times he says these functions should be left to the political system). Generating and weighting outcome criteria are more important and problematic in social than in biological evolution. Is Campbell's neglect of these important matters a consequence of how unproblematic they are in the evolutionary theory he uses as a framework for thinking about program evaluation, or is it a function of his desire to leave these matters to the political system?

The biological model emphasizes retaining knowledge of solutions. Campbell wants the repositories of science to contain our best current approximations to truth so that when the reform wheel turns again, some needed knowledge will be available. But textbooks and archives in social science often contain more false positive than false negative findings and systematic overestimates of effects. Campbell's evolutionary theory is not detailed in describing how scientific archives operate and might be improved. Related to this is the issue of retrieval. Many evaluation reports are not in libraries but in diverse depositories that vary in efficiency and organization. Many evaluation reports are fugitive, not carefully evaluated, and most readily available to those with a keen interest in the topic and resources to match. They can control information flow to their advantage. As one example, we might expect advocates of early childhood education to monitor the relevant information environment constantly and to be better positioned than their opponents or neutral parties to summarize evaluation reports to politicians and professionals when needed.

The issue is: How well has Campbell worked through his evolutionary analogy for evaluation? Should he place so little emphasis on problem description and on retention of evaluation results when these are more problematic and important in social change than in biological evolution? Evolutionary theory is most relevant to evaluation in generating and selecting programs that work through the results of experiments. Thus:

> What is characteristic of science is that the selective system which weeds out among the variety of conjectures involves deliberate contact with the environment through experiment and quantified prediction, designed so that outcomes

quite independent of the preferences of the investigators are possible. It is preeminently this feature that gives science its great objectivity and its claims to a cumulative increase in the accuracy with which it describes the world. (Campbell, 1974a, p. 434)

The history of science reveals many such resolutions of knowledge disputes (Laudan, 1981; Moyer, 1979); however, some theory- and data-based resolutions are socially agreed upon in one generation but subsequently turn out to be wrong—for example, Spence's behaviorist theory gained a data-dependent victory over Tolman's cognitive learning theory, but 20 years later was largely discredited, with cognitive theory in ascendancy (Gholson & Barker, 1985). Moreover, science sometimes stalemates progress. For instance, when behavioral and cognitive psychotherapies are pitted against each other, behavioral researchers produce data supporting their theory while the obverse is true for cognitive theorists (Miller & Berman, 1983). In accounts like these, science does not resolve debates very clearly.

Campbell might contend that these examples come from social sciences where quantified predictions are rarely made, so experiments are more ambiguous in their results; and also that the errors of the past in these examples were detected by science. He might also point to meta-analyses that have been widely accepted and have changed the thinking about some particular class of solutions—as in psychotherapy. In these cases social science experiments can sometimes resolve debates—but rarely and unpredictably.

Thus the criticism is not that social sciences fail to progress in ruling out alternative theories and contributing to policy debates; it is that falsification, being a long-winded, multistudy, fallible process, is more credible in the long than the short term. But many theorists claim evaluation is a short-term enterprise designed to produce results for immediate use. Eventual truth is a fine goal for science and an ancillary goal for evaluation; but it provides an ideal beacon for the future more than a justification for today.

Dunn (1982) urges Campbell not to see experiments as mechanisms for showing what works, but as arguments that depend on many factors other than the alternative interpretations ruled out. Threats to validity are part of Dunn's framework, but they cannot and should not replace sociopolitical decisions. Issues of values and ethics stand next to issues of scientific warrant, but where in biological evolution is the place for values and ethics? Campbell sees the need for values and ethics in evaluation, but he does not tell how values and ethics fit into his evolutionary theory as a comprehensive description of evaluation.

Much sociology and history of science deals with basic research in physical sciences. Since Campbell's theory of knowledge construction depends on this literature, he may have constructed a theory that better describes natural science than social science, especially not an applied social science like evaluation. Applying his theory to evaluation assumes the legitimacy and primacy of scientific evaluations. Critics are vocal on this, challenging the priority given to internal over external validity (Cronbach, 1982a; Cronbach et al., 1980), to truth over short-term utility (Wholey, 1983), to testing over discovery (Guba & Lincoln, 1981), and to elitism in construing social science as different from ordinary knowing (Lindblom & Cohen, 1979). The issue is neither the internal coherence nor the relevance of Campbell's evolutionary theory for science; it is its relevance to evaluation if evaluation need not always be scientific in its priority goals (the best approximation to truth) or methods (quantification and/or experimentation).

Theory of Valuing

Scriven says that "value-phobic" researchers believe that facts can be separated from values and that evaluation seeks only to establish facts. Campbell holds no naive conception that facts are pure readings of reality, but he defends a distinction between facts and values. He ascribes factlike status to any observations that have been repeated despite many differences being incorporated in the observation process. Any successful new theory must subsume these stubborn observations. The proposition is that observations differ in how well they approximate facticity; degree of facticity depends on how many plausible alternative interpretations remain to be ruled out. In defending the factlike status of some beliefs, Campbell can appear to hasty readers to be a naive believer in value-free science.

However, he advocates that the valuing of evaluation results be left to the political process, not researchers. When asked in an interview what evaluators could do to get Congress to use evaluation more, he replied:

> I have to trust democratic populism. I do think it is up to the public, however ill-educated, and up to the Congress, however imperfect a representative of that public, to make decisions. . . . We should inform Congress and the public as best we can about social science, and be willing to be informed by them as well. (Tavris, 1975, p. 55)

Evaluators should not enter the policy world as arrogant guardians of the truth. Rather, they should learn from the policy world about values, and political and administrative feasibility. Campbell knows evaluations cannot be value-free. Early in study design he builds as many values as possible into the evaluation, particularly in selection of criteria of merit. He tells evaluators to use multidimensional outcome measures rather than the few measures preferred by some policymakers. Valuing cannot be avoided, but it can be heterogeneous. There are limits to his heterogeneity, though. Campbell would not incorporate undemocratic values into programs or evaluations, as "The Experimenting Society" makes clear.

Campbell places great store in truth seeking, but in his pantheon of values truth seeking is not paramount. He castigates administrators who sponsor evaluations to postpone action even though postponement may enhance truth seeking. The need to alleviate suffering underlies this preference, as does the notion from natural selection that action is paramount when faced with intractable situations that risk survival or breeding advantage. In "The Experimenting Society," Campbell denounces those truth-seeking methods of science that conflict with sociopolitical values of an open society. His model for the experimenting society is the voting booth, not the more coercive and elitist experimental laboratory.

Questions of epistemology and methodology are paramount in Campbell's work, but, unlike Scriven, he makes no explicit attempt to develop and justify either an intellectual system for assigning value or any particular theory of values, though a democratic theory of open decision making and a materialist theory of need can be inferred in Campbell's thinking. His work is also sparse about describing values of different stakeholders, deciding which values to represent in research, or determining how to represent values. He is most concerned with establishing the consequences of programs. Explicitly *assigning* value—saying that the program is good or bad—is not part of his evaluator's task, but somehow representing heterogeneous values in research is. Yet, apart from measuring multidimensional outcomes, he provides few concrete clues about selecting particular outcomes. But once again he sees the lacuna, writing in the 1971 "Methods for the Experimenting Society":

> As has been already been touched upon in discussion of indicators, the issue of values, of which criteria, will become of preeminent importance in the experimenting society. . . . Methods determining value priorities and of value pooling for collective decision making represent developed social science skills. . . . We need to make contact with the logico-mathematical puzzles provided by theorists such as Arrow. We need subjective-utility theory from psychological economists, and the scaling of social values in the psychometric tradition. (pp. 53-55)

Theory of Use

Campbell fears two potential misuses of evaluation findings. One is the biases in evaluations that lead to false positive or negative conclusions about program effects. This fosters the use of wrong information. The other is the way interested parties can control the content or dissemination of findings to further their own welfare rather than the truth. To counteract such biases, he wants more public scrutiny of findings, and more public and legal support for whistle-blowers. He encourages evaluators to write honest reports for peers even if they cannot do so for funders or the public, and he encourages all of us to press for a more open society in which findings are routinely debated by evaluators and all interested members of the public.

But ultimately for Campbell, use is the concern of the political process, not the evaluator. He does not want evaluators to promote use actively, since this detracts from the credibility of the more factlike findings. Campbell also thinks few evaluation results have such strong warrant that they deserve wide dissemination and discussion. In 1973, when asked why evaluations are not used more often, he said:

Well I think I'll pass on that question. I don't see the store of red hot findings that are being neglected and I really don't think the state of our art, either in the academic recommendations for research design or in the actually implemented designs, is all that advanced. Myself, I think we should continue to get as good findings as we can. But at the moment I'm not panicked by the failure to utilize them. (Salasin, 1973, pp. 9-10)

The danger is that Campbell's truth-driven, hands-off approach to use might lead to fewer evaluations and greater reliance on the prescientific evaluation methods that Campbell esteems less highly. He might not object to fewer evaluations, since he works for a future when political conditions for evaluation might be more favorable. He may even believe that evaluators are no less self-serving or preservation-minded than others. Nonetheless, the major pragmatic justification for evaluation is use; the more use deviates from modifying current programs, the less useful evaluation may be to those who must vote to support it.

Campbell's theory supposes that findings are worth using only if they have withstood the most rigorous tests. But the world of political action may have a different risk calculus from the world of science. It may tolerate more risk about being wrong in causal conclusions for the sake of lesser cost, enhanced timeliness, or more knowledge about program implementability, generalizability, or causal explanation. Why should the risk calculus of traditional science prevail over other ways of calculating the costs and benefits of information for practical action?

Finally, how realistic is it to expect evaluators to work on a problem for years, write a final report, and then disappear while others interpret, disseminate, and use it? Some evaluators become convinced partisans both for the data and for a policy position they derive from the data. They may want to use their expertise to enlighten those in the intellectual and practical worlds. On these matters Campbell is mute, and so risks conveying a scientific elitism rather than the pragmatism of improving a program at the margin with information that reduces uncertainty. The puniness Campbell sees in social science theories and methods makes it unrealistic to restrict use of evaluation findings to those at high certainty. We agree that the world of social policy prefers more certain knowledge; we would disagree that only that information should be used for which no alternative interpretations now exist. Campbell never explicitly makes this second argument, but his beliefs about the importance of truth and his pessimism and lack of urgency about use might all be interpreted this way.

Theory of Practice

Campbell's first theory of practice. Campbell's earliest and best-known theory of practice relied on experimental design to answer summative questions. This position was widely accepted in the decade after 1965 because (a) it fit existing conceptions of scientific knowledge and respectability, (b) it was thought to be widely practical in the field settings where evaluators operate, and (c) it promised clear causal conclusions worth using in policy. The theory depended on the importance of a particular type of causation, and on experiments being a practical, adequate way to achieve such knowledge. Randomized experiments were the preferred type of study, but some quasi-experiments were acceptable backup. Campbell emphasized that implementing randomized experiments in politicized field contexts is simple in design but problematic in execution. In discussing quasi-experiments, the emphasis was on improving and evaluating designs. To help this he invented a language of validity types and threats. Thus he developed a theory of practice that was not revolutionary, seemed feasible, and promised quality knowledge about important causal connections. Moreover, experiments seemed amenable to improvement. When demonstration-type randomized experiments were launched in the 1960s and 1970s, Campbell watched their progress closely to identify difficulties in implementing them and to improve them. His writings of the period leave the impression that the most scientifically distinguished methods for causal inference are practical at their core and can be improved (Campbell, 1969; Riecken et al., 1974).

This first theory of practice also made evaluation conceptually simple. Trade-off questions had clear answers. Although he coined the term *external validity* and explicated threats to it, Campbell was adamant that since evaluation is about the *causal* effectiveness of programs, internal validity had priority. Otherwise, incorrect causal conclusions might be used to modify programs. Other trade-offs that worry evaluation theorists were also given short shrift. For example, should the evaluator be the distant student of a program or the advocate for the program results? Campbell aimed to publish the best approximation to truth, attend to the resulting scholarly debate, but let the political process handle the rest. Trade-offs about answering different types of questions — about implementation, targeting, or explanation — in the same study also did not concern him. His near-exclusive emphasis was on describing effects. He left assessing their theoretical explanation to basic researchers, and their policy relevance to decision makers. This made evaluation seem easy, doing good experiments or quasi-experiments pretty much like in graduate school. The difficult trade-offs are resolved just as they are in experimental methods courses.

He also simplified evaluation by focusing resources on evaluating pilot programs that do not challenge bureaucratic and professional dominance as much as reforming ongoing programs. The lower profile of pilot and demonstration programs makes it easier to implement novel services *and* technically superior evaluations. When government funds for social amelioration increase rapidly and political leaders are willing to try novel approaches, pilot programs may be widespread. But change the conditions, and pilot projects can be dramatically curtailed. This happened often after the Nixon years, although job training and health education are two salient exceptions. After the mid-1970s evaluators had to work mostly with existing programs and projects. In such a climate the relevance of Campbell's preference for pilot programs declined somewhat.

The decline in Campbell's influence on evaluation also occurred because randomized field experiments were less attractive to managers than had been hoped; when approved, they were not easy to implement well; and when completed, they were not definitive in the clarity of causal results achieved. Many criticisms of experiments applied to all quantitative research — for example, poor measurement of outcomes or poor implementation of treatment. But other criticisms spoke directly to the rationale for randomized experiments. These were (a) frequent administrative reluctance to allow inequalities between experimentals and controls; (b) treatment-correlated attrition that occurs when treatments differ in desirability; (c) compensatory rivalry arising when members of the control group compete to make up for receiving fewer resources; (d) the reduction of external validity caused by creating random experimental groups if, for example, assignment is restricted to volunteers; and (e) the great fiscal expense of experiments. In these and other ways randomized experiments were more problematic than advertised. In many sectors their frequency of use was disappointing. Since it is difficult to have at the pinnacle of one's methodological repertoire a technique that can be used only infrequently, experiments lost popularity. Practice requires methods that can be used regularly, not occasionally, and that do not leave significant questions unanswered about program implementation and the causal mediation of results.

When evaluated, most Great Society programs were disappointing in the frequency and magnitude of effects. But it was unclear if disappointment arose from inadequate program theory, inadequate program implementation, or poorly designed or implemented evaluations. Campbell acknowledged the limits of substantive theory but concentrated on inadequate design. But other scholars believed that poor program implementation was the major cause, and they called for rich descriptions of social and individual processes in programs even if this took resources away from clear analysis of causal effects. This moved implementation and process centrally onto the agenda of evaluation theory and method and highlighted the black-box nature of much of Campbell's writing on experiments. He did sometimes write on qualitative methods, and sometimes said that implementation and process questions were legitimate. But he gives no advice on how to use qualitative or quantitative methods to describe implementation or to link process to outcome. The comparison with his work on experiments, where he was much more thorough and explicit, is striking.

Cronbach et al. (1980) claim that, in placing highest priority on causal inference, Campbell inadvertently downplays the practical utility of explanation. Understanding the mechanisms by which causes influence effects is crucial to Cronbach; he believes that such knowledge tells the necessary conditions for a cause to influence its effect. Cronbach is convinced that highly generalized causal connections from one variable to another are rare and that complex interactions are the norm in social life. If so, then future utility requires causal knowledge that is multivariate-explanatory, not bivariate-descriptive, so evaluations should be designed to enlighten program stakeholders instead of being tailored to specific political decisions. Weiss makes a similar argument, but she does not challenge Campbell as directly as does Cronbach.

While sharing similar assumptions about ontological complexity (Campbell, 1987b), Campbell wants evaluation to identify manipulable forces that generally (but not invariably) cause a particular effect. He understands *generally* to mean a common causal sign across most units, not a common sign across all units or the same size of effect across them. Campbell's justification for this is that national policymakers cannot often use fine-grained knowledge of causal contingencies to tailor specific services to specific groups or settings. It is hard enough for teachers to provide one kind of service to some children in their classes and another kind to others; it is often impossible for policymakers to legislate such action, and if they did it would probably not be carried out. Such selectivity of application is sometimes possible, but often not; and both political and logistical pressures incline toward comparable treatment.

The "postpositivist" zeitgeist of the 1980s heavily favored multivariate causal explanatory relationships that include situational, temporal, social, and cognitive factors. This search differs from that implied by the traditional positivist goal of discovering parsimonious general laws, even if the latter is understood in the weakest sense as a robust tendency over many particulars (as in meta-analysis). Some postpositivist critics argue that Campbell's failure to incorporate causal explanation into evaluation practice is wrong in ontological assumptions about the world, is too pessimistic about currently available techniques for causal modeling (here the critics' arguments do not convince us), and overlooks the fact that the use of evaluation results may be linked to causal explanation because such information facilitates enlightenment (Weiss, 1977b).

Another critique of Campbell's theory of experimental practice is that it does not fit much of the world of social programming. He emphasizes the causal effects and pilot programs of interest to legislators and senior managers who seek genuine reform. They want to know what works. Yet this perspective may not be widely shared by those responsible for daily operation of programs at the service delivery level. They are at least as concerned with program process, improving operations, maintaining the client base, facilitating billing and referrals, or ensuring fiscal accountability. They often assume effectiveness and feel threatened if more is demanded than head counts or client testimonials.

Campbell offers no rationale for prioritizing on the concerns of legislators and senior-level managers. Campbell could invoke the public interest and the information needs of senior government officials, but he never does. He wants evaluations to be multidimensional and to reflect the interests of different stakeholders. But he is vague about how to do this. He presents no exemplary case of evaluation from which to infer how to identify relevant stakeholders or deal with their preferences, especially if they do not want information about program outcomes. Yet his broader political commitment to an emancipatory world and his belief in the desirability of client interviews suggest that he would not consider only the interests of legislators and senior managers. Nonetheless, that flavor persists because he emphasizes summative experiments and because the interests of some groups may inhere more than others in these methods.

All this suggests that Campbell's theory of practice is restricted in coverage since (a) it depends on a form of social change — the pilot program — that fluctuates in frequency of use and consumes few resources compared to existing programs; (b) it advocates a technique — experiments — that may be very difficult to implement in some sectors; (c) it does not consider comprehensive evaluation criteria; (d) it prioritizes on the information needs of some stakeholder groups over others; and (e) the summative criteria it emphasizes may be less useful than knowing implementation processes and causal explanation.

Yet there are places in evaluation where experimental studies that Campbell advocates are routinely carried out. One is job training and employment, where economists implement and evaluate pilot programs at the state level with random assignment, where employment and wages are not controversial criteria, and where measures are often added to the design to probe moderator variables (Stromsdorfer, 1987). Economists even produce data to suggest that randomized experiments produce more credible effect size estimates than the alternatives (LaLonde, 1985, 1986). A similar story holds in applied medicine, where randomized clinical trials are the norm for assessing the effects of drugs and technology. Even where control is more difficult, experiments and quasi-experiments are routinely done, in community health promotion (Farquhar et al., 1977, 1984), smoking prevention (Flay et al., in press), and AIDS prevention (Leviton & Valdiserri, in press). It is unwise to generalize about the restricted utility of experiments from negative comments in journals with *evaluation* in their titles, most of which cater to members of the American Evaluation Association, which is composed mostly of educators and psychologists. Experiments in labor economics and public health journals closely adhere to Scriven's logic of evaluation, and are experimental in exactly the ways Campbell advocates.

Campbell's second theory of practice. Campbell has increasingly emphasized the social side of science in the 1970s. He describes how knowledge claims are generated and edited in multiple programs of research by scholars who are passionately committed to truth and fame and are organized to facilitate criticism and reinforcement. Campbell thinks that evaluation practice would improve if it systematized and implemented these social procedures. Out of these conjectures emerged his contagious cross-validation model and other techniques for increasing replication and critical commentary.

The early Campbell wrote about experiments to those who would authorize and conduct studies. His work on social procedures for critical commentary also speaks to both constituencies, but is more relevant to evaluation policymakers than to individual evaluators. These procedures depend on research programs conducted by different investigators and on stimulating critical commentary from scholars. Any one study is just part of the whole required for responsible inference about program effects and transfer. The role of individual evaluators in such research programs may be less attractive compared to believing they can do the definitive study. Campbell does not believe the definitive study exists — certainly not the randomized experiment.

How Campbell might implement the social side of science in evaluation practice is best seen in an evaluation plan he designed (1987a) for monitoring the scientific competence of the Preventive Intervention Research Centers (PIRCs) of the National Institute of Mental Health. Since he is pessimistic about the links among monitoring, indicators, and corruption, he resisted developing indicators to be monitored. But his first draft was judged incomplete and returned for the requisite suggestions. He then offered a number, but noted how each was corruptible and so untrustworthy for actual use. Instead he focused on designing social arrangements in each PIRC to optimize critical interchange, and suggested how each center's interventions might be structured and evaluated. He advised: Better many smaller interventions than one large one; better to use different but overlapping methods in each independent evaluation; better to reanalyze all evaluation data; better to allow dissenting opinions in evaluation reports. Campbell rejected conventional evaluation monitoring. He encouraged multiple evaluations of each center's products. The feasibility of all this in money, time, and technical and interpersonal skills is unclear (Neimeyer & Shadish, 1987). The eventually funded evaluation did not conform to Campbell's plan (Saxe & Bickman, 1987), for the plan prioritized so much on truth that short-term implementability and responsiveness to sponsor took a backseat. Campbell (1987a) has acknowledged that his plan was critically and "self-consciously utopian" (p. 395). In most social sectors, the patience and foresight required for multistudy, multiyear funding are often absent.

In some sectors administrators seem willing to meet these requirements. Evaluating new drugs is an example, especially where the Food and Drug Administration sponsors studies that do not rely exclusively on pharmaceutical companies. In public health, a five-year series of three-community quasi-experiments examined how community-based health promotion efforts influence cardiovascular risk factors (Farquhar et al., 1977, 1984). The National Heart, Lung and Blood Institute then funded three replications — one each in California, Minnesota, and Rhode Island — for eight or more years of data collection. Conclusions about community-based prevention efforts will presumably depend on all this evidence. Moreover, the first study led to replications in other countries and in the United States with funds from other sources. These cases will also go into the record. The program was planned to last.

Still, some policy sectors will tolerate more uncertainty than public health to get information when the issues are still being debated. The world of practical action prefers highly validated, uncontroversial knowledge (Boeckman, 1974); but the best available knowledge will often do, even if its conclusions are controversial and debatable. In Campbell's search for truth and intellectual dispute, he has evaluators forgo occasions to introduce useful information into debates. Cronbach (1982a) believes that Campbell's scientific superego, designed to protect against false positive findings, stifles use of imperfect evaluation evidence that is still better than the alternatives.

Campbell's utopian theory of practice. Managers and similar professionals control program design and redesign more than anybody else. Campbell's image of these stakeholders is consistently negative. It is hard to imagine him endorsing the same task as Wholey (1983) — to develop methods for managers to use. Campbell's evaluators stand apart from managers in owing primary allegiance not to agency budget or public relations, but to an open society, truth, and the social arrangements of dispute and support that promote the truth. Unfortunately, the interests of politicians, managers, and professionals are not likely to change in the near future; nor is their control over program and evaluation design. Yet Campbell does not create methods for trapped administrators, preferring a theory of practice designed for the utopia to which he wants us to aspire.

Campbell's experimenting society may be the continuously self-adapting-to-the-world-as-it-really-is society in which many would like to live, with commitment to political democracy and republican science — no hierarchy, bold ideas, hardheaded reality tests, and open, critical debates with enlightened and passionate colleagues. These seem nobler values than those of the current world of social programming dominated by hierarchy, survival, putting out fires, and expediency. Campbell does not want to accommodate to such a world. For that he pays a price in immediate relevance. Most sectors bought for a while his idea of conducting experiments, and some still do so. But his larger idea of an experimenting society has been less influential. Most evaluation policymakers respect experiments as a scientific form but not as a political ideology. Few politicians and senior managers seem as committed to communitarian democratic values, to the open republic of science, and to the harsh fitting to reality that evolution demands. As late as 1983, Campbell still hoped this might change. What he offers is the ultimate in management by results.

He believes his aspiration will be repeatedly reinvented in the future and that science will be its prototype, because science gives less biased results than the alternatives. He urges us to improve scientific methods and to reflect more about the politics of evaluation that will be needed when politics again favors reforms that adapt us better to the world. Campbell the fallibilist would agree that these methods and attitudes will be imperfect, but they still might be better. Through his utopia Campbell makes us think about evaluation for tomorrow, not today. Surely this is sound advice. Even if we then rejected his experimenting society, his critical utopia would have achieved its goal.

CONCLUSION

Scriven and Campbell set the tone of evaluation in its early years. Looking back, this tone reflected the high ideals of the 1960s, its social idealism and reformist zeal. But their theories had significant weaknesses, especially in assumptions about social programs, social change, and the use of evaluation findings. In Part III, we present several theories of evaluation that differ significantly from Scriven and Campbell in these two respects.

PART III

Stage Two Theories: Generating Alternatives Emphasizing Use and Pragmatism

Many expectations of early evaluators were dashed against the realities of social programs. Information judged poor by traditional scientific standards is often judged perfectly acceptable by policymakers and managers. Some theorists argued that rigorous scientific standards made it less likely evaluations would be completed in a timely, useful manner. Many social problems were more resistant to change than first thought. In short, the theses proposed by first-stage theorists were perceived to have failed to produce useful knowledge for improving programs.

A second stage in evaluation theory followed in the 1970s. Theorists such as Carol Weiss, Joseph Wholey, and Robert Stake proposed new ways of doing evaluation to remedy their predecessors' shortcomings, especially regarding use and social programming. They focused primarily on how information is used in the design and modification of social programs. Great diversity was generated during this period. While all emphasized use, they suggested different ways of obtaining it, and they looked to different stakeholders to whom to be useful. The main characteristics of these second-stage theories are as follows.

THEORY OF USE

Use became the dominant concern among these theorists. Others had mentioned the matter before, of course. In the earliest text in the field,

171

Suchman (1967) wrote: "The 'success' of an evaluation project will be largely dependent upon its usefulness to the administrator in improving services. . . . Unlike the basic researcher, the applied researcher must be constantly aware of the potential utility of his findings" (p. 21). But early theorists like Suchman did not discuss use in detail, nor did they recognize potential conflicts between providing useful results and using randomized experiments in evaluation. All this began to change in the early 1970s.

A wider array of kinds of use should be considered. Second-stage theorists take a two-pronged approach to improving use. First, they propose a more deliberate approach to instrumental use. Instrumental use does not occur spontaneously very often. The evaluator must promote such use by determining information needs of those stakeholders who can use information. So Weiss focuses partly on pending decisions of policymakers and senior managers, while Wholey promotes instrumental use among middle-level bureaucrats who are willing to manage for results. Stake goes to local stakeholders, listens to their concerns, and gathers relevant information.

Second, both Stake and Weiss advocate an increased role for "enlightenment" and question the primacy of instrumental use. Weiss says that emphasizing instrumental use leads to incremental changes that are often just minor variations that make little difference beyond what is already done. Instead, she sometimes prefers to see evaluation used to provide enlightening information about the nature and causes of social problems, or why some social programs have made such small dents to date. Such information can help us make better policies in the future, whether about the program under review or some other program. This change takes longer and is not as easy to plan as instrumental use, but can be more important in the long run. Wholey prefers to improve existing programs in the short term. He is not as pessimistic as Weiss about the yield from social programs. Unlike Weiss, he does not address the social importance of the changes he seeks in programs, nor does he justify the marginal changes on which he sometimes works. We presume he is optimistic that the changes he promotes are important, given that he has pursued his theory consistently over 20 years in the face of competing ideas.

More explicit attention should be paid to identifying the intended users of evaluation. Early theorists had some users in mind — policymakers and senior managers for Campbell and consumers for Scriven. Second-stage theorists claim this focus is inadequate. They want evaluators to identify specific users for each evaluation and to work closely with those users to increase the probability of creating useful information. Wholey and Weiss orient their work to federal and state managers, while Stake expands the list to include clients, service providers, and local administrators. This broadening reflects growing understanding of the limits of senior managers and policymakers. While evaluations could be used to modify regulations from a program central office, these regulations do not always influence local practices, which are also shaped by other, more immediately pressing forces. Each theorist hopes that stakeholders with input into forming issues and interpreting data will have more opportunity and incentive to use results in the short term.

THEORY OF SOCIAL PROGRAMS

Incremental program improvement as an alternative to program change. Campbell and Scriven stressed program improvement through implementing demonstrations that were effective in local tests and replacing ineffective programs. But such changes are rare, tied more to politics than evaluation results. Programs change more through improvement than through replacement, through gradual rather than sudden and uniform shift. Change is nearly always incremental rather than radical.

Second-stage theorists take several approaches to coping with this conservative context. Some emphasize gradual improvement of existing programs or of things people already do. Wholey follows this rationale most closely, working with managers to improve programs by changing mixes of services and resources. Stake takes this incrementalist approach to the local level, letting local program stakeholders make decisions about what to change. His emphasis on gradual program improvement is similar to Wholey's. These theorists recognize the marginalism of this incrementalism, but are not apologetic, given the presumed failures of first-stage approaches.

At first, Weiss (1972b) also took an incrementalist approach, telling evaluators to find out what policy decisions are pending, and to use evaluations to improve that process. But she became disillusioned with the conservatism of such change. Although she thought evaluation needed a place for incrementalism, she sought a less conservative alternative that still made realistic assumptions about social programming and social change. She chose to do research that challenges programs and policies in important ways, even though such research will be used in a longer time frame. She hopes the time frame will not be too long:

> Just as scientific research is being translated into practical technology more rapidly now than it was in the past, so too do good evaluation findings more rapidly influence program design. The influence may be blocked at the site that was studied, because managers and sponsors, staff and clients, all have interests and beliefs tied up in one way or another with things as they are. But down the

road at the next program, in programs just starting up, in the state capital, in the foundation office, and maybe soon again in Washington, evaluations influence how people think about programming and the kinds of programs they are ready to support. (Weiss, 1988b, p. 28)

Social change is more likely if evaluators locate change agents. Second-stage theorists claim that their predecessors failed to consider who would make program changes. Focusing on this, Wholey and Weiss have been concerned with decision makers at state and federal levels, and Stake is concerned more with local stakeholders. Wholey and Weiss prioritize on important program decision makers and policymakers because society has entrusted them with power and responsibility for social policy. Both clearly approve of an active federal role in social affairs. Stake focuses on the local level because he feels that federal and state involvement in social affairs hampers rather than helps. He thinks creating solutions is the job of citizens, not of evaluators or policymakers in a distant bureaucracy. For Stake, the evaluator does not provide solutions but provides stakeholders with better understandings of their program so can design their own solutions to their own problems.

THEORY OF KNOWLEDGE CONSTRUCTION

What is the nature of the world, and can we know it truly? Early evaluation theorists were sophisticated critical realists who believed that an external world exists though it can never be fully known. They were committed to depicting the "true" state of program affairs, especially about program effects. But some evaluators questioned if true knowledge should always be the highest priority. Perhaps, they suggested, the best knowledge must be both true and useful. Some theorists gave useful knowledge higher priority than truth. Since constructing true knowledge requires different methods and resource allocations than constructing useful knowledge, the epistemological priorities of first-stage theorists were questioned. Stake and Wholey are more willing than Campbell or Scriven to trade uncertainty about knowledge claims for utility.

This is most explicit with Stake, for whom concerns with truth are second to fairness, pluralism, and use. Wholey is also willing to settle for less certainty about truth. His stance is pragmatic. He does not ask if something is the best knowledge possible; he asks only if users think the knowledge will suffice given the situation. Campbell wanted scientifically certain knowledge; Wholey would allow program managers to decide if available knowledge is certain enough for their use. If approximate methods are sufficiently reassuring, then such information will do.

Weiss is closest to Campbell and Scriven in epistemological and ontological assumptions. Particularly influential was her study of policymakers' use of knowledge. She found that quality of knowledge sometimes
made a difference to its use, but so did other factors. Low-quality knowledge sometimes was used if it was consistent with what policymakers
knew already or if it pointed to obvious action to improve policy. She did
not abandon truth, but took the more humble stance that evaluation reveals
one "truth" among many.

This second stage, then, gave us Stake's doubts about whether scientists
make better knowledge than laypeople, Wholey's pragmatism in giving
policymakers and managers the final say over knowledge, and Weiss's
belief that useful knowledge is more than just true. In each case, new
ontological and epistemological concerns arose. The net result is that
second-stage theories gave science less absolute authority for placing an
imprimatur on evaluation products than was the case in the first stage.

What priority should be given to different kinds of knowledge? Second-
stage theorists differ from their predecessors about the priorities they
assign to causation, generalization, explanation, program description, and
discovery. Campbell and Scriven both gave priority to the causal inference
that a social program had certain effects. They believed that confident
knowledge of a cause logically precedes explaining or generalizing it, and
is more important than describing implementation. These priorities came
under intense criticism. Second-stage theorists are less hopeful that evaluators can specify important issues in advance, and do not think causal
questions should be paramount. Many evaluators came to share in a
pessimism about solving social problems; for them, discovery took on a
higher priority — the highest priority for Stake. Second-stage theorists also
assign a higher priority to describing how a program is implemented, since
quality of implementation cannot be taken for granted.

Second-stage theorists also differ among themselves. Stake assigns priority to discovery and program description, leaving it to stakeholders to
draw other inferences. He believes evaluators usually know too little about
the crucial variables to develop realistic and important hypotheses about
effects. Wholey assigns less priority to causal inference than Campbell,
about the same as he assigned to describing implementation. He claims
that managers and policymakers find implementation information useful for improving programs. Like Stake, Wholey studies particular cases
instead of trying to generalize to other locations and times. Weiss's concern with use makes her emphasize (a) program description to provide
useful information about the intervention and its functioning, (b) causal
explanation to enlighten policymakers and managers about why programs
and problems function as they do, (c) discovery to generate interesting new

perspectives, and (d) generalization to guide future policy. Truth about causal connections is less important for all these theorists.

What methods should evaluators use? Scriven and Campbell did not agree on which methods evaluators should use, but they agreed that methods for probing cause-effect relationships were important. Campbell emphasized experiments, and Scriven an array of methods, including his own *modus operandi* method.

This consensus disappeared in second-stage theories. Wholey monitors outcomes, but rarely recommends stronger methods. Stake thinks causality can be described to the satisfaction of most stakeholders using case studies. Methodological pluralism characterizes the recommendations these theorists make, whether about causal inference or anything else. In describing program implementation, Stake (1978) prefers intensive, on-site, qualitative observation, but Wholey (1979) prefers procedures amenable to quantification. Indeed, the "quantitative-qualitative" debate was born in the second stage, exemplifying these differences even while oversimplifying them (Cook & Reichardt, 1979).

Several factors account for this move toward methodological diversity. Some second-stage theorists believe that evaluation requires less certain knowledge than demanded in basic social science. Some disagree about which methods produce high-quality answers to particular types of questions. For instance, some qualitative theorists (Guba & Lincoln, 1981) think the case study is just as good as other methods for causal inference, and so is preferable because it also answers a broader range of questions. If questions about program description, explanation, generalization, and discovery have the same priority as questions about causation, then experiments are too limited a tool. A wider array of methods was needed.

THEORY OF VALUING

Campbell and Scriven treated values similarly. Both selected similar criteria of merit relevant to program effectiveness in solving social problems; both advocated comparative standards of performance, especially comparing the evaluand to alternatives; and both agreed that assessing program performance must be as unbiased as possible. Only on the last of Scriven's steps — synthesizing a value judgment — did they disagree, with Campbell asking readers to make their own synthesis.

Criteria of merit. Weiss, Wholey, and Stake all advocate constructing criteria from the values and goals that stakeholders hold. Some stakeholders believe the program is good if it meets congressional intent, if it serves needy clients regardless of effects, if it provides jobs to important constituencies, or if it simply demonstrates a novel idea. Evaluators should include these criteria of merit, Weiss, Wholey, and Stake believe, because they better reflect the political context than do the social problem-solving criteria that Campbell and Scriven use.

Standards of performance. Scriven and Campbell said a good program does better than its alternatives. If not, it should be replaced. Stage two theorists say a program could *also* be good if it meets specified levels of performance, as when minimum safety standards are set for cars. The results of such tests do not depend on how alternative cars do on the same test. The difference between absolute and comparative standards can be crucial. An automobile can pass absolute standards but not be recommended if it performs less well than an alternative. Wholey prefers absolute standards and looking at just one program regardless of its competitors — since social programs are fixed, it is not worth evaluating alternatives that cannot replace them.

Synthesizing results into a final value judgment. For Scriven, valuing is incomplete until a synthesis about merit is made; Campbell was more ambivalent, but shared some of this concern. But nowhere in Wholey, Weiss, or Stake do we find systematic attention to this final judgment. They prefer to let each conclusion stand alone so policymakers, managers, or stakeholders can assign their own weights to findings. They want to rid the process of evaluators' preconceived notions about such matters as social needs, or to identify them clearly as such, deferring value judgments to program stakeholders.

THEORY OF PRACTICE

First-stage theorists recommended outcome-based practices to evaluators — experiments for Campbell and goal-free evaluation guided by the Key Evaluation Checklist for Scriven. Second-stage theorists increase the diversity of recommended practices. They search for alternatives to experiments, for new practices. But they disagree among themselves about what those new practices should be. Wholey and Stake, like Campbell and Scriven, recommend only a few preferred practices, but Stake prefers case studies while Wholey recommends a sequential purchase of information. Of the second-stage theorists, only Weiss does not offer a single set of practices. She wants the evaluator to use multiple methods. The practices of second-stage theorists involve close contact with program plans, operations, and consequences; go beyond traditional concerns with design and measurement; and legitimate practices for question formation and knowledge use.

5

Carol H. Weiss:

Linking Evaluation to Policy Research

KEY TERMS AND CONCEPTS

Stakeholders:	Those whose lives are affected by the program and its evaluation.
Uses of Evaluation:	Evaluations are used in many ways; one must do different things to facilitate different uses.
Instrumental Use:	Specific evaluation findings point to a specific answer, and policymakers implement that answer as policy.
Enlightenment:	Use of evaluation to think about issues, define problems, and gain new ideas and perspectives.
Truth Test of Use:	Evaluation is more useful if it is of high quality or conforms to prior knowledge and expectations.
Utility Test of Use:	Evaluation is more useful if it suggests feasible action or challenges current policy.
The Politics of Evaluation:	Evaluation is a political activity in a political context.
Organizational Resistance to Change:	Organizations resist unwanted information and change.
Decision Accretion:	Decisions and actions accumulate over stakeholders to result in policy action.
Incremental Change:	Change that disturbs few social arrangements and interests.
The Inhospitable Context of Social Programs:	Organizational, political, and social obstacles to doing evaluation research.

179

| *I-I-I Analysis:* | Analysis of ideology-interest-information linkages in policy, to clarify effects of social science research. |
| *Process Model of the Program:* | A model of a program that explicates inputs, implementation, and immediate, intervening, and long-term outcomes. |

BACKGROUND

Carol Weiss has been professor at the Harvard Graduate School of Education since 1978. Her interests in evaluation started in the 1960s, when she was a researcher at Columbia University's Bureau of Applied Social Research. She worked with Associated Community Teams (ACT) in Central Harlem as research director from 1963 to 1965, and with the Housing and Redevelopment Board of New York City, the National Council on Crime and Delinquency, and the Bedford-Stuyvesant Youth-in-Action Project. Such agencies were feeling demands to produce evaluations, and turned to Weiss for help. She soon began consulting with the Office of Juvenile Delinquency and Youth Development of the U.S. Department of Health, Education and Welfare, the Model Cities Administration in the Department of Housing and Urban Development, and the U.S. Office of Economic Opportunity. She began writing about evaluation, became widely known among evaluators, and participated in the early professional development of evaluation. She is widely influential as a theorist and a consultant. Cronbach (1982a) acknowledges using Weiss's (1972b) text for evaluation, and says "her view of evaluation as a means to illuminate the complex working of institutions surely influenced me" (p. xvi).

Weiss brought a new perspective to bear on evaluation. Perhaps because she was a sociologist, she saw the political and organizational difficulties that beset evaluation. She tells of attending a 1969 evaluation conference at the American Academy of Arts and Sciences:

> For two days, a group of evaluation bigwigs talked about every evaluation topic under the sun. Except politics. They talked about the pros and cons of experimental design and cost-benefit analysis, the perils of measurement, the need for qualitative descriptions of program process, necessary training for evaluators, and many other fascinating topics, but not a word about the political aspects of the evaluation enterprise. As I recall, I made a timid but totally unsuccessful effort to introduce the subject. (in press)

As a counterbalance, she published "The Politicization of Evaluation Research" (1970), a classic statements on this topic.

Her early work endorsed the methods and strategies of Campbell and Stanley (1963). But over time, she moved away from such idealistic, effect-focused theories. She thought these approaches failed to produce results that were used, or to appreciate the political and social realities of social policy. She developed a theory of evaluation to remedy such shortcomings.

OUR RECONSTRUCTION OF
WEISS'S THEORY OF EVALUATION

The Early Weiss

Weiss summarized her initial theory in two highly influential books (1972a, 1972b; see also Shadish & Epstein, 1987). She started with the premise that "the purpose of evaluation research is to measure the effects of a program against the goals it set out to accomplish as a means of contributing to subsequent decision making about the program and improving future programming" (1972b, p. 4). Her early theory stressed experimental methodology to assess program goal achievement, since

> systematic evidence on the effects of each project would show which programs worked well and should be expanded, which ones were failures and needed to be abandoned, and which were marginal and needed to be modified. Once systematic and objective data were available, the assumption was that policy-makers would use the information to improve the effectiveness of programs and thereby improve the lot of the poor. It was a thoroughly rational approach. Unlike the hit-or-miss efforts of earlier reform waves, the Lyndon Johnson War on Poverty would learn from both its successes and its mistakes and go on to more effective and efficient programming. (Weiss, 1987b, p. 40)

Many evaluators began conducting such outcome evaluations:

> Soon findings began to pour in. The news was dismaying. Nothing seemed to be working as expected. . . . Evaluators occasionally noted positive effects here and there. Some programs showed small gains. . . . In later years, evaluation results were not quite so uniformly dismal. Some studies found reason for hope and even occasional rejoicing. . . . But even the most recent evaluations using reasonable criteria and more sophisticated methods of study tend to find only marginal success. (1987b, p. 41)

Such findings caused many evaluators to question their commitment to outcome evaluations:

> Those of us who were engaged in evaluation research in the 1960s and 1970s were dismayed by the results. We seemed to be messengers of gloom and doom. However neutral we were supposed to be as evaluators, and methodologically responsible as we in fact were, we were caught up in the excitement and enthusiasms of the antipoverty program. We had signed on as evaluators with the intent of contributing to the improvement of social programming, but we seemed to wind up giving aid and comfort to the barbarians. (1987b, p. 41)

The perception that "evaluative data seemed to have little effect on either budgetary allocations or the selection of programs for expansion or reduction" (Weiss, 1987b, p. 42) led evaluators to consider a variety of options. These included

> a neoconservative response that questioned the effectiveness of "throwing money at social problems", especially when the federal government does the throwing; a methodological response that aimed to make evaluation research better equipped to identify those changes that did in fact occur; and a rethinking of the place of evaluation research in policymaking. (1987b, p. 42)

Weiss considered all three responses. She questioned the wisdom of "throwing more money" at social problems. She examined how evaluations could better identify program effects. But these two responses were ancillary to the main thrust of her work—rethinking the place of evaluation in policy.

In particular, Weiss reconsidered how evaluation results are and should be used in policy. Most early evaluators assumed evaluations would be routinely used to make directly indicated changes. As she put it, unless evaluation "gains serious hearing when program decisions are made, it fails in its major purpose" (1972d, p. 318):

> Evaluation is intended for use. Where basic research puts the emphasis on the production of knowledge and leaves its use to the natural processes of dissemination and application, evaluation starts out with *use* in mind. In its ideal form, evaluation is conducted for a client who has decisions to make and who looks to the evaluation for answers on which to base his decisions. Use is often less direct and immediate than that, but it always provides the rationale for evaluation. (1972b, p. 6)

But often this assumption did not hold; for example, "no-effect" findings were rarely used to terminate programs. Because Weiss saw use as centrally justifying evaluation, she was disturbed to note that "a review of evaluation experience suggests that evaluation results have generally not exerted significant influence on program decisions" (1972a, pp. 10-11). She found that "few examples can be cited of important contributions to policy and program. Part of the reason for this lies in the remarkable resistance of organizations to unwanted information — and unwanted change" (1972b, p. 3). Such findings vitiate a theory of evaluation justified by the use of evaluation in improving social programs. Hence rethinking of the use of evaluation results became central to her work.

Understanding What Went Wrong with Early Evaluations

Weiss initially tried to use traditional experimental methods in evaluation, but the political and organizational problems she encountered in doing so sensitized her to the need to consider such problems more realistically. Armed only with methodology, the evaluator is ill prepared to cope with the harsh realities of social programming and policy, and can produce evaluations that are not used or are politically naive:

What looks elementary in theory turns out in practice to be a demanding enterprise. Programs are nowhere near as neat and accommodating as the evaluator expects. Nor are outside circumstances as passive and unimportant as he might like. Whole platoons of unexpected problems spring up. (Weiss, 1972b, p. 25)

Those obstacles to evaluations occur because social programming exists in a "context that is intrinsically inhospitable to them" (Weiss, 1972b, p. vii). Those who do not see this are naive, and Weiss starts one book by noting, "This book is dedicated to overcoming the kind of naivete that I began with" (1972a, p. 13).

Incompatibilities between social science and social programs. Social science and social programming are incompatible in many ways (Weiss, 1972a). Weiss focused many of her early criticisms on experimental methods, but the lessons she learned hold over many more social science methods. The lab researcher can control experimental treatments and dependent variables. But research is not the primary goal of social programs; program changes are rarely made to make research easier or better. When evaluation needs and program needs conflict, the program gets priority. Evaluators must compromise their methodological standards when it suits the program, and often forgo questions that program personnel and managers do not see as legitimate.

The goals of experimental treatments are often clearly specified and operationalized; the goals of social programs are often global, diffuse, diverse, and inconsistent, vary over stakeholders, and may have little to do with program functioning (Weiss, 1973a). "One reason for this sorry state is that it often requires coalition support to secure adoption of a program. Holders of diverse values and different interests have to be won over, and therefore a host of realistic and unrealistic promises are made in the guise of program goals" (Weiss, 1973a, p. 181). It is often hard to formulate questions based on ambiguous program goals. The program can then reject evaluation results by saying the evaluation measured something the program was not trying to do.

Laboratory staff cooperate with researchers; program staff are often reluctant to do so. Program staff like to provide service; they dislike delays in that task, despite needs of evaluators. Staff may not see evaluation as needed at all, already believing in the worth of their work. If staff think the evaluator is judging them, they may cooperate even less. Lack of staff cooperation can "have baleful consequences on the evaluation" (Weiss, 1972a, p. 7).

Control groups are feasible in the laboratory; they are more difficult to obtain in programs. Practitioners and managers may resist random assignment for many reasons. They may feel it is unethical to deny treatment to needy clients. So few clients may apply for treatment that all are accepted by program staff. Staff may undermine even nonequivalent control groups by accepting control clients into treatment when treatment clients drop out. Attrition is likely to occur from treatment and control groups in field settings, vitiating true experiments.

Laboratory treatments can be standardized over subjects, and controlled in content and form. Few social treatments have this simplicity (a social security check or housing allowance voucher); most are more complicated. "At the most elementary level, some programs are never put into operation at all. A regulatory program may never be enforced. A service program may remain a paper phantom" (Weiss, 1973a, p. 182). Interventions often vary from client to client, or from site to site; it is difficult to view their entire content and form comprehensively. Moreover, "an over-all average may mask important variations. Even when across-the-board impact is negligible, certain sites, strategies, or modes of operation may be highly successful" (1973a, p. 182). Programs can shift form and content in midstream, with new directors, new regulations, or changing treatment ideologies. Some programs are "a conglomeration of shifting activities that require enormous efforts to specify and describe" (Weiss, 1972a, p. 9). Evaluators of complex programs have difficulty just describing them, much less explaining which components were responsible for effects.

Experimenters can wait until the experiment ends before initiating changes in the treatment; this stability helps them measure what components of treatment are responsible for outcome. Program managers and staff may want immediate feedback to improve their services or the overall functioning of the program. They may want early results, and may change the program midstream to get more positive results.

When a laboratory treatment fails it can be replaced quickly with an alternative, even a radically different one. Programs rarely turn over completely; the opportunities to try any alternative, much less a radical alternative, are rare. Innovations must usually be consistent with ideologies and interests of program constituents, another reason radically different changes are often rejected. For all these reasons, changes "are likely to be incremental rather than massive" (Weiss, 1980a, p. 25), no matter how good the change is by other criteria.

Experimental methods in early evaluations may also have been poorly designed to detect results. The effects of social programs often take years to emerge; hoping that experiments would find immediate results was unrealistic. Programs act slowly to ameliorate problems: "In fact, some recent evaluations (for example, of the Perry pre-school program) have found positive effects ten and fifteen years after the program ended" (Weiss, 1987b, p. 43). Additionally, "measures used to assess effectiveness were excessively crude" (p. 43), too insensitive to detect effects. Statistical models "tended to assume that the program itself would be powerful enough to cancel out all contrary influences in participants' lives" (p. 43). But those influences are often so strong that weak program effects require powerful statistical procedures to detect. Even when solutions to such methodological problems were proposed,

> given the pressures under which evaluators were forced to work, many of the design changes fell by the wayside. Because of short deadlines, limited budgets, shifting program strategies, changing political priorities, multiple program goals, program attrition, difficulties of managing multisite evaluations, noncooperation, and other such problems, evaluations in the field never attained the sophistication of evaluations on the drawing board. (p. 43)

Weiss (1987b) says the emergence of qualitative methods at this time aimed partly to remedy such problems with experimental methods. She notes, however, that qualitative methods also had their limits:

> Many of the virtues of qualitative evaluation were realized, but its major shortcoming in the late 1970s and early 1980s was its lack of credibility in important places. Without hard data, it was often difficult to convince potential

users that the results represented more than the opinions of a sensitive and usually sympathetic observer. (1987b, p. 43)

Yet Weiss respects the flexibility of qualitative methods, their dynamic quality, and their ability to show the world from others' perspectives. She recommends that evaluators use both qualitative and quantitative methods so that "studies done in the future should be considerably better, if the lessons of the last twenty-five years are not lost" (p. 43). The evaluator who ignores difficulties will do a poorer evaluation:

> This is an awesome list of obstacles to the effective conduct of evaluation research. The aim in presenting it is not to discourage the aspiring evaluator, but rather to alert him to the difficulties of the terrain ahead. There are few sadder sights than a well intentioned researcher embarking on an evaluation study, armed only with his research methods textbook and his experience in laboratory or survey research, who comes a-cropper on the organizational, interpersonal, and political barriers in the program setting. (1972a, p. 11)

The political context of social programs. Political factors also intrude between social science and social programs: "Many of the problems that still bedevil the evaluation enterprise are not so much failures of research expertise as they are failures to cope adequately with the political environment in which evaluation takes place" (Weiss, 1973a, p. 179). The problem arises clearly in decision making. The early Weiss wrote that "evaluation assists decision-makers to make wise choices among future courses of action. Careful and unbiased data on the consequences of programs should improve decision-making" (1973b, p. 37). But this benign theory of use is compromised by the political context of evaluation: "Evaluation is a rational enterprise that takes place in a political context. Political considerations intrude in three major ways, and the evaluator who fails to recognize their presence is in for a series of shocks and frustrations" (1973b, p. 37). One intrusion stems from the fact that programs "are the creatures of political decisions. They . . . remain subject to pressures — both supportive and hostile — that arise out of the play of politics" (p. 37). Programs develop loyal constituencies who fight for program survival, concerned more with whether their interests are served than whether the program achieves its goals. Opponents of a program have similar self-interests. Hence even "devastating evidence of program failure has left some policies and programs unscathed, and positive evidence has not shielded others from dissolution. Clearly, other factors weigh heavily in the politics of the decision process" (1973b, p. 40).

Second, "because evaluation is undertaken in order to feed into decision-making, its reports enter the political arena. There evaluative evidence of program outcomes has to compete for attention with other factors that carry weight in the political process" (Weiss, 1973b, p. 37), particularly ideology and interests (Weiss, 1983c). Criteria of success other than program outcomes are often more valued by decision makers and have more influence on policy: "A considerable amount of ineffectiveness may be tolerated if a program fits well with prevailing values, if it satisfies voters, or if it pays off political debts" (1973b, p. 40). For example, "if a decision-maker thinks it is important for job trainees to get and hold on to skilled jobs, he will probably take negative evaluation findings seriously, but if he is satisfied that job training programs seem to keep the ghettos quiet, then job outcome data mean much less" (1973b, p. 41). To help remedy this naivete, Weiss (1973b) suggests that "just as economic cost-benefit analysis added the vital dimension of cost to analysis of outcomes, *political-benefit* analysis might help to resolve questions about political benefits and foregone opportunities" (p. 40).

Third, "evaluation itself has a political stance. By its very nature, it makes implicit political statements about such issues as the problematic nature of some programs and the unchallengeability of others, the legitimacy of program goals and program strategies, the utility of strategies of incremental reform, and even the appropriate role of the social scientist in policy and program formation" (Weiss, 1973b, p. 37). Evaluating a program while accepting other features of organizational and social life as "given" diverts attention from important structural and institutional problems, and is thus conservative. Accepting evaluation contracts from government offices can lead to accepting policymakers' and professionals' concerns, diverting attention from clients' views. Evaluators sometimes respond to poor program performance by incrementally tinkering with the same ingredients in different configurations; this diverts attention from radically different alternatives. Hence "it does appear that evaluation research is most likely to affect decisions when the researcher accepts the values, assumptions, and objectives of the decision-maker" (1973b, p. 41).

Yet Weiss notes that "the basic proclivity of evaluation research is reformist. Its whole thrust is to improve the way that society copes with social problems" (1973b, p. 42). Evaluators, as social scientists, tend to be more politically liberal than many agencies. Weiss wants evaluators to retain their reformist proclivities despite this conservative political environment. Especially in the face of seemingly intractable problems and ineffective programs, she wants evaluators to create knowledge about possible *fundamental* changes in policy.

Limits on short-term social problem solving. Early evaluators thought social programs would make important changes in social problems, but

> the earliest and most enduring lesson from the last twenty-five years of evaluation is that people are very difficult to change. Unlike our expectations at the start of the Great Society, poverty is not readily overcome by a program, a budget, well-meaning professionals, and good intentions. Even when government policies manage to improve significant elements in poor people's lives, many vital things stay the same. People are anchored to their accustomed ways by personal, family, and community ties that prove remarkably resilient. They remain attached to old patterns of behavior through friendships, mutual patterns of expectation, connections to place, habits, and attitudes of long standing. (Weiss, 1987b, p. 45)

Given slow and incremental program change, evaluations that emphasize short-term instrumental use tinker with more of the same. When a program is conceptually flawed, incremental improvements may not help the program do much better. This is often true for programs that have repeatedly been found ineffective in coping with social problems:

> It seems to me that now in some fields there is a limit to how much more evaluation research can accomplish. In areas where numbers of good studies have been done and have found negative results, there seems little point in devoting significant effort to evaluations of minor program variants. Evaluation research is not likely to tell much more. There is apparently something wrong with many of our social policies and much social programming. We do not know how to solve some of the major problems facing the society. (Weiss, 1973b, p. 44)

In fact, the last 20 years have taught us that

> current day government problems are rarely "solved" once and for all, or even for long periods of time. Any solution is temporary, as likely to generate new problems as to remove the condition that it is intended to solve. And many problems, such as poverty or insufficient oil resources, are so deep-rooted and intractable that government action can at best make modest inroads. Therefore, I have selected the word "coping" rather than "solving" to characterize the kinds of alternatives that officials consider. (Weiss, 1982, p. 626)

At our best, we often only cope with problems, and inadequately at that.

The context of multiple program stakeholders. Programs have multiple stakeholders, "members of groups that are palpably affected by the program and who therefore will conceivably be affected by evaluative conclusions about the program or the members of groups that make decisions about the future of the program" (Weiss, 1983b, p. 84). Each group has different interests in the program, will ask different questions about it, and will have different power to use results. Different stakeholders face different decisions and so want different information. For example, policymakers (members of Congress, federal executives, local school board members) need to know whether to continue, expand, or reduce program funding. They are particularly interested in program outcomes. Program managers (national program staff, program designers) want to know how to improve the program by, say, changing the number and kind of staff or clients. They want more fine-grained information than do policymakers, about different outcomes for different clients, different types of services, and staff. Practitioners (teachers, psychotherapists) want to know how to help clients. They often don't want much evaluative information, relying on their professional training, experience, and credentials to justify what they do. Clients (students, parents, community groups, patients) want to know if the program helps them to decide whether to continue to attend, but they may also value their own experience of treatment more than evaluative data about it.

Many stakeholders have little interest in knowing if programs work:

> How well do the host of programs, new and old, succeed in achieving the goals for which they were established? That seems a rational question, but not everyone is interested in the answers. Some people justify a program because it is "doing something" to deal with an obvious need. Others declare themselves content if a program saves one youth from crime, prepares one pupil for college. Agencies, staff, and constituencies form around a program, and they often develop an interest in perpetuating the program — and expanding it. As program advocates, they are interested in assessing the program only for the purpose of demonstrating its worth and justifying further funding. Long-established programs seldom see the need for rigorous proof of success since they "know" that they are doing good. (Weiss, 1972a, p. 4)

A study of program outcomes is not of much interest to such stakeholders. They may not support or cooperate with it, and may argue against its conclusions when the evaluation report enters the policy-making arena.

Stakeholder diversity also makes defining evaluative questions more difficult. The evaluator first needs some means to identify all the stakeholders systematically, but "no procedural mechanisms appear capable of identifying, let alone representing, the entire set of potential users of evaluation results or the questions that they will raise" (Weiss, 1983b, p. 87). Even if all groups are identified and contacted, "people do not always know in advance what they will need to know in order to make a decision" (p. 87). Such problems make Weiss (1983b) pessimistic that some assumptions about the benefits of diverse stakeholder participation in evaluation hold up under scrutiny.

Stakeholder diversity complicates the use of results. Not all stakeholders have decisions to make "of the kind for which evaluation has much to offer" (Weiss, 1983b, p. 89). Those with such decisions often draw competing implications from the data about what should be done in their interests. They will fight in political arenas for their own interpretations of the data: "Unless and until the evaluator finds out specifically who wants to know what, with what end in view, the evaluation study is likely to be mired in a morass of conflicting expectations" (Weiss, 1972b, p. 6).

The Later Weiss:
Uses of Social Science Research in Policy

In view of all these difficulties, Weiss (1979) concluded that the traditional view of "evaluation itself is problematic. . . . Its decline is not the worst of the alternative futures we can imagine" (p. 243). She began to consider alternatives to this view:

> For the social scientist who wants to contribute to the improvement of social programming, there may be more effective routes at this point than through evaluation research. There may be greater potential in doing research on the processes that give rise to social problems, the institutional structures that contribute to their origin and persistence, the social arrangements that overwhelm efforts to eradicate them, and the points at which they are vulnerable to societal intervention. (1973b, pp. 44-45)

After the mid-1970s, Weiss rarely discusses "evaluation," mostly discussing policy research or social science research. This, and her assertion that there may be more effective routes to social problem solving than evaluation, might lead readers to think she abandoned evaluation. This is not so. Weiss simply stopped making distinctions among program evaluation, policy research, and applied social science. Her works on social science and policy *are* her current theory of evaluation; it is different from the goal-based, decision-driven, experimental model of her early works, but retains an emphasis on use and on political sophistication.

The Nature and Facilitators of Use

The starting point for Weiss's later theory is the concept of use. She gave a paper on the topic at the American Sociological Association convention in 1966. The paper was reprinted in a House of Representatives report, *Use of Social Research in Federal Domestic Programs*, by the Committee on Governmental Operations, in April 1967 (C. H. Weiss, personal communication, May 25, 1989). By the 1970s she was studying use empirically. Her early theory emphasized instrumental use: "that specific findings point to a specific answer and that responsible policy makers proceed to implement that answer in policy or practice" (Weiss & Bucuvalas, 1980, p. 10). But Weiss decided this expectation was naive:

> Uses of this type are relatively rare, because they require an unusual concatena- tion of circumstances. Among the requisite conditions appear to be: research directly relevant to an issue up for decisions, available before the time of decision, that addresses the issue within the parameters of feasible action, that comes out with clear and unambiguous results, that is known to decision makers, who understand its concepts and findings and are willing to listen, that does not run athwart of entrenched interests or powerful blocs, and that is implementable within the limits of existing resources. (Weiss & Bucuvalas, 1980, p. 10)

Weiss (1978) distinguishes several more kinds of use. Under a "knowl- edge-driven model" of use, scientists identify a problem, and find the knowledge to solve the problem; it then enters the marketplace of ideas for whomever wants to use it. This model overestimates the cogency of social science knowledge, wrongly expecting that the marketplace knows how to use it.

In the interactive model, research findings are passed back and forth among policymakers, part of a complex process including experience, political insight, pressure, social technologies, and judgment. This model requires close working relationships among the major actors, which is hard to achieve in large countries. Research is also used to conceptualize policy or redefine its agenda. Such use requires accumulation of many studies over the long term. One can also use research as political ammunition to support a position; to manipulate the environment (highlighting the frail- ties of social science more often than not); to advance self-interests, including the interests of scientists; and to create a "language of discourse" (p. 33) for stakeholders to use to conceptualize problems and solutions.

Each of these uses occurs in policy-making. But all suffer from a flawed shared assumption — that use is rare, so the problem is to make *more* use of research in policy. Weiss denies this, saying the problem is to make *better* use of research:

> How to increase the use of social research in policy making is only one way to conceptualize the problem. An alternative is: how can public policy making be improved, and what role can the social sciences play in that improvement? (1978, p. 78)

She has devoted her work to this task. A distinguishing feature of her work is the empirical research she conducted to understand how social science can play a better role in policy.

Toward more realistic theories of policy-making and decision making. Weiss wanted to understand how policymakers make policy, and the role that research plays in doing so, to clarify the kind of research that facilitates that process. In research with Michael J. Bucuvalas (Weiss & Bucuvalas, 1977, 1980, 1981), she found that "researchers apparently have a simplistic view of the decision-making process inside large organizations, and because they conceptionalize decision-making as a series of discrete problem-solving choices, they fail to appreciate the variegated contributions that research can make" (1980, p. 260). Researchers think policymakers have the power to implement policy. This is not so:

> Policies are not made at a single point in time; they seem to happen as the result of gradual accretions, the build-up of small choices, the closing of small options and the gradual narrowing of available alternatives. Small choices over time, each one barely noticed and made with little rational review, leave few options open; they lead with seeming inevitability to "the only thing we could do under the circumstances." Even in legislatures, where votes on legislative provisions look like clear-cut decisions, the main decisions have usually been made before-hand—in a series of minor choices in committee deliberations, in the original drafting of the legislation, or even earlier, in the executive bureau or interest grouping that designed the key features of the bill. (Weiss, 1976, p. 226)

This process is better called *decision accretion* than decision making (Weiss, 1980b). Policy is not the result of stop-go decisions about alternatives; it emerges from custom and implicit rules about what can be done, improvisation in new situations, mutual adjustment to the actions of other policymakers, negotiation of conflicts, countermoves when bargaining breaks down, opportunity, and as a by-product of other decisions (Weiss, 1982). In the midst of this diffusion, no single decision maker makes policy.

Even if policymakers have more leverage, they tend to avoid the battles that would be caused by advocating a major policy initiative costing considerable money, requiring significant change, or threatening accepted values:

> Policy makers are looking for answers, preferably inexpensive solutions that satisfy the most people with the least disruption of the status quo. What they usually seek from policy research is an incremental change in policy or program that disturbs few social arrangements and institutional interests and yet does away with obvious social ills. (Weiss, 1976, p. 225)

In all this, policymakers value social science research "as a device of control":

> Only when the federal agency has good information about what local services are doing — their structure, the processes of service delivery, and the outcomes for clients — can it begin to exercise the authority that rule making and resource allocation allow. (Weiss, 1982, p. 630)

Research can provide support and vindication for current policies, help them appear to make rational decisions, help them to renew their sense of mission and adapt to change (Weiss, 1982), and appear to endorse the rationality traditional to Western culture (1983c).

But "most policymakers are very busy people. More issues come at them each day than they have time to consider very carefully" (Weiss, 1987a, p. 275):

> They have little time available for reading. Members of the House of Representatives spend about 11 minutes a day reading — and their greatest complaint is that they do not have time to study and analyze. When they do read something other than staff memos, it tends to be summaries of pending bills, crucial mail, and newspaper headlines. Just about nobody in high office reads social science journals. (p. 276)

Further:

> There is relatively little *search* for evidence or analysis. People tend to make do with what they already know — or at least know about. . . . The occasions that give rise to search for evidence are (1) new issues, something the policymaker has not dealt with before and therefore needs to get an orientation to, (2) big questions with important or expensive consequences, (3) issues on which they feel inadequately prepared, and (4) situations where their judgement may be challenged and they want authoritative support. But again, neither policymakers nor their aides are likely to embark on a library search, however computerized the system may be, unless they have prior awareness that a category of useful information on the topic actually exists. (p. 276)

Policymakers most value data that come naturally to them, not those they have to work to obtain. These include the mass media:

> Policymakers prick up their ears, not only because *Time* or the *Washington Post* reaches them with a brief and simple version of social science, but even more important, because they know that that same story reaches all the other players

in the policy game. They will be asked about it. They had better know about it. They can't sweep it under the rug. (Weiss, 1987a, p. 279)

They value data provided by lobbies and interest groups:

> Congressmen and congressional staff appear to be more receptive to social science that arrives in this form, interlocked with argumentation and proposals for action, than they are to social science that arrives under the guise of pure and objective evidence. . . . They tend to be suspicious of academics who come bearing objective research; they want to know "What's in it for them?" (Weiss, 1987a, p. 279)

Finally, they get information from "issue networks":

> Around many major issues in contention, there has grown up a set of people who have long-term interest and knowledge in shaping policy. These people include members of Congress and their staffs, leaders of major executive-branch agencies charged with developing and implementing policy, some state and local leaders in the field, academics, consultants, interest group representatives, and think-tank experts. As policy on the issue develops and is modified over time, these people maintain contact, circulating material and exchanging ideas. Since many of the most active issue networks, such as those concerned with welfare reform and energy policy, include researchers and analysts among their participants, they become an active channel for the dissemination of social science research and analysis. (1987a, p. 280)

Evaluators must learn how to put their results into these windows of opportunity.

In summary, "agency decision makers are bombarded with information, not only from social science research but from a host of other sources" (Weiss & Bucuvalas, 1980, p. 249). They cannot attend to it all.

> They screen the research that they read or hear about through a series of implicit filters. If it fails to pass the filters, they tend to discard it. If it passes, it deposits a residue that becomes incorporated into their stock of knowledge, which they draw upon when action is called for. (1980, p. 249)

Decision makers use certain filters to make this screening:

> Analysis of responses of 155 decision makers in mental health fields to 50 actual research reports reveals . . . that, in essence, decision makers apply a "truth test" and a "utility test" in screening social science research. They judge truth on two bases: research quality and/or conformity with prior knowledge and expectations. They also assess utility on alternative bases: feasible direction for action

and/or challenge to current policy. The ways in which they apply research conclusions to their work is a broader, more diffuse, and wider-ranging process than many earlier investigators have recognized. (Weiss & Bucuvalas, 1981, p. 695)

Truth tests. The truth test filter has two components, Research Quality and Conformity to Expectations. Research Quality is the perception that a study is methodologically and theoretically "state of the art." Common lore is that decision makers rarely attend to research quality. To the contrary:

> Research Quality is of value not only because of adherence to the norms of science but perhaps more importantly because it increases the power of research as ammunition in intraorganizational argument. To change minds and mobilize support, it is valuable to have research evidence of sufficient merit to withstand methodological criticism and convince others of one's case. (Weiss & Bucuvalas, 1980, p. 253)

Decision makers are also influenced by Conformity to User Expectations, "which represents the compatibility of research with people's prior knowledge, experience, and values" (Weiss & Bucuvalas, 1980, p. 255). These truth test factors interact:

> The more a study Conforms to Expectations, the less important is the effect of its Research Quality on decision makers' likelihood of using it. Conversely, the more it departs from User Expectations, the more important it is that it be high in Research Quality. When a study yields counterintuitive findings, Research Quality becomes more essential for decision makers' willingness to pay attention to it. (Weiss & Bucuvalas, 1980, p. 256)

Utility tests: This filter also has two components, Action Implications and Challenge to the Status Quo. "Action-oriented research gives explicit guidance and clear direction for feasible reform. Challenging research suggests more fundamental change" (Weiss & Bucuvalas, 1980, p. 256):

> Where studies that support current agency practice have a ho-hum quality about them, challenging studies create a sense of operational discomfort that can stimulate new thinking, new planning, and a motivation to act. Another function served by Challenge is the conceptual function of providing alternative perspectives, alternative constructions of reality. . . . Challenging research can thus not only make decision makers ready to change but can also restructure the questions they ask, the evidence they seek, the analyses they respond to, and the range of options they consider. (Weiss & Bucuvalas, 1980, pp. 253-254)

There are limits to which research can challenge existing arrangements and still be useful: "None raised fundamental questions about the social or economic order. We are dealing with Challenge to the Status Quo within a limited range" (Weiss & Bucuvalas, 1980, p. 254). Weiss also found that

> the effects of Action Orientation and Challenge to the Status Quo on decision makers' likelihood of using a research study are contingent upon each other. Action Orientation is more important for usefulness when a study does not challenge existing practice, and a challenging study is more likely to be taken into account when it is not action-oriented. When a study provides feasible direction for incremental modifications, it does not add much to its likelihood of use to show fundamental deficiencies in current practice. Similarly, when a study implies a need for basic redirection of policy, decision makers may be receptive to its ideas but they get little added push to use it from clear instructions for implementation. There is a tradeoff between the two types of utility. (Weiss & Bucuvalas, 1980, p. 256)

Many differences about preferred kinds of use are a function of this trade-off. For example, Wholey opts to emphasize Action Orientation. Weiss emphasizes Challenge to the Status Quo.

Toward an enlightenment theory of use. From her early emphasis on decision-driven evaluations, Weiss came to emphasize conceptual uses. She questions whether instrumental use (a social engineering model of evaluation; Weiss, 1978) produces much relevant information:

> Information specifically geared to "decision points," "decision deadlines," and "decision makers" may be relevant in a surprisingly limited number of instances. When most people most of the time operate from the knowledge base that they have acquired informally and haphazardly over time, research and analysis have to become incorporated into that base if they are to be influential. (Weiss & Bucuvalas, 1980, p. 268)

If so, facilitating instrumental use is not the most productive route:

> To accept officials' formulation of the problem or to limit the study to alternatives that are politically and organizationally feasible often represents undue constraint on the scope and focus of investigation. Studies too tightly tied to current operating "realities" rapidly become obsolete. If they lose their one shot at immediate application, they have little left to say. (Weiss, 1982, p. 643)

Social engineering can only "operate within narrow limits" (Weiss, 1978, p. 78) defined by the conservative nature of short-term change. It is best limited to "those topics on which there is consensus" (p. 78) about the nature of the problem and desirable solutions. But many conditions "block this type of use in the world of policy" (p. 29), so Weiss is now less sanguine about the model than before. Especially in state and federal policy-making:

> Concern about pleasing — or at least satisfying — the immediate client is second-ary when dozens of other actors will affect the shape of policy. Being practical and timely and keeping the study within feasible boundaries may be unimportant, or even counterproductive. If the research is not completed in time for this year's budget cycle, it is probably no great loss. The same issues, if they are important, will come up again and again. Keeping the study within the accepted constraints of one set of actors will often imply irrelevance to the concerns of other sets of policy actors. (Weiss, 1982, p. 637)

Lindblom (1986) makes a similar argument, that policymakers need infor-mation that is not immediately useful to keep an eye on the "big picture," so as not to be surprised by coming crises, and so as to think creatively about solving stubborn problems.

As an alternative, Weiss proposes "enlightenment" (1977b, p. 535; from sociologist Morris Janowitz); or "knowledge creep" (1980b; from Deborah Shapley): "The diffuse process of research use that we are calling 'enlightenment' is highly compatible with the diffuse processes of policy-making" (Weiss, 1982, p. 635). The enlightenment model gives less short-term use, but "may be the wisest use of the social sciences" (p. 78) for intractable problems: "In the enlightenment tradition, the researcher is well advised to broaden the scope of the question and take time to do quality research" (Weiss, 1982, p. 637).

Her data suggest enlightenment is more frequent than instrumental use:

> As the decision makers whom we interviewed reported, a much more common mode of research use is the diffuse and undirected infiltration of research ideas into their understanding of the world. They reported few deliberate and targeted uses of the findings from individual studies. Rather, they absorbed the concepts and generalizations from many studies over extended periods of time and they integrated research ideas, along with other information, into their interpretation of events. This gradual sensitization to the perspectives of social science, they believe, has important consequences. Over time it affects what they think and what they do. It is not planned and conscious use, not directed toward immediate applications, but the research information and ideas that percolate into their stock of knowledge represent a part of the intellectual capital upon which they draw in the regular course of their work. (Weiss & Bucuvalas, 1980, p. 263)

She thinks enlightenment is "the most important contribution that social research makes to government policy" (Weiss, 1977b, p. 535):

> The enlightenment model of research . . . sees a role for research as social criticism. It finds a place for research based on variant theoretical premises. It implies that research need not necessarily be geared to the operating feasibilities of today, but that research provides the intellectual background of concepts, orientations, and empirical generalizations that inform policy. As new concepts and data emerge, their gradual cumulative effect can be to change the conventions policymakers abide by and to reorder the goals and priorities of the practical policy world. (p. 544)

Enlightening research "does not solve problems; it provides evidence that can be used by men and women of judgment in their efforts to research solutions" (Weiss, 1978, p. 76):

> Research evidence does sometimes serve to reduce conflict by narrowing the zone of uncertainty. It establishes which variables are implicated in outcomes, something about their relative importance, and the interrelationships among them. It keeps people from arguing about what actually is, and saves them time to deal with the issue of values—with what ought to be. Although it does not resolve the policy issue, it focuses debate more sharply on its problematical and value-related facets. (p. 76)

Outcome research has a role in this theory: "By showing that some actions work well and others have little effect, social science can recast the type of alternatives considered as solutions" (Weiss, 1987a, p. 278).

Doing Useful Research for Policy-Making

The decision to evaluate. Evaluators should not immediately accept an evaluation commission. Too many biases are present in social programs to be sure that all such requests are legitimate:

> Lesson No. 1 for the evaluator newly arrived on the scene is: Find out who initiated the idea of having an evaluation of the program and for what purposes. . . . If the real purposes for the evaluation are not oriented to better decision making and there is little commitment to applying results, the project is probably a poor candidate for evaluation. (Weiss, 1972b, p. 13)

To help evaluators assess the likelihood that evaluation results might be used in any specific evaluation, she recommends I-I-I analysis. The three letters stand for ideology, interests, and information:

Public policy positions taken by policy actors are the resultant of three sets of forces: their *ideologies*, their *interests* (e.g., in power, reputation, financial reward) and the *information* they have. Each of these three forces interacts with the others in determining the participants' stance in policymaking. (Weiss, 1983c, p. 221)

Ideology "encompasses a broad range: philosophy, principles, values, political orientation" (p. 224). Interests "are defined primarily in terms of self-interest" (p. 224) — being reelected, accumulating power, and increasing budgets. Information "is basically descriptive" (p. 225), including science but also "the partial, biased, or invalid understandings" (p. 225) of direct experience, craft lore, secondary reports, media, and organizational sources.

Information is usually least important when taken by itself:

The imperative of democratic decision making is to accommodate the interests and ideologies represented in the society. In the nature of the system, it is more important to negotiate decisions that are at least minimally satisfactory to significant segments of the population than to reach some scientifically "best" solution that will provoke significant cleavages. (Weiss, 1983c, p. 222)

But the three factors interact to produce policy. Information can be influential when people hold conflicting ideologies and interests, when new information clarifies interests and ideologies, or when interests and ideologies are stalemated (Weiss, 1983c).

Weiss (1983c) proposes a rudimentary diagnostic framework for evaluators who want to know if gathering information will make a difference:

We can draw on an understanding of ideology-interest-information linkages to develop hypotheses about the likely effects of social science research under different circumstances. For example, if ideological commitments and strong interests are joined in a compelling way, they probably represent a combination too formidable to be overcome by an infusion of social science knowledge. If ideologies are weak or confused or if there are divisions in interest among key policy actors, then social science knowledge is likely to stand a better chance of consideration and even of action. (p. 243)

More specifically:

Starting with policy situations in which ideological commitments are powerful, interests arrayed on one side of the issue, and existing knowledge supportive, we would hypothesize that new information incompatible with the current constellation would make little headway. As we move toward configurations with less internal consistency — for example, when ideologies and interests coincide but available information discloses severe problems in implementing the preferred policy or when available information is sparse or of doubtful validity — then new information is likely to receive a marginally more receptive hearing. When important policy actors have divergent ideologies and interests and existing information can be interpreted to support a variety of positions, then new information is likely to be used to strengthen one or another of the sides in contention. As ideologies and interests become less salient or conditions make old commitments untenable, we would hypothesize that information would have greater influence. (pp. 243-244)

If ideologies and interests conflict, social science can provide key information to resolve the conflict.

But I-I-I analysis is too underdeveloped to be as useful as it could be:

To predict with any assurance whether research will influence policy, either in the short term or through gradual redefinition of interests and ideologies, is a difficult and complex undertaking. What I propose is that future investigations that try to tackle the question give explicit attention to the configuration of ideologies, interests, and existing information. Unless these factors are taken into account, I doubt that we will gain much cumulative understanding of when and how research makes a difference. (Weiss, 1983c, p. 245)

Organizing and managing the evaluation. Weiss reconceptualizes the role of the evaluator to be more consistent with her theory of use:

What evaluators should aspire to achieve in the area of use is influence, not the status of philosopher-kings whose dictates determine program futures. . . . In essence, evaluation should be continuing education for program managers, planners, and policymakers. (1988b, p. 18)

She notes that "an evaluation study can be staffed and structured in different ways. A research unit or department within the program agency can do the evaluation, or special evaluators can be hired and attached to the program" (1972b, p. 19) — that is, internal versus external evaluators. Weiss lists some advantages and disadvantages of each, but does not have a preferred choice: "There is no one 'best site' for evaluation. The agency must weigh the factors afresh in each case and make an estimate of the way which the benefits pile up" (1972b, p. 21).

To obtain the critical cooperation of program personnel, Weiss (1972b, pp. 104-107) suggests obtaining support from program administrators, involving practitioners in designing the evaluation, minimizing disruptions to staff, emphasizing interest in the program rather than in evaluating program personnel, feeding back useful information as the evaluation progresses, and clearly defining the roles and authority of practitioners, administrators, and evaluators.

Next, Weiss (1978) identifies "three major stages in the policy research process" (p. 40). First is research formulation: "Questions that research will address are identified. This involves identifying a policy issue and a need for knowledge about the issue; it requires translating the knowledge needs into research questions" (p. 40). Second is conducting the study: "Data sources are selected, measures developed, samples drawn, and data collected and analyzed" (p. 40). Third is drawing policy implications: "Research results are translated back into the realm of policy. At this stage, the implications of the data for resolution of the policy issue are made explicit, and the results are disseminated to potential users" (p. 40). Each stage is a link in a causal chain from research to policy. If one weakens, use is vitiated. Often, the chain will weaken or break at each stage. It is hard to formulate good questions that bear on real information needs of decision makers. Studies to answer such questions can be so complicated that results may be subject to heated debate concerning validity. Translating results into policy action depends on political, ethical, and organizational complexities that shift from time to time, place to place, and stakeholder to stakeholder. All this makes use more difficult, so evaluators should lower expectations about immediate and important contributions to policy.

Research formulation. For the early Weiss, the most important questions concerned either program goal achievement or pending decisions. She had a broad view of formulating program goals. The evaluator should "read everything," "talk to practitioners," "observe the program," and collaborate with staff in obtaining "successive approximations of goal statements . . . until agreement is reached" (1972b, p. 28). She also wanted information about intervening variables, about "differences that evolve between groups, between activities, and so on [because they] give increasing information about what works and does not work in reaching program goals," and about program inputs (p. 25). The evaluator should then "construct a model of the intended processes of the program" (p. 50). The model helps the evaluator find out what is occurring, how well people move along, and where things break down. Such information points to program elements that need to be fixed, and allows the evaluator to test the theory underlying the program. In so doing, the study can generalize to other programs that operate under similar assumptions.

But over time, Weiss became more concerned with questions that affect policy more conceptually. She captures this change in the distinction "between the social engineering model of research use and the enlightenment model" (1978, p. 77). Her early work used a social engineering model, in which "researchers as social engineers are expected to answer specific requests for information and knowledge in a straightforward manner. . . . Since research is planned, done, and transmitted, it is expected to be applied" (p. 77). Her later work emphasizes enlightenment, which "assumes social science research does not so much solve problems as provide an intellectual setting of concepts, propositions, orientations, and empirical generalizations. No one study has much effect, but, over time, concepts become accepted" (p. 77).

Both models have a place in Weiss's evaluation. Under the social engineering approach, during research formulation there are "some things that researchers can do to facilitate the use of their research" (Weiss, 1982, p. 633):

> In the local case, there are undoubtedly acts that can lead participants in decision making to pay greater attention to research results. The literature is replete with admonitions: locate the potential users of research in advance, understand which policy variables they have the authority to change, concentrate the study on the feasible (manipulable) variables, involve the potential users in the research process, establish a relationship of trust, demonstrate awareness of the constraints that limit their options, report promptly, provide practical recommendations, write results clearly and simply, and communicate results in person. All of these prescriptions are directed at influencing one decision maker, or a small group of decision makers, to use research in making a direct, concrete, immediate choice. (pp. 633-634)

Research will not always carry the day, but these actions increase the chances of its immediate impact.

But Weiss (1982) reminds evaluators that they may not "always want to abide by the restrictions embedded in the traditional prescriptions for influence" (p. 643). She has shifted her theory of question formation toward enlightenment: "Let us try to ask the right questions — the key questions — the pregnant questions — questions that have important implications for the future of programming" (1988b, p. 27). To begin: "The pivotal phase in developing relevant research is framing the questions. The most important choice is to decide: whose questions?" (1978, p. 76). The evaluator should identify potential users as early as possible. This search extends to all stakeholders "whose lives are affected by the program and its evaluation" (1983a, p. 9). Involving multiple stakeholders

> can improve the fairness of the evaluation process. It can probably make marginal improvements in the range of information collected and in the responsiveness of data to participant requests. It can counter the federal tilt of many previous evaluations and give more say to local groups. It can democratize access

to evaluative information. If stakeholder groups take an active role, it can make them more knowledgeable about evaluation results and equalize whatever power knowledge provides. (1983b, pp. 91-92)

Involving multiple stakeholders is demanding on resources and patience. It may distract stakeholders from acting, bogging them down in discussions and debates about evaluation when they really care about the program: "A Machiavellian mind could conceive of the stakeholder approach as a way to mire stakeholders (particularly powerless groups) in the details of criteria definition and item wording, while the powers that be go blithely on with decisions as usual" (1983b, p. 93). Weiss fails to prescribe an answer to this dilemma, simply highlighting the trade-offs.

The evaluator uses this input to clarify the needed knowledge. This "hinges on better prediction of policy issues. More thought should go into looking ahead so that newly funded research is not concentrating on last year's problems but addressing those that loom ahead" (1978, p. 63). Weiss is now "less exercised over the problem of timing than I used to be" (p. 63) because "most domestic issues are not resolved once and for all" (p. 63). Rather, "research is relevant not only to the original making of policy but also to the inevitable remakings of policy and even (maybe especially) to the unmaking of policy" (p. 64). Research focused on small present decisions quickly outlives its usefulness. She prefers broad-ranging research that

can contribute to reconsideration of (1) the basic goals of a policy ("Should the federal government assume responsibility for improving the mental health of the populace?"); (2) the means through which goals are to be achieved ("Should the federal government encourage and support the community mental health centers?"); (3) the amount of public funding allocated to the activity ("How much should the government pay toward the establishment and support of centers?"); and (4) its ongoing administration ("What activities of treatment, prevention, and education should be conducted and how can they best be carried out?"). (1978, pp. 63-64)

In another work she says:

I would like to see evaluation research devote a much larger share of its energies to tracing the life course of a program: the structures set up for its implementation, the motivations and attitudes of its staff, the recruitment of participants, the delivery of services, and the ways in which services and schedules and expectations change over time, the responses of participants and their views of the meaning of the program in their lives. (1987b, p. 45)

She reasons that "more wide-ranging work . . . can be generalized beyond the immediacies of the present situation" (1978, p. 64), which helps it "retain its relevance long beyond the use-life of specific-problem-oriented studies" (p. 64).

The researcher must be intimately familiar with the policy issues:

> This is not a call for retreat to the ivory tower. Researchers need to be sophisticated about the shape and contour of policy issues if their work is to be relevant to current debates. They need to recognize that decision makers cannot wait for certainty and authoritativeness (which social science may in fact never be able to provide), but must proceed on the basis of the best knowledge available at the time. As social scientists, their responsibility is to convince government agencies to allow them the opportunity to do the best social science of which they are capable. (Weiss, 1982, p. 638)

Policy research is further improved when it is a systematic, long-term, programmatic effort: "Probably only continuous contact with decision makers and involvement in policy questions will help planners to choose appropriate areas for research emphasis" (Weiss, 1978, p. 64). There are many obstacles to such programmatic research; many require institutional remedies from funding agencies that can provide more stable sources of funding for social scientists:

> Researchers with long-term support can select issues, or topics within issues, that are most suitably investigated given current knowledge and available research methodologies. They can also select issues that hold the greatest promise for generalizable and theoretically relevant findings, so that they have high motivation to do capable research. (Weiss, 1978, p. 65)

The feasibility of mechanisms for doing this is just now being explored.

Conduct of the study. Next, the evaluator must develop "a plan to select people to be studied, set the timing of the investigations, and establish procedures for the collection of data" (Weiss, 1972b, p. 60). Design options are numerous, so "the purpose of the evaluation study, the use to which results will be put, should determine the study design" (p. 66). Weiss's early work was specific: To assess program goal achievement, she preferred experimental and quasi-experimental methods. She is less specific in her later work about methods, preferring to concentrate on research formulation and on drawing out policy implications. But she states:

> The conduct of research, Stage 2, cannot be ignored, for, at the least, it has spillover effects both fore and aft. If appropriate concepts and methodologies

are lacking, research cannot be formulated in ways that snugly fit the policy problem. If the research methods used compromise either internal validity or external generalizability of conclusions, the reception of those conclusions in the policy world may well be skeptical. (1978, p. 40)

She concludes forcefully that "Research Quality . . . is the single most significant factor for both measures of usefulness" (Weiss & Bucuvalas, 1980, p. 252). She is "committed to improving the methodological quality of evaluations, both quantitatively and qualitatively, so that they have something valid to say" (Weiss, 1988b, pp. 26-27).

An emphasis on high-quality methods is common to Weiss's early writings on design and her current work. In discussing quasi-experimentation, she emphasizes: "They are in no sense just sloppy experiments. They have a form and logic of their own. Recognizing in advance what they do and do not control for, and the misinterpretations of results that are possible, allows the evaluator to draw conclusions carefully" (1972b, p. 68). Today, her advice on design is broader, emphasizing high-quality work but accepting diverse methods, including the "experiment, survey, historical case study, observation, or whatever," as long as it is "careful and sound research" (1981a, p. 400).

She tells government staff to "put a great deal of emphasis on monitoring research performance" (Weiss, 1978, p. 68): "Close contact with research in progress tends to keep it honest, on time, and technically competent. It also smoothes the way through the booby traps of forms clearance, requirements for the use of government computers, and other such time-taking snares" (p. 68). Final reports should routinely be sent to experts for review that "gives the reader a sense of the strengths and limitations of the research" (p. 69), and "limits smoke-screen claims of 'poor research quality' as an excuse for policy makers' ignoring good research if they dislike the message" (p. 69). Scriven makes similar recommendations concerning metaevaluation.

Drawing policy implications from research. From the start, Weiss has emphasized drawing policy implications from research. In her early work, she advocated cost-benefit analysis for this: "It does introduce elements of clarity, comparability, and simplification into complex situations and in so doing, helps policy makers express their value preferences more accurately" (1972b, p. 88). She elaborates: "An allure of this type of analysis is that it moves evaluation conclusions from the realm of interesting description into the value system and terminology that make sense to many policy makers" (p. 88). She also discusses the limits and misinterpretations of cost-benefit analysis.

Her later work acknowledges the need to summarize evaluations:

> The important need . . . is that many people who take research and evaluation
> seriously, under many auspices, engage in synthesizing available research and
> continually try to bring the best knowledge to the attention of people who shape
> policy. (Weiss, 1981a, p. 401)

But she differs from Scriven. Multiple stakeholders may each want a
summary geared toward their own interests, so that separate summaries
may be computed for each group (Weiss, 1972b, p. 88).

Weiss then tells the evaluator to draw out recommendations from the
data: "There does seem to be recognition of a function that is largely
unfilled in social programming. Somebody or some body should fill the
gap of translating the evaluation research results into explicit recommendations for future programs" (1972a, p. 26). She adds: "There is even a
step beyond suggesting alternative courses of action. The conscientious
evaluator can proceed to an analysis of the likely consequences, good and
bad, of the alternative courses he recommends" (1972b, p. 126). But this
task is riddled with problems:

> Even where data are relatively clear and consistent, to move from data to
> recommendations requires a leap guided by values. The researcher's sense of
> what the data imply for action may be at variance with the judgement of
> policy-makers. What Paul Lazarsfeld calls the "road to recommendations" is
> uncertain ground where science is rapidly left behind. (Weiss, 1976, p. 225)

Evaluators bring their own biases to this task; Weiss reminds them to be
open about this:

> While social scientists' concern with the utility of social research rests on a
> belief in its potential as a rational guide to policy, it is likely to be buttressed
> by (1) interest in the status and rewards that accrue to social science, (2) desire
> for influence in the corridors of power, and/or (3) reformist zeal to move
> public policy in the direction of their own beliefs, which are usually economic
> liberalism and social egalitarianism. They are not disinterested bystanders.
> (1977a, p. 8)

All of these efforts are diminished if results are not disseminated. The
most common form of dissemination is a final report given to the client;
according to Weiss, the evaluator should "start a report with a brief
summary of results, avoid jargon, write graceful prose, use charts, maps,
and other attractive graphics, interpret the meaning of statistical statements, and write in terms that have meaning to the policy audience" (1978,

p. 69). There should be "systematic procedures for getting research to users" (p. 69), including "(1) development of organizational channels for linking research to decision processes, especially through offices of planning and analysis; (2) disseminating integrated 'state of knowledge' reviews of research rather than the results of one study at a time; and (3) using the mass media more effectively to report policy-relevant research" (p. 73). But there is a limit to the evaluator's right to expect research to be used: "A democratic system does not want technocratic solutions imposed on decision makers; a pluralistic society does not want political controls on the freedom of research" (pp. 73-74).

Many of Weiss's recommendations "include tighter control by federal staff" (1978, p. 74) at all three stages. Control is warranted, but its problems are severe enough to require care. To avoid deleterious effects, she recommends that,

> to the extent possible, research should be funded at many levels of government and by sponsors of many kinds outside government. . . . When the expense of research makes government the only likely funder, planners should purposefully canvass many groups for their perceptions of the policy issue and the questions in need of answers. (1978, pp. 75-76)

Communication among interest groups before, during, and after research helps clarify its usefulness.

OUR ANALYSIS OF
WEISS'S THEORY OF EVALUATION

Scriven and Campbell are somewhat idealistic. Politically they believe scientific knowledge has a special claim to validity in debates about public interest. They emphasize the evaluator's special role in judging which solutions to social problems are best. They want society to strive to solve its social problems in a sometimes utopian way, and they hope the policy-making process will attend significantly to objective, evaluative knowledge about what works. Weiss shares some of this idealism, particularly in her theory of knowledge. But her theory reflects a shift in evaluation in the 1970s toward a more pragmatic view more in tune with a realist view of the public interest. Her value theory emphasizes understanding stakeholder values rather than, say, material needs. Her theory of social programming lacks the utopian flavor with which Campbell challenges us; she is sophisticated if diffident about important short-term change. More than anything, she has struggled toward a realistic theory of use. These shifts started a debate in evaluation that goes on to the present day about the role in evaluation of idealism and pragmatism.

Theory of Knowledge

What little Weiss says about this is consistent with Campbell and Scriven. She seems to endorse similar ontological and epistemological assumptions. For example, she says that evaluators "will help to reveal one or more of the several realities that surround the program" (in press), so she is certainly not a naive realist. Her advocacy of strong social science methodology suggests that she thinks some constructions of reality are more defensible than others. She is not bound to any methodological orthodoxy; rather, she recommends a wide array of social science methods for the evaluator's repertoire.

Like Campbell and Scriven, Weiss assumes that the evaluator has a special responsibility for endorsing the validity of evaluative knowledge, and for conveying the strength of that endorsement to the users of the evaluation. When forced to choose between traditional scientific rigor versus other goals such as use, she seems to lean in the former direction. Some of her contemporaries who also aimed to increase use, like Wholey and Stake, seem to lean in the latter direction. Weiss's choice might have two sources. Since she was employed in academia most of her career, she may have an academic's predilection for such traditional standards. More important, her research on use found that policymakers attend to research quality as a factor influencing use (Weiss & Bucuvalas, 1980). As a result she concluded that evaluation practitioners ought to emphasize research quality to facilitate use.

A difference between Weiss and both Campbell and Scriven is important. The latter theorists were mostly interested in valid knowledge about causal manipulanda. They looked for social interventions that worked, that reduced social problems and led to desirable outcomes. Their methods reflected this interest. The early Weiss shared this interest. But later, this interest receded in her theory to become just one of many useful kinds of knowledge. Others were knowledge about the nature and origins of problems; about program clients and their needs; about program implementation and costs; about intervening variables that explain program effects; about the social, political, and economic contexts in which the program exists; about implicit assumptions; and about the social ramifications of the program.

Weiss emphasizes such diversity for many reasons. One is pragmatic; experiments are often difficult to implement in field settings. More fundamentally, she questions whether causal knowledge is the most useful knowledge. Campbell argues that it is useful, suggesting practical actions to bring about effects. But in Weiss's experience, constraints often prevent policymakers from taking many of those actions. If decisions are accreted rather than made, if the opportunity for action fails to match the availability of information about which actions work, and if such information is anyway only a small input into decisions compared to interests and ideologies, then knowledge of causal manipulanda is not always useful to policy. In the policy environment, knowledge about more diverse matters stands the best chance of being used. Such knowledge is also more generalizable: Knowledge of program context and implementation gives information to decide if evaluation results apply to other cases not directly studied. Stake and Cronbach make similar arguments.

This bifurcation between Campbell and Weiss reflects a divergence of opinion that continues to this day. Campbell says if social problem solving is the goal, then the direct route is to find the solution. Weiss argues for an indirect route premised on the notion that direct solutions are hard to find, and, when found, are often not usable in policy. Campbell's goal is social problem solving. Weiss's goal is better policy-making. These two goals are related but are not isomorphic, and can be so divergent that knowledge aiding one goal fails to aid the other.

Theory of Valuing

Weiss claims that evaluation is about judging merit: "What all the uses of the word have in common is the notion of judging merit" (1972b, p. 1). But she breaks with Scriven, and to some degree from Campbell, about the process of valuing. Scriven prefers a narrow definition of value: A thing is valuable if it meets needs. His approach tends toward the prescriptive because his material criterion of need has roots in egalitarian theories of justice. Campbell is not explicitly prescriptive, but might be called "semiprescriptive" in that he prescribes a limited criterion of merit — solving important social problems — in judging program worth.

Weiss differs from Campbell and Scriven in two ways. First, she is a descriptive theorist rather than a prescriptive theorist of valuing. Weiss believes of decision making:

> At its core are ethical and moral values. . . . People's ideologies are sometimes carefully constructed and internally consistent, but often they are haphazard and makeshift. However weakly integrated they may be, they provide an emotionally charged normative orientation that provides a basis for position taking. (1983c, p. 224)

But for Weiss, stakeholder values should dominate the decision-making process, not those of the evaluator. To be useful, evaluators must provide information to decision makers that speaks in the language of valuing they themselves use. Evaluators' liberalism and reformist proclivity can threaten their credibility, and so their usefulness: "It does appear that evaluation research is most likely to affect decisions when the researcher accepts the values, assumptions, and objectives of the decision-maker" (1973b, p. 41). This latter statement from Weiss's older work reflects her early emphasis on serving decision makers. Today, with the greater role she gives to more stakeholders (Weiss, 1983a, 1983b), she would undoubtedly use the values, assumptions, and objectives of more stakeholders.

Weiss says it is important to use descriptive values rather than ethical theory or preconceived notions of what is good because doing so increases the use of results. Scriven's notion of meeting needs and Campbell's notion of solving social problems are attractive in their egalitarian ethics and political rationalism, but neither reflects the values that drive policy. When stakeholders make decisions or act in the policy arena, their actions are colored more by their ideologies and self-interests (Weiss, 1983c).

Stakeholder interests are rarely "needs" in the material sense in which Scriven uses the word; nor are they communally motivated concerns about whether social programs solve important problems. Self-interest often reflects not "needs" but "wants," or, in the worst case, "pork barrel" projects that few prescriptive theorists would justify as high priority. People rarely assign their own self-interests a lower priority than the needs of other stakeholders, and these contending self-interests are viewed by many political scientists as the basis of public interest (Downs, 1967). In contrast to Weiss, Scriven and Campbell seem to suggest a real substance to the public interest that is independent of self-interests.

Weiss (1983c) essentially contends that information that is not about political self-interest gets a lower priority in decisions. She may underestimate how much such information comes into play in negotiating, or when lawmakers see a chance to make a name for themselves by championing something not obviously in their own interests. Nonetheless she may be right that to maximize the chances that information will be used in policy, evaluators must gather information about the interests of the stakeholders in that process. Evaluators often face stakeholder interests in their most aggressive form when uncomplimentary reports on programs threaten such interests. It is a mistake to denigrate this because there is such a thing as legitimate self-interest. Failure to consider such interests arrogates better judgment about valuing to the evaluator than is often warranted. Weiss sensitizes us to this fact.

Weiss also differs from Campbell and Scriven about which criteria of merit deserve high priority. The latter theorists mostly use criteria that bear on outcomes. Weiss allows more criteria to be considered in judging whether the program is good. We have noted this difference already in her theory of knowledge; Campbell and Scriven emphasize causal knowledge, but Weiss emphasizes broader knowledge for fostering generalization. This preference for diverse criteria of merit is also justified under a descriptive approach to valuing. Stakeholders care about things other than outcomes; the evaluator cannot limit information to outcomes if the results are to be most useful. Finally, since funding of evaluation includes a mandate to be useful in the short term, this shift was probably necessary.

For all these reasons descriptive theories of valuing ought to hold center stage in theory of valuing. Nonetheless, we risk losing some things we may not want to lose in the transition. One is loss of an explicit tie to social problem solving. For both Scriven and Campbell, constructing criteria of merit always begins with a version of what it would take to solve a social problem. To link up with social problem solving, descriptive approaches must hope that some important stakeholders have social problem solving in mind. But the self-interests of many stakeholders do not include such criteria. We will drive this point home more strongly in discussing the work of Wholey and Stake, where the tie to social problem solving is further eroded to serve the values of stakeholders.

The other potential problem is a loss of perspective provided by the accumulated wisdom of ethical theorists. If evaluation is a science of valuing, then evaluators ought to know the implications of various criteria of merit for the values served by the political process, or the kind of society we build. The best example concerns the hidden implications in Scriven's choice of material needs to drive criteria of merit. From the perspective of ethics one sees this is a value-laden choice in its implications for distributing resources, for alternatives such as individual liberty, or for implied stances against utilitarianism in a society that has been driven by utilitarian values since its inception. All these implications would be noted faster, and with less error, with knowledge of ethics. Nonetheless, if descriptive valuing must hold center stage, most evaluators will not have time to delve deeply into the ethics relevant to evaluation. We suspect that remedying this loss will occur over a long period of time as scholars like Bunda (1985) or Lane (1986) show us how to resolve some important problems or errors in our work.

The potential loss of a tie to social problem solving, however, is serious. Weiss offers a remedy to this loss that seems plausible in a theory emphasizing use. Her remedy is policy analysis: "to be sophisticated about the shape and contour of policy issues" (1982, p. 638). She advises the evaluator to study closely and know well the entire policy context surrounding the evaluand. This includes "the basic goals of a policy" (1978, p. 63), presumably including the problems implied by those goals. In the same way that ethics gives us perspective on the worth of programs, policy analysis provides another "big picture." Evaluation is moving closer to policy analysis anyway (Cronbach et al., 1980); efforts to understand program generalization, methods like cost-benefit and cost-effectiveness analysis, and techniques like multiattribute utility analysis are close to policy analysis already. In these senses, Weiss's recommendations are well taken.

But we are not sanguine this solution always works well; its limits need to be explored. Will most evaluators have any more time to read policy analysis than they have time to read ethics? Or to read the many other relevant topics — political science, methodology, economics, social change theories, and epistemology, to name a few? The demands on evaluators to act limit the time they have to read, reflect, and reconsider. Weiss's advice may be differentially realistic in different employment situations. Academic evaluators, or those working close to the policy-making process, have more opportunity to study policy than the evaluator at a local community mental health center or a small contract research firm. There may be good policy-analytic skills we could be teaching evaluators even at the local level (Stokey & Zeckhauser, 1978). But in general, it will be only partly realistic to expect most evaluators to know policy analysis. For those evaluators, the tie between their practice and social problem solving may often be tenuous. Finally, even if they did all this, policy analysis does not explicitly capture all the dimensions of social problem solving that Scriven and Campbell emphasize. Explicit needs assessments, for example, are practical actions that Weiss's theory mostly lacks, and that evaluators may need to make the tie concrete.

Theory of Use

Neither Scriven nor Campbell assumes that stakeholders will use evaluations instrumentally. Their evaluator has little responsibility to facilitate use beyond reporting results. The use of results is up to the marketplace of ideas. Weiss questions this assumption, partly because of her perception that evaluations are not used (but see Leviton & Boruch, 1983, 1984), and partly because of what she learned about how information is used in policy. So where Campbell and Scriven make truth and social problem solving their central organizing concepts, Weiss emphasizes use. Without use, evaluation loses the tie to policy that gave rise to the field.

Weiss (1972b, 1972d) first aimed to improve instrumental use by making decision making the source of evaluation questions. If evaluators could anticipate decisions, study the value of alternatives, and recommend choices based on data, odds were increased that decision makers would use the results instrumentally. But she abandoned this approach given her impressions that decisions were accreted, not made; that the opportunity to feed into decisions existed rarely; and that decisions often concerned minor variations unlikely to have major impact.

Weiss's enlightenment model holds a middle ground between social problem solving and instrumental use. It allows the evaluator to address important social problems and pose challenging alternatives, and yet still influence decision making by influencing how people think. However, Weiss takes this preference a bit far by making it her nearly exclusive focus. She is vulnerable to criticism that she lost the tie to short-term social problem solving because enlightenment contributes to problem solving in the long term. She is also open to criticisms that she has given instrumental use short shrift.

Enlightenment is a vulnerable goal for a field that first promised more instrumentally useful information. It is an admission of possible inability to achieve that goal, and an attempt to salvage a use-based rationale with a concept that is plausible but hard to verify. Weiss acknowledges this when discussing how policymakers identify when they were enlightened:

> Because the link between their intake of social science research and their output of actions is so tenuous and ill defined, they find it difficult to cite particular studies that influence particular actions. The connection is underground, shielded even from their own awareness. Yet they have a firm sense that a link exists—that research does indeed influence action. (Weiss & Bucuvalas, 1980, p. 264)

If the connection is out of awareness, how does one know it exists? Again, Weiss anticipates:

> Outsiders may scoff. It sounds like a courteous tale told to fob off a visiting social scientist and maintain their own claims to intellectual rectitude. Observers may scoff at us for taking the stories seriously. It sounds like the usual rejoinder of policy researchers when confronted with the lack of evidence of the use of their research. . . . But we do take it seriously. Looking at changes in the definitions of issues and the kinds of policies considered and adopted in many fields over the last two decades, we believe that the influence of the social sciences has been considerable. (Weiss & Bucuvalas, 1980, p. 264)

Our gut reaction is to agree that enlightenment occurs and influences policy; and Weiss and Bucuvalas (1980) provide plausible evidence to that effect. Yet one wishes for more frequent and tangible evidence of the effects of enlightenment. Such a demonstration would require explicit listing of issues and policies that have changed due to enlightenment, showing clearly that they originated in social research, and that they were used by decision makers. The technology needed to do such research might be drawn from cognitive psychology—to construct cognitive maps of knowledge structures and to examine how those structures change over time given new information (Graesser & Clark, 1985).

If one grants that enlightenment occurs, one still wonders if Weiss shortchanges short-term instrumental use. Enlightenment occurred more frequently in the Weiss and Bucuvalas study than did instrumental use. But this may be an artifactual finding: "Internal policy analysis, *which we did not study*, is probably better suited (in style, timing, and definition of parameters) to influence the single decision than is outside social science research" (Weiss & Bucuvalas, 1980, p. 264; emphasis added). Weiss and Bucuvalas could not clearly support enlightenment being more frequent than instrumental use if the latter were not much studied.

Many researchers assume that instrumental use has great value. Wholey built an entire career and theory of evaluation around facilitating instrumental use through internal policy analysis of the kind Weiss did not study. The longevity of his approach and of ones like it (Patton, 1978), and their popularity with managers and policymakers, suggests it is possible to build a viable theory around instrumental use. Weiss thinks such a theory addresses less important issues than enlightenment, and is of passing relevance in the long run to trenchant policy issues. Her own findings indeed suggest that facilitating Action Orientation was useful only if it did not result in serious Challenge to the Status Quo, and vice versa (Weiss & Bucuvalas, 1980). Our own experience is similar—too much emphasis on instrumental use limits one to problems and interventions that are feasible and implementable in existing political, social, and economic arrangements (Cook & Shadish, 1982; Shadish, 1984). Such limits harm problem solving because they imply the intervention may not be very different. Enlightenment can consider all the options considered by instrumental use, and more. With more options, the enlightenment-oriented evaluator may be more likely to find those that solve problems.

One wonders how much this works in practice, however. If enlightening evaluations find options that solve problems, those options must still be accepted by politicians and practitioners. They must still be refined and tested for feasible implementation and effectiveness—a long and chancy process. The Great Society programs illustrate public ambivalence about programs that depart too much from the status quo. Weiss assumes that enlightening information will be used to improve policy, and that improved policy translates into implementable programs. But will better understanding of social problems change ideologies to permit adoption of better policy? It is not likely.

Even if one agreed with the thrust of arguments for enlightenment, they still have a major flaw. They contain an implicit *ceteris paribus* (other things being equal) clause that limits the claim that enlightenment is more important than instrumental use to situations where all other factors are equal. But it is rare for all things to be equal for most evaluators. Evaluators work in different settings, on different problems, with different interventions, and these factors interact to limit the range of possibilities for study so that, in many cases, an instrumentally oriented evaluation can yield information that may be more important than an enlightenment-oriented evaluation. The importance of an evaluation hinges on more than its orientation to use. It also hinges on the importance of the problem and the potential impact of the solution. An enlightening study of a trivial problem or of impractical solutions is plausibly less important than an instrumentally usable study of a small but practical solution to an important problem. An example is the development of the phenothiazine medications for treatment of psychotic disorders (Crider, 1979; Shadish, 1987b). Had an evaluator spread resources over possible solutions to enlighten policy 20 years from now, development of phenothiazines might have been significantly delayed. In reality, different researchers pursued both instrumentally useful research (clinical trials of phenothiazines) and enlightenment-oriented research (basic biological research into the causes of schizophrenia). The same simultaneous strategy is being used today in AIDS research.

All this is even more complicated since different evaluators in different employment situations have access to different resources and authority to pursue inquiry. Academic evaluators, like Weiss, can pursue enlightening strategies with no fear that superiors will object. Since enlightenment is more compatible with development of social science theory than is instrumental use, pursuing enlightenment is more compatible with the social role of an academic. By contrast, consider a local community mental health center evaluator with a request from the center director for data about how many clients insured by third-party payers were seen in the previous month. That evaluator has little latitude to enlighten the director that there are more socially important questions to be asked, and more important problems in the long run to be studied. Even the evaluator in a major federal executive-branch department often works under serious constraints concerning options that can be considered.

A reading of Weiss's work over 20 years suggests that she is aware of the value of both approaches, even if she emphasizes enlightenment more today. For those who want an instrumental approach, her early work (1972b) is a good guide, albeit developed more fully by evaluators such as Wholey and Patton. Her later work (1977b, 1978) presents a guide for enlightenment. In the middle years (1973-1976), during her transition between the two approaches, she said conciliatory things about the need for both approaches:

> To have an immediate and direct influence on decisions, there is a vital place for "inside evaluation" that is consonant with decision-makers' goals and values — and perhaps stretches their sights a bit. There is also a place for independent evaluation based on different assumptions with wider perspectives, and for the structures to sustain it. (1973b, p. 45)

But she never spells out the trade-offs, or suggests how to choose given personal interests, employment, resources, and authority. It would help that local mental health center evaluator to pursue enlightenment if she showed how to deal with the trade-offs. Otherwise, the evaluator will choose on the basis of personal interests and environmental demands — perhaps not so bad, given our inability to predict all the local contingencies that shape practice.

Theory of Social Programming

Weiss has introduced two important advances into thinking about social programming. Scriven and Campbell focus on studying the effects of possible solutions to problems; Weiss makes a role for studying all activities associated with social problem solving. Evaluation is part of a set of social problem-solving activities that includes problem formation, generation of possible solutions, implementation of solutions, evaluation of implemented solutions, and use of the results. The worth of the evaluation depends on how well the other activities are done — a highly internally valid study of the effects of a solution to an unimportant problem is less important. Campbell implicitly acknowledges this dependency through the importance of blind variations in evolutionary epistemology; Scriven's frequent pleas to consider critical competitors is similar acknowledgment. But neither Scriven nor Campbell makes it the evaluator's main job to gather data about all aspects of problem solving. Weiss does, through enlightenment, and her theory is stronger for it.

Second, Weiss has a more realistic view of how social programs work and change. Scriven and Campbell wrongly assume that programs will be significantly responsive to rational information, that ineffective programs will be replaced and effective ones retained, and that programs can be treated as uniform wholes implemented similarly across sites and times. Weiss explicitly rejects such assumptions. She criticizes theories that assume

> that organizations make decisions according to a rational model: define problems, generate options, search for information about the relative merits of each option, and then, on the basis of the information, make a choice. As our colleagues who study organizations tell us . . . this is a patently inaccurate view of how organizations work. When we implicitly adopt this as our underlying theory of organizations in studying research use, we inevitably reach distorted conclusions. (1981b, p. 26)

Weiss understands that problem solving in organizations is guided by a different rationale than the one scientists attribute to them, and that stakeholders, political considerations, and organizational characteristics interact to complicate each problem-solving activity. This leads her to more realistic advice about how social programs change. Since program implementation is heterogeneous and incomplete, evaluators must describe implementation to make clear statements about the causes of effects (Weiss, 1972c).

Above all, Weiss understands that policy resists major change, so the evaluation is conservative to the extent that it serves as handmaiden to policymakers. Evaluators thus must choose between major policy innovation and incremental program improvement. Evaluations oriented toward instrumental use tend to suggest incremental program improvements. Results are more instrumentally usable when they describe changes that are consistent with existing structural and ideological arrangements — usually changing elements within projects. Those changes are mostly procedural ones in how services are provided or administered — adopting a new intake procedure in a mental health center, or issuing a new regulation changing eligibility standards for welfare. Incremental changes are more practical, and are more likely to be adopted in the short term. Wholey built his entire theory around the value of such changes.

Weiss (1972b) was enthusiastic about incremental changes when she wrote about decision-driven evaluations. But she became disillusioned with them, perceiving them as doing little to solve important problems. Enlightenment allows her to examine problems and solutions that depart significantly from the status quo; she can study new policies and programs rather than new elements or projects that would be variants of existing programs. She hopes that, eventually, novel policies and programs will yield better problem amelioration. But new policies and programs are less likely than incremental changes to be adopted; their adoption requires so many changes in existing arrangements that many stakeholders will resist.

Weiss's enlightenment-oriented evaluation sacrifices short-term incremental change for long-term policy change. Evaluators who follow her lead must do so with clear understanding of the infrequency of major policy change. The conditions that favor such changes occur rarely and unpredictably (Polsby, 1984; Quirk, 1986), and it is hard to predict their emergence. When they do emerge, policymakers propose their preferred innovation and cite evidence in its favor. If they have no favorite innovation, they search through the "garbage can" of innovations that accumulated over the years from enlightening research until they find one that seems relevant and consistent with their interests and ideologies. They then compete to get their program adopted, hoping that politics, circumstance, and luck will make their favorite innovation the chosen one. Any given innovation stands a tiny chance of being adopted in the competition. Aiming for long-term change can mean not having much impact, if any at all.

Weiss does, of course, want evaluators to produce short-term incremental changes in the way policymakers think about policy. The difference is that theorists like Wholey propose incremental changes in programs and policies, whereas Weiss proposes incremental changes in people's cognitive structures in the hopes that such changes will lead to changes in policy. Such an interpretation of Weiss is properly treated as a theory of use rather than a theory of social programming. The two theories are related, but meeting social needs and meeting information needs are not always the same thing.

Just as Weiss may have prematurely minimized instrumental use in evaluation, so also she may have prematurely minimized the role of incremental change in her theory of social programming. We know little about the cumulative effects of many incremental changes relative to the effects of major policy shifts. Weiss (in press) acknowledges this cumulative potential in her most recent work:

> I am somewhat more impressed with the findings that evaluation studies have provided. Perhaps they have not led to massive breakthroughs and revolutionary insights, but they have increased our understanding of how programs operate, what effects they have, and what the consequences are of different program strategies. In many agencies and in many countries, policymakers, program managers, and planners have paid attention. Incremental improvements have been made, and cumulative increments are not such small potatoes after all.

She should elaborate this position further, for three reasons. First, the field has little clarity about when an incrementalist approach is worth doing compared with enlightenment, and about the ultimate limitations on the capacity of an incrementalist approach to solve important political, economic, and social problems (Dahl, 1983; Lindblom, 1983; Manley, 1983). If existing social programs do ameliorate problems, then perhaps a responsible strategy is to help them work better. Public managers can contribute greatly to this by making implementation more uniform or better tailored to local reality in ways that enhance effectiveness (Bardach, 1977; Pressman & Wildavsky, 1984). If the program theory is worthwhile, then a responsible strategy is to increase effective implementation of it — exactly those minor incremental changes Weiss tends to forgo. Second, many evaluators work in situations where incremental change is what they are encouraged to do, either by authorities or by financial arrangement. They need guidance about how to do such work better, and their morale would benefit from demonstration that incrementalist strategies can have important benefits.

A third objection concerns Weiss's definition of *conservative*. One definition of a conservative is one who "conserves" the best of the past. In this sense a conservative stance on policy has merit. Not all radical departures from the status quo are automatically desirable. Even leaving political ideology out of the picture, there is good reason to be careful about change in the status quo. Radical change may look good in plan, but cause negative side effects that are hard to anticipate (Braybrooke & Lindblom, 1963; Lindquist, 1988). Deregulation of the airline and banking industries are cases in point. Even if radical departures were chosen, tinkering at the margins will still be required in implementing those departures. Etzioni (1967) observes that incremental changes often either anticipate or elaborate more fundamental changes.

Finally, Weiss's view that social programs are an inhospitable context for evaluation might have been dramatized by the coincidence that much of her early work was in sectors such as antipoverty programs or mental health. Objectives and goals in antipoverty programs were highly politicized. The programs were politically unacceptable to entrenched interests, and were not implemented properly or uniformly partly for those reasons. Objectives and goals may well be more fuzzy and dependent on politics in those sectors than in others. Public health does so more easily for prevention, and extremely easily for Black infant mortality or AIDS prevention. Similarly, in fields like public health that may have had greater success than antipoverty programs, short-term incremental change may be more desirable because standard operating procedures already make sense.

Theory of Practice

Why demote instrumentalism? Weiss has a theory of practice that would be difficult to use for many evaluators who work in situations where short-term instrumental use is encouraged, and where incremental changes are the most likely target. Such situations are common in evaluation, and incrementalist approaches evolved precisely because they are an appropriate response (Shadish & Epstein, 1987). Weiss grants part of this argument, noting that "if we acknowledge that evaluation doesn't routinely lead to program improvement, we risk the loss of clients" (1988b, p. 26)—an argument she attributes to Patton (1988) but seems to endorse at least partly. Her response is to question why Patton puts more emphasis on evaluation's "salability than on its integrity" (p. 26). Ignoring the questionable association of instrumental use with low integrity, Weiss's response simply avoids the key question of what is to be done by all those evaluators who, like it or not, cannot ignore the salability of their work to their local supervisors.

To convince the field that enlightenment should shape the most common form of evaluation, Weiss has to show that incrementalism mostly fails to produce worthwhile information, and that the enlightenment approach provides a viable fiscal base for the field. We doubt she can do this. First, many reports of instrumental, incrementalist approaches to evaluation have been important contributions (Shadish & Reichardt, 1987). Second, to judge from the dollars they award in contracts, managers often place great value on the incrementalist approach. If an evaluator insists on an enlightenment approach, the funder may reject him or her for one who provides more immediately and instrumentally useful results.

How can evaluators build a politically and fiscally viable profession, which requires serving the information needs of decision makers who fund them, without removing the practice of evaluation too far from important social problem solving? Weiss settles on a middle ground with enlightenment, trying both to report important information and to give decision makers information they can use. But other use-oriented theorists propose alternative theories of practice that place instrumental use at center stage. Patton (1987, 1988), in a speech to the annual convention of the American Evaluation Association, has criticized Weiss (1988a) directly on this point. He claims that the instrumental use approach is more successful than Weiss acknowledges, and that evaluation practitioners are not well served in adopting Weiss's approach. Patton (1978) is the author of one of the most popular evaluation books, a book premised mostly on instrumental use. Wholey (1979, 1983) built a successful career as an evaluation theorist and practitioner partly by emphasizing instrumental use. Given this evidence of the popularity of an instrumentalist approach, the fact that the fiscal base of evaluation requires an instrumentalist option, and Weiss's (in press) own acknowledgment that "cumulative increments are not such small potatoes after all," we cannot see a compelling case for rejecting the instrumentalist approach. By all means, complement instrumental use with enlightenment, highlight the failures of instrumentalism to produce important changes, and point to the successes of enlightenment in providing information that policymakers want to buy. But relegate instrumentalist approaches to a minor position? No. They can and should play an important role in evaluation practice. In a very real sense they are the most practical of evaluation theories.

Weiss (1988b) has responded that Patton (1987) ignores the political factors making instrumental use problematic:

> I doubt that we can ever persuade stakeholders to make evaluation results the overriding consideration in program decisions. For one thing, program people know a lot more about their programs than simply the things the evaluator tells them. They have firsthand experience in the operating organization; they know the site, the clients, the staff, the problems, the budgets, the conflicting directives from sponsors and funders, the state of relationships with other organizations that refer clients or receive clients, the history, the complaints and kudos, and the prospects for the future. (p. 17)

This is a daunting list of obstacles. But it is also only partly relevant. These obstacles mean there is no guarantee that instrumental use will occur; but the same is true of enlightenment, which may not occur because the potential user never sees the report or is quickly offended by something said early, or because the user has changed since the evaluation started. The point is not to guarantee the outcome, but to find a process that makes it more likely. Local evaluators, with no guarantees that either instrumental or conceptual use will result from their work, still must make choices about which use to *try* to facilitate. Many of them work in situations where the choice to try to facilitate instrumental use is more appropriate.

We are not endorsing Patton or Wholey in preference to Weiss; demoting enlightenment would be as shortsighted as demoting instrumentalism. Patton's (1987) claim that evaluators would not be well served by adopting Weiss's approach is as narrow a vision of evaluation, in its own way, as Weiss's. In some ways it is even more narrow, since Weiss expresses willingness to consider the alternatives that Patton fails to reciprocate. Narrow vision is a sometimes virtue, but in prescribing practices appropriate to a field as large and diverse as evaluation, narrow vision is fatal.

The need for more specific guides to practice. Weiss's (1972b) book was admirably specific in its advice to evaluators about how to practice. No doubt partly because of this, it is among the best known works in the field (Shadish & Epstein, 1987). Problematically, Weiss has changed much of her advice to evaluators since that book was written almost two decades ago. Since then, she has not written a comprehensive revision that just as specifically tells evaluators what she would have them do today. Hence it is not clear exactly how one would do an evaluation consistent with her modern theory.

Most aspects of this ambiguity are not too problematic. Compared to Rossi and Freeman (1985), Weiss does not describe social science methods in sufficient detail to guide practice. But it is probably not necessary for her to do so, since evaluators can get this guidance from other sources. Still, one central part of her theory is still so ambiguous as to need more attention—question formation. Weiss is not specific about either how to generate an important array of questions to ask in evaluation or how to select a tractable subset of questions for study. She says one should construct a process model of the program—a model of the theory underlying the program that lays out the intermediary steps that move participants toward the program goal. She also says that evaluation

> can contribute to reconsideration of (1) the basic goals of a policy ("Should the federal government assume responsibility for improving the mental health of the populace?"); (2) the means through which goals are to be achieved ("Should the federal government encourage and support the community mental health centers?"); (3) the amount of public funding allocated to the activity ("How much should the government pay toward the establishment and support of centers?"); and (4) its ongoing administration ("What activities of treatment, prevention, and education should be conducted and how can they best be carried out?"). (1978, pp. 63-64)

Equally general is her statement:

> I would like to see evaluation research devote a much larger share of its energies to tracing the life course of a program: the structures set up for its implementation, the motivations and attitudes of its staff, the recruitment of participants, the delivery of services, and the ways in which services and schedules and expectations change over time, the responses of participants and their views of the meaning of the program in their lives. (1987b, p. 45)

This advice is too general. It implies asking a very large set of questions; many evaluators will not have the time or resources to do so. They must narrow the set, and Weiss is not specific about how to do that. Also, it is hard to get high-quality answers to so many questions, making it hard to follow her other advice emphasizing research quality.

Weiss (1972b) is pessimistic about the wisdom of offering evaluators such specific advice about these choices:

> There is no cut-and-dried formula to offer evaluators for the "best" or most suitable way of pursuing their study. Much depends on the uses to be made of the study, the decisions pending, and the information needs of the decision makers. Much also depends (unfortunately) on the constraints in the program setting — the limits placed on the study by the realities of time, place, and people. Money is an issue, too. Textbooks rarely mention the grubby matter of funding, but limited funds impose inevitable restrictions on how much can be studied over how long a period. Thus evaluation methods often represent a compromise between the ideal and the feasible. (p. 9)

Very specific consideration of these trade-offs and choices is the essence of a theory of practice. Other theorists have discussed them better than Weiss has. Few evaluators will use Weiss's new theory until she has done so.

The political context of evaluation is both good and bad. Weiss tells evaluators only about how political context interferes with evaluation practice. Hedrick (1988) provides a fuller, more accurate picture with which Weiss would probably agree. Hedrick agrees that politics interferes in many ways:

- Political pressure may be exerted in ways that bias the scope of evaluation research. . . .
- Political pressure may be exerted to press for unrealistic time frames for completion of research. . . .
- Political pressure may be exerted on evaluators to distort study results. . . .
- Political entities may disseminate or use evaluation results selectively. . . .
- Political pressure may suppress the release of an evaluation report. (pp. 7-8)

But Hedrick also notes that politics can be a positive force in evaluation:

- Political disagreements can serve as stimuli for the initiation of evaluative studies. . . .
- Political maneuvering sometimes includes using evaluation research as a delaying tactic. . . .
- Political disagreements, by their very adversarial nature, can be a major factor in supporting the existence of organizational entities that conduct evaluation studies. . . .

- Political disagreements can be responsible for replications of evaluation studies, thereby increasing the confidence in the conclusions reached. . . .
- Political disagreements can serve to increase the visibility of the results of evaluation studies. (pp. 9-10)

Finally, Hedrick (pp. 11-13) provides strategies to use in political contexts to increase the credibility of evaluation:

- specification of the full scope of the issues
- maintenance of continuous communication
- formation of advisory groups
- clear statements of the study's limitations in final reports and summaries
- nontechnical statements of findings in final reports and summaries

Some of these are identical to recommendations Weiss makes; the rest are consistent with the spirit of her work.

CONCLUSION

Weiss improved upon the early theories of evaluation, especially with her superb analysis of political context and her penetrating studies of use. The next two chapters review two other theorists who share her concerns — Joseph Wholey and Robert Stake. All three theorists first advocated the centrality of experimental methods in evaluation but then left that tradition for one emphasizing methods to construct evaluations that are used by stakeholders. But each sought to reach these goals in different ways. Weiss took an enlightenment approach, mostly at the federal level. Wholey also worked at the federal level, but for social engineering rather than enlightenment. Stake agrees with Weiss's emphasis on enlightenment, but stresses local rather than federal evaluation. This conceptualization of Weiss (federal enlightenment), Wholey (federal social engineering), and Stake (local enlightenment) suggests a fourth use-oriented approach — local social engineering. Patton (1978) could be characterized as taking this fourth approach. In a longer book, we would devote a chapter to the many important things he has to say, as well. Although the reader can intuit much of his approach from the use-oriented theorists we do cover, such intuitions are no substitute for reading Patton's work. We commend his work to you. In the next two chapters, however, consider the use-oriented theories of Wholey and Stake.

6

Joseph S. Wholey:

Evaluation for Program Improvement

KEY TERMS AND CONCEPTS

Results Oriented Management:	The purposeful use by management of resources and information to achieve measurable progress toward program outcome objectives related to program goals.
Performance-Oriented Evaluation:	Partner to results-oriented management, evaluation to help managers achieve high organizational performance.
Sequential Purchase of Information:	Buying increments of timely information when its likely usefulness outweighs the costs of acquiring it. It consists of the next four activities.
Evaluability Assessment:	Assessing whether the program is ready to be managed for results, what changes are needed to do so, and whether the evaluation would contribute to improved program performance.
Rapid Feedback Evaluation:	A quick assessment of program performance in terms of agreed-upon objectives and indicators; also provides designs for more valid, reliable, full-scale evaluation.
Performance Monitoring:	Establishment of ongoing process and outcome program monitoring system.
Intensive Evaluation:	Rigorous experimental evaluations to test the validity of causal assumptions linking program activities to outcomes.

Service Delivery Assessment: A goal-free method of rapid feedback evaluation; documents important program outcomes without the constraints of a predetermined set of objectives and indicators.

BACKGROUND

Wholey earned a master's degree in mathematics and a doctorate in mathematical philosophy from Harvard in 1962, but he has spent his entire career in and around government. Wholey developed a theory of evaluation that is responsive to the desires of government agencies and decision makers. He began his government career during the Kennedy administration as an operations research analyst in the Defense Department from 1962 to 1966. When demands for program evaluation increased during the Johnson administration, he moved to the Department of Health, Education and Welfare (HEW) as special assistant to the deputy assistant secretary for program analysis (1966-1968). From 1968 to 1978 he was director of program evaluation studies at the Urban Institute, consulting closely with government agencies (Bell, 1988). In 1978 he became deputy assistant secretary for evaluation at HEW, continuing until 1980. Since then, he has been professor of public administration with the University of Southern California's Washington (DC) Public Affairs Office.

At HEW and the Urban Institute, Wholey helped shape federal evaluation for years to come: "We proposed legislation that stimulated the subsequent growth of the program evaluation industry" (1982, p. 259). His influence was particularly strong in HEW (now Health and Human Services — HHS) (Abramson & Wholey, 1981; Windle & Woy, 1983), which implemented key aspects of his theory of evaluation:

> In the Carter Administration, my colleagues and I were able to refocus a good deal of the department's evaluation resources on "program performance evaluations" designed to clarify program goals and get policy-management agreement on realistic program objectives and appropriate program performance indicators. (1982, p. 259)

Other examples of adoption of his approach at the federal, state, and local levels are listed in Wholey (1979, 1981, 1983). At the federal level, especially in HEW/HHS, where most major U.S. social programs reside, Wholey may be the most influential theorist covered in this book.

OUR RECONSTRUCTION OF
WHOLEY'S THEORY OF EVALUATION

Evaluation for Good Government

Wholey wants evaluation to foster good government:

> Our goal is good government. "Good government" used to mean not stealing money and not filling public payrolls with political hacks. Today, the term means much more: it now means producing public services that efficiently and effectively respond to the needs of an increasingly complex, increasingly interrelated society. (Wholey, 1983, p. 204)

A focus at the federal program level. Most of Wholey's work is about *program* evaluation for *federal* evaluators, but he provides examples from local and state levels and intends his theory to transfer across all three levels (Wholey, 1981). Federal evaluators are usually asked to respond to three markets: (a) the *individual consumer* market (requests from those in government for specific information about programs), (b) the *program management* market (demands to evaluate programs to find out how to manage them better), and (c) the *policy* market (questions about general policy issues) (Wholey, 1979). He values each of these, but most of his theory is about the second. He says little about doing the first or third kinds of work. Hence we treat the bulk of Wholey's theory as aimed primarily at this program management market, and criticize his theory from that perspective.

For Wholey, evaluation is "the comparison of actual program performance with some standard of expected program performance, and the drawing of conclusions about program effectiveness and value" (1986b, p. 6). This goal is "to make certain that these policies and programs meet the needs of society, [so] it is necessary to analyze programs to determine their consequences — that is, to measure their successes and failures in meeting the nation's goals" (Wholey et al., 1970, p. 11). He focuses on government social programs for two reasons. First, government programs are society's primary means of addressing social problems: "Most government programs . . . were created to respond to real public needs" (1983, p. 29); improving those programs is thus central to social problem solving. Second, social programs are rarely terminated given the political, social, and economic factors involved in their initial creation and maintenance: Even "in very tight budget environments, some programs may be cut, but few programs are eliminated" (1982, p. 258). So Wholey "assumed the continued existence of the programs and organizations produced by the political process" (1982, p. 260). Therefore, in recommending how to evaluate the Title I compensatory education program, he notes that "the Title I program or similar support for compensatory education is here to stay for some considerable period," so that "in order to have value, evaluation must affect program decisions and, if the decisions change program operations, must enhance program effectiveness or efficiency" (Wholey & White, 1973, p. 76).

Improving program management. Wholey hopes to help program management evaluate and improve government social programs: "Evaluators and other analysts should place priority on management-oriented evaluation activities designed to facilitate achievement of demonstrable improvements in government management, performance, and results" (1983, p. 8). He might disagree with Scriven's (1983a) prioritization on consumer-oriented evaluation, and especially with Scriven's avoidance of management. He feels so strongly about this priority that he says at the end of one chapter: "If you're not part of the solution, you're part of the problem" (1983, p. 30).

By *management*, Wholey does not mean only those people who occupy designated management positions. Rather, he refers to the half dozen or so people with greatest influence on a program. This always includes managers, but also includes executives, budget analysts, and legislative staff. To reflect this he has recently adopted broader phrases, such as "policymakers and managers" (Wholey, 1987). We try to mimic his usage, so that reference to managers also includes the broader group of people Wholey intends.

To explain the need for public sector evaluation, Wholey uses an analogy with the private sector (Wholey, Abramson, & Bellavita, 1986). Private sector firms are evaluated by their profitability. But "government organizations are radically different from for-profit firms because government organizations are paid out of budget allocations rather than being paid for satisfying taxpayers or customers by producing results" (Wholey, 1983, p. 189). Partly as a result,

> government is too often wasteful, ineffective, or unresponsive to public needs. Without the type of accountability that directs profit-making firms to seek out needs and to meet them efficiently, government agencies often appear as self-perpetuating bureaucracies primarily interested in growth, salaries, and benefits. (1983, p. 4)

Evaluation does for government what profit does in the private sector — provides critical feedback about whether programs meet their goals, much in the manner "that audit and control do for budgeting and that compliance checks do for administration" (Horst, Nay, Scanlon, & Wholey, 1974, p. 305).

Policymakers and program managers need this feedback quickly because

> any course of action has many possible outcomes and any act has inherent error associated with it. We cannot predict with certainty which results will follow from particular policies, nor should we be confident that policy implementation will conform to plan. Both factors imply that early determination of effects is necessary in order to meet, and possibly redirect, program goals. The limited resources available to meet grave social needs and the significant but largely unpredictable impact of federal domestic policies require timely feedback about both positive and negative effects from on-going programs to assure productive program planning and management. (Wholey et al., 1970, p. 21)

Evaluation provides feedback that is immediately useful to policymakers and managers as they try diverse strategies for meeting social needs. This is reminiscent of Campbell's hope that policymakers and managers will experiment with strategies for solving social problems; but Campbell is suspicious of these groups, whereas Wholey has faith in them.

Wholey's theory of evaluation was "born out of the frustrations of the evaluator in seeking to meet management needs — and the frustrations of the manager in trying to get useful progress reports on program results" (Wholey, Nay, Scanlon, & Schmidt, 1975b, p. 194). For Wholey, program evaluation helps meet these management needs: "*Program evaluation* is the measurement of program performance, the making of comparisons based on those measurements, and the use of the resulting information in policy-making and program management" (1979, p. 1).

The Development of Wholey's Theory

The early Wholey. In the late 1960s, Wholey and his colleagues at the Urban Institute did a study of federal ability to evaluate social programs (Buchanan & Wholey, 1972; Wholey et al., 1970). As with Weiss, Wholey's early work was consistent with that of Suchman (1967) and Campbell (1969); it had not developed its current unique characteristics. He advocated assessing program effects using traditional experimental methods, relying extensively on Campbell and Stanley (1963). The randomized experiment was particularly prominent: "Federal money should not be spent on evaluation of individual local projects unless they have been developed as field experiments, with equivalent treatment and control groups" (Wholey et al., 1970, p. 93). But as with Weiss, experimental methods receded in prominence from his theory over the years.

That early work did contain kernels of his current theory. Wholey et al. (1970) deplored evaluation for its own sake, and called on evaluators to examine critically when evaluation is really needed:

> Not everything one might want to investigate in federal programs can be evaluated. There will be questions that should not be pursued — study cost may be out of line, results might not be obtainable by the time answers are needed, or feasible methods may not exist for tracing certain kinds of effects. It is essential, therefore, to know the limits of what evaluation can accomplish. (p. 16)

Wholey's later theory explicates this early concern with when evaluation should be pursued. Leaving experimental methods mostly behind, he developed a theory to make evaluations maximally useful to policymakers and managers.

Why are evaluations not used by policymakers and managers? The key to his subsequent theory was the observation that evaluations should be *used* by policymakers and managers, but are not. Buchanan and Wholey (1972) note that "the primary justification for evaluation research is its usefulness to policymakers and program managers" (p. 22); "evaluation efforts can only be justified if they result in products that are used" (Abramson & Wholey, 1981, p. 42). But evaluation was not often used in this manner, making it difficult to institutionalize it into federal decision making. So he cajoled evaluators to "move from their present preoccupation with evaluation as an end in itself and begin to think in terms of evaluation as part of policy planning and management systems" (Buchanan & Wholey, 1972, p. 22).

By 1974, his views solidified further. Evaluations had proliferated throughout the federal government since their 1970 survey, but "there is little evidence to show that evaluation generally leads to more effective social policies or programs" (Horst et al., 1974, p. 300). Horst et al. (1974) describe the critical management problem confronting government agencies and evaluation: "Why have those in charge of programs and those who evaluate them not been able to join their efforts in a way that leads more frequently to significant improvements in program performance?" (p. 300). In answer, they blame three problems: lack of definition, lack of clear logic, and lack of management. Lack of definition implies that "the problem addressed, the program intervention being made, the expected direct outcome of that intervention, or the expected impact on the overall society or on the problem addressed are not sufficiently well defined to be measurable" (p. 301). Lack of clear logic means that "the logic of assumptions linking expenditure of resources, the implementation of a program intervention, the immediate outcome to be caused by that intervention, and the resulting impact are not specified or understood clearly enough to permit testing them" (p. 301). Lack of management suggests that "those in charge of the program lack the motivation, understanding, ability, or authority to act on evaluation measurements and comparisons of *actual* intervention activity, *actual* outcomes, and *actual* impact" (p. 301). When any of these problems is present, evaluation is unlikely to cause significant improvement in program performance.

Good management of social programs is hard. These management and evaluation problems are inherent in programs that "operate in complex political environments, pushed and pulled in many directions by legislative bodies and by a multitude of funding and regulatory organizations, grantees, and interest groups" (Wholey, 1983, p. 15). Consider some implications of this environment for evaluation and management. Social programs are variable in implementation over sites. Wholey et al. (1970) distinguish between programs and projects. A program is "the provision of federal funds and administrative direction to accomplish a prescribed set of objectives through the conduct of specified activities. Typically, the money goes to intermediaries rather than to final recipients of services" (p. 24). A project "is the implementation level of a program — the level where resources are used to produce an end product that directly contributes to the objectives of the program" (p. 24); "an examination of 20 projects in the same program will often reveal 20 very different program intervention designs, different in activity and purpose" (Horst et al., 1974, p. 303). This distinction between programs and projects is like one we have made (Cook et al., 1985; Cook & Shadish, 1986).

This variability makes evaluation and management of programs difficult:

> Evaluations of large programs are difficult, both because of the cost of data collection and because wide variations in local activities or objectives often complicate the task of collecting comparable data at different sites. The diversity at local level also makes it difficult to summarize what is being accomplished in a large program. (Wholey, 1983, p. 124)

Complicating this further is "the fact that most are administered by State and local governments" (Wholey et al., 1972, p. 120) with long traditions of autonomy without federal monitoring. Setting clear objectives and activities for diverse projects is an overwhelming management task.

Moreover, statements of program goals and activities are vague for political reasons:

> Many federal social programs are simply envelopes for a large federal investment in a problem area. A program may be deceptive in the sense that it has enough content to allow it to be described in the media, lobbied into existence, and established as a federal effort — and yet the program interventions are not spelled out in any detail. (Horst et al., 1974, p. 303)

"Federal policy-makers and program managers operate in an environment that tends to inhibit effective program management" (Wholey, Nay, Scanlon, & Schmidt, 1975a, p. 89), an environment of poorly defined objectives and priorities; insufficient staff, resources, and authority; and rapid turnover or reorganization.

Such complexities cause the three problems that interfere with using evaluation to improve programs — lack of definition, clear logic, and management. But "these three factors are not the responsibility of the evaluator" (Horst et al., 1974, p. 301); they are management problems. If "we define management as the purposeful application of resources to tasks in order to achieve specified objectives" (Wholey et al., 1975b, p. 175), then those who must manage cannot do so without clear objectives; without plausible, testable assumptions between resources and objectives; and without the motivation, ability, or authority to manage. Therefore, evaluators must work with management to remedy these problems, sharing responsibility between evaluator and manager. Wholey writes of the evaluation of Title I (compensatory education):

> At local and state levels, the routine evaluation activities that exist in the Title I program have generally been imposed on local and state program officials from above. Rather than being an integral part of program management, these Title I evaluation activities have been isolated from program operations. Particularly at local and state levels, education officials still tend to view evaluation as "just more paperwork required by the feds" — as a condition to get their Title I allocation. In short, the main purpose for evaluation, *i.e.*, to feed back information about how a program is working to improve its operation, is missing from most local and state evaluation activities. (Wholey & White, 1973, p. 75)

Such experience led Wholey to develop a theory aimed at working with management to ensure such problems do not hinder successful use of evaluation. Stake takes a similar rationale to develop a very different kind of theory.

Wholey's approach is good for the field of evaluation, too. Policy-makers and managers control much evaluation funding, so the profession increases its viability by making itself needed by these groups. As funds become scarce, evaluation must continue to prove its worth: "Evaluators will have to produce more relevant, less expensive evaluations if evaluators are to have roles in the constrained resources environments of the 1980s and beyond" (Wholey, 1983, p. 205):

> In the late 1970s and 1980s, some disenchantment with evaluation became apparent. Led by the Senate Appropriations Committee, Congress began to set limits on contracts for consultant services, including contracts for evaluation. "It seems as though, year after year, the same programs get re-evaluated, yet never change," the Committee complained. (Wholey, 1986b, p. 7)

He hopes his approach to evaluation partly counters such complaints.

Results-Oriented Management

Over time Wholey has expanded his management-oriented focus. In *Evaluation and Effective Public Management* he writes: "As a result of my experience and the experience of others over the last twenty years, I believe that much more policy-level attention and analytical talent should go into activities designed to improve the management and performance of agencies and programs" (1983, p. xv). Wholey, who rarely says any-thing negative about other approaches to evaluation, called for evaluators to limit their role as social critics and to be team players working with management to improve programs: "It has been argued that evaluators have contributed to the public's negative image of government by accen-tuating their role as critics" (Bellavita, Wholey, & Abramson, 1986, pp. 285-286). Wholey is dismayed by this image:

> Although evaluators clearly should not be asked to be cheerleaders for govern-ment, there is a legitimate point that they can play a more positive role in both shaping public opinion about government and helping agency managers run their programs. Although there have been instances where evaluators have also helped policymakers and managers decide realistically what their programs can do, there need to be more instances of evaluators playing this constructive role. Evaluators have also helped policymakers and managers improve their programs while those programs were underway, but it is argued that this role should become the norm for evaluators, rather than the exception. Finally, evaluators have provided timely, convincing evidence about program effectiveness in the past and should continue to play that role. (Bellavita et al., 1986, p. 286)

He clarifies this role:

> The new evaluator is a *program advocate*—not an advocate in the sense of an ideologue willing to manipulate data and to alter findings to secure next year's funding. The new evaluator is someone who believes in and is interested in helping programs and organizations succeed. At times the program advocate evaluator will play the traditional critic role: challenging basic program assumptions, reporting lackluster performance, or identifying inefficiencies. The difference, however, is that criticism is not the end of performance-oriented evaluation; rather, it is part of a larger process of program and organizational improvement, a process that receives as much of the evaluator's attention and talents as the criticism function. (Bellavita et al., 1986, p. 289)

Wholey's recent work is as much a theory of management as a theory of evaluation. Evaluation is not sufficient for improving government performance. Improving performance requires effective management:

> Government needs a special kind of management, result-oriented management, directed at producing demonstrable improvements in the performance and results of government agencies and programs. As we are using the term here, *results-oriented management* is the purposeful use of resources and information to achieve measurable progress toward program outcome objectives related to program goals. (Wholey, 1983, p. 11)

Evaluation is just one resource for this purpose.

Levels of results-oriented management. Results-oriented management (or performance-oriented management; Wholey et al., 1986) is achieved to different degrees in different programs. Wholey (1983) suggests seven levels of achievement. At Level 0, policymakers and managers define the program and responsibility for managing it. At Level 1, management gets policy agreement about realistic, results-oriented program objectives, and about qualitative or quantitative performance indicators to use in assessing and managing the program. At Level 2, management establishes a means to assess program performance and intraprogram variations in performance in terms of the indicators from Level 1. At Level 3, management obtains policy-level consensus on realistic targets for program performance on the program objectives at Level 1 and the measurement system at Level 2. At Level 4, management establishes a way to use this information to improve program performance. At Level 5, management gets better program performance on the targets from Level 3. At Level 6, management communicates program performance to parties at policy levels and to the general public.

Any existing program is at Level 0. Evaluation activities associated with each of the other six levels, respectively, are as follows:

1. Working with program managers, policymakers, those delivering services, and relevant interest groups to identify program goals and agency priorities; to diagnose program potential; to get policy and management agreements defining the sets of program objectives and program performance indicators that will be used in assessing program performance and results; and to identify options for improving program and agency performance.
2. Developing systems for assessing program performance in terms of agreed-on program objectives and performance indicators.
3. Working with managers and policymakers to establish realistic target levels of expected or improved program performance, in terms of agreed-on program objectives and performance indicators.
4. Developing systems for using information on program performance, and intra-program variations in performance, to stimulate and reward improvements in program and agency performance and results.
5. Assessing program performance and results in terms of agreed-on program objectives, performance indicators, and performance targets; in particular, documenting program performance and intra-program variations in performance, comparing program performance with prior or expected performance, documenting how especially good performance is achieved, and identifying factors inhibiting better program performance.
6. Communicating program performance to policy levels and to the public. (Wholey, 1983, pp. 14-15)

With coordination between management and evaluator, Wholey says a program can move to Level 1, and probably Level 2, in one year; by the second year it could move to Levels 3 and 4; and by the third year, to the final levels (1983, p. 202).

Sequential Purchase of Information About Programs

Managers may not want or benefit from all these evaluation activities:

Policy makers and managers already receive unsystematic feedback on program performance *without* formal evaluation: from telephone calls, letters, meetings with constituents, the press, professional opinion, public interest groups, and officials at other levels of government. In any given instance, the value of systematic program evaluation is uncertain. (Wholey, 1981, p. 93)

Managers have limited time and resources to spread among many activities, of which evaluation is only one. They may wish to minimize evaluation costs to fund more of these other activities. Finally, different programs are at different levels of results-oriented management; not all programs need all evaluation activities. So, Wholey suggests that

> the concept of expected value of information is crucial to evaluation planning. Evaluation information can be very expensive but has the characteristic of diminishing marginal returns. In deciding which information to buy, the evaluation planner must be able to explicitly consider, and trade off, confidence and expected impact within constraints set by the use to which the evaluation will be put. Estimation of information cost and value is the mechanism for tying the evaluation design steps together. (1977, p. 42)

So Wholey proposes that managers "purchase sequential increments of timely, useful information on program promise and performance" (1979, p. xiii). Evaluation should be purchased only "when the likely usefulness of the new information outweighs the costs of acquiring it" (1983, p. 119)—similar to Scriven's (1976a) "cost-free" evaluation. Wholey changes Scriven's idea from urging that evaluation yield a positive cost-benefit to urging that it be cost-effective, recognizing the difficulties that have plagued attempts to translate effects into dollars.

Wholey (1979) describes four evaluation tools that can be sequentially applied if managers wish to purchase them: evaluability assessment, rapid feedback evaluation, performance monitoring, and intensive evaluation:

> Program managers and policy-makers can use each increment of information as it becomes available, while the evaluator can use the information to further explore the users' information needs and the feasibility and cost of meeting those needs. At each stage in the evaluation process, evaluators and those in charge of the program are free to decide either that sufficient program performance information is available or that additional information is likely to be useful. Using this "sequential purchase of information" strategy, the evaluator can increase managers' and policy-makers' familiarity with evaluation and their confidence in it; show managers and policy-makers where further evaluation work is feasible and likely to be useful; and stop evaluation when it is clear that further increments of information are unlikely to have sufficient impact on program performances. (Wholey, 1979, p. 14)

Wholey encourages flexibility in applying these four steps, which we consider now.

Evaluability assessment. Horst et al. (1974) end their article by presenting a tool to help ameliorate the problems of lack of definition, clear logic, and management—evaluability assessment (see also Nay & Kay, 1982; Schmidt, Scanlon, & Bell, 1979; Strosberg & Wholey, 1983). This tool has also been called "preassessment of evaluability" (Horst et al., 1974, p. 307), "pre-evaluation design" (Horst et al., 1974, p. 307), "accountability assessment" (Wholey, 1981, p. 96), and "exploratory evaluation" (Wholey, 1981, p. 96; 1983, p. 35). Evaluability assessment helps remedy problems that hinder the usefulness of evaluation by asking:

> Are the problems, intended program interventions, anticipated outcomes, and the expected impact sufficiently well defined as to be measureable? In the assumptions linking expenditures to implementation of intervention, intervention to the outcome anticipated, and immediate outcome to the expected impact on the problem, is the logic laid out clearly enough to be tested? Is there anyone clearly in charge of the problem? Who? What are the constraints on his ability to act? What range of actions might he reasonably take or consider as a result of various possible evaluation findings about the measures and assumptions discussed above? (Horst et al., 1974, p. 307)

One should evaluate only those programs about which affirmative answers can be given to these questions; only such programs are evaluable. For programs that may never yield positive answers, the evaluator should decline the commission. For those that yield remediable negative answers, the evaluator can work with management to develop an evaluable program.

Evaluability assessment does not tell if a program can be evaluated: "Evaluability assessment answers the question, not whether a program can be evaluated (every program can be evaluated), but whether the program is ready to be managed for results, what changes are needed for results-oriented management, and whether evaluation is likely to contribute to improved program performance" (Wholey, 1983, p. 35). It tells if evaluating a program might help managers improve the program. It is cheap and quick, a considerable advantage in policy: "By quickly providing objective, credible information relevant to problems that managers face, the evaluability assessment process tends to overcome managers' skepticism" (Wholey, 1983, p. 87). Evaluability assessment helps programs at Level 0 move to Level 1.

Evaluability assessment has three purposes: to clarify program intent; to explore program reality; and to assist policy, management, and evaluation decisions. To clarify program intent, the evaluator examines program documentation, interviews a few managers and policymakers in the executive and legislative branches, and interviews representatives of interest groups. From this, the evaluator constructs two products. One is a program design model that presents "the resources allocated to the program, intended program activities, expected program outcomes, and assumed causal linkages" (Wholey, 1983, p. 42). Including intermediate outcome objectives to connect activities with outcomes is crucial. The evaluator constructs a model in some detail, but presents a condensed version to policymakers and managers.

The second product is agreed-upon program performance indicators. Getting consensus on indicators is difficult:

> There will usually be political and bureaucratic resistance to clear definition of the program activities, objectives, and performance indicators that would signal "good" (or "bad") performance in a public program. A broad coalition was needed to bring the program into existence and is still needed to maintain it. Those who make up the coalition might be "turned off" by establishment of priorities that they do not share; there may be political trouble in putting aside program goals even when those goals are unattainable because of resource constraints or lack of needed technology. (Wholey, 1982, p. 264)

"Decisions on policy questions such as definitions of program objectives, measures of progress toward objectives, and important program assumptions should be made by the managers, not by the evaluators" (Wholey, et al., 1975b, p. 186).

The second purpose of evaluability assessment is exploring program reality: "the evaluator documents the feasibility of measuring program performance and estimates the likelihood that program objectives will be achieved" (Wholey, 1983, p. 46).

> By documenting flows of resources, flows of clients (or other entities of interest), and flows of program performance information, evaluators learn what program performance information could be developed in a full-scale evaluation or management system; and they can estimate the likelihood that program objectives will be achieved. Examination of program operations may reveal that program reality is far from the program design envisioned by those at higher management and policy levels. (p. 46)

The emphasis is on actual, not intended, activities. Sometimes only informed opinion is available about this; Wholey views opinion as a poor substitute for actual data. Site visits may be necessary to observe activities and outcomes, and to see whether it is realistic to expect the program to achieve its objectives — a decision ultimately made by management with the evaluator's input.

The third purpose of evaluability assessment is assisting policy and management decisions. The evaluator takes the previous information "to work with management, clarifying the implications of what has been

learned and exploring options for program change and program improvement" (Wholey, 1983, p. 51). The evaluator presents an evaluable model
of the program: "that portion of the program which is currently manageable in terms of a set of realistic program objectives and agreed-on
program performance indicators" (p. 51). Then the evaluator helps management explore possible improvements:

1. Options for changes in program resources or objectives (now called "policy
   options");
2. Options for changes in program activities ("management options");
3. Options for changes in collection and use of program performance information ("information options"). (Wholey, 1983, p. 52)

Consider an example from a hypothetical drug abuse treatment program:

Those in charge are challenged to specify in advance how decisions might vary
with the range of possible evaluation findings. For example, will a task force
convene for program redesign if national program cure rates average 5 per cent,
15 per cent, or 50 per cent? Will technical assistance be given to projects whose
average cure rate falls below 5 per cent? Is there technical assistance to give?
Can projects be closed down? Will a stated national objective of a 30 per cent
cure rate be adjusted downward, if the actual average cure rate found is 15 per
cent? This type of dialogue would permit the evaluator to assess the potential
value of evaluation information by identifying plausible and practical uses of it
and also permit the evaluator to assess the specific type and accuracy of the
information required. (Horst et al., 1974, p. 306)

As these options develop, the evaluator clarifies the "dollars, staff time,
management time, and other resources" (Wholey, 1983, p. 90) needed to
implement the change, and should have much contact with program reality
to ensure that options can be realistically implemented. Management
decisions about which options to attempt are elicited and documented. All
findings of evaluability assessment can be given to management in a series
of memoranda, briefings, and meetings. The steps in evaluability assessment are often iterative, with new data leading to continued revision of
models and recommendations.

One possible decision is that evaluation is premature because the program is not manageable for results. If so, management should "embark
on a *program design* effort to define the measurable objectives and explicit, testable assumptions linking expenditures, program activities, intended outcomes, and intended impact on the problem addressed by
the program" (Wholey et al., 1975b, pp. 186-187). Such work may be
resisted because it may restrict freedom of managerial action, require more

accountability than managers want, or require politically sensitive objectives to be specified.

Wholey (1979, 1983) provides many examples of evaluability assessment, complete with an array of methods for practice. Evaluability assessments are cheaper for simple programs or those with much prior information. A simple state-level project he describes took seven calendar weeks to complete, and cost $11,000 and several staff days. Complex federal evaluability assessments cost from $50,000 to $120,000, used 6 to 18 staff months, and took 3 to 10 calendar months. That Wholey reports these time and cost data is a testimony to his sensitivity to economic and organizational realities.

One study of manager opinion of evaluability assessment in HHS (Scanlon & Bell, 1981) found "that the executives and managers were far more positive about evaluability assessment than about evaluation in general" (Wholey, 1983, pp. 102-103), and that "seven of nine program managers and three of the three executives involved in evaluability assessments stated that they found evaluability assessment useful" (p. 103). A positive but more cautious endorsement is provided by Rog's (1985) study of 57 evaluability assessments. These studies were implemented with good fidelity but varied in cost considerably; they produced information about which programs were evaluable or which changes might make them evaluable; and many of these studies, particularly the costly ones, were used. But the frequency of use of evaluability assessment dropped off dramatically after Wholey left government in 1980 (this is confounded with the dramatic cutbacks of the Reagan years), and some evidence suggests that evaluability assessments were used to substitute for evaluations rather than to precede them.

Rapid feedback evaluation. After evaluability assessment, program management may want more evaluative information. An intermediate step between evaluability assessment and more intensive evaluation is a rapid feedback evaluation, which provides "(1) a quick preliminary assessment of program performance in terms of agreed-on program objectives and performance indicators; and (2) designs for more valid, more reliable full-scale evaluation" (Wholey, 1983, p. 119). Compared to intensive evaluation this strategy shortens the time for managers to get some data, forces evaluators to test the feasibility of designs, and is often sufficient for management and policy purposes. Rapid feedback evaluation has five steps: "(1) collection of existing data on program performance, (2) collection of new data on program performance, (3) preliminary evaluation, (4) development and analysis of alternative designs for full-scale evaluation, and (5) assisting policy and management decisions" (1983, p. 121). Existing data include agency records, program data systems, and monitoring reports, as well as past research, evaluation, and audits. Only data on agreed-upon performance indicators is used. New data can be gathered by interview, survey, or site visit. Quick and practical methods are preferred over time-consuming methods:

> Existing data sources should be used before evaluators create new information systems or request staff and others to collect data that are not already being gathered. Evaluators can look for rough approximations instead of precise answers and can reduce sample sizes for the sake of timeliness. Triangulation, blending qualitative and quantitative data, and other techniques can be used to minimize the likelihood of gross errors. Methodologies that are simple should be preferred over ones that are complex. Evaluators should pursue data collection strategies that emphasize quality over quantity of data, inexpensive over expensive data collection strategies, and clear performance measures over the complex and the subtle ones. . . . Working closely with people who have more intimate knowledge of the program is another protection against major errors. (Bellavita et al., 1986, pp. 290-291)

With this information, the evaluator produces "a preliminary evaluation of program performance in terms of the agreed-on program performance indicators" (Wholey, 1983, p. 122). Rapid feedback evaluation "supplements the preliminary evaluation with statements of the degree of uncertainty in the preliminary assessment and statements of the time and effort required to get more conclusive information" (p. 122). More intensive designs can be compared for costs, time, and strengths. Management can then decide on changes in program resources, activities, or objectives, or can make an informed commitment to full-scale evaluation.

One other approach complements rapid feedback evaluation — service delivery assessments (SDA), developed in HHS (Champion, 1985; Hendricks, 1981, 1982). SDA was developed independently; its inventors did not require it to follow evaluability assessment. Rapid feedback evaluation is "goal-oriented, directed at the identification of agreed-on program objectives and performance indicators, and at the evaluation of program performance in terms of agreed-on objectives and indicators" (Wholey, 1983, p. 139). SDAs are goal-free, documenting "important program outcomes without the constraints imposed by a predetermined set of objectives and performance indicators" (p. 139). Service delivery assessment has five steps: "(1) preassessment, (2) design, (3) data collection, (4) analysis of data, and (5) presentation of findings and recommendations" (Wholey, 1983, pp. 141-142).

SDAs "are typically initiated when problems are suspected or policy changes are planned, or when the Secretary is interested in a particular program or issue" (Wholey, 1983, p. 142). SDA preassessment takes four

to six weeks, and moves the SDA "from a fairly general one-page assignment to decisions on the set of issues and questions to be addressed in
the assessment" (Wholey, 1983, p. 142). The questions come from available program materials and data, and from discussions with stakeholders.
Step 2 is design: specifying the number of respondents (typically several
hundred respondents over 15-30 states), sampling scheme (typically purposeful but sometimes random), and methods (typically personal interview, on-site observation, and inspection of documents). The third step,
data collection, takes two to three more weeks. The fourth step takes five
to six weeks—results are synthesized in preliminary reports, and staff
are debriefed. This results in "descriptions of local operations and local
environments, comparisons among local sites, comparisons with standards
of expected performance, early warnings of emerging problems, descriptions of best practices observed, and recommendations for operational
improvements" (1983, p. 144). Finally, a 12- to 15-page report is prepared.
Illustrative quotes and case studies often figure prominently in it. The
report is then discussed with the services and top department managers.
SDA thus helps top-level decision makers to understand operating program reality better, and to initiate changes to improve the program. These
managers are isolated from program reality, and information they receive
is filtered by many levels, each with its own agenda (Downs, 1967);
evaluators are part of this filtering process. Part of the attraction of SDAs
is their unfiltered nature.

Wholey (1983) says that "service delivery assessment provides much
richer data on program reality than is obtained in the typical goal-oriented
evaluation, though service delivery assessment suffers from lack of direction as to which questions are of greatest interest" (p. 152). SDAs are best
used "when policymakers or managers need clearer perceptions of program reality or early warning of emerging problems" (p. 140). Future
combinations of evaluability assessment and service delivery assessment
could combine advantages of both; evaluability assessment has over time
incorporated the emphases of SDA on program reality as well as program
intent.

Performance monitoring. Successful completion of evaluability assessment moves a program to Level 1. Managers may then wish to purchase
even more evaluation: "Establishment of an appropriate outcome monitoring system moves programs to Level 2 on the results-oriented management scale . . . and lays the basis for policy and management agreement
on realistic performance targets (Level 3 performance)" (Wholey, 1983,
pp. 154-155). Wholey uses performance monitoring and outcome monitoring interchangeably, but "whatever term is used, both process measures

and outcome measures will be important in the types of monitoring systems with which we are concerned" (p. 155).

Certainty that the program caused the outcome is compromised in performance monitoring: "Outcome monitoring simply measures program outcomes and progress toward program objectives, leaving to others the task of estimating the extent to which program activities have caused the observed results" (1983, p. 155). But this uncertainty is not fatal, for two reasons. First, performance monitoring is useful to policymakers and managers even without valid causal inference: "Government managers manage public programs as they manage their own lives, attempting to improve performance by adjusting activities when performance leaves too much to be desired" (1983, p. 154). They use performance monitoring as a "signaling system" (Wholey et al., 1975b, p. 188) that an intervention is needed, although "the appropriate corrective management actions are often not obvious" (Wholey et al., 1975b, p. 188). Second, "together with qualitative case studies, . . . outcome monitoring is usually the most feasible evaluation alternative" (Wholey, 1983, p. 155). It is often cheaper and easier to implement compared to the randomized experiment.

Performance monitoring has four steps: "(1) establishment of data sources; (2) collection of data on program outcomes; (3) comparison of program outcomes with prior or expected outcomes; and (4) assisting policy and management decisions" (Wholey, 1983, p. 156). Data sources "include agency and program records, existing data systems, use of trained observers, and conduct of special surveys . . . or site visits" (1983, p. 156). Data collection is ongoing and repetitive. Such data can be corrupted if used for decision making, but this can be minimized "by securing prior agreement with intended users on the data to be collected" (Wholey, 1979, p. 146), and by letting managers "know what kind of performance is expected and what kinds of data will be required" (1979, p. 146).

Program outcomes can be compared to program performance during a previous period, to expected performance if such standards have been developed, and among different units within a program. The last of these can "trigger qualitative case studies to document how the high performers achieved especially good results — and to trigger management actions to stimulate improvements in program and project results" (Wholey, 1983, p. 158). Controversy may ensue over appropriate standards:

> Agreement on the events to be monitored is much more important than the establishment of performance standards, however. If necessary, management can omit the establishment of expected performance levels in the early years, simply establishing the most important measures of program performance and collecting data on those measures. (1979, p. 146)

Intensive evaluation. Next, policymakers and managers can decide whether to purchase intensive evaluation, where "the major evaluation design choice is whether to test the validity of causal assumptions linking program activities to program outcomes" (Wholey, 1979, p. 149). The preferred methods are randomized experiments or quasi-experiments. These designs are more costly than performance monitoring. True "experiments can provide much more compelling evidence on program effectiveness than is provided by more typical evaluation designs" (1979, p. 152). Quasi-experiments, especially time series, can yield convincing evidence about cause and effect "when an experiment is considered infeasible or too costly (the usual situation!)" (1979, p. 159). The ability to do a time series depends on the rare availability of many pre- and postprogram data points, and on implementing the program quickly so effects are not dissipated. Randomized experiments are more feasible in demonstration programs than ongoing programs (Wholey, 1983). Often,

> plausible assumptions cannot be formulated given present knowledge (how do you teach disadvantaged children? stop child abuse? reduce crime?) or the actual program design does not lend itself to definitive tests of program assumptions (sufficient replications are not available to yield convincing evidence on whether treatment A is better than treatment B, or no treatment at all, under condition C). (Wholey et al., 1975b, p. 189)

Given such reservations, Wholey's opinion about the worth of intensive evaluation is guarded. Some resources should be devoted to it: "If the government spent just 10 percent of *demonstration* funds doing experiments and quasi-experiments, evaluators could often get convincing evidence on whether or not particular programs cause hoped-for results or unwanted side-effects" (Wholey, 1979, p. 166). But simple outcome monitoring is the "most feasible and the least expensive" (1983, p. 117), more "cost-effective" (Wholey et al., 1975a, p. 93), and "much more useful to managers" (Wholey et al., 1975b, p. 189); and "rapid feedback evaluation may well obviate the need for more expensive, time-consuming evaluation by producing adequate information to satisfy management" (Wholey et al., 1975a, p. 92). Intensive evaluation is not even mentioned in many of Wholey's works (Wholey, 1983); and he presents few examples of it actually following from a sequential purchase of evaluability assessment, rapid feedback evaluation, and performance monitoring — the only exception is an evaluation of the Tennessee prenatal care program (Wholey, 1987). The experiments that illustrate intensive evaluation in Wholey (1979) come from other authors, even though Wholey usually illustrates his theory with his own work. The evaluator might present the design to the manager as an option, but Wholey implies that rapid feedback evaluation or outcome monitoring is usually preferred because it is cheaper, more feasible, and provides adequate information.

The Evaluation Product

At all steps, the evaluator should report to the manager about progress and results: "Final reports and exit briefings ought not to be the places where significant findings are revealed for the first time. Evaluators should continually be sharing their insights, findings, and conclusions with staff, managers, and policymakers" (Bellavita et al., 1986, p. 291). Additionally:

Evaluators' ideas about how programs and organizations can be improved should not ignore political, organizational, or fiscal realities. Evaluators should aim first to provide ideas that require no new personnel, data collection requirements, or spending. Recommendations that do require new resources are more likely to be adopted if evaluators can show how existing resources can be reallocated without reducing a program or organization's effectiveness in other areas. (Bellavita et al., 1986, p. 291)

Managing Evaluation

In organizing and managing evaluation, the first task is to work with high-level managers and policymakers to establish evaluation policy — "how evaluation resources are to be used, what types of evaluation activities are to be given priority, and what results are expected from evaluation" (Wholey, 1983, p. 168). Then, resources are mobilized; evaluation staff and contractors are hired; and the evaluation office is integrated with the program. Such integration helps evaluators increase their leverage by working with other management groups in "operational planning systems, financial management systems, computer support programs, personnel systems, audit and evaluation programs" (1983, p. 174).

Regarding hiring, "performance-oriented evaluators need skills not typically taught in evaluation training programs or courses" (Bellavita et al., 1986, p. 289). These include ability to work in uncertain, ambiguous, and complex situations; negotiation skills; a bias for the pragmatic; flexibility and skills to respond quickly to requests; and good speaking, visual communication, and listening skills (Bellavita et al., 1986).

Subsequently, "managing a useful evaluation program requires both strategic and tactical decisions. The former include decisions on evaluation office objectives: which evaluation markets will the evaluation office serve, what resources will be allocated to each of these markets, how will success be measured?" (Wholey, 1979, p. 180). These strategic decisions are made with program managers and policymakers. A particularly important decision is the location of the evaluation office in relationship to the program being evaluated: "It makes obvious sense to place the responsibility for evaluation at a level appropriate to the decisions which the evaluation is to assist. No program manager should be expected to evaluate the worth of his program, for example, nor should a member of the manager's staff be put in the position of having to criticize his boss" (Wholey et al., 1972, p. 119). Wholey et al. (1972) also describe the kinds of questions appropriately addressed by evaluation offices at different levels.

Evaluation also involves tactical decisions, which "include decisions on which evaluation activities to undertake, decisions on whether to do the evaluations through in-house staff or through contractors or grantees, and decisions related to the implementation and use of specific evaluations" (Wholey, 1979, p. 180). The conduct of evaluation—formulating plans, implementation, utilization—must be monitored for compliance with policy. The evaluation office can be a repository of completed evaluations; can publicize, disseminate, and synthesize completed works; and can prepare memos and briefings (Abramson & Wholey, 1981).

Finally, when a new evaluation office is first established, the evaluators must quickly establish the worth of evaluation so as to solidify funding and administrative support for the program. Early efforts should be kept tractable, focusing on a limited number of programs where the evaluation policy can be implemented and its worth demonstrated. Evaluators should also have frequent and productive meetings with program management to report results—meetings in which evaluators are "informally marketing their product line" (Wholey, 1983, p. 176).

Using Evaluation to
Stimulate Effective Management

Good evaluation is stymied by poor coordination with management, since many of the problems in using evaluation are controlled by management. Simply doing evaluation will not promote the use of evaluation. The evaluator must actively facilitate such use. For example, when interacting with management during evaluability assessment:

> The keys to getting the necessary policy and management decisions appear to be (1) holding the interest of management through provision of early evaluability assessment products; (2) continuing interaction with management at frequent intervals; (3) briefing key individuals on evaluability assessment findings and

options to clarify the findings and options and to get their positions on the options; and (4) providing the additional information needed to clarify the options and prepare for implementation of the highest-priority options. (Wholey, 1983, p. 91)

But these tasks are not enough. Management must be motivated to implement results-oriented management; but in government, structural problems in government often preclude such motivation. So evaluators must help management do so:

Existing incentives (the budget process, paths to promotion, and media attention) tend to pull policymakers and managers toward actions that inhibit rather than promote efficient, effective government. Before needed improvements in government management and performance can be achieved, changes in government incentive structures appear to be required. (Wholey, 1983, p. 178)

Such changes will not be quick or easy; rather, "sustained, creative effort is needed to produce better incentive systems and better government performance" (p. 179). The private sector routinely uses incentives such as perks, pay, and vacations to motivate improved performance. These same kinds of incentives could be used in public programming, within the limits of government regulations, linked to progress in results-oriented management. Intangible incentives include public recognition, media attention, awards, interesting assignments, more responsibility, removal of constraints, and delegation of authority; perks include travel to conferences, selection for training programs, educational leave, flexible working hours, better office space, free parking, more annual leave, and sabbaticals; financial incentives include promotions, bonuses, cash awards, and pay raises. Some such incentives can be given to organizations, too, including increases in program budget, allocation of discretionary funds, discretionary use of savings, staff allocations, allocation of overhead resources, and renewal of discretionary grants. Power to implement these incentives is not in just one set of hands; it requires the cooperation and coordination of many groups, personnel offices, inspectors general, auditors, evaluators, and public affairs offices.

OUR ANALYSIS OF
WHOLEY'S THEORY OF EVALUATION

The major key to Wholey's theory is working with management—those policymakers, managers, and others who most directly influence a program. The approach has many advantages, and provides a viable funding base for the profession. It provides evaluators with quick legitimacy, and ensures a future for evaluation in proportion to how useful evaluators can be to management. When budgets for evaluations are on the decline, the viability of evaluation may well lie in "making evaluation an active, powerful tool for local managers" (McLaughlin, 1983, p. 57). Wholey's theory seems to be just this kind of tool, hence it is a major option for practice — productive, thoughtful, and enduring. But the centrality of management in his theory brings problems, as well. Wholey submits important evaluation decisions to management above other stakeholders — especially about what counts as knowledge and about values. Yet policymakers and managers are like any other stakeholder groups, with special interests and a limited perception of social problems and solutions. Many of the problems of relying exclusively on management can be avoided by widening the scope to include other stakeholders. But doing so risks losing management power and authority to use information in improving programs. Some evaluators compromise by including managers as a central interest group, but subjecting their views to external criticism (Kanter & Brinkerhoff, 1981). Wholey's recent works endorse such tactics, but policymakers and program managers still hold center stage. These problems and trade-offs figure prominently in the critique that follows.

Theory of Knowledge

Because Wholey received his Ph.D. in philosophy, one might expect his theory to address philosophical epistemology, much as Scriven has used his background to elucidate valuing. But this is not the case. Such philosophical discussions are nowhere to be found in his work. Wholey's theory is about *action* and *change*, not reflection on abstract matters. Unlike Campbell, he does not discuss epistemology; unlike Scriven, he does not elaborate the nature of values; and unlike Weiss, he does not discuss the nature of use or social change. Wholey, more than any theorist, has a theory of *practice*. The reader is left to ferret out the implicit theories underlying those practices.

The implicit epistemology underlying Wholey's approach to knowledge seems logical positivist in general tenor. It requires evaluators to observe the program using operational definitions of dependent variables. But Wholey says so little about epistemology that any characterization is too speculative, and his endorsement of such postpositivist features as threats to validity drawn from evolutionary epistemology suggest his work is more complex. He is also not fairly criticized on many other grounds on which logical positivists have been criticized — mono-operationalism, expectation of constructing generalizable laws, or value-free assumptions. In fact, he departs from the logical positivism tradition in which truth obtained warrant from application of rigorous methods; he clearly says that evaluative knowledge need not meet traditional scientific standards of rigor. He accepts approximate knowledge, prefers quick and practical methods, and sacrifices accuracy and precision for timeliness and relevance. This is a distinct departure from Campbell and Weiss, and to a lesser extent Scriven, theorists who want the highest-quality methods to be used when possible. Wholey rejects such methods unless management would really use the results.

Wholey's work might best be characterized as pragmatist. He suggests that such matters as truth depend on what works in practice, especially as decided by management. Pragmatism is the most dominant theme in all his work, not just epistemology. Pragmatism can be a credible, useful guide to the construction of knowledge. But it makes Wholey's theory subject to the same criticisms that any pragmatist theory receives. One such criticism is that it "appears to be more a theory of the social acceptance of ideas, not about how one must make sure that one's ideas, beliefs, or theories are correct" (Machan, 1977, p. 111). Pragmatists must always be on guard against this; Wholey succeeds only partially.

Consider Wholey's treatment of causality. His early work endorsed notions of causal inference drawn from Campbell and Stanley (1963):

Essential conditions for successful evaluation of a federal program are the existence of the methodology and sound measurements that will make it possible to distinguish the program's effects, if any, from the effects of all the other forces working in a situation — to isolate what happened as a result of the program from what would probably have happened anyway. (Wholey et al., 1970, p. 86)

But Wholey moved away from Campbell's approach and toward pragmatism. For example, he now says about the validity of causal inference:

The second part of the analysis concerns the assumed causal relationships linking activities to process objectives and process to program objectives. Ideally, these assumptions could be isolated through appropriate tests to provide feedback to a manager or policy maker, indicating that an observed effect was attributable to a particular set of activities and to no other variables. *Practically, however, we must settle for substantially less in virtually all federal programs. An assumption is considered "testable" if there exists test comparisons that the manager/intended user would consider adequate indication that observed effects were attributable to program activities.* (Wholey, 1977, p. 51; emphasis added)

This latter interpretation of valid causal inference is clearly pragmatic—causal inference is valid if the practical consequences of assuming causality satisfy policymakers and managers.

The danger of pragmatist theories is that they inform us about only the social acceptance of causality. Sometimes the inference is still plausible; for example, a program model includes clients arriving at treatment because clients who fail to show cannot be affected by treatment. But managers are not always well versed in causal inference, so such inferences can be vulnerable to naïveté or manipulation. Wholey advises the evaluator to guard against it:

> Such collaboration does not mean the evaluator simply serves as a technician on behalf of program managers. Rather, in this collaborative process, there is the opportunity for the evaluator to carry out an analytical function by raising relevant questions, searching for clarification of the program and its goals, identifying potential side effects which merit study, and assisting the manager to view the program more critically. (Wholey, 1977, p. 42)

But such qualifications are rare, and he never tells how the evaluator can strongly criticize management while working for management. Yet the validity of the resulting knowledge depends greatly on how well the evaluator acts as critic.

Such general qualifications are overshadowed by the specific advice he gives about doing evaluation, advice that does not display this critical perspective. Consider this discussion of performance monitoring:

> Much has been written on the problems of getting valid program performance data. Those problems are real—and are not removed by this study. Our evaluation strategy is intended to *minimize* the problems of getting valid data by securing prior agreement with intended users on the data to be collected and by early investigation of the feasibility and cost of data collection. If program performance data are to be obtained through program staff, prior agreement on program objectives can establish a "management contract" that lets operating-level managers know what kind of performance is expected and what kinds of data will be required. (Wholey, 1979, pp. 145-146)

His solution to the validity problem is to rely on managers and staff to work together to provide valid data. Relying on managers may bias program performance data with management perspectives. What if those biases are toward making program managers look good to advance their careers and programs? What if letting managers know what performance is expected and what data will be used to assess that performance maximizes rather than minimizes validity problems (Campbell, 1975a, 1984b; Cochran, 1978; Shadish, 1979; Tabor, 1977)?

Managers may find it expedient to see that program performance data make their program look good. As two mental health evaluators have noted in discussing a form of local-level mental health evaluation that resembles Wholey's approach: "The assumption that this is an accountability mechanism is akin to providing the fox with the key to the henhouse, while admonishing him to resist temptation" (Neigher & Windle, 1979, p. 229). Wholey acknowledges such influence on managers often in his theory: "A good image counts for a great deal in government; good performance gains little currency in the media" (1983, p. 180). He never confronts the damaging effect of this observation on his theory.

Wholey acknowledges that making causal inference from performance monitoring data is problematic. But he lets management decide if problematic inference is acceptable: "Outcome monitoring does not attempt to determine whether the program caused observed changes in performance measures; instead, it allows managers and policymakers to make those judgements" (1983, p. 117). Management will make such judgments, and results may appear to be positive. But skepticism of such judgments may be required. Consider another example from mental health. Performance monitoring was the major form of evaluation proposed in the 1980 Mental Health Systems Act (later rolled into a block grant during the Reagan administration; Windle & Woy, 1983). But clients come to mental health professionals when they are most distressed, often due to an infrequently occurring combination of extreme causal factors. Those factors may ease up quickly, leaving the client under less distress with no intervention at all. Performance monitoring would suggest that even a totally ineffective program is effective through regression to the mean. This is an extreme example; but Wholey never discusses such plausible alternative hypotheses, so it is never clear that managers would be told this as part of the evaluation. Managers are unlikely to know about such problems; even if they do know, they have little incentive to acknowledge them.

Hence Wholey's pragmatism is insufficiently critical in what it allows as valid knowledge. He is often remiss in suggesting tools evaluators can use to criticize the knowledge they construct. Some parts of Wholey's theory are critical — Wholey's recommendations for examining the rhetorical versus actual program model are a fine example of critical thinking. In some respects criticism is the essence of evaluability assessment, as the evaluator criticizes the hypothesis that it is worth evaluating a program. But even in these cases, Wholey's criterion for true knowledge — about causality, entitivity, generalizability, or certainty — is that knowledge is true when managers are satisfied.

These criticisms apply with somewhat less force to Wholey's recent writings, in which he acknowledges that policymakers and interest groups can play a role in evaluation. Such groups broaden the critical perspectives brought to bear on findings. But compared with Cronbach or Rossi, Wholey says little about who those groups are or how one involves them; management still dominates the process. Wholey disagrees with the theorists who preceded him (Campbell, Scriven, Weiss) about who puts the final warrant on the validity of knowledge. Contrast Wholey to Weiss on this matter. Weiss shares Wholey's goals about facilitating use, and has developed realistic theories of use and social programming. Wholey continues those developments. Weiss moved from a prescriptive to a descriptive mode in representing values in evaluation. Wholey shares that movement, too. But Weiss, like Scriven and Campbell, reserved it to evaluators, not policymakers, to judge the validity of knowledge. Wholey lets go of this remnant. Wholey vests the final authority in policymakers and managers to decide if knowledge is valid. To borrow the terminology we used to describe value theory, where Campbell, Scriven, and Weiss have a prescriptive theory of knowledge in which the theories and methods of science give warrant to the validity of knowledge, Wholey has a descriptive epistemology in which evaluation is ultimately given its warrant through the social authority of policymakers and managers. This is a descriptive criterion of true knowledge—knowledge is valid if policymakers and managers say it is. Stake uses a similar descriptive criterion, except he routinely extends this authority to all program stakeholders, not just policymakers and managers.

Is this a good criterion for true knowledge? A descriptive theory of knowledge will have the same advantages and disadvantages incurred by a descriptive theory of valuing. Wholey does a fine job of outlining its advantages. It gives policymakers and managers exactly what they most want—empirical data about their programs, and the sense that they know satisfactorily enough what is happening in them. A descriptive theory of knowledge may produce knowledge that is accepted as valid by stakeholders, for the same reasons that descriptive theories of valuing produce value judgments most likely to be accepted. Descriptive theories are couched in terms used by management, speak to issues of current concern to management, and have intuitive credibility that more esoteric methods do not. House (1980) argues that such credibility ought to be a key criterion for the validity of knowledge.

Criticisms of a descriptive criterion of knowledge should also be the same as those of descriptive theories of valuing. The validity of knowledge under the descriptive approach is constrained by biases managers have. Managers may resist close, critical examination of data quality. An example of this is provided by a former HEW manager discussing Wholey's role in working out a compromise between the needs of management for flexibility and the needs of evaluators for scientific control:

> Joe Wholey tried to put a respectable face on SDAs but, in my view, he succeeded only to the extent that he helped make them something they never were intended to be – semirigorous, statistically defensible, and firmly anchored in disciplinary analysis. Well, I'd rather have that than what we started with, but, in my view, the evolution of SDAs lost more than it gained. It lost the anecdote and sometimes the whole larger story. Its analytic edges had been hardened and its accessibility and resonance had been largely lost. It has gone the way of GAO and Eleanor Chelimsky, which is not a bad way to go if you are an adviser and question-answerer for Congress. But if you are trying to help a hands-on manager, you might wish for more freedom to decide which evidence is admissible. (Champion, 1985, pp. 37-38)

Service delivery assessments are about as far from traditional, rigorous evaluations as any method currently in use, so this remark is pregnant with implications for the relationship between evaluation and management. There may be a conflict between management and evaluator control about which evidence is worth admitting. The manager wants data with as few filters as possible; the evaluator wants to filter the data for reliability and validity.

Any theory that depends so heavily on a descriptive criterion of knowledge construction, especially one that limits stakeholders primarily to management, should address such problems cogently. Wholey does not. His work is not based in a theory of knowledge, but rather a theory of what policymakers and managers think knowledge is. This theory is practical, credible to policymakers and managers, and likely to produce relevant and useful knowledge. It may even work well when managers are in a position to know – about the objectives and intended activities of the program, for example. But it may work poorly when managers are in a poor position to know – for example, about the causal efficacy of large social programs in achieving objectives. Various versions of this problem recur throughout the rest of Wholey's theory.

Theory of Valuing

Wholey's apparatus for inferring value is a simple one: *"Program evaluation* is the measurement of program performance, the making of comparisons based on those measurements, and the use of the resulting information in policy-making and program management" (1979, p. 1). Like Scriven's, this definition refers to assessing performance and making comparisons. Unlike Scriven's, it does not refer to constructing criteria of merit as an integral part of valuing. Wholey has such criteria — the extent to which programs meet objectives: "Unless goals are precisely stated, there is no standard against which to measure whether the direction of a program or its rate of progress is satisfactory" (Wholey et al., 1970, p. 15). Wholey's later work is less tied to goals and more to program realities, but still without clearly linking realities to criteria of merit.

Management is the major source of criteria of merit for Wholey. This is most apparent in evaluability assessment: "The first evaluation design task, analysis of the decision-making system and clarification of the questions to be answered, is carried out to define the program to be evaluated in terms that agree with the manager's or policy maker's intentions" (Wholey, 1977, p. 41). And also: "The key question is who should develop the measures of success. The assessment process discussed here rests on the belief that ambiguous objectives should not be rendered unambiguous by an evaluator; that, we believe, is a management or policy question" (1977, p. 51). Other stakeholders sometimes have input as well:

> When program objectives are to be examined, it is logical to ask whose objectives they are. In many instances, potential users may also include groups with varying abilities to have impact on the program: other administrators, legislators, public interest groups, professional groups, the general public, etc. It may be a question of what feedback loop you are designing your evaluations for or of what loop the findings may be picked up in. (Wholey, 1977, p. 44)

Wholey has been especially likely to refer to such groups in his recent writings (1987). He also recommends inspecting program documentation to get criteria. But selection of criteria is always up to management. He says a merit of this approach is that

> it captures all of the activities and their objectives, while avoiding the temptation to insert what might appear to be missing or "necessary" objectives or activities. The rhetorical model should represent the program that has been defined by the manager, policy maker, or other intended user and defined in legislation, internal plans, and program justifications. (1977, p. 49)

Yet Wholey seems to want the value of social programs to be connected to social needs. One of the rare uses of words like *good* and *valuable* in his theory occurs in a remark about this connection:

> Our goal is good government. "Good government" used to mean not stealing money and not filling public payrolls with political hacks. Today, the term means

much more: it now means producing public services that efficiently and effectively respond to the needs of an increasingly complex, increasingly interrelated society. (1983, p. 204)

But it is a long road from meeting social needs to meeting management-interpreted program objectives. The following quote suggests how he got there:

> Many new missions that the Federal government has been called upon to undertake (e.g., lowering hard core unemployment; reducing crime, poverty, or inflation) involve problems in which the proper mechanism of program intervention is not well understood, or defined, or in some cases even known. Since in these cases no one knows exactly what detailed program intervention will be of value, greater management discretion is allowed and exercised. The newer programs are characterized by *uncertainty* and *discretion*: uncertainty as to the nature of the problem and what constitutes effective strategies of intervention, and discretion in how the problem and the intervention are defined and how the intervention is implemented. (Wholey et al., 1975b, p. 194)

Social needs are too strict a criterion of merit because social programs are insufficiently developed and not powerful enough to affect those needs much. Society does not know how to reduce crime, poverty, inflation, or unemployment, so holding managers to this criterion is unfair. Wholey relies on the policy-making process to force the manager to generate useful program objectives, and then simply uses those objectives as criteria of merit.

If one accepts Wholey's focus on goals, then his proposals for constructing criteria of merit make sense. Program goals are often vaguely specified and irrelevant to program activities. He provides a solution to this problem. Evaluability assessment forces the manager or policymaker to list specific goals that bear on actual activities, to which the manager is willing to be held accountable. The evaluator tests and refines program theory by contrasting it to program reality through available documents, site visits, observed side effects, and apparent local obstacles. When model and reality conflict, the model may have to be changed. So his use of program objectives and goals as criteria of merit is not naive—a good program meets a realistically formulated set of objectives.

But to be relevant to social problem solving, this approach depends on how well policymakers and managers formulate program goals and objectives, and how well they tie the program to social problems and needs. Managers suffer from obvious limitations in this regard. They are under pressure to look good; good performance is less highly valued. They often shy away from controversy (Windle & Woy, 1983). They may formulate goals that will make them look good, are noncontroversial, and avoid important but difficult goals. The connection between management formulations of program objectives and social needs is not obvious. The trail from social needs to policy agendas to legislation to management formulation of objectives is mediated by public opinion, elections, lobbyists, committee reports, legislation, executive orders, and regulations. Management exercises discretion in interpreting all of these mediating mechanisms. The connection to needs can quickly get lost. The evaluator must hope that policymakers and managers formulate credible and reasonable program objectives that they know will be available for public scrutiny, so they will be under some pressure to consider social needs.

To illustrate how the tie to social problems can get lost, consider Wholey's example of an evaluability assessment of the community mental health center (CMHC) program (Wholey, 1977). He first constructed a *rhetorical* program model consisting of six program objectives and more than 40 process objectives. But the *evaluable* program model was much smaller, and

> excludes all of the special and continuing objectives of the four branches and all but one of the program objectives, because they were not stated in measurable terms. One set of program activities, intended outcomes, objectives, and program objectives *did* appear to satisfy the evaluability/manageability criteria: those intended to result in "economically viable CMHCs, independent of Federal support." These activities and objectives appear to be measurable, and the assumed causal links to be testable. (Wholey et al., 1975b, pp. 177, 181)

He notes "that over *three dozen* objectives vanished during the evaluability assessment" (Wholey et al., 1975b, p. 181). How can this happen? Not because such objectives are unmeasurable: "The analysis of objectives for measurability is not, then, a test of the evaluator's ingenuity in defining measures. It is, rather, a test to determine whether the manager or policy maker has defined what he or she wants the program to accomplish and what evidence is needed to determine this" (Wholey, 1977, p. 51). But if managers want to look good and avoid controversy, they might leave out definitions — even important ones — that might yield controversial or poor results (such a decision might return to haunt them if those to whom managers are accountable ask why important definitions were left out, somewhat mitigating this problem). Was anything important left out of the evaluable program model for CMHCs? Yes:

> Missing from the evaluable model is what might have been considered the most important objective — the reduction of inappropriate use of mental hospitals.

> Unless it were known that CMHCs did have this impact, it might be argued, there would be little justification for having economically viable CMHCs. The evaluability assessment has concluded, at this time, it would not be appropriate to conduct an evaluation of the program's effectiveness in reducing inappropriate use of mental hospitals since no acceptable measures of progress toward this objective have yet been defined. The onus is therefore on the program manager and analysts to identify and develop appropriate measures if the manager needs such evaluation information. (Wholey, 1977, p. 54)

This remark incorrectly suggests it is not feasible to evaluate CMHC effectiveness in reducing mental hospital use because there are no appropriate measures. But several such analyses have appeared in the literature (Delaney, Seidman, & Willis, 1978; Doidge & Rogers, 1976; McNees, Hannah, Schnelle, & Bratton, 1977; Scully & Windle, 1976; Spearly, 1980; Windle, Goldsmith, Schambaugh, & Rosen, 1975). None of the measures they used is without flaws; but they yield a pessimistic picture of the effectiveness of CMHCs in reducing state hospital admissions. Management reluctance to evaluate on this objective may reflect concern with whether results would be positive and noncontroversial. The CMHC program had been widely criticized as not meeting this and other important objectives by Nader's Raiders (Chu & Trotter, 1974) and by the U.S. General Accounting Office (1974). CMHC management probably knew of such visible critiques (Windle & Woy, 1983). While the burden is on management "to identify and develop appropriate measures if the manager needs such evaluation information" (Wholey, 1977, p. 54), management has little incentive to do so if it makes the program look ineffective. (Also eliminated from the evaluation were such CMHC objectives as increasing the quality of services by CMHCs and national mental health care systems, increasing the funding base of CMHCs and national mental health care systems, and increasing the quality and level of services to special target groups — all of which could and should be measured if one wanted to know if CMHCs were good.)

Weiss uses criteria suggested by a policy analysis as a perspective from which to judge the value of that program. Another CMHC example points out the merits of Weiss's suggestion and the limits of Wholey's focus on management objectives. Reviewing the history of evaluations of the CMHC program, Windle and Woy (1983) conclude:

> The origins of the CMHC Program are found in criticisms of the mental health service system in the United States during the 1950s, particularly the undesirable conditions in state mental hospitals at that time. The primary goal of the CMHC legislation was to improve and upgrade the overall network of care for mentally ill and disabled citizens in this country. To evaluate progress toward that major

goal requires information not only about the specific achievements of the CMHCs themselves, but also information about other major components in the network of mental health services, including state and county mental health services, not-for-profit mental health services, and the private sector, the relationships among these components of the mental health service system, and the relationships of these service components to improved care for clients. However, as described earlier in this paper, the history of evaluation of the CMHC Program reveals a narrow concern with the operations and performance of the CMHCs themselves. Our emphasis on a narrow meaning of the term "program" evaluation has not served us well. (p. 64)

Management excluded the criteria that Windle and Woy said were essential to understanding the value of CMHCs. Windle and Woy say evaluation should never focus just on programs, but also on the policy system to understand the value of the program.

Wholey's most recent writings recommend increasing involvement of policymakers, and sometimes other interest groups, providing some counterbalance to the shortcomings of management goals. But his theory is still mostly management oriented. Perhaps this is inevitable in a theory that starts with the values of policymakers and managers, that formulates a model based first on those values and that is only later adjusted by criticism. The bias is built in by these front-end assumptions, and can be modified only by starting with other assumptions.

Just as Wholey has a theory of what management thinks knowledge is, he has a theory of what management thinks is valuable. It works well when management knows what makes social programs valuable; and it produces results that maximally speak to the values of management—no small advantage in public policy. But his value theory may work poorly when those in management do not bring to bear values besides their own, or consider the policy issues invoked by their program. Over the range of federal, state, and local programs, it is difficult to know how much these circumstances hold. At the federal level, program managers are pressured by Congress, lobbyists, GAO, client organizations, and professional organizations to take multiple value perspectives into account. But such pressures must also be reflected in interactions between management and evaluation staff. The reflection is probably incomplete, imbued with the particular flavor of management interests.

Our commentary on Wholey's theories of knowledge and valuing implies a more critical attitude toward program managers than we really feel. The vast majority of managers are well intentioned, really care about the programs they run, and work extremely hard to respond to social and political demands. The same is true of evaluators who work for them.

Further, cogent reasons argue for working with managers. Still, an orientation toward management has potential liabilities. Those liabilities may never occur if the evaluator is diligent and vigilant, and management responds in kind. We need to know more about when those conditions hold, and to what effect.

Theory of Social Programming

Wholey has a theory of social problem solving through incremental program improvement. Existing programs, for better or worse, are our main vehicles for social problem solving. Wholey assumes that the cumulation of many small improvements eventually results in a greatly improved ability to solve social problems. This is just the opposite of Weiss, who would avoid incremental change in favor of examining major policy variations that might produce large changes in social problems.

Hence the strengths and weaknesses of Wholey's approach are largely opposite those of Weiss's theory. Weiss relies on the rare occasions when policy agendas change to allow new policies and programs to be adopted and implemented. In the meantime she hopes to influence what policymakers think through enlightenment. Her approach would not quickly change the status quo, but she hopes the changes she eventually does produce will be major and important compared to incremental change. Wholey's theory has the opposite qualities. His incremental changes are likely to be immediately implementable, fitting nicely into the status quo. He can produce many such changes since none is likely to consume the amount of resources a new policy or program would require. But incremental changes are worth doing only if the program as a whole could significantly dent the relevant problems. It makes little sense to improve a program that is fundamentally flawed to begin with; and tying evaluation to incrementalism makes it eminently conservative in serving the status quo. Major social problems caused by the structure of society itself, or not addressed well by any current program, might never be addressed well through Wholey's approach.

Hence Wholey, and all theorists who advocate incrementalism, should discuss why they believe that many incremental changes can cumulatively solve the problems facing our nation. Although Weiss abandoned an incrementalist approach early in her career, she has recently asserted that perhaps these incremental changes might not be "small potatoes" after all. But she does not present the evidence or experiences that left her with that impression. Similarly, Wholey does not tell the reader how incrementalism eventually results in solving the problems that Weiss says have proven so intractable.

Since neither Weiss nor Wholey presents these arguments, we will construct one that may be compatible with Wholey's strategy. We remind the reader that this is our argument, not Wholey's; Wholey reminds us that such considerations are the province of academicians with the leisure and warrant to examine such abstract questions. Most evaluators do not have that luxury; rather, they probably work in exactly the kind of situation that Wholey describes in his theory — for managers of programs, if not at the federal level then at the state or local level (Patton, 1978; Shadish & Epstein, 1987). Wholey would undoubtedly say he has given such evaluators exactly the theory they need, a practical one that managers welcome and purchase. His theory proves its merits not by theoretical justification, but by survival in the jungle of government policy-making: "Performance-oriented evaluation is one strategy that has demonstrated its utility in real-world situations" (Bellavita et al., 1986, p. 291).

Nonetheless, here is the argument for working with management. In the United States, government policymakers and managers are vested with responsibility, authority, and power to implement programs passed by the legislative branch, ratified by the pluralistic interests the legislative branch represents. Elected representatives delegate to these policymakers and managers the authority to influence the implementation of social programs. Particularly since use of evaluation is facilitated by close contact with a user (Leviton & Hughes, 1981), Wholey's theory fosters use by centrally powerful groups of users — policymakers and managers.

Social programs are largely here to stay whether or not they are ideal vehicles for change. They rarely die to be replaced by other programs. When they do start or end, it is largely for political or economic reasons, not because of a primary influence of evaluation findings. Wholey's strategy recognizes this reality by working with programs to improve them. Wholey might add that judgments about whether or not programs are fundamentally flawed are not his to make; they belong in the political arena. If the program was passed and implemented, then a significant set of interest groups must have thought it worthwhile.

Additionally, good governmental management may be *necessary* (but not sufficient) for government programs to produce positive outcomes. A number of Brookings Institution publications in the 1970s, in which one social program after another was deemed a failure, highlighted the many implementation failures of federal programs. Implementation failures are partly a management problem. In such a climate, it is difficult not to prioritize on federal implementation questions, and so on management questions. Some local projects might produce positive outcomes without federal assistance, but the number of such projects might be small in many cases — the problems that projects address are not so simple that projects could do it alone. Wholey's assumption is that federal coordination and assistance are needed for their solution. This assumption may be wrong, but it deserves a fair test.

To increase the number of "good" local projects, federal coordination may be necessary. Vague federal goals, sloppy monitoring, mistaken assumptions about logistics, and hazy regulation can impede the creation of adequate local projects and thus prevent a fair test of social interventions. Lack of good federal coordination produces some effects that are intrinsically undesirable, regardless of the eventual impact of local projects on recipients. Resources are wasted that could be used by other social programs (Pressman & Wildavsky, 1984). Such waste can have a chilling effect on social innovation (Weiss, 1973a) — inadequate management has led to government graft or recipient fraud in defense, food stamps, Community Action Programs, and Medicaid. It has led to logistical problems in distribution of needed services — improper targeting of resources, and distribution delays in programs like the Federal Emergency Management funds. It has led to the diversion of resources to serve local rather than national goals (bilingual education, Community Development Block Grants), an effect that Bardach (1977) says is inevitable and desirable in some respects, but also controllable so that a balance between the two can be achieved. It has led to active interference with federal intent, as in desegregation. One could opt for less federal control, given this spotty record; or one could admit that we are still learning about how to solve social problems using federal programs, and part of that learning involves better program management.

A mature social program will have dealt with many of these problems of implementation — a good example is social security. A mature social program of the 1960s is Title I (now Chapter 1) of the Elementary and Secondary Education Act — federal legislation is clearer about uses of funds, about responsibilities of all parties, and about types of activities permitted in local projects (Leviton & Boruch, 1983). Programs that are still evolving include some federal health care programs. Other programs may always be immature if they contain flaws of goal definition or program logic; Wholey's approach helps remedy this. To the extent that programs are immature, a focus on management information needs is a priority. We may disagree with an *exclusive* emphasis on management, but this approach should play one key role in evaluation. Wholey's methods may not be sufficient for effective social problem solving, but they may be necessary to give social interventions a fair test.

But even if all these arguments are correct, they do not respond to the fundamental problems with incrementalism. Critics say that incrementalism is insufficiently self-critical about what it can accomplish with existing programs and policies, that it fails to help policymakers formulate new policies and programs when opportunities arise, and that it has a poorly articulated sense of which incremental changes are worth pursuing (Lindblom, 1983; Manley, 1983). Some examples of incrementalist evaluation systems have had very little to do with social problem solving (Cook & Shadish, 1982). These criticisms must receive fair hearing and response if we are to know when incrementalism is the strategy of choice.

Wholey really does not have a theory of social policy and social change; rather, he has a theory of management—which is, of course, all he claims to have. He outlines the difficulties of managing—vague objectives, lack of incentives to manage effectively, and lack of clear logic linking resources, implementation, and outcome. Compared with most evaluators, he makes the evaluator an active participant in management. Where Weiss's theory overlaps program evaluation with policy analysis, Wholey's theory overlaps program evaluation with organizational development. But his connections between program management and social problem solving are left vague. Compared to Weiss, Wholey's theory does not so much serve policy-making as it serves management. To the extent the two processes are not isomorphic, his theory is limited in its ability to improve policy-making.

One can formulate theories of evaluation that serve other parts of policy-making. Weiss is one example; similarly, Chelimsky (1981) and Hedrick (1981) describe policy-relevant evaluation at the U.S. General Accounting Office. Boruch, Cordray, and Pion (1981) and Zweig (1979; Zweig & Martin, 1981) describe evaluation that is responsive to legislative needs. Cronbach et al. (1980) describe several proposals for independent evaluative examinations of policy. All of these approaches serve policy-making, and none focuses primarily on management. None takes into account the full range of interfaces between evaluation and policy-making. But to the extent that each approach has merit, the connection Wholey champions between effective government and working with management is not exclusively desirable. There are other routes to good government, as well. Wholey's is an excellent theory of how to improve programs, but it is not the only good theory of how to improve government. What is missing is discussion of when evaluators ought to try to improve programs, versus using other strategies.

Compared to Scriven and Campbell, Wholey displays political and organizational sophistication about how social programs operate and change. Like Weiss, he understands the complications of conducting evaluation in a highly politicized environment. He could discuss further, however, the fact that policymakers and managers are themselves interest groups. Managers are not neutral servants of other interest groups, and they are subject to pressures to look good. Wholey places trust in policy-makers and managers that might sometimes be unwarranted given their vested interests. As a result, his theory walks a fine line between cooperation with and co-optation by management. Wholey mentions this only once, and then briefly: "To have something to offer, evaluators must preserve their credibility and independence. But independence need not conflict with cooperation and service" (Bellavita et al., 1986, p. 287). Sometimes they do conflict, however; Wholey says little about recognizing and dealing with such instances. Practicing evaluators could benefit from his advice about this.

Theory of Use

Wholey, Weiss, and Stake share a concern with increasing the usefulness of evaluations. Wholey takes an instrumental use approach. This was also a goal of early evaluation theories. Campbell hoped that positively evaluated programs would be retained and disseminated, and negatively evaluated ones replaced. When this outcome did not materialize, and when programs were retained or eliminated on grounds that had little to do with their evaluated effectiveness, many theorists assumed that instrumental use was itself unrealistic, and they looked to other kinds of use. Weiss pursued enlightenment, hoping to influence the way policymakers think about problems and solutions. Stake sought use in the form of naturalistic generalizations from case studies to new situations, similar to enlightenment.

Wholey assumed that instrumental use was a worthy goal that was not achieved because evaluators pursued that goal with inadequate methods. His methods, especially evaluability assessment and rapid feedback evaluation, were specifically tailored to producing instrumentally usable results. To judge from available reports, he succeeded. Anecdotal evidence suggests that policymakers and managers use his evaluations to make changes in program activities, and that legislative bodies have used information about program effects, along with other information, to make decisions about continued funding of some programs. The latter programs include Job Corps, NIMH's Community Support Program, and the Special Supplemental Food Program for Women, Infants, and Children (WIC); the State of New York's decision to fund the Harlem Valley Psychiatric Center; and the State of Tennessee's decision about funding its prenatal care program (Wholey, 1986a, 1986b, 1986c, 1987). Thanks to these and similar reports by other evaluators (Leviton & Boruch, 1984), instrumental use has a rejuvenated respectability in evaluation. Wholey deserves much credit for this.

These evaluations achieved instrumental use without always using the most rigorous methodologies for investigating cause-effect relationships. One of the evaluations that helped keep funding for Job Corps used a non-equivalent control group design (Wholey, 1986a). The authors of that evaluation presented several analyses with different assumptions about biases, and then showed that positive conclusions about Job Corps held up under all these assumptions. Evaluations of WIC were mostly not rigorous either (Chelimsky, 1984), but decision makers found these evaluations compelling enough to base funding decisions on them, at least in part. As Wholey (1986a) puts it, "WIC's effectiveness has been demonstrated to the satisfaction of members of Congress and congressional staffs" (p. 281), whether or not the evidence passes the muster of traditional scientific canons. Although Weiss found that research quality was positively related to usefulness, in these examples we see that evaluations can be useful without meeting the rigorous standards proposed by Campbell.

It is worth exploring factors that facilitated these instances of instrumental use. Evaluation is part of a problem-solving sequence that includes problem definition, solution generation, solution implementation, solution evaluation, and solution dissemination. Compared to earlier theorists who strove for instrumental use, Wholey's approach is more intensive at each one of these steps. He instructs the evaluator to resolve each step in the context of useful options, and to work extensively with intended users at each step to provide "information about issues a manager can influence" (Bellavita et al., 1986, p. 291). In contrast, earlier theorists did not routinely address each of these problem-solving steps, and did not limit themselves to options at each step that could be instrumentally used.

We especially appreciate Wholey's attention to the social, organizational, and behavioral variables that reinforce an individual's decision to use results. His discussion of incentives and rewards to encourage improved organizational performance based on evaluation results is virtually unique in evaluation. If evaluators want to facilitate instrumental use, they must move out of the traditional evaluator's role into an organizational development role, vicariously learning about and helping to change the contingencies that impinge on use. The role of the evaluator in Scriven's and Campbell's theories is comparatively passive.

In the context of instrumental use, we can easily understand why Wholey rarely recommends the fourth stage of the sequential purchase of information — intensive evaluation of program effects. Managers do not have much control over the continuation of programs, so they will not use that information instrumentally. Hence Wholey's evaluator would rarely recommend the fourth stage when working with program management. But there are occasions when moving to the fourth stage might provide management with information it needs. For example, management sometimes decides which programs to terminate or decrease when Congress cuts the agency budget but leaves discretion about how to implement the cuts. Such exceptions are not well documented, but they deserve to be in today's stringent fiscal environment.

It is less clear what role Wholey would give to enlightenment. He says that "evaluators can help government managers to identify and sort through policy goals" (1985, p. 43), and acknowledges a role for criticism in evaluation (Bellavita et al., 1986). But he downplays this critic role, claiming that "for the balance of this century, we need to give greater attention to the constructive roles that evaluators can play helping programs, organizations, and society itself make the transition from its current struggle with malaise to excellence" (Bellavita et al., 1986, p. 287). Wholey is clearly saying that evaluators, for the balance of this century, should adopt his incrementalist, instrumental use approach. But he is never clear about why. Weiss justifies enlightenment by pointing out that instrumental use is tied to transient rather than persistent problems, that it gains timeliness by losing long-term relevance, and that it can result in so little change from the status quo that it may make little difference to problem solving. Wholey does not provide any such arguments to contrast the worth of instrumental use to alternatives like enlightenment.

One might say that the arguments for incremental change we constructed in the last section are reasonably compelling, and emphasizing instrumental use is the best way to achieve incremental change. Hence incremental change is practical, it wins the favor and the funding of policymakers and managers who want program improvement, and it is faithful to the original promise of evaluation to provide useful results in the short term. Wholey would be joined in this argument by theorists like Patton (1978) at the local level.

But still, we are reminded by Lindblom (1986) that policymakers and decision makers need the critical perspective provided by enlightenment to gain perspective on current problems and policies. Instrumental use simply cannot achieve this. Just as Weiss ought to make a place for instrumental use in her theory, so Wholey might consider incorporating a role for enlightenment, or some similar policy-analytic approach, to complement his own instrumental inclinations. Both theorists strive to facilitate use. Both have created intelligent, interesting, yet apparently opposed theories of use and practice. Greater dialogue between them might help evaluators to understand the contingencies that govern the choice of the two approaches across situations.

Theory of Evaluation Practice

Wholey's theory of practice is more detailed than that of any other theorist discussed in this book. We have already presented in detail his choice of program management as the primary stakeholder group. Those who might not agree with that choice need not reject his other methods. Those methods are mostly orthogonal to choice of client, and would transfer across clients with little change. His methods are generally commendable, as are the concepts he uses to guide method choices.

The most meritorious of those concepts is the sequential purchase of information. The concept captures the trade-offs among timeliness, cost, and quality of information, trade-offs that have plagued evaluators over two decades — the better the information, the more time it takes to produce and the more it will cost. The sequence Wholey prescribes — deciding if it is worth evaluating, providing a rapid assessment of the program to get a sense of how it is doing, troubleshooting the program on an ongoing basis by monitoring performance and outcome, and testing causal assumptions that seem particularly critical — is sequentially logical in evaluations of program effects, and reasonably comprehensive in the kinds of information it provides about effects. Since Wholey explicitly encourages flexibility in applying these tools, both in sequence and in local adaptation of methods, his advice is worth considering by most evaluators.

Two points might improve Wholey's suggested activities. The first concerns improved or alternative methods for doing the sequential purchase of information. Other methods can fill the same function as the methods he prescribes, but offer slightly different advantages and disadvantages. Wholey considers one other method — Hendrick's service delivery assessment method — to provide rapid feedback. But in general, his methods have remained rather solidly cast in the same form as first proposed. Further improvements could probably be located. For example, providing rapid feedback to management might be done by meta-analyses of projects or components of the program (Cook, 1984), or by operations research or simulations. Intensive evaluation could cautiously explore causal modeling techniques, particularly given the success of econometric methods in federal policy. These latter methods fit with Wholey's desire to provide rapid data-based feedback. Wholey's theory could benefit from more catholicity in methods.

Also needed are data-based studies of the strengths and weaknesses of the methods he actually does prescribe. He has done little of this kind of analysis. Take evaluability assessment, for example. Does evaluability assessment have weaknesses, in addition to its strengths? Rog's (1985) study suggests it might. Wholey (1983) reports a critical review of evaluability assessment that includes an empirical study of managers' views. They said many positive things about evaluability assessment; but negative comments also emerged, as with the manager who said, "I never received useful information" (p. 104). Other managers said, "I wouldn't use (evaluability assessment) if I knew the program was troubled by longstanding, difficult policy questions" (p. 102). Wholey reports these comments, but never addresses their conceptual implications for evaluability assessment. He seems to draw only the following simple inference:

> Evaluability assessment is one way to get policy and management agreement on a set of objectives and performance indicators in terms of which a program is to be assessed and managed. In some cases, evaluability assessments produce sufficient information to stimulate policy and management decisions designed to improve program performance. (Wholey, 1983, p. 105)

More could be said.

Similarly, Wholey fails to examine in much detail the differences between rapid feedback evaluation and SDAs. He notes that the former is goal-based and the latter goal-free, and suggests that "though not the answer in every situation, service delivery assessment can be very helpful when policymakers or managers need clearer perceptions of program reality or early warning of emerging problems" (Wholey, 1983, p. 140). But he provides little help in choosing between the two. By comparison, Scriven might say more about why goal-free strategies are preferable — the need to know program effects irrespective of goals, so that the program can be judged according to whether its effects meet social needs. Wholey provides very little such conceptual detail, more as an afterthought than as systematic analysis. A goal-free approach might be highly advantageous at the federal level; "people at the federal level, often isolated from any systematic view of program reality, tend to have imperfect knowledge of the effects of their policy choices and management decisions" (Wholey, 1979, p. 3). Why rely on their imperfect knowledge to set goals and objectives; why not rely on a goal-free approach to help them discover effects? Perhaps this is why Wholey's most recent writings place so much more emphasis on program *reality* relative to the emphasis on program *intent* in his early work.

A final example concerns his ambiguity about using intensive evaluation. When it comes to specific recommendations about when to do intensive evaluation, Wholey is less helpful than he could be. He says that spending 10% of demonstration funds on experiments might be useful (Wholey, 1979, p. 166), but does not say how to pick that 10%, nor why he picked 10%. How would evaluators know that they are facing a situation that might call for expenditure of such funds? The problem may partly be that intensive evaluation really does not fit logically into the sequential purchase of information. The sequence notion connotes the idea that one purchases better information later in the sequence. But intensive evaluation adds a requirement that is not present anywhere in the first three steps, that the evaluator gather information only about *program effects.* Wholey only recommends the randomized experiment (or related methods) in this fourth step, and the experiment provides better information only about effects. In the fourth step of the sequence, one could gather better information about other matters as well by expending more resources and using higher-quality methods to describe the evaluand, study its generalizability, or provide a better answer to any other question of interest.

This omission is more obvious when one asks how Wholey treats generalizability or the assessment of social needs. He seems interested in generalizability, but devotes little attention to how to know if evaluative findings might be generalizable. In one discussion of rapid feedback evaluation, he advocates using case study methods to identify "health systems agency (HSA) programs that appeared to have high potential for influencing the health care system" (1983, p. 128); such "examples were to be used in development of federal regulations and guidelines and in development of technical assistance products likely to be effectively used by other health systems agencies" (p. 128). But this method has an important flaw; each instance of a project can depend heavily on idiosyncratic circumstances that contribute in important but unrecognized ways to project effects — a charismatic leader, a particularly loyal funding source, or a fortuitous location. Such instances may not transfer with the same success unless all important causes of success are identified, or unless some mechanism ensures that the important causes are transferred, too. The likelihood of such identification is low if the evaluator relies on single instances; larger samples of projects would be beneficial. Another example: Wholey suggests that evaluators can identify successful types of projects that share common elements leading to success (1983, p. 83). These types could be transferred across projects by virtue of this empirical robustness. But he does not tell how to construct these types.

If Wholey really values the fourth step of his sequence, he should outline an array of high-quality methods to address these purposes, such as sample surveys or meta-analysis. Doing so would make the fourth step more useful to program management by answering a wider array of questions. Management might then be more prone to purchase this fourth step. It would also help to remedy the impression that Wholey is interested only in program effects. Cronbach (1982b), for example, complains that the newly developed standards for evaluation practice, by endorsing evaluability assessment early in evaluation, implicitly endorse an experimental approach to evaluation concerned only with program effects. Since Wholey in fact rarely recommends a randomized experiment, and since the first three steps clearly address a sizable bandwidth of questions about clients, implementation, costs, and impacts, Cronbach's conclusion about Wholey is probably wrong. Broadening the fourth step of the sequence would help remedy this perception. Wholey could argue that program effects are the only question about which it is worth gathering high-quality information; we doubt he intends this implication, though it would be consistent with Cronbach's reading of him.

CONCLUSION

If we were going to take a job under program management in government settings, we would rely on Wholey's theory and methods as much as on any other theorist. No other theorist has had to do what Wholey has — survive in government by doing evaluation. He not only survived but prospered, and in the process provided a sound professional base for the field. Like those of the other theorists, his theory continues to evolve in ways we probably have not reflected in this chapter as fully as they warrant. Evaluability assessment has developed a broader focus to include policymakers as well as managers, and program reality as well as program intent. But still, his theory's strength is the instrumentally useful information it provides to program management. Nobody does it better.

Both Weiss and Wholey began their careers by endorsing the experimental methods that dominated evaluation during the 1960s; both then became disillusioned with the results of using those methods and so found ones that better facilitated use. Weiss and Wholey did this in different ways, with Weiss striving for enlightenment and Wholey for instrumental use, but both worked primarily at the federal level. In the next chapter we review another theorist who abandoned the experimental model in favor of methods to facilitate use — Robert Stake. Stake's solution is quite different from Wholey's or Weiss's. Where they work mostly at the federal level, he works mostly at the local level; where they use mostly quantitative methods, he uses qualitative methods, like the case study, nearly exclusively. Stake's theory again illustrates the diversity of variations in doing evaluation that emerged during the 1970s in response to perceived failures of the theories of the 1960s. Evaluators were trying many different things, and none was clearly dominant during this time.

7

Robert E. Stake:

Responsive Evaluation
and Qualitative Methods

KEY TERMS AND CONCEPTS

Preordinate Evaluation:	Evaluations that emphasize program goals as evaluation criteria, using objective tests for data collection, standards or program personnel to judge programs, and research-type reports. Preordinate evaluations are determined by the evaluator early in the evaluation, and imposed on the program based upon an a priori plan.
Responsive Evaluation:	Opposite of preordinate evaluation, these evaluations orient to program activities rather than program goals, respond to audience information needs rather than predetermined information categories, and consider different values of people interested in the program when judging its adequacy. Questions and methods are not imposed but emerge from observing the program during the evaluation.
Case Study Methodology:	Use of interviews, observation, examination of documents and records, unobtrusive measures, and investigative journalism, resulting in a case report that is complex, holistic, and involves many variables not easily unconfounded. Writing is informal, narrative, with verbatim quotations, illustrations, allusions, and metaphors.

Naturalistic Generalization: Responsive evaluations using case study methods give readers vicarious experience of the evaluand in context, detailing situations in which the reader usually has no firsthand experience. The reader, not the researcher, provides reference population and comparison groups. The researcher describes the new case in ways that facilitate reader interpretation. The evaluator interprets, but considers facilitating the reader's intuitive analysis and generalization to be of equal responsibility.

BACKGROUND

Robert Stake, an educational evaluator, was an early advocate of qualitative methods for evaluating social programs (Stake, 1975a, 1975b; Stake & Gjerde, 1974). Such methods were present in some predecessors of evaluation, such as action research and ecological psychology (Barker, 1968; Barker & Gump, 1964; Marrow, 1969). Stake helped legitimate them in evaluation, and evaluation will never be the same. Since Stake, every major evaluation theorist discusses such approaches. Their ability to generate a rich bounty of novel data is no longer even debated. Theorists regularly rely on them for a discovery capacity in evaluation, and sometimes for other tasks as well, even impinging on turf where traditional quantitative methods dominate, such as causal inference (Campbell, 1975b; Scriven, 1976c). Stake's work helped to catalyze productive debates about epistemology, ontology, and disciplinary myopias (Cook & Reichardt, 1979). When program evaluation began in the 1960s, such developments were not foreseen, and might not have been taken seriously if they had been. We suspect that after 20 more years have passed, the addition of well-reasoned qualitative approaches will be seen as a major accomplishment of applied social sciences and of evaluation in particular.

Along with Wholey and Weiss, Stake has reacted to the early failures of Campbell and Scriven by emphasizing use. But he takes different means to this end. Stake advocates that case study methodologies be used to improve local practice. He pays little attention to indicators of program success, wanting local projects to bear primary evaluation responsibility. He acknowledges public curiosity, even a national need to know, but is not confident that social science designs can find useful input-output relationships. He urges instead that social scientists describe individual situations that can be understood by nonscientists.

Stake's doctoral training was in psychometrics, his early research was in student learning, and his early teaching was in training school counselors. He was disappointed that his quantitative skills seemed to contribute so little to judging the quality of post-*Sputnik* curriculum reform efforts. His beliefs resulted from a convergence of forces and his arguments for case study methodology are complex, sophisticated, and subtle — far more so than he is generally given credit for. A key experience was his 1966 consultation with the Follow Through staff and the U.S. Office of Education. He persuaded them to consider a national evaluation using organizational process studies of local projects in which local staff members observed their situations. Stake hoped this approach might reveal local events, and perhaps a bit about what was and was not working. The proposal was not funded for logistical reasons. Eventually Stanford Research Institute designed and executed an extensive, comparative, psychometric study that Stake saw as a futile effort to be respectable social science, particularly given lack of agreement as to criteria for success. From this point on, Stake increasingly began to do and to write about case study methods.

Until recent works by Guba and Lincoln (1981; Lincoln & Guba, 1985) and Patton (1980), Stake wrote more about qualitative methodology than any other evaluator. Guba and Lincoln (1981) describe their naturalistic inquiry as descending from Stake. House (1980) and Patton (1980) cite Stake's work when they advocate case study methods. All these authors have contributed to qualitative methods in evaluation. We will cite them where they provide a particularly useful articulation of issues, but we focus primarily on Stake as the pioneer in the area.

OUR RECONSTRUCTION OF
STAKE'S THEORY OF EVALUATION

Evaluation as Service

"People expect evaluation to have many different purposes" (Stake, 1975b, p. 15), such as documenting events, recording change, aiding decisions, seeking understanding, or facilitating remediation:

Each of these questions deals, directly or indirectly, with the values of the program and is a legitimate evaluation question. The questions reflect different purposes and information needs of different audiences. Unfortunately, only a few questions can get prime attention in a formal evaluation study. The evaluator has to decide what to attend to. Will he rely on his preconceptions; on the formal plans and objectives of the program; on actual program activities; or on reactions of participants, as the primary basis for choosing the key questions? Most evaluators can be faulted for over-reliance on preconceived notions of success. I advise the evaluator to pay attention to what is happening in the program, then to choose the value questions and criteria. (Stake, 1975b, p. 15)

As in Scriven's goal-free evaluation, Stake emphasizes letting evaluation emerge from observing the program. But Stake is more inclined than Scriven to let program stakeholders influence the purpose and conduct of evaluation: "There are different ways to evaluate programs and no one way is the right way. I prefer to think of ways that evaluation can perform a service and be useful to specific persons" (1975b, p. 13).

Stake sees the purpose of evaluation more as service than as critical analysis: "I like the evaluator more in the role of civil servant than of civil philosopher" (1975a, p. 36); "the evaluator should have a good sense of whom he is working for and their concerns" (1975b, p. 13). He contrasts himself specifically with Scriven:

I admire most the modest evaluator, playing a supportive role, restraining his impulses to advocate, unlike the crusading evaluator, however honestly and forthrightly he announces his commitments. I think that I differ with Mike Scriven in this preference. I think that he designs evaluation for the "visiting philosopher" . . . who can deliver insights beyond the reach of the ordinary educator. . . . I emphasize the facilitator-role more than the deliverer of insights. (1975a, pp. 36-37)

Unlike Wholey, however, Stake does not emphasize management concerns, although management views are also reflected in the evaluation. Underlying his approach is concern for stakeholder well-being, identification of the particular stakes that persons have in a program, and a desire to serve those whom the program is supposed to be helping. Another purpose of evaluation is supporting the practitioner: "As educational researchers and program evaluators, we are interested in improving instructional practice" (Stake, 1986a, p. 89). He is dismayed about the quality of teaching (Stake & Easley, 1978; Stake, Raths, Denny, Stenzel, & Hoke, 1986), and often sees arresting deterioration rather than improvement as the immediate task. He aims for increased practitioner understanding, letting the ordinary political processes work out any action that should follow (Stake, 1986a, 1986b). He often describes practitioners in detail and gives focus to the quality of learning opportunities the educational system is providing. Yet none of these responses is always best. In responsive evaluation, evaluators size up the particular situation to see which issues and stakeholders can best be served by evaluation inquiries.

Evaluation as Reflecting Values

"To layman and professional alike, evaluation means that someone will report on the program's merits and shortcomings" (Stake, 1980a, p. 86). "All evaluation is presumed to be value-oriented" (Stake, 1975b, p. 15; see also 1970, 1979). But Stake wants evaluation clients, not evaluators, to make those value judgments. He disagrees that the evaluator's job is to render summative judgments: "Seldom will the evaluator's obligation be to choose between blue ribbon and red, to assign a grade, or to provide any single indicator of worth" (1975b, p. 26; 1982a). Stake feels that no single, correct value system exists; rather, "the evaluation encounters a pluralism of values" (1975b, p. 26). In discussing the evaluation of an arts program, Stake (1975b) says "a work of art has no single true value. A program has no single true value. Yet both have value. The value of an arts-in-education program will be different for different people, for different purposes" (p. 25). So, "whatever consensus in values there is . . . should be discovered. The evaluator . . . should not create a consensus that does not exist" (p. 26).

Stake prefers to describe values rather than to make value judgments. The evaluator performs services for a client, and has ethical responsibilities to all who even indirectly acknowledge the evaluation — these are more important than identifying which values are correct:

> I am less inclined to have the evaluator do battle with illogical value-positions held, consciously or unconsciously, by clients and audiences. They should be reminded (or taught) that others value things differently, but not told they are wrong. (1975a, pp. 37-38)

He elaborates by an example:

> When a community expresses a desire for, or a tolerance of, some form of discrimination the evaluator can fight it or study it. He can look for and report the injury that results. As a human being he may choose to oppose the discrimination but his contract to evaluate is not a license to undermine the local practices. The social reformer role is one I admire, but I would like it recognized as only overlapping, not synonymous with, the evaluator role. I do not admire school systems that are discriminating in the way they distribute privilege and opportunity. I am not impressed, however, with the ability or the sensitivity of evaluators to set matters right. Of course, they should tell the story of what is happening, no matter how unpopular the message. (1975a, p. 38)

Stake says that the evaluator should "reveal minority value-positions" (1975a, p. 37)—that is, the values of stakeholders who are so few in number that they might otherwise not be heard.

Responsive Evaluation

Stake advocates responsive evaluation:

> I prefer to work with evaluation designs that perform a service. I expect the evaluation study to be useful to specific persons. An evaluation probably will not be useful if the evaluator does not know the interests and language of his audiences. During an evaluation study, a substantial amount of time may be spent learning about the information needs of the persons for whom the evaluation is being done. . . . To be of service and to emphasize evaluation issues that are important for each particular program, I recommend the *responsive evaluation* approach. It is an approach that sacrifices some precision in measurement, hopefully to increase the usefulness of the findings to persons in and around the program. (1980a, p. 76)

He distinguishes "between a preordinate approach and a responsive approach" (1980a, p. 75): "Many evaluation plans are more 'preordinate', emphasizing (1) statement of goals, (2) use of objective tests, (3) standards held by program personnel, and (4) research-type reports" (p. 76). Most educational evaluation is preordinate, resembling basic research (Stake, 1969). But many educators, including Stake, became disenchanted with the preordinate approach; "the designs preferred by (traditional quantitative) researchers did not focus on the variables that educational administrators have control over" (p. 73). Administrators cannot control the gender or age of teachers, but can influence distributions of budgets or class schedules. Stake wants evaluation to respond to these management concerns. But "the rewards to an evaluator for producing a favourable evaluation report often greatly outweigh the rewards for producing an unfavourable report" (p. 74). Stake prefers evaluations designed to resist management biases. Finally, traditional quantitative methods often do not address the value of the intervention.

In place of the preordinate approach, Stake advocates responsive evaluation: "An educational evaluation is *responsive evaluation* (1) if it orients more directly to program activities than to program intents, (2) if it responds to audience requirements for information, and (3) if the different value-perspectives of the people at hand are referred to in reporting the success and failure of the program" (1980a, p. 77). The term *responsive* refers to a stimulus-response relationship; Stake believes "that the preordinate evaluator conceptualizes himself as a stimulus, seldom as a response" (1980a, p. 82). The preordinate evaluator generates standardized stimuli (treatments, dependent variables) to which the program responds. But the responsive evaluator "considers the principal stimuli to be those naturally occurring in the program, including responses of students and the subsequent dialogues" (p. 82). The responsive evaluator responds to these stimuli.

Advantages of Responsive Evaluation

Advantage 1: allowing important program variables to emerge. Preordinate evaluation requires the evaluator to specify in advance which treatments and outcomes are the most important to study. Stake is pessimistic that evaluators can do this often. In social programs "there are few 'critical' data in any study, just as there are few 'critical' components in any learning experience" (1980a, p. 78); "few, if any, specific learning steps are truly essential for subsequent success in any of life's endeavours" (p. 86). It is unrealistic to expect evaluators to identify important treatments and outcomes prior to observing the program. Moreover, preordinate evaluation "usually is not sensitive to ongoing changes in program purpose, nor to unique ways in which students benefit from contact with teachers and other learners, nor to dissimilar viewpoints that people have as to what is good and bad" (1980a, p. 85). Responsive evaluation accommodates ongoing changes in the program and its evaluation, focuses more on observing teacher-student interactions, and reports multiple views about what people think is good or bad.

Advantage 2: encouraging change efforts in local stakeholders. "One's design of evaluation research indicates much about one's belief in social change and improvement of services" (Stake, 1986b, p. 141). Stake is pessimistic that federal and state social programs have caused many beneficial results:

> During these thirty years we had across the country major federal projects and institutional pressures aimed at producing new knowledge to improve our universities and schools; *and* within their faculties a desire to change. One might expect this combination to assure a significant change. Lay observers and professionals alike ... concluded, however, that it did not happen.... The federal programs resulted in much less desired change than hoped for. I think the dominant research and development model was partly at fault. (1986a, pp. 91-92)

The evaluation of the Cities-in-Schools program had the effect of "quieting reform," of focusing practitioners so much on meeting evaluation requirements that they ceased doing reform activities that might have benefited the children (Stake, 1986b).

Stake sees a tension between the role of the social reformer and that of the social scientist. With the Cities-in-Schools evaluation, he protested the plight of the social reformer. In *Quieting Reform* (1986b), he speaks of the disillusioning effect of evaluation:

> In a minor way formal evaluation research contributes to the disillusionment. And so it strives. It seeks to help us shed our illusions. But without illusion we would find little worthy of attention. A world without curiosity and the aspiration to change, without the hope of "doing good," would rival any prospective calamity. (p. 163)

The line between enlightenment and disillusionment is a fine one, especially when remaining problems are intransigent and change efforts occur only at the margin.

Stake wants to combat the disillusionment by championing evaluations that describe programs comprehensibly, avoid mystification, and arrest the drift of responsibility from local to state and federal levels. "As educational researchers and program evaluators, we are interested in improving instructional practice" (Stake & Trumbull, 1982, p. 1), and such improvements are best identified by local stakeholders:

> When you hire an evaluator you aren't hiring a person who has a great deal of wisdom about your problems. You aren't going to get somebody who will capture a truth that is really crucial to your program. It is much more likely that whatever truths, whatever solutions there are, exist in the minds of people who are running the program, those participating in the program, those patrons of the program. . . . He is making his greatest contribution, I think, when he is helping people discover ideas, answers, solutions, within their own minds. (Stake, 1975a, p. 36)

When evaluating educational programs and classroom instruction, "the alleviation of instructional problems is most likely to be accomplished by the people most directly experiencing the problem, with aid and comfort perhaps (but not with specific solutions or replacement programs) from consultants or external authorities" (Stake, 1980a, p. 86).

Advantage 3: increasing local control. Preordinate evaluation takes power from local stakeholders by imposing treatments and measurements on them. It encourages them to abdicate control to "experts" who will solve problems for them (Stake, 1980b). The increasing influence of federal and state governments over local life has had the same effect. In education, "the subtle political and managerial message to the schools has been, 'You are incompetent, you need to be directed' " (Stake, 1980b, p. 161). When

> schools failed . . . each unfulfilled expectation brought about a new renovation, a new quest for the technology that would remedy our schools. And each new idea placed less reliance on the competence of the neighborhood and school staff to solve their problems. Much local control was yielded willingly, even advocated, as political leaders saw the schools as an instrument for social reform and as the citizenry became increasingly aware of the shortcomings of the schools. (p. 162)

Thus,

> as with many institutions in our society, the public schools have become increasingly oriented to state and federal standards, less oriented to the standards of family and neighborhood. Although state and federal standards are not indifferent to the concerns of family and neighborhood, they are not pluralistic, but rather emphasize uniformity and interchangeability, characteristics which often lend themselves to more effective review and control of the schools. (p. 162)

Increasing pressure toward uniformity results, but unfortunately,

> the quality of education is diminishing in this country partly because uniform standards of skill and performance are overemphasized and teachers and parents are not left sufficiently free to bear the burden and exercise the opportunity to decide what is best for the individual student. (Stake, 1980b, p. 163)

Such pressures occur "even when uniformity is not in the best interests of school children" (p. 163). Such uniformity is fundamentally undemocratic:

> We probably would be better off with less subordination of the education purposes of schools to economic and political purposes of the country. The schools need more help with their formal mission, to provide educational opportunity. It might help to formalize two "rights": the right of a parent to the kind of teaching he or she wants for his or her child; and the right of a student to a learning situation where other students are ordinarily serious about (at least tolerant of) academic learning. Current priorities would have to change to accommodate those rights, and the most likely way of getting those changes would be to re-establish local control. (Stake, 1980b, p. 167)

Responsive evaluation helps stakeholders recover as much control as possible over interventions:

> The argument that vicarious experience data are neglected knowledge for the understanding and improvement of practice has a political rationale too. To return emphasis to classroom *events* is to return a certain control to the classroom teacher . . . not assurance of democracy, but an enablement of democracy. And practically speaking, even in situations where teachers are pleading for someone else to specify what their curriculum responsibilities are, it is likely that neither parent nor state will be served if external demands on the teachers are inconsistent with their convictions. (Stake & Trumbull, 1982, p. 11)

Stake urges evaluators to resist unquestioned acceptance of state goals and service to policymakers, but also to resist using evaluation to empower favored stakeholders:

> The ethics of the evaluation specialist should be such that the mere act of carrying out an evaluation study should not in itself result in a change in the power structure. The degree of control over social programs should not be altered . . . for any constituent member merely because an evaluation study has occurred. (1979, p. 56)

Evaluation findings can change the power structure; but Stake is "not talking about the study's findings at all. I am talking about the condition of having an evaluation study — that condition alone should not cause a change in power" (1979, p. 56). By serving only decision makers, evaluators would violate this principle; "in so doing they contribute in a small way to the technologizing and disintegration of our society" (p. 56). Hence the responsive evaluator includes all program stakeholders to ensure the political fairness and justice of the evaluation (Stake, 1983a).

Advantages of preordinate evaluation. Preordinate evaluation is sometimes warranted; but "the investigator should remember that such a preordinate approach depends on a capability to state the important purposes of education and a capability to discern the accomplishment of those purposes, and those capabilities sometimes are not at our command" (Stake, 1980a, p. 85):

> Preordinate evaluation should be preferred to responsive evaluation when it is important to know if certain goals have been reached, if certain promises have been kept, and when predetermined hypotheses or issues are to be investigated. With greater focus and opportunity for preparation, preordinate measurements made can be expected to be more objective and reliable. (1980a, p. 87)

Stake concludes that

> it is wrong to suppose that either a strict preordinate design or responsive design can be fixed upon an educational program to evaluate it. As the program moves in unique and unexpected ways, the evaluation efforts should be adapted to them, drawing from stability and prior experience where possible, stretching to new issues and challenges as needed. (p. 87)

Doing Responsive Evaluation

Emphasis on observation and flexibility. Twelve events occur in a responsive evaluation. In some articles he has presented these as 12 hours on the face of a clock (adapted from Stake, 1980a, p. 81):

> 12 o'clock: Talk with clients, program staff, audiences.
> 1 o'clock: Identify program scope.
> 2 o'clock: Overview program activities.
> 3 o'clock: Discover purposes, concerns.
> 4 o'clock: Conceptualize issues.
> 5 o'clock: Identify data needs, issues.
> 6 o'clock: Select observers, judges; select instruments if any.
> 7 o'clock: Observe designated antecedents, transactions, and outcomes.
> 8 o'clock: Thematize; prepare portrayals, case studies.
> 9 o'clock: Validate; confirm; attempt to disconfirm.
> 10 o'clock: Winnow, match issues to audiences.
> 11 o'clock: Format for audience use.

In discussing this clock, Stake notes:

> My responsive-evaluation plan allocates a large expenditure of evaluation resources to observing the program. The plan is not divided into phases because observation and feedback continue to be the important functions from the first week through the last. I have identified twelve recurring events. I show them as if on the face of a clock. I know some of you would remind me that a clock moves clockwise, so I hurry to say that this clock moves clockwise and counter-clockwise *and* cross-clockwise. In other words, any event can follow any event. Furthermore, many events occur simultaneously, and the evaluator returns to each event many times before the evaluation ends. (1980a, pp. 80-81)

Program activities and stakeholder interests influence which responsive evaluation activities are engaged in at any time.

Stake summarizes how to do a responsive evaluation:

> To do a responsive evaluation, the evaluator conceives of a plan of observations and negotiations. He arranges for various persons to observe the program, and with their help prepares brief narratives, portrayals, product displays, graphs, etc. He finds out what is of value to his audiences, and gathers expression of worth from various individuals whose points of view differ. Of course, he checks the quality of his records; he gets program personnel to react to the accuracy of his portrayals; authority figures to react to the importance of various findings; and audience members to react to the relevance of his findings. He does much of this informally — iterating and keeping a record of action and reaction. He chooses media accessible to his audiences to increase the likelihood and fidelity of communication. He might prepare a final written report, he might not — depending upon what he and his clients have agreed on. (1975b, p. 14)

Preordinate evaluators do some of these tasks, but preordinate and responsive evaluators spend different amounts of time on each task. Preordinate evaluators spend more time on preparing instruments, administering tests, processing formal data, and preparing formal reports. Responsive evaluators spend more time observing the program, gathering judgments, learning client needs, and preparing informal reports (Stake, 1980a) — more time in actual contact with the program.

Letting questions emerge and change. Responsive and preordinate evaluators approach question formation differently. The preordinate evaluator relies too much on "preconceived notions of success" from academic theories or past research. In education, preordinate evaluators might thus use standardized achievement tests. But the responsive evaluator should be sure to

> give careful attention to the reasons the evaluation was commissioned, then to pay attention to what is happening in the program, then to choose the value questions and criteria. He should not fail to discover the best and worst of program happenings. He should not let a list of objectives or an early choice of data-gathering instruments draw attention away from the things that most concern the people involved. (Stake, 1980a, p. 78)

The responsive evaluator lets questions emerge and change during the evaluation, rather than be set at the beginning and remain fixed. We cannot know all important questions at the start of evaluation, so we need a means to discover important questions that are not apparent initially.

The primary source of questions for the responsive evaluator is direct contact with the program and its stakeholders:

> After getting acquainted with a program, partly by talking with students, parents, taxpayers, program sponsors, and program staff, the evaluator acknowledges certain issues or problems or potential problems. These issues are a structure for continuing discussions with clients, staff, and audiences. These issues are a structure for the data-gathering plan. The systematic observations to be made, the interviews and tests to be given, if any, should be those that contribute to understanding or resolving the issues identified. (Stake, 1980a, p. 79)

Stake (1980a) suggests another tool to help the evaluator know what data to gather, in "The Countenance of Educational Evaluation" (1967, 1982b). The countenance approach emphasizes "use of multiple and even contradictory sources of information" (1980a, p. 79). Drawing from a 1966 discussion with Scriven, Cronbach, Hastings, and Glaser, Stake identifies 13 kinds of data. The evaluator could gather (1) data on program rationale; (2-7) data on intended or observed antecedents, transactions, and outcomes; (8-10) data on standards regarding antecedents, transactions, and outcomes in this type of program; or (11-13) data on judgments of quality of the programs' antecedents, transactions, and outcomes. At first, he said the processing of these data is a matter of "finding the contingencies among antecedents, transactions, and outcomes and finding the congruence between intents and observations" (1967, p. 532). Today he ties it more to responsive methods.

Portrayal and holistic communication. "One of the principal reasons for backing away from the preordinate approach to evaluation is to improve communication with audiences" (Stake, 1975b, p. 22). Preordinate evaluators write large, technical final reports; but "from a report of such analytic inquiry it is very hard, often impossible, for a reader to know what the program was like" (1975b, p. 22). Technical reporting is inappropriate to the skills of most readers: "Unlike research reporting, evaluation reporting is communicating with an audience that does not share the technical qualifications and special interests of the investigator" (1970, p. 199). Responsive evaluators aim for accurate portrayal of the program, being less concerned with formal reporting than with "the responsibility for writing in a way that is maximally comprehensible" (1980a, p. 83). Evaluation findings should be stated in the "natural ways in which people assimilate information and arrive at understanding" (1980a, p. 83); "the evaluator will often find that case studies of several students may more interestingly and faithfully represent the educational program than a few measurements on all of the students" (1975b, p. 25). He does not limit reporting to case studies. Stake and Balk (1982) use a briefing panel to communicate evaluation results to stakeholders. Reports may be written in several forms appropriate to the needs and interests of different stakeholder groups. They should include "charts and products and narratives and portrayals" (Stake, 1980a, p. 86). He encourages diverse ways of presenting evaluations (Smith, 1982; Stake, 1979).

A Preference for Qualitative Methods

Stake likes to use case studies: "The case need not be a person or enterprise. It can be whatever 'bounded system' . . . is of interest. An institution, a program, a responsibility, a collection, or a population can be the case" (1978, p. 7). The case study approach is distinguished "in the first place by giving great prominence to what is and what is not 'the case' — the boundaries are kept in focus" (1978, p. 7). Case studies can be statistical, but

> most case studies feature: descriptions that are complex, holistic, and involving a myriad of not highly isolated variables; data that are likely to be gathered at least partly by personalistic observation; and a writing style that is informal, perhaps narrative, possibly with verbatim quotation, illustration, and even allusion and metaphor. Comparisons are implicit rather than explicit. Themes and hypotheses may be important, but they remain subordinate to the understanding of the case. (1978, p. 7)

Knowledge from case studies "is different in that it is more concrete, more contextual, more subject to reader interpretation, and based more on reference populations determined by the reader" (Stake, 1981, p. 36).

In case studies, "human observers are the best instruments we have for many evaluation issues" (Stake, 1980a, p. 80). They exercise critical judgment with more sensitivity to program realities and accomplishments than could preordained measurements: "Students, teachers, and other purposively selected observers exercise the most relevant critical judgements, whether or not their criteria are in any way explicit" (1980a, p. 86). Direct observation of the case, whether by participants or trained professionals, is the cornerstone of responsive evaluation. These observers use interviews, observation, examination of documents, records, and unobtrusive measures, and even investigative journalism (Guba, 1981; Guba & Lincoln, 1981; Lincoln & Guba, 1985; Patton, 1980). They allow the evaluator to respond to the program and participants without introducing new stimuli, such as achievement tests, into the program. Such methods are best suited to the workplace, the activity place where researchers make observations.

An Emphasis on Improving Local Practice

Evaluation is dedicated to improving local practice, not to producing and disseminating new knowledge: "Directing attention to knowledge production and utilization diminishes attention to practice. Building dissemination mechanisms diminishes emphasis on practice" (Stake & Trumbull, 1982, p. 4). Improving local practice is central:

> Traditionally, researchers have had scant interest in studying the entwining, personalistic, and crisislike problems of daily practice. Rather, they conceptualize new systems expecting orderly circumstances and dispassionate practitioners. They fiddle with models. But for practitioners, and the helpers of practitioners, the well-being of daily practice is the goal. Sometimes that well-being requires changed practice, sometimes preserved practice, but always practice. The end product desired is not knowledge-about-practice or knowledge-about-subject-matter. Formal knowledge is not necessarily a stepping stone to improved practice. This knowledge may be helpful in the long run, but in each teaching dilemma the importance of formal knowledge about teaching or about curriculum remains to be shown. We maintain that practice is guided far more by personal knowings, based on and gleaned from personal experience. And change in practice, or resistance to change, are often directly related. Because of this personal aspect it will sometimes be more useful for research to be designed so that *research* can evoke *vicarious experience* which leads to *improved practice*. (Stake & Trumbull, 1982, p. 5)

Formal theory and codified data can also affect practice. But:

> We speak not against such knowings but claim they are too often exclusively relied upon, too regularly presumed to be the preferable messages. If we look on the sketch the leverage point for change too often neglected is the disciplined collection of experiential knowledge. (Stake & Trumbull, 1982, pp. 8-9)

Case studies help rectify this historical neglect of vicarious experience in producing change.

The Role of Naturalistic Generalization in Improving Practice

We commonly think of two means of changing practice: incorporating new developments suggested by others, and better understanding ourselves and our relationships to others (Stake & Trumbull, 1982). The former approach relies on producing and disseminating new knowledge that is generalizable to situations in which practitioners work. The latter approach requires the practitioner to be in some activity such as psychotherapy, where an expert guides change or improvement. Stake argues that both approaches rely on a third way of change: "One may change by adding to one's experience and re-examining problems and possible solutions intuitively" (Stake & Trumbull, 1982, p. 2):

> We maintain that this third method of planned change . . . is at least as important as the other two and that program improvement efforts should more often rely upon the experiences or intuitions of the practitioners involved. We believe that program evaluation studies should be planned and carried out in such a way as to provide a maximum of vicarious experience to the readers who may then intuitively combine this with their previous experiences. The role of the program evaluator or educational researcher would then be to assist practitioners in reaching new understandings, new *naturalistic generalizations.* (Stake & Trumbull, 1982, p. 2)

Naturalistic generalization resembles Polanyi's (1966) tacit knowledge:

> Tacit knowledge is all that is remembered somehow, minus that which is remembered in the form of words, or other rhetorical forms. It is that which permits us to recognize faces, to comprehend metaphors, and to "know ourselves." Tacit knowledge includes a multitude of unexpressible associations which give rise to new meanings, new ideas, and new applications of the old. (Stake, 1978, p. 6)

Tacit knowledge helps us generalize from our experience to new situations. This is like "*naturalistic generalization,* arrived at by recognizing the similarities of objects and issues in and out of context and by sensing the natural covariations of happenings" (Stake, 1978, p. 6). Naturalistic generalizations "guide action, in fact they are inseparable from action" (p. 6).

Sometimes stakeholders gain tacit knowledge directly:

> *Direct* personal experience is an efficient, comprehensive, and satisfying way of creating understanding, but a way not usually available to our evaluation-report audiences. The best substitute for direct experience probably is *vicarious experience* — increasingly better when the evaluator uses "attending" and "conceptualizing" styles similar to those which members of the audience use. Such styles are not likely to be those of the specialist in measurement or theoretically minded social scientist. Vicarious experience often will be conceptualized in terms of persons, places, and events. (Stake, 1980a, p. 83)

Responsive evaluation creates tacit knowledge for people who do not experience the program directly: "As readers recognize essential similarities to cases of interest to them, they establish the basis for naturalistic generalization" (Stake, 1978, p. 7).

Case study reports are uniquely suited to conveying vicarious experiences: "Case studies will often be the preferred method of research because they may be epistemologically in harmony with the reader's experience and thus to that person a natural basis for generalization" (Stake, 1978, p. 5). Readers can then generalize to their own situations to help solve problems. Consider the clinical psychologist dealing with a presenting problem she has not dealt with before. A case study of another therapist's work with a similar patient can give her vicarious experience about techniques and approaches that might work with the present client.

Naturalistic generalizations produce actions that probably "lead to evolutionary change rather than the replacement or re-creation kind of change implied in most literature on the reform of social and educational practice" (Stake & Trumbull, 1982, p. 2; see also Stake, 1986a). Evolutionary change is a more realistic goal than revolutionary change. Still, "it should be an empirical matter, as well as an intuitive one, to consider whether or not the case reports offering portrayals and vicarious experiences contribute to valid understandings of the workings, costs, and impacts of a program" (Stake, 1981, p. 33).

Case Studies and a Complex World

"One of the problems of the case study report is that it dismays readers with the fluidity and complexity of interactions" (Stake, 1981, p. 34). But this complexity reflects the fact that "education is a complicated business" (p. 34); "some educationists and evaluators say that the determinants of learning are relatively few and robust; and that if we provide those critical conditions, desired learning will occur. . . . But some others say that the vital conditions of learning are innumerable" (pp. 33-34). Moreover: "We do not know what causes what. We also do not know whether we in schools live in a simple world magnificently obscured to our weak vision or in a complex world where multitudes of causes take turns evoking success or failure" (p. 37). Stake leans toward the second option:

> Lee Cronbach noted that it is fourth- or fifth-order interactions, those beyond our analysis, perhaps interactions with a factor we failed to measure, that defy our explanations of educational achievement. . . . If the world is complex then, even though our explanations may have little predictive power, many of our descriptions should be complex. Not only should we put lots of variables in the

checklist, but we should keep the contingencies among individual data outside
the computer where the reader can pursue them. (1981, p. 37)

He reiterates this in his *Case Studies in Science Education* (CSSE; Stake
& Easley, 1978): "We believe that in reality, reality is multiple, rooted in
the different perceptions of people. . . . In a project such as this, we wanted
to encounter as many realities as we could" (p. A:5). If you "advocate
pluralism and relativism" (Stake, 1975a, p. 36), then the complexity of the
case study in a complex world is a virtue, not a vice.

Referring to "constructivist reality," Stake clarifies his epistemological
and ontological beliefs (R. E. Stake, personal communication, March 14,
1989; the remaining paragraphs in this section are taken directly, or para-
phrased, from that communication). Knowledge is a human construction
that begins with sensory experiences of external stimuli that are then
given meaning and interpreted by the recipient. Only the interpretations
are knowable, although not always conscious or rational. The human mind
can generate knowledge entirely from internal deliberation, but no knowledge is ever purely of the external world, devoid of human construction.

Stake then posits three realities. Reality 1 stimulates us in simple
ways but we know little else of it. Reality 2 is formed of interpretations of
stimulation; we know it so well that we seldom doubt its correspondence
to Reality 1. Reality 3, which blends into the second reality, is devised of
our most complex interpretations, our rational reality. Each person's versions of the second and third worlds are constantly changing. But just as
a person's world remains largely the same from one day to the next, two
people sharing experience devise largely the same realities.

Many stimulations come from other people. Some suggest generalizations others also hold. Views held by many people or respected people are
more credible, appearing factual. A common human view, for example, is
that an outside reality, Reality 1, exists, corresponding nicely to our notion
of it, Reality 2. This correspondence cannot be tested because that outside
reality cannot register independent of our constructed interpretation. But
the view that Reality 1 exists is esteemed, partly because the extreme
counterclaim, that the world is entirely illusory, is unpopular. Denying an
independent reality is both unsupportable by evidence and socially discon-
certing. The price of believing in reality is small, even if there is none.

The most appealing conclusion is the nonparsimonious view that all
three realities exist and affect us. The question of which reality is more important is academic. We jeopardize our lot by neglecting any of the three.
The aim of research is not to discover Reality 1, for that is impossible, but
to construct a clearer Reality 2 and a more sophisticated Reality 3, that

will withstand disciplined skepticism. Science strives to build universal understanding that is partly unique to the beholder and partly common. In this process, each person's personal reality is not of equal importance. Some interpretations are better than others. People have ways of agreeing on which are the best. Of course, they are not always correct. Even among people fully committed to a constructed reality, not all constructions are of equal value. One can believe in relativity, contextuality, and constructivism without believing all views are of equal merit. Personal civility or political ideology may call for respecting every view, but scientific study does not.

Belief in independent reality is not belief in a simple world. Realists, too, believe that generalizations are regularly limited by local condition. Nor does belief in construction fix belief in a heterogeneous, particularist world. Though idealists, relativists, situationalists, and contextualists often resist broad generalization and support constructivist ontology, their support for a contextualist epistemology is a correlate, not a derivative, of that ontology. Contextualists value case studies because the design allows extra attention to physical, temporal, historical, social, political, economic, and aesthetic contexts. Contextualist epistemology requires in-depth studies, leaving less time for refining theme and construction. Many realists, too, are fond of case studies. However, naturalistic, phenomenological, and hermeneutic case studies are more likely to be done by constructivist researchers. It would be a mistake to conclude that a constructivist logic promotes case study methodology more than does a realist logic. Case study researchers often espouse a constructivist view of reality, but the two persuasions are not the same.

Case Studies and Reader-Centered Knowledge

Case studies give readers power to form opinions and judgments about the case:

> Something has been wrong with evaluation studies more than their inability to measure impact and to isolate critical ingredients. They poorly serve different value positions. Different audiences, of course, are not treated equally. Michael Scriven invented the goal-free approach to dissociate us from program advocates. Urging more concern for consumers, he opposed Lee Cronbach's early orientation to curriculum developers. Marcia Guttentag coined the term "stakeholder" to help the evaluator answer the question "Whose side are you on?" It has been no secret that each evaluation approach favors certain points of view more than others. (Stake, 1981, p. 38)

Stake offers a remedy in the case study:

> A partial alternative to asking or forcing the evaluator to be more equitable is to give leverage to the reader. The case study that provides portrayals capable of different interpretations, hewing to what is commonly observed and relevant to an array of concerns, may do more for justice than it loses in efficiency. (1981, p. 38)

He concludes that

> readers have enormous power, though it is not infallible, to recognize what is relevant and what is irrelevant to their own circumstances. For those matters that are greatly influenced by context, the responsibility of a case study researcher is to provide the contingency and contextual data that enhance and constrain those intuitive powers. The population of cases most relevant to decision-oriented research and program evaluation is the population that the reader already has experience with. (1981, p. 39)

Stake dislikes using researcher-defined reference populations and the search for discipline-based knowledge, exemplified in Cronbach's (1982a) *Designing Evaluations of Educational and Social Programs*. He prefers to let readers define their own reference groups from personal experiences.

Case Studies and Theory Development

Although the case study is primarily a tool for improving practice, it can be "useful in theory building" to the basic researcher, and "for exploration for those who search for explanatory laws" (Stake, 1978, p. 7). However:

> Although case studies have been used by anthropologists, psychoanalysts, and many others as a method of exploration preliminary to theory development, the characteristics of the method are usually more suited to expansionist than reductionist pursuits. Theory building is the search for essences, pervasive and determining ingredients, and the making of laws. The case study, however, proliferates rather than narrows. One is left with more to pay attention to rather than less. The case study attends to the idiosyncratic more than to the pervasive. The fact that it has been useful in theory building does not mean that that is its best use. (1978, p. 7)

Here Stake suggests that case study methods are stronger for discovery than for confirmation tasks in science. Such emphasis is usually warranted in responsive evaluation.

Difficulties with the Case Study

The case study and validity. Case studies succeed in giving valid portrayals if they give "an accurate and useful representation of the case in a certain setting" (Stake & Easley, 1978, p. C:28). "To be validated a report needs to be confirmed through other observers, it needs to survive deliberate efforts to disconfirm it, and it needs to be credible" (p. C:28). He includes credibility

> to acknowledge that previous experience can contribute something to the confirmation, and that it is validity, "for use by persons" that we are most concerned about. If a report strains credulity, then it will need much more confirmation to attain a certain level of validity. (Stake & Easley, 1978, p. C:28)

Recall that Weiss found something similar, that "Challenge to the Status Quo" was more credible if based on high-quality research.

Stake subscribes to some traditional notions of assessing validity: "One of the primary ways of increasing validity is by triangulation . . . trying to arrive at the same meaning by at least three independent approaches" (Stake & Easley, 1978, p. C:27). This takes place within a case study, and between case studies of the same program at different sites. In his CSSE evaluation:

> The field observers sought out informants having different positions, roles, experience, attitudes, and goals in order to check the perceived constance of a phenomenon. The observers themselves observed, interviewed, and analyzed documents. Their findings were reviewed by site visit teams, site coordinators, and on-site educators. . . . Many taped interviews were analyzed by a specialist in linguistics well experienced in science education research. . . . Survey data were added to the site visit and case study data. Triangulation occurred across CSSE sites as multiple researchers examined the issues manifest in data from multiple sources at the eleven sites and from the national sample. (Stake & Easley, 1978, p. C:27)

These procedures do not yield a number to index validity, but "naturalistic observation reports have the great advantage that the readers can participate in the determination of validity" (p. C:27):

> Accuracy of observing and reporting is more than a matter of everyone seeing the same thing, for many observations cannot be made independent of the observer's point of view. The validity of a case study then is dependent on the observer's point of view, and its utility to a reader will be dependent on

recognition of that point of view. To some this sounds hopelessly relativistic, but it is consistent with Lee Cronbach's 1971 definition of validity. (p. C:28)

If there are multiple realities mediated by the perceptions of each individual, then different observers may see different things, and attach different meanings to the same thing. So "we are not willing to claim that in order for a report to be valid the observations reported need to be those another observer would have reported" (Stake & Easley, 1978, p. C:28):

> During an extended visit to a complex site, only a small portion of happenings will be seen, and only a small portion of those seen will be reported. An important isolated event may occur. The idea of *inter-observer reliability* of reporting may be pretty nearly lost in such a situation but the idea of validity holds. (p. C:28)

The validity of case study methods will continue to be hotly debated; but Stake thinks they have sufficient validity to continue their use. The primary criterion against which to judge the case study is the increase in understanding it offers the reader: "It seems less important to ask if these case studies met scientific standards than to ask if they added to understanding. Neither one depends on the other" (Stake & Easley, 1978, p. C:56).

Difficulties generating more global questions. Because naturalistic inquiry "attends to the issues which emerge from the situation studied, it may pay little heed to the momentous issues confronting Society" (Stake & Trumbull, 1982, p. 10). One critic (Fox, 1981) of *Case Studies in Science Education* has suggested that CSSE in particular, and naturalistic inquiry in general, ignores such great curricular questions as the following: Does the fate of society depend on correct analysis of science education? How much effort should go into discovery and perpetuation of the common culture, and to what extent is it properly represented by the schools' curricula? To what extent does a teacher owe something to a child's future beyond that which the parents choose and prefer? Stake responds:

> In naturalistic studies a few questions on such a global scale arise, but many would not unless the fieldworker were to push and probe for them. And such pushing and probing is considered by many to be inappropriate for naturalistic research. In the *Case Studies* a great many global questions were raised, but too infrequently to aggregate across sites, or across teachers within a site. These are not questions important, or at least discussed, in daily practice. Some research does need to address the global questions, but we hope we have made a case for research which addresses the emic issues, the issues of importance within the individual case studied. (Stake & Trumbull, 1982, p. 10)

Naturalistic inquiry is good at seeing the obvious, but it

> is not sufficiently mature to pursue diligently the subtle, especially when interesting — and more spectacular — social, political (and methodological) issues emerge. It is important for us to continue to report what is dominant and what is emergent, but we also need to be able to focus on more subtle dynamics and their culture, context, and history. Case study research has yet to show that it can do this. (Stake, 1983b, p. 74)

Difficulties when abstraction is needed. Case studies are more concrete than abstract, so they are not best when abstraction is needed:

> There will be some audiences and some occasions, of course, for which experimental observations will be more valued; but there will be others where a less personal, more sophisticated conceptualization will be preferred. It depends on the audience and on the purpose. (Stake, 1981, p. 36)

Case studies are not good vehicles for publication in scientific journals where theoretical abstractions are valued (Stake, 1978). Similarly, "any reader may recognize the political force of highly abstract language. When the purpose of evaluation is advocacy or legitimation, the abstract, even the more mystifying, may be preferred" (Stake, 1981, p. 37).

Weakness for some traditional goals. Preordinate evaluation using surveys, experiments, and testing may sometimes be preferred to responsive evaluations using case studies, especially when important goals and issues can be specified ahead of time. The case study is weaker than traditional research methods for some other goals of science:

> When explanation, propositional knowledge, and law are the aims of an inquiry, the case study will often be at a disadvantage. When the aims are understanding, extension of experience, and increase in conviction in that which is known, the disadvantage disappears. (Stake, 1978, p. 7)

The case study is best when important issues cannot be specified ahead of time, and when understanding a specific local program is more important than developing scientific theories about it.

Aggregating multiple case studies. A difficult problem arises when the evaluator conducts multiple case studies and then collects them for interpretation:

> Obviously multiple case studies demand a form of linkage — a manner in which to discuss their differences and similarities. The methodology for aggregating wholistic data from multiple observers at multiple sites and comprehending the

overview is one that is little examined in the methodological literature. (Stake & Easley, 1978, p. C:45)

If reality, or knowledge of reality, is relative to each knower, if each case is unique, then finding communalities inevitably distorts each case. If so, integrating case studies may be epistemologically reprehensible. Yet evaluators often face demands for such integrations. Stake did in the CSSE evaluation; his federal funders wanted integrated interpretations and conclusions as well as case studies:

> We tried to restrain interpretation during data gathering and not to impose our interpretations too much during the assimilation. Only under pressure from the NSF did we prepare an executive summary. . . . We found this to be an opportunity to make one synthesis and encouraged readers to make others. (Stake & Easley, 1978, p. C:54)

Case studies place responsibility on the reader to synthesize and interpret. In one case study evaluation, the evaluators presented conflicting arguments about the positive and negative aspects of the project, and then said that "the reader is left with responsibility of resolving these conflicting arguments" (Stake & Gjerde, 1974, p. 2). Similarly, in the CSSE evaluation, "we wanted the reader to summarize all these things for himself or herself" (Stake & Easley, 1978, p. A:3). Ultimately, "the study cannot be the arbiter. As one of the other panelists [who reviewed the CSSE study] noted, it leaves it up to the reader and the policy maker to make their own comparison, interpretations, and policy decisions" (Stake & Easley, 1978, p. C:56). If the reader does not interpret and integrate, those tasks may not get done.

Some solutions to the problem of aggregation are being developed by case study researchers. One method is "use of a computerized coding system, converting ethnographic data to bits of natural language reports coded and stored in a computer" (Stake & Easley, 1978, p. C:46). Another method

> is to analyze the context of case studies with a closed-ended questionnaire containing questions regarding pertinent issues. The resulting analysis becomes "case survey method." It may allow an analyst to aggregate the case study across sites. Cases that do not have information for the questionnaire are dropped. (p. C:46)

Lofland and Lofland (1984), Miles and Huberman (1984), and Patton (1980) elaborate such methods. But aggregation is partly antagonistic to

Stake's theory of locally responsive evaluation: "This may be more suitable for developing theory than for understanding a particular group of situations. It neglects key information that is available in a case study report—the context of a situation. Context is utilized more for decision making" (Stake & Easley, 1978, p. C:46).

The Limits of Stake's Advocacy of the Case Study

Stake deliberately overstates his advocacy of the case study method: "I see it as unfortunately necessary to overstate the distinction between academic research and practical inquiry as a step toward improving and legitimizing inquiries that are needed for understanding and problem solving but which are unlikely to produce vouchsafed generalizations" (1978, p. 7). He is trying "to make an alluring plea for the inclusion of case studies in the evaluation research arsenal" (1981, p. 32). But ultimately, he notes that he really does not know the limit of his argument:

> The responsive evaluator is guided largely by the particular situation. How much to emphasize the particular or the general is a relative matter. Of course, there will be the day when I will say, "We went too far." And there is a danger that we will become too "situation-specific," too willing to serve an immediate audience and not willing to serve some more distant audiences enough. (1975a, p. 34)

But for now, he does not know exactly how close that danger is.

OUR ANALYSIS OF STAKE'S THEORY OF EVALUATION

Stake's preference for case study methods and responsive evaluation stems from his understanding of how social programming should take place, how knowledge is best constructed and conveyed, how the evaluator should approach valuing, and how people use information to generalize and act. In this section, we examine the nature and adequacy of such assumptions, concluding that his arguments are sometimes cogent, but often too one-sided to yield a complete theory of evaluation.

Theory of Social Programming

Throughout this book we have stressed the conservative, incremental nature of most social change. Stake takes this perspective to its extreme.

He works almost exclusively at the local project level, eschewing federal intervention efforts as failures; he sees project heterogeneity as so important as to almost preclude interesting generalizations about programs; and he makes a virtue of conservative, evolutionary, incremental change initiated by local stakeholders to meet their own needs (Stake, 1986a). Many of his points are not sufficiently emphasized in evaluation. One example is Stake's emphasis on working with practitioners who actually intervene with clients; these are the people who most directly control program implementation. The success of many initiatives hinges on whether or not the practitioner will adopt them. Evaluations that overlook this link may find that evaluation results cause little program change.

Stake is virtually unique among evaluators in raising one argument. Program evaluation owes much of its existence to funding that accompanied large federal social programs. But Stake, so to speak, bites the hand that feeds us, arguing that federal and state influence is too great, has disenfranchised local stakeholders, and has discouraged them from solving their own problems. Stake asks, "In the process of change how much should we give people opportunity to approve, to participate in controlling, the changes we would make in their lives?" (1986a, p. 90). This is an uncommon perspective among evaluators, but is respectable among some politicians and political theorists who believe, as President Reagan said, "Government is not the solution to our problem; government is the problem" (Moynihan, 1985, p. 9). Murray's (1984) treatise on social welfare policy, *Losing Ground*, argues that federal social welfare programs have made matters worse. Murray's work has become a handbook for those who argue there is too much government. Theorists from other parts of the political spectrum sometimes argue similarly (Mansbridge, 1983; Rahman, 1985). In either case the argument is that local social problem solving can be stunted when government intervenes. Evaluations that cooperate with these federal efforts can inhibit local change efforts.

Stake's (1986b) review of the Cities-in-Schools evaluation documents an exemplar of such "quieting of reform": "The evaluators were trying to help – but they were trying mostly to get a research study going. Getting that pregnant girl back in school was not the highest priority for them" (p. 151). Local practitioners focused so much on doing research activities that they stopped doing activities like getting that pregnant girl back in school. This example helps us to understand a possibly pernicious effect of a narrow focus on federal and state interventions. Locally responsive evaluation is a partial remedy to this bias, increasing local power over social change.

This study, *Quieting Reform* (Stake, 1986b), is a qualitative meta-evaluation – an evaluation of evaluation using qualitative methods. Stake evaluates the *social* and *political* value of evaluation, topics that most metaevaluations eschew in favor of critiquing methodology. Evaluation can have negative as well as positive social and political effects; assessing them should be an essential part of metaevaluation. We need more studies like *Quieting Reform*.

We admire the moral courage of this study, and the forthrightness of Stake's views about federal and state intervention. We do not entirely agree with his conclusions about the nature of social programming, or about the relationship of evaluation to programming. His analysis is interesting and thought-provoking; it is also too one-sided and uncritical to be convincing. His theory of social problem solving has an important internal contradiction. Stake's theory is a "call for aid to the *self*-correction of practice" (1986a, p. 91) at the local level. His problem-solving model starts with practitioners encountering problems: "This person is moved to act, to change an activity, to refrain from acting, or to resist acting, only when sufficient external demand or internal conviction arises" (1986a, p. 96). Responsive evaluation somehow helps solve the problem through naturalistic generalization when the practitioner reads the case study. But that case study is about the very practitioner (and local colleagues) who has the problem but no solution to begin with, and who already has probably discussed the problem with colleagues. Some broadening of perspective may occur if the practitioner has not discussed the problem widely with local colleagues—although such benefit might be had more efficiently with organizational development techniques than evaluation. But solutions might be more novel if they were imported from new places that do things differently. By this rationale, evaluators should spread case study resources over multiple sites and import multiple succinct summaries from those sites, as did the U.S. Department of Education (1986) report, *What Works: Research About Teaching and Learning*. Reflecting back to stakeholders the details of their own cases seems to be least likely to produce novel solutions.

His theory is fundamentally conservative in another sense. Unlike, say, Rahman (1985), Stake does not endorse theories of social change drawn from the left of the political spectrum. Stake does not emphasize helping needy stakeholders, or educating stakeholders about socioeconomic causes of their plight. His approach is laissez-faire, characteristic of a traditional "rightist" or libertarian perspective. His approach fits well in an educational system characterized by local social and political decision-making processes. Stake's funding often probably comes from local school districts whose primary interests are not in championing the disenfranchised. But the economically and educationally disadvantaged do not participate in local decision making at the same level as other stakeholders. Thus Stake's approach to evaluation implicitly endorses a conservative, incremental approach to social change. Responsive evaluation leaves power for social change in the hands of those who already have it. Where the distribution of power is part of the problem, responsive evaluation contributes to maintaining the problem rather than resolving it. Some evaluators are reluctant to endorse such a conservative approach to evaluation, even if they agree that federal and state interventions generally have not been helpful.

But the latter assumption may not be warranted. We are not convinced that federal social programs failed in the social welfare area or in any other area. Evidence in favor of Murray's (1984) conclusions for the failure of social welfare policy is not at all conclusive (Shadish & Cook, 1985). First, those who perceive a failure focus on income maintenance programs for the poor and on outcomes like economic independence and stability of households or elimination of poverty (Murray, 1984). Those who perceive more success focus on in-kind service programs that improve material conditions, especially in health, nutrition, or housing (Aaron, 1984; Jencks, 1984; Lynn, 1977). Second, success is easier to document with some evaluative criteria than others. For example, social welfare is often justified to make households more stable in composition and more economically self-sufficient. Yet these are difficult criteria to modify in reality and to measure in practice, less amenable to social interventions compared to health access and status, nutritional intake, housing expenditures, or educational access and achievement.

Third, many apparent program failures were failures of implementation. Nevasky and Paster (1976) prevented a premature conclusion that the idea behind the Law Enforcement Assistance Administration did not work by showing that it had never been implemented in originally promised form. Starfield and Scheff (1972) showed the same thing in preventive child health care. Larson (1976) pointed out that low implementation levels of the Kansas City Police Patrol Experiment contributed to its failure to find significant effects in preventing crime. Both the bilingual education program and the Push-Excel program were not implemented in any reasonable way (American Institutes for Research, 1977, 1980). The study of implementation has now become a major task for social scientists (Bardach, 1977; Berman, 1980; Pressman & Wildavsky, 1984; Williams, 1980).

Fourth, some apparent failures may have been due more to failures of evaluation than to failures of the programs. In the 1960s and 1970s, social scientists were new to the study of large social interventions; their methods were unproven. When early evaluations showed few program effects, evaluations rarely told *why* — because of inadequate program theory

(Levin, 1977), poor implementation of a good program (Pressman & Wildavsky, 1984), or poor research design (Boruch & Gomez, 1977). Early researchers expected large effects from social programs, and so failed to ensure enough statistical power (Boruch & Gomez, 1977; Rossi & Wright, 1984). Early evaluations also made errors in estimating the size and direction of causal relationships. Cicirelli et al. (1969), for example, studied the effects of Head Start by comparing program participants to nonequivalent control children, adjusting for selection biases using covariance analysis; results suggested no effect, or even harmful effects, especially for the summer component of Head Start. But this analysis was later shown to underestimate the effects of Head Start (Campbell & Erlebacher, 1970), partly because of an inability to specify the true selection model and partly because of unreliability in measuring the selection model that was used. More appropriate linear structural modeling techniques suggest modest, statistically reliable effects for the program in raising academic achievement (Magidson, 1977; Rindskopf, 1981).

For these reasons we reject Stake's assumption that federal interventions are failures. We can draw an analogy to psychotherapy research. In the early 1950s, Eysenck (1952) reviewed the literature and concluded that psychotherapy did not work. His challenge caused a storm of controversy (Eysenck, 1954; Luborsky, 1954) and 30 years of outcome research to assess the validity of his claim (Smith, Glass, & Miller, 1980). The claim, it turns out, was premature and probably wrong. We should not repeat that mistake in program evaluation. It is premature to conclude that federal programs do not work. In another 30 years we will probably have a more finely differentiated analysis that acknowledges different degrees of success depending on factors like those described above.

Even if federal interventions were not stellar successes, Stake provides no reason to think that local problem solving is superior. Arguments about the conservative nature of social change apply just as much at the local level as at the state and federal levels. Moreover, federal interventions often occurred precisely because local problem solving failed for lack of expertise, political and social will, or resources. From this perspective, Stake does not criticize local-level problem solving as vigorously and fairly as he criticizes the state and federal levels. To take as narrow an approach as Stake does is too one-sided to be successful in the complex environment in which evaluators work.

Theory of Use

Stake's theory of use is closer to Weiss's enlightenment approach than to Wholey's instrumental use: "Decision making and policy setting are important consequences of evaluation study, but *understanding* alone is a consequence that indicates utility in evaluation studies" (Stake, 1986b, p. 141). Where Weiss is vague about psychological processes leading to enlightenment, Stake says more: Use occurs when people read material that elicits vicarious experiences that they intuitively understand. He argues that case studies are the best means to elicit these experiences.

One line of research in clinical psychology supports his argument. Since the late 1940s that field has used the "scientist-practitioner" model for training professionals. Under that model, psychologists are trained to conduct professional activities such as psychotherapy and testing, and to be active consumers and producers of research. Yet practicing clinical psychologists rarely use traditional research in an instrumental fashion to change their practice (Barlow, 1981). Rather, such changes come primarily from on-the-job experiences, discussions with colleagues, and workshops where training in a technique is offered (Barrom et al., 1988; Cohen, Sargent, & Sechrest, 1986). The only scholarly writing that much influences practitioners is the thick description of contextual material in case studies:

> Therapists were critical of research that ignored the complex realities of the therapy situation. They favored research on typical populations and modes of treatment, especially if it described the treatment carefully and focused on process-outcome links, significant change events, and the therapeutic alliance. (Morrow-Bradley & Elliott, 1986, p. 188)

And another study found that

> the instrumental use of psychotherapy research is not a frequent occurrence, but the psychologists' responses suggest that conceptual research use is more widespread. Specific factors that seem to influence the adoption of a positively evaluated treatment include a detailed description of the tested treatment, training in that treatment, and the compatibility of the treatment with a clinician's usual intervention strategy. (Cohen et al., 1986, p. 198).

This literature supports Stake's general argument that case studies are a relatively effective means of eliciting vicarious experience and increasing use. Our own experience is consistent with this argument. Case studies about our research and clinical work (Estroff, 1981; MacKinnon & Michels, 1971) have been both informative and influential on our thinking and practice. Other researchers often share this view (Bachrach, 1981).

Even so, Stake overstates the case for his approach to use. In the process of embracing enlightenment, Stake underestimates the prevalence and value of instrumental use. Leviton and Boruch (1983) document numerous examples of instrumental use of evaluations in shaping educational programs and policy. Wholey (1979, 1983; Wholey et al., 1986) presents anecdotal evidence suggesting that instrumental use occurs as a result of his evaluations. A growing literature suggests that at least some instrumental use can and does occur (Kirkhart & Attkisson, 1986; Majchrzak, 1986; Rossi & Wright, 1985; Saxe, 1986; Shadish & Reichardt, 1987). If so, we err if we focus evaluation *solely* on enlightenment or tacit knowing.

One use of evaluative findings falls under neither enlightenment nor instrumental use — the influence of evaluation on practitioners during their initial training or continuing education. Evaluation findings are frequently reported in education and social work textbooks, although the time lag between the initial findings and their inclusion in texts could not be characterized as short-term use (Leviton & Cook, 1983). This other route to influencing practice should be considered, as well. Case studies are not the only way to get use.

Case study *reporting formats* can facilitate use. That does not mean that only case study *methods* can produce information for case study reporting formats. It is only a tiny but sensible departure from Stake's recommendations to intersperse quantitative information throughout a case study to put local contextual information into perspective. Moving somewhat further, final reports could contain both case study material and results of quantitative studies (e.g., Segal & Aviram, 1978), complementing each other's strengths and weaknesses, as service delivery assessments do (Hendricks, 1981; Wholey, 1983). Case study material need not exclude the joint use of quantitative information, and vice versa. Stake acknowledges this: "Formal research reports may contain the detailed description necessary to generate vicarious experience for readers" (1986a, p. 94). We join Stake in wishing that all traditional evaluations would include qualitative, case study material, resources allowing. But this is a two-way street; we wish all qualitative evaluators would incorporate quantitative information, as well. We are greatly impressed with cases that have done so (Maxwell, Bashook, & Sandlow, 1986; Trend, 1979); reports of either approach by itself now seem incomplete compared with multimethod reports.

If the goal were *only* to facilitate use of results — as opposed to, say, valid portrayal of real cases — one could do so with fictionalized case studies created to give life and context to quantitative data. Case studies can be used like Kuhnian "exemplars" — "concrete problem-solutions that students encounter from the start of their scientific education . . . that also show them by example how their job is to be done" (Kuhn, 1970, p. 187). Each exemplar is a case study of methods and theories applied to a particular problem. It may describe an actual historical instance, but may also be partly fictionalized as long as the essential details of theory and method convey the paradigm being taught. But it would be a bad idea to use case studies primarily in this way in evaluation if evaluation should be primarily concerned with *valid* portrayals of *real* cases — as we think it should. We make this observation only to highlight the fact that Stake's claim is not that case study *methods* facilitate use, but that case study *reporting formats* do so. His arguments about facilitating use with case study reports are not arguments for case study methods unless only case study methods are valid input into case study reports. He does not make this case, and such arguments would be subject to serious empirical and logical question.

Further, we see no reason to think that *only* case study reporting formats produce either enlightenment or instrumental use. Many apparently useful studies are not in case study format (Kirkhart & Attkisson, 1986; Leviton & Boruch, 1983; Majchrzak, 1986; Rossi & Wright, 1985; Saxe, 1986; Wholey, 1979, 1983, 1986a, 1986b, 1986c). The traditional final report has itself evolved means of facilitating use — for example, an executive summary. The U.S. Department of Education (1986) report *What Works: Research About Teaching and Learning* is another way to translate research into usable suggestions for practice; there is not a case study in its 65 pages. It simply summarizes an array of mostly quantitative studies. Finally, the written final report, in either traditional or case study form, is certainly not the only way of communicating useful results (Smith, 1982). By all means we should incorporate the case study into our repertoire of methods for facilitating use; but we see little evidence that we should depend mostly or totally on it.

The major problem with Stake's theory of use is that it is unduly parochial, relegating many kinds of use and numerous methods of facilitating use to second-class status. We now have every reason to believe that there are many legitimate kinds of use in evaluation, and many ways to achieve each kind.

Theory of Knowledge

The quantitative-qualitative debate has engendered many important discussions of knowledge construction in evaluation (Cook & Reichardt, 1979). Stake's persistent advocacy of case study methods played a seminal role in making these issues salient. However, compared with Guba and Lincoln (1981) or Patton (1980), Stake has not much articulated the ontological and epistemological arguments in favor of qualitative approaches. Indeed, given the importance he places on practice, he might regard such discussions as unduly abstract and philosophical: "Directing attention to knowledge production and utilization diminishes attention to practice" (Stake & Trumbull, 1982, p. 4). Lincoln and Guba (1985; Guba & Lincoln, 1981) justify their preference for case study methods more through onto-logical and epistemological arguments than through arguments about social programming and use. Specifically, they claim that there is no Reality 1, in Stake's terms; there are only the realities that we construct. They conclude that valid knowledge is that which best portrays the rich-ness and individual variations of each person's created reality; the case study is best suited to such portrayals.

Lincoln and Guba's (1985) epistemological and ontological arguments do not justify the case study. Even if radical constructivist assumptions were accepted, use of case study methodologies does not necessarily follow (Reichardt & Cook, 1979) — a point widely granted today, even among qualitative theorists (Guba & Lincoln, 1981, p. 244). More impor-tant, Lincoln and Guba (1985) base their arguments on a number of questionable propositions: that (a) the fact that philosophers (and physi-cists) criticize concepts such as external reality and causality implies that the critics want such concepts dropped, (b) the consensus is growing that naturalistic epistemology is the best current approach to knowledge con-struction, and (c) the assumptions of naturalistic inquiry are themselves less subject to criticism than past assumptions. Each point is suspect. Concepts like external reality or causality are alive and well in philo-sophical discourse, albeit in more sophisticated form (Humphreys, 1986; Leplin, 1984; Putnam, 1984). Complex findings in modern particle phys-ics do not imply dropping causality and reality, at least not as far as most participants in that debate are concerned (Davies, 1984; Davies & Brown, 1986; D'Espagnat, 1983; McMullin, 1984). No consensus exists in philos-ophy that naturalistic inquiry — or any other paradigm — is the paradigm of choice. The only way one can perceive a consensus in the disputatious philosophical literature is to ignore all of one's opponents. Finally, the assumptions of naturalistic epistemology are themselves quite assailable. For example, the contention that reality and truth are created entirely by the perceiver is partly self-defeating, for the authors are claiming we should accept their theory as true when they also claim there is no truth (Machan, 1977).

The popularization of knowledge construction. Stake does not en-dorse or use these assumptions in justifying the case study. In fact, he disavows any strong connection between case study methods and his epis-temological and ontological beliefs. But we can speculate about one inter-esting epistemological implication of his work. His theory of knowledge construction — like his theory of values — owes a considerable debt to his theory of social programming. Stake wants to use evaluation to help stakeholders determine what social changes they want to implement. He believes in the disciplined skepticism of science, but he also wants stakeholders to have more say about what counts as knowledge. So he says, "Whatever truths, whatever solutions there are, exist in the minds of people who are running the program, those participating in the program, those patrons of the program" (1975a, p. 36). The evaluator's job is to help local people discover and construct their own truths, their own definitions of the problem, and their own solutions. He is like Wholey in this regard. Wholey allows managers to determine what counts as an effective program improvement. Stake would disagree about Wholey's choice of stakeholder and methods, but agree that in our political system stakeholders should substantially control what counts as knowledge in political and social decisions.

We might call this the popularization (or democratization) of evaluative knowledge. Most theorists agree that the use of evaluation in policy and responsibility for social change are properly the purview of social and political institutions rather than professional evaluative ones. Stake also wants to give more responsibility for decisions about what counts as valid knowledge (and values) to laypersons, not evaluators. Popularization is contrasted with professionalization of knowledge, which emphasizes scientific control of decisions about valid knowledge. Popularization denies that evaluators have a privileged position in constructing knowledge, or that they produce knowledge that is more *socially* or *politically* warranted than that produced by laypersons (Stake, 1986b).

We see two potential problems with popularization of knowledge. First, sometimes Stake suggests that not all constructions of knowledge are equally good: "One can believe in relativity, contextuality, and constructivism without believing all views are of equal merit. Personal civility or political ideology may call for respecting every view, but scientific study does not" (R. E. Stake, personal communication, March 14, 1989). This puts scientific study in a privileged position to judge other views, but leaves many questions unanswered about the criteria and procedures through which science makes these judgments, and about any limits on this privilege. Stake's elevation of *stakeholder credibility* to the status of a criterion for good knowledge suggests this analysis is not far off base.

Stake's endorsement of popularization also explicitly disempowers some groups. The concerns of stakeholders are diverse, reflecting different problems and agendas that are sometimes greatly at odds with each other, or with credible evidence about what should count as knowledge.

The evaluator who too quickly accepts the constructions of any single stakeholder group risks drawing dysfunctional or incomplete conclusions; we have criticized Wholey for this. Stake minimizes such occurrences by presenting multiple constructions from different stakeholders with diverse perspectives. He is not explicit about exactly which groups he would include, but he tends toward inclusion rather than exclusion, with two exceptions. He rejects the constructions of two important groups with a legitimate perspective on the program — nonlocal stakeholders such as federal managers, and evaluators with different beliefs about how to construct knowledge.

Stake thinks nonlocal stakeholders can thwart the change efforts of local stakeholders, as with the Cities-in-Schools example (Stake, 1986b). But he does not claim that the perspectives of, say, federal managers are illegitimate, wrong, or less valid — only that they can be disruptive. Why is it not a valid knowledge construction, for instance, for the U.S. General Accounting Office (GAO) to criticize community mental health centers (CMHCs) for not meeting congressional implementation expectations, even though the GAO is far removed from the local CMHC? Local stakeholders do not have a pipeline to validity just because they are physically close to a program. They may lack exactly the perspective that federal and state stakeholders have gained through dealing with multiple local projects over places and time. This may have happened with one model of local CMHC evaluation that was locally controlled, with the evaluator trying to be responsive to local CMHC interests (Cook & Shadish, 1982). That model produced evaluation results that were used, but that were also criticized by many observers as producing relatively unimportant results compared with other ways the money might be spent (Cook & Shadish, 1982; Jerrell, 1986). As one well-placed observer put it: "We frittered away our potential in many, badly flawed, little studies of small problems of local agencies" (Windle, 1982, p. 296). Outside perspectives help compensate for local myopia (and vice versa, of course — as indicated by desegregation, where local stakeholder views about implementing desegregation in their communities could have received more attention to help ameliorate backlashes against busing).

The other group whose knowledge Stake omits is made up of preordinate evaluators, whom Stake says interfere too much and present an incomplete picture of the program from stakeholder perspectives. But an evaluation that leaves out constructions of preordinate evaluators may be no more complete than an evaluation that leaves out the constructions of responsive evaluators. Are not both perspectives worth having? Even if the preordinate evaluator changes the program by acting as stimulus, knowledge based on those changes is not necessarily invalid. If both perspectives are worth having, then one naturally would consider the joint use of responsive and preordinate methods — a development some qualitative theorists resist.

Stake might respond that the benefits of the preordinate evaluator's perspective are outweighed by the harm done in intruding into the natural ecology of the program (1986b). This harm is the same as that caused by federal and state agencies that impose social programs on the local level — the "quieting" of local-level reform efforts. But Stake's criticism is again one-sided. In balancing local stakeholder self-determination against the interests of other parties, Stake neglects the harm done to those other interests when they are excluded. Federal and state representatives, policymakers, and managers have a political warrant from local voters to inquire into, form opinions about, and even intervene in local affairs. When acting responsibly, preordinate evaluators share in this warrant when they are directly commissioned through grants and contracts, or are indirectly legitimated through provision of tax dollars to fund university research. Their legitimate interests, and indirectly the interests of the nation, can be harmed in a responsive evaluation that excludes them. Inequities can occur when these sometimes conflicting interests are joined together in a single evaluation. Such trade-offs are an intrinsic part of an interest group democracy. Their resolution is not always easy, but excluding one set of interests by decree is hardly a functional solution, especially since the decree could not be enforced because the community of preordinate and responsive evaluators is just as much an interest group democracy as is American society as a whole.

Credibility as a criterion for knowledge. Stake subscribes to some traditional notions of checking validity, including triangulation, confirmation, and disconfirmation (Stake & Easley, 1978). But he adds a new requirement, that a report must be credible before it is valid (Stake & Easley, 1978, p. C:28). Credible reports are more likely to be used, and case studies are the best way to produce credible reports. But credibility is not a matter of validity; it is a matter of whether the report is *perceived* to be true rather than whether it *is* true. Sometimes the truth is not credible — witness Galileo's contention that the earth was not the center of the universe, or modern particle physics' findings about causation over large distances (Davies, 1984). Sometimes what is credible is not true — witness Orson Wells's infamous radio broadcast of *War of the Worlds*, which apparently convinced many of a Martian invasion. In principle, credibility is orthogonal to validity.

Nor is it clear that case studies *best* facilitate credibility. Other formats facilitate use; to the extent that use implies credibility, other formats can be credible. Moreover, case studies can suffer from lack of credibility compared with more traditional, quantitative methods (Johnson, 1985; McClintock & Greene, 1985). Methods such as the sample survey fit more readily into the expectations of many stakeholders for what counts as "scientific" work, and seem to be perceived as more fairly representing a broad array of perspectives than the case study. McClintock and Greene (1985) say that one reason their evaluation client attended more to their survey than to their case study "was the symbolic value of a questionnaire. Because the questionnaire would sample widely within the organization and would quantify the findings, it had political and scientific credibility" (p. 354). When credibility is a desirable goal, the case study may not always be the best way to achieve it.

Stake's constructivist reality. Stake's discussion of a constructivist reality is preliminary and tentative; a meticulous analysis of it may be premature. Its general tenets—that there probably is an external reality that we cannot know directly, that all knowledge is a human construction, and that the disciplined skepticism of science is good for knowledge development—are reasonably consistent with modern epistemology and ontology in evaluation (Campbell, 1977, 1984c, 1986b; Cook, 1985) and philosophy (Brown, 1977; Fuller, 1989). However, his discussion contains ambiguities that might be worth discussing in more detail should Stake ever return to the topic. First, Stake alludes to a privileged position for scientific study that is not clear in nature, and may be inconsistent with the popularization of knowledge implicit in his work. Second, Stake notes that the price of believing in reality, if there is no reality, is small. But the price is potentially large if one person imposes a particular construction of reality on another through social, political, economic, or military means. We have social institutions to ameliorate such disputes, but even science is not immune to them. Conversely, the price of not believing in reality, if there is one, is potentially enormous if we then overlook real dangers that threaten our very existence, or real opportunities for progress. The choice about believing in reality is partly about which of these two dangers to risk.

Third, Stake asserts that the aim of research is not to test the correspondence between his Reality 1 and Reality 2, and that it is impossible to discover reality. Granted, we may never know if and when we have succeeded in these tasks. But we can try to do science in such a way that, if there is an external reality, we seem to be most likely to tap into it (Campbell, 1977). This is short of the goal of discovering reality, but does allow science to explore possible correspondences between Reality 1 and Reality 2. Because Reality 2 depends on Reality 1 *definitionally*, it is difficult to see how Stake's conception cannot allow Reality 1 a role in science.

Theory of Valuing

Stake treats values exactly as he treats all knowledge. Just as he says, "Whatever truths, whatever solutions there are, exist in the minds of people who are running the program, those participating in the program, those patrons of the program" (1975a, p. 36), so he also says, "A program has no single true value. . . . The value of an arts-in-education program will be different for different people, for different purposes" (1975b, p. 25). Just as he subordinates professional standards about knowledge to local stakeholders' standards, so too he subordinates evaluators judgments about value to local stakeholders' values. Stake has a nearly pure form of descriptive valuing. He lets local stakeholders describe the criteria of merit by which they judge the program, the standards of performance to which they hold the program, what they will count as valid measures of program performance, and how they weight criteria in forming a final value judgment. Scriven might say that Stake totally abrogates his responsibility to make value judgments; Stake might respond that Scriven usurps local stakeholders' prerogative to make their own judgments on matters that affect their own lives.

Given the parallels between Stake's theories of knowledge and values, all the advantages and disadvantages of his theory of knowledge apply directly to his theory of values. Hence we do not repeat those arguments here, but summarize highlights. Stake's approach (a) focuses attention on the crucial importance of reflecting local stakeholder values, (b) empowers local stakeholders to judge the worth of their own programs, and (c) creates a good match between the values expressed in evaluation and the values that hold sway in local decisions. But his approach (a) ignores the values of some stakeholders who are distant from the program but who have legitimate interests in it; (b) provides a less critical perspective on the value of the program than if prescriptive ethical theories were considered, such as House's (1980) application of Rawls's theory of justice to social programming; and (c) may be biased by whatever biases local stakeholders share about program value.

Stake's descriptive approach to values is similar to that of most other theorists, Scriven being the salient exception. This descriptive approach is both politically practical and ethically warranted in an interest group democracy where multiple values contend freely against each other. Unlike Wholey's reliance on a limited set of stakeholders such as program managers to nominate value judgments, and unlike Campbell's reliance on a limited kind of criteria of merit such as program effectiveness, Stake's reliance on multiple stakeholders and multiple criteria of merit is likely to generate an extremely wide array of perspectives for judging a program.

We disagree with Stake's limited approach to using the case study to generate these perspectives, but we endorse his emphasis on diversity of perspectives (Shadish, 1986a; Shadish et al., 1982).

Theory of Practice

Responsive evaluation is logically distinct from case study methods since it is quite possible to use a case study without doing responsive evaluation. Nearly all evaluation theorists make a place today for the case study even though they do not endorse responsive evaluation generally (Rossi & Wright, 1984). They use the case study for reasons other than those Stake gives, predominantly because it generates and maintains a discovery capacity in evaluation. Conversely, one can do responsive evaluation without using case study methods. Wholey does not give case study methods a major role, but might well do responsive evaluation according to Stake's definition: "*responsive evaluation* (1) . . . orients more directly to program activities than to program intents, (2) . . . responds to audience requirements for information, and (3) . . . different value-perspectives of the people at hand are referred to in reporting the success and failure of the program" (1980a, p. 77). Wholey attends greatly to program activities, probably more so than to program intents. He certainly responds to audience needs for information, albeit more management needs than other stakeholder information needs. Finally, there are few conceptual or logistical obstacles to implementing Wholey's approach in the more diverse mode to reflect different value perspectives. Evaluators could do responsive evaluation with a small adaptation of Wholey's methods.

To be or not to be responsive most of the time? Stake says evaluators should be responsive most of the time. Being responsive implies not being preordinate — not imposing treatments on local programs, not using traditional tests, not emphasizing the information needs and values of management, not issuing traditional research reports. Being responsive also implies letting questions emerge, attending to diverse values and information needs, and examining program activities rather than intents. But one can think of many situations in which these prescriptions would hinder evaluators. For example, federal and state public sector evaluators are often involved in implementing and evaluating certain regulations that will be imposed on the local level, are given prior questions to answer by legitimate authorities, are told to limit attention to certain information needs and values, or are required to assess whether program implementation mirrors the intents of Congress. In the private sector, similar demands are even more pressing; to ignore them is to risk seriously one's ability to respond to requests for proposals and contracts from funders. Academic

evaluators routinely do many things that are the antithesis of or orthogonal to responsive evaluation; they would find Stake's restrictions an unwanted fetter on their work. Whether or not Stake is in principle right or
wrong about the merits of responsive evaluation, his proposal is just not
practical for many evaluators.

All these evaluators could be wrong. Perhaps the pressures of evaluation practice mislead them into doing evaluations that are not responsive.
But this assertion is plausible only if the demands on and concerns of these
evaluators are illegitimate — for example, if legislators and program managers have no right to impose questions and regulations, if private sector
evaluators should not respond to requests for proposals (RFPs) that request
"preordinate" evaluation (note the irony here — doing "responsive" evaluation means not being responsive to the RFP), or if academic evaluators
should not study program effectiveness using the randomized experiment
or meta-analytic reviews. These contentions seem only plausible if we
agree with all of Stake's theoretical rationales — that there is too much
federal and state intervention, that local stakeholders are the only legitimate judges of programs, that these stakeholders are also the best judges
of what is to count as legitimate knowledge, and that the most important
use evaluators can pursue is naturalistic generalization. Since these theoretical rationales are questionable, the prescription to be responsive most
of the time is greatly weakened.

The responsive-preordinate distinction is superficially attractive. The
jargon is simple and memorable, and implies a comprehensive symmetry
capturing the domain of possible evaluation practices in a pair of all-
inclusive opposites. It is no surprise these terms have joined the list of
popular technical evaluation jargon like Campbell's internal and external
validity, or Scriven's formative and summative evaluation. Jargon plays
a central role in popularizing theory. But the virtues that may contribute
to the coining and adopting of successful technical jargon also create
hazards. Terminological simplicity may fail to capture the complexity
underlying the term. The seeming comprehensiveness of the symmetric
terms may not capture all of the domain at issue. The internal and external
validity distinction proposed by Campbell and Stanley (1963), for example, was expanded by Cook and Campbell (1979) into four terms to capture
the domain better; then Campbell (1986a) proposed completely new terminology that he felt more accurately described the underlying concepts —
replacing *internal validity* with *local molar causal validity* and *external
validity* with the *principle of proximal similarity*. The replacement terms
do not have the same beneficial characteristics of the original ones: They
are not simple, memorable, or obviously symmetric, and so they may not

be widely adopted. Such trade-offs between accuracy and popular adoption of jargon are not well understood, and are worth further study.

The preordinate-responsive distinction may not do justice to either Stake's or others' theories of evaluation practice. Responsive evaluation is not responsive in providing a tailored, contingency-driven response to varying situations that evaluators encounter. It is quite nonresponsive in this ordinary language sense: it imposes the same method on all evaluation situations regardless of whether it best meets the client's wants or needs. A label such as *case study evaluation* more accurately conveys the underlying construct. *Preordinate evaluation* describes only one alternative to responsive evaluation, evaluation that primarily relies on stated program goals, uses objective tests, emphasizes standards held by program personnel, issues research-type reports, and imposes treatments onto programs (Stake, 1980a). Other alternatives to responsive evaluation exist — as illustrated by practically any evaluation theorists we cover in this book. The responsive-preordinate distinction implies a comprehensiveness belied by the diversity of evaluation practice. It might be wise for Stake to reconsider the responsive-preordinate distinction, just as Campbell has done with internal-external validity.

Should evaluators use case study methods most of the time? The answer to this question does not depend on whether one should do responsive evaluation most of the time. Evaluators ought to rely on the case study to the extent that it gives them information they need. Under many legitimate circumstances, case studies do not provide such information. They provide information that is characterized by bandwidth rather than fidelity (Cronbach et al., 1980) — providing answers to a wide array of questions rather than a single question. Stake wants case studies to be responsive to diverse stakeholders, and diverse stakeholders have diverse questions. The higher the quality of information one wants in answer to a question, the more it will cost. But attending to all local stakeholder information needs requires spreading scarce evaluation resources thinly over all questions, providing poorer-quality answers to many questions rather than better answers to a few questions. This strategy is sound sometimes, but often it is distinctly undesirable to spread one's resources so thin — for example, when a program manager wants to monitor a specific category such as service hours or costs, when a federal policymaker wants to know if a program is implemented as intended, or when an academic evaluator wants to judge whether or not a program has been effective.

Moreover, the case study is not the only method that can produce high-bandwidth information. Surveys can do the same thing. Case studies are more discovery oriented, whereas surveys require forming questions ahead of time; and case studies excel at providing contextual information to aid naturalistic generalizations, while surveys can excel at providing statistically generalizable results. To prefer the case study, the evaluator must not only want bandwidth rather than fidelity, but must also decide that few questions are known ahead of time to be interesting, and that the primary use of the evaluation is by readers who cannot experience the program themselves and who want extensive contextual information about that particular case to decide how relevant the evaluation is to their own local situations. These conditions may occur individually from time to time, but the simultaneous conjunction of all these events seems unlikely — some questions are often known ahead of time, higher-quality answers to fewer questions are sometimes wanted, and the primary use might be something other than providing contextual information to those who cannot experience the program directly themselves.

Note an odd implication in one of these assumptions. Responsive evaluations focus on local stakeholder information needs and values. Yet local stakeholders are the least likely to need the vicarious experience of their own program that is provided by a case study's contextual information. The case study reporting format primarily benefits those who will not have direct contact with the program. If this is so, Stake's justification for the case study reporting format implies that people other than local stakeholders are likely to be an audience for the evaluation results, an audience whom Stake must think are too important to be ignored if case study formats are primarily for their benefit. If so, one wonders why their needs are not taken into account sooner than at the reporting point. This reinforces a point made earlier in our discussions of use — advocating case study reports to increase use is separate from advocating case study methods for creating knowledge.

The evaluator who chooses the case study must accept other losses as well. One is that high-quality answers to some questions are better provided by other methods. When confirmations of causal relationships are desired in social research, most methodologists prescribe some form of experiment, although case studies can be used for confirming causal hypotheses in very rare circumstances (Campbell, 1975b; Cook et al., 1985; Scriven, 1976c). When descriptions of a population are desired, most methodologists recommend sampling methodology. Evaluators face these circumstances often enough to question a routine reliance on case studies.

Another problem is how to analyze and summarize case study data once they have been gathered. Several books help evaluators approach this task, including works by Miles and Huberman (1984) and Patton (1980). In both these books, however, numbers begin to find a place, blurring the distinction between quantitative and qualitative methods. This quantification may be happening for similar reasons that account for why meta-analysis is widely used in literature reviews. Numbers make it easier to keep track of large amounts of data. Other summarization techniques for case studies are not quantitative. But in either case, some summarization is almost required the more material is presented in a single case study, and the more case studies are presented. The capacity of humans to process large amounts of data is just too limited for us to cope with the task otherwise (Faust, 1984). The case study report may facilitate naturalistic generalization, but it may not be the most efficient, practical means of summarizing and presenting results.

A related problem concerns constructing generalizations over sites from case study methods that presume idiosyncratic site uniqueness. Few federal and state evaluation clients will be satisfied with an approach to evaluation that fails to attempt some generalizations. They might rebel entirely against the notion that no generalization is possible, since policymaking requires making some generalizations about what is likely to happen if certain policies are implemented. Such stakeholders rarely have time to read one case study from cover to cover, much less to read several case studies from a multisite study and then to struggle long with drawing their own generalizations. Unless it copes with this problem, case study methodology will have limited federal and state appeal.

Finally, there is the problem of credibility. Stake believes that evaluators and clients "will often find that case studies of several students may more interestingly and faithfully represent the educational program than a few measurements on all of the students" (1975b, p. 25). But the evidence may not favor this claim. We have only a small literature documenting experience with qualitative methods, especially when used with quantitative methods, and the accumulation of more such literature (for all evaluation methods) is a high priority (Shadish & Epstein, 1987). Sometimes the use of qualitative methods seems quite successful (Maxwell et al., 1986; Trend, 1979), but in other instances (Johnson, 1985; McClintock & Greene, 1985) qualitative approaches have been *less* credible and useful to the client than quantitative ones. Granted, in both instances the client was imbued with quantitative methodology and so had difficulty accepting the relatively foreign paradigm of case study inquiry. But this was not the only problem. In the federal study, when resources were short and clients had to choose, they rejected the qualitative inquiries as providing merely redundant illustrations of the more credible and generalizable survey results.

Stake wants evaluators to use case study methods most of the time, but this choice makes sense only when the following conditions are met routinely in an evaluator's practice:

(1) The evaluator wants bandwidth rather than fidelity.

(2) Few if any questions are known ahead of time to be interesting.

(3) The evaluation is primarily going to be used by readers who cannot experience the program themselves and who want extensive contextual information to help decide how relevant that local site is to their own.

(4) The evaluator can forgo higher-quality answers to specific questions that might be yielded by other methods.

(5) A succinct summary of evaluation results is not a high priority.

(6) Succinct generalizations over sites are also not needed.

(7) Case studies will be seen as sufficiently credible to the client.

(8) Discovery is a higher priority than confirmation.

There are probably some circumstances in which these conditions are met, perhaps at the early stages of implementation of a new program, where goals and procedures are in flux (Rossi & Wright, 1984). But it is unlikely that most of these conditions will be met most of the time in most of the situations evaluators commonly face. The fewer of these conditions that are met, the more likely it is either that the case study ought to be used in conjunction with other methods or that the case study ought to be dropped entirely in favor of other methods that provide better information for the evaluation situation at hand.

CONCLUSION

Evaluation owes Stake a deep debt for his persistent advocacy of case study methods. All our criticisms should not detract from that fact. But frankly, we cannot think of any evaluator to whom we would routinely recommend doing only responsive evaluation using the case study method, with one pragmatic exception. An evaluator might specialize in this approach in order to corner the local market in it, as at least one private sector firm has done. But this evaluator must recognize that such a specialization might well preclude getting many evaluation contracts and grants where the responsive approach is not appropriate or desired, and that a wide array of interesting evaluation situations would probably remain unavailable except perhaps through subsidiary contracts with primary investigators.

In most cases, we would advise evaluators to incorporate the case study approach as one part of a more integrated repertoire that includes all of the more traditional methods. Achievement of this integration requires several more developments in evaluation theory. First, we need a better understanding of the relative strengths and weaknesses of the case study approach. Its premier strength is in facilitating naturalistic generalization, but it is also more "expansionist than reductionist," and advantageous for "theory building" and "for exploration" (Stake, 1978, p. 7) as opposed to theory confirmation and hypothesis testing. Presumably in these quotations Stake is endorsing the common perception that case studies are relatively stronger for discovery than for confirmation tasks in science. Similarly, Stake recognizes the difficulties of drawing generalizations from individual case studies—a task that is probably essential if his approach is to be used widely. More such elaborations are needed to help establish case study methodology in its rightful place in evaluation.

Stake might agree with us. He is aware of many limits of case study methods, and admits to overstating the case for how often such methods ought to be used in evaluation (Stake, 1975a, 1981). Since early evaluation traditions made no place for the case study approach, he understandably might have felt a need to advocate the case study so as to counteract the inertia of the status quo. But that time has passed. Case study methodology now has a place in nearly all evaluation theories; to argue that we still need to overstate the case for case study methods simply is not credible anymore. Stake, who so rightly points out the importance of credibility in facilitating the use of evaluation findings, overlooks the role of credibility in facilitating the use of his own theory. A credible evaluation theory needs a place for multiple methods, and must make explicit the contingencies that guide selection of one method over another when time, circumstances, and resources force the choice. Just as a narrow focus on experimental and quasi-experimental methods proved insufficient to the task in evaluation's early years, so today a narrow focus on any one other method, be it case study or anything else, is equally insufficient to the complexities of the field. In the next chapters, we examine the theories of two evaluators who have tried to integrate case study methods—indeed, all the methods of the first two stages—into comprehensive theories of evaluation.

PART IV

Stage Three Theories:
Trying to
Integrate the Past

Scriven and Campbell made definite recommendations about "what evaluators ought to be doing." By substituting one dogma for another, Wholey and Stake abandoned the strengths of the early idealists and precluded the formation of cumulative theories of evaluation. Weiss did not succumb as much to the "what evaluators ought to be doing" mentality. After abandoning sole reliance on an experimental paradigm, she focused more on theoretical than practical problems, on overall issues like use and the intransigence of social problems. She tried to retain an emphasis on truth and social problem solving while remedying problems that first-stage theorists encountered in being useful. She did not entirely succeed in this, given her silence about methods for practice. But she exemplified the concerns to which the third-stage theorists have responded.

Third-stage theories have as their major focus the synthesis of work from preceding stages. They attend not just to descriptive knowledge about use and social programming, but also to requirements for valid knowledge about which the first-stage theorists were so concerned. Foremost among these synthesizing theorists are Cronbach and Rossi. Both have developed theories of tailored, comprehensive evaluation that confer legitimacy upon methods and concepts that came before, but conditionally, so that the legitimacy of a method or concept depends on the circumstances. Cronbach and Rossi are integrators. They survey the diverse prescriptions that have appeared since the 1960s, and try to fit the puzzle together into a coherent whole. They try to leave no legitimate position out of that whole, denying that all evaluators ought to be doing one thing always and everywhere. They have created contingency theories, trying to specify under which circumstances and for which purposes different practices make sense.

THEORY OF SOCIAL PROGRAMMING

Third-stage theorists agree that social programs are politically affected, that they change gradually, that improving existing programs offers the best chance to contribute to short-term social change, and that radical change requires a longer-term perspective. But Cronbach and Rossi disagree with Wholey and Stake that programs and policies turn over too rarely to make policy change a central topic of study. Incremental change may be more feasible and practical, but we must *also* know about program and policy effects since abrupt and novel changes do sometimes occur. Weiss would agree with Cronbach and Rossi.

Cronbach claims that evaluations are primarily used to justify and improve *future* programs, not the program being evaluated. On rare occasions, some of these uses will be about decisions to replace policies or programs. So Cronbach gives some resources to evaluations that study which programs work if the evaluation probes the conditions under which it works, if such information is not available, and if it bears on issues that will reoccur on the political agenda. Cronbach distinguishes between incremental improvements that are more and less important; more than Wholey or Stake, he would not do work he judges to be less important. For him, importance depends on the money at stake, how many people and sites are affected, whether beneficial side effects might occur, and how many related programs and projects might benefit from the information. Cronbach, albeit implicitly, counters the notion in some second-stage theories that judgments of importance are solely the business of stakeholders. To Cronbach, some second-stage theorists carried the emphasis on incremental change too far, making it an end in itself regardless of the importance of the change.

Rossi acknowledges the central role of incremental change in a practical theory of evaluation. He accepts the fixity of existing programs, and prescribes practices that facilitate program improvement. But he also wants evaluation to have a role for bold program changes. His solution is very Campbellian — evaluating novel demonstration projects as trial runs for new social programs. He wants to ensure that evaluative information about bold innovations is available to policymakers when, in the future, they have the latitude to introduce new programs and policies (Polsby, 1984). Furthermore, Rossi's experimental evaluations of demonstration projects place more emphasis on theoretical explanation and on causal mediating processes than would Campbell, for Rossi ascribes a larger role to explanation in facilitating generalization.

THEORY OF USE

The naive instrumentalist theory of use from the first-stage evaluation theorists is, and should be, gone forever. Cronbach and Rossi try to integrate the positions of second-stage theorists—enlightenment and a more sophisticated instrumental use where stakeholders set evaluation questions and monitor evaluation progress. Weiss mostly preferred enlightenment. Stake emphasized enlightenment, but he had no problems with stakeholders using information instrumentally. Wholey was concerned almost exclusively with instrumental use, never addressing enlightenment.

Rossi and Cronbach integrate these two kinds of use in similar ways. To facilitate instrumental use, they follow a generalized version of Wholey's theory, with instrumental use being assisted when the evaluator identifies potential users prior to the study, discovers issues currently of most instrumental concern to them, maintains frequent contact during an evaluation, focuses on things stakeholders can control, and does all this in a timely manner even at the cost of lowering the quality of information. Both Rossi and Cronbach assume that some evaluators are better placed than others to facilitate instrumental use, especially those who work routinely with those responsible for making changes—for example, the evaluator who works for a federal program manager or the local evaluator who answers questions of staff.

Cronbach and Rossi also make a similar place for enlightenment (Berk & Rossi, 1977; Cronbach et al., 1980). Like Weiss, they tell evaluators to study questions that deal with root causes of social problems, and why our efforts at changing them have met with such difficulties. They both note that evaluation for enlightenment should be bolder than evaluation for incremental change. Cronbach discusses institutional arrangements to facilitate enlightening evaluations—for example, task force panels that summarize what is known about a problem and its solutions to help inform and guide policy-making. Compared to evaluation for instrumental use, evaluation for enlightenment is more likely to be conducted by evaluators who are not under immediate pressure to respond to requests for specific information, to provide answers about pending decisions, or otherwise to make their evaluations immediately useful. Such evaluations may be more often conducted by academic evaluators, or perhaps evaluators located in "think-tank" research centers that are well-enough funded to afford the luxury of reflection.

THEORY OF KNOWLEDGE CONSTRUCTION

Rossi and Cronbach recognize that no single paradigm for knowledge construction has sufficient empirical or theoretical support to dominate the field. Both recognize that evaluation is characterized by multiple epistemologies, multiple methods, and multiple priorities for the kinds of knowledge that are important.

Rossi is more traditional in his epistemological thinking, approaching evaluation as a quantitatively trained social scientist with a realist inclination. He writes little on epistemology or philosophy of science, so it is difficult to ascribe a position to him with confidence. Over time, Cronbach has incorporated less and less traditional epistemological and ontological concepts into his writing. One now sees more explicit doubts about the nature and quality of knowledge construction in social science. Neither Cronbach nor Rossi proposes a new paradigm for the field; neither offers a resolution of epistemological conflicts in evaluation. Rather, their work is characterized by serious doubt about old ways of thinking, by openness to new ways, and by skepticism toward anyone who claims to have *the* answer. They are epistemologically humble.

Campbell and Scriven prioritized on causal knowledge. Second-stage theorists still gave priority to certain kinds of knowledge. Wholey nearly always prioritized on program description, and Stake on discovery. Cronbach and Rossi avoid assigning across-the-board priorities about which kinds of knowledge are most important. In the early stages of program development, when little is known about the problem and its solutions, they prioritize on discovery and on describing program implementation. For new programs, their theories share concepts and methods with Stake and with parts of Wholey's sequential purchase of information that are more discovery oriented. When a program is large and has been in place for a long time, they propose the kinds of descriptive monitoring techniques suggested by Wholey, including descriptive analyses of program outcomes. When the evaluator has specific causal hypotheses worth investigating, Cronbach and Rossi recommend experimental methods or sophisticated causal modeling techniques.

Rossi and Cronbach want evaluators to study program description, causation, explanation, and generalization, sometimes including all of them in the same study, albeit with different priority depending on circumstances. Neither would conduct an evaluation that has no capacity for discovery, that provides no descriptive information about the program, or that does not help future users determine how well present findings might generalize. Rossi and Cronbach do not agree completely, however. Cronbach would give explanation and generalization a higher priority than Rossi, and Rossi would more often prioritize on causal inference.

First- and second-stage theorists had favorite methods they recommended most of the time. No third-stage evaluation theorist has this characteristic. Methodological pluralism unites Rossi and Cronbach. In their work one finds a place for all methods espoused by previous theorists — case study, sample survey, and randomized experiment. For them, method choice depends on the strengths and weaknesses of methods for meeting the information need.

Rossi and Cronbach discuss the strengths and weaknesses of different methods in terms of feasibility, validity, and capacity for exploration versus confirmation. Within this framework they agree that the case study provides thick description, is discovery oriented, but is relatively weak for confirming causal hypotheses and providing generalizable results; that the randomized experiment answers a narrow cause-effect question at particular sites in the past, and is weak for discovery, for explaining observed causal relationships, and for helping the evaluator know if an established causal connection generalizes; that the sample survey and the case study can both provide answers to many kinds of evaluation-relevant questions, but that the sample survey is less discovery oriented than the case study. They do not agree on everything; Rossi is less critical of causal modeling, while Cronbach is less critical of the case study. Both also agree it is desirable to use multiple methods when possible because no single method provides a complete and unbiased answer (Cook, 1985). So Rossi advocates joint use of randomized experiments and causal modeling, and Cronbach advocates the joint use of quantitative and qualitative techniques.

THEORY OF VALUING

Criteria of merit. First-stage theorists rendered judgments about how good a program was. Second-stage theorists denounced this because evaluators' values are bound to intrude, and because the American political system is built upon giving stakeholders the right to make these judgments. Third-stage theorists take a middle ground between these positions. Cronbach is closer to second-stage theorists than Rossi, advising the evaluator to be sensitive to the values of the "policy-shaping community" that evaluators serve. Yet he also asks evaluators to be educators of stakeholders, to sensitize them to the needs and values of other stakehold-ers, and to show them alternative perspectives about the program. Rossi advises evaluators to reflect the values of stakeholders, but he also brings needs assessments back into evaluation as a criterion against which pro-gram value should be measured. Rossi calls for substantive social science theories to provide independent perspectives on what the program should be doing (Chen & Rossi, 1983). In third-stage evaluation theories, reliance on stakeholders is complemented by the use of independent sources of values.

Rossi and Cronbach draw on many sources in constructing criteria of merit: (a) examination of the claims that clients, service deliverers, and program managers make about program effects and about factors respon-sible for effects; (b) factors that feed into decisions that policymakers or managers are likely to make in the near future; (c) assessment of substan-tive models to explain how program inputs should be transmuted into subsequent processes and from there into outcomes; (d) estimation of how much the material needs of clients are met; and (e) searches for all program effects, whether intended or not, harmful or beneficial. Cronbach and Rossi intend these multiple sources to inform the evaluator about the range of values relevant to the program, so that no important values are overlooked.

Scriven and Campbell judged programs against critical competitors. Second-stage theorists varied on this issue. Wholey judged program worth against absolute performance levels set by program management; Stake let stakeholders construct standards; Weiss endorsed both comparative and absolute standards depending on the circumstances. The third-stage theo-rists are less clearly integrative on this issue. Cronbach has long advocated absolute standards, having publicly disagreed with Scriven about this. Rossi uses both absolute and comparative standards. Rossi and Freeman (1985) invoke absolute standards when discussing whether a program is meeting needs, but invoke comparative standards by their use of compar-ison groups in experiments.

Scriven combined results into a single value judgment about the worth of the program; Campbell agreed with the sentiment, but disagreed that this had to combine the results of all variables. Second-stage theorists said evaluators who render summative value judgments interfere in the busi-ness of stakeholders; evaluators should merely report how programs do on each criterion. Cronbach and Rossi mostly argue that separate summative conclusions should be presented for each criterion, because different conclusions warrant different confidence, and individual conclusions are less likely to be challenged if they stand alone than if they are part of a synthesis that depends on a weighting system with which stakeholders will disagree. Neither shies away from judgments about the program within this constraint; Rossi has devoted a full chapter to cost-benefit analysis.

THEORY OF EVALUATION PRACTICE

With the exception of Weiss, first- and second-stage theorists told evaluators to conduct a specific set of practices most of the time, but those practices differed across theorists. Weiss recommended a large array of practices, but was less clear about when one ought to do each. Third-stage theories try to remedy this latter deficiency in Weiss, and to integrate the practice of other theorists, by specifying contingencies under which certain practices ought to be used. One major variable that controls these contingencies is the stage of program development. In Rossi's "tailored" evaluation theory, practices are tailored to a program still in the planning process, a demonstration project, or an existing program. Cronbach has a similar category system, but adds his notion of the leverage of different questions to specify these contingencies further. Both theorists arrive at similar recommendations. For each kind of program, their recommendations resemble those of previous theorists who wrote about how to do evaluation for that kind of program.

For example, when evaluating an existing program, both Rossi and Cronbach recommend program monitoring designed to improve programs incrementally. Their recommendations for evaluating existing programs are quite like Wholey's. When working with a new program, they recommend heavy investment in discovery-oriented techniques, including needs assessment techniques, case study methods, and the quantitative techniques that Wholey suggests for quickly gaining information about program implementation. The goal is to catch implementation problems, ensure the program is designed to meet relevant needs, and discover unexpected problems. In evaluating demonstration projects, both Rossi and Cronbach suggest methods for probing cause-and-effect relationships, including experimental and quasi-experimental methods and causal modeling techniques. Both want to maintain a descriptive capacity in such evaluations to describe mediating processes and assist generalizations.

These contingency theories have in common an effort to specify the conditions under which different evaluation practices make sense. After all, theorists of the first and second stage were reasonable, intelligent people. None of them was entirely wrong. Contingency theories assume that all past theories were reasonable solutions to some problems that evaluators faced. We endorse that assumption and its corollary of finding the good in past work and specifying how it can best be adapted. We much prefer this to assuming that one group of theorists is right and the rest wrong, or that we should pick a winner from among the first two stages of theory. Progress in evaluation theory will be facilitated best by such integrative efforts, by finding ways to create a coherent, useful whole out of apparently disparate parts.

8

Lee J. Cronbach:

Functional Evaluation Design for a World of Political Accommodation

KEY TERMS AND CONCEPTS

Social Inquiry: The class of study to which evaluation belongs, it seeks knowledge about the social world using quantitative social research, history, ethnography, journalism, and critical reflection.

Political Accommodation: How decisions are reached in policy settings, in contrast with a model of decision making as "command" in which a decision maker facing a specific decision takes relevant information and decides.

Policy-Shaping Community: Stakeholders who shape policy through interaction; may include legislators, officials at program central office, officials at the local service level, program constituents, and scholars, journalists, and others who do social inquiry.

Generalizability Theory: A measurement theory to estimate the influence of factors irrelevant to the construct.

Generalization Through Explanation: A central task of evaluation is to facilitate the transfer of knowledge from some programs or sites to other programs or sites through explaining the processes that cause or prevent the outcomes achieved.

Functional Evaluation Design:	Evaluations fulfill multiple functions, so trade-offs must be made when allocating evaluation resources. By contrast, structural theories of design create measures, treatment groups, and treatment assignment to justify a single causal inference, directing attention away from important trade-offs.
Bandwidth and Fidelity:	Bandwidth denotes the range of issues broached, while fidelity denotes the accuracy of an answer. They are negatively related; for a fixed budget the resources for increasing fidelity reduce bandwidth.
Aptitude-Treatment Interactions:	Specify the types of persons one treatment serves better than another, and the settings and times that condition treatment effects.
utos:	The sample of units, treatments, observations, and settings in a research project.
UTOS:	The population of units, treatments, observations, and settings actually represented in the observed sample.
*UTOS:	Units, treatments, observations, and settings that manifestly differ from UTOS. Generalization to *UTOS is the main function of evaluation, permitting transfer of knowledge across diverse localities, times, and programs.
sub-utos:	Subsamples of the data, such as breakdowns by ethnicity, one treatment realization versus another, one operationalization of outcome rather than another, or one class of setting versus another.

BACKGROUND

Cronbach is a giant of social science methodology. He took the Stanford-Binet at age 4, attaining a remarkably high score that led a psychologist-mentor to want to further his talents (Cronbach, 1989b). He completed high school at 14, and graduated from Fresno State College at 18 with dual majors in mathematics and chemistry. Fresno State was a teacher's college; after he evaluated an idea to improve a course, the professor asked whether he might like to be an educational researcher. But he wanted to be a schoolteacher, so he next earned a teaching credential and a master's in education at the University of California, Berkeley. He took a doctorate in 1940 in educational psychology at the University of Chicago, concentrating mostly on measurement. Subsequently he taught at Washington State University (1940-1944), briefly did wartime naval research, and then taught at the University of Chicago until 1948, at University of Illinois, Champaign-Urbana (1948-1964), and Stanford (1964-1980), from which he retired. In his early career he cemented his reputation in education and measurement theory. Later, he extended his reputation with papers on the achievements and promises of social sciences in general. He has won awards in education, psychology, and evaluation; he is a member of the National Academy of Sciences, and was president of the American Psychological Association when holding that office still constituted scholarly recognition.

Four overlapping aspects of Cronbach's intellectual career will concern us: (a) measurement theory, (b) combining individual differences and experimental treatments in the study of aptitude-treatment interactions, (c) program evaluation, and (d) understanding what social scientists should aspire to know, and how well purely quantitative techniques allow social scientists to achieve these ends. These four themes are interdependent in time and content, and do not exhaust Cronbach's work. Even with these four themes, we cannot do justice to the constancies and changes of his 50-year career. His views on evaluation concern us most. Though he wrote only three works explicitly on evaluation, they are partly products of his other work, which we need to describe lest we misunderstand the intellectual framework from which he criticized evaluation and offered recommendations to improve it.

OUR RECONSTRUCTION OF
CRONBACH'S THEORY OF EVALUATION

The Intellectual Context

The earliest concerns with theories of measurement. Cronbach wrote much about measurement theory in his early career. A major contribution was the reliability coefficient now called Cronbach's alpha (Cronbach, 1951). Reliability was mostly estimated earlier by split-half techniques, alternate-forms reliability, or test-retest. Cronbach developed a general formula for the mean of all possible split-half coefficients for a test. Alpha remains the most used measure of internal consistency in the social sciences.

Cronbach and colleagues also developed a more ambitious generalizability theory (Cronbach, Gleser, Nanda, & Rajaratnam, 1972; Cronbach, Rajaratnam, & Gleser, 1963). This deemphasized the view that there is only one true score for an "entity" and only one true reliability coefficient for a test. Observed scores reflect variance due to many facets—characteristics of a physical test, testers, time, or circumstances of testing. Each facet has multiple conditions; if one test facet is observers, its conditions are the sample of observers in the study. Classical test theory diverts attention from such systematic sources of variance, relying instead on the assumption that all error is random. Potential test users at the local level are less interested in general statements about reliability than in how reliable a test is under the conditions in which they work: "An investigator asks about the precision or reliability of a measure because he wishes to generalize from the observation in hand to some class of observations to which it belongs" (Cronbach et al., 1963, p. 144). Generalizability theory inquires about the suitability of a test for particular users and purposes.

A generalizability study estimates variance components for measurements across facets and conditions that may influence test performance. A decision study collects data for making specific decisions. For example, the decision maker may need to know how many items to use in a job selection test. The generalizability study—which may or may not be conducted by the decision maker—might use, say, 10 items to estimate variance components from which generalizability coefficients are computed. If these coefficients suggest that 10 items yield insufficient reliability, the generalizability study can estimate how many more items are needed for acceptable reliability. The decision study then uses that number of items (probably after pilot testing) in deciding who to hire. Explaining sources of variability in test scores drives generalizability theory.

Generalizability theory has not been as widely used as Cronbach's alpha (Weiss & Davison, 1981), except among measurement theorists (Jones & Applebaum, 1989). Its statistical presentation in Cronbach et al. (1972) is daunting, and few researchers have been willing to spend the time to conceptualize the relevant facets and conditions and then collect and analyze the needed data. Practitioners find classical test theory adequate. Yet generalizability theory displays Cronbach at his most typical: identifying the limits of current theory; trying to understand the local, user-oriented determinants of the phenomena that interest him; and then proposing an alternative to the conventional wisdom. He did this on a smaller scale with coefficient alpha, and it is also what he tried to do with evaluation.

Cronbach's concern with reliability is interlocked with his concern with validity. With Paul Meehl he wrote a highly influential paper on construct validity (Cronbach & Meehl, 1955); Cronbach credits Meehl with much of the originality in the paper (Cronbach, 1986). Their starting point was the need to validate instruments when no adequate criterion is available. Concurrent and predictive validity correlate test data with such a criterion; content validity systematically samples items from a criterion domain. But it is hard to specify many social science constructs in order to sample items from them. Anxiety would be a case in point. For such cases Cronbach and Meehl proposed that validity depends on the fit between obtained data and the network of relationships in which a target construct is embedded in relevant theory. No single prediction is sufficient, since no one hypothesis adequately differentiates a construct from its cognates. At stake is a predicted pattern of results, including hypotheses about determinants and consequences of the construct. Thus Cronbach and Meehl used the positivistically tinged, hypothetico-deductive philosophy of the day to advocate a greater role for substantive theory in validation.

Most experimentalists presumably welcomed this, but perhaps not Cronbach's espousal of the need for both correlational and experimental evidence in the construct validity, which implied indifference about whether one style of research is superior — a key issue in the psychology of the 1950s. Cronbach preferred meeting a need to adhering to a method. And in making construct validation contingent on understanding theoretically specified sources of variation attributable to a construct, Cronbach linked validation to explanation — probably the most esteemed function of science. He rejects the notion that mere adherence to any particular method constitutes science.

The 1955 paper with Meehl remained the classic and most-cited paper on construct validity for decades. Cronbach (1989a) later expressed doubts about its hypothetico-deductivism, its overtones of confirmationism rather than falsificationism, and its certainty about differentiating construct validity from predictive and content validities. He also noted that this approach to construct validation is honored more in the breach than in the observance. Except for a few instances in personality assessment, measures are selected more for their content validity or prior use than for their grounding in theory. The multivariate substantive theories that Cronbach and Meehl's approach needs are often lacking, and may not be reasonable aspirations for social scientists. In a climate of careerist science, few researchers can devote years to the theoretical and empirical development of well-validated measures. Pressures exist to move ahead with novel theory, using the best available measures. It is not that Cronbach had abandoned the idea of concepts. He merely had doubts about the epistemological and sociological assumptions buttressing Cronbach and Meehl (1955). But no better theory of construct validation exists, and his early work remains the ideal in fields that deal with hypothetical, multidimensional, and unobservable phenomena.

Aptitude-treatment interactions. Cronbach and Meehl treated the correlational study of individual differences and the experimental study of
averages as companion tributaries to knowledge. Cronbach (1957) used
aptitude-treatment interactions to show how these two methods might join
in more powerful inquiries. He argued that such interactions are frequent;
predicting more outcome variance in experiments demands attention to
those features of individuals, situations, and times that interact with
treatments. He also argued that public policy offers opportunities to provide different treatments to groups with different needs. He opposed public
policy prescriptions (and experimental methods) that homogenize society
in favor of prescriptions that respond to the strengths and weaknesses of
different people. Twenty years later, he wrote:

> "Should the school group its students by ability?" is much too limited a question;
> research cast in this mold has inevitably given conflicting and useless results.
> *What* is done for the "fast" and "slow" groups has to be the focus of attention.
> Grouping will have negligible consequences for learning unless the treatment is
> redesigned to fit each kind of student. Streaming plans intended merely to
> simplify the teacher's task are properly condemned as perpetuating social strat-
> ification. Stratification in school is even more objectionable when the plans force
> different *kinds* of educational goals upon students with different abilities. For
> most purposes the school needs a plan that directs all learners in the same
> intellectual and developmental directions, but using procedures designed to fit
> each one's characteristics. Such a plan could hope to *reduce* social stratification.
> It is socially indefensible to give some children good education and some poor
> education. (Cronbach & Snow, 1977, p. 2)

In an explicit follow-up to the 1957 paper, Cronbach (1975) extended
the 1957 argument. He regretted that the earlier paper had not discussed
statistical interactions beyond first-order ones. A review of the education literature (Cronbach & Snow, 1977) convinced him that two-way
interactions are unstable, and that higher-order interactions are required
for dependable knowledge. If the explanation of events requires third-,
fourth-, or *n*th-order interactions, then social research should discover
and explain such interactions. In such a complex social world, dependable
knowledge will be hedged by multiple conditionals.

In both his monograph with Snow and the 1975 paper, he denied that
molar complexity was necessarily temporary, since general laws might
be developed to explain the complexity of higher-order interactions. Such
general laws operate in physical and biological sciences, providing parsimonious explanations of phenomena that seem complex at the molar level.
But he doubted that such laws are available to the social sciences because
the social world is in constant flux. Humans interpret their world and react

to these interpretations. Scholarly theories are interpretations to which humans react both individually and collectively, and in so doing they reduce a theory's explanatory power. If scholars learn about teacher expectancies and then teachers in training learn about them, teacher expectancies may no longer operate as they first did. For Cronbach, attainable theories will be local in time and space, and simple explanatory theories of any generality will be rare. He wants research to explain a complex world of human interaction. Aptitude-treatment interactions are one form of ontological complexity that Cronbach assumes for all social life.

Learning about a complex social world requires strong substantive theories and powerful methods, both of which social scientists currently lack. Referring to Mischel's (1973) hypotheses of seven factors that modify reactions to experimental treatments on delay of gratification, Cronbach (1975) notes that to probe all possible interrelationships among these seven factors requires 120 interactions! How can this be done? Cronbach and Snow's (1977) analysis does not offer much hope to practicing researchers, given (a) the many possible interacting variables that often can be invoked, (b) statistical power loss that accrues when testing interactions, (c) limits to traditional statistical methods—"Closure in the end will have to come more from the theoretical coherence of results than from the statistics alone" (Cronbach & Snow, 1977, p. 104)—(d) confounding of interaction effects within and between aggregate units (e.g., school classes) when multiple individuals make up the aggregate, and (e) practical difficulty of studying interactions involving time. No one can read Cronbach's work on aptitude-treatment interactions and conclude that they are rare, stable, or easily studied. After discussing why interactions of the form ability × age × subject matter × treatment × outcome should be common in education, Cronbach and Snow write:

> A program of research to track down the fourth-order interactions of any aptitude would require prohibitively large amounts of investigator and subject time. Furthermore, even if a fourth-order interaction were established, it would have so narrow a field of application that it could play little part in school policy. Furthermore, any real treatment is multidimensional and more than one ATI [aptitude-treatment interaction] may be relevant. (p. 518)

Cronbach (1975) ends with an exhortation to pay less attention to the null hypothesis when probing interactions, to pay more attention to Brunswik's theory of representative sampling, and to spend more time describing uncontrolled local details that provide contextual variables interacting with treatments to provide greater explanation and control. Not all contextual variables can be evaluated statistically, but the relevant data should be collected and presented to readers. Such details are the grist from which future theorists construct dependable interactions. But the resulting generalizations are tenuous:

> When we give proper weight to local conditions, any generalization is a working hypothesis, not a conclusion. The personnel tester, for example, long ago discovered the hazard in generalizing about predictive validity, because test validity varies with the labor pool, the conditions of the job, and the criterion. . . . Personnel testers are taught to collect local data before putting a selection scheme into operation, and periodically thereafter. . . . Intensive local observation goes beyond discipline to an open-eyed, open-minded appreciation of the surprises nature deposits in the investigative net. This kind of interpretation is historical more than scientific. I suspect that if the psychologist were to read more widely in history, ethnology, and the centuries of humanistic writings on man and society, he would be better prepared for this part of his work. (1975, p. 125)

In Cronbach and Snow (1977) and Cronbach (1975) we see Cronbach using experience to react against a dominant metatheory predicated upon discovering robust, lawlike main effects. He proposes a new metatheory predicated on multivariate explanatory complexity more appropriate for social inquiry than searching for general laws. But such complex, dependable, explanatory knowledge requires substantive theory and methodology not generally available, and requires long research programs. Given his purposes and this appraisal, Cronbach is forced to urge researchers to place more weight on interpretative, thick-descriptive methods (Cronbach, 1975) rather than methods traditionally espoused in social sciences—systematic sampling, experimentation, and quantitative data analysis. Some might think this advocacy is inconsistent with the hardheaded methods Cronbach developed for reliability, construct validity, and generalizability. But Cronbach's views on theory and method evolved. By the 1970s he began to use the phrase *social inquiry* rather than *social science* or *social research*—connoting the need for history, ethnography, and journalism to complement quantitative social science.

Throughout Cronbach's work run relentless, trenchant, thorough analysis; persistent emphasis on fundamentals; desire to learn from experience; and creativity in proposing new methods that respect the complexity of nature—if not the dedication and perseverance of most researchers. There are no free lunches in Cronbach's intellectual world, only pressures to specify more sources of variance in data, and to specify the processes through which one force affects another so as to yield generalized knowledge for transfer to new settings and persons. If traditional methods do not do this, then Cronbach would use or develop untraditional methods.

This is part of the intellectual journey Cronbach had made when he began working on his two evaluation books, and it had an impact on his thinking about evaluation. Before we explore such influences in his theory of evaluation, we first describe his earlier evaluation paper, which presaged some of the later themes.

"Course Improvement Through Evaluation" (1963): The Primacy of Formative Evaluation

In the preface to *Designing Evaluations of Educational and Social Programs* (1982a), Cronbach reflects on what propelled him to write that book:

> My training under Ralph W. Tyler from 1938 onward introduced me to a then-unorthodox view of evaluation; nearly two decades of close association with J. Thomas Hastings at the University of Illinois, another Tyler alumnus, reinforced those ideas. Although I wrote directly on program evaluation only once during that period, the paper (Cronbach, 1963) precipitated debate by encouraging the heresy now called formative evaluation. Outside the Tyler group, social scientists and policy makers had seen the central task of program evaluation to be the summing up of treatment effects. That view dominated the studies of instruction in science and mathematics that the National Science Foundation was sponsoring in the 1960's. Following Tyler, I argued that assessing the impact of a fixed plan is not the best use of evaluation; improving plans and operations is a higher goal, and one to which formal quantitative comparisons usually contribute little. The 1963 paper, stimulated by my conversations as consultant to the foundation and some of its projects, was an attempt to balance out the prevailing emphasis on summative evaluation. (p. xii)

The 1963 paper begins with an exposition of the multiple functions evaluation can play in curriculum evaluation:

> To draw attention to its full range of functions, we may define "evaluation" broadly as the *collection and use of information to make decisions about an educational program*. The program may be a set of instructional materials distributed nationally, the instructional activities of a single school, or the educational experiences of a single pupil. Many types of decisions are to be made, and many varieties of information are useful. It becomes immediately apparent that evaluation is a diversified activity and that no one set of principles will suffice for all situations. (p. 672)

This passage reveals the multiple functions and actors we usually find in Cronbach's analysis of issues (e.g., with generalizability theory) and the description and critique of the dominant orthodoxy that he frequently uses to advance his thinking. Here is the 1963 description and critique:

> Measurement specialists have so concentrated upon one process — the preparation of pencil-and-paper achievement tests for assigning scores to individual pupils — that the principles pertinent to that process have somehow become enshrined as the principles of evaluation. "Tests," we are told, "should fit the content of the curriculum." Also, "only those evaluation procedures should be used that yield reliable scores." These and other hallowed principles are not entirely appropriate to evaluation for course improvement. (p. 672)

And then:

> When evaluation is carried out in the service of course improvement, the chief aim is to ascertain what effects the course has — that is, what changes it produces in pupils. This is not to inquire merely whether the course is effective or ineffective. Outcomes of instruction are multidimensional, and a satisfactory investigation will map out the effects of the course along these dimensions separately. To agglomerate many types of post-course performance into a single score is a mistake, because failure to achieve one objective is masked by success in another direction. Moreover, since a composite score embodies (and usually conceals) judgments about the importance of the various outcomes, only a report that treats the outcomes separately can be useful to educators who have different value hierarchies.
>
> The greatest service evaluation can perform is to identify aspects of the course where revision is desirable. Those responsible for developing a course would like to present evidence that their course is effective. They are intrigued by the idea of having an "independent testing agency" render a judgment on their product. But to call in the evaluator only upon the completion of course development, to confirm what has been done, is to offer him a menial role and to make meager use of his services. To be influential in course improvement, evidence must be available midway in curriculum development, not in the home stretch, when the developer is naturally reluctant to tear open a supposedly finished body of materials and techniques. Evaluation, used to improve the course while it is still fluid, contributes more to improvement of education than evaluation used to appraise a product already placed on the market. . . .
>
> Insofar as possible, evaluation should be used to understand how the course produces its effects and what parameters influence its effectiveness. It is important to learn, for example, that the outcome of programmed instruction depends very much upon the attitude of the teacher; indeed, this may be more important than to learn that on the average such instruction produces slightly better or worse results than conventional instruction.
>
> Hopefully, evaluation studies will go beyond reporting on this or that course and help us to understand educational learning. Such insight will, in the end,

contribute to the development of all courses rather than just the course under test. (p. 675)

Here are vintage themes that Cronbach decants 20 years later: the need for multidimensional outcomes, the fact of multiple stakeholders with different interests, the primacy of improving programs over certifying their worth, the explorations of how to improve a program and to generate knowledge-transferring programs. The wines not worth drinking are also the same — experiments and comparative judgments of worth:

> The aim to compare one course with another should not dominate plans for evaluation. . . . Formally designed experiments, pitting one course against another, are rarely definitive enough to justify their cost. Differences between average test scores . . . are usually small. . . . At best, an experiment never does more than compare the present version of one course with the present version of another. A major effort to bring the losing contender nearer to perfection would be very likely to reverse the verdict of the experiment. . . . It is quite impossible to neutralize the biases of teacher. . . . It is thus never certain whether any observed advantage is attributable to the educational innovation as such, or to the greater energy that teachers and students put forth when a method is fresh and "experimental." . . . Ours is a problem like that of the engineer examining a new automobile. He can set himself the task of defining its performance characteristics and its dependability. It would be merely distracting to put his question in the form, "Is this car better or worse than the competing brand?" (p. 676)

Cronbach distinguishes four types of data collection for evaluation. First are process studies describing events happening in the classroom; he values them for their relevance to course improvement, his premier goal. Second is assessing attitudes, how pupils and teachers feel about the educational experience. Third, he studies pupil proficiency, particularly (a) assessing proficiency by comparison to a standard, not to a comparison group; (b) examining item responses for diagnostic feedback; (c) administering different subsets of the items to different pupils so one can ask more research questions; and (d) selecting some items tailored to both the developer's understanding of a course's aims and other stakeholders' understandings. Finally, Cronbach mentions the follow-up study. He does not devote a separate section to this topic because it is of minor value for course improvement and because its interpretation depends on comparison with control groups that Cronbach does not favor. Cronbach acknowledges summative studies but assigns them less value than formative evaluations — the opposite of Scriven's preferences.

Cronbach is dissatisfied with conventional achievement tests, particularly to assess proficiency. They fail to measure important cognitive skills that schools should be imparting. They assess how much pupils have learned of what the tests measure; teachers know this, so tests also assess what teachers choose to teach because of the tests. Cronbach prefers to emphasize understanding principles, transfer of knowledge, and learning how to learn. No course can cover all relevant materials; a course can motivate pupils and impart the skills they need to learn on their own. His perennial concern is to ask the "right" questions, not to be caught up in trivial research that is easy, available, or common:

> Asking the right questions about educational outcomes can do much to improve educational effectiveness. Even if the right data are collected, however, evaluation will have contributed too little if it only places a seal of approval on certain courses and casts others into disfavor. Evaluation is a fundamental part of curriculum development, not an appendage. Its job is to collect facts the course developer can and will use to do a better job, and facts from which a deeper understanding of the educational process will emerge. (Cronbach, 1963, p. 683)

"Toward Reform of Program Evaluation" (1980)

Cronbach wrote this book with a number of his Stanford faculty colleagues, who joined him in the Stanford Evaluation Consortium, a particularly influential theory group in evaluation.

The problematic conventional wisdom in evaluation. Toward Reform of Program Evaluation is explicitly grounded in evaluation and policy research:

> We see evaluation as an integral part of policy research, and we therefore blend ideas appearing in the policy-research literature with ideas about evaluation itself. The distinction between evaluation and policy-research activities is beginning to disappear, as members of one subcommunity come to appreciate the ideas springing up in the other. (Cronbach et al., 1980, p. 19)

Cronbach and his coauthors use empirical research and substantive theories from policy analysis and evaluation to analyze the political context of evaluation, to detail how evaluation results are used, and to highlight trade-offs practicing evaluators face. The hope was to develop a theory of evaluation that is more contextually realistic and more likely to produce useful results in the short term.

Cronbach et al. (1980) note the pessimism of the day about the achievements of evaluation, particularly concerning use. They ask whether prevailing assumptions about evaluation might be responsible for this, being based upon a flawed rational model. That model assumes a decision maker who understands the social problem and the alternatives that might solve it; who keenly appreciates exactly what new information is needed, and when, to make a decision; and whose decision is of a stop-go variety that requires evaluative knowledge about how well a program meets its goals relative to alternatives. Under this flawed model, the evaluator conducts a study that meets the highest standards of science: random selection of respondents, random assignment to treatments, and the use of highly valid measures. A report is then issued to the decision maker, who awaits it eagerly and uses it to decide on action.

Toward Reform of Program Evaluation criticizes this model on many counts. Drawing upon empirical research on organizations and political decision making, Cronbach and colleagues claim that rarely are decisions made rather than slipped into; rarely is there a single decision maker; rarely do data about optimal decisions take precedence over politics; rarely are stop-go decisions made about programs; rarely does time permit adequate attention to all phases of research; rarely do all stakeholders give the project the same attention and meaning as evaluators; rarely is a report ready on time; rarely are decisions made on particular days; rarely are the decision makers who get the results the same as those who commissioned the work; rarely is a report suitably prepared for managers; and rarely are evaluation results used to modify programs in ways that instrumentally link the modifications to the evaluation. Cronbach and his coauthors depict a world of politics and administration that undercuts the rational model and its image of clear command and optimal decision making.

Alternative assumptions about public policy and social programs. A better theory of evaluation requires a better theory of the political world of programs:

> Perhaps it was the Williams-Evans (1969) review of the Head Start evaluation that first said emphatically that a theory of evaluation must be as much a theory of political interaction as it is a theory of how knowledge is constructed. Acceptance of this view has come slowly. (Cronbach et al., 1980, pp. 52-53)

Social programs must be politically embedded to gain initial funding, with powerful constituencies willing and able to influence votes. Since different constituencies want different things, there is an art to putting together winning coalitions. Program goals must be deliberately vague to accommodate multiple interests whose differences might be salient with clear goals.

Cronbach and colleagues divide the "policy-shaping community" into five groups, three groups of public servants and two of members of the public. Among the former are *responsible officials at the policy level*, often in the legislature or the executive branch in senior policy positions. Their concern revolves around expected program outcomes and how they contribute to policy. Next are *responsible officials at the program level*, public officials in action agencies who have the name of a particular program on the office door. Their responsibility is for the daily running of the program and for representing it in the policy-shaping community. They need information to monitor program inputs and outputs to ensure that regulations are adhered to and the program is generally on course. Next is a heterogeneous collection of *program officials who operate at the local level* to administer and dispense services. In health, these include hospital administrators, nurses, doctors, or social workers, who want to know how the delivery and effectiveness of services can be improved.

Of the two groups of members of the public, one is *program constituents* — those individuals and groups for whom program services are intended. They want to know how their interests might be affected by the evaluation. The second public group is *illuminators* — scholars, journalists, and others who interpret and disseminate information about a program. Their interest is in having access to data, discovering puzzles and insights, and summarizing what is known.

Programs have different stages of maturity; each stakeholder group's knowledge needs depend on the stage of maturity. The *breadboard* stage comes first. The ideas for a program have been provisionally incorporated into field activities on a small scale and are being routinely tinkered with to improve design. The *superrealization* stage is when a suitable design has been constructed and a demonstration study is initiated under conditions that maximize the likelihood of success — designers of the model deliver services with no slippage from the plan, expenditures per recipient are high, service recipients are carefully chosen for cooperativeness, and the catchment area is partly cut off from outside perturbations. In the *prototype* stage a program plan is implemented under conditions that mimic those under which the program would be introduced as policy. Finally, the *operating program* stage is when the program is permanently up and running.

Each of the five stakeholder groups will have different expectations for evaluation depending on the maturity of the program. Five constituencies and four stages of maturity yield twenty possible priorities in evaluation question preferences (fewer than this in practice, however). Moreover, many programs have internal elements at different levels of maturity. So this combination of constituencies and stages of program maturity rapidly escalates to highly complex questions that reflect the political world of social programs.

Evaluation must be crafted to the political system as it is rather than to an abstract model of how it should be. Although a program name may be constant over sites, program activities are not. Programs are not immutable or clearly bounded; individuals receive services from multiple programs simultaneously. This makes it hard to judge which gains come from which programs. The demarcation problem is most acute when the funds given to an agency for one purpose substitute for funds from other sources for the same purpose, creating a new program in name but not in fact. Evaluations should respond to the complex forms and purposes of local program inputs; they should reject the naive experimentalist's assumption of the treatment as a stable black box; and they should study program implementation and process for clues to program improvement. Program goals are vague, numerous, and often mutually contradictory so as to accommodate the different interests of stakeholders. Any theory of evaluation should be rejected if it uses program goals to generate evaluation questions; it is unwise to focus on whether or not a project has "attained its goals" (Cronbach et al., 1980, p. 5).

Cronbach paints an unremittingly conservative image of the political system, and evaluation has a modest (but important) role within it:

> The phrase *adjustment at the margin* sums up the characteristics of most of the actions taken in a context of accommodation. Participants who wish to take a large step in a certain direction find few allies, but some small step will be welcomed by many interest groups, even groups with conflicting motives. The proposals themselves are trimmed to fit the players' assessment of the political situation. As a consequence, most social change is gradual. Still, successive small repairs and added fixtures do accumulate over time to create a different edifice. (Cronbach et al., 1980, p. 116)

In choosing the term *policy shaping* over *policy-making*, Cronbach and colleagues are also attacking the rational decision model because of its normative implications. Democracy evolved to protect against tyranny rather than to promote the efficiency postulated by rational models; democracy seeks to resolve tensions between the rationalist's elitism and the true democrat's participation in favor of the latter. Such priorities justify political processes promoting accommodations among stakeholder interests, downplaying the contributions of technocrats whenever their advice conflicts with accommodation. "Rational" decision making smacks of totalitarianism. Though Cronbach's thinking about political interactions among stakeholders (and between evaluators and stakeholders) is largely the product of descriptions of current policy, it also has clear roots in the Enlightenment and British empiricism.

Proper and improper evaluation purposes. Cronbach and his coauthors reject the notion of evaluation to serve decision choices or to hold managers accountable for program performance. Demands for such accountability are a sign of pathology in a political system; they are backward- and not forward-looking; they hold managers responsible for outcomes they cannot control rather than for the inputs they can control; and they embody system-level distrust of managers who will only perform to their full ability if they know they are being watched. They also challenge evaluations to answer any one question precisely, including causal questions. Cronbach (1982a) prefers less dependable answers about a broad set of questions, and calls this the trade-off between fidelity and bandwidth, terms he used 30 years earlier in a humorous article on the relationship between psychometrics and clinical psychology practice (Cronbach, 1954) and developed more seriously a few years later (Cronbach, 1957). For Cronbach, evaluation is a pluralist enterprise, with the fidelity of each research conclusion balanced against the absence of information on other matters:

> It is self-defeating to aspire to deliver an evaluative conclusion as precise and as safely beyond dispute as an operational-language conclusion from the laboratory. It is unrealistic to hope to tell the PSC [policy-shaping community] all it needs to know. When the evaluator aspires only to provide clarification that would not otherwise be available, he has chosen a task he can manage and one that does have social benefits. (Cronbach et al., 1980, p. 318).

Rather, evaluations should contribute to enlightened discussions of alternative paths for social action, clarifying important issues of concern to the policy-shaping community. This often entails identifying and analyzing program assumptions — how a social problem is understood; what is known about the program or ones like it; how political, social, and organizational contexts influence program functioning; what the processes are within a program; and what program processes contribute to program outcomes. This last is particularly important; many processes should be transferable to other, superficially quite different, sites. Evaluation should help design better future programs rather than record past achievements: "The better and the more widely the workings of social programs are understood, the more rapidly policy will evolve and the more the programs will contribute to a better quality of life" (Cronbach et al., 1980, pp. 2-3). If so, then "what counts in evaluation is external validity, that is, the plausibility of conclusions about one or another *UTO [unsampled universe of persons, treatments, outcomes, or settings] that is significant to the PSC" (1980, p. 314). Though evaluation addresses alternative social actions, Cronbach opposes explicit experimental contrasts of such alternative treatments.

How does Cronbach learn about alternatives if he prefers evaluation within programs over evaluation between them? First, evaluations can examine the consequences of natural variability within programs, even though evaluators will not know whether selection differences are fully controlled (Cronbach, Rogosa, Floden, & Price, 1977). For example, different ways of structuring intake or outreach procedures might be studied using naturally occurring variability, as might the consequences of different degrees of exposure to a curriculum. Experiments are preferable for such purposes, but formal contrast groups are expensive, are not definitive in conclusions, and are associated with opportunity costs elsewhere in the research. Second, comparison occurs as details accumulate across a set of evaluation studies; illuminators can review a literature to see which programs have better or worse substantive theories, or achieve better client approval, utilization, or implementation. Experimental methods are not necessary for these evaluation issues, although Cronbach will endorse experiments if a causal issue has considerable leverage and if the need to reduce uncertainty about the issue is high.

Flexible evaluation design. Cronbach and his coauthors see a pluralistic policy world, with each potential user emphasizing different issues that require different methods. Since Cronbach et al. (1980) do not want evaluations to be tailored to the parochial interests of a few members of the policy-shaping community, they outline how research can be done to meet the needs of multiple stakeholder groups. Three principles loom large. The first is to avoid doing a single large evaluation study; instead, evaluators should conduct several smaller studies that are programmatically linked, most being rapid efforts with only modest yields but that contribute to better questions and more refined designs in later studies. The second principle is that evaluators should rarely allocate resources to providing highly precise answers to a narrow range of issues. Better to provide less clear answers to a larger range of pluralistically responsive questions — a point of view at odds with design traditions that emphasize precise, unbiased inferences.

The third principle is detailed more in Cronbach's second book — an algorithm for prioritizing evaluation issues in two phases. In the *divergent* phase the concern is to generate possible issues to investigate through canvassing the policy-shaping community to find issues with leverage because many constituencies care about them, because they could sway a noncommitted group, or because they could clarify why a program works. For each issue, an assessment is then made of uncertainty in existing knowledge about it. Cronbach is an implicit Bayesian; he prefers to allocate resources where prior uncertainty is high. Finally, judgments must be made about anticipated information yield; imagine identifying an issue of great leverage and high uncertainty about which nothing meaningful can be learned through evaluation at reasonable cost.

The divergent phase yields many more issues than can be tackled. In the *convergent* phase, a determination is made of the most important questions for which a reasonable answer can be expected. Cronbach has a recipe for this, though he calls it "crude":

1. A question with high leverage and high prior uncertainty merits close attention. Without investment in each such question somewhere in the sequence of investigations, the other findings . . . may have little merit.

2. If leverage is low but not negligible, a question with high prior uncertainty deserves some investment.

3. If leverage is high and prior uncertainty low, low-cost information should be collected. If it confirms the sharp priors, it will help to muzzle the kind of critic who, at the end, raises doubts for the sake of doubting. . . .

4. If leverage is low and uncertainty is low, the investigator should do no more than keep open the channels for incidental information.

Among questions with leverage, the first basis for assigning priority is prior uncertainty. Then one moves on to balance posterior uncertainty against cost, while continuing to give preference to the high-leverage options. Judgment is to be made in the light of a tentative sampling plan and a probable analytic procedure. (1982a, p. 240)

The above prioritization is imperfect, and issues deemed important initially may not retain that status. Evaluators should be flexible, prepared to rework questions and design as early feedback accumulates from program sites. Cronbach wants to see more evaluation planning and more replanning. Here is yet another area where his concept of research design differs from that of experimentalists; few of the latter would deliberately replan a study as new issues emerge or as the intellectual context of the study changes.

Evaluation roles. Cronbach and his coauthors see the evaluator as part of a system of political interaction that influences program design. They carefully delineate what the evaluator's role should and should not be. Evaluators should be educators rather than the philosopher-kings of Scriven, the guardians of truth of Campbell, or the servants of management of Wholey. Cronbach et al. (1980) "advise the evaluator to be multi-partisan, to make the best case he can for each side in turn" (p. 210):

The evaluator has a political influence even when he does not aspire to it. He can be an arm of those in power, but he loses most of his value in that role if he does not think independently and critically. He can put himself in the service of some partisan interest outside the center of power, but there again his unique contribution is a critical, scholarly habit of mind. He can, we assert, render greatest service if he becomes an informant to and educator of all parties to a decision, making available to them the lessons of experience and critical thinking. Since information produces power, such diffusion of information is power equalizing. (p. 67)

Evaluators are active information brokers who bring information to bear and provide interested participants with it. This information might throw new light on assumptions about the nature of a social problem or about the theory implicit in program activities; it might teach stakeholders what is known about a program or programs of its type; or it might detail how constituencies construe the program's latent and manifest rationales. In transmitting such information the evaluator is not restricted to a particular reporting style. Cronbach favors informal, frequent, unplanned communication, being influenced by Weiss's empirical work on factors promoting use and his own belief that instrumental use is rare but enlightenment is common. When he cites Sproull and Larkey (1979) about stimulating use, the position is very near to Weiss:

> *Be around.* . . . Managers exchange information mostly with "insiders." An evaluator may never actually become an "insider," but the benefits . . . can be approximated simply by being present and available.
> *Talk briefly and often.*
> *Tell stories.* The evaluator should always be prepared with a stock of performance anecdotes to illustrate the points.
> *Talk to the manager's sources.* . . .
> *Use multiple models.* . . .
> *Provide publicly defensible justifications for any recommended programmatic changes.* (Cronbach et al., 1980, p. 175)

Cronbach sometimes likens the evaluator to the historian and the engineer. He chooses the historian to stress evaluating a program on its own terms, documenting important contextual and process factors. Evaluators should sometimes write program histories as part of their task. Engineers evaluate objects, particularly at the breadboard stage, to diagnose problems and fix them. Their purpose is to develop a better automobile or whatever else they are working on; rarely is their purpose to assess merit to help potential purchasers know which car to buy. According to Cronbach, their justification is for doing formative and not summative evaluation.

"Designing Evaluations of
Educational and Social Programs" (1982)

Scope and purposes. Cronbach's analysis of social programming and use convinced him that evaluation should be pluralist in both the constituencies and issues it dealt with. It also convinced him of the utility of generating knowledge that permitted extrapolating the persons, settings, treatments, and observations studied to related but unstudied populations and classes. Existing treatises on research design are too narrow for this, being focused on precision and bias reduction rather than on generalization. Cronbach needed a new theory of research design; his 1982 book presents it. He called his theory "functional" to differentiate it from the theories of Fisher (and Campbell), where valid inference largely depends on structural factors such as control groups, pretests, and treatment assignments. In Cronbach's approach, evaluation questions are paramount, and evaluators ask many different types of questions. He explicitly rejects those who think experiments are *the* model for evaluation under the dual assumptions that molar causal questions are central to evaluation's purpose and that the structural design features of experimentation provide the best answers.

However, Cronbach carefully delineated the scope of application of his theory of design. It applies mostly to evaluating prototypes — plans for future programs that are being implemented in trials that mimic the conditions of future implementation. In the 1980 book this was one of four contexts where evaluation had a role, the others being the breadboard stage, the superrealization stage, and when the program is established. Cronbach does not consider the last of these, contending that "established programs are comparatively immune to serious evaluation, save as proposed modifications lead to a new study of prototypes" (1982a, p. 3). He assumes that evaluation has most leverage for affecting social change when a prototype is under study as opposed to when a superrealization has been achieved or the program has been established.

Internal and external validity. As in so much of his writing, Cronbach (1982a) uses a dominant orthodoxy to further his critical thinking. He acknowledges in the preface that his book was written to push

against the writings of Campbell and his team-mates. Let me explain. The Campbell-Stanley monograph (1963) had a profound influence on evaluators. It said that research should strive for both internal and external validity, but internal validity was its main theme. I reverse the emphasis that a generation of social scientists, students of education, and commissioners of evaluations took from Campbell and Stanley and the later monographs of Cook and Campbell. (p. xiv)

To make his case, Cronbach needed to describe internal and external validity. To do so he invented a set of symbols introduced in the 1980 book but developed further in the 1982 book. In lowercase letters, *utos* refers to data actually collected in terms of units (often people), treatments, observations, and settings. Uppercase *UTOS* refers to the populations of units, treatments, observations, and settings around which the research questions were formulated and to which the particular u, t, o, and s are supposed to correspond. **UTOS* (pronounced "star UTOS") refers to populations of people, treatments, observations, and settings that are manifestly different from those to which the obtained samples (utos) correspond. The populations in any one study are not homogeneous; *sub-UTOS* refers to observed subpopulations of persons, subtypes of settings, and subcategories of treatments and outcomes.

For Cronbach, *UTOS is the most relevant domain of application for social inquiry because it deals most with transfer of research findings beyond their contexts of generation. Sometimes study sampling particulars are designed to meet the anticipated knowledge needs of particular users, so internal inferences from utos to UTOS are then important. Some users want certain subanalyses of the data to maximize the proximal similarity between sampling details and people, settings, treatments, or outcomes that interest them. Multiple extrapolations are useful, but none more than to *UTOS for its potential for meeting the interests of present and future stakeholders.

This terminology helps specify different targets of knowledge and raises questions about their relative utility. It does not describe validity itself. For Cronbach, validity is not a property of research design, data collection, or data analysis, as in most traditional theories of method. He rejects the claim that because a particular method was used — random assignment, for instance — the resulting study outcome is valid. All procedures are incomplete given the multiple inferences and extrapolations that researchers must make. Cronbach details the limits for random assignment — small samples, differential attrition, weak treatment contrasts — but one has the sense he could do just as critical an analysis of any method for any purpose. For him, validity is a property of conclusions, not research procedures; it makes little sense to speak of valid methods or a valid study. At issue is justifying a conclusion to a critical audience, for Cronbach believes that "validity is subjective rather than objective: The plausibility of the conclusion is what counts. And plausibility, to twist a cliche, lies in the ear of a beholder" (1982a, p. 108). Validity is assimilated to credibility.

In *Designing Evaluations of Educational and Social Programs*, Cronbach understands internal validity differently from Campbell. For

Cronbach, internal validity concerns inferences from utos to UTOS, from samples to intended targets of generalization. For Campbell, internal validity concerns the nature of the relationship between t and o at the sample level — in particular, whether it was causal. Campbell's conception is historical and local; a study can be internally valid even if one cannot characterize the class of treatment and observation into which the sample fits. Cronbach considers this conception of internal validity trivial:

> I consider it pointless to speak of causes when all that can be validly meant by reference to a cause in a particular instance is that, on one trial of a partially specified manipulation t under conditions A, B, and C, along with other conditions not named, phenomenon P was observed. To introduce the word *cause* seems pointless. Campbell's writings make internal validity a property of trivial, past-tense, and local statements. (1982a, p. 137)

He argues instead for a conception of cause like Mackie's (1974), achieving greater predictability and control over causal connections by discovering more causal contingencies on which the connection depends. He does not espouse the full essentialist position that one cannot claim causation until all the necessary and sufficient conditions for an effect are known. He does reject Campbell's manipulability or activity theory of causation that one can detect many simple causal connections at the molar level that are dependable enough to be useful even though far from inevitable. Cronbach is committed to ontological complexity and to explaining more of this complexity than Campbell; he criticizes experimentalists who claim a treatment caused a particular effect. A treatment is logically embedded in, and cannot be differentiated from, the U, O, and S through which it was varied and on which its replication depends. For Cronbach, the activity theory of causation is too dependent on simple assumptions about main effects.

Cronbach adds a further critique of internal validity. Campbell maintains that internal validity takes precedence over external validity. Of what use, Campbell argues, is generalizing a causal connection if there is plausible doubt about the connection itself? Cronbach argues that in an applied field like evaluation it is not important to assuage the last shred of plausible doubt about causation. Invoking Moynihan (1969), he claims that policymakers do not pay as much attention to causation as basic researchers; they act on the best information available, whatever its merits according to traditional scholarly criteria. Campbell's validity priorities are useful for basic research, but Cronbach argues they are less useful for applied research:

Campbell's writings on method have been chiefly concerned with basic science and the long-term evolution of scientific explanations. Approaching evaluation from the standpoint of an applied psychologist, I am concerned with knowledge for short-term use. If our roles were interchanged, perhaps each of us would make the other's arguments. Throughout his career, Campbell has advocated hardheaded research, but that advocacy is tempered by his desire to see inquiry into social concerns, including those about which definite answers cannot be expected. I have advocated investigating what is important, whether or not the questions fit conventional paradigms. That advocacy has in turn been tempered by a desire to reduce overconfident interpretation and misinterpretation. (1982a, pp. xv-xvi)

According to Cronbach, many relevant stakeholder groups value a particular segment of the space within *UTOS that reflects their local information needs. To be maximally useful to such heterogeneous needs requires knowledge that transcends any limited set of persons, settings, treatments, or outcomes. If meeting such needs is the major purpose for evaluation, then externally valid knowledge extrapolating from UTOS to *UTOS takes precedence over internally valid knowledge. We must re-call the potential terminological confusion here. Campbell's starting point is the sample of units, treatments, observations, and settings actually studied (utos). His external validity asks to what targets these can be generalized, whether intended or not; and it definitely includes (but is not limited to) reference to how well sampling particulars (utos) corre-spond to populations and classes specified in a guiding research ques-tion (UTOS). But while links from utos to UTOS are part of Campbell's description of external validity, they are internal validity for Cronbach! By contrast, internal validity for Campbell asks if the connection be-tween t and o is causal. Without attention to this difference, it is not easy to follow Cronbach's discussion of validity priorities.

Cronbach maintains that external validity is important because indi-vidual stakeholders often want to apply existing knowledge to persons, settings, treatments, and observations for which they are responsible. Rarely will all these particulars be contained in the existing base of knowledge, so potential users often must extrapolate beyond the data available. Such extrapolation is difficult and has not been the central focus of any recognized theory of research design and interpretation. A crucial question, in many ways the core of Cronbach's (1982a) book, is: How can we achieve knowledge transferable to populations of persons, set-tings, treatments, and outcomes that differ from those examined? Since Cronbach does write about the traditional inference from utos to UTOS, we examine this before analyzing what he has to say about the less traditional UTOS-to-*UTOS link.

Methods for generalizing to UTOS. Cronbach's discussion of the links between utos and UTOS is mostly not original. He emphasizes (1982a, p. 246):

- clear specification of plans and acts that generate or harvest data and develop a conclusion from them
- controls on sampling or realization of program events and evaluative operations
- restriction of inquiry and inference to a comparatively narrow, homogeneous UTO

Internal validity as Cronbach understands it is promoted by a clearly specified research question around which sampling takes place, by homogeneous populations and categories, by the use of formal sampling theory in generalizing from u to U, by the use of content validity in generalizing from t and o to T and O, and by experimental designs to probe whether a relationship between t and o (and hence T and O) is causal. (Generalizing from s to S is more problematic because for Cronbach each situation is unique. However, others may well believe it possible to draw a random sample of sites to represent a population, albeit a population that may be somewhat different next year.) Internal validity is difficult to foster in practice because it is hard to specify research questions fully and implement sampling designs in accordance with formal sampling theory—particularly for occasions of measurement, where, "in practice, formal sampling of conditions is rare" (Cronbach, 1982a, p. 267).

Cronbach's discussion of internal validity makes many important practical points that evaluators should consider. For instance, he discusses the utility of designs when sample sizes are unbalanced, arguing that such imbalance is often responsive to concerns about financial cost (e.g., when treatments of less importance are expensive) and political salience (e.g., when larger sample sizes in important treatment groups enhance credibility). He acknowledges that treatment standardization advocated in most experimental design texts reduces error variance, but opposes it in general. Standardization detracts from external validity when diverse treatment realizations are found, reducing the meaningfulness of research questions predicated on a standard treatment. Cronbach notes other adverse consequences of homogeneity. He cites the case where breeding ever-purer rat strains reduced individual differences but led to aptitude-treatment interactions that were harder to detect. Strains responded differently to the same stimuli in a context where no theory explained when each strain would react idiosyncratically. Finally, he notes that experimental research using group means does not require measures whose reliability is as high as individual testing requires. Each outcome can be assessed with fewer items, making it possible to measure more outcomes. This is not trivial, given Cronbach's interest in evaluative questions that respond to multiple stakeholder concerns.

*Methods for generalizing to *UTOS*. Methods for extrapolating to unstudied populations — Cronbach's external validity — are much more conceptually problematic than methods for generalizing from samples to target populations:

> No investigation can answer all questions. The variety of U*, T*, and O* that will concern the different sectors of the audience is endless, and future settings can be only dimly foreseen. The planner seeking relevance aims at a target that becomes visible only after he has fired off his best shot. The task is so demanding as to make the aspiration seem almost foolish, but there is room for optimism. The task is not radically different from that of suppliers of business information, who try to provide executives and investors with facts applicable in fast-changing circumstances, or from the task of educators supplying facts and concepts for their students' future use. . . . Social scientists lack the tightly articulated [models] that would generate firm statements about *UTOS. Many lines of reasoning about the differences between utos and *UTOS are pursued simultaneously. Conclusions about a social program are not derived directly and exclusively from evaluations of that program. Other sources of social knowledge — folklore, history, anecdotes, research on tangential topics — flow into the interpretation (Weiss, 1977; Lindblom and Cohen, 1979). (Cronbach, 1982a, pp. 289-290)

Cronbach discusses three strategies for extrapolating beyond studied populations. The first is shortening the extrapolation, especially by examining subpopulations in the data to select instances with the most proximal similarity to populations that interest stakeholders. Thus, if I have an early childhood program emphasizing self-worth in the South Bronx, I would try to find instances involving early childhood programs having this primary goal, and whose clienteles were composed of very poor Black children in a very large city. At issue here is similarity of appearances, though supplementary data would be useful if they help explain findings from the subanalysis. Such subanalyses presuppose heterogeneous sampling in any one study or across a set of studies. While subcategorization promotes the UTOS to *UTOS link, it conflicts with the standardization and control that promote inferences from utos to UTOS. Cronbach frankly admits this, but he leaves no doubt as to his choice.

The second strategy is extrapolating to the *UTOS level through causal explanation. By this Cronbach means explaining how a treatment has a particular effect. He discusses both quantitative and qualitative analyses. The former include causal modeling, partitioning a treatment into components and testing their efficacy, and using multiple indicators of a particular causal construct. Qualitative methods include detailed on-site observation and the use of diaries or narrative histories that generate the thick description of program context and history that helps identify important variables for explaining the conditions under which a program is more effective. Explanation promotes transfer because it tells what processes must occur for an effect to be realized, and it stimulates thinking about the different molar ways in which one could activate a particular mediating process. Mediating processes and other contingencies are a major means of promoting Cronbach's external validity.

But note that we have come full circle. When is a research conclusion internally valid? asked Cronbach. His answer: When other investigators repeat it using their best reconstruction of the original procedures or when it can be reliably brought about using different procedures from the original investigator's that activate the same mediating processes. What makes a causal conclusion externally valid? Cronbach answers: When we understand most of the contingencies on which a causal relationship is based, especially the micromediating processes! The keys to internal and external validity are thus very similar: Gain more knowledge of causal mechanisms, the traditional goal of science. When the question is, Why should we fund basic research? a common answer is because it achieves explanatory knowledge likely to apply in contexts we cannot yet imagine that will be different from those of the original research.

The third strategy for extrapolating to *UTOS relates to how evaluation findings are disseminated. Cronbach urges evaluators to present information more as narratives than as hypothesis tests, as lively, colorful, frequent, informal, and sensitive to the unique needs of each audience. He favors creating study groups of experts in a particular area who will acquaint themselves with past evaluations, and who are willing to use them along with their substantive knowledge and background wisdom to give advice about a host of matters, including the transfer of knowledge to unstudied contexts. Such bodies would be in a special position to think through the supplementary theoretical work that extrapolation requires — for instance, explicating what might explain the success of a past treatment and then analyzing whether these factors might be present in future contexts to which transfer is desired. As Cronbach says:

> The argument leading to a conclusion about *UTOS has to be abstract. There is no direct way to convert findings about schools in California into a prediction about schools in New Jersey; only by bringing to bear concepts about kinds of communities, or curricula, or taxation systems can the transfer be made credible

or criticized. A strict defense of [my model for extrapolation] would require an impracticable effort toward construct validation. In the natural sciences, the validation of propositional networks proceeds slowly. The pace of social events is far too swift to allow a comparable sharpening of thought about proposals for intervention. The networks used in considering social programs have to deal with ever new institutions and conditions; hence, much of [my model for extrapolation] will always be conjectural. It would be wrong, however, to dismiss either common experience or accumulated social research merely because it is undependable. Current experts on contraception or delinquency or early education are vastly better informed than those of a generation ago. Much of the added knowledge consists of complications, of additional factors for planners to consider. Such knowledge rarely signals what is right to do, but it can warn against numerous shortsighted courses of action. Replacing unwarranted certainty with uncertainty is a contribution. (1982a, p. 175)

Research design as art, not science. We do not have perfect methods for extrapolating beyond the factors that have been directly studied, so Cronbach cannot provide extended mathematical or logical discussion of design in the manner found in textbooks on research methods. Still, he believes it better to ask important questions than to give precise answers to minor ones. Since his most important evaluative questions are about knowledge transfer, he probes the less well-developed methods for doing so. But he probes them under the assumption useful evaluation does not require as much uncertainty reduction as basic research, trying to take the edge off critics who maintain that Cronbach's methods for transfer are "soft."

In *Designing Evaluations of Educational and Social Programs*, Cronbach is dragged by his conception of social program realities toward methodologically looser conceptions of evaluation design. Its guiding principles are relevance for getting results used in the short term in a political setting characterized by stakeholder pluralism and a need for knowledge that can be generalized. Relevance requires considering each evaluation assignment as a novel challenge, not as a pretext for implementing techniques that the evaluator knows best or that are dominant in the day. A design must be crafted to encompass multiple questions differing in priority, with generalization to a population or a category that is not directly studied. Designing evaluations to meet such purposes requires deviating from the methods and standards of orthodox science. Cronbach does not want a particular conception of scientific method to trivialize the process of asking important questions, so he throws down the intellectual gauntlet in the very first words of the 1982 book: "Designing an evaluative investigation is an art" (1982a, p. 1). His last chapter reiterates the point:

Advice on evaluation design cannot be packed into a few maxims that would enable the evaluator to make ideal use of resources, although maxims of a kind could be extracted from earlier chapters. Two will suffice to lead off this recapitulation:

- Evaluation is an art.
- There is no single best plan for an evaluation, not even for an inquiry into a particular program, at a particular time, with a particular budget. (p. 321)

OUR ANALYSIS OF
CRONBACH'S THEORY OF EVALUATION

Cronbach's books on evaluation appeared in the early 1980s, though many of the points in them were presaged in the 1963 paper. The books also reflect influence from his theoretical work in the 1960s and 1970s, particularly about making research methods responsive to different knowledge needs of scholars and practitioners (Cronbach et al., 1972; Cronbach & Suppes, 1969) and about ontological, epistemological, and methodological assumptions required for sensitive studies of aptitude-treatment interactions (Cronbach & Snow, 1977). He was also influenced by his participation in evaluations from 1939 onward, by his discussions with practicing evaluators, and by his extensive reading of evaluation reports and commentaries on these reports.

Also important was his immersion in empirical and theoretical studies of organizational realities in the policy world into which evaluation must fit to be useful. These influences, and the late date at which he wrote these books, meant that Cronbach called upon a richer array of experience than his predecessors — albeit mostly vicariously — and a larger body of empirically influenced theory about evaluation practice and its relation to policy. Hence his judgments about what was worth assimilating and rejecting in others' theories are particularly well grounded.

Cronbach is also unusual in the extent to which his thinking about social programming, knowledge construction, use, and valuing interconnect to form a comprehensive theory of evaluation practice — so interwoven that it is hard to discuss his major ideas under a single one of our category headings. For instance, he argues that evaluators should primarily draw conclusions about improving a program's internal processes. This argument depends on hypotheses about (a) where change is possible in social programs, (b) how evaluation findings are more and less likely to be used, and (c) why it is so hard to gain definitive knowledge about the causal connections that loom paramount in competing evaluation theories. Hence the theories we discuss as separate are integrated into more of a whole in Cronbach's case. We assign this or that idea to a single one of our categories with reluctance, consoled by the notion that discussing his ideas is more important than pigeonholing them.

Theory of Social Programming

Leaning heavily on Carol Weiss, James March, and Charles Lindblom, Cronbach and his colleagues thoroughly and convincingly describe social programs and the policy contexts in which they are embedded. For him, evaluation is part of policy studies. No program is usefully evaluated unless one knows how stakeholder groups came to approve of it, influenced its design, implementation and monitoring, and helped modify it at federal, state, and local levels. All evaluation theories require thorough grounding in the political and administrative realities that create, sustain, and constrain each program.

Hence Cronbach rejects many ideas impregnated with naive normative expectations of social policy and programming. He rejects the rational choice model of decision making along with its idea of centralized command, since individual policymakers rarely make policy decisions alone, since there are rarely specific dates for decisions, and since scholarly knowledge is rarely the sole impetus for policy changes. Important authority resides not just at the federal level. He also doubts that accountability enhances efficiency or that program goals are clear and widely agreed upon.

Cronbach assumes a policy world of ceaseless political accommodation characterized by decisions that are slipped into rather than made; by policy-making that takes place in decision-shaping communities rather than by individual decision makers; by community members who promote their own interests in conflict with others' priorities; by decisions made piecemeal over many different occasions; by decision-shaping communities that want and use many kinds of information; by knowledge used for different purposes at the federal, state, and local levels; by programs that are modified mostly at the margin; by high variability in local program implementation; and by programs at such different stages of development that different questions are relevant to them. The important point is that he has learned the sad lessons of the first years of evaluation, when prescriptions for evaluation practice were not closely linked to knowledge about how programs are designed, implemented, and modified. As he sees it, the core of social programs and policy is political accommodation among conflicting stakeholders, not rational decision making.

If we use organizational research as a benchmark, there is little to fault in Cronbach's theory of social programs, but there are some problems of emphasis. He assumes that programs go through four stages: the breadboard, the superrealization, the prototype, and the ongoing program. He further assumes that the prototype stage is most important, for it is then that an evaluation can have maximal leverage:

> This book is chiefly concerned with prototype trials. At the breadboard stage, a program is in such flux that the evaluation must be reoriented frequently and can scarcely be "designed." I shall not ignore ideal conditions ("superrealizations"), but they are too rare to be the main concern here. Established programs are comparatively immune to serious evaluation, save as proposed modifications lead to a new study of prototypes. (1982a, p. 3)

But this relative neglect of evaluation at the other three stages is unwarranted. Evaluation is less useful if it is almost exclusively oriented toward prototypes. Superrealizations occur when a treatment is delivered and evaluated under conditions designed to maximize its efficacy: a scale of operations less than is required for an established program, research conducted in settings with atypical levels of control, program developers intimately involved in program activities, levels of financial expenditure that cannot be duplicated in an established program, and levels of monitoring of treatment implementation that would otherwise be obtrusive. Because of their atypicality, Cronbach rejects their usefulness as targets of evaluation. But superrealizations play an important role in policy. They are precursors of the prototypes on which Cronbach prioritizes; it makes little sense to implement prototypes that do not work as superrealizations. More important, without evaluations of superrealizations it is hard to tell, when a program yields disappointing results, whether underlying theory was wrong, whether program activities were poorly implemented, or whether the evaluation was so poorly implemented that sensitive findings could not be expected. If a superrealization has been evaluated and judged successful, this helps rule out a flawed basic concept — not totally, however, since superrealizations contain irrelevant features that might influence study outcomes — hovering evaluators who communicate social desirability that inflates treatment estimates. Even so, carefully appraised superrealizations are not trivial; Cronbach may understate their importance.

Cronbach's work tells us little about how evaluations of superrealizations differ from evaluations of prototypes. A key question is whether different theories of question and method choice are required for evaluating superrealizations. Evaluations of superrealizations might look more like summative than formative evaluations. There is no point in improving the implementation of a superrealization whose artificiality is acknowledged anyway. The enhanced control associated with superrealizations permits the experimental designs and contrast groups that are inconsistent with Cronbach's conception of evaluation's major purpose. Has his low opinion of experiments influenced his evaluation of superrealizations?

Cronbach also ignores superrealizations because they are rare; but much depends on the definition of a superrealization. We know of no systematic description of the frequency of superrealizations, however defined, making it doubly unrealistic to expect informed debate about them. Yet if one examined theses in schools of education, public health, medicine, and social work and in programs of clinical psychology, one would find many instances of students implementing and evaluating superrealizations. Indeed, in its guidelines about the studies that should precede a randomized clinical trial, the National Institutes of Health propose a stage, called an "efficacy study," that seems to be a superrealization (Flay, 1986). Superrealizations may not be as rare as Cronbach implies. His relative neglect of them may have thus led him to limit the leverage that evaluation might have for promoting program change. Cronbach also does not concern himself with established social programs. He reasons that they are so affected by politics as to be "immune to serious evaluation" except when a new component is added to an existing program. Cronbach hardly discusses the strategies that Wholey uses — monitoring performance in established programs to examine the numbers and types of persons served, the quantity and quality of services, or financial costs. Such information helps many different stakeholders think about an ongoing social program, increasing their enlightenment and enlarging their options about what can or should be done — the consequences Cronbach desires from evaluation.

Moreover, some elements in ongoing social programs, while perhaps conceptually marginal, are amenable to change and far from trivial in aggregate impact. In programs that serve millions of people, a modest change might influence thousands of lives or save millions of dollars. Programs also contain naturally occurring variability that evaluators can exploit without setting up prototypes. Thus one might study which ways of, say, processing an application or conducting client outreach are more effective and worth transferring within a program. These are not intellectually glamorous issues, but, given the large numbers involved, such research has considerable potential.

Even in small programs, natural variability can be exploited. Cook et al. (1985) propose identifying the major models of practice in a program and then using natural variability in local implementation of each model to probe how effective each is. Pitfalls of this strategy include the following: (a) There is potential inaccuracy in preliminary model identification, (b) few outcome criteria are genuinely relevant to all models, (c) variance between models may be swamped by variance within them, and (d) selection problems inevitably arise in the study of natural variability. It is clearly preferable to follow such exploitation with demonstration projects incorporating the major models. Cronbach does not favor such studies, but there have been successful instances (e.g., Connell, Turner, & Mason, 1985).

Since established social programs are so heterogeneous in local implementation, we should pay particular attention to sources of variability that other sites might adopt to promote the transfer that Cronbach so esteems. Of the many reasons a particular activity is done at some sites but not others, some are remediable. For instance, it may not be difficult to introduce an attractive new activity into some sites where no one knew of it before, to teach specific skills to those who do not know about them, or to provide minor incentives for introducing a new, low-cost activity. Can we afford to neglect evaluation of established social programs when so much social investment takes place in them, when some marginal changes are possible in them that might affect many people?

To be fair, Cronbach says established programs can be improved by adding elements evaluated as prototypes, but he does not tell how to do this and otherwise explores sources of leverage in established programs very little. To a management-centered theorist like Wholey, or a practitioner-centered theorist like Stake, neglect of these programs is a major theoretical lacuna. Cronbach is probably correct that considerable leverage for program change and evaluation lies at the prototype stage. It may even be the major source of leverage. But he may be wrong to assign so little leverage to superrealizations and established programs.

Theory of Valuing

Cronbach mostly restricts his analysis of values to descriptive concerns, rejecting most other value concerns:

> Some writers, notably Scriven (1967), call upon the evaluator to value the program, that is, to tell the public whether the program is good enough. Our position is more in line with that of an international group of evaluators who met in England in 1972 (MacDonald and Parlett, 1973): "It is the reader's task (in digesting the report) to 'evaluate' in the literal sense of the concept, and the evaluator's task to provide the reader with the information which he may wish to take into account in forming his judgment." (Cronbach et al., 1980, p. 154)

Prescriptive values play only a small role in his thinking. They are not used to justify weights for outcome criteria. Instead, a few related values are used to critique rational decision making in policy analysis. Specifically, Cronbach is suspicious of urges to remove decision making from the public clash of conflicting interests where the framers of the U.S. Constitution placed it. Like Cronbach, the founding fathers mistrusted calls for managerial efficiency that often concealed latent attempts to promote self-interest. Instead, the founding fathers (and Cronbach) favored a theory of democratic control that assigns open debate among multiple interests a higher value than efficiency or rationality.

Hence Cronbach advises evaluators against using their own prescriptive theories for criteria selection, instead linking that selection to stakeholder values. He wants evaluation to serve the whole social system, not just particular stakeholder interests. The appropriate evaluator role is that of educator, not lawyer or debater. Individual evaluators can never be value-free, but they can minimize how much their values intrude when they offer advice within a political system where values clash and where they play a major role in decision shaping.

Cronbach acknowledges that sometimes stakeholders do not get to formulate their own versions of the evaluation issues, and so is not averse to representing interests with no effective political voice. The economically disadvantaged and racial minorities are often left out of question formulation. In this context he comments favorably on the evaluation of *Sesame Street* by Cook et al. (1975). They showed that children from poor and racial minority backgrounds view the program less often than children from more advantaged backgrounds. The show is modestly successful in teaching, hence when poor children enter first grade, the viewing difference results in their being even further behind their more advantaged counterparts than they would otherwise have been. The superordinate principle is representing all the political voices in evaluation; if some are not represented, evaluators must represent them the best way they know how. The optimal position is to canvass all voices and not be forced to represent one vicariously.

Cronbach is concerned more with descriptive than with prescriptive valuing. He wants evaluators to resist generating simple summary statements about the value of a program. He is not a fan of cost-benefit analysis, meta-analysis, or other schemes to achieve a single easily understood conclusion about returns on the dollar, average effect sizes, or utility-weighted effects. He fears that such conclusions obscure individual findings that he wants to be inviolate because stakeholders will differ in how they weight each finding, the findings themselves will differ in validity, and the relevance of some findings might not be apparent until later. He also fears that summaries gloss over important contingencies that limit a finding's scope of applicability. His final fear is that summaries compromise the evaluator's educator role because, in deciding what weights to attach to different findings, the evaluator must implicitly take sides.

The key question is whether it is possible to construct summaries that respect the integrity of lower-order findings and avoid unrealistic assumptions implicit in the weighting techniques. No easy answer is forthcoming, since, by their very nature, summaries simplify and, in adding another set of techniques to those that generated lower-order findings, summaries are more assumption riddled than lower-order findings. Nonetheless, summaries can be constructed that are faithful to lower-order findings and can educate audiences rather than bamboozle them.

Consider again the evaluation of *Sesame Street* by Cook et al. (1975); they laboriously presented findings for each achievement test and population group. Only then did they attempt to synthesize, highlighting how dependent the valuing of *Sesame Street* is on assumptions one makes about the importance of improving the preschool achievement of all preschoolers versus economically disadvantaged preschoolers, and of disadvantaged preschoolers knowing more versus narrowing the achievement gaps that separate their achievement from that of others. *Sesame Street* is "good" if one values millions of preschoolers from different backgrounds — including the poor and racial minorities — knowing more, but is "bad" if one values reducing the achievement gap between richer and poorer children. The summary asked whether *Sesame Street* is part of the solution or part of the problem for economically disadvantaged children. Individual findings were respected and a sensitivity was shown to social values and the assumptions of the summary. Does Cronbach have too undifferentiated a view of what a summary statement contains? Or is this more contingent and educative type of summary contained in his concept of the evaluator as educator? We are not sure — this is an uncertainty in his theory.

Stakeholder groups will create their own evaluative summaries, whether evaluators do so or not. If so, might it be better for evaluators to do some form of summary? Evaluators are not necessarily more likely to be correct, but, being acquainted with multiple criteria and weights for valuing results, they might produce summaries that are educative and that could help stakeholders consider factors they might otherwise overlook. In our experience in policy we often hear the question, Is Program X any good? and hear global evaluative rejoinders of yes or no. Cronbach wants evaluators to respond to such questions by "educating" the questioners about assumptions on which such verdicts rest and about different verdicts that result if different criteria are used. But it might sometimes be useful for evaluators to answer the summative question carefully — not as a single good/bad judgment or estimate of effect size, but a small set of summaries based upon different plausible assumptions. Such an answer would not be perfect, but might be less imperfect than no summative answer or inundating readers with all lower-order findings.

Careful attempts to construct summary statements might alter the terms of public debates or sharpen the evaluator's analysis of evaluative claims. Cronbach ignores this possibility in his general antipathy to evaluative summaries. This reluctance is inconsistent with his belief that, when specific information is needed by the policy-shaping community, evaluators should respond to these needs even if the methods for generating an answer are imperfect. If stakeholders value summary statements, why should responsive evaluators not provide such statements if (a) individual findings are also presented, (b) summaries are hedged with discussions of how outcomes are weighted, and (c) a range of estimates is presented? Cronbach has not yet specified contingencies under which different forms of a summary might be helpful to stakeholders. His blanket disavowal of summaries fails some of the needs of the policy-shaping community to which Cronbach wants to respond.

All current techniques for generating summaries are flawed — cost-benefit analysis, meta-analysis, subjective utility scaling, and even non-quantitative reasoning. We prefer some of these techniques to others, and have the gravest misgivings about cost-benefit analysis. We have been impressed by the warm reception of meta-analysis in public policy. Part of this may be due to the easily memorized summaries meta-analysis provides, rarely modified by more contingencies. But for these very reasons Cronbach objects to it. Meta-analysis does not reflect ontological complexity, and so has little of the transfer-facilitating explanatory knowledge that Cronbach values highly (Cook, 1990). Also, meta-analysis usually aggregates data across so many variables that it is unclear to users how much overlap exists between the studies that were synthesized and the populations and classes of local interest. Finally, if a single direction of bias exists across meta-analyzed studies, a biased average effect size results.

These objections should give pause to naive users of meta-analysis. Nonetheless, a critically assessed meta-analysis is useful; its results are more robust than most single studies could achieve, with obvious advantages for reassuring central decision makers that, in the past, a particular class of treatment usually had a particular type of effect. This does not guarantee the future, but does promise well for it. The heterogeneity also helps local users to generalize. They might adopt a treatment, not because it was effective in contexts like their own, but because it repeatedly caused a particular class of effect despite large heterogeneity in the circumstances studied. The theory of generalization implicit in meta-analysis is heterogeneous replication rather than proximal similarity (as with Campbell) or reproducible micromediating processes (as with Cronbach). Cronbach is no fan of meta-analysis because its major rationale is brute-empirical replication, which he values less than theory-contingent transfer.

Cronbach is also no fan of subjective utility scaling techniques (Edwards et al., 1975) to facilitate summary judgments. The uses they illustrate are in contexts where managers attach preferences/utilities to particular outcomes; Cronbach would object to such narrow application. But the technique could be used with a broader array of stakeholders. Different summaries could be constructed using the weights of each group. Nothing prevents broader use of utility techniques in ways that are commensurate with Cronbach's pluralistic conception of policy in the United States. Stakeholder-specific weighting schemes would not result in the single value judgments that Cronbach fears, and would enlighten stakeholders about how program achievements relate to furthering stakeholder interests. Cronbach's attitude about constructing overall summary statements is so negative that he ignores many situations where summary judgments might be not only feasible but also useful in ways that are not parochial.

To be fair, Cronbach favors building multiple perspectives into evaluations; summary statements that reflect multiple perspectives are in line with this principle. At issue is the inevitability he assumes between summaries and pushing a single view that is insensitive to stakeholder differences. Stakeholder-sensitive summaries could add to the liveliness and memorability of communication that Cronbach seeks, and could respond to a need for summary statements that some consumers express. It will help evaluators adopt an educator rather than a pontificator role as they outline different weights that characterize stakeholders and lead to differences in the lens through which the program is judged.

Theory of Use

Cronbach's theory of use depends heavily on the work of many empirical researchers, especially Weiss. He postulates that use occurs mostly in an enlightenment rather than an instrumental mode and ensues not just from knowledge gained at particular evaluation sites but also from past literature on programs like the one under analysis and from what is known in basic research about substantive theory undergirding a program. He further assumes that many uses occur in the long term to influence the design of future programs rather than simply to modify the program under evaluation. So a key question is, How can evaluators plan for such use?

Cronbach is, of course, interested in short-term use of knowledge in policy debates, but says it is unrealistic and undesirable to expect that knowledge to dictate any decision. He counsels evaluators to participate in debates to which evaluation knowledge might pertain, even if they can bring to bear only critically appraised impressions rather than systematic data. He urges evaluators to release information whenever asked, whether fully digested or not, provided it is as well assessed as it could be at that stage and does not violate confidentiality. He counsels against evaluators remaining silent until the final evaluation report is available. Such reports usually represent a communication overload, are often self-defeating in their thoroughness, and have opportunity costs stemming from the failure to speak out at opportune times before the report was ready. He stresses the importance of personal factors in knowledge dissemination and use, including the accidents that locate evaluators in some information networks but not others. Be open, be around, he suggests; never forget that expertise is relative, that the evaluator with grounded, on-line program experience has access to important knowledge that others do not have, even if it fails to meet the traditional canons of social science. In this pragmatic theory, evaluators' judgments matter.

In evaluating evaluations, "scientific quality is not the principal standard; an evaluation should aim to be comprehensible, correct and complete, and credible to partisans on all sides" (Cronbach, et al., 1980, p. 11). Users of evaluation rarely place most stress on the technical quality of the methods. Hence Cronbach resolves the trade-off between bandwidth and fidelity in favor of bandwidth, and lower-quality methods are warranted for some questions if bandwidth requires this. His algorithm for selecting questions invokes leverage and prior uncertainty, but is mute about how much uncertainty reduction various stakeholder groups need for taking results seriously. But in our experience, quality of evidence matters to many stakeholders and is one criterion by which they evaluate evidence (Weiss & Bucuvalas, 1980). The primary focus may be on action, but decision shapers can have personal and political reasons for acting in accord with the best available scientific evidence. Indeed, if this were not true, we would not find federal agencies using National Academy of Science panels for reviews. Chelimsky (1987a), from her vantage point as director of the Program Evaluation and Methodology Division of the General Accounting Office, says technical quality is of the highest importance for legislative bodies that receive evaluations from her staff. And in some debates — like that on the effects of television violence on children — technical issues predominate in public and political discussions, and the debate languishes unresolved because an appropriate methodology is unavailable.

Technical quality may be valued more at the federal than at the local level and more by managers than by service deliverers. The counterinstances cited above have this flavor. Cronbach's own experience is very broad, including much federal work; but education is a specialty of his, and is a field with a long tradition of local rather than state control and with an emphasis on changing teacher behavior (rather than formal policy) to improve educational programs. But even if technical quality of evidence counts less as one moves from the central heights of planning to the trenches of implementation, teachers, principals, and superintendents may still presume that novel practices brought to their attention have passed muster technically. Cronbach's theory of use acknowledges some situations where technical quality is especially important — if few questions are important and collecting fine-grained data to answer them may reduce uncertainty to a satisfactory level. Yet in straining against the dominant apotheosis of technical quality, his contingent approach is sometimes overshadowed by his own prose, which downplays fidelity and technical quality and emphasizes bandwidth and looser methods that probe many issues in the same evaluation study.

Cronbach posits that much use is unplanned, in the distant future, and concerns programs other than the one under study. The difficult issue thus arises of how to plan for such diffuse and unanticipatable usage. His algorithm for selecting questions involves estimating the degree of leverage a question has, assessing how much prior uncertainty about it exists, and then judging how much uncertainty evaluation will reduce. Though difficult in practice, this is a reasonable theory of question choice. But it applies more to the short than the long term, and to the program under analysis rather than some other program. For such issues Cronbach asserts that maximal utility comes from probing the substantive program assumptions. Knowing about their general validity and about the specific conditions under which they are valid should help modify both the program on hand and the class of programs designed around a similar theory. A Cronbach-influenced evaluation will include probes of causal mediating mechanisms through which a program influences outcomes. To do this, evaluators should lay out the program's substantive theory and test those parts of it where prior uncertainty is greatest and system dependence is highest.

This emphasis on theory-based explanation is presumed relevant to all officials and practitioners. The relevance to central government officials is obvious. Rarely will users at the local level look at national-level (or even state-level) research and recognize the particulars of their sites;

rarely will evaluative data be collected at their sites. How can evaluations help local practitioners if the particulars of a past evaluation differ from those to which the heterogeneous array of local officials and practitioners wants to generalize? How can we generalize from UTOS to *UTOS to help the army of local officials and practitioners in the thousands of sites that characterize any one sector?

Cronbach responds that once causal mediating mechanisms are known, local users can ask if the elements identified in the causal model are or could be present at their site. The degree of proximal similarity between their site and those where research was conducted is irrelevant. A second response is that analyses at the sub-UTOS level might suggest some conditions under which program theory is differentially effective. A third response is that evaluators can look to supplementary sources for knowledge about mediating processes, such as various extant substantive theories or the practical experience of those who know program design and implementation quality. Planning for evaluation use depends on learning about explanatory knowledge:

> Knowing this week's score does not tell the coach how to prepare for next week's game. The information that an intervention had satisfactory or unsatisfactory outcomes is of little use by itself; users of the study need to know what led to success or failure. Only with that information can the conditions that worked be replicated or modified sufficiently in the next trial to get better results. (Cronbach et al., 1980, p. 251)

How well placed is Cronbach's faith in knowledge of causal generative processes and contingencies as means of generalization? There is no sure way of knowing. But such a belief is regularly reiterated to the public in defense of basic science budgets; for instance: "Let us basic researchers study whatever we want — usually generative causal processes — and we promise that our results are likely to be usable in different ways and contexts we cannot now conceive." Stable knowledge of causal mediating processes will often be useful in informing present and future program design. But does this justify Cronbach's silence about how to facilitate instrumental use? He acknowledges that instrumental use sometimes occurs, and urges evaluators to stay close to constituencies, feeding them relevant information for decisions. But we join Rossi and Freeman (1989) in noting that, while instrumental usage contributes to the program modification less often than other forms of use, it is still worth planning for. A comprehensive, contingency theory of use should specify pathways for both.

Cronbach assumes that useful knowledge of generative causal mechanisms can be found in the social sciences. Is this accurate? Cronbach likes Mackie's (1974) essentialist theory of causation, which assumes causal relationships exist of the type "When A varies, B inevitably results." But Mackie's theory also postulates that such knowledge is virtually unattainable in practice. At best, a long series of studies might slowly reduce some uncertainty about a causal relationship that stems from multiple conditions and partial causes that are inevitably present in causal propositions. In this formulation, single tests of unconditional causal propositions are impossible; even programs of research are unlikely to rule out all contenders as partial causes. Reading Mackie, one cannot believe it easy to generate definitive and complete causal information about social events. Nor can causal mediation be definitively established with conventional social science techniques of causal modeling. Cronbach writes favorably about the Transitional Aid to Released Prisoners (TARP) evaluation by Rossi, Berk, and Lenihan (1980), which used such techniques to explain the absence of effects in a randomized experiment. But his approval is conditional; he is fully aware of the high likelihood of misspecifying any causal model, including those about the substantive theory undergirding a program.

How does Cronbach recommend doing this crucial, but almost impossible, task of extrapolating to *UTOS? For single evaluation studies, Cronbach recommends an eclectic set of quantitative and qualitative tools, all to reduce uncertainty without aspiring to total certainty. Included are firsthand, qualitative knowledge of program operations and knowledge of relevant substantive literature. He never expects certain knowledge of causal mediating processes; useful knowledge is the goal. But we do not know what features of single studies convince national and local audiences about mediating processes, whether through Cronbach's techniques or those of others. We are also apprehensive that the techniques Cronbach prefers for individual studies increase the likelihood of incorrect knowledge that might be more harmful than beneficial in its consequences.

Fortunately, Cronbach places more faith in the accumulated knowledge base than in the results of single studies. Crucial is the slow accumulation of research as knowledge of causal processes enters into general circulation, including into textbooks about effective practice. How the existing knowledge is to be synthesized is not clear from Cronbach's work. He advocates standing committees of experts within topic areas that would offer advice based on their knowledge of research, their command of substantive theories, and their general experience and wisdom. To prevent parochialism, Cronbach would rotate members regularly. These standing committees might well operate from the essentialist notion of complete theory to which Cronbach aspires; it is less clear that they can speak clearly to local needs for tailored advice. They are more relevant to "what works in general" or "what the crucial components of any local program should be." Nor could such standing bodies be very active, given how busy substantive experts are. Finally, who would fund them? The closest approximation today is National Academy of Science panels, but they do not have the continuity and intensity that Cronbach's vision calls for. His standing committees would help synthesize knowledge, but might not be sufficient for identifying transferable program-relevant knowledge.

Cronbach is leery of meta-analysis for generating these syntheses. It usually makes use of outcome data, and has been insensitive to micro-mediating processes. It presents an average effect size relating a global manipulandum to outcome measures lumped into very general categories, limiting scope for the treatment-aptitude interactions his theory values. Cronbach believes the social system needs causal explanatory knowledge, not knowledge of things that work on average under a set of diverse conditions. His characterization of meta-analysis as insensitive to micro-mediating process is a fair description of the recent past. But there are a few exceptions. Harris and Rosenthal (1985) meta-analyzed intrapersonal processes that mediate teacher expectancy effects; and the Russell Sage Foundation is currently putting together a casebook of explanatory meta-analyses. These efforts explore the considerable promise of meta-analysis for gaining information about causal moderators, causally efficacious components of the independent variable, causally affected components of the effect, and demographic, setting, and temporal factors that condition the effect. Cronbach may not have paid enough attention to this developing potential.

Cronbach's faith in causal mediation as the path to extrapolation may cause him to underestimate other useful theories of generalization. He sees a role for formal sampling theory, but only when inferences from samples of people to populations are involved — from u to U. He also sees a role for Campbell's proximal similarity, when subgroup analyses are conducted on samples deliberately chosen because their characteristics resemble those of particular local populations. But he pays less attention to generalizations based on a robust causal connection, as when meta-analysis demonstrates an effect across a heterogeneous collection of populations of persons, settings, times, treatments, and outcomes. Even if the achieved heterogeneity in meta-analysis does not warrant extrapolation to all possible contexts, the leap of faith inherent in extrapolation is less troublesome if the causal connection is probabilistically stable across heterogeneous instances. The key issue in meta-analytic generalization is how globally the cause and effect are specified. The danger is that so many variants are combined that the global constructs lose all trace of the things practitioners might actually vary and the attributes of clients or circumstances that might actually change. Cronbach's neglect of meta-analysis and its brute empirical theory of causal generalization limits his analysis of useful causal generalizations.

The obvious contrast here is between Cronbach and Campbell. Campbell believes that multiple evaluations help converge on a general estimate of effect. He limits the analysis of causal conditions to those that policy actors can affect. He is less convinced than Cronbach of our ability to tailor at the local level, arguing that it is rarely possible to provide different instruction to different children in the same school, different prenatal services to healthy pregnant women, or different forms of juvenile detention to different young people convicted of similar offenses. Cronbach, by contrast, regretted that his work with Snow considered first-order interactions instead of fourth-order interactions involving aptitude, age, subject-matter, treatment, and outcome factors. Cronbach wants different treatments for children of different aptitude levels at different ages for different school subjects and for different outcomes. Campbell's approach is simpler, asking if a particular class of treatments is generally effective across outcome measures and across aptitude, age, and subject-matter levels. Campbell would not factorially cross all of Cronbach's variables, though from a God's-eye view Campbell's formulation is contained in Cronbach's. But Campbell does not believe that policymakers can use or wait for the complex knowledge Cronbach requires. Highly differentiated services can make policy actors uncomfortable if they have to justify differences in treatment to those receiving the less desired alternatives. Moreover, many local practitioners have neither motivation nor skill to implement the differentiated set of services that a causal contingency theory suggests.

Both Campbell and Cronbach could be correct if a high degree of service differentiation is more feasible in some contexts than in others — say, more in education than in policing, or more with special classroom pull-outs than with instruction in intact classes. Unfortunately, we rarely know about factors facilitating the provision of different services to different persons in the same institution — except hospitals, where differential diagnoses predominate and are socially legitimated. Cronbach may inadvertently exaggerate the amount of differentiation in service delivery that can be politically justified and locally implemented. His experience in education, and his long search for full prediction of complexly determined performance, may have led him to a belief in service differentiation that generalizes poorly across sectors or is too fine-grained for the coarse-grained implementation of social change.

Here, then, is a key issue in Cronbach's theory of use. For stimulating long-term use, should the preferred strategy be to create highly differentiated knowledge about causal contingencies, even if these theories are less well established because of problems with social science methods for causal explanation and because, from within these, Cronbach advocates those that are technically less perfect — the methods of journalists, historians, and ethnographers? Or should the strategy be to identify types of treatment that usually work with target populations, substituting replication across heterogeneous instances, as in meta-analysis, for understanding causal process? No easy answer is forthcoming; we need both in some measure. But still, the choice leads to important issues of research priority; it affects how one does evaluation. The social sciences have not been very successful with their most esteemed methods for causal explanation, let alone with the looser methods that Cronbach generally prefers. They have had more success identifying robust and manipulable causal agents through brute empirical paths such as meta-analysis.

There is a profound irony at this intersection of theories of use and method. Campbell gives up on the full explanation of essentialist theories of causation, including Mackie's theory. Cronbach believes in an essentialist notion of causation and believes that full causal explanation remains the traditional goal of knowledge in general and in science in particular. Cronbach retains the traditional scientific aspiration to causal explanation but uses nontraditional scientific methods for this end, while Campbell retains the stellar scientific method — the experiment — but abandons the traditional scientific aspiration to full causal explanation. Campbell substitutes the aspiration to identify with great confidence robust, molar causal connections, while Cronbach is reconciled to achieving only marginal decreases in uncertainty whenever many questions are asked in a single study.

Theory of Knowledge Construction

Cronbach's generalizability theory is predicated on several assumptions: that test performance is multiply determined, that it helps to know about determinants of test performance, and that some users are interested in only a subset of determinants that help them make decisions. His theory of aptitude-treatment interactions makes similar assumptions. So does his work on evaluation: that program performance is multiply determined, that it is best to know about all determinants of performance (*UTOS), but some users are interested in only the subset of determinants that characterize their work setting. Throughout all these areas he pays explicit attention to (a) the ontological assumption of causal complexity that can be captured only by multivariate explanation, (b) the traditional scientific aspiration to perfect knowledge of this world, and (c) a pragmatic concern to provide knowledge based on proximal similarity or causal explanation to help practitioners shape local practices and judge them intelligently.

The theme that most characterizes Cronbach's intellectual endeavors is this: how to construct methods to explain multiply determined complex phenomena so that one can respond to general and local circumstances with knowledge of the likely limits of application of a given relationship. It is our distinct impression that the younger Cronbach was more hopeful than the older Cronbach about the likelihood of achieving such knowledge. His experiences as theorist and researcher, and the antipositivist trend in philosophy of science, may have played some role in these growing doubts. The older Cronbach had no clear epistemological stance to adopt as a replacement for the earlier positivist tinge in his work. Mackie's (1974) theory of "gappy universal propositions" is not a replacement epistemology, for it offers no recipe to learn about causal processes; rather, it brilliantly explains why it is so hard to learn such things. Cronbach may have liked Mackie's work precisely because it does not oversimplify the intellectual problem or peddle a practical but partial solution.

Nor can Cronbach find certainty in the methods of our day. Using the highest standards of methodological rigor, his 1980 and 1982 books trenchantly critique experiments and quasi-experiments, concluding that many experiments have undesirable side effects and that data analysts can never know if they have successfully adjusted initial group nonequivalence statistically (Cronbach et al., 1977). He notes the limits of sampling with known probability, not because it is biased — it is not! — but because it often cannot be used when generalizing causal relationships involving social program manipulanda. Resources rarely permit taking a random sample from some clearly designated population of settings or persons, and then assigning these elements to different treatment conditions. Cronbach also criticizes causal modeling, is sensitive to the limits of qualitative studies, and even criticizes his own early work on construct validation (1989a). For him, no method is perfect, even for its primary task. Such techniques are even less perfect in evaluation because evaluations should, in his view, usually try to answer many different kinds of questions. No simple methodological advice emerges from Cronbach's pen. He wants evaluators to study inferences of many kinds, with many ways of generating the evidence to support or challenge each inference. Evaluation has no overwhelmingly dominant knowledge needs (like molar causation for Campbell) and no single method appropriate to meet those needs (such as the experiment and quasi-experiment for Campbell).

Campbell's preferences reduce the complexity of choices; Cronbach's increase them.

Cronbach adds to the complexity by advocating multiple methods for generating any one type of knowledge; he might propose a different method for the same type of inference in different studies. His choice of method depends on priority knowledge needs and how one method intersects with another in fulfilling multiple needs within budget and time. If resources are considerable and causal inference is paramount, he might recommend a randomized experiment; if cause is important but description of process is even more so, he might prefer on-site observation linked to conceptual analysis of causes. Techniques for causal explanation might differ from study to study — causal modeling in one case, on-site observation in another, a literature review in another, a combination of these, or something completely different. Which method to choose in each instance is a matter of trade-offs, not of the method's reputation in the scholarly community. Method choice is cut adrift from traditional scientific practice, which, in our view, links a particular class of question to a particular preferred method for providing an answer.

In addition, Cronbach further asserts that evaluators must modify guiding research questions when original questions become less relevant than originally thought. Designing for shifting questions has never been the strong point of quantitative social science. If current methods are not so flexible, Cronbach urges us to replace or complement them with other methods. To find them, Cronbach looks to professional groups that traditionally deal with questions that evolve in time and have methods to answer many different types of questions in the same study — journalists, qualitative social scientists, and historians. From these disciplines he draws an eclectic set of methods capable of multifunctional and fluid evaluation work. This preference transcends the usual notion of research design predicated on a single method providing the best answer for a particular inference, whether about causal connections (the experiment), causal explanation (modeling techniques), or generalization to populations (sampling theory). Cronbach's functional theory of design is radical when compared to traditional structural theories of design. He writes:

> The central purpose of evaluation differs from that of basic social research, and evaluations fit into a different institutional and political context. . . . Many recommendations appropriate for long-term programs of scientific research are ill suited to evaluation. Hence, general writings on design and scientific method are inadequate to guide the evaluator. General recommendations on evaluation can also mislead; evaluations should not be cast in a single mold. For any evaluation many good designs can be proposed, but no perfect ones. (1982a, p. 2)

Yet this functional model of plastic method choice is not unbounded; it is not the case that "anything goes." For instance, Cronbach adamantly rejects Campbell's argument that internal validity (in Campbell's sense) is the *sine qua non* of evaluation because describing causal connections is evaluation's central task. Cronbach says external validity — generalizing to unobserved persons, settings, treatments, and outcomes — is the *sine qua non*. For him, the field's central task is to generate knowledge that transfers to heterogeneous local projects where services are or might be delivered. Cronbach is also not averse to suggesting types of method that might generally be used, though no method is always best. Thus, if most evaluations should answer many questions, the best methods will not be experimental; they might be quasi-experimental or nonexperimental and include an extensive qualitative analysis of program process. Cronbach wants methods to suit questions, and so avoids peddling method recipes.

It seems to us that a theory as explicit as Cronbach's about the need to design and redesign studies might recognize that sometimes the need for high-quality inference about a particular type of knowledge is important to many potential users and points toward a particular design. This could be the case when needs analysis is crucial that might well lead to selection of a survey; or it might be the case if causal descriptive knowledge is paramount, so a randomized experiment is needed. Cronbach is adamant that such knowledge is rarely paramount, citing Moynihan's assertion that policy shapers assign a lower priority to causation than academics. They need to act, and so use whatever evidence is at hand, irrespective of technical quality. Our experience of congressional debates has not convinced us that Moynihan's position is widely shared in the policy-shaping community. Debates about violence on children's television and about the effects of the Women, Infant, and Children Special Supplemental Food Program (WIC), and the experience of evaluators in the legislative branch (Chelimsky, 1987c), convince us that Cronbach overgeneralizes this point. Even if he were correct, this would not imply that knowledge of molar causal connections is usually irrelevant to the policy-shaping community.

Cronbach cites Mackie and his own reanalyses of studies to show that, even for those who believe causal connections warrant high priority in evaluation, their favored technique for attaining such knowledge, the experiment, is imperfect. This argument obscures the fact that the rationale for experiments has always been that they promote internal validity (in Campbell's sense) better than the alternatives — not that they are perfect. No one claims that single experiments provide clear causal inferences of the near-essentialist sort that Mackie (and Cronbach) esteems. Experiments promote a different, more modest but nontrivial, type of causation as embodied in the manipulability theory (Collingwood, 1940; Gasking,

1955; Whitbeck, 1977). Indeed, the popularity of meta-analysis attests to the perceived value of the manipulability theory undergirding many meta-analyses. We find it difficult to give internal validity a low priority just because it is not fully attainable in open system studies, including those that use experimental methods.

But Cronbach is right that experiments are irrelevant to some other functions that evaluations must fulfill, especially generalization and measurement; he is also right that they sometimes require trade-offs with methods for fulfilling other functions. But none of this implies that experiments are incapable of the type of causal inference for which they were designed. Even if they were, that would not require relegating them to a minor role in the armamentarium of evaluation methods, for in Cronbach's own theory method choice does not depend on generating *perfect* knowledge. Reducing uncertainty is the criterion, if priorities among questions are clear and if methods fit the list of prioritized questions. Sometimes the experiment might fit into such a package; sometimes not. To judge by the omnipresence of experiments in health promotion under the National Institutes of Health, or by the Department of Labor's espousal of experimental studies of job training programs (Stromsdorfer, 1987), many policy shapers think experiments are highly valuable for providing reassurance about the causal connections that are so central in their thinking about policy. Such policy shapers show little inclination to prefer methods from history, journalism, or qualitative social science. They prefer the quantitative experimental option, which today provides more legitimacy for an answer than alternatives. The policy shapers may be wrong in this. But since evaluation is a short-term pragmatic exercise in Cronbach's theory, their method preferences and the needs for credibility these preferences reflect should count in method choice.

Though he recognizes that evaluation involves exploring options for action, Cronbach does not favor comparative studies of the relative value of a small set of options. This is because (a) they often deal with options for programs rather than with options for changes within a program; (b) outcomes often differ in relevance to the options under evaluation, being biased toward some options more than others; (c) some past comparisons show more variability in outcomes within each option than between options; and (d) the worse variants might have done better than the superior ones if minor improvements were made in program design. Cronbach leans toward exploring the naturally occurring options within a program instead of doing experiments.

However, we were impressed by a recent comparative experiment explicitly designed to consider the mistakes of early comparative experiments (Connell et al., 1985). This study contrasted four curricula for teaching health education. The sponsors of each curriculum helped select outcome criteria, noting measures that were less relevant to their program. Each option was then tested against all the others and a control group to assess both absolute and relative efficacy. Each option was tested both as an established program in a school where it had already been in place for some time and as a novel option in new schools. Detailed information was collected about how much the planned curriculum was actually implemented. Finally, since some curricula were more extensive than others, options were compared to each other on the amount of time spent on each in the schools.

Results showed that curricula did not differ initially; that gains over controls subsequently occurred in knowledge, attitude, and reported health behavior in both the established and the novel instances; and that programs with greater inputs gained more, but no program gained more than any other per time unit of input. According to Cronbach, such comparative studies are difficult or impossible to execute. Yet, if they carefully take cognizance of the lessons of the past, they are sometimes feasible (Cook & Walberg, 1985). Since comparative experimental studies speak directly to the issue of exploring options, we wonder at the mismatch between Cronbach's stated aim for evaluation, to "contribute to enlightened discussions of alternative plans for action" (Cronbach et al., 1980, p. 2), and his recourse to means of learning about alternative paths for action that are manifestly less direct than the comparative study.

Cronbach's pessimism about the certainty yielded by existing social science methods, and his hope that each evaluation would answer many different types of questions, led him to suggest that successful evaluation requires less uncertainty reduction than successful science. He wrote with approval about the evaluation by Rossi et al. (1980) of a demonstration program for ex-offenders that seemed to produce no effects on prison recidivism. The authors found that this no-difference finding might have resulted from two countervailing forces that canceled each other out. One was a treatment effect. To Cronbach, Rossi et al. were exemplary because they explored why no differences resulted from the experimental contrast, since such knowledge generates understanding of TARP and related programs. Other scholars were less impressed by the attempt to interpret a null finding. Zeisel (1982) said Rossi et al. capitalized on chance, uncovering a spurious contingency that only seemed to make the program look effective. Cronbach's approval and Zeisel's disapproval are not necessarily inconsistent. They may reflect different standards about what constitutes a valid knowledge claim, highlighting the basic point: When will harm result from the looser standards for knowledge that Cronbach builds into his functional theory of research design?

One could argue about TARP that accepting the null hypothesis is harmful if the program reduces recidivism under some conditions. But the opposite argument is also plausible: Less stringent standards make one spend longer identifying effects that are trivial or that occur under such rare circumstances they are not of much value. Social science methodologists traditionally prefer to defend against false positive over false negative findings, and might not be impressed by arguments for increasing the risk of false positive findings in evaluation. Cronbach's stand on this matter moves evaluation further from the social sciences and closer to management consulting by emphasizing credibility over validity, situational specificity of data, eclecticism of methods, consideration of knowledge from past consultations, and counseling timely action with information on hand irrespective of how well it meets scholarly standards. Cronbach would not approve of consulting only in the interests of management; he wants to serve a broader set of stakeholders. But in rejecting the standards of inference that predominate in science, Cronbach points evaluation toward the need to develop and justify its own standards.

A key issue is to identify the standards underlying the methods of the historian, journalist, and qualitative social scientist that Cronbach endorses, and then to justify these standards on grounds other than the purely pragmatic. Unfortunately, these methods are not comprehensively described and analyzed in Cronbach's work. Few evaluators are schooled in their use, and few practicing scientists will lay down the tools and standards that worked for them in the past, especially without easily implemented and socially legitimated alternatives. Hence Cronbach's advocacy is not likely to shake faith in the standards now dominant among evaluators. Moreover, many scientists do not share Cronbach's assumptions about ontological complexity, the limited role that underspecified substantive theories can play, and the limits of current quantitative techniques for achieving knowledge of a complex social world. Still, Cronbach has an unusual grasp of the history of social science. Perhaps one day we will witness the transition from social science to social inquiry he advocates, from a more sciencelike practice to a more artlike practice. However, as of 1990 many areas resist this notion, largely because it implies so radical a change in practice. It loosens evaluation's ties with the more esteemed social sciences, and it involves unclear standards of inference.

Theory of Practice

Cronbach's theory of practice is constructed around his assumptions about types of questions worth asking and the degree of certainty worth attaining if evaluation is to contribute to improving the program under test and programs superficially dissimilar to it. He wants evaluators to be eclectic in choice of methods, avoiding slavish adherence to any particular methods, and adopting the role of educator rather than judge, philosopher-king, or servant to a particular stakeholder group. Program improvement that benefits all is the goal. To this end evaluators must ask many types of questions, so bandwidth has primacy over fidelity. Important roles in evaluation are played by wisdom, judgment, reflections on impressions, purposive sampling, and case study designs. If evaluation should probe multiple issues simultaneously, then the starting point for any theory of evaluation is: Which sorts of questions are most important, and how does one know this?

Cronbach offers both all-purpose and particularistic answers. The all-purpose answer depends on the evaluator's assessment of the leverage associated with a particular issue, the degree of prior uncertainty about the answer, and the degree of possible and desirable uncertainty reduction in light of trade-offs among questions, methods, and resources. This all-purpose algorithm results in different types of issues gaining primacy in different program contexts. Cronbach offers no solace to those who want concepts and operations they can easily plug into their evaluations; he offers no "evaluation program kit," no "checklist of evaluation questions." His grasp of issues is complex and contingent on the many different situations in which evaluation occurs. But this respect for uniqueness in the heterogeneous world of social programs forces Cronbach to great abstraction in the concepts undergirding his theory of selecting evaluation issues. Concepts such as leverage, prior uncertainty, and degree of desired uncertainty reduction are hard to conceptualize, let alone operationalize. Practicing evaluators cannot read his work and say, "Now that I know about leverage and uncertainty, I have a 'tool' to justify and prioritize evaluation questions." Cronbach's work generally sensitizes evaluators to questions of leverage and uncertainty reduction, but it does not as clearly help practicing evaluators do a persuasive analysis of leverage and uncertainty reduction. The abstraction is persuasive; the tools for its implementation are not.

Even if leverage and prior uncertainty were easily assessed, in most evaluations many questions are important and it is hard to sustain fine distinctions among them. Multiplicity of important questions makes method choice even more complicated. No single method can be paramount; evaluators have to mix and match methods in unique ways for each study. The method for inferring, say, molar causation might differ from one evaluation to the next depending on the context. In breaking the link between particular kinds of questions and the small set of clearly ranked methods appropriate for answering them, Cronbach seriously complicates the task facing practicing evaluators. They must now command a large repertoire of methods for answering each kind of question, with no methodological justification for preference among them, whatever social science methodology textbooks might say to the contrary. This ambiguity is partly on target, and may even reflect how the most creative scientists operate. But it is an impediment to practicing evaluators accepting Cronbach's theory if they want tools that simplify rather than complicate their work.

The situation is even more complicated than this, because Cronbach suggests that evaluation questions should be malleable and modified as circumstances change. New issues and questions entail midstream redesign. Notice the invitation that Cronbach makes to practicing evaluators. He claims that arriving at original questions is time-consuming and fallible; that many different designs can answer any particular set of questions but without clear criteria for differentiating among these designs; and that original method choices might need changing as evaluation questions and issues are revised in midstream. This may accurately state the stances required of evaluators by the reality of multiple stakeholders, of fallible methods, and of social programs in constant flux, but it is hardly an inviting portrayal of the evaluator's task. It is an invitation into a world with few clear methods for raising or answering questions, with little hope of certainty about anything, devoid of foundations or clear prescriptions about practice. Evaluators who crave clear priorities or who expect clear answers will find it easy to reject Cronbach's all-purpose theory of question choice based on leverage, prior uncertainty, and the degree of anticipated uncertainty reduction.

His more particularistic theory of question choice offers more psychological supports and better-known paths to practical evaluation activities. Cronbach says that most important evaluation questions are often about substantive theory undergirding program design. From this follows the primacy of investigating why a program appears to be more or less successful, so such knowledge can feed into improving the program under evaluation or others like it. He realizes that some stakeholders are not interested in such knowledge; they legitimately want either the kind of outcome knowledge that Scriven and Campbell value or the stakeholder-specific knowledge to which Wholey and Stake aspire. But in general he believes that causal process issues are most important to aid transfer to other programs. Thus some readers might ignore his all-purpose algorithm for question generation, and the dilemmas of method choice to which it gives rise, and concentrate instead on the more clearly defined task of identifying causal mediating processes. This is, after all, not just any task. In the pantheon of scientific gods, it may be the most important deity of all. Cronbach's emphasis on identifying causal processes gives evaluators not just a specific task that is missing from his all-purpose theory, but also scientific respectability and policy utility. What more potent promise could one imagine?

However, this promise has not resulted in a horde of acolytes paying homage to his theory. It has captured more attention for its critique of summative evaluation and experiments than for its particular evaluation alternatives. This may be due to some readers' doubts about answering questions of micromediation and multivariate causal contingency when legitimate doubts exist about whether there is any significant causal impact at all. It is one thing to cite Moynihan about the policy world being less concerned than academics with standards of evidence about causal description. It is quite a different thing for practicing evaluators to attribute little importance to reducing uncertainty about a causal connection, given their training and the norms of the general scientific community. Part of the small response to Cronbach's theory may occur because he assigns less weight to the most highly esteemed methods for analyzing causal contingency theories, such as path analysis or structural equation modeling. Cronbach has doubts (which we share) about the quality of extant theory for specifying causal models correctly. Some of the small response may be due to his call for evaluators to adopt the explanatory methods of journalists, historians, and cultural anthropologists. These are often considered exploratory methods, prone to spurious findings that could enter into deliberations in the policy-shaping community. In retaining explanation as the most general goal of evaluation, Cronbach emphasizes what many practicing evaluators would endorse as central. But in detaching explanation from traditional techniques for studying it, Cronbach invites answers widely thought to be less clear-cut and that move evaluators further from their training, reducing their communality with mainstream social science practice.

Cronbach wants evaluators to be educators; his writings may make obvious to practicing evaluators what the central behavioral requirements of that role are. The essence of traditional education includes a clear curriculum and authority structure and a captive audience. None of these is obviously present between the evaluator and stakeholders. Indeed, the relationships are often reversed. Evaluators have much less status and authority than some political stakeholder groups; they are lucky to get much time with them. It is rarely clear what stakeholders are to be taught about a program if they have different knowledge needs to be answered by different kinds of information with different degrees of intellectual warrant. Some educational contexts can also be characterized this way, but they are rare. Cronbach's discussion of evaluator as educator also makes clear what roles are not expected of evaluators — they should not be judges, servants, or philosopher-kings. Cronbach also makes clear that the evaluator's first duty is to represent the knowledge base. But otherwise his discussion is mostly mute about what characterizes the behavior of educators, leaving many evaluators unclear about what to do.

Cronbach's theory of practice does not arm evaluators with blueprints for doing their work, but Cronbach probably never had such an instrumental purpose in mind. In evaluation he aspires to enlightenment, not instrumental use; his theoretical work is consistent with this priority. He elucidates in incomparable fashion many dilemmas and trade-offs that bedevil the evaluator's life. He presents stimulating critiques of others' works, creatively developing and justifying alternatives to what they have done. This cannot help but create enlightenment in evaluators who take the time, and devote the cognitive energy, required to master his two volumes on evaluation. It would be inconsistent for Cronbach to have a theory of evaluation based on enlightenment and rejecting instrumental use and then to write about evaluation in a cookbook way, specifying lower-order instrumental procedures and failing to enlighten readers about major issues and trade-offs in evaluation. Cronbach's intellectual books will be read long after we stop reading the works of other theorists with narrower assumptions and purposes. But his purposes do not create an army of followers who put theory into practice. His work is too complex and contingent for that, too free-thinking and independent in the paths he explores, perhaps too rigorous in letting the analysis of purposes dictate the advocacy of means without considering the capacities of this generation's practitioners.

His theory of evaluation may incur the same fate as his theories of construct validation, treatment-aptitude interactions, and generalizability of measures. Each is a brilliant tour de force, unusually rewarding if closely read, intellectually rigorous, trenchant in analysis of the status quo, and creating truly unique alternatives sensitive to the scholarly need for general knowledge and the practitioner need for local application. But in each case his complex suggestions for improved practice are not widely used among practicing social scientists. Rare is the construct validation study à la Cronbach and Meehl — indeed, rare is the program of validation even approximating what they lay out; rare is the systematic program of research pursuing replicable fourth- and fifth-order interactions; rare is the formal generalizability study compared to simpler alternatives in psychometrics. Our fear is that the same fate has already befallen Cronbach's theory of evaluation. In most respects it far surpasses the theories we have considered thus far, being more comprehensive and empirically grounded, better advised about social programming and about how social science information is used. But his work is not readily attuned to what evaluators might do. It is too general and complex to provide the tools for practice that many evaluators want. For those who delve deeply into his theory, it may be too revolutionary in how it cuts evaluators off from old certainties in social science about question and method choice. But we would also guess his theory will have a more enthusiastic reception tomorrow, as seems to be the case with generalizability theory today, two decades after its initial presentation (Jones & Applebaum, 1989).

9

Peter H. Rossi:

Comprehensive, Tailored, Theory-Driven Evaluations — A Smorgasbord of Options

KEY TERMS AND CONCEPTS

Tailored Evaluation: Evaluation questions and research procedures depend on whether the program is an innovative intervention, a modification or expansion of an existing effort, or a well-established, stable activity.

Comprehensive Evaluation: Studying the design and conceptualization of an intervention, its implementation, and its utility.

Theory-Driven Evaluation: Constructing models of how programs work, using the models to guide question formation and data gathering; similar to what econometricians call model specification.

Demystification: Use of evaluation to influence thinking about an issue without using the information for a specific, documentable purpose.

The "Good Enough" Rule: Choose the best possible design, taking into account practicality and feasibility.

The Metallic and Plastic Laws of Evaluation: A review of the last two decades of evaluation research on major social programs in the United States does not sustain the proposition that the American establishment of policymakers, agency officials, professionals, and social scientists knew how to design and implement social programs that were at all effective, let alone spectacularly so.

BACKGROUND

Peter Rossi is a sociologist, currently professor of sociology at the University of Massachusetts, Amherst. Few evaluators have had more distinguished careers. He has been on the faculties of Harvard University, Johns Hopkins University, and the University of Chicago. He has been a consultant to most major federal agencies. He has been president of the American Sociological Association and the recipient of major awards in sociology, evaluation, and public policy analysis.

In evaluation, Rossi is best known for his widely used text on evaluation, coauthored with Howard E. Freeman, now in its fourth edition (Rossi & Freeman, 1989). In one recent survey, the second edition of that book (Rossi & Freeman, 1982) was rated third in impact among 21 different scholarly works in evaluation written by the theorists covered in the present book (Shadish & Epstein, 1987) — particularly impressive because, relative to the two most highly rated works (Campbell & Stanley, 1963; Weiss, 1972b), the Rossi book is of recent vintage. Clearly, through widespread use of this text in training evaluators, he has had a major impact on the field. Moreover, some subsequent editions (Rossi & Freeman, 1982, 1985, 1989) of the initial text (Rossi et al., 1979) were not mere cosmetic revisions. Rossi and Freeman often added new substance to new editions, and always reflected the subtle influence of previous theorists.

Many evaluators would be satisfied with just one success like the Rossi and Freeman text, but Rossi has had many more successes. He has been directly or indirectly involved in many important evaluations in the last 20 years (Berk, Lenihan, & Rossi, 1981; Rossi et al., 1980; Rossi & Lyall, 1976, 1978). He has edited major reference works on methodological topics like survey research (Rossi & Nock, 1982; Rossi, Wright, & Anderson, 1983), and he has written seminal articles and chapters in evaluation (Rossi, 1971a, 1971b, 1972; Rossi & Wright, 1977; Rossi & Williams, 1972). He has been around evaluation for a long time; he has seen a lot and learned a lot. That experience and wisdom is reflected in his theory.

Rossi collaborates extensively with colleagues who are major figures in their own right — Freeman, Berk, Chen, and Wright. Freeman and Berk have coedited *Evaluation Review* since its inception. As with Campbell's colleagues at Northwestern, Stake's at Illinois, or Wholey's at the Urban Institute, Rossi's colleagues could each be the topic of a chapter. While this chapter is about Rossi, the references we cite make it clear the work is often that of both Rossi and a collaborator.

Rossi's work is so diverse that it is hard to know which works are most central to his theory of evaluation. If all one had read was a recent treatise Rossi coauthored on social policy experimentation (Berk, Boruch,

Chambers, Rossi, & Witte, 1985), one might think him a narrow advocate of Campbellian experimentation. If all one had read were the articles by Chen and Rossi (1981, 1983, 1987) on theory-driven evaluation, one might take that as his theory, noting similarity between Rossi and Cronbach. We use Rossi and Freeman (1985) as the exemplar for Rossi's theory, for three reasons. First, it is the most comprehensive of his works on evaluation, the best big picture of his views on it. Second, the volume incorporates most of Rossi's other, more narrow lines of work into a coherent whole. Rossi's works are prolific and appear bewilderingly diverse and scattered on first glance, but they have a unity and coherence we hope to demonstrate in this chapter. Finally, we use the 1985 rather than 1989 edition of this text because little changed between the two that would change our description or critique of Rossi's theory.

OUR RECONSTRUCTION OF
ROSSI'S THEORY OF EVALUATION

Rossi's theory is a comprehensive attempt to incorporate the lessons of the last 20 years in evaluation, yet do so in a way that includes past theories without distorting or denying the validity of what they said. When he first wrote about evaluation, Rossi heavily emphasized the randomized experiment as a method of choice (1971a, 1971b); he called Campbell's work the "Bible for evaluation" (Rossi & Wright, 1977, p. 13). But his recent works are considerably broader (Chen & Rossi, 1983; Rossi & Freeman, 1982, 1985; Rossi & Wright, 1984). Gone is reference to Campbell's work as the Bible of evaluation. He now asks a comprehensive set of questions not limited to traditional effect questions (Rossi & Wright, 1984). He now incorporates Scriven's emphasis on needs assessment, Campbell's highlighting of experimenting with innovative programs, Weiss's understanding of the politics of evaluation and of the value of enlightenment, Wholey's advocacy of incremental improvement of existing programs, some of Stake's uses of case study methods, and Cronbach's emphasis on external validity, complex interactions, and the study of causal mediation.

Integrating the work of past theorists is, implicitly and explicitly, what Rossi does. His integration is more or less successful from topic to topic, but the effort to integrate is more ambitious than any other attempt. He comments on some past debates between theorists like Cronbach and Campbell, and he incorporates the work of other theorists into his overall theory. He offers three concepts to facilitate integration: comprehensive evaluations, tailored evaluations, and theory-driven evaluations.

Comprehensive Evaluations

Theorists often express quite different preferences for the kinds of questions evaluators should ask, and for methods to answer those questions. Campbell, for example, focuses on program effects; Wholey attends more to implementation. Rossi thinks all major questions are important, and should be asked in one form or another in all evaluations—comprehensive evaluation. Evaluators can do three kinds of activities, each aimed at answering different questions: "analysis related to the conceptualization and design of interventions, monitoring of program implementation, and assessment of program utility" (Rossi & Freeman, 1985, p. 38) (program utility includes program effects, impacts, and cost-efficiency). Rossi and Freeman want all three activities to be done in all evaluations: "Although it is not always possible to do so fully, the evaluation of social programs may need to include all three classes of activities. Evaluations that do so are termed 'comprehensive evaluations' " (p. 38). Comprehensive evaluation is "the systematic application of social research procedures in assessing the conceptualization and design, implementation, and utility of social intervention programs" (p. 19).

Why program conceptualization is important. "The essential premise of human services systems is that there are pockets of deficiencies in our social structure that can be corrected through such encounters, or that naturally occurring processes accompanying human development can be speeded up or made more efficient with the use of human services delivery" (Rossi, 1979, p. 71). Since social programs respond to social needs, "systematic documentation of program need must be undertaken in order to plan, refine, implement, and evaluate social action efforts" (Rossi & Freeman, 1985, p. 103). Such information helps target an intervention appropriately, and helps assess whether the intervention reached a needy audience and remedied the need.

Why program monitoring is important. "Program monitoring information is often as important or more important than information on program impact" (Rossi & Freeman, 1985, p. 144), for two reasons. First, like Wholey, Rossi believes that "if evaluation is ever to develop as a profession, it seems likely that . . . administrative monitoring . . . will be at its core" (1981, p. 236). Second:

> A treatment that is not being delivered or is being delivered in a defective way obviously cannot be effective, although correct delivery is not any guarantee of effectiveness. . . . A monitoring system is useful not only for evaluation but also for correcting administrative faults. A human services systems administrator who does not know whether his program is operating as designed is obviously an inefficient administrator who has to operate largely in the dark. (1979, p. 89)

Forms of accountability and monitoring dealing with finances and law are best left to other professions. But the evaluator can help by monitoring "(1) whether or not the program is reaching the appropriate target population, and (2) whether or not the delivery of services is consistent with program design specifications" (Rossi & Freeman, 1985, p. 139). These evaluations may be undertaken for accountability purposes, to rule out faulty implementation as a culprit in poor program outcome, or to supplement utility assessments. Monitoring particularly aids the program development process in new programs. The operational data it provides help later program diffusion; and it assists management in making programs meet specifications.

Why program utility is important. Rossi and Freeman's rationale for examining program utility seems traditional: "Unless programs have a demonstrable impact, it is hard to defend their implementation and continuation" (1985, p. 40). Yet Rossi recognizes that political and social factors can play a more important role than evidence about impact in deciding whether a program continues. Rossi extends his argument about program effects to a corollary need to know about program cost-benefit. Too few evaluators emphasize this important factor in social programming; Rossi and Freeman devote a chapter to it.

Rossi and Freeman (1985) present six chapters about how evaluators can do each of these three activities. We will not repeat these detailed methodological discussions because we agree that "the problem presented by evaluation research lies not in research methodology, but in the politics of research" (Rossi, 1971a, p. 99):

> Evaluation research is more than the application of methods. It is also a political and managerial activity, an input into the complex mosaic from which policy decisions and allocations emerge for the planning, design, implementation, and continuance of programs to better the human condition (Rossi & Freeman, 1985, p. 27)

The key to this betterment is not methods, but knowing when, where, and why to use them in productive policy research. Rossi's other concepts, tailored evaluation and theory-driven evaluation, help answer these questions about when, where, and why.

Tailored Evaluations

By itself, comprehensive evaluation is not too practical; limited time and resources preclude evaluators from doing all activities. Hence Rossi developed a complementary concept — tailored evaluations — to narrow the focus. Any particular method for answering a question is not uniformly applicable over all programs. For example, in examining program effects, the randomized experiment will often not be feasible or desirable. It might be logistically infeasible if the program covers so many eligible recipients that it is impossible to form a random control group. It might not be desirable in a new program that is still working out implementation bugs that make assessing program effects premature. Such evaluations should still be comprehensive, but methods must be tailored to the stage of program development. Tailoring is a process of "fitting evaluations to programs" (Rossi & Freeman, 1985, p. 102):

> The ways the evaluation questions are asked and the research procedures undertaken depend on whether or not the program under evaluation is an innovative intervention, a modification or expansion of an existing effort, or a well-established, stable human service activity. (Rossi & Freeman, 1985, p. 38)

Tailoring is not a narrowing of questions and methods at different stages of development; the evaluator would ask questions about program conceptualization, implementation, and impact for all programs at all stages. But the evaluator should ask those same questions in different ways or with different procedures depending on the stage. So tailoring is partly a process of determining "the level of effort and technical procedures undertaken during the evaluation" (Rossi & Freeman, 1985, p. 46).

The conjunction of stages of programs (innovations, modifications, ongoing programs) and evaluation activities (conceptualizing, implementing, assessing utility), yields a 3 × 3 matrix of possible evaluative activities tailored to stage of program development. These are illustrated in Table 9.1, which summarizes all the kinds of evaluations that Rossi and Freeman envision.

The interplay outlined in the table is summarized in the following passage:

> In planning social intervention programs, the focus of evaluation is on the extent and severity of problems requiring social intervention, and on the design of programs to ameliorate them. In the conduct of ongoing and innovative programs, the concern is that programs are reaching their intended target populations and are providing the resources, services, and benefits envisioned. As interventions are implemented and continued, there is interest in whether they are effective and, if so, what the magnitudes of their impacts are. For accountability purposes, and for decision-making on the continuance, expansion, or curtailment of programs, it is important to consider costs in relation to benefits, and to compare an intervention's cost-efficiency to that of alternative resource allocation strategies. (Rossi & Freeman, 1985, p. 13)

Table 9.1 Rossi and Freeman's Overview of Evaluation Activities

Conceptualizing
  for innovative programs
    (1) problem description
    (2) operationalizing objectives
    (3) developing intervention model
    (4) defining extent and distribution of target population
    (5) specifying delivery systems
  for fine-tuning
    (1) identifying needed program
    (2) redefining objectives
    (3) designing program modifications
  for established programs
    (1) determining evaluability
    (2) developing evaluation model
    (3) identifying potential modification opportunities
    (4) determining accountability requirements
Implementing
  for innovative programs
    (1) formative research and development
    (2) implementation monitoring
  for fine-tuning
    (1) R&D program refinements
    (2) monitoring program changes
  for established programs
    (1) program monitoring and accountability studies
Assessing
  for innovative programs
    (1) impact studies
    (2) efficiency analyses
  for fine-tuning
    (1) impact studies
    (2) efficiency analyses
  for established programs
    (1) impact studies
    (2) efficiency analyses

In new interventions, for example, Rossi and Freeman recommend that few resources be devoted to estimating program effects; any resources in that direction might fund methods like forecasting, meta-analyses of results of similar programs, and gathering expert opinion about likely effects — not program monitoring or experiments that are either infeasible or undesirable in innovations.

Evaluations across programs at different stages of development are not entirely distinct from each other; "the designs of all evaluations have many generic qualities" (Rossi & Freeman, 1985, p. 64). Many of Rossi and Freeman's points about innovative programs also apply to evaluating established programs and to fine-tuning programs by modifying them. Still, the concept of tailoring evaluations integrates much past evaluation theory. It makes a place for the diverse activities and questions that past evaluation theorists have advocated; it allows methodological diversity in implementing those activities; and it prioritizes exactly which questions and methods might be selected depending on program development. It fits many past theories into a coherent picture without distorting or denying the validity of what past theorists said. Consider Rossi's treatment of Wholey, for example. Rossi recommends using Wholey's methods for monitoring stable, established programs, and occasionally for fine-tuning those programs—exactly the kind of situation about which Wholey writes. He recommends variants of Campbell's methods when assessing the effects of innovations. In both cases, he tells when monitoring or assessing outcomes might be important. Such integration is not completely successful, nor does Rossi admit the validity of all past theorists' work—he dislikes some uses of qualitative approaches. But the effort is ambitious, unique in evaluation, and successful enough to warrant close scrutiny.

Theory-Driven Evaluation

Comprehensive evaluation and tailored evaluation are closely related concepts. The third concept that Rossi uses to integrate past work, theory-driven evaluation, is less closely related to the other two. The idea is to introduce more substantive theory into evaluations. Campbell's and Scriven's approaches to evaluation attended little to substantive theory about programs and interventions. Neither theorist used much theory about how programs worked, about the nature and causes of social problems, or about the kinds of educational, social, health, or economic concepts and techniques that compose social interventions. This influenced the field in a somewhat atheoretical direction ever since. Weiss and Cronbach have loosely advocated for more substantive theory in evaluation, but many observers still see the field as largely atheoretical: "Evaluation research is an applied, largely (and unfortunately) atheoretic, multidisciplinary activity" (Wortman, 1983b, p. 224). Rossi notes this trend with dismay:

> The domination of the experimental paradigm in the program evaluation literature has unfortunately drawn attention away from a more important task in gaining understanding of social programs, namely, developing theoretical models of social interventions. . . . An unfortunate consequence of this lack of attention to theory is that the outcomes of evaluation research often provide narrow and sometimes distorted understandings of programs. (Chen & Rossi, 1983, p. 284)

Rossi believes expanded theoretical understandings of social programs are crucial to further progress in solving social problems. To understand why he takes this position, one must first know how Rossi sees our past successes and failures in social problem solving.

Rossi's Pessimism:
The Conservative Nature of Program Evaluation

Rossi sees the ultimate purpose of program evaluation as being "to better the lot of humankind by improving social conditions and community life" (Rossi & Freeman, 1985, p. 13). To do so, evaluators study social programs "aimed at helping the disadvantaged segments of our society" (Berk & Rossi, 1977, p. 79). But Rossi cautions against excessive optimism that evaluations will produce important or major social change. Evaluation is rarely the deciding factor in social programming:

> In any political system sensitive to weighing, assessing, and balancing the conflicting claims and interests of a number of constituencies, one can expect an evaluation to play the role of expert witness, testifying to the degree of a program's effectiveness. A jury of decision makers and other stakeholders may give such testimony more weight than uninformed opinion or shrewd guessing, but it is they, not the witness, who reach a verdict. (Rossi & Freeman, 1985, p. 375)

Change results from the interplay among interests of these multiple stake-holders, not from evaluation. For Rossi, that is as it should be: "While evaluation research is political, it is no substitute for politics. Social science can demystify, but it remains the task of politics to interpret the meaning of demystification for direction of political policy" (Berk & Rossi, 1977, p. 85).

Evaluations bring about only small social changes: "Evaluation methodology in usual practice implicitly endorses an incremental notion of social change" (Berk & Rossi, 1977, p. 82). Part of the problem is that it is rare to produce large results in the United States, where many important advances have already been made in solving social problems. "Diminishing returns set in: the more we have done in the past, the more difficult it becomes to add new benefits" (Rossi, 1971b, pp. 276-277). Just to propose radical changes in society is hard enough, so "social programs rarely exceed the limits of dominant political ideologies" (Berk & Rossi, 1977, p. 80). Even innovations "typically had only incremental and segmental change as their objective, tinkering with the system rather than addressing fundamental redesign" (Berk & Rossi, 1977, p. 83). Most innovations "go little beyond conventional wisdom" (Berk & Rossi, 1977, p. 80), making it even harder to evaluate the effects of radical change.

Aspects of evaluation methods are themselves potentially conservative in nature. Existing social science methods cannot cope with the full array of problems: "Applied social researchers are more technically proficient in the study of individuals than in the study of organizations, and therefore, social research tends to be more social psychological than social structural" (Berk & Rossi, 1977, p. 81). But if the problem is social structural, such evaluations produce results that do not contribute to a solution. Hence "it is simply impossible to be a neutral technician; applying the technology necessarily implies ideological positions with political consequences. Evaluation researchers are *always* choosing sides even before empirical findings are produced" (Berk & Rossi, 1977, pp. 89-90).

The metallic and plastic laws of evaluation. Hence Rossi became increasingly pessimistic "about the state of our knowledge about how to improve the lot of personkind" (Rossi, 1985, p. 1). In an only partly tongue-in-cheek paper, Rossi (1985) coined a series of pithy laws that capture the difficulties of social change that have been noted and quoted by powerful figures in social policy (Moynihan, 1985). The Iron Law states:

> The expected value of any net impact assessment of any social program is zero. That means that our best a priori estimate of a net impact assessment of a program is that it will have no effect. It also means that the average of net impact assessments of a large set of social programs will crawl asymptotically toward zero. (Rossi, 1985, p. 2)

The Stainless Steel Law says:

> The better designed the impact assessment of a social program, the more likely is the net impact to be zero. This means that the more technically rigorous the net impact assessment, the more likely are its results to be zero — or no effect. This also means that controlled experiments with programs, the avowedly best approach to estimating net impacts — are more likely to show zero effects than other less rigorous approaches. (p. 3)

The Copper Law states:

> The more social programs are designed to change individuals, the more likely the net impact of the program will be zero. This law means that social programs designed to rehabilitate individuals by changing them in some way or another are more likely to fail. (p. 3)

Finally, the Plastic Law claims:

> Only those programs that are likely to fail are evaluated. The plastic law has an optimistic slant to it since it states that there are effective programs: it's just that they are never evaluated. It also implies that if a social program is effective, that characteristic is obvious enough and hence policy makers and others who sponsor and fund evaluations decide against evaluation. (p. 3).

Rossi notes that other laws could be mined from this metallic vein, such as the Plutonium Law: "Program operators will explode when exposed to typical evaluation research findings" (p. 3). He concludes:

> The laws claim that a review of the history of the last two decades of evaluation research on major social programs in the United States does not sustain the proposition that over this period the American establishment of policy makers, agency officials, professionals and social scientists knew how to design and implement social programs that were at all effective, let alone spectacularly so. (pp. 3-4)

Rossi acknowledges some exceptions to these laws, cases where evaluations revealed effective programs.

> But even in the case of successful programs, the sizes of the net effects have not been spectacular. In the social program field, nothing as good has yet been invented which was as effective in its way as the small pox vaccine was for the field of public health. In short, as we all know (and deplore), we are not on the verge of wiping out the social scourges of our time: Ignorance, poverty, crime, dependency, or mental illness show great promise to be with us for some time. (Rossi, 1985, p. 5)

Is evaluation worth doing? Given these difficulties, Rossi asks the same question Weiss asked earlier: "Is there any point then to undertake serious evaluations of social programs?" (Berk & Rossi, 1977, p. 83). He replies, "In many cases the answer is yes" (p. 83). Evaluation, particularly theory-driven evaluation, provides conceptual knowledge upon which new understandings of social problems and solutions can be built. Social science serves a "demystification" function by questioning common assumptions about society, particularly the assumption that we can easily solve our social problems: "To the degree that skepticism and understanding can be widely communicated, social science may even be subtly subversive" (p. 83). In that case, the scientific character of evaluation research makes results a bit harder to dismiss. In other words, competent evaluation research practitioners can play the game under rules which all sides will likely take as fair (at least in theory) and often correctly show that most programs make little difference. (Berk & Rossi, 1977, p. 84)

"No effect" findings might be due to poor evaluation methods. While Rossi thinks there is much shoddy methodology in the field, he does not think the methods are mostly at fault. He believes that most social programs, in fact, have little effect, and evaluations correctly show this. This conclusion has radical implications:

> Such null outcomes are exactly what we would expect, given our critique of current social programs as piecemeal and lightweight. The failure of program after program if *effectively* documented, can contribute to an empirically grounded critique of American society. (Berk & Rossi, 1977, p. 83)

Rossi cites three specific program failings to account for "no effect" findings; all could be remedied using theory-driven evaluation. First is "in our understanding of the social processes that give rise to the problem to which the social program is ostensibly addressed" (Rossi, 1985, p. 8). Second is "in our understanding of how to translate problem theory into specific programs" (p. 8). The third "failure is organizational in character and has to do with failures properly to implement programs" (p. 9). These three failures taken together restate the first three social problem-solving activities outlined earlier in this book — problem generation, solution generation, and solution implementation. Rossi blames the first two failures partly on the tendency of social scientists to ignore policy-related variables in their theories, partly on the fact that many people who design programs know less than social scientists about social theory, and partly on the failure of everyone involved to estimate accurately the complexity of social, community, and individual processes giving rise to problems. He is pessimistic that these shortcomings can be remedied quickly since we lack the requisite social science theory, condemning us to trial-and-error efforts in solving social problems (Rossi, 1985). Rossi is committed to evaluating those trial-and-error efforts in the experimental manner advocated by Campbell (Berk et al., 1985), but he also wants evaluators to build a strong theoretical component into evaluation to remedy shortcomings in both problem theory and program theory.

Back to Theory-Driven Evaluation

Theory-driven evaluation helps remedy all these problems of lack of knowledge. Rossi's purpose in introducing the concept

> is to bring the theory back into program evaluation. Our aim is not to make a case for basic research — there is enough justification for that goal — but to make a case that neglect of existing theoretical knowledge and of thinking theoretically has retarded both our understanding of social programs and the efficient employment of evaluation designs in impact assessment. (Chen & Rossi, 1983, p. 284)

Social science theory is poorly developed for this task: "With the possible exception of economics, the social sciences have yet to develop an adequate set of theories that are relevant to social problems" (Chen & Rossi, 1981, p. 42). What Rossi proposes is

> not the global conceptual schemes of the grand theorists, but much more prosaic theories that are concerned with how human organizations work and how social problems are generated. . . . What we are strongly advocating is the necessity for theorizing, for constructing plausible and defensible models of how programs can be expected to work before evaluating them. Indeed, the theory-driven perspective is closer to what econometricians call "model specification" than are more complicated and more abstract and general theories. (Chen & Rossi, 1983, p. 285)

Model building is within the grasp of evaluators. Rossi's advocacy of theory-driven evaluation

> does not argue for postponing evaluations until the most adequate theory and knowledge have been constructed. It argues, rather, that we make do with what we have, at least for the time being, drawing upon existing stocks of theory and knowledge to the extent relevant. (Chen & Rossi, 1983, p. 300)

The evaluator studies program inputs and causal mediating processes, in addition to studying the existence of cause-effect relationships (Rossi & Wright, 1984): "A very seductive and attractive feature of controlled experiments is that it is not necessary to understand how a social program works in order to estimate its net effects through randomized experiments" (Chen & Rossi, 1983, p. 284). But then if controlled experiments show no effect, it is not usually clear whether the recorded failures of programs are due to the fact that the programs were built on poor conceptual foundations, usually preposterous sets of "causal" mechanisms (e.g., the Impact Cities program); or because treatments were set at such low dosage levels that they could not conceivably affect any outcomes (e.g., Title I); or because programs were poorly implemented. Note that the emphasis in the above statements is on deficiencies in the theoretical underpinnings of the treatment or of the treatment delivery systems. (Chen & Rossi, 1983, p. 284)

Therefore:

> We have argued for a paradigm that accepts experiments and quasi-experiments as dominant research designs, but that emphasizes that these devices should be used in conjunction with a priori knowledge and theory to build models of the treatment process and implementation system to produce evaluations that are more efficient and that yield more information about how to achieve desired effects. (Chen & Rossi, 1983, p. 300)

Chen and Rossi (1981, 1983, 1987) have written extensively on theory-driven evaluation, tying it closely to the method of linear structural equation modeling (Bollen, 1989; Hayduk, 1987; Jöreskog & Sörbom, 1979; Loehlin, 1987), a methodology that models correlational and causal relationships among latent variables inferred from multiple observed variables. Rossi uses this method in his own evaluations (Berk et al., 1981) to complement the randomized experiment, there being no inherent conflict between the two methods. From the experiment he gains strong inference about the existence of a cause-effect relationship, and from structural modeling he gets more theoretical information about program inputs and causal mediating processes. When forced to choose,

> if we know very little about the subject in question, randomization is superior to model specification. However, if we have more knowledge on the problem or phenomenon under study, we need not rely on the use of randomization for handling the threats to internal validity. (Chen & Rossi, 1987, p. 98)

However, he is not much more specific than that about how often he would make one choice over the other.

To summarize, the theory-driven evaluator constructs a theoretical model of program inputs, mediating processes, and outputs; devises measures of all these parts; and gathers and analyzes these data. Theory-driven evaluation is a specific case of comprehensive evaluation, so it is integrative in the same sense that comprehensive evaluation is integrative. But

Chen and Rossi use it to propose a very specific integration of a prominent debate between Cronbach and Campbell.

Trying to Integrate Cronbach and Campbell

Campbell prioritizes on internal validity through the randomized experiment; Cronbach prioritizes on external validity through functional evaluation design. Rossi's earliest writings were committed to Campbell's view (Rossi, 1971b), and much of his best-known work uses experiments (Berk et al., 1981, 1985; Rossi et al., 1980; Rossi & Lyall, 1976, 1978). But recently he has dropped the primacy he first gave to randomized experiments. For one thing, "the concept of evaluation as applying primarily to the quantitative assessment of net impacts of social programs has hardly diffused to all who use the term nor to those who call themselves evaluators" (Rossi, 1981, pp. 230-231). Moreover, "the realization quickly emerged . . . that randomized, controlled experiments could only be done correctly under very limited circumstances and that the demand for evaluation covered many programs that simply could not be assessed in this way" (Rossi & Wright, 1984, p. 335). Third, Rossi considered the arguments of other theorists, particularly Cronbach, about whether internal validity should have priority. Both Cronbach and Campbell assume it is logistically and logically difficult to design evaluations that facilitate both internal and external validity. Rossi reframes the problem, claiming that if one uses a theory-driven perspective and sophisticated causal modeling procedures, the tension may not be as extreme as past theorists have suggested:

> Both internal and external validity are important in evaluation research. . . . We propose a perspective we call the theory driven approach to deal with issues of validity. The central thrust of our approach is that theory, model, or knowledge are important in dealing with the various types of validity. We are not convinced that the tradeoff problem between internal and external validity, which is so sharply portrayed by Campbell, Cronbach, or others, that dealing with one type of validity must seriously sacrifice the other types of validity. In many situations both internal and external validity (and other types of validity) can and should be dealt with simultaneously. We believe to some extent our approach is a synthesis of Campbell and Cronbach's approaches. (Chen & Rossi, 1987, pp. 96-97)

Theory-driven evaluation allows one to address internal validity by building an accurately specified program model — a complete and accurate model of relationships among variables and of selection biases that normally vitiate quasi-experiments. Chen and Rossi "do not think that model specification is necessarily better than randomization" (1987, p. 98); they would prefer to see the two methods combined if possible. But they prefer model specification because they are optimistic that satisfactory program theory can usually be constructed, and because "randomization benefits only the internal validity, while model specification is also helpful in improving other types of validity" (1987, p. 99).

Model specification also fosters Cook and Campbell's (1979) statistical conclusion validity: "Adding adequate model specification to randomization can reduce the size of residuals of outcome variables and thus improve the ability of an experiment to avoid both Type I and Type II errors" (Chen & Rossi, 1987, p. 99); hence "confidence intervals will be smaller and the real effects will be more likely to be detected" (p. 99). Construct validity is facilitated by use of multiple indicators of theoretical constructs; those indicators reduce the effects of unique bias in any particular measure, and distinguish between common and error variance so the latter can be removed from the analysis.

Chen and Rossi (1987) propose reconceptualizing external validity into two parts that seem isomorphic with Cronbach's UTOS and *UTOS, but that Chen and Rossi (1987) call explicit generalization and implicit generalization, respectively. *Explicit generalization* "refers to an evaluation in which the designer has a clear expectation of the system in which a program may operate in the future, and builds that expectation into the research" (p. 100). Model specification facilitates explicit generalization by forcing the evaluator "to define the population to be sampled, a decision that should be based upon a theory derived model of the program, treatment, contingencies, and possible interactions" (p. 101). In contrast, *implicit generalization*

> refers to researches the designs of which do not include by intent, variables characterizing any particular system which is expected to be the target system for the program in question. Instead implicit generalization characterizes the researches which simply attempt to provide relevant information about a number of alternative targets that might turn out to be the target. (p. 100).

Theory-driven evaluation facilitates implicit generalization by thoroughly investigating

> the ways in which the researched system resembles and is different from the future program operating system to which the results of the evaluation are to be generalized. The researcher's concerns should cover such issues as the future implementing organization's structure and operating procedures, potential contingencies that could affect the operation of the treatment, possible shifts and

changes in the intervening processes and possible interactions among all these elements. (p. 102)

Chen and Rossi see theory-driven evaluation as "a balanced approach . . . to validity" (p. 102) that includes "the identification of potential threats to validity in research" and that relies "less on randomization as a safeguard to internal validity if the threats in a research can be adequately identified and controlled" (p. 102).

Evaluation Practice: Some Orienting Remarks

The preceding discussion has concerned general concepts that Rossi uses to organize his theory of evaluation. But Rossi and Freeman (1985) are also very specific about how to do evaluation, presenting strategies, tactics, methods, and method trade-offs that are too numerous and detailed to review completely here. Instead, we provide an overview mostly at the strategic and tactical level, with little attention to the specifics of methods themselves.

Which stakeholders to serve? Multiple parties are typically involved in evaluation: policymakers and decision makers, program sponsors, evaluation sponsors, target participants, program management, program staff, evaluators, program competitors, and other stakeholders of the program. Each has unpredictable but often strong investments in the program, which leads to three consequences for evaluators. First, "evaluators are often unsure whose perspective they should take in designing an evaluation" (Rossi & Freeman, 1985, pp. 375, 378). Second, "the evaluator must realize that sponsors of evaluations may 'turn' on evaluators when their results contradict the policies and programs they advocate" (p. 378). Third, "strain is introduced because of the difficulties in establishing proper modes for communicating with different stakeholders" (p. 379).

Rossi gives a special place to stakeholders most involved in "decision-making processes" (Rossi & Freeman, 1982, p. 32) about programs, in part because they provide major funding for the field. This group wants evaluation for many reasons: "Legislators and high-level civil servants who came into office during the Kennedy and Johnson administrations had been exposed to social science in the course of their educational training" (Rossi, 1981, p. 223); they were open to evaluations based on social science methods. They needed evaluation because "our society and particularly its decision makers are no longer sure about what they are doing and are skeptical that theirs is an obviously correct and effective set of ways to accomplish a given social end" (Rossi, 1983, p. 22). And decision makers needed "internal intelligence on the functioning of our society and its central public institutions" (Rossi, 1983, p. 24) to plan and adjust policies.

This favoring of policymakers is less pronounced in Rossi's later work. In early work he said that "the independent and dependent variables of evaluation research are determined by the policy-makers and the problem being addressed, not by the evaluation researcher" (Rossi & Wright, 1977, p. 8). Later, however, he suggested a more evenhanded treatment of stakeholder groups:

> All perspectives are equally legitimate. The clients' or target's perspective cannot claim any more legitimacy than that of the program or the government agency funding the program. The responsibility of the evaluator is not to take one of the many perspectives as the legitimate one, but to be clear from which perspectives a particular evaluation is being undertaken and to give recognition explicitly to the existence of other perspectives. (Rossi & Freeman, 1985, p. 378)

Diversity of perspective is important because narrow loyalty to policymakers creates problems. Evaluators may be co-opted by decision makers, producing biased results. Evaluators who work for the program being evaluated are well positioned to do evaluations that "may have a higher rate of impact on organizational decisions" (Rossi & Freeman, 1985, p. 368), but they are also more likely to be co-opted. This problem has led "some experienced evaluators . . . to state categorically that adequate evaluations could rarely, if ever, be undertaken within the organization responsible for the administration of a project. Hence, outside evaluations were to be preferred" (pp. 367-368). Rossi disagrees, partly because external evaluators are not in as good a position to achieve use of results, and partly because "given the increased competence of staff and the visibility and scrutiny of the evaluation enterprise, there is no longer any reason to favor one organizational arrangement over another" (p. 368).

Rossi advocates working within the system, but not simply incorporating the biases of those who employ evaluators:

> To avoid evaluations unless one can work comfortably with the people for whom the research is being undertaken is clearly a political and moral decision with political and moral consequences. By failing to participate one has loaded the dice so that results will likely reflect the preferences of the active parties. Clearly, withdrawal may be equivalent to implicit support. . . . [But] to see oneself simply as a hired hand and incorporate the values of employers into research designs is to abdicate one's moral and political responsibilities to others. All professionals place limits on the uses to which their skills may be put. . . . We are simply arguing that social scientists engaged in applied research exercise similar judgements. (Berk & Rossi, 1977, p. 89)

Policy time and evaluation time. Decision makers also tend to want information about programs "in a matter of weeks or months" (Rossi & Freeman, 1985, p. 380), but good evaluation can take years. Rossi suggests three rules for handling this pressure. First, "a long-term study should not be undertaken if the information is needed before the evaluation can be completed. It may be better in such circumstances to rely on expert opinion or another of the more judgmental evaluation methods" (p. 382). Second, "confine technically complex evaluations to pilot or prototype projects for interventions that are not likely to be implemented on a large scale in the near future" (p. 382). Third, "anticipate the direction of programs and policy activities, rather than be forced, within heavy time constraints, to respond to the demands of other parties" (p. 382).

Quantitative versus qualitative methods. Rossi recommends qualitative methods as part of program conceptualization, design, and monitoring; but his overall preference is for quantitative techniques. His discussion of qualitative methods is brief by contrast to the thorough work of other authors (Guba & Lincoln, 1981), and to Rossi's thorough discussion of quantitative methods. Even when Rossi recommends qualitative techniques, he moves them toward standardization and quantification. Regarding use of key informants, for example:

> It is also useful to construct a data guide in advance — that is, a questionnaire that each informant is asked to complete or that is filled in after an informal discussion with the key informant. . . . Using a data guide facilitates more rapid collating of the responses of the key informants and helps to standardize information across all informants. After all the informants have been contacted and interviewed, the information should be summarized and, if possible, put into tabular form. (Rossi & Freeman, 1985, p. 127)

More traditional qualitative theorists might prefer a case study rather than tabular form (Guba & Lincoln, 1981). Similarly, Rossi and Freeman's discussion of participant observation in monitoring programs suggests that structured approaches are more reliable and practical.

Rossi is skeptical about the feasibility of qualitative methods, especially the less structured ones. In talking about program monitoring, for example, he says:

> Although direct observation methods appear to be attractively simple, they are not easily taught to untrained observers, they are highly time-consuming, and they produce data that are difficult to summarize and analyze. These problems are particularly troublesome the less structured the observation method used and the more complex the program services. (Rossi & Freeman, 1985, p. 172)

In other places he says qualitative methods are generally too expensive, too difficult to use and analyze, and too imprecise to warrant widespread use.

Rossi is clearly unsympathetic to using qualitative methods for impact assessments (Rossi, 1982a):

> The revisionists propose to replace current methods with procedures that have even greater and more obvious deficiencies. The procedures which they advance as substitutes for the mainstream methodology are vaguely described and constitute an almost mystical advocacy of the virtues of qualitative ethnology and of adopting program operator perspectives on effectiveness. Although many of their arguments concerning the woodenness of many quantitative researchers are cogent and well taken, still their main argument for an alternative methodology I find unconvincing. (Rossi, 1985, p. 7)

He concludes:

> While impact assessments of the structured variety . . . could be conducted qualitatively in principle, considerations of costs and human capital usually rule out such approaches. Assessing impact in ways that are scientifically plausible and that yield relatively precise estimates of net effects requires data that are quantifiable and systematically and uniformly collected. (Rossi & Freeman, 1985, p. 224)

Practice: Evaluations of Innovative Programs

Tailored evaluation organizes practice around the evaluation of innovations, of established programs, or of "fine-tuning" changes in established programs. Hence we discuss Rossi's theory of practice separately for these three modes, although he notes that all evaluations share similar generic qualities; for example, assessment of program implementation for innovations and existing programs shares many methodological features. Because we discuss evaluation of innovations first, the discussion is somewhat longer than the discussion of established programs or fine-tuning changes.

Like Campbell, Rossi gives a special place to the evaluation of innovative programs. Much of his own work has been with innovative programs (Berk et al., 1981; Rossi & Lyall, 1978). When possible, the evaluator should work closely with those who implement an innovative program, optimizing the development of both a good intervention and a good evaluation of it. The evaluator helps plan the intervention:

The planning process includes the following: identification of the goals of the organization sponsoring and implementing the intervention, and of the other stakeholders involved; the assessment of the extent to which actual conditions under which the program will operate limit the realization of these goals; the development of a general framework or strategy for achieving the desired goals by modifying conditions or behavior; and specification of necessary human and financial resources, designation of individuals responsible for carrying out intervention activities, and creation of a schedule for meeting objectives. (Rossi & Freeman, 1985, p. 64)

The evaluator does not play the major role in providing a precise plan: *"One distinctive feature of evaluation research is that this precision, in most cases, cannot be supplied by the researcher*; rather, it must be supplied by the policy-makers themselves" (Rossi & Wright, 1977, p. 8).

Setting goals and objectives. Rossi distinguishes goals from objectives:

Social intervention programs can be developed only in relation to one or more goals. Goals are generally abstract, idealized statements of desired social program outcomes. For evaluation purposes, goal-setting must lead to the operationalization of the desired outcome; that is, it is essential that there be detailed specification of the condition to be addressed and identification of one or more measurable criteria of success. Evaluation researchers often refer to these operationalized statements as *objectives*. (Rossi & Freeman, 1985, p. 65)

Objectives are relatively specific; goals are relatively broad and vague. Rossi agrees with Scriven that goals are not a trustworthy source of criteria for program effectiveness (Chen & Rossi, 1981). Hence programs cannot be designed around goals, but only objectives. To set goals and objectives, one needs to know both the existing state of affairs and the desired state of affairs. Programs aim to reduce the discrepancy between the two. To help establish objectives, Rossi recommends the decision-theoretic approach (Edwards et al., 1975), Wholey's (1979) evaluability assessment, and goal-attainment scaling (Kiresuk, 1973).

Rossi's strength, relative to Scriven, is his discussion of methods for such value-related matters as needs assessment, including specifying direct and indirect targets of the program; procedures to distinguish between target and nontarget units during program implementation; assessing problem incidence and prevalence; disaggregating problem rates by, say, age and sex; and examining trade-offs among methods for needs assessments. Scriven's admirable discussion of the conceptual nature of needs might well be complemented by Rossi's thorough discussion of technical matters.

Unlike Scriven, Rossi says little about the conceptual nature of valuing, or about such related matters as needs. Rossi defines a population of targets at need as "a group of potential targets who currently manifest a given condition" (Rossi & Freeman, 1985, p. 119), and says that "need must be distinguished from demand" (p. 119):

> Some needs assessments undertaken to estimate the extent of a problem and to serve as the basis for designing programs are "at-risk assessments" or "demand assessments," rather than true needs assessments. . . . This is the case because it is either technically infeasible to measure need or impractical to implement a program that deals only with the at-need population. (pp. 119, 121)

But Rossi is unclear about *how* to distinguish need from demand. He is probably a descriptive theorist in these matters; he lets a pluralistic group of stakeholders decide what is to count as a need, and as an appropriate program objective in response to that need.

Stakeholder roles in defining objectives. Evaluators should obtain stakeholder agreement about criteria for evaluating whether goals and objectives have been achieved:

> Failing such agreement, the evaluation may be confronted with rancorous conflict between evaluators and project planners, staff, and policymakers when evaluation results are presented. . . . If adequate resources are available, sometimes the solution is to include multiple criteria that reflect the interests of the various parties involved. (Rossi & Freeman, 1985, p. 67)

Including as many sensible outcomes as possible increases "the chances that the goals of tomorrow will be included as well as the goals of today" (Chen & Rossi, 1981, p. 45).

Some stakeholders have more power in defining goals than do others: "Because evaluation research is usually financed by one of the parties to the decision-making process — usually a government agency with administrative responsibilities for the program in question — one set of goals tends to dominate" (Rossi & Wright, 1977, p. 12). But such domination can interfere with successful evaluation:

> The acceptance of the research may hinge not only on the administrative agency in question but the legislature and organized representatives of citizen groups. To accept the goal definition of the sponsoring agency is to become to some extent a partisan in the policy-making process, an outcome that tends to compromise the broader acceptance of the results of the evaluation. (Rossi & Wright, 1977, p. 12)

He has no easy answers for this dilemma:

> Hence, a critical issue an evaluator faces at the outset is how to define the goals to be evaluated in order to retain the support of the sponsor and also to attain the support of other interested parties. The achievement of widespread support for the evaluation effort is a major political problem faced by an evaluator. (Rossi & Wright, 1977, p. 12)

The theory-driven evaluator can also appeal to social science theory as a source of program goals: "Another solution is to include objectives in addition to those originated by the stakeholders, based on current viewpoints and theories in the relevant substantive field" (Rossi & Freeman, 1985, p. 67):

> The perceptive evaluator, drawing on his or her general knowledge of the workings of our society and its organizations, can make rather reasonable inferences about what effects a program can be expected to have, given the working assumptions of the program and the relevant body of social science knowledge. (Rossi & Freeman, 1985, p. 188)

When evaluating a program to reduce crime by ex-felons, Rossi and colleagues borrowed "from criminology, sociology, and economics" (Berk et al., 1981, p. 343) in designing the program and its evaluation.

Rossi's theory-driven evaluation and Scriven's goal-free evaluation (Chen & Rossi, 1981; Rog & Bickman, 1984) are both aimed in part at helping the evaluator with a difficult problem: "The researcher must anticipate results that initially are either unknown or obscure—for example, secondary effects and unintended consequences" (Rossi & Wright, 1977, p. 8). But theory-driven evaluation provides a partial answer to a problem with goal-free evaluation, that the latter is "procedurally vague and does not provide guidance in deciding what effects to examine" (Rog & Bickman, 1984, p. 169). Rossi uses social science theory as a source of potential effects:

> The approach proposed in this paper resembles Scriven's goal-free evaluation ideas in emphasizing that programs have some effects that do not necessarily coincide with the intentions of designers and administrators, but differs from that approach by suggesting ways in which such effects may be discerned. Our approach entails *defining a set of outcomes as potential effects of a program, some given by the official goals of the program and others derived from social science knowledge and theory concerning the subject matter in question.* (Chen & Rossi, 1981, p. 40)

Program design and development. Evaluators are usually not major figures in designing programs. Nonetheless, "in order to undertake a successful evaluation, both explicit, agreed-upon objectives and a detailed description of how they are to be achieved are required" (Rossi & Freeman, 1985, p. 71). The evaluator should construct an impact model of the relationship between program objectives and activities:

> The absence of a well-specified impact model severely limits opportunities to control a program's quality and effectiveness. . . . By analogy, a computer software package is useless if it has not been documented adequately. Even if a program is successful in delivering services and achieving the objectives set for it, without an explicit impact model there is no basis for understanding how and why it worked or for reproducing its effects on a broader scale in other sites and with other targets. (Rossi & Freeman, 1985, pp. 71-72)

The impact model is another instance of theory-driven evaluation.

Impact models contain a causal hypothesis, an intervention hypothesis, and an action hypothesis. The causal hypothesis is "about the influence of one or more processes or determinants on the behavior or condition that the program seeks to modify" (Rossi & Freeman, 1985, p. 72); it "must be stated in a way that permits testing, or measurement" (p. 72). It is critical because,

> assuming that pockets of deficiency exist, then whether a treatment can be devised that will reduce the size of such pockets depends clearly on whether or not the conditions generating the deficiencies are properly understood. In short, treatment depends on the existence of a valid model of how deficiency is produced or maintained. (Rossi, 1979, pp. 74-75)

The intervention hypothesis "specifies the relationship between a program, what is going to be done, and the process or determinant specified as associated in the causal hypothesis with the behavior or condition to be ameliorated or changed" (Rossi & Freeman, 1985, p. 73). The action hypothesis "is necessary if one is to assess whether the intervention, even if it results in a desired change in the causal variable, is necessarily linked to the outcome" (p. 73). The action hypothesis is somewhat obtuse. Rossi explains that although the causal hypothesis might be correct under naturally occurring circumstances—for example, unemployment may cause ex-felons to commit new crimes—it may be impossible to manipulate the relevant circumstances directly to have the same effect, because manipulation of the variable is not possible or because "although a natural change in existing conditions may cause a desirable chain of events, the introduction of that change by means of an intervention may not result in the behavioral and social processes that occur naturally" (p. 73).

Hypotheses about an impact model could come from past experiments or well-developed social theories:

> The evaluator should actively search for and construct a theoretically justified model of the social problem in order to understand and capture what a program really can do for a social problem — social science knowledge and theory become crucial in the evaluation process. (Chen & Rossi, 1981, p. 43)

But we generally lack either strong social theories or past experiments. So impact models are more often constructed from causal modeling of correlational data, from the results of similar programs, and from meta-analyses and metaevaluations.

Delivery system design. It is crucial to assess how well the innovation is implemented: "The components of the delivery system must be explicated and criteria of performance developed and measured" (Rossi & Freeman, 1985, p. 77). This includes assessment of the target problem and population; service implementation; qualifications and competencies of the staff; mechanisms for recruiting targets; means of optimizing access to the intervention, including location and physical characteristics of service delivery sites; and referral and follow-up (Chen & Rossi, 1983). Formative evaluations can be particularly useful to assess such program elements so as to improve program performance. The rigor and sophistication of such formative evaluations might vary. Ideally it includes impact assessments of program components with implementation assessments designed to improve program delivery. If resource limitations preclude this, simulations of program operations can provide useful information.

Such studies benefit from an implementation model that includes characteristics of the organization, procedures for obtaining cooperation from target groups, relationships with other programs, political context of the environment, treatment characteristics, required resources, and interorganizational transactions required to implement treatment (Chen & Rossi, 1983). Evaluators should assess "whether or not a program is reaching its target units, those with specified and appropriate characteristics" (Rossi & Freeman, 1985, p. 146), and should assess overcoverage, undercoverage, and bias in coverage. This includes efforts "to compare individuals who participate in a program with those who drop out, those who are eligible but do not participate at all, or both groups" (Rossi & Freeman, 1985, p. 156), for a "treatment that works well with one type of client may not work well with another" (Rossi, 1979, p. 79). Monitoring can detect program "creaming" of targets: "delivering treatments to individuals who are most likely to recover or to households that are most likely to rise spontaneously out of their deficient state" (Rossi, 1979, p. 77). Methods for monitoring program coverage include inspection of records, surveys of participants, and community surveys; analyses include "description of the project, comparison between sites, and program conformity" (Rossi & Freeman, 1985, p. 182).

Outcome evaluations of innovations. Rossi includes "assessing impact and estimating efficiency" (Rossi & Freeman, 1985, p. 84) in his summary of activities appropriate for innovations. But program diagnostic and monitoring procedures must precede impact evaluation or occur concurrently with it:

> The prerequisites of assessing the impact of an intervention are as follows: First, either the project should have its objectives sufficiently well articulated to make it possible to identify measures of goal achievement or the evaluator must be able to establish what reasonable objectives are. Second, the intervention should have been sufficiently well implemented for there to be no question that its critical elements have been delivered to appropriate targets. (Rossi & Freeman, 1985, pp. 187-188)

Impact evaluations are inappropriate for innovations that have not met these prerequisites.

Complex experiments with many facets are "especially appropriate for testing new policies, because it may not be clear in advance what exact form the new policy should take" (Rossi & Freeman, 1985, p. 255). Such experiments should include options that are likely to be implemented if found effective:

> Experimentation is not likely to be a promising technique for approaching short-term or cyclical issues; by the same token, the half-dozen areas likely to be of national policy concern three to five years ahead are generally distinguishable and can, with enough foresight, be amenable to experimental techniques. (Rossi & Lyall, 1978, p. 421)

Innovations are more amenable than established programs to use of the best outcome evaluation designs. With innovations, it is more feasible to form comparable control groups because innovations, unlike established programs, are usually partial-coverage rather than total-coverage programs:

> For programs with total coverage (as in the case of long-standing, ongoing programs), it is usually not possible to identify a group that is not receiving the intervention and that is, in essential senses, comparable to the subjects who are beneficiaries. . . . In such circumstances, the main strategy available is the use of reflexive controls and before-and-after comparisons. . . . For partial-coverage programs, a larger variety of strategies are available. (Rossi & Freeman, 1985, pp. 208-209)

Fine-tuning changes in established programs usually fall in between; it is sometimes possible to give the change to a limited number of targets, using other targets as a control.

Adequate construction of a control group is usually central to impact assessment. Such groups should consist of multiple units comparable to the treatment group in composition, experiences, and dispositions. The preferred option is use of randomized controls, something that is often more feasible with innovations than established programs. When randomization is not feasible, other options are (from most to least preferred): matched controls, statistically compared controls, reflexive controls (in which subjects are their own baseline), generic controls from established norms, and shadow controls constructed from the opinions of knowledgeable stakeholders about what would be expected without an intervention. The evaluator should use more than one of these controls when possible. These control options are not mutually exclusive. Their joint use provides multiple sources of information about how much confidence can be placed in conclusions. Rossi also advises increasing the precision of impact evaluations by adding multiple pre- and postmeasures and using large sample sizes.

Choosing among impact assessment methods. Rossi prefers the randomized experiment for assessing impact, but he concludes his discussion of impact assessments with a caveat:

> Whenever possible, we advocate the use of randomized experiments. . . . [But] the choice of a design strategy cannot be made simply on the basis of rigor alone. There are many other conditions and circumstances that must be taken into account, including generalization potential, time, resources, human subject considerations, and the expertise of the evaluator. Thus, the evaluator must be practical as well as a proponent of rigor. The appropriate design is the one that provides the most plausible estimate of net effects, that stands the greatest chance of being carried out successfully, and that provides results most useful for administrative, planning, and policy purposes. (Rossi & Freeman, 1985, p. 227)

Rossi advocates the "good enough" rule for choosing designs: "The evaluator should choose the best possible design, taking into account

practicality and feasibility" (Rossi & Freeman, 1985, p. 190) and "the
resources available and the expertise of the evaluator" (p. 167). "In some
cases . . . evaluations may be undertaken that are 'good enough' for
answering the policy and program questions, although from a scientific
standpoint they are not the 'best' designs" (p. 35). This rule applies to all
evaluations, not just impact evaluation.

Practice: Evaluating Established Programs

"While the evaluation of innovative programs represents an important
activity for the field, by far the greater proportion of program resources,
and thus evaluation efforts, goes into the assessment of established, ongoing programs" (Rossi & Freeman, 1985, p. 84). However, established
programs are less open to change in their basic structures. Their roles and
procedures are institutionalized, and program advocates are invested in
their continuation. Nonetheless, pressure to scrutinize these programs is
strong.

In evaluating innovative programs, program conceptualization and design are paramount. Much of this work has already been done for established programs. Even if it has not been done, reconceptualizing or
redesigning the program is rarely feasible. In evaluating established programs, therefore, Rossi advocates a program conceptualization activity
aimed at assessing what exists rather than reconceptualizing — an initial
evaluability assessment (Wholey, 1979) that involves managers and also
increases the likelihood of use of results. The recommended steps closely
parallel Wholey's — preparing a program description, interviewing program personnel, scouting the program, developing an evaluable program
model, identifying evaluation users, and achieving agreement to proceed.
While much of evaluability assessment is quantitative and fairly standard
procedurally, "the evaluability analyst often finds it necessary to let each
'discovery' lead him or her along whatever pathways are required" (Rossi
& Freeman, 1985, p. 91). Wholey's discussion of methods for evaluability
assessment is more thorough than Rossi's — as expected since Rossi and
Freeman (1985) is in good part a reference text that guides the reader to
more specific readings.

Monitoring innovations involves assessments of what inputs, activities,
and processes occur in the new program so as to improve their fidelity to
program intent, and to provide a base for relating causal mediating processes to outcomes. Monitoring established programs involves similar
activities, but the methods and purposes are different. Established programs are more likely to be subject to evaluations for accountability,

including whether the program has the planned impact, reaches the intended targets, provides planned services, is cost-efficient, uses funds properly, and meets legal responsibilities:

> The scope of a program's accountability activities is determined by both external and internal requirements. For example, many laws, including "sunset" legislation, require reports of program impact prior to approval of funding for subsequent years. Program managers and the executives to whom they report are concerned with accountability evaluation in order to improve and modify efforts and to administer their interventions efficiently. (Rossi & Freeman, 1985, p. 95)

Implementation of established programs is often studied continuously when a management information system is used; but this commits funds for a long period of time, so the anticipated payoff must be high. The alternative is a cross-sectional survey, which has expensive start-up costs, and can be resisted by staff. The choice between these alternatives ought to be made in cost-benefit terms; many evaluations mix both methods.

A key issue in serious accountability studies is "whether programs should undertake their own evaluations or contract with outsiders to do so" (Rossi & Freeman, 1985, p. 97). Independence of evaluators from pressure to make the program look good is crucial: "In large programs, where evaluators can operate as a semiautonomous group, it is probably beneficial and economical for accountability evaluations to be internal. Smaller programs may be better served by outside assessments approximating the methods of fiscal audits" (p. 97). Evaluating the outcome of established programs is more difficult than doing so for innovative programs. The latter often allow use of randomized controls that are rarely feasible with established programs that must use inferior controls described previously, except in rare cases where interrupted time-series designs can be used. Joint use of several kinds of controls helps minimize the biases associated with any one of them.

Despite the differences between innovative and established programs:

> In the end, the planning of evaluations of established programs is not qualitatively different from what occurs in innovative interventions. Perhaps the three key distinctions in style are (1) the increased emphasis on creating a program evaluation model from existing, ongoing program activities; (2) much more deliberate attention to stakeholders' views, responsibilities, and influence; and (3) recognizing that there may be important discrepancies between how programs are seen formally and how they are in fact undertaken. (Rossi & Freeman, 1985, p. 97)

Practice: Fine-Tuning Established Programs

A fine line exists between an innovation and a fine-tuning modification of a program. The latter is a "program modification that has marked impact on intervention efforts" (Rossi & Freeman, 1985, p. 97). Such modifications are introduced "to increase the magnitude of their impact or to decrease their costs per unit of impact" (p. 49), "to provide equitable service delivery" (p. 49), or "because program sponsors and staff are dissatisfied with either the effectiveness or the efficiency of their interventions, or with both" (p. 97). Fine-tuning does not involve accountability, although it might follow an accountability assessment that has shown basic failings in an established program. Fine-tuning of evaluations requires the following steps (Rossi & Freeman, 1985, pp. 100, 102):

(1) reappraising objectives
(2) identifying possible program modifications by drawing on the data of previous evaluations as well as information about program progress gathered as part of the service delivery
(3) undertaking reputability assessments
(4) participating in program replanning and redesign
(5) planning and implementing evaluation designs to monitor the program changes and their impact

"Fine-tuning efforts, like innovative programs, are responses to existing conditions. In the case of fine-tuning, however, action focuses on conditions adhering to the program itself, rather than on a new and untreated problem" (Rossi & Freeman, 1985, p. 98). Often, the need for fine-tuning changes "becomes apparent after program implementation, particularly as innovative programs stabilize and emerge as established ventures" (p. 99). The need for such changes can also come from reputability assessments—asking stakeholders to suggest improvements—or from discussions with program clients, staff, and management about problems.

The activities involved in fine-tuning are often similar to those used for innovative and established programs. For example, a management information system can facilitate program conceptualization, monitoring, and outcome activities in much the same way that these would be done in established programs. Like innovations, fine-tuning changes can sometimes be implemented on a partial-coverage rather than full-coverage basis, so that the methods for evaluating innovations can sometimes be implemented as well.

Cost-Efficiency Analyses

One of the unique contributions of the Rossi and Freeman (1985) text is its chapter on cost-efficiency concepts and methods. More extended discussions of the matter exist in the literature (Levin, 1983; Thompson, 1980), but Rossi's is the most extended discussion in a comprehensive evaluation theory. Cost-efficiency questions are constantly "faced by planners, funding groups, and policymakers everywhere. Over and over again, they must choose how to allocate scarce resources in order to put them to their optimal use" (Rossi & Freeman, 1985, p. 325). Cost analyses

> may be appropriate at two pivotal points in program efforts. In the planning and design phases, *ex ante* cost-benefit analyses may be undertaken on the basis of anticipated costs and benefits of programs. . . . Most commonly, efficiency analyses in the social program field take place after the completion of an impact evaluation, when the net impact of a program is known. The focus of ex post cost-benefit and cost-effectiveness assessments may be on examining the efficiency of a program in either absolute or comparative terms. (Rossi & Freeman, 1985, pp. 327-328)

Ex ante methods are not mentioned by other evaluation theorists, yet are particularly important because they are one of the few cases where evaluators try to predict alternative futures — Cronbach's *UTOS being the other major discussion of this kind.

Cost-benefit analysis. The two major forms of efficiency analysis are cost-benefit and cost-effectiveness analyses. Cost-benefit analysis computes all program costs, and compares them to program outcomes expressed in "a common measure, usually a monetary unit" (Rossi & Freeman, 1985, p. 329). Such analyses "raise two distinct problems: first, the identification and measurement of all program costs and benefits; second, the expression of all costs and benefits in terms of a common denominator" (p. 340). Costs are easiest to identify and compute, including direct, indirect, and opportunity costs. Costs can be imputed using market prices of similar goods or services. If market prices are unavailable or might not reflect real costs, the evaluator can construct "shadow prices . . . derived prices for goods and services that reflect 'true' benefits and costs" (p. 344). Benefits include both tangible and intangible outcomes. Both costs and benefits must be discounted for the effects of time on money — inflation, compounded interest, and lost opportunity costs. But the translation of program outcomes into fiscal terms is hard "in social programs, where only a portion of program inputs and outputs reasonably may be valued in monetary terms" (p. 330). Hence "cost-benefit analysis is least controversial when applied to technical and industrial projects, where it is relatively easy to place a monetary value on benefits as well as costs" (p. 329).

Five conditions should be met prior to doing an ex post cost-benefit analysis (Rossi & Freeman, 1985, p. 349):

(1) "The program has independent or separable funding. This means that its costs can be separated from other activities."

(2) "The program is beyond the development stage and it is certain that net effects are significant."

(3) "Program impact and magnitude of impact are known or can be estimated validly."

(4) "Benefits can be reduced to monetary terms."

(5) "Decision makers are considering alternative programs, rather than simply whether or not to continue the existing project."

Cost-effectiveness analysis. If the fourth condition is not met, an alternative is cost-effectiveness analysis, which "requires monetizing only program costs; benefits are expressed in outcome units" (Rossi & Freeman, 1985, p. 330). In other respects, the methodologies for the two approaches are the same. With cost-effectiveness analysis, "programs with similar objectives are evaluated and the costs of alternative programs for achieving the same goals are compared" (p. 349), but "because the benefits are not converted to a common denominator, one can neither ascertain the worth or merit of a given intervention nor compare which of two or more programs in different areas produces better returns" (p. 351).

Design Trade-Offs

Comprehensive evaluation includes activities concerned with program conceptualization, implementation, and effects. But such comprehensiveness can rarely be attained in one evaluation. The evaluator must put more resources into some activities than others: "The basic point is that design tradeoffs always exist, subjective judgments must necessarily intrude, and therefore one should consciously consider these complexities in planning research" (Berk & Rossi, 1977, p. 87). Three concepts help evaluators make these trade-offs. First is the "good enough" rule previously discussed. Second is "use of broadly *political* desiderata in the design of evaluation research" (Berk & Rossi, 1977, p. 87); "one might choose seriously to jeopardize some aspects of scientific validity if a 'greater good' is served. Note however, that both the probability and worth of that greater good are clearly subjective assessments laden with moral and political judgments" (p. 87). The evaluator should try to anticipate the social and political costs associated with program outcomes, and then design the evaluation to maximize the chances of detecting a socially important or costly outcome, sacrificing the ability to detect outcomes of less importance or cost. Third is "tailoring." However:

> There are limits to how fully the process of tailoring can be explained formally — given that it involves not only the orderly formulation and refinement of ideas with data integration but also dialogue, discussion, and interaction with relevant stakeholders. (Rossi & Freeman, 1985, p. 102)

We might like the resolution of these trade-offs to be through straightforward application of scientific methods; but Rossi agrees with Cronbach that evaluation design is an art, and that "certainly via the written word, there are limits to how much of an art form can be taught" (Rossi & Freeman, 1985, p. 37):

> The principles of trade-offs are hard to formulate. Of course, one may trade off a good sample for a good interview guide, but it is difficult to conceptualize how one would make such a decision and to state such decisions as conforming to a general rule. (Rossi, 1982b, p. 5)

Trade-offs are "a neglected concern" (p. 5) in evaluation, and Rossi has no easy answers for them.

Interpreting Evaluation Findings

Generalizable, statistically significant results are not always policy-relevant results. In addition to cost-efficiency methods, to facilitate policy relevance, evaluators should judge the social worth of a change: "Small magnitudes of change have policy significance when social worth is high; but larger magnitudes are necessary when social worth is low" (Rossi & Freeman, 1985, p. 383). Second, "the availability of alternative interventions must also be taken into account" (p. 383); an intervention is less valuable if another program gives the same results at lower cost. Finally, research should "be sensitive to the various policy issues involved" (p. 383); to do this, the evaluator should "consult the proceedings of deliberative bodies . . . interview decision makers' staffs, or consult decision makers directly" (p. 384) and conduct evaluability assessments.

Use of Evaluation Findings

Use is central to the evaluator's responsibilities:

> There are, of course, intrinsic rewards for evaluators, who may derive great pleasure simply from satisfying themselves that they have done as nearly perfect a technical job as possible. . . . But that is not really what it is all about. Evaluations are a "real-world" activity. In the end, what counts is . . . the extent to which it leads to modified policies, programs, and practices — ones that, in the short or long term, improve the human condition. (Rossi & Freeman, 1985, p. 357)

"The rationale for doing applied work is to influence the actions and thinking of the broad category of persons who effect social change, and who in their policy and action roles use the findings and conclusions provided by evaluators" (Rossi & Freeman, 1985, p. 372). Hence "successful evaluators are those who have made clear to themselves, and to their sponsors and program staffs, how the evaluation is to be used and its level of application" (p. 56).

Citing Leviton and Hughes (1981), Rossi discusses three kinds of use: instrumental, conceptual, and persuasive. Instrumental use "refers to the documented and specific use of evaluation findings by decision makers and other stakeholders" (Rossi & Freeman, 1985, p. 387). Rossi first thought instrumental use was rare. But now "it would appear that there is a fair degree of instrumental utilization, contrary to the views expressed when the earlier editions of this book appeared" (p. 389). However, "a pessimistic view of the amount of direct utilization is still widely held among both evaluators and potential consumers of evaluations" (p. 389). As more reports of such use are documented and conveyed to evaluators, this pessimistic view may diminish.

To increase instrumental use, evaluators should follow five rules (Rossi & Freeman, 1985, pp. 392-394). First, they must understand the work styles of decision makers; this implies presenting results briefly and simply. Second, evaluation results must be timely and available when needed. Third, evaluations must respect stakeholders' program commitments by allowing "wide participation in the evaluation design process to ensure sensitivity to stakeholders' interests" (p. 392). Fourth, utilization and dissemination plans should be part of evaluation design. Fifth, evaluations should assess utilization.

Since utilization requires dissemination, "dissemination is a definite responsibility of evaluation researchers" (Rossi & Freeman, 1985, p. 394). The key is to identify relevant stakeholders. The primary client for the evaluation is usually provided with a summary of results. But the evaluator should also "be a secondary disseminator" (p. 397):

> "Secondary dissemination" refers to the communication of research results and any recommendations they yield in ways that meet the needs of stakeholders (as opposed to "primary" dissemination, which in most cases is the technical report). Secondary dissemination takes many forms: abbreviated versions of technical reports (often called "executive summaries"), slick "special reports" that are issued regularly by evaluation groups of the evaluation responses, memos, oral presentations complete with slides and graphic displays, and sometimes even movies or videotapes. (Rossi & Freeman, 1985, pp. 397-398)

Rossi advises hiring experts in these areas to make sure dissemination is done well.

Conceptual use "is the use of evaluations to influence thinking about issues in a general way" (Rossi & Freeman, 1985, p. 388). This kind of use "often provides important inputs into policy and program development, and should not be compared with ending the race in second place" (p. 389); "conceptual utilization may not be as visible to peers or sponsors as direct utilization, but it may in the end have important impacts on the community as a whole or on critical segments of it" (p. 389). Rossi calls this the "demystification" function of evaluation (Berk & Rossi, 1977). His description of demystification is quite similar to Weiss's description of enlightenment. But "it is more difficult to design efforts to maximize conceptual utilization" (Rossi & Freeman, 1985, p. 391). Rossi's best advice to the evaluator who wants to facilitate demystification is in his discussions of theory-driven evaluation.

Persuasive use "refers to enlisting evaluation results in efforts either to defend or to attack political positions" (Rossi & Freeman, 1985, p. 388). An example is the Reagan administration's use of the lack of clear findings of positive impacts from evaluations of social programs to justify cutting social programs. Such "persuasive use of evaluations is, for the most part, out of the hands of either program evaluators or sponsors and will not concern us further" (p. 388).

OUR ANALYSIS OF
ROSSI'S THEORY OF EVALUATION

The only really essential component of evaluation theory is theory of practice. Rossi's work, to an extent exceeded only by Wholey, primarily consists of theory of practice, albeit a much more broadly applicable theory of practice than Wholey's. Rossi steers clear of most theoretical debates, so we have less to say about his theories of knowledge, valuing, use, and social programming. His explicit discussions of these four components are rather pedestrian, and he makes few novel implicit assumptions about them. Our only significant criticism concerns his theory of practice, which is not sufficiently explicit about how to choose from among the many options he presents. Our criticisms of his theories of knowledge, valuing, use, and social programming are mostly precursors of this criticism of his theory of practice.

Theory of Knowledge

Rossi is realist and empiricist in tenor, but with strong doses of fallibilism and multiplism. His fallibilism is seen in his frequent reminders that all social science methods have flaws, and that all rely on ancillary assumptions that might be wrong. So, for example, he says, "All beliefs about what works are held tentatively and subject to many caveats. The findings from social policy experiments are certainly no different in principle" (Berk et al., 1985, p. 397); and "As is the case with all research activities, such estimates cannot be made with certainty, but only within limits of error and with varying degrees of plausibility" (Rossi & Freeman, 1985, p. 185).

Rossi's solution to fallibility is to prescribe joint use of multiple options, each of which sheds a different kind of light on the topic. For example: "The analyst is required, at the very least, to state the basis for the assumptions that underlie his or her analysis. Often analysts do more than that: They may undertake several different analyses of the same program, varying the assumptions made" (Rossi & Freeman, 1985, p. 329). Regarding methods: "The research designs described earlier may sometimes be used jointly, usually to the considerable enhancement of the credibility of conclusions" (p. 220). Regarding impact assessment: "The general point made here is that the plausibility of an impact assessment can be enhanced considerably through the employment of several approaches, provided, of course, that those approaches yield results that are complementary and not contradictory" (p. 221).

Such movement toward multiplism of assumption and method is, we think, a salutary development in evaluation. Experience suggests it is rare in social science for a single way of approaching a theoretical or methodological problem to be always optimal. This observation seems unlikely to change in the future. Since each approach has strengths and weaknesses, the choice of a particular approach introduces systematic theoretical and methodological biases at the same time that it contributes useful information. Such biases especially threaten the validity of knowledge when shared by many investigators working on a problem. Rossi's multiplism can help prevent the introduction of such systematic biases into evaluation. This entails the planned use of multiple heterogeneous options, all reflecting different kinds and directions of biases, coupled with a commitment to seeking and using criticism to find biases in the options chosen.

Unfortunately, Rossi only alludes to these possibilities. He conveys a general impression of familiarity with epistemology, but appears disinterested in and even disdainful of debating it:

> For those who care, positivism is an outdated philosophy of science that no one familiar with the issues takes seriously any longer. Yet, positivism has been adopted as a rallying cry by many of those who object to quantification, statistics, or scientific methods more generally. Although quantification, statistics, and scientific methods are hardly flawless and do overlook or fail to capitalize on other ways of "knowing," no one has yet proposed in any detail what the alternative might be. Serious statements that have appeared are either broadly philosophical (and, therefore, offer little on how concretely to proceed) or are more properly thought of as complements to experimental approaches. (Berk et al., 1985, p. 427).

His distaste is particularly apparent in his observations about the quantitative-qualitative debate, which has continued "ad nauseam" (Rossi & Freeman, 1985, p. 223), resulting in "a rich, although somewhat pointless, literature" (p. 367), with the theoretical arguments of qualitative theorists amounting to an almost "mystical advocacy" (Rossi, 1985, p. 7).

We share Rossi's misgivings about the accuracy and cogency of epistemological and ontological analyses by many qualitative theorists. But we would not dismiss them as mystical, pointless, and nauseating. Many evaluators have adopted predominantly qualitative approaches to their work (Shadish & Epstein, 1987); we hope they have not done so based on inaccurate epistemological and ontological arguments that *only* qualitative approaches have serious philosophical warrant. They are unlikely to change their minds and practices if those of us who disagree with those arguments do not present a detailed and cogent alternative. Presenting such alternatives would help prevent the impression that these issues are regarded as unimportant in evaluation. In addition, many scholars in evaluation and other disciplines find these debates exciting, productive, and critically helpful to understanding the epistemological and ontological bases of our field. When informed, productive scholars take a position seriously, we feel compelled to understand why, and to try to reconcile those views with our own. To do otherwise is to risk overlooking important theoretical and factual matters that could render our own views inaccurate, incomplete, or wrong. One must study and understand these matters to understand fully why different theorists advocate the methods they do. Rossi's dismissal of these matters may be the root cause of some practical and epistemological infelicities in his work.

Consider his treatment of causation, for example. Rossi tries to integrate Campbell's and Cronbach's positions on causation in a way that resolves the conflicts between them. However, because he is insufficiently clear about relevant epistemological and ontological arguments, his effort is not entirely successful. Campbell buttresses his arguments for the randomized experiment in evolutionary epistemology. Cronbach supports his method choices in part by explicit assumptions about the widespread existence of interactions that mitigate the success Campbell can have in finding robust causal main effects (Cronbach, 1957, 1975). Consequently, Cronbach emphasizes causal mediating processes and external validity over internal validity. Rossi explicitly avoids such arguments: "There are many deep and thorny issues surrounding the concept of causality that need not concern us here. Rather, we shall accept the view that the world is orderly and lawful and that 'A is the cause of B' can be a valid statement" (Rossi & Freeman, 1985, p. 188). But those deep and thorny issues cannot be ignored if Rossi's arguments are to be theoretically convincing. Rossi's advocacy of strong causal inference through the randomized experiment seems to acknowledge Campbell's intellectual heritage (e.g., Rossi & Freeman, 1985, p. 243): "Social experimentation on prospective social policies is unquestionably here to stay. . . . Whether Campbell's (1971) 'experimenting society' will ever be achieved is still an open question, but it is quite clear that we have begun to move in this direction" (Rossi et al., 1979, p. 180). But Rossi ignores the theory of knowledge buttressing the experimenting society, and so fails to appreciate why theory (as in theory-driven evaluation) has little place in Campbell's tradition. Evolutionary epistemology requires "blind variations" — radically different alternatives to what already exists. Campbell would not incorporate the a priori constraints of any kind of theory; to do so would limit variations to those our theories suggest. Hence theory-driven evaluation has little place in evolutionary epistemology — one need not know why a cause-effect relationship holds to know that it does hold.

Rossi's integration of Cronbach and Campbell is not practically successful either, again because he ignores the underlying theoretical differences between the two authors about trade-offs in evaluation. Chen and

Rossi recommend (a) doing randomized experiments to study causal efficacy, and simultaneously (b) studying causal mediation using structural modeling procedures (Bollen, 1989; Hayduk, 1987). This is a fine ideal to strive for, (a) if resources can support such an ambitious endeavor, (b) if the evaluation team has the requisite statistical skills to understand and do causal modeling, and (c) if interest in causation is so high that it is worth investing time and effort into a randomized experiment. The first two points are formidable, but the last point is often the largest obstacle to following Chen and Rossi's advice. An ideal theory-driven evaluation is so costly that it takes resources away from the widespread search for successful solutions to problems that Campbell advocates. Rather than fund a few large, expensive experiments, Campbell (1979b, 1986b, 1987a) would fund many small evaluations by different investigators using different designs to foster different perspectives on the program. Theory-driven evaluation is a bit monolithic by contrast.

If the evaluator cannot do the Chen and Rossi ideal, any fallback options result in a very unsatisfactory integration of Campbell and Cronbach. One would have to compromise the theoretical analysis or the experiment; Chen and Rossi mostly do the latter. Falling back to a quasi-experimental design usually results in significant degradation of internal validity — something Campbell would prefer not happen. Chen and Rossi (1987) place great faith in the evaluator's ability to specify a causal model correctly. But evidence about the accuracy of such causal models is quite mixed (Freedman, 1987; Stolzenberg & Relles, 1990; Stromsdorfer, 1987). Hence Chen and Rossi's fallback options provide quite unsatisfactory integrations of Campbell and Cronbach.

Another example is Rossi's discussion of internal and external validity. Rossi has endorsed the latter terminology and concepts, and seems to understand that the essence of internal validity is the idea that " 'A is the cause of B' can be a valid statement" (Rossi & Freeman, 1985, p. 188). But in his recent work he seems to prefer the new terminology that Cronbach (1982a) introduced to replace Campbell's concepts of internal and external validity — namely, *reproducibility* and *generalizability*:

> The paramount purpose of an impact assessment is to make possible valid statements about whether or not a program results in significant net effects. To accomplish this end, an impact assessment must have two desirable characteristics: (1) reproducibility and (2) generalizability. "Reproducibility" refers to the ability of the research design employed to produce findings that are robust enough to be reproduced with substantially the same results, if repeated by another researcher using the same design in the same setting. "Generalizability"

refers to the relevance of the findings to the program in question, or to similar programs in comparable settings. (Rossi & Freeman, 1985, p. 224)

Similar language is found in Chen and Rossi (1987). In this terminological transition, Rossi fails to note that Cronbach changes the meaning of internal validity. Reproducibility and internal validity are not the same thing because in reproducibility, "causal language is superfluous" (Cronbach, 1982a, p. 140). Causal language is the essence of internal validity; reproducing a wrong causal conclusion would not count as internal validity for Campbell. Moving from internal validity toward reproducibility is not an integration of Campbell and Cronbach; it is a move from Campbell to Cronbach in epistemological assumptions and in practical implications for the activities evaluators should be doing.

Theory of Valuing

In several respects Rossi is closer to Scriven on valuing than any other theorist. First, Rossi would agree with Scriven that neither science nor evaluation can be value-free. Particularly noteworthy is Berk and Rossi's (1977) superb discussion of the values inherent in the endeavor of social program evaluation — that social programming generally involves only minor variations in existing programs and so is essentially conservative; that evaluation, by studying those programs, endorses the moral and political values implicit in them; and that the evaluator makes moral choices throughout the design of evaluation.

Second, only Rossi and Scriven devote much attention to needs assessment. In fact, Rossi is more explicit than Scriven about technical and methodological aspects of that topic. Like Scriven, Rossi acknowledges social need as a criterion of merit that drives the valuing of social interventions, talking about how social programs deal with "unresolved defects in social conditions" (Rossi & Freeman, 1985, p. 107). Just as Scriven makes clear that social needs have priority over wants and ideals, Rossi says that "need must be distinguished from demand" (Rossi & Freeman, 1985, p. 119) so the former can have precedence.

Third, Rossi implicitly endorses Scriven's second step in the logic of valuing, constructing comparative standards of performance:

Indeed, there is much to be gained in the way of useful information for policy-makers and project managers if evaluations of several interventions are undertaken comparatively, so that a given intervention is compared not only to the condition in which no intervention is made but also to alternative interventions. (Rossi & Freeman, 1985, p. 235)

Finally, to judge from Rossi's attention to cost-benefit analysis, he also acknowledges value in the fourth step of Scriven's logic — synthesis of results over different criteria into an overall value statement.

A subtler similarity between Scriven and Rossi is that it is difficult to tell if they are descriptive or prescriptive value theorists. Both have a prescriptive edge that makes them very different from the decisively descriptive theories of valuing held by most other theorists. In Scriven's case, the roots of his definition of need lie in egalitarian theories of justice. Rossi is not as clearly prescriptive as Scriven. When he is prescriptive, he appeals to more than one theory, some of which are not entirely compatible with each other. Sometimes Rossi's advice sounds like it is based in egalitarian theories of justice:

> A deficient human being or household lacks or is deprived of experiences and/or resources that are essential to adequate functioning. Thus, according to this view everyone should have a chance at a reasonable job, or a reasonable chance to recover from an illness or injury. In short, we hold to concepts of *social minima* for units of our society. (Rossi, 1979, p. 72)

And:

> If a lowered minimum wage for teenagers increases total family incomes of the most disadvantaged households but decreases the family incomes of the moderately disadvantaged, the dollars gained and lost could be weighted differently, depending on the degree of disadvantage to the families. Some accomplishments are worth more to the community, both for equity reasons and for the increase in human well-being, and should therefore be weighted more heavily. (Rossi & Freeman, 1985, p. 345)

Other times he endorses a utilitarian theory: "While other factors, including political and value considerations, come into play, the preferred program often is the one that produces the most impact on the most targets for a given level of expenditure" (Rossi & Freeman, 1985, p. 325).

As is typical of his relatively atheoretical approach, Rossi overlooks possible tensions between egalitarian and utilitarian positions. The egalitarian theorist would give resources to the most disadvantaged, and not spread them out to create the greatest good for the greatest number (Bunda, 1985; House, 1980). The egalitarian evaluator would follow that lead, judging program merit by how much it meets needs of the most disadvantaged. In community mental health center (CMHC) evaluation, for example, worth might vary dramatically under egalitarian versus utilitarian perspectives. A typical egalitarian critique of CMHCs during the 1970s is that they failed to serve one of the neediest populations, the chronically mentally ill. This omission might not much bother the utilitarian evaluator because CMHCs might do much good for many clients even if they paid no attention to the chronically mentally ill. Should needs really drive judgments of worth? Rossi leaves neither the evaluation theorist nor the practitioner with a clear answer.

At other times, Rossi sounds like a descriptive theorist: "Evaluations provide only superfluous information unless they are designed to draw on the values and preferences involved in policymaking, program planning, and management" (Rossi & Freeman, 1985, p. 384):

> What is seen as a human or social problem by some persons and groups may not be perceived as such by others. . . . While research obviously cannot settle the issue of which perspective is "correct," it can eliminate conflicts that might arise from groups talking past each other. (Rossi & Freeman, 1985, p. 113)

He is influenced by the practical merits of descriptive valuing, and of ensuring that different value perspectives are included:

> The consequences of proceeding under the illusion that there is consensus when in fact there is considerable conflict can be seen in the fate of the urban renewal program. . . . This program was predicated on presumed agreement regarding important criteria of housing dilapidation and obsolescence by planners, residents, and institutions. The criteria used by planners often did not correspond with those of residents. Consequently, urban renewal projects in city after city created rancorous conflict—so much that in many cases the programs were gradually abandoned." (Rossi & Freeman, 1985, p. 117)

Yet he does not wholeheartedly endorse descriptive valuing since its major limitation "is that it has the built-in biases of the individuals and organizations surveyed" (Rossi & Freeman, 1985, p. 126), something best remedied by "bringing together a cross section of stakeholders" (p. 127). But even the latter remedy falls short: "Especially problematic are the reactions of beneficiaries (targets) of a program. Although in many programs beneficiaries would appear to have the strongest stake in an evaluation's outcome, they are often the least prepared to make their voices heard" (p. 374).

One might view Rossi's discussion of valuing as a salutary attempt to integrate descriptive and prescriptive positions in evaluation. But Rossi is never explicit about how this might be done (see Stokey & Zeckhauser, 1978, pp. 155-158). Hence these different comments can confuse the evaluator who wonders which value perspective to take. If we had to select a quote that would best represent Rossi's position on valuing, therefore, it is this:

> All perspectives are equally legitimate. The clients' or targets' perspective cannot claim any more legitimacy than that of the program or the government agency funding the program. The responsibility of the evaluator is not to take one of the many perspectives as *the* legitimate one, but to be clear from which perspectives a particular evaluation is being undertaken and to give recognition explicitly to the existence of other perspectives. (Rossi & Freeman, 1985, p. 378)

This statement could integrate descriptive and prescriptive theories if one includes prescriptive perspectives among the many equally legitimate ones while retaining the pragmatic advantages of descriptive valuing (Cook & Shadish, 1986). Still, the contention that all perspectives are equally legitimate may need tempering to account for obvious counterexamples, and for the fact that equally legitimate perspectives are not the same as equal needs.

Theory of Social Programming

Rossi has a finely articulated sense of the political and economic constraints on social programming. He understands how the worth of evaluation is constrained by the goodness of the larger social problem-solving context in which it fits. He notes, for example, that problems addressed by programs are long-standing and relatively intractable, so even the best evaluations may find small effects (Rossi & Wright, 1977). Evaluations are also constrained by the worth of the intervention that is implemented: "Completely new interventions are relatively rare. Most programs introduced as 'new and innovative' are ordinarily modifications of existing practices. What makes an intervention 'innovative' in our sense is that the 'treatment' has never been applied to the population specified" (Rossi & Freeman, 1985, p. 46). Such innovations are a far cry from the radical "blind variations" that Campbell would study. Rossi says that "experiments should concentrate primarily on program variations that are clearly within the policy space defined by policymakers and administrators, perhaps extending a bit beyond, but not too far" (Rossi & Freeman, 1985, p. 257). This endorses an incrementalist notion of change, as illustrated in Rossi's discussion of the Negative Income Tax Experiments:

> Regardless of the accuracy of incremental perspectives, their ideological values are clear. First, attention may be diverted away from fundamental issues of power and privilege to detailed debates over the relative merits of minor variations in

negative income tax plans. Income Maintenance in turn becomes solely a question of appropriate minimum and maximum levels of support for the needy, rather than consideration of income redistribution across all levels of American society. Second, if change is incremental, it is far more difficult to accuse society of being unresponsive to the needs of all its citizens. One can argue that "meaningful" change occurs every day. Finally, and perhaps most important, the astructural, ahistorical biases of evaluation methodology reinforce the idea that the rationale for social change can rest on impartial and objective assessments of societal performance. Evaluation findings are put forward as judgments above politics, based on scientific data, not organized interests. The implicit message is that if the "truth" can be revealed, decision makers will respond to it. Again, whether this is accurate or not, it is clearly a political statement in which social change becomes increasingly a technological question to be decided by the outcome of scientific investigation, conducted by dedicated scientists who are above "mere politics." (Berk & Rossi, 1977, pp. 82-83)

Here Rossi points out the intimate connection between values and change—that incremental change serves the interests and values of those who currently benefit from existing arrangements.

The metallic and plastic laws are the epitome of social incrementalism in Rossi's work, or his perception that social programs have very small, often null, effects due to the conservative nature of social programming. However, the evidence to support the laws is far from clear. We outlined a number of relevant arguments in criticizing Stake's theory of social programming. Weak evaluation methods may be as much at fault here as weak social programs, since the first 20 years of evaluation were not as methodologically sophisticated in detecting effects as is the case today (Shadish & Reis, 1984). Indeed, Rossi cites some evidence of at least partly effective programs in his own work (Berk et al., 1981; Rossi et al., 1980; Rossi & Freeman, 1985; Rossi & Lyall, 1976, 1978), and acknowledges that our methods are far better now than when we started (Rossi & Wright, 1984). Both Rossi and Weiss proclaim program ineffectiveness publicly and frequently, but neither presents a thorough and systematic review of the relevant evidence, or points to an author who has. Such pronouncements have the character of professional lore rather than of demonstrated fact.

At one international conference on evaluation, one of us confidently cited the Iron Law in a discussion of social experimentation (Shadish, 1987a). But a well-known and knowledgeable policy analyst quickly made two cogent responses. One was that it is dangerous to foster the idea that social programs don't work, since such contentions give "aid and comfort to the barbarians" (Weiss, 1987b, p. 41). Rossi should be sympathetic to this criticism given his sensitivity to moral choices in evaluation (Berk &

Rossi, 1977). The other, more important, objection was the existence of obvious counterexamples of apparently large and dramatic successes, particularly social security and Medicare. Anyone who cannot see the dramatic changes these programs have wrought in the condition of the elderly is, in the words of this policy analyst, blind.

In part we agree with Rossi that social interventions are conservative and incremental (Cook, 1981; Shadish, 1984). Yet the metallic and plastic laws are overstated and underjustified—perhaps deliberately, to provoke thoughtful response. Still, Rossi might consider discussing these objections and counterexamples more thoroughly, and reviewing more thoroughly the evidence bearing on them.

Rossi is unclear how much he wants evaluators to do evaluations that produce usable but incremental change in the short term, versus evaluations of more comprehensive changes to the status quo. Wholey opts for the former; Weiss opts for the latter. Rossi opts for both in that tailored evaluation prescribes both, depending on the kind of program one is evaluating. He does not discuss the relative merits of each option or any criteria evaluators should use in making the choice of the kind of program to evaluate. This failure is of little consequence to evaluators when the program to be evaluated has already been chosen. But if an evaluator or evaluation policymaker can *choose* whether to evaluate an innovation, an established program, or a fine-tuning adjustment, Rossi offers no help in making the choice. The problem is not whether one choice is always best; important problem solving has resulted from evaluations of programs at all three developmental stages. The problem is more subtle—to predict the circumstances under which choosing one option rather than another will be beneficial.

It is tempting to infer that Rossi personally prefers to evaluate the impact of innovations. When he has actually conducted an evaluation (Berk et al., 1981), he evaluated the impact of the innovative TARP (Transitional Aid to Released Prisoners) project, an experiment that provided temporary unemployment insurance to recently released felons so they would not need to commit crimes to obtain money. When he critiqued past evaluations (Rossi & Lyall, 1978), he critiqued the innovative Negative Income Tax Experiments. Rossi may think that evaluating such innovations is more likely to result in important change than alternative kinds of evaluation.

Compare Rossi to Wholey on this. Both suggest a similar range of activities for practice—obtaining agreement on objectives prior to evaluation, monitoring program performance, and using randomized experiments to get good estimates of impact. Rossi's discussion of evaluating existing programs incorporates much of Wholey's theory. Both agree on the need for scrutiny of existing programs: Rossi says that "there will continue to be intensive scrutiny of existing programs, because of the pressure to curtail or dismantle those for which there is limited evidence of program efficacy and efficient delivery of services" (Rossi & Freeman, 1985, p. 32); Wholey says that "the public demand for better government performance has been growing" (1979, p. 7). Both prescribe the use of evaluability assessments and performance monitoring.

But despite their agreement on all this, the two authors part ways in choosing options for practice. Wholey cites many examples from his own work of monitoring existing programs, but never reports having done an impact experiment. Rossi devotes more resources to high-quality impact assessments of innovations. But the divergence in these practical choices is striking. Wholey seems more comfortable in practice than Rossi with the incrementalism implicitly endorsed by monitoring existing programs.

Rossi may be caught between his liberal ideals and his experience of how those ideals are best implemented in a stable political and economic system:

> I regard myself as a liberal, especially on issues involving welfare programs. In the times of the regimes of Kennedy and Johnson, I was certainly to their left, and have found more space to my right in every presidential regime since those times, a fact that reflects not my moving to the left but the rightward drift during the Nixon and Carter regimes and the decided acceleration in that direction in the Reagan Presidency. . . . I believe firmly that the state — our national government and its subdivisions — has an obligation to put a floor under every individual in our country, below which no individual should be let sink. . . . The floor should consist of decent minima of income, housing, education, personal safety, and medical care. . . . I could say more about equality and liberty, but that would take too long. The main point is that I am a staunch supporter of social programs that are designed to achieve those ends. The central intellectual task for left of center applied social scientists such as myself is how to design the appropriate programs, minimizing undesirable side effects. (Rossi, 1985, pp. 1-2)

We would rephrase the dilemma in this last sentence somewhat: The central intellectual task is how to design programs that serve the disadvantaged well, given the trenchant resistance of the status quo to such changes. No evaluation theorist does a good job of resolving this dilemma.

Theory of Use

Rossi's theory of use explicitly borrows Leviton and Hughes's (1981) differentiation among instrumental, conceptual, and persuasive use. He tries to make a place for both instrumental and conceptual use, and is most like Weiss on this topic. Both started their careers hoping for instrumental use, but were disappointed with what little they saw occur. They both moved toward conceptual use — Weiss calling it enlightenment and Rossi calling it demystification. Both acknowledged this was a move away from short-term use toward long-term use, but both felt evaluators could legitimately make this move. Both Weiss and Rossi have recently seen cause for optimism about the amount of instrumental use that occurs, but both theorists still lean heavily toward preferring conceptual use.

Rossi is not very clear about contingencies to guide the evaluator's choice of what kind of use to facilitate. Weiss is much clearer. She tells evaluators to aim for enlightenment most of the time. Rossi is less clear, sometimes telling evaluators emphatically to facilitate instrumental use, and other times equally emphatically encouraging demystification. This could result from tailoring evaluations to different stages of program development, but tailoring is never tied to use. Theory-driven evaluation is a particularly instructive example of the resultant problems. Rossi criticizes some experiments for not being sufficiently interactive with social science theory, and he has defined social policy experiments as "*theoretically based*" (Berk et al., 1985, p. 407) efforts that "must exploit social science theory" (p. 407). Theory-driven evaluation brings social science theory to the forefront of evaluation practice, which increases its potential for demystification about the nature of social problems and their amelioration. But this subordinates user information needs to social science theory needs, and it is difficult to meet both needs well. Chelimsky (1985) questions

> the ability of policy experiments (or any other type of research, for that matter) to conciliate over the long term the two objectives of satisfying user needs while simultaneously advancing social science theory and knowledge: Experience has not been encouraging in this area. Can these two objectives be jointly pursued and balanced without resulting in what has so often happened in the past — the subordination of user information needs to those of research producers? (p. 431)

In many situations the evaluator's goal is to foster instrumental use; theory-driven evaluation may be the wrong choice in those situations.

The Leviton and Hughes (1981) conceptualization of use seems tacked on to Rossi's theory of practice as an afterthought; it is not integrated logically into the theory to guide evaluator practice. Lacking advice about how expectations about use can guide practice, Rossi's preference for demystification will be criticized by theorists who think that goal is too "scientistic" for evaluators — Patton (1988) has criticized Weiss (1988a) on exactly this point. Rossi may not mean to discount the value of instrumental use, but his lack of clarity about when it should be pursued leaves him vulnerable to such criticism.

Theory of Practice

Consider Rossi's theory of practice in light of how well it describes options for practice, constraints on the implementation of those options, trade-offs among options as a result of those constraints, and priorities among options when trade-offs must be made. Rossi does well in listing options for practice, and in discussing constraints on each option. The Rossi and Freeman (1985) text is full of such discussion, covering far more options than any other theorists. Rossi is often not given enough credit for this catholicity. McLaughlin (1983), for example, criticizes Rossi and Freeman (1982) for giving scant attention to qualitative methods. But that book relies heavily on qualitative methods during program conceptualization and monitoring, although they do not always call those methods qualitative, and they do not endorse such methods for impact assessments. Similarly, Rossi is often mistakenly characterized as a narrow advocate of experiments (Guba & Lincoln, 1981; McLaughlin, 1983), but his theory is far more complex than that. Of the eight chapters in Rossi and Freeman (1985), only three deal with impact assessment, and only one is about the experiment.

Yet Rossi's comprehensiveness leads to other problems, for his theory of practice does less well in describing trade-offs and priorities among the options he lists. He discusses trade-offs and priorities of different methods for conducting the *same* evaluation activity. For example, his analysis of different methods for answering impact questions suggests clear trade-offs and priorities regarding the differential feasibility, desirability, and advantages of different methods for this task. His preferences are clear: Randomized experiments are best for assessing impact, followed by time series, statistical controls, other nonequivalent controls, and reflexive, shadow, and generic controls.

But when Rossi moves beyond methodology to trade-offs and priorities about other aspects of evaluation, his theory is less clear. For example, in a comprehensive evaluation Rossi is unclear about when an impact assessment is preferred over monitoring, diagnostic procedures, or efficiency analysis. Rossi's theory presents the evaluator with many options but too little advice about when and why to choose each option. The impression is of an only partly disciplined eclecticism that succeeds in integrating the work of past theorists at the cost of losing some internal coherence. Rossi's answer to this criticism may be that designing evaluation is an art that cannot be guided by tidy rules. We partly agree with this response, but still believe he could do more to clarify some inconsistencies in his theory.

Should evaluations be comprehensive? The problem is epitomized by comprehensive evaluation — that all evaluations should answer a comprehensive set of questions about program conceptualization, implementation, and utility. Yet Rossi acknowledges that "it is not always possible" (Rossi & Freeman, 1985, p. 38) to conduct comprehensive evaluations that provide valid and reliable findings, given "political and ethical constraints and the limitations imposed by time, money, and human resources" (p. 13). All things being equal, comprehensive evaluations will sacrifice fidelity to obtain bandwidth. Rossi recognizes this trade-off when discussing program monitoring: "As with records on target populations, a few items of data gathered consistently and reliably are generally much better for monitoring purposes than a more comprehensive set of information of doubtful reliability and inconsistent collection" (Rossi & Freeman, 1985, p. 174). The same arguments apply to his theory as a whole. To the extent that evaluators try to do everything Rossi recommends, they will do little well. To the extent that they pick and choose among the options, they will not be comprehensive. Some priorities are needed.

Good reasons exist for evaluations *not* to be always comprehensive. A completely comprehensive study would be large and expensive; a few mistakes or misfortunes could seriously detract from its overall utility. It might also prevent evaluators from being closely acquainted with substantive issues and sites under study, leaving the evaluation deficient in contextual knowledge that improves the design, implementation, and interpretation of studies. A single comprehensive study may not be logically desirable. Asking some questions may be premature if others have not been answered. It might not make sense to explore service implementation if the program is not reaching its intended beneficiaries, or to judge a program ineffective if one is not sure it was implemented (Rossi & Wright, 1984). Evaluators sometimes examine novel programs, projects, or elements that are still undergoing a shakedown period; such evaluators might prefer to provide feedback about service targeting and implementation rather than about effects. Finally, sometimes the funder does not want a comprehensive look at the program, as is often the case in the General Accounting Office's relationship to the Congress (Chelimsky, 1987a). In all these cases, it makes more sense to do programmatic sequences of smaller, noncomprehensive studies instead of single large studies with comprehensive purposes (Cronbach, 1982a). Tailored evaluation seems to acknowledge these points, except that even tailored evaluations are supposed to be comprehensive in Rossi's scheme.

Tailored evaluation as a tool for deciding trade-offs. The concept of
tailoring evaluations epitomizes the kind of theorizing about trade-offs
and priorities that we think is necessary in a theory of evaluation practice.
We placed Rossi last among the theorists discussed in this book in large
part because the concept of tailoring is the kind of direction we want
evaluators to consider. Tailoring is a contingency device—a heuristic
concept that specifies how evaluation practices vary over situations. Contingency devices stand in contrast to focusing devices that reduce the
scope of activities by routinely focusing on some practices rather than
others—an example of which might be Stake's concept of responsive
evaluation, which basically tells all evaluators always to be responsive,
nearly always with the case study.

Contingency devices are superior to focusing devices because they can
unite the diverse practices described in this book. Moreover, implicit in
tailoring is a theory about how diverse practices evolved in evaluation,
and about what the political and organizational context of evaluation will
allow evaluators to do. For example, Rossi notes that it is easier to form
an independent control group for an innovation or program modification
than for an existing program, since programs are larger and more likely to
have achieved full coverage. In the past, evaluators who tried to form a
control group for an existing program quickly encountered this problem,
and so developed their own tacit theory that they should be reluctant to try
to form such a group in such a situation again. Similarly, accountability is
more at issue with existing programs than with innovations or modifications, since the experimental nature of the latter allows more leeway as
new procedures are ironed out. Finally, active participation in program
design is more feasible in an innovation than in an already-designed,
existing program. Tailoring simply warns evaluators about these constraints so evaluators do not do activities that experience has shown to be
self-defeating. Focusing devices are self-defeating in this latter respect;
by prescribing the same approach to all situations, they risk applying a
limited or misleading approach to a problem better addressed by some
other approach, or risk restricting evaluation practice to those situations
where the focus is appropriate.

Tailoring is the end result of a process of evolutionary epistemology
resulting in knowledge about what practices work in the world of evaluation. The ideas behind tailoring may seem familiar or mundane today, but
20 years ago they were not so obvious. Then, it seemed feasible to do an
immediate impact assessment of innovations without detailed attention to
program conceptualization and implementation; or to do randomized studies of existing programs without realizing how difficult it is to find comparable controls. Early evaluators learned the hard way that such ideas

were not functional. So Wholey, for example, gave up his Campbellian notions of experimentation for his contextually pragmatic theory emphasizing program monitoring and improvement. So the concept of tailoring has much value — for saving future evaluators from the mistakes of past evaluators, and for explaining how certain theories of evaluation (like Wholey's) are an almost necessary response to the context in which the theorists operated.

Although Wholey's theory of evaluation can be explained as a reasonable response to Rossi's "existing program" stage of program development, other theorists discussed in this book are not neatly pigeonholed into program stages. By implication, something else is required to explain why theorists differ from each other. Stake's theory is not clearly a response to innovations, modifications, or existing programs, but is potentially applicable to all three; the same is true about Weiss's emphasis on enlightenment. Hence Stake and Weiss are responding to influences other than stage of program development. Knowledge of those other influences would allow us to write a theory that more fully identifies important influences evaluation practice. This is the most significant criticism of Rossi's theory of practice: It fails to consider the many other contingencies that have *just as important an influence* on evaluation practice as does stage of program development. Rossi and Freeman spend a full chapter on how stages of program development affect decisions about practice; one could write a chapter about how each of the following contingencies has similar effects.

First, evaluators are often constrained by factors associated with their employment. Rossi and Freeman note in passing that this factor can influence evaluative work: "Certainly evaluators, whether insiders or outsiders, need to cultivate clear understanding of their relationship to sponsors and program staff. Evaluators' full comprehension of their roles and responsibilities is one major element in the successful conduct of an evaluation effort" (1985, p. 369). But the influence of employment is far more dramatic than this. Cook and Buccino (1979) differentiate among evaluators in the public sector, the private sector, and university settings. Evaluators in these settings tend to do evaluations in different ways and to produce different kinds of evaluations because available resources, skills, authority structures, and time pressures are different in each setting (Shadish & Epstein, 1987). Academic evaluators tend to work in isolation; they cannot access the team of experts that a private research firm can quickly hire; they are unaccustomed to having to meet short deadlines, preferring a long-term perspective for understanding root problems and solutions; and they often want to fit the evaluation assignment into their theoretical interests even if this compromises the client's question somewhat. From this perspective, it is no accident that Chelimsky (1985) has criticized Rossi—who is an academic—on exactly these points regarding social experimentation (Berk et al., 1985). Similarly, knowing that Weiss is an academic helps us to understand her penchant for social science theory-driven evaluations—even for Rossi's "existing programs," which tailored evaluations would advise studying with program monitoring methods.

Is the influence of employment any less than the influence of the stage of program development? We doubt it. For example, under tailored evaluation Rossi advises evaluators who examine existing programs to put most resources into program monitoring and improvement, with less attention to the other questions that comprehensive evaluators look at. But the situation of the academic evaluator of existing programs is quite different from that of the public sector evaluator who works for the program, which in turn also differs from the private sector evaluator brought in by program management on contract. The academic evaluator has more freedom and time to pursue critical questions about program outcome. An example is Murray's (1984) critique of welfare programs—an outcome evaluation of existing programs that is one of the more influential evaluations of the 1980s. It may well be that academic evaluators *should* take advantage of their opportunities to exercise independence of inquiry, because they are the best placed to do so and such inquiries are badly needed. Similar but opposite arguments could be made about public and private sector evaluators, that they should tailor their efforts somewhat to the strengths that their situations give them—fast response time and great flexibility in the private sector, and access to powerful decision makers, managers, and funding mechanisms in the public sector. An ideal theory of evaluation practice cannot ignore such influences.

Second, evaluation practice is constrained by the structural heterogeneity of programs—our distinctions among policies, programs, projects, and elements. Policy expresses intentions about executive and legislative actions that have priority and may buttress a host of programs. Programs are administrative umbrellas for distributing and regulating funds for a particular initiative under a policy. Programs consist of locally implemented projects where service delivery takes place, and projects usually differ widely from each other even in the same program. Projects consist of service and administrative elements, so they are internally heterogeneous as well. Structural heterogeneity is orthogonal to stage of program development, since one can have innovative or existing elements, innovative or existing projects, innovative or existing programs, and innovative or existing policies. Hence structural heterogeneity adds a different kind of information to that provided by stages of program development. As one goes down the list from policies to elements, fewer people are affected.

The opportunity to affect many people is greatest with programs, but turnover is fastest with elements, so the opportunities for evaluative information to be used occur more frequently with elements than with programs and policies. Whether programs are innovative or established, they reach more people but turn over less often than projects or elements.

Organizing a theory of evaluation practice around structural heterogeneity incorporates information about the leverage of evaluative information for subsequent use (a point elaborated by Cook et al., 1985); Rossi's organization around existing programs, modifications, and innovations does not do this well. For example, it is worth distinguishing between established programs and established elements because many methods are more feasible in the latter case than in the former case, and because the latter are replaced often enough that they offer leverage points for change. Similarly, it is worth distinguishing between innovative elements like a new psychotherapy and innovative projects like TARP, because the use of evaluations of TARP will be hamstrung by the fact that TARP is a project, and projects turn over so rarely and cost so much to start up that it seems far less likely that TARP will be implemented than that a new form of psychotherapy will be implemented. Hence a good theory of practice is incomplete without an extended discussion of this contingency, as well.

Third, Wholey and Cronbach note that evaluation practice is also constrained by the "leverage" that certain information would have if gathered. Wholey's theory mostly concerns Rossi and Freeman's established program stage of program development. Within Rossi and Freeman's questions about program conceptualization, implementation, and impact, Wholey points out that some versions of these questions are more worth asking than others if their answers are more useful in changing the program. Cronbach agrees with Rossi that stage of program development should influence practice, but he thinks some stages of programs are not worth evaluating at all. His theory claims that *even within the same stage*, some questions are more worth asking than others because they are currently receiving attention from the policy-shaping community, because they could sway an important group, or because they could clarify why a particular program works. He also points out that the questions most worth asking may be those about which there is greater uncertainty; and that the evaluator should consider the anticipated information yield, because some issues with great leverage and high uncertainty could be answered well only at too high a cost.

Finally, evaluators' personal inclination will also influence the kinds of evaluations they do — and rightly so. Some evaluators like to do academic studies of the underlying causes of and solutions to social problems; others delight in serving management information needs in federal settings. In evaluation, as Popper (1972) says of science generally, "nothing will ever be achieved without a modicum of passion" (p. 12) — and passion is facilitated when evaluators pursue personal inclinations that fit into a reasonable and ethical scheme of practice. Bringing personal passions out into the open is probably beneficial for another reason — it is an honest admission that our choices are often underjustified by the reasons we give for them.

Clearly many possible concepts could be used to organize advice about priorities for evaluation practice. Each of these contingency devices provides information about the merits of different choices we made in evaluation practice, information that is orthogonal to that provided by knowing stages of program development, and that is just as powerful a determinant of what can be done. These concepts add a crucial kind of information that Rossi's theory lacks — concepts that evaluation *policymakers* can use to understand the relative merits of evaluating innovations, fine-tuning adjustments, or established programs.

There is a possible contradiction between comprehensive and tailored evaluation. Rossi claims that all evaluations should strive to be comprehensive; tailored evaluations seem to imply the contrary. The evaluator who tailors evaluations according to Rossi's recommendations will often not have the resources to ask questions about program conceptualization, implementation, and utility. At best that evaluator could be comprehensive over a program of research, a laudable goal but not often within the realistic grasp of many evaluators who control neither the questions they ask nor the resources they use. Tailored evaluation is probably the better route to pursue, so we would minimize prescriptions for evaluations to be comprehensive, and look instead to better ways to organize choices that must be made in practice.

We speak of tailored evaluation as a concept developed from years of experience with what does and does not work in different situations. Not so oddly, various versions of the concept have been around for years, although few evaluators have paid much attention to them. This includes use of the term *tailored evaluation* to refer to a different concept (Cook, 1974b), and use of a different terminology to describe a similar concept. The latter case occurs in the earliest text in the field, in which Suchman (1967) distinguishes among programs *past, present,* and *future,* pointing out that past programs were often fixed and mostly changeable at the margins, that present programs make important implementation decisions to which evaluation could contribute, and that the evaluator can significantly affect planning for future programs so that major alternatives might be tried. Suchman notes that methods for doing different evaluation activities are differentially feasible for past, present, and future programs. The interesting question is why it took evaluators so long to appreciate this lesson. Did they first have to try narrow models to test their limits, given the lack of experience with evaluation that might have proved Suchman correct? Was it that Suchman's work was so quickly eclipsed by Campbell's and Scriven's, given Suchman's untimely death shortly after his book was written? Or was it that evaluation has not been theoretically cumulative, with tailored evaluation being simply a passing fad soon to be replaced by another? Such questions are worthy of more study.

Theory-driven evaluation. Rossi has written so much about theory-driven evaluation, and has incorporated it into so much of his theory, that one must take it seriously as a major component of his theory of practice — even though Rossi and Freeman (1985) rarely if ever mention it by name. Theory-driven evaluation is Rossi's third alternative to guide evaluation practice. Problematically, it is not entirely consistent with comprehensive evaluation or tailored evaluation. Theory-driven evaluation is most like comprehensive evaluation; both advise the evaluator to ask many kinds of questions, to construct a program model, and to take advantage of social science theory. But Rossi usually advises the theory-driven evaluator to ask only a subset (program inputs, mediating processes, conditioning variables, outcome) of the questions asked in comprehensive evaluation (program conceptualization, implementation, utility). Moreover, the theory-driven evaluator prefers to use structural modeling methods; the preferred questions are usually those that fit neatly into causal modeling. The comprehensive evaluator has no such methodological preference. If Chen and Rossi (1987) would loosen the ties between theory-driven evaluation and causal modeling, theory-driven evaluation would be more similar to comprehensive evaluation. But doing so would weaken Chen and Rossi's other arguments about the ability of theory-driven evaluation to address different kinds of validity at once.

Theory-driven evaluation is quite different from tailored evaluation. Theory-driven evaluation relies heavily on causal modeling, and makes little mention of the eclectic panoply of methods that Rossi offers in tailored evaluation. Many options for tailored evaluations, such as needs assessment, have little or nothing to do with program theory, and would be difficult to fit into causal modeling. Theory-driven evaluation is yet a third piece that we must fit into the jigsaw puzzle of Rossi's theory of practice.

Rossi seems to intend theory-driven evaluation to be subordinate to tailored evaluation, and to be of primary use in evaluating innovations. His examples of theory-driven evaluation concern innovations like TARP (Chen & Rossi, 1987), no doubt because theory-driven evaluation is more feasible in that context than at other stages of program development. He has never recommended it as the primary strategy for evaluating an existing program. But this assumption could be wrong. Nothing in theory-driven evaluation precludes evaluating an existing program by surveying program participants and nonparticipants; gathering data about the characteristics of clients, treatments, process, and outcome; and modeling the causal connections among all these. But given Rossi's endorsement of such methods as monitoring when evaluating existing programs (Rossi & Freeman, 1985), methods that require procedures different from those used in theory-driven evaluation, it seems doubtful that he intends theory-driven evaluation to have such overall priority across all stages of program development. Nonetheless, the matter warrants closer attention from Rossi than it receives.

If theory-driven evaluation is subordinate to tailored evaluation, and has particular use in evaluating innovations, some problems with the notion still remain. First, Chen and Rossi (1987) argue that theory-driven evaluation addresses all of Cook and Campbell's (1979) four kinds of validity at once — internal validity, external validity, statistical conclusion validity, and construct validity. Ignoring Chen and Rossi's (1987) equation of internal validity in Campbell's sense with reproducibility in Cronbach's sense, there are problems with this claim. First, it is inconsistent with Rossi and Freeman's claim that "because randomized experiments require such tight controls on treatments and selection, they are not likely to have high generalizability or external validity" (1985, p. 262). This latter remark might be an oversight left over from Rossi's earlier understandings of these trade-offs in previous editions. We assume that Rossi's claim about solving these trade-offs with theory-driven evaluation accurately reflects his understanding of the matter.

If so, theory-driven evaluation faces two problems. One is that it relies on modeling a single instance of an intervention, or at most a small number of cases. In all the examples Rossi cites, great resources are devoted to few cases to facilitate internal validity by using random assignment to conditions. But these single cases may not provide a methodologically sound or credible base from which to draw generalizations. Rossi might respond that it is the theoretical basis, not the sampling of cases, that facilitates generalization. But this response relies on the unlikely presumptions that the purportedly active causal processes were correctly identified, that those identified in the first case are common to all cases, and that the theory-driven evaluator can know the idiosyncratic characteristics of each case and differentiate them from those that generalize over multiple cases. The implausibility of such assumptions significantly weakens the argument that theory-driven evaluation facilitates generalization. Actually, it facilitates theory; the connection of the weak theory that Chen and Rossi discuss to the strong theory needed to facilitate generalization is not a confident one.

The other problem occurs when theory-driven evaluation is implemented without a randomized experiment, so Rossi must place great faith in causal modeling. This faith is belied by evidence that such technologies do not yield accurate results compared with experiments (Haveman, 1986; LaLonde, 1985, 1986). Rossi rarely acknowledges such codicils; their absence is particularly salient in a proposal to solve validity problems (Chen & Rossi, 1987). The solution is not compelling if the major problem is not well addressed. This particular problem becomes even more intense if the tie between theory-driven evaluation and causal modeling is loosened, for then Chen and Rossi give the evaluator little methodological advice about addressing all four kinds of validity at once. Their fallback position is that theory-driven evaluation "should include the identification of potential threats to validity in research" (Chen & Rossi, 1987, p. 102). This is hardly new, being essentially the quasi-experimental logic that Campbell outlined decades ago (Campbell & Stanley, 1963), with the attendant trade-offs between internal and external validity that Cronbach and Campbell noted. Campbell always opts for strong design features, like randomization or interrupted time series, to rule out these threats. Cronbach argues for measuring aspects of "utos" that foster generalization and address threats to validity. Out of the context of a randomized experiment or similar design feature, theory-driven evaluation is just a measurement procedure like Cronbach's. Unlike Cronbach, Chen and Rossi (1987) seem unwilling to admit the fragility of causal modeling or our inability to identify and measure all the important threats to validity.

Rossi's theory-driven evaluation of TARP was a randomized experiment, and he has said that "the time is right to launch a major and coordinated effort in social policy experimentation" (Berk et al., 1985, p. 390), making it clear in that article that this should occur in a theory-driven mode. Perhaps he would implement theory-driven evaluation only in such contexts. But this would not be realistic for most evaluators to do, given the enormous costs of social experimentation (Haveman, 1986). Evaluators rarely have the money to invest in both strong design features and intensive measurement. Such funding is available to only a few evaluators, like Rossi, as he seems to realize:

> In reviewing the profession of evaluation, it should be noted that a small group, perhaps no more than a thousand evaluators, constitutes an "elite" in the field by virtue of the scale of the evaluations on which they work. . . . They are, to some degree, akin to the elite physicians who practice in the hospitals of important medical schools. They and their settings are few in number but powerful in setting the norms for the field. (Rossi & Freeman, 1985, p. 370)

Theory-driven evaluation in the context of randomized experiments may be for this elite, those with sufficient money to do it all well. It may not be at all practical for most practicing evaluators, at least not if it is to address all kinds of validity at once. If so, then the elite may not set the norms for the field. The norms for most evaluators might well be set by theorists who, like Patton (1978), offer advice that can be implemented with the limited resources most evaluators have.

Can rules be made to guide trade-offs? The most important criticism of Rossi is that he endorses too many options without recognizing the trade-offs among them, and without adequately telling how to prioritize when choices must be made. Rossi might respond that it is difficult to formulate such normative rules. In commenting on the Standards for Evaluation Practice of the Evaluation Research Society (ERS), he has noted that design trade-offs are not well clarified in the standards, and need future research (Rossi, 1982b). He has also said it may not be productive to state such priorities, given the youth of the field and the constant emergence of new knowledge about it:

> There are many ways in which standards can inhibit creativity, but one of the best is excessive specificity. Methodological procedures change with time, and the state of the art at one time may be an anachronism at another. Methods can also be rehabilitated after a lapse of time. (Rossi, 1982b, p. 4)

The ambiguity of the standards

> means that ERS stands for tolerance within the evaluation community, gathering unto itself all the tribes of evaluations — hard and soft, formative and summative, academic and commercial — regardless of creed or discipline of origin. Another positive feature is that it does not harden evaluation practices into any one specific mode, allowing for change, innovation, and progress. (pp. 5-6)

It may be that Rossi wants to foster a diversity of experience and practice in evaluation that will ultimately lead to more informed priorities.

We are sympathetic to this position. Diversity of perspective in evaluation, and in social science, helps identify important omissions and commissions of fact and logic (Cook, 1985; Houts et al., 1986; Shadish, 1986a; Shadish et al., 1986; Shadish & Epstein, 1987). We encourage this diversity, and admire Rossi's work because it is so diverse. But diversity is most helpful when accompanied by critical scrutiny. Arguing only for diversity in evaluation would argue against formulating evaluation theories as we have studied them in this book. Those theories are tentative hypotheses about productive ways of doing evaluation — corrigible and presumptive but critical analyses of where the field has been and where it needs to go.

Fostering diversity should be encouraged; but critical theorizing about diversity is equally important to separate the wheat from the chaff. Therefore, once rules are formulated they should be subject to criticism and debate from diverse logical and empirical perspectives. But evaluators need such rules; that they are difficult to formulate is no reason not to attempt to do so.

Rossi might agree with this point. He notes the impediments to professionalization of evaluation that result from the diversity in the field:

> This diversity of evaluative activities, accompanying skills, and associated basic disciplines would not be such an impediment to the development of evaluation as a profession were it not for the fact that evaluators differ in their emphases on one as opposed to another facet of evaluative activities. These internal divisions within the body of evaluators would make it difficult to develop consensus on qualifications for legitimacy and on standards for performance, as well as on appropriate training for evaluative activities. (1981, p. 232)

He criticizes the heterogeneity of what is often offered as evaluation, calling for "ways of evaluating evaluation services" (p. 234). It is difficult to see how such metaevaluation could be done without concepts that guide trade-offs.

Second, Rossi has moved more toward concepts to guide trade-offs as his work has matured. Rossi and Freeman (1982) is a revision of an earlier book (Rossi et al., 1979). Unlike the earlier edition, the revision included a chapter on tailoring evaluations to suggest trade-offs and priorities. Perhaps Rossi sees the need for concepts that help prioritize among evaluative activities. In addition, Rossi's argument about theory-driven evaluation of social programs could also be applied to theories of evaluation—with social programs, Rossi wants to "bring the theory back into program evaluation" (Chen & Rossi, 1983, p. 284): "Most important of all, it is necessary to think theoretically, that is, to rise above the specific and the particular to develop general understandings of social phenomena" (p. 285). If so, we would add that evaluations are social phenomena, too. Evaluations also deserve theoretical attention aimed at developing general understandings of better and worse ways of conducting them.

Perhaps Rossi has not attended to trade-offs because he has focused on well-funded evaluations of a large scope, such as TARP (Berk et al., 1981) or NIT (Rossi & Lyall, 1978). Rossi alludes to this possibility in a self-criticism of his own work:

> A second gap in this coverage is that we have not dealt in any great detail with evaluations of small programs or projects. In principle, there is no difference between the logic of evaluation research for a large as compared with a small

project. In practice, there may be considerable differences. Resources devoted
to small projects may be very limited, the relationships between evaluator and
project personnel may be more intimate, and so on. (Rossi & Wright, 1977, p. 45)

Rossi writes for large-scale evaluation; McLaughlin (1983) criticizes him
for not discussing methods for local, small-scale evaluations as well. But
the methods used in small-scale evaluation are logically the same as those
that Rossi discusses. Hence we would reformulate McLaughlin's criticism;
Rossi covers methods for small-scale, local evaluation, but he does not
address trade-offs due to resource constraints in those situations. Rossi
acknowledges this point, even though he does nothing to address it.

Where rules to guide trade-offs are lacking, we agree with Berk and
Rossi (1977) that the evaluator must make decisions using his or her own
subjective judgment, with particular attention to the moral and political
consequences of design decisions. Berk and Rossi's article, although brief
and necessarily underdeveloped, is one of the best and most convincing
discussions of how one might tie moral and political judgments more
explicitly to design decisions. Methodological rules can never completely
replace moral and political judgments in evaluation; any such rules will
themselves have political and moral consequences. Such consequences
must be examined; they are as much a matter for systematic study as any
other aspect of the discipline (Cook & Shadish, 1986; Shadish, 1984).

CONCLUSION

If one wanted to acquaint a student with the range of practice in
evaluation, one would be hard-pressed to find a single theorist who
portrays that range better than Rossi. We hope our treatment of him fairly
portrays the breadth of his thinking, and his conscientious efforts to move
away from experimentation to a more comprehensive theory of evaluation
practice. On the other hand, Rossi's theory succeeds so well at being
comprehensive that it leaves a host of critical unanswered questions about
resolving trade-offs that most evaluators face. Tailored evaluation helps
guide these choices. But most evaluators will still not have the time,
resources, and expertise to do well all of the things Rossi wants them to
do because (a) tailored evaluation demands a comprehensiveness that may
exceed available resources, (b) they will wonder how much they should
be theory-driven, and (c) the concept of stages of program development
only partly addresses the trade-offs that evaluators face, so other concepts
and heuristic devices are needed to resolve these trade-offs. However, the
successive editions of the Rossi and Freeman books have progressively

deemphasized the role of comprehensive evaluation in favor of tailored evaluation, and theory-driven evaluation has never played much explicit role in those books. Perhaps in subsequent editions, the first two of the reasons mentioned above will be a problem only for those who try to make sense of the corpus of Rossi's works on evaluation rather than just the Rossi and Freeman books. Perhaps we have located some of the problems we have because we have tried to understand his works as a whole. But even if future editions of Rossi and Freeman continue to deemphasize comprehensive evaluation and theory-driven evaluation, others of these problems will still remain, to the extent that they continue to rely so exclusively on tailored evaluations when so many other important contingencies exert such powerful influences on evaluation practice.

PART V

Conclusions

10

Summary and Implications for Evaluation Theory and Practice

By closing this volume with a summary, we risk being pedantic and repetitious. But without one, we risk ending without a concise review of the state of evaluation theory and of the challenges it faces. Hence this chapter summarizes the major lessons of this book. In addition to the work of the seven theorists discussed in previous chapters, we consider related work, including our own, to bring wider perspectives to bear. For each of the five components of evaluation theory, we (a) discuss a set of component-specific questions that evaluators should ask when starting an evaluation (Tables 10.1 through 10.5); (b) analyze the lessons learned about the component, for such lessons provide necessary background for generating useful answers to the questions; and (c) briefly summarize agreements and disagreements theorists have about the component. We do not provide "answers" because few of the questions have a single correct answer. Indeed, our summary of theoretical disagreements constitutes a list of unanswered questions that deserve further study. Lacking such research, evaluators must answer these questions for themselves, choosing from diverse strategies that have unique advantages and disadvantages that our extended discussion helps make apparent.

THEORY OF SOCIAL PROGRAMMING

The Questions

Most early evaluators came from academia and had little direct exposure to policy formulation and modification. Hence they were unprepared for the characteristics of social interventions that make them difficult to control and improve. Table 10.1 presents questions about social programs that will help evaluators better understand forces they must confront in learning how a social intervention is linked to social problem solving.

Table 10.1   Questions to Ask About Social Programming

---

(1) What is the problem to which the intervention is a response? For whom is it a problem? How big a problem is it, according to what criteria? Has the problem reached crisis proportions so that a short and timely evaluation needs to be done? Is the problem so trenchant that even a long-term evaluation will eventually be useful? Is the problem important enough to spend your time and evaluation resources studying?

(2) Is this intervention just a minor variation on how things are usually done, or does it represent a major departure from common practice or common thinking about solutions to the problem?

(3) What are some of the alternative interventions to address this problem that have not been tried? Why have they not been tried? Would it be worth trying to locate, implement, and evaluate some of these alternatives instead of the current intervention?

(4) Is this intervention a program, a project, or an element? How rapidly does it change in the natural course of things, and does it have constituent parts that are quickly and easily changed? How big an impact could the intervention or its parts have, both as they are and if they were changed? Is the evaluation worth doing given the answers to these questions?

Early evaluators either did not think to ask such questions or made overly optimistic assumptions about their answers: (a) that social science theory would point to causes of social problems and suggest solutions, (b) that these solutions would be implemented and evaluated in ways that gave clear answers, and (c) that powerful stakeholders would welcome these answers and adopt them, (d) leading to significant amelioration of the social problem (Suchman, 1967). But reality treated these assumptions poorly. Early optimism about the role of social science and evaluation in promoting social reform gave way to disillusionment.

Lessons Learned

The difficulty of changing social problems and social programs. Part of the problem is the difficulty of creating major changes in advanced societies where many problems have already been greatly ameliorated. Remaining problems are stubborn ones for which inexpensive or feasible solutions do not yet exist. Consequently, most evaluators now aim for incremental rather than radical improvements in remaining problems. Another problem is that multiple groups have stakes in how social policies and programs are organized and changed. Each group lobbies for the priorities it assigns to problems and proposed solutions. Since most of these priorities differ, plans for action are often diluted as a political precondition to their implementation as policy. Few policies are approved that call for more than marginal changes in the status quo; few widely implemented social change efforts are conceptually bold (Shadish, 1984).

Disillusionment has also resulted from increased understanding about how implementation difficulties can thwart program intentions. Part of these difficulties stem from the complex, heterogeneous structure of social policies and programming. Social policies are given "flesh and blood" form through social programs. Programs are mostly administrative umbrellas for funding and regulating local projects where services are provided. In the United States, those projects are implemented differently across 50 states and in tens of thousands of local governments (Lindblom, 1977). Local projects typically differ in the mix of services provided, in client characteristics, in staff training, and in the mix of funding sources. Just as programs consist of heterogeneous projects, so also each project is internally heterogeneous, consisting of service and organizational elements that not all clients receive or experience equally. The Special Supplemental Food Program for Women, Infants, and Children (WIC) provides medical checkups, nutrition counseling, well-baby care, outreach, intake, record keeping, and service coordination. Few women and babies experience these services in the same way and in the same concentration, even within a WIC center. Professionals often have much discretion in what they do, so that services with the same name can be quite different over professionals. Hence a complex chain connects policymakers and central program officials to local managers, service providers, and local consumers of services that the program aims to influence.

Complicating the chances of social change still more, all social programs need political constituencies to be funded; once funded, they attract additional constituencies from among those whom the program employs, empowers, or services. The result is program political impactedness, making most social programs permanent features of the policy world rather than temporary features that can be canceled after a negative evaluation. Local projects are also entrenched, but not as much as programs. Some projects occasionally end for want of sufficient resources, and some new projects are added as a program's budget expands. This turnover allows modifying the mix of program-funded projects to improve the program as a whole. But any local project reaches a fraction of a program's total clientele, so its potential for program improvement is limited unless the project proves widely transferable. Elements are less influenced by politics than programs or projects, so more latitude exists to change them. But even manipulable, transferable elements have only a tiny potential to influence individuals because they are just a small part of the services a client receives.

This is a great paradox in evaluation. Programs reach more people and promise larger effects than projects and elements, but are so politically entrenched that evaluation results contribute little to starting or ending them. Projects turn over more than programs, so changing the number and mix of projects influences the program itself. Yet project turnover is slow relative to element turnover, especially when the latter can be added to the repertoires of service providers or managers without much disruption of routine. Unfortunately, elements usually promise relatively little change in individual clients; and those with greater impact may not be transferable across a wide range of projects. There is a mismatch among (a) the ability to introduce new practices — lowest with programs and highest with elements; (b) the number of people receiving services — lowest with elements and highest with programs; and (c) influence on individuals — lowest with elements and highest with programs and projects. This mismatch increases the difficulties of social problem solving.

The nature of social problem solving. Early hopes were that evaluation would be part of a rational problem-solving effort in which (a) problems are clearly defined, (b) an array of potential solutions is generated, (c) some solutions are implemented and (d) evaluated, and (e) knowledge of successful solutions is disseminated to (f) people who use it to make decisions. But the real world of social problem solving is not so rational. Its problems are ill defined, and stakeholders disagree about problem priority (Bryk, 1983); program goals can be vague or contradictory (Wholey, 1983); implemented change attempts are marginal in potential impact (Shadish, 1984); heterogeneous program structures hinder accurate spread of information from programs to projects (McLaughlin, 1985); and authority for decision making is diffuse, with program directives often playing a minor role in determining local decisions about service implementation (Weiss, 1978). Such realities have forced evaluators to adjust their rational models to compensate for their descriptive inaccuracy and for the limited role that evaluation plays in most social problem solving.

Evaluators have also realized more clearly that policymakers, program officials, and project employees assign higher priority to improving their jobs and promoting their beliefs than to evaluators' goals of identifying technically superior options for problem definition or program design. They have also learned that large program effects are rare because bold new programs and fundamental changes in existing programs are rare. Finally, they have come to understand that project heterogeneity means that effects obtained in some projects will not necessarily be found in other projects in the same program. Since the most difficult effects to find are those that are small on average and variable in manifestation, evaluators saw that their work might be drawing too many false negative conclusions.

The merits of various change strategies. Evaluators have adopted different strategies to cope with these problems. A frequent strategy, represented by Wholey and Stake, is to improve existing social programs incrementally, by improving or changing their elements or projects. Such change is needed when budgets shift, clients complain, service providers seek better techniques, or managers and auditors spot problems. A critical assumption of incrementalism is that modifying projects or programs at the margin will increase their effectiveness enough to help ameliorate a social problem. Yet if the basic assumptions of a program or project are flawed, marginal changes may not be enough to improve client welfare. A major challenge to incrementalists is to identify the types of marginal change with significant potential for problem amelioration. Some such elements may exist, but they may be rare. In mental health, examples include the phenothiazine medications for treating psychosis, or systematic desensitization treatment of phobias. They are manipulable (Campbell, 1969), difficult to implement incorrectly (Sechrest et al., 1979), consonant with the values of professionals who use them (Fullan, 1982), keyed to easily identified problems (Williams, 1980), robust in effects across clients and service providers (Cronbach, 1982a), inexpensive, can influence many lives, and seem to enhance individual functioning by important criteria (F. L. Cook, 1982).

But incrementalism is often criticized as too modest, or even conservative, in aspiration. An alternative adopted by Campbell and Rossi is to use demonstration projects to test bolder innovations that might be introduced later as part of a new policy. For instance, experimental demonstrations of a negative income tax were based on the notion that each needy citizen should be guaranteed an income rather than social services (Rossi & Lyall, 1976). Fairweather's (1980) Lodge project assumed that chronic mental patients can care for themselves in small group settings without much professional help. Demonstrations are explored in circumscribed settings without taking resources from current policy, so they can be bolder than incremental changes. Demonstrations are often funded when existing programs are widely seen as ineffective and difficult to improve, and when the political climate favors exploration of bold alternatives.

Demonstrations have drawbacks. They are initiated less often than changes in elements. They do not clearly show what would happen if a demonstration became policy because their time frame is limited and staff motivation often exceeds that of those who would implement the activities as a routine job. In addition, due to rapid turnover of federal officials, persons receiving results are sometimes not those who initiated the demonstration. Policy issues are also subject to turnover, so demonstration results are sometimes provided after a window of opportunity has closed. Many demonstrations are contaminated by other social programs, so attributing effects exclusively to the demonstration is hard. In the first negative income tax experiment, local welfare authorities wanted demonstration households to report benefits when filing for regular welfare entitlements; this pressure may have affected demonstration results (Rossi & Lyall, 1976, 1978). Finally, the transition from demonstration to funded program is tenuous, as the fate of Fairweather's Lodge illustrates. Despite positive evaluation results and efforts to disseminate the project, we still have relatively few Lodges (Shadish, 1984). Successful evaluation may raise the chances that a demonstration will be used in new policy, but this outcome is tenuous.

Given these limits, evaluators such as Weiss, and sometimes Campbell, opt for a third strategy — to question fundamental assumptions of existing programs and policies, and to search for radical alternatives that might fit with the fundamental values of society. They avoid incrementalism by going beyond existing policies and programs that may be flawed or of limited capacity for ameliorating a problem. They avoid demonstrations that are not manifestly different from the status quo. They want evaluators to explore all important questions about a social program, problem, or policy, irrespective of its immediate or practical use. Although few evaluators take it this far, this strategy can also question such basic matters as the nature and locus of political authority, the form of the economy, and the distribution of income and wealth (Rahman, 1985). By reserving few alternatives from consideration, such evaluators hope to find the programs and policies best suited to solving a social problem.

However, this strategy may not find changes that can be implemented in existing social systems that share the assumptions under attack. This strategy can change how people think and can lead to diluted adaptations of radical ideas, but it is limited because fundamental social change is rare — for example, as when the 1930s Depression forced major changes in U.S. beliefs about the structure and responsibilities of the federal government. Such changes are not part of the routine government functioning most evaluators seek to improve, but are more the purview of historians, sociologists, and political scientists.

Summary of Theory of Social Programming

To summarize, most evaluation theorists now hold the following beliefs about social programming:

- Social programming ameliorates social problems incrementally rather than radically.
- Social programming exists in a political and organizational context that makes uniform, planned change difficult to implement.

- Phasing social programs in or out promises more impact on problems than phasing projects or elements in or out, but fundamental shifts in programs are less likely than shifts in availability and mix of projects and elements.
- Evaluation is an omnipresent political activity in social programs even when no formal evaluation occurs.
- The quality and utility of evaluation depend on other social problem-solving activities, such as deciding on an important intervention to evaluate or defining a social problem well.

However, major disagreements about social programming still remain to be resolved in evaluation:

- To maximize helpful social change in the public interest, is it more effective to modify the philosophy or composition of whole programs, or to improve existing programs incrementally — perhaps by modifying regulations and practices, or influencing which local projects are phased in or out?
- Should the evaluator identify and work with change agents, or merely produce and explain evaluation results without forming alliances with change agents?
- Should evaluators try to change present programs or test ideas for future programs?
- Under what circumstances should the evaluator refuse to evaluate because the relevant social problem is not very important or the social program is not likely to ameliorate the problem?

Evaluators probably choose among these options mostly on the basis of personal values, political inclinations, and their technical skills. This fosters a healthy diversity of approaches befitting a pluralistic, interest group democracy. But we hope evaluation theory could develop more grounded, empirical understandings of the effects of different answers to these questions so that choices could be better informed about the likely consequences of each choice. We return to this theme at the end of this chapter.

THEORY OF USE

The Questions

In basic social science, little explicit thought is given to how results are used. Scientific peers are the primary intended users, and journal or book publication is the primary mode of communication. Past decades have taught evaluators that this traditional model of use is inadequate; evaluators must take active steps to increase the use of their results. Table 10.2 summarizes the kinds of questions evaluators must ask if they want their work to be used.

Table 10.2 Questions to Ask About Use

---

(1) What kind of use do you want to produce? Why? Given that it is hard to do an evaluation that facilitates all kinds of use equally well, what balance between instrumental and conceptual use would you like to produce?

(2) If you want to produce instrumental use, have you identified potential users? Have you talked with those users to find out what kind of information they want? Is the information they want to know about already available? Have you found out how potential users might use the results? When do they need results in order to use them, and can you provide the results by then? Will circumstances allow you to maintain frequent contact with users?

(3) If you want to produce enlightenment, who do you want to enlighten? How do you want to affect their thinking about the problem and the intervention? How can you reach them? Are the problem and intervention to be studied of lasting significance, or likely to be of transient interest? What do we know least about the problem and intervention?

(4) What are the characteristics of the particular intervention being evaluated? For instance, is the intervention a program, project, or element? What do its stakeholders want to know? Given these characteristics, what questions would be most useful to ask?

(5) How should results be communicated? Should interim results be reported periodically to users? In any final report, should you include an executive summary? Action recommendations? Should oral briefings be used? Should reports of evaluation results be communicated in forms tailored to the specific information needs of different stakeholder groups? Can results be disseminated through mass media outlets?

Lessons Learned

The concept of use. In retrospect, early answers to these questions were naive, especially in assuming that evaluation results would be used instrumentally. The most grandiose hope was to use results to expand effective social programs and to discontinue or radically change ineffective ones (Suchman, 1967). Discontinuing programs based on evaluation results is virtually unheard of. Evaluations are never so compelling, often causing dispute rather than consensus (Lindblom & Cohen, 1979). Evaluation is a political act in a context where power, ideology, and interests are paramount and influence decisions more than evaluative feedback.

Evaluation results sometimes affect program budgets. This is a less stringent criterion of use than discontinuance, but is still important and an instance of results being used instrumentally in decisions. An example may be the initial decision to end the summer component of Head Start (Weiss & Rein, 1969). In the short term, however, evaluations rarely influence program budgets significantly; given the complexity of politics, it is difficult to attribute budget decisions to evaluation findings alone.

Evaluations can change internal program priorities, affecting service mix and manner of provision, preferred targets, and enforcement of regulations. Such instrumental changes are less political than shifts in budget levels, for the latter send powerful symbolic messages about problem priorities and about client groups and professional guilds that will benefit from a program. We know little about how often, and under what conditions, evaluation results lead to such changes in internal program priorities.

The foregoing discussion has stressed instrumental use of evaluations of national programs and demonstrations. Another model of short-term instrumental use is local. Some federal programs have mandated all their local projects to evaluate themselves, hoping such evaluations would identify better where evaluative results would have leverage, and so collect more relevant data. The hope was to improve each project and thereby enhance overall program performance. Outside of educational television (Cook & Curtin, 1986), there is little empirical support for the efficacy of this approach. In community mental health (Cook & Shadish, 1982), community crime prevention (Feeley & Sarat, 1980), and local Title I education projects (David, 1982), the theory ran afoul of reality. Few project managers wanted social science information, instead preferring ammunition for public relations. In-house evaluators often had little power, multiple responsibilities, and little evaluation training, being named "evaluators" because they knew something about methods and because someone had to have the title. Such evaluators were often seen as allies of project managers; competing factions viewed evaluators as taking sides, negating some of the advantages of internal over external evaluators. The organizational conditions that foster this local project model of use may not occur often.

Immediate instrumental use is now less salient than it used to be in evaluation, largely because few clear incidents of such use are documented, except where government bodies request specific studies (Chelimsky, 1987a; Leviton & Boruch, 1983, 1984; Shadish & Reichardt, 1987). Even when evaluation results and government decisions coincide, the evaluation results sometimes justify decisions already made on other grounds. Clear demonstrations of abundant, short-term instrumental use are still rather rare, giving pause for concern to those who would construct a theory of evaluation on this particular kind of use.

Normative expectations about use shifted when evaluators began to ask: What should the role of evaluation be in an open, democratic society (Cook, 1983)? Shouldn't cultural values and political action influence decisions as much as or more than professional evaluative feedback? Such reflections decoupled use from exclusive emphasis on results constituting decisions to a wider emphasis on results being cited in policy deliberations as one of many inputs to a decision. This decoupling was furthered by the realization that prior choices often leave decision makers with little discretion (Weiss, 1980b); to call their choices "decisions" exaggerates their freedom to select options. If many political decisions are preempted, and evaluation feedback should not determine political decisions in a democracy, then no rationale exists for limiting evaluation to instrumental use.

Second, decision makers are exposed to information from sources that use evaluation findings to suit their own purposes; such use may not be closely linked to the evaluator's major stated conclusions. Thus lobbyists or journalists might refer to findings about one program in deliberations about another. Knowledge influences cognitive frameworks, as when it clarifies a program's theoretical assumptions, highlights relationships among stakeholder values, or illuminates priorities among problems. In altering cognitive frameworks, conceptual uses of evaluation decouple use from the "facts" about a program, from dependence on reports about a single program, and from the notion that use should occur quickly. For Weiss (1977b), Cronbach (1982a; Cronbach et al., 1980), Stake (Stake & Trumbull, 1982), and sometimes Rossi (Berk & Rossi, 1977; Chen & Rossi, 1987), evaluation is socially justified by conceptual use as much as by instrumental versions.

A further shift decoupled use from use by particular decision makers, especially program managers and funders. Multiple groups have a stake in a program, so other stakeholders came to be seen as equally important, especially those who deliver (Cronbach et al., 1980; Stake, 1986a) or consume services (Scriven, 1980). While evaluations sometimes modify central program regulations, local stakeholders do not comply with these regulations perfectly because more pressing forces influence the design and delivery of services. So evaluators have become increasingly interested in how local practitioners use evaluation results to improve their services, as with in-service training, books and journals, talks with colleagues (Leviton & Boruch, 1983), and initial training (Leviton & Cook, 1983). These themes assume that use of evaluations should not be expected only in the short term and only from senior program and project managers.

A further shift decoupled use from dependence on presenting an evaluation report. Potential users sometimes require knowledge synthesized from multiple prior studies, from incidental observations made by evaluators during their work, or from evaluators reflecting on the intervention that was studied (Leviton & Hughes, 1981; Mielke & Chen, 1981). Such circumstantial knowledge enlarges the number of ways in which evaluations are used, transcending the short-term instrumental use of findings first advanced in the 1960s.

Today, the concept of use encompasses evaluations constituting decisions, playing a joint role in constituting decisions, being cited in debates, being used in in-service training of professionals, being used in educating future practitioners, and being used to reconceptualize social programs and problems. The agent of influence is no longer a single evaluation report presented to formal decision makers. Literature reviews are also involved, as is knowledge from incidental reading and interactions with experts and practitioners. Sources for disseminating knowledge now include not only evaluation reports and briefings targeted at funders, but also reports aimed at scholars and practitioners, ad hoc media presentations, and unanticipated conversations at informal events.

Promoting use. Understanding of how to facilitate use has also broadened. Use is promoted in three major, related ways: through choice of issues addressed, through roles the evaluator adopts toward potential users, and through the communication channels chosen for disseminating results. Our descriptive language for discussing how these issues are framed includes a number of distinctions. One concerns whether issues are framed at the program, project, or element level. Second is the priority accorded to various issues: (a) targeting (Who receives or distributes services?), (b) implementation (What are program inputs, processes, and costs? How can the treatment be specified?), (c) effectiveness (What changes occur in the units receiving services?), and (d) impacts (How do the services influence persons and systems with which clients interact — families, neighborhoods, other projects?). A third distinction is between issues framed in a descriptive mode and those framed in an explanatory mode. Examples of the former include, Which types of clients receive services more often? What are the effects of the program? Examples of the latter: Why did some types of clients receive services more often? Why did the intervention have certain effects? We use these distinctions to discuss how methods to stimulate use depend on framing the evaluative question.

Facilitating use through choice of issue addressed. Describing effects and impacts at the program level (as distinct from the project or element level) provides little leverage for short-term instrumental use. Large social programs begin and end too rarely to use such information. Describing or explaining targeting and implementation of services produces more leverage for programs through (a) identifying implementation problems across many projects in a program, and (b) generating practical suggestions to improve projects through common sense, current professional practice, and knowledge of what was done at superior sites. Knowledge of such improvements can be disseminated for adoption or adaptation by projects (Wholey, 1983).

A second source of leverage about programs comes from explanatory studies that model the theoretical and operational logic of a program. The hope is to trace the relationships through which inputs influence processes and then change clients and ultimately social indicators. Such explicit models can suggest whether the required resources are available and whether the hypothesized relationships among inputs, processes, and outcomes are congruent with background knowledge. Such model building can reveal failures of program planning prior to collecting data. Collecting relevant data helps in assessment of correspondence between program operations and assumptions, useful because armchair analysis and ad hoc reports from practitioners do not always provide comprehensive or veridical description of what happens in a program (Rossi & Freeman, 1985).

A third source of leverage about programs is describing effects of elements that program administrators can control. (These may differ from elements that project officials control.) Many program elements are puny in effects, but reach many clients, so their aggregate impact is high; for example, a minor change in program application forms for free and reduced-price school lunches reduced fraudulent applications by only a small percentage, but, with a billion lunches served each year, first-year savings amounted to about $7 million (Applied Management Sciences, 1984). The need is to identify the types of program elements that can be changed and that can result in socially significant improvements.

Moving from programs to projects, considerable leverage was once anticipated from describing the targeting, implementation, and effects achieved in the individual projects. The anticipated payoff was once enough to lead some programs to mandate local project evaluations. But this path to program improvement now appears less promising. More emphasis is now placed on identifying particularly successful projects that can be used to modify the mix of projects and to change the mix of service elements that local personnel provide. However, most past procedures for identifying successful projects concentrate on *single* exemplary instances that may be unique in ways that precluded effective transfer — for example, because the charisma of the original project developer could not be transferred. Also, disagreements emerged about criteria of success and methodological standards used to identify exemplary projects. Moreover, procedures for identifying successful instances rarely emphasize microlevel elements responsible for success, even though such explanatory knowledge might particularly aid transfer to other projects.

Given such limits, it might be more useful to identify *types* of projects that are so effective as to deserve wider distribution throughout a program (Cook et al., 1985). After all, the number of local projects in a program waxes and wanes as projects are replaced or change operating philosophy. But it is hard to identify successful types of projects because the task requires a typology of project types from which individual projects are sampled, and considerable variability within each type will often exist. The more within-type variability there is, the less useful is the concept of type.

Turning from projects to elements, some novel elements of practice might improve projects and so enhance a whole program. In times of fiscal stringency, much leverage can come from identifying manipulable elements practitioners can adapt without changing the essence of their practice (McLaughlin, 1985). One could locate such practices by identifying elements responsible for success in exemplary projects. This research might also be aimed at identifying successful elements in ordinary projects where data on service implementation are used to explain results.

Other sources of knowledge about transferable project manipulanda include developers who improve the tools practitioners use, practitioners who experiment with better procedures, and new substantive theories with implications for practice. Each can lead to a clinical trial or demonstration to identify successful elements that should be made available for general practice (Bunker, 1985; Pacht et al., 1978). Clinical trials of possible future practices do not link current practice to effectiveness criteria and so are less threatening than trials of present practice. Independent, on-site monitoring tends to be expensive and obtrusive; but monitoring by fellow professionals employed by the same agency or by self-reports from practitioners are often biased toward exaggerated levels of compliance.

The preceding discussion has dealt mostly with framing evaluation issues to influence instrumental use. Evaluation theory has less to say about framing issues to facilitate enlightenment. Some theorists recommend facilitating enlightenment by drawing questions from a detailed program model. But such information can be instrumentally useful as well, leaving little sense of how explicit program models exclusively promote enlightenment. Other theorists recommend probing basic program assumptions, but they rarely provide enough specific advice for evaluators to implement the suggestion. Given the importance that conceptual use has assumed in justifying evaluation, this paucity of advice needs remediation.

Influencing use through choice of evaluator roles. Leverage is also influenced by the persons setting evaluative questions, and by the role relationships evaluators adopt toward these persons. Wholey (1983) says program managers have special opportunities to change program guidelines, and so tells evaluators to look to those managers for questions, helping managers formulate questions that are clear, important, and answerable in the constraints of time and budget.

Most theorists agree that frequent, close contact between evaluators and users stimulates use. The type of contact they recommend varies. Campbell (1969) favors the evaluator as servant to honest administrators but whistle-blower to dishonest administrators; Wholey (1983) sees evaluators as faithful retainers who educate managers about evaluating usefully; Cronbach (Cronbach et al., 1980) also favors an educator role that takes theory and research into greater account than does Wholey and that also represents those who deliver or manage local services; Berman and McLaughlin (1977) see the evaluator as an information broker; Scriven (1983a) sees evaluators as consultants who tell prospective consumers about best buys. Some work suggests that short-term use is fostered when the evaluator plays a proactive rather than a reactive role, responding flexibly if user information needs change, and invoking background knowledge about the social problem and program instead of sticking only to preformulated evaluative issues (Leviton & Boruch, 1983; Leviton & Hughes, 1981).

Influencing use through communication of results. Some ways of communicating may be more likely than others to lead to dissemination and eventual utilization of results. Among the most common pieces of advice are (a) to write informal reports in simple language, (b) to present reports in different forms tailored to specific information needs and communication styles of different stakeholder groups, (c) to make action recommendations, and (d) to publicize evaluation findings in mass media and professional outlets to increase the number of stakeholders who learn of them.

Summary of Theory of Use

To summarize, we offer the following list of likely agreements among evaluation theorists:

- Many kinds of use occur; evaluators are concerned with both instrumental and conceptual use.
- Short-term use is the most compelling justification for funding evaluation.
- Evaluations rarely determine decisions instrumentally; enlightenment occurs more often.

The following questions summarize major disagreements about use that are still unresolved:

- Should conceptual or instrumental use have priority?
- Should the evaluator identify and attend to intended users of evaluation? If so, which users?
- What increases the likelihood of use, especially for instrumental versus conceptual use?

Table 10.3 Questions to Ask About Valuing

---

(1) What would a thing like this intervention do to be good, and how would it accomplish those ends? What do other interventions like it do? What needs might it meet, and what harm would be done if those needs were not met? What do its stakeholders want it to do? What social values does this intervention foster, and what values does it potentially harm? Might there be any negative side effects?

(2) How well does it have to do these things? Is it possible to construct any absolute standards in answer to this question? Are there any other interventions like the one being studied to which it could be compared? Are there any other interventions that could do what this intervention does, even if the two interventions do not seem much alike?

(3) How will you measure program performance?

(4) At the end of the evaluation, do you plan to summarize all your results into a statement about whether the intervention is good or bad? If so, how will you weight the different criteria in summing them to reflect which criteria are more or less important? Is it possible or desirable to construct a different value summary for each stakeholder group?

THEORY OF VALUING

The Questions

In its early years, evaluation paid scant attention to values, perhaps because evaluators naively believed their activities could and should be value-free (Scriven, 1983b). But experience showed that it is impossible to make choices in the political world of social programming without values becoming salient in choices about evaluative criteria, performance standards, or criteria weightings. Evaluators will do a better job of judging the value of programs if they explicitly consider the questions outlined in Table 10.3, and the many different kinds of answers that could be provided.

Lessons Learned

Descriptive, prescriptive, and metatheoretical approaches to valuing. Scriven's (1980) metatheoretical approach constructs value statements about any entity. His four steps are as follows: (a) Justifiable criteria of merit are developed that specify what a good evaluand would do; (b) justifiable standards of performance are selected that specify how well the evaluand should perform on each criterion; (c) performance is measured on each criterion to see if those standards have been reached; and (d) with multiple criteria, results are integrated into a single statement about the value of the evaluand.

A logic like this is widely used in product evaluation, and is implicit in much program evaluation. In evaluating automobiles, criteria of merit include purchase price, gas mileage, passenger capacity, and comfort. Absolute standards of performance specify minimum standards of safe handling under emergency conditions. Relative standards compare several automobile models in the same size and price range from which consumers will choose. Measurement of performance includes test drives, owner surveys, interviews with automobile engineers, and laboratory tests. Results are synthesized to recommend the "best buy" from among the automobiles tested. Much traditional research follows the same logic — criteria are called dependent variables, standards of performance are called comparison or control groups, data collection retains the same name, and synthesis is achieved through decision-making statistical procedures.

Metatheoretic approaches do not specify which criteria to use in the first step of the logic. *Prescriptive* ethical theories could generate such criteria, because evaluators participate in a moral act by evaluating programs aimed at problems such as poverty, racism, and crime (Warnock, 1971). For instance, Rawls's (1971) egalitarian theory of justice implies that programs should be evaluated on their capacity to meet the material needs of the disadvantaged that, if not met, cause unacceptable harm. Scriven leans toward this approach, with his concept of needs-based evaluations. House (1980) argues explicitly that Rawls's theory should guide selection and weighting of evaluative criteria.

Few evaluators may use prescriptive ethics for criteria selection because no compelling reason exists for preferring one prescriptive theory over another. For example, many credible alternatives to Rawls's theory of justice are available (Nozick, 1974), and justice is just one moral concern in evaluation, along with human rights, equality, liberty, and utility. In addition, few data have been advanced to indicate that a better society will result if one ethic is followed rather than another. Finally, the U.S. political system traditionally fosters pluralism of values, so promoting a prescriptive ethic is inconsistent with that political context. Even Scriven's appeal to material needs, which may have more political support in American society than more abstractly argued prescriptive ethics, is largely inconsistent with values that drive policy. That is, we rarely set political priorities according to whose material needs are largest. Evaluators may benefit from knowing about prescriptive implications of criteria selection for the kind of society that particular choices imply or for the kinds of needs that are not being met. But it is difficult to justify a more extensive role than this relative to descriptive valuing.

Descriptive valuing is simple description of stakeholder values. It is better suited to the political context of evaluation, since decision making depends more on coping with values held by legislators, managers, voters, and lobbyists than on a prescriptive ethic. Knowledge of stakeholder values helps ensure that no criteria are overlooked that are of crucial importance to some groups. More is at issue than conformity with pluralism; not understanding stakeholder values can make doing evaluation more difficult. Stakeholders may not cooperate with data collection and may challenge evaluation findings as partisan.

Descriptive approaches are limited by the wisdom of the various stakeholders consulted. Many are handicapped because they do not have the time, interest, or experience to express their values as clearly or carefully as theorists of ethics or even some organized stakeholder groups such as professional lobbies. Further, many U.S. citizens are socialized to endorse the priority of certain values — for example, life, liberty, and the pursuit of happiness — and may not fully understand how promoting these hinders attaining others. Knowledge of stakeholder values may be enlightening, but does not automatically lead to selecting some criteria and standards over others. Describing values yields a list, not a justified procedure for setting priorities. Priority setting is partly prescriptive, so a purely descriptive approach avoids the hard choices that prescriptive approaches face head on.

The distinction among descriptive, prescriptive, and metatheoretic approaches has conceptual appeal in suggesting overall advantages and disadvantages of different approaches, but it tells little about the specifics by which evaluators actually answer questions about values in evaluation. We turn to this topic now.

Selecting criteria of merit. Early practice was to use program goals as criteria; after all, such goals are usually formulated through political compromise, and so reflect a conjunction of many interests. But exclusive reliance on goals proved to be an error because (a) goals are often vague, contradictory, or latent; (b) program implementation is so heterogeneous and locally controlled that central program goals do not overlap heavily with local goals; (c) programs have unintended effects that can be just as important as planned goals; and (d) managers often specify modest goals so as to succeed at something less important rather than fail at something more important, or else (e) they find themselves stuck with unrealistically high goals that overpromised to secure initial funding.

No replacement for goals is agreed upon. Candidates include (a) claims by clients, service deliverers, and managers about program achievement and factors leading to success or failure (Stake, 1978); (b) factors feeding into decisions that policymakers or managers must make (Weiss, 1972b); (c) systems models that explain how inputs relate to processes and outcomes (Chen & Rossi, 1983); (d) the degree to which material needs of clients are met (Scriven, 1980); and (e) information needs of stakeholders (Bryk, 1983) or of managers and policymakers (Wholey, 1983).

Procedures exist for prioritizing over these options (Edwards et al., 1975), but they are more easily implemented with few stakeholder groups. But in many other cases, especially with multiple stakeholder interests, no widely accepted method exists for generating prioritized criteria of merit.

Goals are just a limited subset of all effects a program achieves, intended or not, harmful or beneficial. A practical problem is how to identify unintended effects. Program models provide clues to such effects by relating program inputs to processes, effects, and impacts (Chen & Rossi, 1983); and side effects may be discovered if evaluators study the evaluand in detail before collecting data (Scriven, 1980). Interviews with stakeholders also serve this purpose, with particular attention to passionate advocates and opponents of the program, since no one is more likely to have thought about potential beneficial or harmful side effects. However, no sure method exists for finding unplanned effects.

Standards of performance. The second step in Scriven's metatheoretic logic of valuing is constructing standards for performance. Absolute standards link performance to specified levels, as when educators use criterion-referenced tests to certify competency for high school graduation. Results of such tests do not depend on how classmates perform. Comparative standards link performance to achievements by other evaluands, as when school grades are assigned on a curve or automobile models are directly compared. With grading on a curve, a student can perform well and still receive a D; an automobile can be satisfactory but not recommended for purchase because it performs less well than an alternative.

Comparative standards are more easily justified and so predominate in evaluation; many such standards are used. Campbell (1969) recommends *no-treatment control group* standards that show what might have happened to respondents in the absence of the evaluand—whether exposure to an intervention is better than no exposure. Such evaluations must vigilantly assess whether control group members get comparable services from nonprogram sources so as to know what baseline level of services is received in the absence of the program.

In a *no-services baseline*, controls receive no ameliorative services, even from sources other than those being evaluated. This control is sometimes used alongside purified treatment groups, where persons receive more or better services—contrasting a "high- or maximal-dosage" group with the "no-dosage" control group.

Scriven (1980) prefers comparisons to *available alternatives* from among which consumers might choose. Few consumers choose between an automobile or no car at all. Similarly, social policy decisions are rarely between a program or no program, or even between a program and a single alternative. Campbell's (1974a) evolutionary epistemology also aims to identify better performers among multiple alternatives, and so advocates evaluations that examine planned variations not restricted to a single plan for a program.

Light (1983) adds another relative standard of performance — a *placebo control group*. In many areas of social welfare the interventions involve attention to clients, so the marginal contribution of an evaluand should be assessed over and above results due to attention. Attention is an intrinsic component of many interventions, but is less expensive than the total package of services, may not have the same long-term effects, and does not define what is unique about an intervention.

Cronbach (1963) opposes comparisons to alternatives, arguing that social problem solving is best facilitated by improving the evaluand. Studies of variants do not tell how to improve current practices, and different variants rarely pursue the same set of goals, rarely prioritize their shared goals the same way, and rarely postulate the same time frames for effects and impacts. Hence Cronbach believes it is misleading to treat social variants as functionally equivalent. Comparative evaluation can engender in project developers and staff a counterproductive apprehension about being evaluated. Project staff may see the services they provide as unique, and fear that their work will be insensitively tested if evaluation activities are limited to studying only consequences that evaluators think all projects should achieve.

In selecting relative standards, (a) a concern for maximizing treatment effects leads to contrasting maximally implemented services with a total absence of services, (b) a concern for detecting effects when control clients get other treatments impels evaluators toward comparing treatments with no-treatment controls who are free to seek out those alternative, (c) a concern for comparing major alternatives impels evaluators toward studying planned or existing variations, (d) a concern for attributing effects to specific and unique treatment services impels the evaluator toward placebo controls, and (e) a concern for improving an existing evaluand impels an evaluator toward before-after measurement, unless maturation or testing increases performance over time. These brief generalizations oversimplify. Since so much depends on choice of comparative standards, since so many standards exist, and since they have not been well discussed in the evaluation literature, more debate on such standards needs to occur. First, no algorithm exists to help evaluators select relative standards. Yet the choice of a standard can have profound implications. For example, the likelihood of large effects is generally lowest when an evaluand is compared to an alternative, next lowest when compared to a placebo control group, and next lowest when compared to a no-treatment group. Effectiveness is more likely when no-services baselines are used or when before-after changes are contrasted with clients who are particularly distressed at pretest, particularly when treatment consists of persons manifestly receiving high-quality services. When resources permit, the preferred strategy is to design a study with multiple controls (Light, 1983); otherwise a choice algorithm is needed.

Comparison standards that yield large effects seem to be preferred by evaluation theorists today. This may reflect a belief that past evaluations chronically underestimated treatment potential because of inadequate designs (Cronbach, 1982a; Light & Pillemer, 1984), suboptimally implemented program activities (Sechrest et al., 1979), and operational plans poorly linked to program theory (Chen & Rossi, 1983). Such concerns give rise to studying implementation, and to emphasis on no-service baselines and before-after changes. However, one must distinguish between impediments to implementation resulting from inherent structural constraints and those resulting from problems that might be corrected with better knowledge, more resources, or keener commitment. Assessing achievement of well-implemented services makes sense if past impediments to implementation were corrigible. Evaluators can then probe how to improve the implementation of factors that improve performance, not factors that are ineffective even when evaluated by standards designed to maximize effectiveness. Sometimes impediments to implementation are based in the structure of the program. If so, it makes less sense to maximize the contrast between no services and best-implemented services, for it may not be possible to implement routinely the conditions leading to highest-quality implementation.

Measuring performance. The vast majority of evaluation practice is about the third step in this metatheoretical logic—measuring performance—so we defer most of its discussion to theory of practice. In Scriven's original conception, he claimed this is a limited task, not including describing the evaluand, assessing opinions about its value, analyzing why it was effective, or suggesting how the evaluation results might be used. For the summative purpose he prizes, only measurement of each alternative on each criterion of merit is required, provided measurement permits valid inference about whether absolute standards were reached or true comparative differences detected. So measurement entails more than performance assessment alone; it must be clear that the evaluand, not some force correlated with it, caused changes in the criteria of merit. Hence inferences about causal connections are necessary to Scriven's concept of measurement.

Many theorists disagree with Scriven's judgment. Cronbach (1963, 1964) countered Scriven's arguments early in the history of the field. He said that analyzing why the evaluand was effective yields useful knowledge for program improvement. Weiss (1972b), Wholey (1979), and Stake (1978) took up this theme and advocated measuring many aspects of the evaluand. Even some of those who once were sympathetic to Scriven's argument now believe some assessment of program implementation is required (Rossi & Wright, 1984). We discuss this more below, in the section on theory of knowledge.

Synthesizing results. For Scriven (1980), valuing is not complete until a final synthesis about merit is achieved. All synthesis requires weighting and summing criteria, so measurements must be converted to a common metric. Benefit-cost analysis converts program inputs and outputs into monetary terms so the ratio of costs to benefits can be computed. But it is hard to assign monetary value to outcomes such as increased marital happiness, decreased fear of crime, or higher self-concept. Weighting schemes used in benefit-cost analysis are thus problematic, so some evaluators prefer cost-effectiveness analysis (Levin, 1983), which converts program inputs into monetary terms but leaves effects and impacts in the original metric. Statements are made about how much financial cost is required to cause the same change in outcome. Syntheses can also be achieved through descriptive weighting techniques that use the values of the persons who might use the evaluation to assign weights to different patterns of results. Common methods for doing this are Bayesian (Edwards et al., 1975).

By putting all outcomes onto the same standardized scale, meta-analysis (Glass, McGaw, & Smith, 1981) is widely used to synthesize results across multiple evaluations of an intervention. Meta-analysis helps evaluators escape from the limited statistical power and contextual uniqueness of single studies, but it requires assumptions about weights, especially as concerns weighting effect sizes by features of their methodology (Hedges & Olkin, 1985; Light & Pillemer, 1984). Techniques are also emerging to integrate studies qualitatively into findings from earlier research and into the knowledge base of professionals (Cronbach et al., 1980). Meta-analysis and qualitative integration both help in drawing conclusions about robustness of findings, in identifying factors on which effects depend, and in providing a comprehensive picture of an evaluand's total functioning.

Many evaluators are not very concerned with synthesizing results. Cronbach (1982a) argues that separate conclusions should be presented for each criterion, because different conclusions warrant different degrees of confidence, and individual conclusions are less likely to be challenged if they stand alone than if they depend on a weighting system with which some stakeholders disagree. When each conclusion stands alone, readers can assign their own weights to findings, drawing an overall conclusion that may differ from the evaluator's. For instance, tall readers of automobile evaluations in *Consumer Reports* may assign more weight to the feature of front leg room than do the magazine's staff. Evaluators can reduce this problem by constructing multiple value syntheses for different stakeholders using different weights.

Despite these reasons for not synthesizing, both benefit-cost analysis and meta-analysis have proven quite appealing in public policy; they lead to simple, quantified results of general application, can be readily remembered, and are not hindered by multiple caveats. Perhaps a good overall synthesis is compatible with the political system's desire for simple answers to complex issues. But individual findings still should be retained, so that readers can construct their own syntheses.

Summary of Theory of Valuing

To summarize, we offer the following list of likely agreements among evaluation theorists:

- Evaluation cannot be value-free.
- Evaluation inevitably mimics the first three steps of Scriven's logic of valuing, but not always the fourth one.
- Considering multiple stakeholder interests increases the chance that all relevant value perspectives will be included.

The following questions summarize the major disagreements about valuing that remain to be resolved:

- By whose criteria of merit should we judge social programs?
- Should prescriptive ethical theories play a significant role in selecting criteria of merit?
- Should programs be compared to each other or to absolute standards of performance?
- Should results be synthesized into a single value judgment?

Evaluations are always potentially controversial and explosive events. Perhaps this suggests why remaining disagreements about value theory have been so little addressed. Taking stands on these disagreements makes evaluations more combustible by increasing the salience of value judgments and associated labels, such as *good, bad, fair, just, better,* and *worse.* Many evaluators avoid such combustibility by ignoring value questions to begin with. For such reasons, these disagreements may be among the most intransigent in evaluation theory.

Table 10.4 Questions to Ask About Knowledge Construction

---

(1) What criteria are you going to use in deciding what constitutes acceptable knowledge? Will you use some traditional scientific set of standards, like the various constructions of validity? Which set, and why that set rather than others, such as fairness or credibility? How certain do you want the knowledge you construct to be? Are you willing to accept less than the most certain knowledge possible?

(2) What kind of knowledge does the client who paid for the evaluation want? What about program stakeholders? How would they answer the questions you just answered about knowledge? Is there a serious mismatch between your standards for knowledge and those held by clients or stakeholders? If so, can you produce the kind of knowledge that stakeholders want, or at least educate them about the advantages and disadvantages of your respective opinions?

(3) What kind of knowledge, if any, do you think should be most important in the evaluation? Knowledge about causation, generalization, implementation, costs, clientele, or something else? Why? How can you maintain a capacity for discovering things you did not think of at first?

(4) Can you produce the required knowledge, at the desired level of certainty, in the time available? Do you have sufficient acquaintance with the methodologies you need to produce this information? If not, can you build a team with such expertise?

(5) What arrangements will you make to carry out critical evaluation of your own evaluation? Can you do this prior to implementing the evaluation? Can outside experts or stakeholders critique your initial design or your final report?

THEORY OF KNOWLEDGE

The Questions

Most early evaluators, like most social scientists of the time, were not well versed in epistemology and ontology. The legacy of logical positivism still had an important if implicit impact on the field, even though philosophers no longer gave it much credence by the 1940s. Between then and now, evaluators have been chastened by their attempts to answer key epistemological questions such as those in Table 10.4. Yet thinking about the answers to those questions is still critical to the epistemological base of the field and, often in concrete ways, to the conduct of any given evaluation.

Lessons Learned

Early emphasis on causality and the experiment. Early evaluators held somewhat naive assumptions about the certainty and ease of constructing scientific knowledge. Consider, for example, the early preference for using program goals to formulate causal hypotheses for testing in experiments (Campbell, 1969; Suchman, 1967). This strategy assumes that programs are homogeneous and have totally explicit goals that can be validly measured and assessed with feasible experiments that rule out all spurious interpretations. All these assumptions have been attacked. Of special importance are three themes popularized by Kuhn (1970): (a) All observations are theory-laden, so no "objective" measurement is possible; (b) to the extent that theories are incommensurable and soft, disconfirming evidence can easily be rejected; and (c) science relies on human intuition and background knowledge, sometimes preferring theories on aesthetic or social grounds rather than scientific ones.

These attacks hit evaluation especially hard. Realization of the vague, contradictory, and latent nature of program goals made it questionable to assume that they function like scientific hypotheses. Alternative sources of evaluative issues did not imply the primacy of causal analysis built into the models to which early evaluators ascribed. One source was multiple stakeholders who must be consulted to learn of their information needs. Program managers are one stakeholder group. They are accountable for program operation, so are interested in descriptive issues of targeting and implementation as much as or more than in assessing effects and impacts. A further reason to deemphasize description of causal connections was the ambiguity of results from early evaluations of Great Society programs. Did these programs achieve so little because (a) substantive theories underlying program design were deficient, (b) program implementation poorly reflected theory, or (c) evaluations were too insensitive to detect small program effects? Such uncertainty led to emphasis on describing program activities and assessing implementation, thus exploring the "black box" of the treatment.

Experiments probe causal connections between manipulanda and outcomes, but do not explain treatment effects. Causal explanation requires describing program process and identifying necessary and sufficient conditions under which causally efficacious program components influence components of outcome measures. Such full explanation specifies the factors that must be present if an intervention is to be effective when transferred elsewhere (Cronbach, 1982a). As program descriptions revealed unexpected variability within and between projects, explanatory knowledge as a guide to transfer became more needed. Today, explaining effects has a higher profile than describing them, especially for Cronbach (1982a), Weiss (1977b), and Rossi and Freeman (1985).

Gradually evaluators began to understand the need for a wider array of methods in their work. For example, they became more sensitive to the utility of letting evaluation issues emerge from on-site observation rather than fixing them prior to data collection. Such openness helps detect unanticipated side effects (Guba & Lincoln, 1981; Patton, 1978). Further, since programs evolve with considerable local discretion, it is presumptuous of evaluators to maintain they always know in advance the most useful research questions or to believe that the most important issues at the beginning of a study will always remain so by its end. This led some evaluation theorists to reject quantitative research in favor of qualitative methods. They use intensive on-site observation and interviews to formulate explanatory hypotheses about processes and effects that can be iteratively tested and reformulated until a satisfactory fit is achieved between data and explanation. These evaluators use ethnographic and hermeneutic techniques (Dunn, 1982; Habermas, 1972), with the latter used to interpret events. Such techniques arise from different epistemological assumptions than those of a hypothetico-deductive research strategy for testing program goal achievement through experimental designs.

Today, evaluators no longer assume that the world they study consists of simple causal connections from programs to outcomes. Some evaluators even abjure realism in favor of an idealism in which humans cognitively create their worlds and, by communicating their creations to others, generate a shared social reality whose links to the outside world are unclear. By assuming humans respond to social constructions of the world rather than to the world itself, some evaluators found the issue of how these cognitive links relate to reality of little interest (Lincoln & Guba, 1985). Even those who retained realist assumptions came to endorse a multivariate world of complex, interdependent causal forces rather than simple, bivariate pushes and pulls. As with epistemological options, the ontological options from which evaluators select today are more numerous and diverse than those of 20 years ago.

New options for knowledge construction also followed from attacks on the assumption of theory-neutral measurement. Historians and sociologists of science showed how scientific observation is theory-impregnated (a) in choice of constructs, (b) in construct definition, (c) in theoretical irrelevancies that measures contain, (d) in components measures fail to include, and (e) in weights implicitly assigned to factors in multidimensional measures that social scientists use. These attacks led many evaluators to endorse the use of multiple operations, multiple methods, and the integration of one study into the multiple relevant studies that preceded it (Cook, 1985). Many evaluators admit to less certainty about their results, especially because commentators often disputed constructs selected for measurement and the ways measures were constructed (Lindblom & Cohen, 1979). Attacks on objective measurement led some evaluators to believe that anthropology and journalism, rather than experimental psychology or economics, are the appropriate models for constructing knowledge in evaluation (Guba & Lincoln, 1981).

Claims also surfaced that evaluation should minimize traditional scientific standards of inference. Cronbach et al. (1980; Cronbach, 1982a) asserts that users of evaluation are less concerned than academics with reducing the final few grains of uncertainty about knowledge; that users are more willing to trust their experience and tacit knowledge for ruling out validity threats; and that they must act on whatever knowledge is available. Cronbach says that each evaluation should generate many findings, even at the cost of less certainty about any one of them — that "bandwidth" of knowledge should be preferred over its "fidelity."

Cronbach particularly objects to the preference for resolving method trade-offs in favor of enhancing valid causal inference (internal validity) over generalization (external validity). Cronbach favors enhancing generalizations from the samples achieved in a study to populations with different characteristics from those studied. Social programs are so heterogeneous that sampling plans cannot assure knowledge applicable to the unique characteristics of single projects not yet studied. Also, evaluation results are often used in unexpected ways, less instrumentally and more for enlightenment associated with general explanations about successful practical procedures and substantive theories that might be transferred to other places.

The need for diversity in methodology. At the same time, many methodological changes occurred as well. In the 1960s, methods for acquiring knowledge in evaluation reflected the following schema: (a) The important question in evaluation concerns causal consequences of programs. To examine such consequences, randomized experiments should be used, or, failing this, strong quasi-experiments based on interrupted time-series or regression-discontinuity designs should be used. (b) Since it can be important to make generalizable statements, evaluators should sample people and settings at random, or, if this is not possible, the samples should be heterogeneous so inferences are not restricted to a small range of settings and persons. (c) For those who seek causal explanation, substantive theory should be used to identify constructs worth measuring and causal modeling should be conducted. If such modeling is impossible, the evaluator should at least correlate potential explanatory constructs with changes obtained on outcome measures. (d) Most important issues about a program are probably known in advance, so confirmatory rather than exploratory methods can predominate in evaluation.

Today, all four elements of this schema have come under attack, leading to a broader, more diverse set of methods in evaluation. First, the experiment lost its hegemony, partly because of the increased importance of noncausal issues and causal explanation for which the experiment was not designed. The loss in hegemony also resulted from growing awareness of the limits of experiments. Randomized experiments were attacked because (a) they are only relevant to causal forces that can be manipulated directly or through assignment of subjects; (b) ethical and political concerns can preclude random assignment in favor of assignment by entitlement, need, merit, or order; (c) most social programs provide valued treatments, so attrition from conditions is often treatment related, which violates a critical assumption of experiments that groups are probabilistically equivalent on all characteristics except treatment assignment; and (d) respondents sometimes compare the treatment they receive with what others receive, leading to compensatory rivalry, resentful demoralization, treatment diffusion, or compensatory equalization (Cook & Campbell, 1979). Quasi-experiments were attacked by advocates of randomized experiments, who focused on the frequently used design requiring pretest and posttest data from groups that are initially nonequivalent. Equivocal causal inferences result from this design because the processes leading to selection into treatment are rarely, if ever, completely understood and so cannot be adequately modeled. In some areas a single source of selection bias may plague all evaluations, creating an impressive convergence of results on the same wrong answer (Campbell & Boruch, 1975)!

Some evaluators claimed that alternative methods could adequately probe causal connections while also probing other relevant issues. In quantitative traditions, the challenge came principally from causal modeling, especially from latent variable models exemplified by LISREL and from econometric methods (Heckman, 1980). In the qualitative tradition, the challenge came from case studies (Yin, 1984), especially after Campbell (1975b) showed how a case study with multiple dependent variables could, under rare conditions, achieve a pattern of results fit by only one cause. The desirability of alternatives to experiments increased because they seemed more widely useful, more flexible in types of knowledge achieved, and, according to their advocates, hardly worse for facilitating causal inferences.

Second, evaluators began to use a wider array of methods for constructing generalized knowledge. The initially preferred techniques required sampling with known probability from a known population. But it is hard to define some populations, particularly times or physical situations. Variability among projects, and among clients and practitioners in projects, requires that samples of them be large, and expensive, if representativeness is to be achieved within reasonable limits. Hence the respectability of purposive sampling increased, particularly those kinds that emphasize selecting presumptively modal or manifestly heterogeneous instances. Use of modal instances helps ascertain whether findings generalize to the most frequently occurring types of persons or settings. Use of heterogeneous instances helps probe whether a finding is robust when different subgroups of persons and settings are separately examined (Cook & Campbell, 1979).

It is a small step from heterogeneous sampling within studies to unsystematic sampling in meta-analysis of studies that are heterogeneous on important attributes. Meta-analysis would be most effective if effect sizes are a random sample of those that could be achieved with a particular treatment. This assumption cannot be sensitively tested, so meta-analysts make the less restrictive assumption that the effect sizes come from studies with considerable heterogeneity in populations and settings sampled. Thus the generalizations that meta-analysis achieves are more a product of purposive sampling than of formal random sampling.

Third, the previously mentioned preference for functionally plastic methods also influenced how causal explanations were studied. At first, primitive forms of causal modeling predominated, principally multiple regression. More sophisticated, multiequation, latent variable models were preferred later, partly because they cope better with unreliability and partial invalidity of measurement and partly because they simultaneously relate client characteristics, program inputs, program processes, third-variable spurious causes, and intended outcomes measured at different times (Flay & Cook, 1982). Also, qualitative researchers emphasize the explanatory power of juxtaposing prior knowledge, expert opinion, practitioner belief, logical analysis, and observational knowledge acquired on site, and to these Cronbach adds knowledge gained from quantitative studies relating input, process, and outcome variables. One can also extend the sampling and measurement frameworks of experiments to probe issues of process. The resulting analysis uses the same explanatory modeling techniques advocated for nonexperimental data. Since so many methodological options are now available to study causal explanation, the formerly preferred option of quantitative causal modeling has lost its hegemony, though not as much as experiments have lost their hegemony for probing causal connections.

Evaluators also realized that causal explanation facilitates generalization (Cronbach, 1982a). The more we know about contingencies on which program effects depend, the more we are able to transfer successful practices to sites not yet studied. Since generalization follows from multiple sampling procedures and from theoretical explanation, it became clear that multiple methods exist for generalizing. Hence the initially favored method of random sampling lost its hegemony.

Fourth, to discover novel issues and questions, the degree of functional blurring among methods is not as noticeable as in the previous cases. On-site observation and interviews have always been, and continue to be, favored for discovering knowledge not formulated in initial hypotheses.

Over time, however, attitudes changed about the priority that discovery deserved, partly because of the demise of goal-centered approaches that had implicitly devalued discovery in favor of hypothesis testing. Evaluators also valued the functional plasticity of methods for discovery, given how Yin (1984) and Campbell (1975b) linked intensive on-site knowledge to causal connections and how Cronbach (1982a) linked it to causal explanation.

The fallibility of all methods. Growing consciousness of the fallibility of observation is reflected in the growth of multiplist methods of data collection, in having multiple investigators analyze the same data set, and in doing data analysis in more of an exploratory than a confirmatory mode (Glymour & Scheines, 1986). A philosophy of data analysis akin to Tukey's (1977) has arisen in quantitative evaluation, with issues being approached several ways predicated on different methodological and substantive assumptions. An analogous development in the qualitative tradition is using multiple observers for each site instead of single observers. In such research, observers struggle to reconcile the different interpretations that result (Stake & Easley, 1978). Sometimes both qualitative and quantitative methods are used in the same study, generating results with different implications for the overall conclusion, leading to a creative tension resolved only after many iterations (Trend, 1979). Whatever the data collection mode, multiple tentative probes are the watchword, replacing conceptions based on theory-free observation, single definitive tests, and crucial single studies.

Recognition of the social components of evaluative knowledge, and the fallibility of evaluative methods, has led to increased interest in methods for critically scrutinizing evaluation questions and methods. These methods include commentaries on research plans by experts and stakeholders; monitoring of the implementation of evaluations by federal program officers and scientific advisory groups; simultaneous funding of independent evaluations of the same program; funding secondary analyses of collected data; including comments in final reports by personnel from the program evaluated; and forcing out latent assumptions of evaluation designs and interpretations, often through some form of adversarial legal process or a committee of substantive experts (Cronbach, 1982a; Hennigan, Flay, & Cook, 1980). Such metaevaluations assert that all evaluations can be evaluated according to publicly justifiable criteria of merit and standards of performance, and that data can help to determine how good an evaluation is. The need for metaevaluation implies recognition of the limitations of all social science, including evaluation (Cook, 1974a).

Summary of Theory of Knowledge

To summarize, we offer the following list of likely agreements among evaluation theorists:

- Epistemology and methodology are essential topics in evaluation.
- All theorists postulate a real world, though they differ greatly as to its knowability and complexity.
- Logical positivism is an inadequate epistemology that no theorist advocates anymore, either in evaluation or in philosophy.
- Program evaluation is an empirical endeavor in a social science tradition.
- Knowledge of many different kinds (about causation, generalization, description of implementation, and so on) must be constructed in most evaluations, but the relative emphasis given to each differs over studies.
- No social science method can be rejected from the evaluator's repertoire.
- All methods are fallible.
- Summaries of multiple studies are preferred to single studies for constructing reliable and valid knowledge.
- The quality of knowledge increases with critical public scrutiny of it.

The following questions summarize major disagreements about knowledge that remain to be resolved in evaluation:

- How complex and knowable is the world, especially the social world? What are the consequences of oversimplifying complexity?
- Does any epistemological or ontological paradigm deserve widespread support?
- What priority should be given to different kinds of knowledge, and why?
- What methods should evaluators use, and what are the key parameters that influence that choice?

Part of what drives these disagreements is the ultimate obscurity of certain ontological matters (e.g., How complex is the world?) that might have great epistemological and methodological import if known. Hence some uncertainty is inevitable in theory of knowledge, and some disagreements may never be resolved. But more could be done to make progress by coupling various pragmatic ontological stands (e.g., it seems to have survival value to assume there is a reality) with those methodological and epistemological matters about which evidence can be gathered (e.g., situations under which describing real-world causes would make sense). Even so, such progress will always depend on obscure basic assumptions, so healthy skepticism and mutual criticism will always be a hallmark of theory of knowledge (Cook, 1985).

THEORY OF PRACTICE

The Questions

The questions in Table 10.5 suggest the many problems with which evaluators must cope in their daily work. A theory of evaluation practice helps them do so, using logic and experience (a) to justify the types of questions worth asking about the evaluand because answers might help improve social programs and ameliorate social problems; (b) to specify critically assessed and practical methods for gathering data about questions; (c) to detail productive roles evaluators can play in doing useful evaluations; (d) to highlight constraints under which evaluators work — budget, time, staff abilities, and sponsor sophistication about evaluation — that restrict the issues, methods, and roles that can be selected for a particular evaluation; and (e) to specify trade-offs in choices about conducting the evaluation once issues, methods, roles, and constraints are understood. This last task is complex, since all evaluations require implementing plans for sampling, measurement, and data collection when there rarely is one right way of doing so. Theories of practice outline the strengths and weaknesses of each option, trade-offs among them, signs that indicate when a preferred option is failing, and fallback positions when a failure occurs in implementing some option. We cannot discuss all these issues in the space available, so we concentrate on the most general level by postulating three general approaches to evaluation practice. These three approaches reflect a higher-order integration of the seven theories covered in the previous chapters, pointing to a few common threads not highlighted elsewhere in this book that unite or divide some theorists. Many lower-order issues about practice can be inferred from these general characterizations.

All theorists agree that evaluation should help ameliorate social problems; they disagree about how to do so. We can identify three general approaches to doing so: (a) identifying manipulable solutions, (b) identifying generalizable explanations, and (c) providing stakeholder service. Many differences among these approaches stem from disagreements about the other four knowledge bases (social programming, use, valuing, knowledge construction), although the differences are sometimes more implicit than explicit. Here we make some important differences explicit so they can be publicly scrutinized on logical and empirical grounds to assess their relative strengths and weaknesses as guides to practice.

Table 10.5 Questions to Ask About Evaluation Practice

---

(1) Why is the evaluation being initiated? Who initiated it? How else could the money currently earmarked for this evaluation be spent? Is it worth spending time and money on this evaluation given other things one could do? Why?

(2) What purposes might the evaluation serve? To measure program effects? To improve the program? To influence decision makers? To judge program worth? To provide useful information? To explain how this intervention, or ones like it, work? To help solve social problems? To help the disadvantaged? Why? How will you choose among these purposes?

(3) What role do you want to play in the evaluation? Methodological expert? Servant to management or some larger set of stakeholders? Judge of program worth? Contributor to program improvement? Servant of the "public interest"? Educator of the client paying for the evaluation? Why?

(4) Where could you get questions? From clients, stakeholders, or those who paid for the evaluation? From past research, theory, or evaluations? From pending decisions or legislation? Why?

(5) What questions will you ask in this evaluation? Questions about real and potential clients, and their characteristics and needs? About how the program is implemented? About client outcome, and impacts on those with whom the client interacts? About the connections among clients, program implementation, and outcome? About costs and fiscal benefits? Why?

(6) What methods will you use? Case study methods like observation, interviews, and inspection of records? Experimental or quasi-experimental methods? Surveys? Needs assessments? Achievement testing? Metaevaluation or meta-analysis? Causal modeling? Why? Do these methods provide good answers to the questions you are asking?

(7) How do you plan to facilitate the use of the evaluation, especially using some of the methods previously outlined under theory of use? Is it your responsibility to do so? Why?

(8) Can you do all this within time and budget? If not, then what has the highest priority, and why?

(9) What are your fallback options if something goes wrong with any of these matters?

Three Approaches to Evaluation Practice

The manipulable solution theory of practice. Campbell's (1969, 1971, 1988) experimenting society and Scriven's (1983a) consumer model epitomize the manipulable solution approach. This mounts a frontal assault on social problems by testing manipulable solutions, postulating that it is less important to know how and why solutions might work than to know that they do work. Campbell and Scriven view evaluation as serving the public interest more than the interests of specific stakeholders; they say a good social program ameliorates social problems; they prefer to study multiple solutions to a problem to increase the chances of discovering one that works better; they emphasize reducing uncertainty about program effects over identifying elements to improve a program; they prefer methods that yield confident causal inference; and they believe the political and economic system should determine how an effective solution is used, with the evaluator playing only a small role in this process.

The manipulable solution model dominated the early years of program evaluation, but its popularity has diminished because many of its assumptions were flawed. One assumption was that evaluation techniques would suggest clear answers about which solutions worked best; but early randomized experiments and planned variation studies did not yield these clear answers. A second assumption was that, once identified, novel solutions would be widely disseminated; but dissemination and adoption were not so easy in the world of social programming. The approach also relegated program implementation and causal mediation to a subordinate position; but such analyses promote explanation, and so also transferring evaluation findings to new settings and populations (Rossi & Wright, 1984). Finally, empirical studies of use suggest that the restricted role Campbell and Scriven adopt may not facilitate use, especially in the short term. By the mid-1970s, the manipulable solution approach was under heavy attack, and alternative models were being formulated. This type of evaluation did not disappear entirely from the field; it is widely used in many instances (Boruch, McSweeny, & Soderstrom, 1978; Fairweather & Tornatzky, 1977; Nathan, 1989). But with the passing from dominance of this approach, evaluators explored two other options — generalized explanation and stakeholder service. Instances of both can be found in the second stage of evaluation theory, a time of searching for alternatives.

The generalizable explanation theory of practice. Cronbach (1982a) and some writings of both Rossi (Chen & Rossi, 1981, 1983) and Weiss (1977b, 1978) represent the generalized explanation alternative. They differ from manipulability theorists in many ways. First, the latter theorists believe that many solutions will show robust effects over many subpopulations. Explanatory theorists believe the world is ontologically complex and best described by higher-order statistical interactions in which a particular effect may be present under some conditions but absent or reversed under others. Hence generalized explanation theorists seek knowledge of complex interrelationships among multiple causal determinants to facilitate transferring findings from samples studied to other projects. Second, manipulability theorists believe that quick, instrumental use of identified solutions can proceed smoothly. Explanatory theorists contend that such instrumental usage is far less likely than enlightenment and that any such instrumental use is more likely to occur at the site of local service delivery rather than in offices of central program officials.

Third, manipulability theorists believe that summative questions about effects and impacts are sufficient to justify evaluation. Generalizability theorists seek answers to a wider array of questions at the cost of increased uncertainty about causal connections. They study program implementation, targeting, or costs in both explanatory and descriptive modes, preferring functionally plastic methods over methods developed for highly specific purposes. Generalizable explanation theorists test the theory and assumptions that underlie the program so as to understand its operations and consequences. They emphasize enlightenment over instrumental use, favor external validity—sometimes more than internal validity—and stress multivariate causal models over simple causal connections from program to effects.

Unfortunately, the generalizable explanation approach requires great faith in our ability to construct well-specified theories relating program inputs, processes, and effects. It also assumes that generalizable knowledge facilitates transfer of knowledge so much so that social problems are eventually ameliorated—an assertion about which there is little evidence. In placing a higher premium on explanation than description, these evaluators may expend great effort explaining complex causal relationships in which the basic causal connection is poorly justified. And Cronbach's exhortation for evaluators to adopt lower standards than academics contradicts some case study findings that suggest federal decision makers prefer findings of higher methodological quality (Boeckman, 1974; Weiss & Bucuvalas, 1980).

The stakeholder service theory of practice. The major alternative approach to practice in the second stage of evaluation theory was the stakeholder service model. As represented by Wholey's (1983) management-centered evaluation, Stake's (1975a, 1980a) responsive evaluation, and Patton's (1978) utilization-focused evaluation, proponents of this approach postulate that evaluations will better ameliorate social problems when tailored to information needs of stakeholders who are close to specific programs being evaluated. These theorists subordinate other aspects of evaluation to producing useful information for stakeholders, but they differ as to who those stakeholders should be. Wholey and, to some degree, Patton focus on program managers who have more control over social programs than other actors. But Stake and Guba and Lincoln (1981) also serve program clients, service providers, local boards, and others. All these theorists agree that evaluations should not try to generalize evaluation findings to other sites. The priority is on the particular program under study. Theorists who favor this approach want stakeholders to play the major role in deciding problems, questions, interventions, and even methods, with the evaluator acting as a consciousness-raising educator. They prefer methods that provide quick, approximate answers to many questions rather than higher-quality answers to fewer questions. They maintain close and frequent contact with stakeholders to respond to changing needs and to maximize use of the results.

Adherents of the stakeholder service approach criticize other theorists on several grounds. One is for being too concerned with traditional social science theory and method at the expense of serving those with a direct stake in a program. Another is for concocting an ambiguous public interest divorced from real people with real information needs. A third is for being insufficiently concerned with providing rapid results for use in the short term. A final criticism is for presuming that evaluators who do not have close contact with stakeholders can construct better understandings of social problems and programs than those with more frequent and direct contact with clients and with the social world from which these clients come.

Several criticisms of the stakeholder service approach can be made. First, its connection to social problem solving depends on locating stakeholders who want information about important social problems and their solution. Stakeholders may ask uninformed, trivial, or self-centered questions, and the resulting information, while usable, may be minimally relevant to important social problems. Second, the idea that evaluators will educate stakeholders about better questions and methods is sometimes inconsistent with political and economic realities. Many practicing evaluators make their livings by securing contracts or responding to superiors' requests. Those contractors and superiors are free to give future work to other evaluators if they dislike the education being provided. Finally, trade-offs among accuracy, timeliness, and comprehensiveness of results are not yet well known, but adherents of the stakeholder service approach risk providing timely information that is wrong or misleading.

Which theory of practice is best? Judging the merit of these three approaches is complex. Proponents often speak as if the three approaches are mutually exclusive. This is incorrect in two respects. First, the contingency theories developed by Cronbach and Rossi during the third stage of evaluation theory allow (to varying degrees) a place for all three approaches to practice, depending on circumstances. Second, proponents often assume the approaches are logically incompatible; but this is only partly true. For example, the generalized explanation approach relies on theoretical explanation to facilitate project transfer. But the manipulable solution approach might approximate this goal by using sampling, meta-analysis, or simultaneous replications (Cook, in press; Cook et al., 1985) to identify main effects that are demonstrably robust. Similarly, the stakeholder service approach can regain a focus on social problem solving through choice of stakeholders who are more actively concerned with social problem solving. For instance, when members of congressional committees request evaluations from the General Accounting Office, the resulting work often has a clearer link to ameliorating important social problems than if a local project manager asked an evaluator to upgrade the record-keeping system for billing purposes.

Judging the merits of these three approaches is also difficult because data bearing on their merits is mostly lacking. Some of their basic assumptions could simply be wrong. For example, advocates of the generalizable explanation approach assume that short-term instrumental use is rare. But some empirical evidence to the contrary exists (Leviton & Boruch, 1983; Shadish & Reichardt, 1987); program managers would probably not have continued funding Wholey's methods for stimulating short-term use if he did not deliver it. Similarly, advocates of the generalized solution and the stakeholder service approaches assume that failures of randomized experiments and planned variation studies are well documented. But early failures of these methods may have been due as much to inexperience in implementing them as to any intrinsic limits they might have (Rossi & Wright, 1984). Recent successful experiments with multiple planned variations warrant study to determine conditions under which such efforts can be undertaken fruitfully (Cook & Walberg, 1985). A similar need for data applies to most other arguments in the field.

Clearly, we are not inclined to pick a "winner" from among these three approaches. Proponents of each approach provide intelligent, persuasive arguments in favor of their position. It is sometimes easy to think that all of them may be correct, that the positions seem inconsistent only because our theories of evaluation are not complex enough to specify the contingencies that would integrate them. Rather than encouraging evaluators to choose just one approach, we hope to encourage them to get to know each approach on its own terms, to explore how well each is grounded in the knowledge bases we outlined, to seek ways to resolve apparent differences among the approaches, and to make their practical choices after considered judgments about the relative strengths and weaknesses of each approach, instead of relying exclusively on a single one. From such efforts, better conceptualized evaluation theories might emerge.

Summary of Theory of Practice

To summarize, we offer the following list of likely agreements among evaluation theorists:

- Evaluation typically occurs under time and resource constraints that require difficult trade-offs.
- At least initially, evaluators are rarely welcomed by many parties to evaluation.

- The single evaluation study is inevitably flawed.
- To facilitate use, evaluators must take active steps toward that end.

The following questions summarize major disagreements about practice that still remain to be resolved:

- What should the role of the evaluator be?
- Whose values should be represented in the evaluation?
- Which questions should the evaluator ask?
- Given limited time and resources, which methods should be used to best answer questions?
- What should the evaluator do to facilitate use?
- What are the important contingencies in evaluation practice that guide these choices?

One recent study suggests that—to oversimplify more complex findings—there are two patterns of answers to these questions (Shadish & Epstein, 1987). One is an academic pattern in which evaluations resemble more traditional academic research that may be less immediately useful but may be enlightening in the long term. The other is a stakeholder service pattern in which the evaluation provides a service that relevant stakeholders want, more likely to result in short-term use but also more socially conservative in problems studied and changes suggested. These two patterns were related to the evaluator's job situation, past training, and exposure to different ways of doing evaluation. Differential patterns of practice may be reasonable responses to these contingencies—not to be integrated into a single pattern to be used always and everywhere, but perhaps to be integrated by better empirical and theoretical explication of contingency heuristic devices to guide choice.

TOWARD MORE
DATA-ORIENTED EVALUATION THEORY

The current state of evaluation theory is much more sophisticated than ever before. Modern theories are more comprehensive and realistic than theories of 20 years ago, incorporating practical and theoretical lessons of previous work. They are more knowledgeable and informed about the problems they face—about how social programs work and change, about how social science results get used, about the complexities that arise when values are invoked in social settings, about the interface between scientific conceptions of knowledge and conceptions held by other stakeholders, and about how to do evaluations in a world of limited resources. Evaluation theories have developed a better sense of the contingencies of practice that help evaluators know which kinds of evaluations to conduct in different situations. Partly because of all this improvement, modern evaluations are much better products than ever before (Rossi & Wright, 1984).

One of the most important but least frequent ways that evaluation theory has improved over the years is by increasing its empirical content. Evaluators take for granted that the data they generate about social programs provide theoretical insights and help illuminate theoretical debates about social programs. Too often, they forget to apply this principle reflexively to their theories of evaluation. Yet the same generativity and illumination might occur if they did.

For example, in 1973 Pressman and Wildavsky first published their classic study of the implementation of a local project aimed at reducing poverty and unemployment in the late 1960s in Oakland, California, funded by the federal Economic Development Administration. Their study found massive implementation difficulties — large sums of money not spent, crucial decisions not made, and blockages and delays resulting from the need to coordinate multiple decision makers — all captured best in the book's pithy title and narrative subtitle, *Implementation: How Great Expectations in Washington Are Dashed in Oakland; Or, Why It's Amazing That Federal Programs Work at All, This Being a Saga of the Economic Development Administration as Told by Two Sympathetic Observers Who Seek to Build Morals on a Foundation of Ruined Hopes: The Oakland Project.* After the Pressman and Wildavsky study, program theory could never be the same. Their findings showed that we could never again assume that social programs would be implemented uniformly — or even at all — from site to site and time to time. The implications for evaluation practice were equally important. Assessing program implementation took on a much higher priority than before, both as a phenomenon to be studied in its own right and as a means in outcome evaluations to prevent faulty conclusions that a program did not work when it had not been implemented well or at all (Rossi & Wright, 1984).

Another example of the power of theoretically relevant empirical study was in theory of use. The early 1970s were a time of disillusionment in evaluation about the likelihood that evaluation results would be used much in helping solve social problems. Few evaluators saw this sooner or more clearly than Carol Weiss, who as early as 1966 sketched a program of research on the use of evaluation (Weiss, 1966, 1967, 1972d). The 1970s saw a spate of traditional, empirical, social science studies of use that gave us a more detailed and realistic picture of the kinds of use that occur in different circumstances, and of the factors that facilitate those uses

(Weiss, 1977b; Weiss & Bucuvalas, 1980). These lessons have been widely adopted in subsequent evaluation theories (Patton, 1988; Rossi & Freeman, 1985; Weiss, 1988a, 1988b), and the prescriptions developed from this research for facilitating use have been widely adopted by practitioners (Shadish & Epstein, 1987).

A third example comes from theory of knowledge. The relative merits of various methods for estimating the effects of social programs have been debated for decades, both in evaluation (Cook & Campbell, 1979; Cronbach, 1982a) and in related disciplines such as labor economics (Haveman, 1986; Heckman, Hotz, & Dabos, 1987). But the debate was affected significantly in 1986 by the publication of an empirical study by Robert LaLonde. He compared results from a randomized experiment of a job training program with results obtained from various econometric approaches to the same data; the two methods yielded different estimates of the causal efficacy of the program. LaLonde concluded that the findings favored the randomized experiment for theoretical reasons, and that such experiments ought to be used more. The study and his recommendation had a significant impact. The Department of Labor charged an advisory panel to discuss the relative merits of various approaches to estimating the effects of job training programs. That panel issued a report that cited the LaLonde results as a major reason the department ought to move toward more extensive use of randomized trials in evaluating its programs (Stromsdorfer, 1987). The department then decided to implement some of its evaluations using random assignment (LaLonde, 1986). Clearly the impact of theoretical debates about randomized experiments versus econometric modeling was increased dramatically as LaLonde's test gave those debates empirical content.

The next example pertains to value theory. Finding any examples of empirical studies of valuing bearing on evaluation theory was difficult. This paucity is a telling signal that more such research is badly needed. One example is the critiques of the early Follow Through evaluation, which was begun by the Stanford Research Institute in the late 1960s. This example is not a planned, empirical study of a problem explicitly framed in terms of value theory; it is a retrospective case report about a broad set of problems in the Follow Through evaluation documented many years after the fact. Nonetheless, as House (1980; House et al., 1978) and others (Haney, 1977) have described, the failure of the original SRI evaluation plan to take sufficiently into account the descriptive values of diverse Follow Through stakeholders — and even of the evaluation sponsors themselves — led to heated protests that continued over several years. Eventually new evaluations had to be commissioned to remedy this failure. Although it is difficult to document the effect this case had on subsequent developments in value theory, it is clear that after the late 1960s concern with descriptive valuing and broad assessment of stakeholder values increased greatly.

The final example is from theory of practice: the survey conducted in the late 1960s by Wholey and his colleagues on existing federal evaluation practices (Wholey et al., 1970). Their study found that many evaluations were conducted for their own sake rather than to provide information to managers and policymakers that they could use to improve program performance. These observations led Wholey to develop a new theory of practice where evaluations are done only when connections between the evaluations and planned changes in the program can be made clear ahead of time (Wholey et al., 1975b).

In view of the power to affect theory and practice exhibited by these empirical studies, evaluation theory should strive to have even more such empirical content. In any science, theories are subjected to empirical tests to see how well their propositions hold, or if they fare better than alternative theories in explaining their domain. Any scholarly specialty that does not subject its theories to such tests, when it can do so, would be regarded by many observers with great skepticism, eventually relegated to the realm of pseudoscience. The type of theorizing currently prevalent in evaluation — generally conceptual with little empirical content — is inappropriate to the developmental stage of the field and to the scientific status to which it aspires. We need empirical study to answer the unanswered questions we outlined in evaluation theory earlier in this chapter.

A move from primarily conceptual theories toward data-based theories of evaluation is part of a natural progression already under way. In the early stages of any field, particularly a field like program evaluation, which had so little large-scale precedent, most theory may be inevitably conceptual. The data on which early theory relies exist in researchers' own personal experiences in doing evaluations, and in their vicarious experiences of watching them being done. No theorist constructs hypotheses entirely in a void; all have some observational knowledge of the matters about which they speculate. To borrow from the language of theoretical physics, early evaluation theory is often more like "thought experiments" than actual experiments. Such analyses are preliminary in the sense that they pioneer in an area in which little is known beyond common sense or the knowledge gained from training in related topics. Empirical studies of evaluation are rarely used in support of such analyses, most likely because few such studies are available. For example, the initial adaptation of theories of experimentation as a model for doing evaluations was based largely on a conceptual guess that evaluation needed a methodology that was good at identifying program effects. Similarly, in the first chapter we pointed out that all practicing evaluators are nascent theorists who, we would now add, do mostly conceptual-experiential rather than data-based theorizing. Examples include not only the first evaluators of the 1960s, who had no developed evaluation theory from which to draw, but also many evaluators today who come to the field from other specialties or professions to "don the evaluator's hat" by request, by change of interests, or by supervisory mandate.

The key weakness of all theory that relies primarily on conceptual analysis, including much of what we have written in this book, is its lack of extensive and systematic *empirical* content. Conceptual argumentation helps resolve some debates, and can sharpen the issues involved. In some cases, such analysis is the only practical tool. In the quantitative-qualitative debate, for example, many key questions about such things as the existence of an external reality, or our ultimate capacity to know the world, may be beyond much systematic empirical test. Good conceptual analysis is also essential to good theory, but it is incomplete without data. The move from speculation to data (and iteratively back and forth) helps improve the descriptive accuracy of a theory, helps set priorities that are more likely to hold up in practice, and helps a field progress from professional lore to scientific theory.

Developmentally, the earliest use of systematic data may occur when a theorist cites some feature of a past evaluation that supports the conceptual point being made. With such citations, little effort is made to gather data systematically to explore or test the tenet being considered. Rather, cases are cited retrospectively and selectively to support the theorist's point. These cases are rarely specifically designed to provide a representative array of available evidence about a theoretical issue, and certainly are not intended to falsify the contention the theorist is making. This use of data is common in evaluation theory; one of the strengths of the Rossi and Freeman (1985) text is its liberal use of such examples. Consider also debates about the relative merits of social experimentation in evaluation. Much of this debate has proceeded with authors citing cases they think support their positions, but with little effort to ensure a systematic sample of cases that are then critically scrutinized to see if the cases really do support the contention when the cases are taken as a group. For example, Riecken et al. (1974) cite the Manhattan Bail Bond Experiment (Ares et al., 1963; Botein, 1965) to illustrate the benefits of social experiments; Cronbach (1982a) criticizes the same case in arguing against social experiments. The case itself was just a report of a study that happened to use experimental methodology, not a prospective effort to investigate systematically the merits of experimentation. Both Riecken et al. and Cronbach cite other examples from time to time, but neither makes any effort to locate a systematic or representative array of experiments to see if the conclusions they want to draw still hold. Neither takes a deliberately falsificationist approach to their own favored hypotheses.

The core of the problem with this approach to data-based theory is that one can always find at least one case that supports the conceptual point at issue. Further, the single case almost always allows great latitude of interpretation (Campbell, 1975b); alternative explanations can rarely be ruled out convincingly. Hence evaluation theorists can say almost anything within plausible reason, and still find some evidence somewhere that seems to be consistent with the assertion. Alternative explanations often abound, but authors usually make little effort to identify those alternative explanations in the first place, much less to rule them out.

This use of case studies is also of unclear generalizability, but evaluation theories virtually require generalizable evidence. The very nature of such theories is to make broad appeals to the practices of many evaluators to whom the conceptual points, and the cases that support them, are alleged to apply. The idiosyncratic characteristics of particular case studies seem less likely to support such generalizations than would a wider selection of cases. Some theorists might counter this claim by saying that some version of Stake's naturalistic generalization (Stake & Trumbull, 1982) is their goal — rather than provide evidence about the generalizability of their theory, their job is only to write a theory that individual evaluators can use to decide for themselves whether the theory fits their situations. This appeal is persuasive enough to convince us that any evaluation theory ought to have the characteristics that Stake claims facilitate that goal. But such a claim still endorses the goal of generalization; if so, such generalizations are even better facilitated by the addition of empirical data to whatever descriptions the theorists would normally write to facilitate naturalistic generalization.

All this is not to say that the citation of past cases to support one's theory is a bad thing. We are engaging in this kind of persuasion right now, citing cases like Pressman and Wildavsky (1973), Weiss (1977b), House (1980), LaLonde (1986), Wholey et al. (1970), Riecken et al. (1974), and Cronbach (1982a) to illustrate our point, without systematically reviewing all evidence on each of our contentions. Such citations illustrate by example those conceptual points that might otherwise be obscure; they begin a process of locating publicly available evidence bearing on a hypothesis, they provide preliminary indication of the plausibility of a theory, and, perhaps very rarely, they eliminate some possibilities because no examples of them can be found even after painstaking search. For instance, we know of no definitive case in which a social program was completely terminated primarily on the basis of a negative evaluation of it by program evaluators (we use the term *program* in specific contrast to projects and elements). To the extent that evaluation theory is still conceptual, a move toward citation of cases to support and illustrate hypotheses is welcomed if for no other reason than to provide these preliminary benefits.

In the long run, however, evaluation will be better served by increasing the more systematic empirical content of its theories, by treating evaluation theory like any other scientific theory, subjecting its problems and hypotheses to the same wide scientific scrutiny to which any theory is subjected. We do not lack for hypotheses worth studying. Indeed, after reviewing all the theorists in this book, one senses that despite great progress, many key questions remain hotly debated. We have outlined some of these disagreements in this chapter, but one can easily think of more. In social programming, more systematic data would help theorists better answer these questions:

- Under what conditions are social problems and interventions important and at the same time feasible to implement or tractable to address with some likelihood of success?
- Under what conditions does a "context of command" exist in social programming?

Regarding knowledge use:

- What are the conditions under which and frequency with which instrumental use occurs, and how often is it a realistic goal in various settings?
- Can the concept of enlightenment be usefully explicated so that we understand better the circumstances under which it is a worthwhile goal for evaluators to pursue in addition to or in lieu of instrumental use?

Regarding knowledge construction:

- Under what conditions does quality of evidence matter by different definitions of quality?
- What is the relative effectiveness and practicality of different means of studying generalization — through sampling, theory-based generalizations, or searching for robust findings over studies?
- Are evaluations with both quantitative and qualitative components better than either by themselves?
- Under what circumstances do social and psychological factors exert a corrupting influence on evaluative data?

Regarding valuing:

- What difference does explicit attention to valuing make?
- Given the greater political practicality of descriptive valuing, what important contributions can prescriptive approaches make?
- Does explicit, prominent attention to discussing money — that ubiquitous metric for synthesizing value judgments — increase the likelihood that evaluations will affect decisions?

Finally, for evaluation practice:

- What are the key factors in evaluation practice that influence the conduct and eventual form of the evaluation?
- What are the consequences of encouraging critical debate about evaluation design and findings?
- Can the practice of evaluation be improved by better training of evaluators?

All these questions could be studied using social science methods — case studies of evaluation (Boruch, Dennis, & Carter-Greer, 1988; Cook & Walberg, 1985; Kytle & Millman, 1986; Lobosco & Kaufman, 1989; Shadish, 1987a; Stake, 1986b), surveys of evaluation (Dennis, 1988; Jerrell, 1986; Shadish & Epstein, 1987; Williams, 1989), experiments and quasi-experiments (Bradburn et al., 1980; Braverman, 1988; Senf, 1987), cost-effectiveness analyses of various methodologies (Detsky, 1989), narrative reviews of literature relevant to evaluation theory (Boruch & Cecil, 1979), meta-analyses of evaluations (Lipsey, Crosse, Dunkle, Pollard, & Stobart, 1985; Lynch, 1988), secondary analyses of evaluations (Boruch, 1978; Boruch & Wortman, 1978; Boruch, Wortman, & Cordray, 1981; Bowering, 1984), and metaevaluations (Cook & Gruder, 1978; Cook & Shadish, 1982; Scriven, 1969).

Such efforts have always been relatively rare in evaluation because so little effort is generally put into developing empirically testable hypotheses based in evaluation theory, and because so few evaluators are both interested in the topic and in a position to undertake such studies. Nonetheless, we need more such efforts, for the future of better-developed evaluation theories lies in these kinds of empirical studies over the broad spectrum of theoretical issues we have raised in this book.

CONCLUSION

Judging from the preceding chapters, evaluation theory is flourishing. More important, we hope we have helped the reader to understand that even in a practice-driven field like evaluation, such theories — especially the comparative study of them — are not only interesting in their own right, but are essential to making the practical decisions most evaluators face. Such theories help to identify where reflexive research on evaluation practice needs to be done; they give evaluators a greater range of conceptual and practical options from which to choose in thinking about and doing their work, along with a better sense of the context in which different practices have been generated; they enhance critical faculties so that evaluators are less likely to adopt practices that we have good theoretical reasons to believe may be inappropriate, that have inadequate conceptual or empirical support, or that comprehensive knowledge of theory would make one suspicious of; and they help evaluators to see that the field is less bewildering in its diversity than first seems. Finally, theory is practically useful to evaluation policymakers who make the decisions about what questions are to be asked, what interventions are studied, and how many resources will be devoted to the task, at least to the extent that they have degrees of freedom to make those decisions — and very few evaluators or evaluation policymakers have no degrees of freedom at all. Improved, data-based evaluation theory would be still more practically useful; we hope this book encourages such tendencies.

References

Aaron, H. J. (1984, Fall). Six welfare questions still searching for answers. *Brookings Review*, pp. 12-17.

Aaronson, N. K., & Wilner, D. M. (1983). Evaluation and outcome research in community mental health centers. *Evaluation Review, 7*, 303-320.

Abramson, M. A. (1978). *The funding of social knowledge production and application: A survey of federal agencies.* Washington, DC: National Academy of Sciences.

Abramson, M. A., & Wholey, J. S. (1981). Organization and management of the evaluation function in a multilevel organization. In R. J. Wooldridge (Ed.), *Evaluation of complex systems* (pp. 31-48). San Francisco: Jossey-Bass.

American Evaluation Association. (1986, September). *Membership directory* (prepared by Evaluation Research Center, School of Education, University of Virginia). Charlottesville, VA: Author.

American Institutes for Research. (1977). *Evaluation of the impact of the EASA Title 7 Spanish/English Bilingual Education Program* (3 vols.). Palo Alto, CA: Author.

American Institutes for Research. (1980). *The national evaluation of the PUSH for Excellence project.* Washington, DC: Author.

American Psychological Association. (1985). *Standards for educational and psychological testing* (2nd ed.). Washington, DC: Author.

Applied Management Sciences, Inc. (1984). *Income Verification Pilot Project Phase II: Results of the quality-assurance evaluation, 1982-1983 school year.* Silver Spring, MD: Author.

Ares, C. E., Rankin, A., & Sturz, H. (1963). The Manhattan Bail Project: An interim report on the use of pre-trial parole. *New York University Law Review, 38*, 67-95.

Austin, D. (1981). The development of clinical sociology. *Journal of Applied Behavioral Science, 17*, 347-350.

Ayer, A. J. (1936). *Language, truth and logic* (2nd ed.). New York: Dover.

Bachrach, L. L. (1981). [Review of *Making it crazy*]. *New England Journal of Medicine, 305*, 1421.

Bardach, E. (1977). *The implementation game: What happens after a bill becomes a law.* Cambridge: MIT Press.

Barker, R. (1968). *Ecological psychology.* Stanford, CA: Stanford University Press.

Barker, R., & Gump, P. (1964). *Big school, small school.* Stanford, CA: Stanford University Press.

Barlow, D. H. (1981). On the relation of clinical research to clinical practice: Current directions, new directions. *Journal of Consulting and Clinical Psychology, 49*, 147-155.

Barrom, C. B., Shadish, W. R., & Montgomery, L. M. (1988). PhDs, PsyDs, and real-world constraints on scholarly activity: Another look at the Boulder model. *Professional Psychology: Research and Practice, 19*, 93-101.

Beauchamp, T. L. (1982). *Philosophical ethics: An introduction to moral philosophy.* New York: McGraw-Hill.

Bell, J. (1988, October). *Evaluation at the Urban Institute.* Paper presented at the annual convention of the American Evaluation Association, New Orleans.

Bell, W. (1983). *Contemporary social welfare.* New York: Macmillan.

Bellavita, C., Wholey, J. S., & Abramson, M. A. (1986). Performance-oriented evaluation: Prospects for the future. In J. S. Wholey, M. A. Abramson, & C. Bellavita (Eds.), *Performance and credibility: Developing excellence in public and nonprofit organizations* (pp. 286-292). Lexington, MA: Lexington.

Berk, R. A., Boruch, R. F., Chambers, D. L., Rossi, P. H., & Witte, A. D. (1985). Social policy experimentation: A position paper. *Evaluation Review, 9*, 387-430.

Berk, R. A., Lenihan, K. J., & Rossi, P. H. (1981). Crime and poverty: Some experimental evidence from ex-offenders. In H. E. Freeman & M. A. Solomon (Eds.), *Evaluation studies review annual* (Vol. 6, pp. 339-359). Beverly Hills, CA: Sage.

Berk, R. A., & Rossi, P. H. (1977). Doing good or worse: Evaluation research politically reexamined. In G. V Glass (Ed.), *Evaluation studies review annual* (Vol. 2, pp. 77-89). Beverly Hills, CA: Sage.

Berman, P. (1980). Thinking about programmed and adaptive implementation: Matching strategies to situations. In H. M. Ingram & D. E. Mann (Eds.), *Why policies succeed or fail* (pp. 205-227). Beverly Hills, CA: Sage.

Berman, P., & McLaughlin, M. W. (1977). *Federal programs supporting educational change: Vol. 8. Factors affecting implementation and continuation.* Santa Monica, CA: RAND Corporation.

Bhaskar, R. (1979). *The possibility of naturalism: A philosophical critique of the contemporary human sciences.* Brighton, Sussex: Harvester.

Bhaskar, R. (1982). Emergence, explanation and emancipation. In P. F. Secord (Ed.), *Explaining social behavior: Consciousness, behavior, and social structure* (pp. 275-310). Beverly Hills, CA: Sage.

Bickman, L. (Ed.). (1987). *Using program theory in evaluation.* San Francisco: Jossey-Bass.

Boeckman, M. E. (1974). Policy impacts of the New Jersey income maintenance experiment. *Policy Science, 7*, 53-76.

Bogatz, G. A., & Ball, S. (1971). *The second year of Sesame Street: A continuing evaluation* (2 vols.). Princeton, NJ: Educational Testing Service.

Bollen, K. A. (1989). *Structural equations with latent variables.* New York: John Wiley.

Boruch, R. F. (Ed.). (1978). *Secondary analysis.* San Francisco: Jossey-Bass.

Boruch, R. F., & Cecil, J. S. (1979). *Assuring the confidentiality of social research data.* Philadelphia: University of Pennsylvania Press.

Boruch, R. F., & Cordray, D. S. (1980). *An appraisal of educational program evaluations: Federal, state, and local agencies.* Final Report of U.S. Department of Education Contract No. 300-79-0467.

Boruch, R. F., Cordray, D. S., & Pion, G. M. (1981). How well are local evaluations carried out? In L. Datta (Ed.), *Evaluation in change: Meeting new government needs* (pp. 13-40). Beverly Hills, CA: Sage.

Boruch, R. F., Dennis, M., & Carter-Greer, K. (1988). Lessons from the Rockefeller Foundation's experiments on the Minority Female Single Parent Program. *Evaluation Review, 12*, 396-426.

Boruch, R. F., & Gomez, H. (1977). Sensitivity, bias, and theory in impact evaluations. *Professional Psychology: Research and Practice, 8*, 411-434.

Boruch, R. F., McSweeny, A. J., & Soderstrom, E. J. (1978). Randomized field experiments for program planning, development, and evaluation: An illustrative bibliography. *Evaluation Quarterly, 2*, 655-695.

Boruch, R. F., & Wortman, P. M. (1978). An illustrative project on secondary analysis. In R. F. Boruch (Ed.), *Secondary analysis* (pp. 89-111). San Francisco: Jossey-Bass.

Boruch, R. F., Wortman, P. M., & Cordray, D. S. (Eds.). (1981). *Reanalyzing program evaluations.* San Francisco: Jossey-Bass.

Botein, B. (1965). The Manhattan Bail Project: Its impact on criminology and the criminal law process. *Texas Law Review, 43*, 319-331.

Bowering, D. J. (Ed.). (1984). *Secondary analysis of available data bases.* San Francisco: Jossey-Bass.

Bowman, M. L. (1989). Testing individual differences in ancient China. *American Psychologist, 44*, 576-578.

Bradburn, N. M., Sudman, S., Blair, E., Locander, W., Miles, C., Singer, E., & Stocking, C. (1980). *Improving interview method and questionnaire design.* San Francisco: Jossey-Bass.

Braverman, M. T. (1988). Respondent cooperation in telephone surveys: The effects of using volunteer interviews. *Evaluation and Program Planning, 11*, 135-140.

Braverman, M. T. (Ed.). (1989). *Evaluating health promotion programs.* San Francisco: Jossey-Bass.

Braybrooke, C. E., & Lindblom, C. E. (1963). *A strategy of decision: Policy evaluation as a social process.* New York: Free Press.

Brewer, M. B., & Campbell, D. T. (1976). *Ethnocentrism and intergroup attitudes: East African evidence.* New York: Halstead.

Brewer, M. B., & Collins, B. E. (Eds.). (1981). *Scientific inquiry and the social sciences: A volume in honor of Donald T. Campbell.* San Francisco: Jossey-Bass.

Brickman, P., & Campbell, D. T. (1971). Hedonic relativism and planning the good society. In M. H. Appley (Ed.), *Adaptation-level theory: A symposium* (pp. 287-302). New York: Academic Press.

Brinkerhoff, R. O., Brethower, D. M., Hluchyj, T., & Nowakowski, J. R. (1983). *Program evaluation: A practitioner's guide for trainers and educators.* Boston: Kluwer-Nijhoff.

Brown, H. I. (1977). *Perception, theory, and commitment.* Chicago: University of Chicago Press.

Bryk, A. S. (Ed.). (1983). *Stakeholder-based evaluation.* San Francisco: Jossey-Bass.

Buchanan, G. N., & Wholey, J. S. (1972). Federal level evaluation. *Evaluation, 1*, 17-22.

Bunda, M. A. (1985). Alternative systems of ethics and their application to education and evaluation. *Evaluation and Program Planning, 8*, 25-36.

Bunker, J. P. (1985). When doctors disagree. *New York Review of Books, 32*, 7-12.

Campbell, D. T. (1950). The indirect assessment of social attitudes. *Psychological Bulletin, 47*, 15-38.

Campbell, D. T. (1957). Factors relevant to the validity of experiments in social settings. *Psychological Bulletin, 54*, 297-312.

Campbell, D. T. (1958). Common fate, similarity, and other indices of the status of aggregates of persons as social entities. *Behavioral Science, 3*, 14-25.

Campbell, D. T. (1959). Systematic error on the part of human links in communication systems. *Information and Control, 1*, 334-369.

Campbell, D. T. (1960). Blind variations and selective retention in creative thought as in other knowledge processes. *Psychological Review, 67*, 380-400.

Campbell, D. T. (1965). Ethnocentrism and other altruistic motives. In D. Levine (Ed.), *The Nebraska Symposium on Motivation*. Lincoln: University of Nebraska Press.

Campbell, D. T. (1966). Pattern matching as an essential in distal knowing. In K. R. Hammond (Ed.), *The psychology of Egon Brunswik* (pp. 81-106). New York: Holt, Rinehart & Winston.

Campbell, D. T. (1967). Stereotypes and the perception of group differences. *American Psychologist, 22*, 817-829.

Campbell, D. T. (1969). Reforms as experiments. *American Psychologist, 24*, 409-429.

Campbell, D. T. (1970). Considering the case against experimental evaluations of social innovations. *Administrative Science Quarterly, 15*, 110-113.

Campbell, D. T. (1971). *Methods for the experimenting society*. Paper presented at the meeting of the Eastern Psychological Association, New York, and at the meeting of the American Psychological Association, Washington, DC.

Campbell, D. T. (1974a). Evolutionary epistemology. In P. A. Schilpp (Ed.), *The philosophy of Karl Popper* (pp. 413-463). La Salle, IL: Open Court.

Campbell, D. T. (1974b, September 1). *Qualitative knowing in action research*. Kurt Lewin Award Address, Society for the Psychological Study of Social Issues, presented at the 82nd annual meeting of the American Psychological Association, New Orleans.

Campbell, D. T. (1975a). Assessing the impact of planned social change. In G. M. Lyons (Ed.), *Social research and public policies* (pp. 3-45). Hanover, NH: Dartmouth College, Public Affairs Center.

Campbell, D. T. (1975b). "Degrees of freedom" and the case study. *Comparative Political Studies, 8*, 178-193.

Campbell, D. T. (1976). Focal local indicators for social program evaluation. *Social Indicators Research, 3*, 237-256.

Campbell, D. T. (1977). *Descriptive epistemology: Psychological, sociological, and evolutionary*. William James Lectures, Harvard University.

Campbell, D. T. (1978). Qualitative knowing in action research. In M. Brenner, P. Marsh, & M. Brenner (Eds.), *The social context of methods* (pp. 184-209). London: Croom Helm.

Campbell, D. T. (1979a). Assessing the impact of planned social change. *Evaluation and Program Planning, 2*, 67-90.

Campbell, D. T. (1979b). A tribal model of the social system vehicle carrying scientific knowledge. *Knowledge: Creation, Diffusion, Utilization, 1*, 181-201.

Campbell, D. T. (1981a). Comment: Another perspective on a scholarly career. In M. B. Brewer & B. E. Collins (Eds.), *Scientific inquiry and the social sciences* (pp. 454-501). San Francisco: Jossey-Bass.

Campbell, D. T. (1981b). Introduction: Getting ready for the experimenting society. In L. Saxe & M. Fine, *Social experiments: Methods for design and evaluation* (pp. 13-18). Beverly Hills, CA: Sage.

Campbell, D. T. (1982). Experiments as arguments. In E. R. House, S. Mathison, J. A. Pearsol, & H. Preskill (Eds.), *Evaluation studies review annual* (Vol. 7, pp. 117-127). Beverly Hills, CA: Sage.

Campbell, D. T. (1983, July). *The role of the psychologist in planning for an experimenting society*. Paper presented at the Nineteenth Interamerican Congress of Psychology, Quito, Ecuador.

Campbell, D. T. (1984a). Can we be scientific in applied social science? In R. F. Connor, D. G. Altman, & C. Jackson (Eds.), *Evaluation studies review annual* (Vol. 9, pp. 26-48). Beverly Hills, CA: Sage.

Campbell, D. T. (1984b). Hospital and landsting as continuously monitoring social polygrams: Advocacy and warning. In B. Cronholm & L. von Knorring (Eds.), *Evaluation of mental health service programs* (pp. 13-39). Stockholm: Forskningsraadet Medicinska.

Campbell, D. T. (1984c). Toward an epistemologically relevant sociology of science. *Science, Technology, and Human Values, 10*, 38-48.

Campbell, D. T. (1986a). Relabeling internal and external validity for applied social scientists. In W. M. K. Trochim (Ed.), *Advances in quasi-experimental design and analysis* (pp. 67-77). San Francisco: Jossey-Bass.

Campbell, D. T. (1986b). Science's social system of validity-enhancing collective belief change and the problems of the social sciences. In D. W. Fiske & R. A. Shweder (Eds.), *Metatheory in social science: Pluralisms and subjectivities* (pp. 108-135). Chicago: University of Chicago Press.

Campbell, D. T. (1987a). Guidelines for monitoring the scientific competence of preventive intervention research centers: An exercise in the sociology of scientific validity. *Knowledge: Creation, Diffusion, Utilization, 8*, 389-430.

Campbell, D. T. (1987b). Problems for the experimenting society in the interface between evaluation and service providers. In S. L. Kagan, D. Powell, B. Weissbourd, & E. Zigler (Eds.), *Family support programs: The state of the art* (pp. 345-351). New Haven, CT: Yale University Press.

Campbell, D. T. (1988). *Methodology and epistemology for social science: Selected papers* (E. S. Overman, Ed.). Chicago: University of Chicago Press.

Campbell, D. T., & Boruch, R. F. (1975). Making the case for randomized assignment to treatments by considering the alternatives: Six ways in which quasi-experimental evaluations in compensatory education tend to underestimate effects. In C. A. Bennett & A. A. Lumsdaine (Eds.), *Evaluation and experiments: Some critical issues in assessing social programs* (pp. 195-296). New York: Academic Press.

Campbell, D. T., & Erlebacher, A. E. (1970). How regression artifacts can mistakenly make compensatory education programs look harmful. In J. Hellmuth (Ed.), *The disadvantaged child: Vol. 3. Compensatory education: A national debate* (pp. 185-210). New York: Brunner/Mazel.

Campbell, D. T., & Fiske, D. W. (1959). Convergent and discriminant validation by the multitrait-multimethod matrix. *Psychological Bulletin, 56*, 81-105.

Campbell, D. T., Hunt, W. A., & Lewis, N. A. (1958). The relative susceptibility of two rating scales to disturbances resulting from shifts in stimulus context. *Journal of Applied Psychology, 42*, 213-217.

Campbell, D. T., Lewis, N. A., & Hunt, W. A. (1958). Context effects with judgmental language that is absolute, extensive, and extra-experimentally anchored. *Journal of Experimental Psychology, 55*, 220-228.

Campbell, D. T., & Mohr, P. J. (1950). The effect of ordinal position upon responses to items in a checklist. *Journal of Applied Psychology, 34*, 62-67.

Campbell, D. T., Siegman, C. R., & Rees, M. B. (1967). Direction of wording effects in the relationships between scales. *Psychological Bulletin, 68*, 293-303.

Campbell, D. T., & Stanley, J. C. (1963). *Experimental and quasi-experimental designs for research*. Chicago: Rand McNally.

Champion, H. (1985). Physician heal thyself: One public manager's view of program evaluation. *Evaluation News, 6*, 29-40.

Chelimsky, E. (1981). Making block grants accountable. In L. Datta (Ed.), *Evaluation in change: Meeting new government needs* (pp. 89-120). Beverly Hills, CA: Sage.

Chelimsky, E. (1983). The definition and measurement of evaluation quality as a management tool. In R. G. St. Pierre (Ed.), *Management and organization of program evaluation* (pp. 113-126). San Francisco: Jossey-Bass.

Chelimsky, E. (1984, March 15). *Evaluation of WIC's effectiveness.* Statement before the U.S. Senate Committee on Agriculture, Nutrition, and Forestry.

Chelimsky, E. (1985). Comments on "Social experimentation: A position paper." *Evaluation Review, 9,* 431-436.

Chelimsky, E. (1987a). The politics of program evaluation. In D. S. Cordray, H. S. Bloom, & R. J. Light (Eds.), *Evaluation practice in review* (pp. 5-22). San Francisco: Jossey-Bass.

Chelimsky, E. (1987b). Retrospective and prospective analysis: Linking program evaluation and forecasting. *Evaluation Review, 11,* 355-370.

Chelimsky, E. (1987c). What have we learned about the politics of program evaluation? *Evaluation News, 8,* 5-22.

Chen, H., & Rossi, P. H. (1981). The multi-goal, theory-driven approach to evaluation: A model linking basic and applied social science. In H. E. Freeman & M. A. Solomon (Eds.), *Evaluation studies review annual* (Vol. 6, pp. 38-54). Beverly Hills, CA: Sage.

Chen, H., & Rossi, P. H. (1983). Evaluating with sense: The theory-driven approach. *Evaluation Review, 7,* 283-302.

Chen, H., & Rossi, P. H. (1987). The theory-driven approach to validity. *Evaluation and Program Planning, 10,* 95-103.

Chu, F., & Trotter, S. (1974). *The madness establishment.* New York: Grossman.

Cicirelli, V. G., & Associates. (1969). *The impact of Head Start: An evaluation of the effects of Head Start on children's cognitive and affective development* (Report to the Office of Economic Opportunity, 2 vols.). Athens: Ohio University and Westinghouse Learning Corporation.

Cochran, N. (1978). Grandma Moses and the "corruption" of data. *Evaluation Quarterly, 2,* 363-373.

Cohen, D. K. (1983). Evaluation and reform. In A. S. Bryk (Ed.), *Stakeholder-based evaluation* (pp. 73-82). San Francisco: Jossey-Bass.

Cohen, L. H., Sargent, M. M., & Sechrest, L. B. (1986). Use of psychotherapy research by professional psychologists. *American Psychologist, 41,* 198-206.

Collingwood, R. G. (1940). *An essay on metaphysics.* Oxford: Clarendon.

Comptroller General. (1980a). *Federal evaluations* (1980 Congressional Sourcebook Series PAD-80-48). Washington, DC: U.S. Government Printing Office.

Comptroller General. (1980b). *Requirements for recurring reports to the Congress* (1980 Congressional Sourcebook Series PAD-80-49). Washington, DC: U.S. Government Printing Office.

Comptroller General. (1980c). *Federal information sources and systems* (1980 Congressional Sourcebook Series PAD-80-50). Washington, DC: U.S. Government Printing Office.

Connell, D. B., Turner, R. T., & Mason, E. F. (1985). Summary of findings of the school health education evaluation: Health promotion effectiveness, implementation, and costs. *Journal of School Health, 85,* 316-317.

Conner, R., & Hendricks, M. (Eds.). (1989). *International innovations in evaluation methodology.* San Francisco: Jossey-Bass.

Cook, F. L. (1982). Assessing age as an eligibility criterion. In B. L. Neugarten (Ed.), *Age or need? Public policies for older people.* Beverly Hills, CA: Sage.

Cook, T. D. (1974a). The potential and limitations of secondary evaluations. In M. W. Apple, M. J. Subkoviak, & H. S. Lufler, Jr. (Eds.), *Educational evaluation: Analysis and responsibility* (pp. 155-235). Berkeley, CA: McCutchan.

Cook, T. D. (1974b). "Sesame Street" and the medical and tailored models of summative evaluation research. In J. Albert & M. Kamrass (Eds.), *Social experiments and social program evaluation* (pp. 28-37). Cambridge, MA: Ballinger.

Cook, T. D. (1981). Dilemmas in evaluation of social programs. In M. B. Brewer & B. E. Collins (Eds.), *Scientific inquiry and the social sciences: A volume in honor of Donald T. Campbell* (pp. 257-287). San Francisco: Jossey-Bass.

Cook, T. D. (1983). Evaluation: Whose questions should be answered? In G. R. Gilbert (Ed.), *Making and managing policy: Formulation, analysis, evaluation* (pp. 193-217). New York: Dekker.

Cook, T. D. (1984). Opportunities for evaluation in the next few years. *Evaluation News, 5,* 20-46.

Cook, T. D. (1985). Postpositivist critical multiplism. In L. Shotland & M. M. Mark (Eds.), *Social science and social policy* (pp. 21-62). Beverly Hills, CA: Sage.

Cook, T. D. (1990). Clarifying the warrant for generalized causal inferences in quasi-experimentation. In M. W. McLaughlin & D. Phillips (Eds.), *Evaluation and education at quarter-century.* Chicago: National Society for the Study of Education.

Cook, T. D. (in press). The generalization of causal connections in research theory and practice. In L. Sechrest, J. Bunker, & E. Perrin (Eds.), *Improving methods in nonexperimental research.* Newbury Park, CA: Sage.

Cook, T. D., Appleton, H., Conner, R. F., Shaffer, A., Tamkin, G., & Weber, S. J. (1975). *"Sesame Street" revisited.* New York: Russell Sage Foundation.

Cook, T. D., & Buccino, A. (1979). The social scientist as a provider of consulting services to the federal government. In J. Platt & J. Wicks (Eds.), *The psychological consultant* (pp. 103-134). New York: Grune & Stratton.

Cook, T. D., & Campbell, D. T. (1976). The design and conduct of quasi-experiments and true experiments in field settings. In M. D. Dunnette (Ed.), *Handbook of industrial and organizational psychology* (pp. 223-326). Chicago: Rand McNally.

Cook, T. D., & Campbell, D. T. (1979). *Quasi-experimentation: Design and analysis issues for field settings.* Chicago: Rand McNally.

Cook, T. D., & Campbell, D. T. (1986). The causal assumptions of quasi-experimental practice. *Synthese, 68,* 141-180.

Cook, T. D., Campbell, D. T., & Perrachio, L. (1990). The design of quasi-experiments for field settings. In M. D. Dunnette (Ed.), *Handbook of industrial and organizational psychology* (2nd ed.). Chicago: Rand McNally.

Cook, T. D., & Curtin, T. R. (1986). An evaluation of the models used to evaluate television series. In G. A. Comstock (Ed.), *Public communication and behavior* (Vol. 1, pp. 1-64). New York: Academic Press.

Cook, T. D., & Gruder, C. L. (1978). Metaevaluative research. *Evaluation Quarterly, 2,* 5-51.

Cook, T. D., Leviton, L. C., & Shadish, W. R. (1985). Program evaluation. In G. Lindzey & E. Aronson (Eds.), *Handbook of social psychology* (3rd ed., pp. 699-777). New York: Random House.

Cook, T. D., & Reichardt, C. S. (Eds.). (1979). *Qualitative and quantitative methods in evaluation research.* Beverly Hills, CA: Sage.

Cook, T. D., & Shadish, W. R. (1982). Metaevaluation: An assessment of the congressionally mandated evaluation system for community mental health centers. In G. J. Stahler & W. R. Tash (Eds.), *Innovative approaches to mental health evaluation* (pp. 221-253). New York: Academic Press.

Cook, T. D., & Shadish, W. R. (1986). Program evaluation: The worldly science. *Annual Review of Psychology, 37,* 193-232.

Cook, T. D., & Walberg, H. J. (1985). Methodological and substantive significance. *Journal of School Health, 55,* 340-342.

Coombs, C. (1964). *A theory of data.* New York: John Wiley.

Cordray, D. S., & Lipsey, M. W. (1987). Evaluation studies for 1986: Program evaluation and program research. In D. S. Cordray & M. W. Lipsey (Eds.), *Evaluation studies review annual* (Vol. 11, pp. 17-44). Newbury Park, CA: Sage.

Crider, A. (1979). *Schizophrenia: A biopsychological approach.* Hillsdale, NJ: Lawrence Erlbaum.

Cronbach, L. J. (1951). Coefficient alpha and the internal structure of tests. *Psychometrika, 16*, 297-334.

Cronbach, L. J. (1954). Report on a psychometric mission to clinicia. *Psychometrika, 19*, 263-270.

Cronbach, L. J. (1957). The two disciplines of scientific psychology. *American Psychologist, 12*, 671-684.

Cronbach, L. J. (1963). Course improvement through evaluation. *Teachers College Record, 64*, 672-683.

Cronbach, L. J. (1964). Evaluation for course improvement. In R. Heath (Ed.), *New curricula* (pp. 231-248). New York: Harper & Row.

Cronbach, L. J. (1975). Beyond the two disciplines of scientific psychology. *American Psychologist, 30*, 116-127.

Cronbach, L. J. (1982a). *Designing evaluations of educational and social programs.* San Francisco: Jossey-Bass.

Cronbach, L. J. (1982b). In praise of uncertainty. In P. H. Rossi (Ed.), *Standards for evaluation practice* (pp. 49-58). San Francisco: Jossey-Bass.

Cronbach, L. J. (1986). Social inquiry by and for earthlings. In D. W. Fiske & R. A. Shweder (Eds.), *Metatheory in social science* (pp. 83-107). Chicago: University of Chicago Press.

Cronbach, L. J. (1989a). Construct validation after thirty years. In R. L. Linn (Ed.), *Intelligence: Measurement, theory and public policy* (pp. 147-171). Urbana: University of Illinois Press.

Cronbach, L. J. (1989b). Lee J. Cronbach [autobiographical statement]. In G. Lindzey (Ed.), *History of psychology in autobiography* (pp. 65-93). Stanford, CA: Stanford University Press.

Cronbach, L. J., Ambron, S. R., Dornbusch, S. M., Hess, R. D., Hornik, R. C., Phillips, D. C., Walker, D. F., & Weiner, S. S. (1980). *Toward reform of program evaluation.* San Francisco: Jossey-Bass.

Cronbach, L. J., Gleser, G. C., Nanda, H., & Rajaratnam, N. (1972). *The dependability of behavioral measurements: Theory of generalizability for scores and profiles.* New York: John Wiley.

Cronbach, L. J., & Meehl, P. E. (1955). Construct validity in psychological tests. *Psychological Bulletin, 52*, 281-302.

Cronbach, L. J., Rajaratnam, N., & Gleser, G. C. (1963). Theory of generalizability: A liberalization of reliability theory. *British Journal of Statistical Psychology, 16*, 137-163.

Cronbach, L. J., Rogosa, D. R., Floden, R. E., & Price, G. G. (1977). *Analysis of covariance in nonrandomized experiments: Parameters affecting bias* (Occasional Paper). Berkeley, CA: Stanford University Press, Stanford Evaluation Consortium.

Cronbach, L. J., & Snow, R. E. (1977). *Aptitudes and instructional methods: A handbook for research on interactions.* New York: Irvington.

Cronbach, L. J., & Suppes, P. (1969). *Research for tomorrow's schools: Disciplined inquiry for education.* London: Macmillan.

Cumming, J. H. (1976). What Congress really wants: A guide to evaluating program effectiveness with examples from the Canadian context. In E. W. Markson & D. F. Allen (Eds.), *Trends in mental health evaluation* (pp. 61-70). Lexington, MA: Lexington.

Dahl, R. (1983). Comment on Manley. *American Political Science Review, 77*, 386-389.

David, J. L. (1982). Local uses of Title I evaluations. In E. R. House, S. Mathison, J. A. Pearsol, & H. Preskill (Eds.), *Evaluation studies review annual* (Vol. 7, pp. 413-426). Beverly Hills, CA: Sage.

Davies, P. (1984). *Superforce: The search for a grand unified theory of nature.* New York: Simon & Schuster.

Davies, P., & Brown, J. R. (1986). *The ghost in the atom: A discussion of the mysteries of quantum physics.* Cambridge: Cambridge University Press.

Delaney, J., Seidman, E., & Willis, G. (1978). Crisis intervention and the prevention of institutionalization: An interrupted time-series analysis. *American Journal of Community Psychology, 6*, 33-45.

Dennis, M. L. (1988). *Implementing randomized field experiments: An analysis of criminal and civil justice research.* Unpublished doctoral dissertation, Northwestern University.

D'Espagnat, B. (1983). *In search of reality.* New York: Springer-Verlag.

Detsky, A. S. (1989). Are clinical trials a cost-effective investment? *Journal of the American Medical Association, 262*, 1795-1800.

Doidge, J., & Rogers, C. (1976). Is NIMH's dream coming true? Wyoming centers reduce state hospital admissions. *Community Mental Health Journal, 12*, 399-404.

Downs, A. (1967). *Inside bureaucracy.* Boston: Little, Brown.

Dunn, W. N. (1982). Reforms as arguments. *Knowledge: Creation, Diffusion, Utilization, 3*, 293-326.

Edwards, W., Guttentag, M., & Snapper, K. (1975). A decision-theoretic approach to evaluation research. In M. Guttentag & E. L. Struening (Eds.), *Handbook of evaluation research* (pp. 139-182). Beverly Hills, CA: Sage.

Estroff, S. E. (1981). *Making it crazy: An ethnography of psychiatric clients in an American community.* Berkeley: University of California Press.

Etzioni, A. (1967). Mixed scanning: A "third" approach to decision making. *Public Administration Review, 27*, 385-392.

Evaluation Research Society. (1980). *Directory of evaluation training.* Washington, DC: Pintail.

Eysenck, H. J. (1952). The effects of psychotherapy: An evaluation. *Journal of Consulting Psychology, 16*, 319-324.

Eysenck, H. J. (1954). A reply to Luborsky's note. *British Journal of Psychology, 45*, 132-133.

Fairweather, G. W. (Ed.). (1980). *The Fairweather Lodge: A 25-year retrospective.* San Francisco: Jossey-Bass.

Fairweather, G. W., & Tornatzky, L. G. (1977). *Experimental methods for social policy research.* Elmsford, NY: Pergamon.

Farquhar, J. W., Fortmann, S. P., Maccoby, N., Wood, P. D., Haskell, W. L., Taylor, C. B., Flora, J. A., Solomon, D. S., Rogers, T., Adler, E., Breitrose, P., & Weiner, L. (1984). The Stanford Five City Project: An overview. In J. D. Matarazzo, S. H. Weiss, J. A. Herd, N. E. Miller, & S. W. Weiss (Eds.), *Behavioral health: A handbook of health enhancement and disease prevention* (pp. 1154-1165). New York: John Wiley.

Farquhar, J. W., Maccoby, N., Wood, P. D., ALexander, J. K., Breitrose, H., Brown, B. W., Haskell, W. L., McAlister, A. L., Meyer, A. J., Nash, J. D., & Stern, M. P. (1977, June). Community education for cardiovascular health. *Lancet, 1*, 1192-1195.

Faust, D. (1984). *The limits of scientific reasoning.* Minneapolis: University of Minnesota Press.

Feeley, M. M., & Sarat, A. D. (1980). *The policy dilemma: Federal crime policy and the Law Enforcement Assistance Administration, 1968-1978.* Minneapolis: University of Minnesota Press.

Feigl, H. (1969). The origin and spirit of logical positivism. In P. Achinstein & S. F. Baker (Eds.), *The legacy of logical positivism* (pp. 3-23). Baltimore: Johns Hopkins University Press.

Feyerabend, P. (1975). *Against method.* London: Redwood Burn Limited Trowbridge & Esher.

Flay, B. R. (1986). Efficacy and effectiveness trials (and other phases of research) in the development of health promotion programs. *Preventive Medicine, 15,* 451-474.

Flay, B. R., & Cook, T. D. (1982). The evaluation of mass media prevention campaigns. In R. E. Rice & W. J. Paisley (Eds.), *Public communication campaigns* (pp. 239-264). Beverly Hills, CA: Sage.

Flay, B. R., Koepke, D., Thomson, S. J., Santi, S., Best, J. A., & Brown, K. S. (in press). Six-year follow-up of the first Waterloo school smoking prevention trial. *American Journal of Public Health.*

Fox, G. T. (1981). *Did we really say influence policy through naturalistic inquiry?* Paper presented at the annual convention of the American Educational Research Association, Los Angeles.

Frankfather, D. L. (1982). Welfare entrepreneurialism and the politics of innovation. In E. R. House, S. Mathison, J. A. Pearson, & H. Preskill (Eds.), *Evaluation studies review annual* (Vol. 7, pp. 603-620). Beverly Hills, CA: Sage.

Freedman, D. A. (1987). As others see us: A case study in path analysis. *Journal of Educational Statistics, 12,* 101-128.

Friedrich, C. J. (Ed.). (1962). *NOMOS V: The public interest* (yearbook of the American Society for Political and Legal Philosophy). New York: Atherton.

Fullan, M. (1982). *The meaning of educational change.* New York: Teachers College Press.

Fuller, S. (1989). *Philosophy of science and its discontents.* Boulder, CO: Westview.

Garfield, E. (1979). Is citation analysis a legitimate evaluation tool? *Scientometrics, 1,* 359-375.

Gasking, D. (1955). Causation and recipes. *Mind, 64,* 479-487.

Gholson, B., & Barker, P. (1985). Kuhn, Lakatos, and Laudan: Applications in the history of physics and psychology. *American Psychologist, 40,* 755-769.

Giere, R. (1985). Philosophy of science naturalized. *Philosophy of Science, 52,* 331-356.

Ginsberg, P. E. (1984). The dysfunctional side effects of quantitative indicator production: Illustrations from mental health care (A message from Chicken Little). *Evaluation and Program Planning, 7,* 1-12.

Glass, G. V. (Ed.). (1976). *Evaluation studies review annual* (Vol. 1). Beverly Hills, CA: Sage.

Glass, G. V., & Ellett, F. S. (1980). Evaluation research. In M. R. Rosenzweig & L. W. Porter (Eds.), *Annual review of psychology* (Vol. 31, pp. 211-228). Palo Alto, CA: Annual Reviews.

Glass, G. V., McGaw, B., & Smith, M. L. (1981). *Meta-analysis in social research.* Beverly Hills, CA: Sage.

Glassner, B. (1981). Clinical applications of sociology in health care. *Journal of Applied Behavioral Science, 17,* 330-346.

Glymour, C., & Scheines, R. (1986). Causal modelling with the TETRAD program. *Synthese, 68,* 37-63.

Goodwin, J. S., & Goodwin, J. M. (1984). The tomato effect. *Journal of the American Medical Association, 251,* 2387-2390.

Graesser, A. C., & Clark, L. F. (1985). *Structures and procedures of implicit knowledge.* Norwood, NJ: Ablex.

Guba, E. G. (1981). Investigative journalism. In N. L. Smith (Ed.), *New techniques for evaluation* (pp. 167-262). Beverly Hills, CA: Sage.

Guba, E. G., & Lincoln, Y. S. (1981). *Effective evaluation: Improving the usefulness of evaluation results through responsive and naturalistic approaches.* San Francisco: Jossey-Bass.

Guttentag, M. (1971). Models and methods in evaluation research. *Journal for the Theory of Social Behavior, 1,* 75-95.

Guttentag, M. (1973). Evaluation of social intervention programs. *Annals of the New York Academy of Science, 218,* 3-13.

Habermas, J. (1972). *Knowledge and human interests.* London: Heinemann.

Haney, W. (1977). *The Follow Through evaluation: A technical history.* Cambridge, MA: Huron Institute.

Harris, M. J., & Rosenthal, R. (1985). Mediation of interpersonal expectancy effects: 31 meta-analyses. *Psychological Bulletin, 97,* 363-386.

Hausman, J., & Wise, D. (Eds.). (1985). *Social experimentation.* Chicago: University of Chicago Press.

Haveman, R. H. (1986). *Social experimentation* and social experimentation. *Journal of Human Resources, 21,* 586-605.

Haveman, R. H. (1987). *Poverty policy and poverty research.* Madison: University of Wisconsin Press.

Hayduk, L. A. (1987). *Structural equation modeling with LISREL.* Baltimore: Johns Hopkins University Press.

Heckman, J. J. (1980). Sample selection bias as a specification error. In E. W. Stromsdorfer & G. Farkas (Eds.), *Evaluation studies review annual* (Vol. 5, pp. 13-31). Beverly Hills, CA: Sage.

Heckman, J. J., Hotz, V. J., & Dabos, M. (1987). Do we need experimental data to evaluate the impact of manpower training on earnings? *Evaluation Review, 11,* 395-427.

Hedges, L. V., & Olkin, I. (1985). *Statistical methods for meta-analysis.* Orlando, FL: Academic Press.

Hedrick, T. E. (1981). Maintaining evaluation quality: CETA local evaluation capacities. In L. Datta (Ed.), *Evaluation in change: Meeting new government needs* (pp. 41-56). Beverly Hills, CA: Sage.

Hedrick, T. E. (1988). The interaction of politics and evaluation. *Evaluation Practice, 9,* 5-14.

Heller, K., & Monahan, J. (1977). *Psychology and community change.* Homewood, IL: Dorsey.

Hendricks, M. (1981). Service delivery assessment: Qualitative evaluations at the cabinet level. In N. L. Smith (Ed.), *Federal efforts to develop new evaluation methods* (pp. 5-24). San Francisco: Jossey-Bass.

Hendricks, M. (1982). Oral policy briefings. In N. L. Smith (Ed.), *Communication strategies in evaluation* (pp. 249-258). Beverly Hills, CA: Sage.

Hennigan, K. M., Flay, B. R., & Cook, T. D. (1980). "Give me the facts": Some suggestions for using social science knowledge in national policy-making. In R. F. Kidd & M. J. Saks (Eds.), *Advances in applied social psychology* (Vol. 1, pp. 113-147). Hillsdale, NJ: Lawrence Erlbaum.

Herman, J. L. (Ed.). (1987). *Program evaluation kit* (2nd ed.). Newbury Park, CA: Sage.

Hites, R. W., & Campbell, D. T. (1950). A test of the ability of fraternity leaders to estimate group opinion. *Journal of Social Psychology, 32,* 95-100.

Horst, P., Nay, J. N., Scanlon, J. W., & Wholey, J. S. (1974). Program management and the federal evaluator. *Public Administration Review, 34,* 300-308.

House, E. R. (1980). *Evaluating with validity.* Beverly Hills, CA: Sage.

House, E. R., Glass, G. V, McLean, L. D., & Walker, D. F. (1978). No simple answer: Critique of the Follow Through evaluation. *Harvard Educational Review, 48,* 128-160.

Houts, A. C., Cook, T. D., & Shadish, W. R. (1986). The person-situation debate: A critical multiplist perspective. *Journal of Personality, 54,* 101-154.

Humphreys, P. (Ed.). (1986). Causality in the social sciences [Special issue]. *Synthese, 68*(1).

Jacobs, R. C., & Campbell, D. T. (1961). The perpetuation of an arbitrary tradition through several generations of a laboratory microculture. *Journal of Abnormal and Social Psychology, 62,* 649-658.

Janousek, J. (1970). Comments on Campbell's "Reforms as experiments." *American Psychologist, 25,* 191-193.

Jencks, C. (1984). The hidden prosperity of the 1970s. *Public Interest, 77,* 37-61.

Jerrell, J. (1986). Evaluation in a down-loaded mental health system. *Evaluation and Program Planning, 9,* 161-166.

Johnson, E. L. (1985). Struck down in their prime: The truncation of five federal longitudinal qualitative impact evaluations. *Evaluation Review, 9,* 3-20.

Jones, L. V., & Applebaum, M. I. (1989). Psychometric methods. *Annual Review of Psychology, 40,* 23-43.

Jöreskog, K. G., & Sörbom, D. (1979). *Advances in factor analysis and structural equation models.* Cambridge, MA: Abt.

Kanter, R. M., & Brinkerhoff, D. (1981). Organizational performance: Recent developments in measurement. *Annual Review of Sociology, 7,* 321-349.

Keller, G. (1983). *Academic strategy: The management revolution in American higher education.* Baltimore: Johns Hopkins University Press.

Kelman, S. (1987). *Making public policy: A hopeful view of American government.* New York: Basic Books.

Kenny, D. A. (1982). Review of evaluating with validity. *Educational Evaluation and Policy Analysis, 4,* 121-122.

Kiresuk, T. J. (1973). Goal attainment scaling as a county mental health service. *Evaluation* [Special Monograph No. 1], pp. 12-18.

Kirkhart, K. E., & Attkisson, C. C. (1986). Characteristics of useful evaluation data: An example from community mental health centers. *American Journal of Community Psychology, 14,* 323-337.

Kuhn, T. S. (1970). *The structure of scientific revolutions* (2nd ed.). Chicago: University of Chicago Press.

Kytle, J., & Millman, J. (1986). Confessions of two applied researchers in search of principles. *Evaluation and Program Planning, 9,* 167-177.

LaLonde, R. J. (1985). *Evaluating the econometric evaluations of training programs with experimental data* (Working Paper No. 183, Industrial Relations Section). Princeton, NJ: Princeton University Press.

LaLonde, R. J. (1986). Evaluating the econometric evaluations of training programs with experimental data. *American Economic Review, 76,* 604-620.

Landsberg, G., Neigher, W. D., Hammer, R. J., Windle, C., & Woy, J. R. (Eds.). (1979). *Evaluation in practice: A sourcebook of program evaluation studies from mental health care systems in the United States* (DHEW Publication No. ADM 78-763). Washington, DC: U.S. Government Printing Office.

Lane, R. E. (1986). Market justice, political justice. *American Political Science Review, 80,* 383-402.

Larson, R. C. (1976). What happened to patrol operations in Kansas City? *Evaluation, 3*, 117-123.

Laudan, L. (1981). *Science and hypothesis.* Dordrecht: D. Reidel.

Lazarsfeld, P. F., & Rosenberg, M. (Eds.). (1955). *The language of social research.* Glencoe, IL: Free Press.

Leplin, J. (Ed.). (1984). *Scientific realism.* Berkeley: University of California Press.

Levin, H. M. (1977). A decade of policy developments in improving education and training for low-income populations. In R. H. Haveman (Ed.), *A decade of federal antipoverty programs: Achievements, failures, and lessons* (pp. 123-188). Madison: University of Wisconsin, Institute for Research on Poverty.

Levin, H. M. (1983). *Cost-effectiveness: A primer.* Beverly Hills, CA: Sage.

Leviton, L. C., & Boruch, R. F. (1983). Contributions of evaluation to educational programs and policy. *Evaluation Review, 7*, 563-599.

Leviton, L. C., & Boruch, R. F. (1984). Why the compensatory education evaluation was useful. *Journal of Policy Analysis and Management, 3*, 299-305.

Leviton, L. C., & Cook, T. D. (1983). Evaluation findings in education and social work textbooks. *Evaluation Review, 7*, 497-519.

Leviton, L. C., & Hughes, E. F. X. (1981). Research on the utilization of evaluations: A review and synthesis. *Evaluation Review, 5*, 525-548.

Leviton, L. C., & Valdiserri, R. O. (in press). Evaluating AIDS prevention: Outcome, implementation, and mediating variables. *Evaluation and Program Planning.*

Lewin, K. (1948). *Resolving social conflicts: Selected papers on group dynamics.* New York: Harper & Brothers.

Lewy, A., & Shye, S. (1978). Three main approaches to evaluating education: Analysis and comparison by facet technique. In S. Shye (Ed.), *Theory construction and data analysis in the behavioral sciences: A volume in honor of Louis Guttman* (pp. 210-234). San Francisco: Jossey-Bass.

Life at the edge. (1987, August). *Consumer Reports, 52*, 504-507.

Light, R. J. (Ed.). (1983). *Evaluation studies review annual* (Vol. 8). Beverly Hills, CA: Sage.

Light, R. J., & Pillemer, D. B. (1984). *Summing up: The science of reviewing research.* Cambridge, MA: Harvard University Press.

Lincoln, Y. S., & Guba, E. G. (1985). *Naturalistic inquiry.* Beverly Hills, CA: Sage.

Lincoln, Y. S., & Guba, E. G. (1986). But is it rigorous? Trustworthiness and authenticity in naturalistic evaluation. In D. D. Williams (Ed.), *Naturalistic evaluation* (pp. 73-84). San Francisco: Jossey-Bass.

Lindblom, C. E. (1977). *Politics and markets: The world's political-economic systems.* New York: Basic Books.

Lindblom, C. E. (1983). Comment on Manley. *American Political Science Review, 77*, 384-386.

Lindblom, C. E. (1986). Who needs what social research for policy making? *Knowledge: Creation, Diffusion, Utilization, 7*, 345-366.

Lindblom, C. E., & Cohen, D. K. (1979). *Usable knowledge: Social science and social problem solving.* New Haven, CT: Yale University Press.

Lindquist, E. A. (1988). What do decision models tell us about information use? *Knowledge in Society, 1*, 86-111.

Lipsey, M. W., Crosse, S., Dunkle, J., Pollard, J., & Stobart, G. (1985). Evaluation: The state of the art and the sorry state of the science. In D. S. Cordray (Ed.), *Utilizing prior research in evaluation planning* (pp. 7-28). San Francisco: Jossey-Bass.

Lobosco, A. F., & Kaufman, J. S. (1989). Working with state and local service delivery systems: The politics of evaluating educational opportunity programs at the community college level. *Evaluation Review, 13*, 141-156.

Loehlin, J. C. (1987). *Latent variable models: An introduction to factor, path, and structural analysis.* Hillsdale, NJ: Lawrence Erlbaum.

Lofland, J., & Lofland, L. H. (1984). *Analyzing social settings: A guide to qualitative observation and analysis.* Belmont, CA: Wadsworth.

Luborsky, L. (1954). A note on Eysenck's article "The effects of psychotherapy: An evaluation." *British Journal of Psychology, 45*, 129-131.

Lynch, K. B. (1988). Evaluation practices of educational programs reviewed by the Joint Dissemination Review Panel, 1980-1983. *Evaluation Review, 12*, 253-275.

Lynn, L. E. (1977). A decade of developments in the income-maintenance system. In R. H. Haveman (Ed.), *A decade of federal antipoverty programs: Achievements, failures, and lessons* (pp. 55-117). Madison: University of Wisconsin, Institute for Research on Poverty.

MacDonald, B., & Parlett, M. (1973). Rethinking evaluation: Notes from the Cambridge Conference. *Cambridge Journal of Education, 3*, 74-82.

Machan, T. R. (1977). *Introduction to philosophical inquiries.* Boston: Allyn & Bacon.

MacIntyre, A. (1981). *After virtue.* Notre Dame, IN: University of Notre Dame Press.

Mackie, J. L. (1974). *The cement of the universe: A study of causation.* Oxford: Clarendon.

MacKinnon, R. A., & Michels, R. (1971). *The psychiatric interview in clinical practice.* Philadelphia: W. B. Saunders.

Madaus, G. F., Scriven, M. S., & Stufflebeam, D. L. (Eds.). (1983). *Evaluation models: Viewpoints on educational and human services evaluation.* Boston: Kluwer-Nijhoff.

Madaus, G. F., Stufflebeam, D. L., & Scriven, M. S. (1983). Program evaluation: A historical overview. In G. F. Madaus, M. S. Scriven, & D. L. Stufflebeam (Eds.), *Evaluation models: Viewpoints on educational and human services evaluation* (pp. 3-22). Boston: Kluwer-Nijhoff.

Magidson, J. (1977). Toward a causal-model approach for adjusting for preexisting differences in the nonequivalent control group situations: A general alternative to ANCOVA. *Evaluation Quarterly, 1*, 399-420.

Majchrzak, A. (1986). Information focus and data sources: When will they lead to use? *Evaluation Review, 10*, 193-215.

Manley, J. F. (1983). Neo-pluralism: A class analysis of Pluralism I and Pluralism II. *American Political Science Review, 77*, 368-383.

Mansbridge, J. J. (1983). *Beyond adversary democracy.* Chicago: University of Chicago Press.

Marrow, A. J. (1969). *The practical theorist: The life and work of Kurt Lewin.* New York: Basic Books.

Maxwell, J. A., Bashook, P. G., & Sandlow, L. J. (1986). Combining ethnographic and experimental methods in educational evaluation: A case study. In D. M. Fetterman & M. A. Pitman (Eds.), *Educational evaluation: Ethnography in theory, practice, and politics* (pp. 121-143). Beverly Hills, CA: Sage.

May, J. V., & Wildavsky, A. B. (Eds.). (1978). *The policy cycle.* Beverly Hills, CA: Sage.

McClintock, C. C., & Greene, J. (1985). Triangulation in practice. *Evaluation and Program Planning, 8*, 351-357.

McLaughlin, M. W. (1983). [Review of *Evaluation: A systematic approach* (2nd edition)]. *Evaluation News, 4*, 55-57.

McLaughlin, M. W. (1985). Implementation realities and evaluation design. In R. L. Shotland & M. M. Mark (Eds.), *Social science and social policy* (pp. 96-120). Beverly Hills, CA: Sage.

McMullin, E. (1984). A case for scientific realism. In J. Leplin (Ed.), *Scientific realism* (pp. 8-40). Berkeley: University of California Press.

McNees, M., Hannah, J., Schnelle, J., & Bratton, K. (1977). The effects of aftercare programs on institutional recidivism. *Journal of Community Psychology, 5*, 128-133.

Meehl, P. E. (1986). What social scientists don't understand. In D. W. Fiske & R. A. Shweder (Eds.), *Metatheory in social science* (pp. 315-338). Chicago: University of Chicago Press.

Mielke, K. W., & Chen, M. (1981). *Children, television, and science: An overview of the formative research for 3-2-1 Contact.* New York: Children's Television Workshop.

Miles, M. B., & Huberman, A. M. (1984). *Qualitative data analysis: A sourcebook of new methods.* Beverly Hills, CA: Sage.

Miller, N., Campbell, D. T., Twedt, H., & O'Connell, E. J. (1966). Similarity, contrast, and complementarity in friendship choice. *Journal of Personality and Social Psychology, 3*, 3-12.

Miller, R. C., & Berman, J. S. (1983). The efficacy of cognitive behavior therapies: A quantitative review of the research evidence. *Psychological Bulletin, 94*, 39-53.

Mischel, W. (1973). Toward a cognitive social learning reconceptualization of personality. *Psychological Review, 80*, 252-283.

Morgan, G. (Ed.). (1983). *Beyond method: Strategies for social research.* Beverly Hills, CA: Sage.

Morris, L. L. (Ed.). (1978). *The program evaluation kit.* Beverly Hills, CA: Sage.

Morrow-Bradley, C., & Elliott, R. (1986). Utilization of psychotherapy research by practicing psychotherapists. *American Psychologist, 41*, 188-197.

Moyer, D. F. (1979). Revolution in science: The 1919 eclipse test of general relativity. In B. Kursunoglu, A. Perlmutter, & L. F. Scott (Eds.), *On the path of Albert Einstein* (pp. 55-101). New York: Plenum.

Moynihan, D. P. (1969). *Maximum feasible misunderstanding.* New York: Free Press.

Moynihan, D. P. (1985, April 8-9). *Family and nation.* Paper presented at the Godkin Lectures, Harvard University.

Murnane, R. J., Newstead, S., & Olsen, M. (1985). Comparing public and private schools: The puzzling role of selectivity bias. *Journal of Business and Economic Statistics, 3*, 23-35.

Murray, C. (1984). *Losing ground: American social policy, 1950-1980.* New York: Basic Books.

Nathan, R. P. (1989). *Social science in government: Uses and misuses.* New York: Basic Books.

Nay, J. N., & Kay, P. (1982). *Government oversight and evaluability assessment.* Lexington, MA: D. C. Heath.

Neigher, W. (1982). Introduction. *Evaluation and Program Planning, 5*, 283-286.

Neigher, W. D., & Windle, C. (1979). Projection for a subversive servant. In G. Landsberg, W. D. Neigher, R. J. Hammer, C. Windle, & J. R. Woy (Eds.), *Evaluation in practice: A sourcebook of program evaluation studies from mental health care systems in the United States* (DHEW Publication No. ADM 78-763) (pp. 227-230). Washington, DC: U.S. Government Printing Office.

Neimeyer, R. A., & Shadish, W. R. (1987). Optimizing scientific validity: Toward an interdisciplinary science studies. *Knowledge: Creation, Diffusion, Utilization, 8*, 463-485.

Nevasky, V. S., & Paster, D. (1976). Background paper. In Twentieth Century Fund Task Force on the Law Enforcement Assistance Administration, *Law enforcement: The federal role* (pp. 25-135). New York: McGraw-Hill.

Nozick, R. (1974). *Anarchy, state and utopia.* New York: Basic Books.

Pacht, A. R., Bent, R., Cook, T. D., Klebanoff, L. B., Rodgers, D. A., Sechrest, L., Strupp, H., & Theaman, M. (1978). Continuing evaluation and accountability controls for a national health insurance program. *American Psychologist, 33,* 305-313.

Patton, M. Q. (1978). *Utilization-focused evaluation.* Beverly Hills, CA: Sage.

Patton, M. Q. (1980). *Qualitative evaluation methods.* Beverly Hills, CA: Sage.

Patton, M. Q. (1987, October). *The evaluator's responsibility for utilization.* Invited address to the annual convention of the American Evaluation Association, Boston.

Patton, M. Q. (1988). The evaluator's responsibility for utilization. *Evaluation Practice, 9,* 5-24.

Polanyi, M. (1962). The republic of science: Its political and economic theory. *Minerva, 1,* 54-73.

Polanyi, M. (1966). *The tacit dimension.* Garden City, NY: Doubleday.

Polsby, N. W. (1984). *Political innovation in American: The politics of policy initiation.* New Haven, CT: Yale University Press.

Popper, K. (1968). *The logic of scientific discovery.* New York: Harper Torchbooks.

Popper, K. R. (1972). *Objective knowledge: An evolutionary approach.* Oxford: Oxford University Press.

Pressman, J. L., & Wildavsky, A. (1973). *Implementation.* Berkeley: University of California Press.

Pressman, J. L., & Wildavsky, A. (1984). *Implementation* (3rd ed.). Berkeley: University of California Press.

Putnam, H. (1984). What is realism? In J. Leplin (Ed.), *Scientific realism* (pp. 140-153). Berkeley: University of California Press.

Quirk, P. J. (1986). [Review of *Public policy*]. *Journal of Policy Analysis and Management, 6,* 607-613.

Rahman, M. A. (1985). The theory and practice of participatory action research. In O. Fals Borda (Ed.), *The challenge of social change* (pp. 107-132). Beverly Hills, CA: Sage.

Rankin, R. E., & Campbell, D. T. (1955). Galvanic skin response to Negro and White experiments. *Journal of Abnormal and Social Psychology, 51,* 30-33.

Rawls, J. (1971). *A theory of justice.* Cambridge, MA: Harvard University Press.

Rayner, M. (1986). Evaluation in Canada. *Evaluation Practice, 7,* 46-56.

Reichardt, C. S., & Cook, T. D. (1979). Beyond qualitative versus quantitative methods. In T. D. Cook & C. S. Reichardt (Eds.), *Qualitative and quantitative methods in evaluation research* (pp. 7-32). Beverly Hills, CA: Sage.

Reichardt, C. S., & Gollob, H. F. (1986). Satisfying the constraints of causal modelling. In W. M. K. Trochim (Ed.), *Advances in quasi-experimental design and analysis* (pp. 91-107). San Francisco: Jossey-Bass.

Rescher, N. (1969). *Introduction to value theory.* Englewood Cliffs, NJ: Prentice-Hall.

Reynolds, P. D. (1971). *A primer in theory construction.* Indianapolis: Bobbs-Merrill.

Riecken, H. W., Boruch, R. F., Campbell, D. T., Caplan, N., Glennan, T. K., Pratt, J. W., Rees, A., & Williams, W. (1974). *Social experimentation: A method for planning and evaluating social intervention.* New York: Academic Press.

Rindskopf, D. M. (1981). Structural equation models in analysis of nonexperimental data. In R. F. Boruch, P. M. Wortman, & D. S. Cordray (Eds.), *Reanalyzing program evaluations.* San Francisco: Jossey-Bass.

Rog, D. J. (1985). *A methodological analysis of evaluability assessment.* Unpublished doctoral dissertation, Vanderbilt University.

Rog, D. J., & Bickman, L. (1984). The feedback research approach to evaluation: A method to increase evaluation utility. *Evaluation and Program Planning, 7,* 169-175.

Rossi, P. H. (1971a). Evaluating educational programs. In F. G. Caro (Ed.), *Readings in evaluation research* (pp. 97-99). New York: Russell Sage Foundation.

Rossi, P. H. (1971b). Evaluating social action programs. In F. G. Caro (Ed.), *Readings in evaluation research* (pp. 276-281). New York: Russell Sage Foundation.

Rossi, P. H. (1972). Boobytraps and pitfalls in the evaluation of social action programs. In C. H. Weiss (Ed.), *Evaluating action programs: Readings in social action and education* (pp. 224-235). Boston: Allyn & Bacon.

Rossi, P. H. (1979). Issues in the evaluation of human services delivery. In L. Sechrest, S. G. West, M. A. Phillips, R. Redner, & W. Yeaton (Eds.), *Evaluation studies review annual* (Vol. 4, pp. 69-93). Beverly Hills, CA: Sage.

Rossi, P. H. (1981). The professionalization of evaluation research in the United States. In R. A. Levine, M. A. Solomon, G. M. Hellstern, & H. Wollmann (Eds.), *Evaluation research and practice: Comparative and international perspectives* (pp. 220-236). Beverly Hills, CA: Sage.

Rossi, P. H. (1982a). Some dissenting comments on Stake's review. In E. R. House, S. Mathison, J. A. Pearsol, & H. Preskill (Eds.), *Evaluation studies review annual* (Vol. 7, pp. 61-64). Beverly Hills, CA: Sage.

Rossi, P. H. (Ed.). (1982b). *Standards for evaluation practice.* San Francisco: Jossey-Bass.

Rossi, P. H. (1983). Pussycats, weasels or percherons? Current prospects for social science under the Reagan regime. *Evaluation News, 4,* 12-27.

Rossi, P. H. (1985, April 17). *The iron law of evaluation and other metallic rules.* Paper presented at State University of New York, Albany, Rockefeller College.

Rossi, P. H., Berk, R. A., & Lenihan, K. J. (1980). *Money, work, and crime: Some experimental evidence.* New York: Academic Press.

Rossi, P. H., & Freeman, H. E. (1982). *Evaluation: A systematic approach* (2nd ed.). Beverly Hills, CA: Sage.

Rossi, P. H., & Freeman, H. E. (1985). *Evaluation: A systematic approach* (3rd ed.). Beverly Hills, CA: Sage.

Rossi, P. H., & Freeman, H. E. (1989). *Evaluation: A systematic approach* (4th ed.). Newbury Park, CA: Sage.

Rossi, P. H., Freeman, H. E., & Wright, S. R. (1979). *Evaluation: A systematic approach.* Beverly Hills, CA: Sage.

Rossi, P. H., & Lyall, K. C. (1976). *Reforming public welfare.* New York: Russell Sage Foundation.

Rossi, P. H., & Lyall, K. C. (1978). An overview evaluation of the NIT Experiment. In T. D. Cook, M. L. DelRosario, K. M. Hennigan, M. M. Mark, & W. M. K. Trochim (Eds.), *Evaluation studies review annual* (Vol. 3, pp. 412-428). Beverly Hills, CA: Sage.

Rossi, P. H., & Nock, S. L. (Eds.). (1982). *Measuring social judgments: The factorial survey approach.* Beverly Hills, CA: Sage.

Rossi, P. H., & Williams, W. (Eds.). (1972). *Evaluating social programs.* New York: Seminar.

Rossi, P. H., & Wright, J. D. (1984). Evaluation research: An assessment. *Annual Review of Sociology, 10,* 331-352.

Rossi, P. H., & Wright, J. D. (1985). Social science research and the politics of gun control. In L. Shotland & M. M. Mark (Eds.), *Social science and social policy* (pp. 311-332). Beverly Hills, CA: Sage.

Rossi, P. H., Wright, J. D., & Anderson, A. (Eds.) (1983). *Handbook of survey research.* New York: Academic Press.

Rossi, P. H., & Wright, S. R. (1977). Evaluation research: An assessment of theory, practice, and politics. *Evaluation Quarterly, 1,* 5-52.

Salasin, S. (1973). Experimentation revisited: A conversation with Donald T. Campbell. *Evaluation, 1,* 7-13.

Salasin, S. (1974). Exploring goal-free evaluation: An interview with Michael Scriven. *Evaluation, 2,* 9-16.

Salasin, S. (1980). The evaluator as an agent of change. *New Directions for Program Evaluation, 7,* 1-9.

Sarason, S. B. (1981). An asocial psychology and a misdirected clinical psychology. *American Psychologist, 36,* 827-836.

Saxe, L. (1986). Policymakers' use of social science research: Technology assessment in the U.S. Congress. *Knowledge: Creation, Diffusion, Utilization, 8,* 59-78.

Saxe, L., & Bickman, L. (1987, December). *Preliminary evaluation of research program activities of preventive intervention research centers.* Preliminary report to National Institute of Mental Health.

Scanlon, J. W., & Bell, J. (1981, May). *Short term study of evaluability assessment activity in the Public Health Service.* Washington, DC: U.S. Department of Health and Human Services, Office of the Assistant Secretary for Health.

Schmidt, R. E., Scanlon, J. W., & Bell, J. B. (1979). *Evaluability assessment: Making public programs work better.* Rockville, MD: U.S. Department of Health and Human Services, Project Share.

Schubert, G. (1960). *The public interest: Critique of a political concept.* Glencoe, IL: Free Press.

Scriven, M. (1966). *Value claims in the social sciences* (Social Science Education Consortium Publication No. 123). Lafayette, IN: Purdue University.

Scriven, M. (1967). The methodology of evaluation. In R. W. Tyler, R. M. Gagne, & M. Scriven (Eds.), *Perspectives of curriculum evaluation* (pp. 39-83). Chicago: Rand McNally.

Scriven, M. (1969). An introduction to meta-evaluation. *Educational Product Report, 2,* 36-38.

Scriven, M. (1971). Evaluating educational programs. In F. G. Caro (Ed.), *Readings in evaluation research* (pp. 49-53). New York: Russell Sage Foundation.

Scriven, M. (1972a). The methodology of evaluation. In C. H. Weiss (Ed.), *Evaluating action programs: Readings in social action and education* (pp. 123-136). Boston: Allyn & Bacon.

Scriven, M. (1972b). Objectivity and subjectivity in educational research. In L. G. Thomas (Ed.), *Philosophical redirection of educational research: The seventy-first yearbook of the National Society for the Study of Education* (pp. 94-142). Chicago: University of Chicago Press.

Scriven, M. (1973). Goal-free evaluation. In E. R. House (Ed.), *School evaluation: The politics and process (pp. 319-328).* Berkeley, CA: McCutchan.

Scriven, M. (1974). Evaluation perspectives and procedures. In J. W. Popham (Ed.), *Evaluation in education: Current application* (pp. 3-93). Berkeley, CA: McCutchan.

Scriven, M. (1976a). Payoffs from evaluation. In C. C. Abt (Ed.), *The evaluation of social programs* (pp. 217-224). Beverly Hills, CA: Sage.

Scriven, M. (1976b). Evaluation bias and its control. In G. V Glass (Ed.), *Evaluation studies review annual* (Vol. 1, pp. 101-118). Beverly Hills, CA: Sage.

Scriven, M. (1976c). Maximizing the power of causal investigation: The modus operandi method. In G. V Glass (Ed.), *Evaluation studies review annual* (Vol. 1, pp. 120-139). Beverly Hills, CA: Sage.

Scriven, M. (1980). *The logic of evaluation.* Inverness, CA: Edgepress.

Scriven, M. (1981a). The good news and the bad news about product evaluation. *Evaluation News, 2,* 278-282.

Scriven, M. (1981b). Product evaluation. In N. L. Smith (Ed.), *New techniques for evaluation* (pp. 121-166). Beverly Hills, CA: Sage.

Scriven, M. (1982). Serious product evaluation: Some field notes. *Evaluation News, 3,* 89-93.

Scriven, M. S. (1983a). Evaluation ideologies. In G. F. Madaus, M. Scriven, & D. L. Stufflebeam (Eds.), *Evaluation models: Viewpoints on educational and human services evaluation* (pp. 229-260). Boston: Kluwer-Nijhoff.

Scriven, M. S. (1983b). The evaluation taboo. In E. R. House (Ed.), *Philosophy of evaluation* (pp. 75-82). San Francisco: Jossey-Bass.

Scriven, M. S. (1986a). New frontiers of evaluation. *Evaluation Practice, 7,* 7-44.

Scriven, M. S. (1986b). *Probative logic.* Paper presented at the First International Conference on Argumentation, Amsterdam.

Scully, D., & Windle, C. (1976). Community mental health centers and the decreasing use of state mental hospitals. *Community Mental Health Journal, 12,* 239-243.

Sechrest, L., West, S. G., Phillips, M., Redner, R., & Yeaton, W. (1979). Some neglected problems in evaluation research: Strength and integrity of treatments. In L. Sechrest & Associates (Eds.), *Evaluation studies review annual* (Vol. 4, 15-35). Beverly Hills, CA: Sage.

Segal, S. P., & Aviram, U. (1978). *The mentally ill in community-based sheltered care: A study of community care and social integration.* New York: John Wiley.

Segall, M. H., Campbell, D. T., & Herskovits, M. J. (1966). *The influence of culture on visual perception.* Indianapolis: Bobbs-Merrill.

Senf, J. H. (1987). The option to refuse: A tool in understanding nonresponse in mailed surveys. *Evaluation Review, 11,* 775-781.

Shadish, W. R. (October, 1979). *Interfaces between management information systems and evaluation research.* Paper presented at the annual meeting of the Evaluation Research Society, Minneapolis.

Shadish, W. R. (1984). Policy research: Lessons from the implementation of deinstitutionalization. *American Psychologist, 39,* 725-738.

Shadish, W. R. (1986a). Planned critical multiplism: Some elaborations. *Behavioral Assessment, 8,* 75-103.

Shadish, W. R. (1986b). Sources of evaluation practice: Needs, purposes, questions, and technology. In L. Bickman & D. L. Weatherford (Eds.), *Evaluating early intervention programs for severely handicapped children and their families* (pp. 149-183). Austin, TX: Pro-Ed.

Shadish, W. R. (1987a, April 15). *American experiences evaluating social and health programs.* Invited address to the conference, Evaluation: Basis for Assessing Social and Health Care Programs, sponsored jointly by the University of Freiburg Department of Psychology and the German Ministry of Youth, Family, Women, and Health, Konigswinter, West Germany.

Shadish, W. R. (1987b). Program micro- and macrotheories: A guide for social change. In L. Bickman (Ed.), *Using program theory in evaluation* (pp. 93-109). San Francisco: Jossey-Bass.

Shadish, W. R. (1989). The perception and evaluation of quality in science. In B. Gholson, W. R. Shadish, R. A. Neimeyer, & A. C. Houts (Eds.), *The psychology of science: Contributions to metascience* (pp. 383-426). Cambridge: Cambridge University Press.

Shadish, W. R. (1990). Criteria for excellence in community research. In P. Tolan, C. Keys, F. Chertok, & L. Jason (Eds.), *Researching community psychology: Integrating theories and methods.* Washington DC: American Psychological Association.

Shadish, W. R., & Cook, T. D. (1985). *Social welfare programs and the material condition of poorer Americans: Towards a differentiated picture of the effects of past and current policies.* Unpublished grant proposal submitted to the Ford Foundation.

Shadish, W. R., Cook, T. D., & Houts, A. C. (1986). Quasi-experimentation in a critical multiplist mode. In W. M. K. Trochim (Ed.), *Advances in quasi-experimental design and analysis* (pp. 29-46). San Francisco: Jossey-Bass.

Shadish, W. R., & Epstein, R. E. (1987). Patterns of program evaluation practice among members of Evaluation Research Society and Evaluation Network. *Evaluation Review, 11*, 555-590.

Shadish, W. R., & Reichardt, C. S. (1987). The intellectual foundations of social program evaluation: The development of evaluation theory. In W. R. Shadish & C. S. Reichardt (Eds.), *Evaluation studies review annual* (Vol. 12, pp. 13-30). Newbury Park, CA: Sage.

Shadish, W. R., & Reis, J. (1984). A review of studies of the effectiveness of programs to improve pregnancy outcome. *Evaluation Review, 8*, 747-776.

Shadish, W. R., Thomas, S., & Bootzin, R. R. (1982). Criteria for success in deinstitutionalization: Perceptions of nursing homes by different interest groups. *American Journal of Community Psychology, 10*, 553-566.

Shaver, P., & Staines, G. (1971). Problems facing Campbell's "experimenting society." *Urban Affairs Quarterly, 7*, 173-186.

Smith, M. L., Glass, G. V, & Miller, T. I. (1980). *The benefits of psychotherapy.* Baltimore: Johns Hopkins University Press.

Smith, N. L. (1981). Classic 1960s articles in educational evaluation. *Evaluation and Program Planning, 4*, 177-183.

Smith, N. L. (Ed.). (1982). *Communication strategies in evaluation.* Beverly Hills, CA: Sage.

Solso, R. L. (1987). Recommended readings in psychology over the past 33 years. *American Psychologist, 42*, 1130-1132.

Spearly, J. L. (1980). Evaluating the impact of community mental health centers on hospital admissions: An interrupted time-series analysis. *American Journal of Community Psychology, 8*, 229-242.

Sproull, L., & Larkey, P. (1979). Managerial behavior and evaluator effectiveness. In H. C. Schulberg & J. M. Jerrell (Eds.), *The evaluator and management* (pp. 89-104). Beverly Hills, CA: Sage.

Stake, R. E. (1967). The countenance of educational evaluation. *Teachers College Record, 68*, 523-540.

Stake, R. E. (1969). Generalizability of program evaluation. *Educational Product Report, 2*, 39-40.

Stake, R. E. (1970). Objectives, priorities, and other judgment data. *Review of Educational Research, 40*, 181-212.

Stake, R. E. (1975a). An interview with Robert Stake on responsive evaluation. In R. E. Stake (Ed.), *Evaluating the arts in education: A responsive approach* (pp. 33-38). Columbus, OH: Merrill.

Stake, R. E. (1975b). To evaluate an arts program. In R. E. Stake (Ed.), *Evaluating the arts in education: A responsive approach* (pp. 13-31). Columbus, OH: Merrill.

Stake, R. E. (1978). The case study method in social inquiry. *Educational Researcher, 7*, 5-8.

Stake, R. E. (1979). Validating representations: The evaluator's responsibility. In R. Perloff (Ed.), *Evaluator interventions: Pros and cons* (pp. 55-70). Beverly Hills, CA: Sage.

Stake, R. E. (1980a). Program evaluation, particularly responsive evaluation. In W. B. Dockrell & D. Hamilton (Eds.), *Rethinking educational research* (pp. 72-87). London: Hodder & Stoughton.

Stake, R. E. (1980b). Quality of education and the diminution of local control in schools in the United States. In U.S. House of Representatives, Committee on Education and Labor, *Needs of elementary and secondary education in the 1980's* (pp. 161-168). Washington, DC: U.S. Government Printing Office.

Stake, R. E. (1981). Case study methodology: An epistemological advocacy. In W. Welch (Ed.), *Case study methodology in educational evaluation*. Minneapolis: Minnesota Research and Evaluation Center.

Stake, R. E. (1982a). How sharp should the evaluator's teeth be? *Evaluation News, 3,* 79-80.

Stake, R. E. (1982b, Summer). Persuasions, not models. *ERS Newsletter, 6,* 8.

Stake, R. E. (1982c). The two cultures and the evaluation evolution. *Evaluation News, 3,* 10-14.

Stake, R. E. (1983a). Stakeholder influence in the evaluation of Cities-in-Schools. In A. S. Bryk (Ed.), *New directions for program evaluation* (pp. 15-30). San Francisco: Jossey-Bass.

Stake, R. E. (1983b). Two observations. *Evaluation News, 4,* 72-74.

Stake, R. E. (1986a). An evolutionary view of education improvement. In E. House (Ed.), *New directions in educational evaluation* (pp. 89-102). London: Farmer.

Stake, R. E. (1986b). *Quieting reform.* Urbana: University of Illinois Press.

Stake, R. E., & Balk, D. E. (1982). Briefing panel presentations. In N. L. Smith (Ed.), *Communication strategies in evaluation* (pp. 259-267). Beverly Hills, CA: Sage.

Stake, R. E., & Easley, J. A. (1978). *Case studies in science education.* Champaign: University of Illinois, Center for Instructional Research and Curriculum Evaluation.

Stake, R. E., & Gjerde, C. (1974). *An evaluation of TCITY: The Twin City Institute for Talented Youth* (AERA Monograph Series in Curriculum Evaluation, No. 7). Chicago: Rand McNally.

Stake, R. E., Raths, J., Denny, T., Stenzel, N., & Hoke, G. (1986, September 15). *Final report: Evaluation study of the Indiana Department of Education Gifted and Talented Program.* Champaign: University of Illinois, Center for Instructional Research and Curriculum Evaluation.

Stake, R. E., & Trumbull, D. J. (1982). Naturalistic generalizations. *Review Journal of Philosophy and Social Science, 7,* 1-12.

Stanford Evaluation Consortium. (1976). Review essay: Evaluating the *Handbook of evaluation research.* In G. V Glass (Ed.), *Evaluation studies review annual* (Vol. 1, pp. 195-215). Beverly Hills, CA: Sage.

Starfield, B., & Scheff, D. (1972). Effectiveness of pediatric care: The relationship between processes and outcome. *Pediatrics, 49,* 547-552.

Stokey, E., & Zeckhauser, R. (1978). *A primer for policy analysis.* New York: W. W. Norton.

Stolzenberg, R. M., & Relles, D. A. (1990). Theory testing in a world of constrained research design: The significance of Heckman's censored sampling bias correction for nonexperimental research. *Sociological Research and Methods, 18,* 395-415.

Stromsdorfer, E. W. (1987). Economic evaluation of the Comprehensive Employment and Training Act: An overview of recent findings and advances in evaluation methods. *Evaluation Review, 11,* 387-394.

Stromsdorfer, E. W., & Farkas, G. (Eds.). (1980). *Evaluation studies review annual* (Vol. 5). Beverly Hills, CA: Sage.

Strosberg, M., & Wholey, J. (1983). Evaluability assessment: From theory to practice in the Department of Health and Human Services. *Public Administration Review, 43*, 66-71.

Stufflebeam, D. L., & Webster, W. J. (1981). An analysis of alternative approaches to evaluation. In H. E. Freeman & M. A. Solomon (Eds.), *Evaluation studies review annual* (Vol. 6, pp. 70-85). Beverly Hills, CA: Sage.

Suchman, E. A. (1967). *Evaluative research: Principles and practice in public service and social action programs.* New York: Russell Sage Foundation.

Tabor, J. G. (1977). The role of the accountant in preventing and detecting information abuses in social program evaluation. In H. W. Melton & D. J. H. Watson (Eds.), *Interdisciplinary dimensions of accounting for social goals and social organizations* (pp. 77-100). Columbus, OH: Grid.

Tavris, C. (1975, September). The experimenting society: To find programs that work, government must measure its failures. *Psychology Today, 9*(4), 46-56.

Thompson, M. S. (1980). *Benefit-cost analysis for program evaluation.* Beverly Hills, CA: Sage.

Trend, M. G. (1979). On the reconciliation of qualitative and quantitative analyses: A case study. In T. D. Cook & C. S. Reichardt (Eds.), *Qualitative and quantitative methods in evaluation research* (pp. 68-86). Beverly Hills, CA: Sage.

Trochim, W. M. K. (1984). *Research design for program evaluation: The regression-discontinuity approach.* Beverly Hills, CA: Sage.

Tukey, J. W. (1977). *Exploratory data analysis.* Reading, MA: Addison-Wesley.

Tyler, R. (1935). Evaluation: A challenge to progressive education. *Educational Research Bulletin, 14*, 9-16.

U.S. Bureau of the Census (1951). *Statistical abstracts of the United States* (72nd ed.). Washington DC: U.S. Government Printing Office.

U.S. Bureau of the Census (1962). *Statistical abstracts of the United States* (83rd ed.). Washington DC: U.S. Government Printing Office.

U.S. Bureau of the Census (1972). *Statistical abstracts of the United States* (93rd ed.). Washington DC: U.S. Government Printing Office.

U.S. Bureau of the Census (1989). *Statistical abstracts of the United States* (109th ed.). Washington DC: U.S. Government Printing Office.

U.S. Department of Education. (1986). *What works: Research about teaching and learning.* Washington, DC: Author.

U.S. General Accounting Office. (1974). *Need for more effective management of community mental health centers program* (Report to the Congress, B-164031-5). Washington, DC: U.S. Government Printing Office.

U.S. General Accounting Office. (1982). *A profile of federal program evaluation activities* (Institute for Program Evaluation: Special Study 1). Washington DC: Author.

U.S. General Accounting Office. (1988). *Program evaluation issues* (GAO/OCG-89-8TR). Washington DC: Author.

Warnock, G. J. (1971). *The object of morality.* London: Methuen.

Webb, E. J., Campbell, D. T., Schwartz, R. D., & Sechrest, L. B. (1966). *Unobtrusive measures: Nonreactive research in the social sciences.* Chicago: Rand McNally.

Weiss, C. H. (1966, September 1). *Utilization of evaluation: Toward comparative study.* Paper presented at the annual meeting of the American Sociological Association, Miami Beach, FL.

Weiss, C. H. (1967). Utilization of evaluation: Toward comparative study. In U.S. House of Representatives, Committee on Government Operations, Research and Technical Programs Subcommittee, *The use of social research in federal domestic programs* (Vol. 3, pp. 426-432). Washington DC: U.S. Government Printing Office.

Weiss, C. H. (1970). The politicization of evaluation research. *Journal of Social Issues, 26,* 57-68.

Weiss, C. H. (1972a). Evaluating educational and social action programs: A treeful of owls. In C. H. Weiss (Ed.), *Evaluating action programs: Readings in social action and education* (pp. 3-27). Boston: Allyn & Bacon.

Weiss, C. H. (1972b). *Evaluation research: Methods for assessing program effectiveness.* Englewood Cliffs, NJ: Prentice-Hall.

Weiss, C. H. (1972c). The politicization of evaluation research. In C. H. Weiss (Ed.), *Evaluating action programs: Readings in social action and education* (pp. 327-338). Boston: Allyn & Bacon.

Weiss, C. H. (1972d). Utilization of evaluation: Toward comparative study. In C. H. Weiss (Ed.), *Evaluating action programs: Readings in social action and education* (pp. 318-326). Boston: Allyn & Bacon.

Weiss, C. H. (1973a). The politics of impact measurement. *Policy Studies Journal, 1,* 179-183.

Weiss, C. H. (1973b). Where politics and evaluation research meet. *Evaluation, 1,* 37-45.

Weiss, C. H. (1976). Using research in the policy process: Potential and constraints. *Policy Studies Journal, 4,* 224-228.

Weiss, C. H. (1977a). Introduction. In C. H. Weiss (Ed.), *Using social research in public policy making* (pp. 1-22). Lexington, MA: Lexington.

Weiss, C. H. (1977b). Research for policy's sake: The enlightenment function of social research. *Policy Analysis, 3,* 531-545.

Weiss, C. H. (1978). Improving the linkage between social research and public policy. In L. E. Lynn (Ed.), *Knowledge and policy: The uncertain connection* (pp. 23-81). Washington, DC: National Academy of Sciences.

Weiss, C. H. (1979). Social science fiction. In G. Landsberg, W. D. Neigher, R. J. Hammer, C. Windle, & J. R. Woy (Eds.), *Evaluation in practice: A sourcebook of program evaluation studies from mental health care systems in the United States* (DHEW Publication No. ADM 78-763) (pp. 242-243). Washington, DC: U.S. Government Printing Office.

Weiss, C. H. (1980a). Efforts at bureaucratic reform: What have we learned? In C. H. Weiss & A. H. Barton (Eds.), *Making bureaucracies work* (pp. 7-26). Beverly Hills, CA: Sage.

Weiss, C. H. (1980b). Knowledge creep and decision accretion. *Knowledge: Creation, Diffusion, Utilization, 1,* 381-404.

Weiss, C. H. (1981a). Doing research or doing policy [Review of *Toward reform of program evaluation*]. *Evaluation and Program Planning, 4,* 397-402.

Weiss, C. H. (1981b). Measuring the use of evaluation. In J. A. Ciarlo (Ed.), *Utilizing evaluation: Concepts and measuring techniques* (pp. 17-33). Beverly Hills, CA: Sage.

Weiss, C. H. (1982). Policy research in the context of diffuse decision making. *Journal of Higher Education, 53,* 619-639.

Weiss, C. H. (1983a). The stakeholder approach to evaluation: Origins and promise. In A. S. Bryk (Ed.), *Stakeholder-based evaluation* (pp. 3-14). San Francisco: Jossey-Bass.

Weiss, C. H. (1983b). Toward the future of stakeholder approaches in evaluation. In A. S. Bryk (Ed.), *Stakeholder-based evaluation* (pp. 83-96). San Francisco: Jossey-Bass.

Weiss, C. H. (1983c). Ideology, interest, and information: The basis of policy decisions. In D. Callahan & B. Jennings (Eds.), *Ethics, the social sciences, and policy analysis* (pp. 213-245). New York: Plenum.

Weiss, C. H. (1987a). The circuitry of enlightenment. *Knowledge: Creation, Diffusion, Utilization, 8,* 274-281.

Weiss, C. H. (1987b). Evaluating social programs: What have we learned? *Society, 25*(1), 40-45.

Weiss, C. H. (1988a). Evaluation for decisions: Is anybody there? Does anybody care? *Evaluation Practice, 9*, 5-20.

Weiss, C. H. (1988b). If program decisions hinged only on information: A response to Patton. *Evaluation Practice, 9*, 15-28.

Weiss, C. H. (in press). Postscript to "Where politics and evaluation research meet." In D. Palumbo (Ed.), *The politics of program evaluation.* Newbury Park, CA: Sage.

Weiss, C. H., & Bucuvalas, M. J. (1977). The challenge of social research to decision making. In C. H. Weiss (Ed.), *Using social research in public policy making* (pp. 213-234). Lexington, MA: Lexington.

Weiss, C. H., & Bucuvalas, M. J. (1980). *Social science research and decision-making.* New York: Columbia University Press.

Weiss, C. H., & Bucuvalas, M. J. (1981). Truth tests and utility tests: Decision-makers' frame of reference for social science research. In H. E. Freeman & M. A. Solomon (Eds.), *Evaluation studies review annual* (Vol. 6, pp. 695-706). Beverly Hills, CA: Sage.

Weiss, D. J., & Davison, M. L. (1981). Test theory and methods. *Annual Review of Psychology, 32*, 629-658.

Weiss, J. A., & Weiss, C. H. (1981). Social scientists and decision makers look at the usefulness of mental health research. *American Psychologist, 36*, 837-847.

Weiss, R. S., & Rein, M. (1969). The evaluation of broad-aim programs: A cautionary case and a moral. *Annals of the American Academy of Political and Social Science, 385*, 133-142.

Weiss, R. S., & Rein, M. (1970). The evaluation of broad-aim programs: Experimental design, its difficulties, and an alternative. *Administrative Science Quarterly, 15*, 97-109.

Werner, O., & Campbell, D. T. (1970). Translating, working through interpreters, and the problem of decentering. In R. Naroll & R. Cohen (Eds.), *A handbook of method in cultural anthropology* (pp. 398-420). New York: Natural History Press/Doubleday.

Whitbeck, C. (1977). Causation in medicine: The disease entity model. *Philosophy of Science, 44*, 619-637.

Wholey, J. S. (1977). Evaluability assessment. In L. Rutman (Ed.), *Evaluation research methods: A basic guide.* Beverly Hills, CA: Sage.

Wholey, J. S. (1979). *Evaluation: Promise and performance.* Washington, DC: Urban Institute.

Wholey, J. S. (1981). Using evaluation to improve program performance. In R. A. Levine, M. A. Solomon, G. M. Hellstern, & H. Wollman (Eds.), *Evaluation research and practice: Comparative and international perspectives* (pp. 92-106). Beverly Hills, CA: Sage.

Wholey, J. S. (1982). Results oriented management: Integrating evaluation and organizational performance incentives. In G. J. Stahler & W. R. Tash (Eds.), *Innovative approaches to mental health evaluation* (pp. 255-276). New York: Academic Press.

Wholey, J. S. (1983). *Evaluation and effective public management.* Boston: Little, Brown.

Wholey, J. S. (1985). Managing for high performance: The role of evaluation. *Evaluation News, 6*, 40-50.

Wholey, J. S. (1986a). The Job Corps: Congressional use of evaluation findings. In J. S. Wholey, M. A. Abramson, & C. Bellavita (Eds.), *Performance and credibility: Developing excellence in public and nonprofit organizations* (pp. 245-255). Lexington, MA: Lexington.

Wholey, J. S. (1986b). Using evaluation to improve government performance. *Evaluation Practice, 7*, 5-13.

Wholey, J. S. (1986c). WIC: Positive outcomes for a demonstrably effective program. In J. S. Wholey, M. A. Abramson, & C. Bellavita (Eds.), *Performance and credibility: Developing excellence in public and nonprofit organizations* (pp. 271-283). Lexington, MA: Lexington.

Wholey, J. S. (Ed.). (1987). *Organizational excellence: Stimulating quality and communicating value.* Lexington, MA: D. C. Heath.

Wholey, J. S., Abramson, M. A., & Bellavita, C. (1986). Managing for high performance: Roles for evaluators. In J. S. Wholey, M. A. Abramson, & C. Bellavita (Eds.), *Performance and credibility: Developing excellence in public and nonprofit organizations* (pp. 1-13). Lexington, MA: Lexington.

Wholey, J. S., Duffy, H. G., Fukumoto, J. S., Scanlon, J. W., Berlin, M. A., Copeland, W. C., & Zelinsky, J. G. (1972). Proper organizational relationships. In C. H. Weiss (Ed.), *Evaluating action programs: Readings in social action and education* (pp. 118-122). Boston: Allyn & Bacon.

Wholey, J. S., Nay, J. N., Scanlon, J. W., & Schmidt, R. E. (1975a). Evaluation: When is it really needed? *Evaluation, 2,* 89-93.

Wholey, J. S., Nay, J. N., Scanlon, J. W., & Schmidt, R. E. (1975b). If you don't care where you get to, then it doesn't matter which way you go. In G. M. Lyons (Ed.), *Social research and public policies: The Dartmouth/OECD Conference* (pp. 175-197). Hanover, NH: Dartmouth College.

Wholey, J. S., Scanlon, J. W., Duffy, H. G., Fukumoto, J. S., & Vogt, L. M. (1970). *Federal evaluation policy: Analyzing the effects of public programs.* Washington, DC: Urban Institute.

Wholey, J. S., & White, B. F. (1973). Evaluation's impact on Title I elementary and secondary education program management. *Evaluation, 1,* 73-76.

Williams, J. E. (1989). A numerically developed taxonomy of evaluation theory and practice. *Evaluation Review, 13,* 18-32.

Williams, L., & Light, E. (1982). Appendix A: Trends over a decade in the NIMH federal evaluation program. *Evaluation and Program Planning, 5,* 299-301.

Williams, W. (1980). *The implementation perspective.* Berkeley: University of California Press.

Williams, W., & Evans, J. W. (1969). The politics of evaluation: The case of Head Start. *Annals of the American Academy of Political and Social Science, 385,* 118-132.

Windle, C. (1982). Limited and limiting perspectives. *Evaluation and Program Planning, 5,* 296-298.

Windle, C., Goldsmith, J., Schambaugh, J., & Rosen, B. (1975). *Demographic differences between areas with and without federal community mental health center grants* (Mental Health Demographic Profile System Working Paper No. 22). Washington, DC: U.S. Government Printing Office.

Windle, C., & Woy, J. R. (1983). From programs to systems: Implications for program evaluation illustrated by the Community Mental Health Centers Program experience. *Evaluation and Program Planning, 6,* 53-68.

Wortman, P. M. (1975). Evaluation research: A psychological perspective. *American Psychologist, 30,* 562-575.

Wortman, P. M. (1982). [Review of *Evaluating with validity.*] *Educational Evaluation and Policy Analysis, 4,* 22-25.

Wortman, P. M. (1983a, October). *Evaluation at the frontier: Some "timely" comments for future use.* Presidential address to the annual meeting of the Evaluation Research Society, Chicago.

Wortman, P. M. (1983b). Evaluation research: A methodological perspective. *Annual Review of Psychology, 34*, 223-260.

Wyatt, D. F., & Campbell, D. T. (1950). A study of interviewer bias as related to interviewers' expectations and own opinions. *International Journal of Opinion and Attitude Research, 4*, 77-83.

Yin, R. K. (1984). *Case study research: Design and methods.* Beverly Hills, CA: Sage.

Zeisel, H. (1982). Disagreement over the evaluation of a controlled experiment. *American Journal of Sociology, 88*, 378-389.

Zuniga, R. (1975). The Experimenting Society and radical social reform: The role of the social scientist in Chile's Unidad popular experience. *American Psychologist, 30*, 99-115.

Zweig, F. M. (Ed.). (1979). *Evaluation in legislation.* Beverly Hills, CA: Sage.

Zweig, F. M., & Martin, K. E. (Eds.). (1981). *Educating policymakers for evaluation.* Beverly Hills, CA: Sage.

Author Index

Aaron, H. J., 297
Aaronson, N. K., 29
Abramson, M. A., 14, 26-27, 226, 228, 230, 233, 246
Ambron, S. R., 16
American Evaluation Association, 29
American Institutes for Research, 297
American Psychological Association, 31
Anderson, A., 378
Applebaum, M. I., 326, 376
Applied Management Sciences, 452
Ares, C. E., 30, 481
Attkisson, C. C., 300-301
Austin, D., 25, 28
Aviram, U., 300
Ayer, A. J., 95

Bachrach, L. L., 299
Balk, D. E., 283
Ball, S., 101
Bardach, E., 219, 261, 297
Barker, P., 159
Barker, R., 271
Barlow, D. H., 55, 299
Barrom, C. B., 55, 299
Bashook, P. G., 300
Beauchamp, T. L., 48, 50, 95-96
Bell, J. B., 226
Bell, W., 22, 240
Bellavita, C., 14, 228, 233-234, 241-242, 260, 263-265
Berk, R. A., 53, 317, 362, 378, 385-388, 390-391, 394, 396, 408, 411-413, 416, 420-421, 423, 428, 433, 435-436
Berman, J. S., 159
Berman, P., 297, 454

Bhaskar, P., 30
Bickman, L., 39, 41, 168, 399
Boeckman, M. E., 169, 474
Bogatz, G. A., 101
Bollen, K. A., 390, 415
Bootzin, R. R., 101
Boruch, R. F., 26, 33, 57, 122, 128, 212, 261-263, 298, 300-301, 378, 449-450, 454, 467, 473, 476, 484
Botein, B., 30, 481
Bowering, D. J., 484
Bowman, M. L., 21
Bradburn, N. M., 484
Bratton, K., 257
Braverman, M. T., 28, 484
Braybrooke, C. E., 219
Brethower, D. M., 34
Brewer, M. B., 121
Brickman, P., 121
Brinkerhoff, D., 248
Brinkerhoff, R. O., 34
Brown, H. I., 306
Brown, J. R., 43, 302
Bryk, A. S., 49, 444, 457
Buccino, A., 29, 427
Buchanan, G. N., 26, 229-230
Bucuvalas, M. J., 14, 54, 57, 191-192, 194-197, 205, 208, 213-214, 359, 474, 479
Bunda, M. A., 48, 96-97, 211, 214, 417
Bunker, J. P., 453

Campbell, D. T., 9, 32-34, 37, 42-43, 45-46, 55-56, 60, 62, 64, 66, 69-71, 74, 89, 103-104, 111-112, 114, 118-170, 172-177, 181, 207-212, 216, 229, 248-250, 252, 262-264, 271, 298, 306-307, 309-311,

Subject Index

518

About the Authors

William R. Shadish, Jr., is Professor of Psychology with the Center for Applied Psychological Research in the Department of Psychology at Memphis State University. His Ph.D. in clinical psychology was taken at Purdue University in 1978, with dual minor areas in statistics and measurement theory. He then spent three years as a postdoctoral fellow in methodology and evaluation research in the Psychology Department at Northwestern University. He has consulted on evaluation to the National Institutes of Health, the National Institute of Mental Health, and the Centers for Disease Control. His research interests include methodology, program evaluation, mental health policy, and social studies of science. His articles and chapters on these topics have appeared in such outlets as the *American Psychologist*, the *Handbook of Social Psychology*, and the *Annual Review of Psychology*. His recent books include *Evaluation Studies Review Annual* (Volume 12, edited with Charles S. Reichardt) and *Psychology of Science: Contributions to Metascience* (edited with Barry Gholson, Robert Neimeyer, and Arthur Houts).

Thomas D. Cook is Professor of Sociology, Psychology, Education, and Public Policy at Northwestern University, where he has been since 1968. He was educated at Oxford University and Stanford University, receiving his Ph.D. at the latter in 1967. He was an Academic Visitor at the London School of Economics in 1973-1974, and a Visiting Scholar at the Russell Sage Foundation in 1987-1988. He has been the recipient of the Myrdal Prize for Science of the Evaluation Research Society and of the Donald T. Campbell Prize for Innovative Methodology of the Policy Sciences Organization. He has two major research interests. The first concerns the roles that family management, residential mobility, better schooling, and local political organizations play in helping inner-city residents of color move closer to the national mainstream, if they so desire. The second line of research is methodological and deals with the design and execution of quasi-experiments, and with methods for promoting causal generalization through both meta-analysis and the explanation of causal processes. In these contexts he has published or edited the following volumes: *"Sesame Street" Revisited* (with H. Appleton, R. F. Conner, A. Shaffer, G. Tamkin, and S. J. Weber), *Evaluation Studies Review Annual* (Volume 3, with M. L. DelRosario, K. M. Hennigan, M. M. Mark, and W. M. K. Trochim), *Quasi-Experimentation: Design and Analysis Issues for Social Research in Field Settings* (with Donald T. Campbell), and *Qualitative and Quantitative Methods in Evaluation Research* (with Charles S. Reichardt).

Laura C. Leviton is Associate Professor of Community Health Services of the Graduate School of Public Health, University of Pittsburgh. She received her Ph.D. in social psychology from the University of Kansas in 1978. She then spent two years as a postdoctoral fellow at Northwestern University, where she participated in a study mandated by the U.S. Congress to critique evaluation research in educational programs at the federal, state, and local levels. She also conducted research and policy analysis for the Health Care Financing Administration while at Northwestern. She specializes in evaluation of health services and, in particular, of prevention in both the AIDS and cancer control areas. Her evaluation studies include a large-scale randomized trial on prevention of HIV infection in homosexual and bisexual men, and a demonstration project to prevent AIDS in injection drug users and their sexual partners. She has also directed studies of risk communication and prevention, in the areas of smoking cessation and medical surveillance for occupational diseases. She is the recipient of a W. K. Kellogg National Fellowship, which is awarded to outstanding early and midcareer professionals primarily in health, education, and agricultural fields.

NOTES

NOTES

NOTES

NOTES

NOTES

NOTES

NOTES

232937